MEDIA THEORY *in* JAPAN

MEDIA THEORY *in* JAPAN

MARC STEINBERG AND
ALEXANDER ZAHLTEN, EDITORS

Duke University Press   Durham and London   2017

© 2017 Duke University Press

All rights reserved

Printed in the United States of America on acid-free paper ∞

Designed by Courtney Leigh Baker

Typeset in Minion Pro and Myriad Pro by Westchester Publishing Services

Library of Congress Cataloging-in-Publication Data

Names: Steinberg, Marc, [date] editor. | Zahlten, Alexander, [date] editor.

Title: Media theory in Japan / Marc Steinberg and Alexander Zahlten, editors.

Description: Durham : Duke University Press, 2017. | Includes bibliographical references and index.

Identifiers: LCCN 2016043543 (print) | LCCN 2016046042 (ebook)

ISBN 9780822363125 (hardcover : alk. paper)

ISBN 9780822363262 (pbk. : alk. paper)

ISBN 9780822373292 (e-book)

Subjects: LCSH: Mass media—Philosophy. | Mass media—Social aspects—Japan—History—20th century. | Mass media—Political aspects—Japan—History—20th century. | Popular culture—Japan—History—20th century.

Classification: LCC P92.J3 M44 2017 (print) | LCC P92.J3 (ebook) | DDC 302.23/0952—dc23

LC record available at https://lccn.loc.gov/2016043543

COVER ART: Photo by Alexander Zahlten

Chapter 11 appeared originally in *Review of Japanese Culture and Society*, vol. 22, 88–103 and is reproduced with permission.

Contents

Acknowledgments

A journey is made by one's traveling companions, as the Japanese expression goes. On the journey that resulted in this volume, we had the benefit of an incredible group of contributors. We thank each and every one of them for taking the time to put their ideas into conversation, and to forge this collective project. We are grateful to them for the journey as well as for the final product. Ken Wissoker and Elizabeth Ault at Duke University Press were immensely supportive of this project from the very beginning, and their continuous advice—and patience—were invaluable in navigating it through its multiple stages. The Reischauer Institute of Japanese Studies was vital in supporting a workshop that allowed the contributors to meet and spend an intense and very rich two days exchanging ideas on all aspects of this enterprise. The current form of this volume started to take shape at the Histories of Film Theories in Asia conference at the University of Michigan in 2012, organized by Markus Nornes, where we benefited from early and immensely sensible advice from Tomiko Yoda. Karen Beckman, Yuriko Furuhata, Joshua Neves, Masha Salazkina, and Haidee Wasson offered guidance and solidarity in the art of creating an edited collection. We extend our deep thanks to our talented research assistants, Peter Bernard, Alain Chouinard, Andrew Campana, Kimberlee Sanders, and Edmund Stenson. We thank everyone in our contexts near and far who offered advice and support during this project.

Finally, there is one contributor who is especially in our thoughts. Ryoko Misono enthusiastically agreed to contribute a central chapter to the volume at a late stage in its development, greatly enhancing the project as a whole. She tragically passed away just days after sending in her essay. With Misono-san the fields of film and media studies in Japan lost one of its most promising young scholars. It is our hope that this volume helps keep her work alive and realizes the intervention about which she felt so deeply.

Note on Names:

Japanese names in this volume appear in the order family name first, given name second, unless the person goes by the given name first, family name second convention. For the sake of consistency, all contributors to this volume are referred to by their given name first, family name second.

Preface (Interface)

AKIRA MIZUTA LIPPIT

The volume that follows is long overdue. Which is not to say that it arrives late, or even too late, but rather that its timeliness appears in the form of a long-anticipated, and thus deferred, actualization. It represents a needed point of contact, or interface, between a media culture and its thought, between the material and conceptual dimensions of media culture in Japan. For too long there has been a perception that visual media cultures are practiced in Japan—film, art, architecture—but understood or thought elsewhere. Practiced within but thought from without, this false rift effects an erasure of those who have thought and continue to think media in Japan from within. Marc Steinberg and Alexander Zahlten's anthology *Media Theory in Japan* brings these dimensions together for the first time, perhaps—certainly in English—and into a present that also, at once, takes the form of a past, hence overdue. A past folded at the same time into a present, arriving in the dual temporalities of a future anterior, or perfect.

This overdue volume portrays a lively media theory in Japan then and now by many of the critics and theorists most active in media studies today. But even with its publication, this volume remains overdue. Past due, past the time of its anticipated arrival, *Nachträglichkeit*, and yet at the same time absolutely timely in its presentation of a coherent interface between media theory and practice in Japan. How is it possible to reconcile postponement with timeliness, and what sort of temporality is invoked in such a temporal schism?

It is perhaps the temporality of a media theorization par excellence. The deferred arrival of such a volume, overdue, reveals the problem of a national media and its theorization as chronic, which is to say, "about time." What sutures the practices and discourses of media within a cultural sphere bound by a single language, however porous, and however multilingual that language (as Japan's frequently is), may be temporal. A temporality marked by the time-liness of delayed arrivals.

In this sense, it is not only history that separates media practices and discourses, nor even languages and cultures, but also times that disjoin the two, times that are born of the material infrastructure of media praxes—of technologies and creativities, technologies of creation, one might say—and of media discourses, in all of the complexities that language interacts with: thought, representation, and expression. The task then may lie in finding the temporality that allows the incommensurate temporalities that define the media to interface, to encounter one another in a temporality other than one's own. It is this temporality that arrives in this volume, overdue.

An overdue volume is also one that acknowledges, and in some cases settles, debts. These debts are to a set of past inscriptions, "a line of credit," to use Derrida's idiom, that makes possible the present. It is not only about settling and closing accounts, of "counter-signing" as Derrida says, but also about acknowledging a past that reverberates in the present, that continues to resonate in the contemporary discourses on Japanese media. A series of such lines throughout *Media Theory in Japan* attribute indebtedness to a present that channels a frequently underacknowledged foundation.

Keisuke Kitano invokes literary theorist Kobayashi Hideo, while Takeshi Kadobayashi and Thomas Looser situate Azuma Hiroki's interventions in subculture studies as modes of media theory. As antecedents to media theory, Anne McKnight traces a lineage through feminist art and criticism; Alexander Zahlten, through "New Academicism"; and Fabian Schäfer, through the Kyoto school, as modes of media philosophy and thought. As critical moments in the evolution of Japanese media theory, Akihiro Kitada inscribes leftist philosopher Nakai Masakazu; Ryoko Misono, the artist Nancy Seki; Marilyn Ivy, NTT's *InterCommunication* project; Marc Steinberg, the reception of Marshall McLuhan in Japan; and Miryam Sas, the mistranslation of poet and theorist Hans Magnus Enzensberger. For Yuriko Furuhata, architecture informs Japan's media theory; for Tomiko Yoda, it is marketing and advertising. For Aaron Gerow, the history of Japanese television theory provides a foundation for contemporary media theory in Japan. Each account offered of media theory in Japan originates from and returns to a place other than the narrow confines of either nation or thought. A portrait of displaced origins and impossible teleologies appears throughout *Media Theory in Japan*.

This volume, then, is as much about an alternative media archaeology as it is about theorizing the eccentric genealogies it reveals; as much about paying dues and giving due to those that make the present visible. The authors of *Media Theory in Japan* settle a debt that goes beyond the field of media studies; one that expands the realm of media in Japan to include philosophy, feminism, literary theory, economics, and art. What makes the nature of these accounts of media archaeology in Japan, these lines of credit extended, remarkable is that they mark the advent of a media theory located not only in media studies. A media theory that takes place not only outside of the nation but also as a discourse of the outside. A media theory that comes from and returns to a Japan dislocated.

In Japan and elsewhere, media studies represents the aggregation of various disciplines, lines of thought, and modes of expression. Its boundaries are located not in national or even postnational contours, nor are they effects of cultural, ethnic, or aesthetico-political practices. Instead, the media and its thought take place as a series of extensions, to borrow McLuhan's idiom, and as what Deleuze and Guattari call "lines of intensity" and extensity, which traverse technology and art, practice and expression, discourse and politics. As intensities, these lines move from without to within Japan; as extensities, from within to without. In this matrix of media praxis and thought, Japan itself becomes a medium, an interface of multiple lines of practice and thought bound by the charges that animate the nation as a temporary and finite media state. Japan itself is not, as the authors reveal, a permanent state, nor is Japanese media a national entity, an infrastructure of phenomenon. Japanese media theory is defined by the authors in this volume not as the delineation of a national practice but rather as the disarticulation of a national discourse; media theory in this sense performs a "dejapanization."[1] To undo the nation, but also to understand the name of the nation not as the culmination of a discourse but as that which is already inscribed in advance, and then erased. *Déjàponisme, déjàpan.*

In this formulation, what is overdue comes to be déjà vu. What arrives late was already there once before. Japan appears and disappears in this work, an organizing principle/unsustainable origin, and destination. Because all media actualized and theorized exceed the terms by which nations are formed. Media practice and theory are no more Japanese than they are classical Greek or modern American, no more "Oriental" than Western: they arrive in the form of translations and mistranslations, transpositions and displacements, taking place between and outside of nations as such. And thus perpetually.

THE CRITICAL PROBLEM taken up by *Media Theory in Japan* is neither media theory nor Japan as such but the conjunction that brings them into contact: *in*. What type of interface does the title's "in" represent? For the chapters that constitute this volume hardly remain within Japan: what takes place in and around media theory in Japan comes from without as well as from within, not only from the registers of national thought but also from within and without the disciplines and practices one might call "media theory." *Media Theory in Japan* is thus neither about media theory nor Japan but rather a phantasmatic possibility of the two together, conjoined by an "in," which is not even or strictly in. The "in" here also means "out," within and without, inside out as much as outside in.

In this sense, the volume undoes the very set of binds, dialectics, and causalities that would ascribe lineage and nationality to ideas, as if such fabrications were even possible. In *Media Theory in Japan*, media theory itself disappears along with Japan, only to return as a series of provocations that begin neither here nor there, and arrive, as it were, only when overdue, ensuring the postponement of a destination that would posit something like a "media theory in Japan." *Déjà*ponisme might describe the trope that undoes the axioms of national thought and practice but also speaks of their simultaneity: media theory in Japan can only be thought, perhaps in advance and *après coup*. As such, any timeliness would require the split temporalities and historicities that this volume performs. To arrive overdue is to arrive on time, *in time*, as a chronic mode of undoing what cannot be done in the first instance, which is to ascribe national identity to thought, particularly to media thought. To be overdue, in this case, is also to invoke déjà vu. A present made possible by the before that appears in every after, the after inscribed in any before.

How then to preface that which is overdue and déjà vu? What does it mean to write before such a volume, to inscribe or prescribe a text before a set of interventions that arrive later than imagined or desired? How to signal that which has already come and returned again? What could such a preface achieve, and in what temporal form?

To preface a work is to stand before it, to speak in advance of that which follows. It is at once a provocation (calling forth) and an utterance a priori: the first word, or rather a word before the first word, facing before any face has appeared. But when the word to come has already come, when what follows is also already past, then any preface can only intervene en route. Because the interventions collected in this volume signal a history of theory in transit as well as transition, the only possible preface would be an interface. That which would arrive in the middle, which is to say never, suspended in a thought in transit, and no longer prefatory. A preface defaced, if not effaced, neither undone nor overdue, in lieu of a proper preface to arrive later, perhaps much later, in due time.

NOTES

1. See, in this connection, Akira Mizuta Lippit, "Playing against Type: On Postwar Japanese Film," *Artforum* (February 2013): 210–17.

INTRODUCTION

MARC STEINBERG AND ALEXANDER ZAHLTEN

Can you name five media theorists from Japan? This is intended less as a confrontational question than a loaded one. If you can, what are you saying about theory? What are you saying about media? If one moves beyond the very specific and circumscribed sociotope of North American and European academic work on media (or Japan), and what is defined as "theory" by *what "we" do*, then questions come crashing in that force a reassessment of some of the goals, assumptions, and methods of a very important inquiry: How can we understand our inescapable relationship to media? How can we understand our attempts to understand media, especially under the wobbly umbrella of "theory"? And how do we move away from a narrowly defined "we" in both of these questions?

In the English-language context both early discourse on media and its recent resurgence have tended to elide engagement with some of the most complex sites of media practice and theorization. Theorists wrote instead from the position of the universal, assuming that the West stood in for the world. This tendency to a degree continues with the rise of the Internet and the spread of digital media, at a moment when media theory in the European and American milieus has gained a new and more speculative life. In the wake of the flurry of work around new media, the retracing of formerly new media, and the subsequent critique of the framework of the "new," there has been a turn to what can now be called media theory or media studies in a novel form. New lines of inquiry emerge from the convergence of film, screen, and video studies; cultural studies; science and technology studies; and new media studies, as these established fields are being reshaped in the process.[1] The objects of media studies are the many forms of media made visible by new media studies, past and present. Its concerns are with format, platform, infrastructure, body, paper, language, and other facets of mediation, ranging from the decidedly abstract to the distinctly material.[2] Scholars wrestling with the affordances of this specific transitional moment in media history are searching for the theoretical tools to engage with a radically shifting media ecology. Forgotten texts from another era of media transformation—most notably Marshall McLuhan's *Understanding Media*, penned at a time when the new medium of television was first turning heads—have developed a renewed influence. Moreover, German media theory represented by the work of Friedrich Kittler and Wolfgang Ernst has had a strong impact on Anglo-American work on new media, even as the scope of this work is still being explored.

However, knowledge of media-theoretical discourse outside of North America and Europe is extremely limited. Japan, with one of the largest and most complex media industries on the planet and a rich and sophisticated history of theorization of modern media, is nearly a complete blank spot on the Euro-American media-theoretical map. If Japanese models of industrial production were the subject of great interest—and much hand-wringing—from the 1980s onward, the lively theorization of media taking place in Japan was markedly not. If media technologies and media cultures from Japan—consider trends in mobile media and miniaturization—exerted immense influence on everyday life around the world, then the specific models of media that thinkers in Japan have developed have remained overwhelmingly unknown even to specialists. Philosopher Nakai Masakazu's theory of film reception, formulated in the 1930s, focuses on the lack of a copula in film aesthetics and the results for corporeal spectatorship; it would have been a fruitful approach for reception theory in the United States and Europe decades ago and remains relevant today—if one had had the opportunity to engage with it (see Akihiro Kitada's contribution in this volume for Nakai's approach). This kind of invisibility is particularly regrettable considering the strong interdisciplinary cross-pollination that the theorization of media has allowed for in Japan. It is also part of a larger and by now familiar structural imbalance in knowledge production itself—something that Mitsuhiro Yoshimoto effectively pinpoints in his critique of the discipline of film studies—between a West that is figured as the site of Theory, and the

Rest as the site of history or raw materials ("texts").[3] As Aaron Gerow further elucidates, this structural imbalance was at times internalized by Japanese film theorists themselves, who lamented the absence of film theory in Japan, despite the country's rich history of film theorization.[4]

Let us be unequivocal at the outset, then: there is media theory in Japan. Even taking a relatively conservative definition of it, the theorization of media in Japan spans a time period from at least the beginning of the twentieth century until today. Sociologists from Gonda Yasunosuke to Miyadai Shinji to Ueno Chizuko to Yoshimi Shunya; philosophers from Nakai Masakazu to Yoshimoto Takaaki (also Yoshimoto Ryūmei); art theorists and critics such as Ishiko Junzō, Hasegawa Yūko, Matsui Midori, and Sawaragi Noi; editors and authors such as Ōtsuka Eiji; film critics and theorists such as Osaki Midori and Hasumi Shigehiko; artists, economists/critics such as Asada Akira; and ethnologists such as Umesao Tadao—the list of writers who have profoundly engaged with media goes on. Japan experienced an intensification and multiplication of media technologies and practices in the twentieth century similar to that in North America and Western Europe. There is accordingly a long history of reflection on these processes. (To give one small example, the term "information industry" was coined in Japan a decade before Daniel Bell introduced his idea of the "information age.")[5] These writers and the debates that they and others have engaged in have formed a heterogeneous yet dense discourse on the relationship of media and life that was eminently aware of global developments in media theorization, even as English-language writing remained almost entirely oblivious to the discussions taking place in Japan. Hence we agree wholeheartedly with Alexander Galloway, Eugene Thacker, and McKenzie Wark when they write, "The story of media theory in the twentieth century has still yet to be written."[6] We would simply add that this is all the more true in the Japanese context— not to mention other sites marginalized within the theory imaginary, from China to South Asia, or Africa to the Arab world.[7]

This volume aims to trace some of the central theoretical and conceptual work around media in Japan from the 1910s to the present day, paying attention to the technological, historical, institutional, and cultural practices that form the ground for its emergence and development. As such, this volume offers, to our knowledge, the first systematic introduction to and contextualization of the history of media theory from Japan in any language, including Japanese. Yet it operates alongside Euro-American frameworks— chronological history, the concept of "theory"—even as it problematizes them. The specter of colonial time, then, which defines Euro-American

Others as continually belated and too late, lurks in the background of the discussions found here.[8] Japan, itself a colonial power for the first half of the twentieth century, has shown the capacity to continually and actively complicate that specter. The temporality of both theorization and its transmission, then, remains a central concern for this endeavor. A different—but not necessarily *belated*—temporality will haunt any discussion of media terminology and theorization. To give but one example, Lev Manovich's landmark volume *The Language of New Media* (2001) was published in Japanese in 2014, which is slow for a publishing industry with a massive translation arm that so quickly responds to global trends in media writing. In fact the translation lag in this case may be explained if we remember that Japan's infatuation with the term "new media"—which referred mostly to VCRs, cable TV, and the computer—had its boom and fizzle in the 1980s, leaving little appetite for the recycled framework of "new media" in the late 1990s and 2000s (even if this time it was used in reference to computational media).[9] Accounting for these differences in uptake and description of media events and their theorization outside the comfortable synchro-functions of "belated" and "advanced" opens up new avenues of exploration, which are undertaken by the essays in this volume.

Two aspects require us to rethink some of our fundamental premises about what exactly we mean by *media theory*. First, this compound is a tenuous link between two moving targets. As David Rodowick describes in great detail in *An Elegy for Theory*, the concept of theory has a long and variable genealogy, and the linking of theory with a medium such as film—in the now naturalized form *film theory*—is intensely historical. As Rodowick notes when referencing the first time this then highly idiosyncratic link was formulated by Béla Bálazs: "What film studies has forgotten in the intervening decades is the strangeness of this word, as well as the variable range and complexity of the questions and conceptual activities that have surrounded it over time like clouds reflecting light and shadow in ever-changing shapes."[10] This variability is joined by the shifting criteria for defining or even just naming "media." Lev Manovich has pointed out some of the ways technological changes have shifted the definitional standards for this qualification, in a manner that simply adds on new categories without revising the existing ones. While film and photography were still distinguishable via the divisions between time- and space-based media going back to Lessing, the advent of television and video did not allow for that framework. Instead they were allotted roles as distinct media by the practices they afforded. The criteria thus shifted to the social sphere and to questions of engagement. The computer, in Manovich's argument, radicalizes that shift and confronts us with a post-medium situation.[11]

Second, media theory is itself profoundly reliant on media—particularly the medium of print, and the circulatory networks of print capitalism (magazines, journals, book volumes, and their publishers), but also the specific configurations of media institutions and their histories, with which media theorization grapples. There is more interaction between media theory and the contexts for this theorization than has been accounted for in most studies of media theory.

The Situation Is Media Theory

We can best illustrate this last point by turning to the very title of this volume, which raises more questions than it answers: *Media Theory in Japan*. As several of our contributors aptly pointed out in a workshop leading up to this volume, all of these terms deserve to be put in quotation marks. Each term within this title raises questions: What are media? What is media *theory*? What is media theory *in* Japan?

Whichever question we grapple with, one thing is clear: media theory as a kind of conceptual work is conditioned by the constellation of media and the practices associated with them. Hence this book's emphasis on "in Japan"; this is not simply a marker of a location but a way of broaching the inevitably *contextual* process of media theorization itself. (Here we bracket the way that "Japan" is a baggy construct that stands in for a series of often geographically circumscribed practices of writing and interaction that sometimes engage the question of the nation but just as often do not. Indeed, the case could be made that media theorization is quite a regional affair, sometimes centered in Kyoto, as in the 1930s, and sometimes in Tokyo. Still, we use "Japan" as a conceptual shorthand for the intersection at which this engagement with media occurs.) As media studies moves away from its exclusive concern with the temporal location of "*new* media," we take the opportunity to pose questions about the spatial locatedness of theory and the specificity of certain kinds of theoretical work. This enables the explication of the geopolitical unconscious (or semiconscious) of media theory, structured among others by university ranking systems, the uneven trickle and flow of translation, military and economic power, and an aesthetic politics of knowledge.

W. J. T. Mitchell and Mark B. N. Hansen's *Critical Terms for Media Studies* offers an inspiring point of departure for moving beyond media theory's recent emphasis on thinking *new media*, showing the continuities between thinking about media new and old. The volume helpfully suggests the terrain encompassed by media studies, and maps out a number of theoretical problems that compose the field of media theory. As Mitchell and Hansen forcefully emphasize in their introduction, media do not simply designate an externality against which to position the human. Rather, "*media* names an ontological condition of humanization,"[12] and for this reason is a perspective from which to think the human-media condition. Hence Mitchell and Hansen propose that we pivot away from Friedrich Kittler's famous dictum "Media determine our situation"[13] to instead situate "media as a perspective for understanding." This shift, they write, "allows us to reassert the crucial and highly dynamic role of mediation—social, aesthetic, technical, and (not least) critical—that appears to be suspended by Kittler."[14]

But what happens if the very conditions of thinking mediation arise from the particular media and media-cultural forms with which we interact? This is an aspect of media theorization that Mitchell and Hansen's volume—and the vast majority of writings on the subject—tends to pass over in silence. Put differently, the contributions to their volume concern media problems often posed in the language of the universal, drawing on texts and traditions that are exclusively from European or American contexts. While the technological and intellectual development of media theory is examined, the geographical or geocultural focus on American, British, French, and German events and writers is all too pronounced.[15] In that sense, media theory has always already been a covert subset of Euro-American area studies on the one hand, and complicit in larger geopolitical power structures on the other. The canon is also a cannon.

In this book we pass from the ontological status of the coconstitution of human and media, to the practical (and historically grounded) problem of how distinct cultural-media configurations give rise to distinct forms of mediation, and distinct kinds of media theorization. That is, we resist the universal language of theory in favor of a contextual and unstable practice of theory, without giving up on the belief that theorization—of media or anything else for that matter—is an indispensable tool with which to grapple with our times.

This volume of essays proposes to make this shift from media theory as universal to media theory as a practice composed of local, medium-specific, and culture-inflected practices. Such practices are as much about performance and the particular dynamics of a given media ecology as the content of a given theory. This volume, then, proposes to reframe certain practices as part of a history of media theorization. Ideas cannot be separated from the economic, historical, and medial conditions of production. This is not simply to say in a materialist vein that ideas are produced by material conditions, however. The essays in this volume also show how the *practices* of theory themselves intervene in and transform these medial and economic conditions. Theory makes the news, and theoreticians sometimes become media celebrities, making theory of media in the media. We acknowledge too that theory may be—or perhaps even habitually is—consumed as a commodity, complete with cycles of novelty and obsolescence that have profound consequences for the ways that theories are produced, circulated, and read.[16] We may go so far as to say that debates and denominational battles between proponents of competing media, theoretical paradigms and the way they are organized tell us as much about these paradigms as the conceptual frameworks they put forward. Theory, as it is understood here, is as much based on the performative as the constative, not to mention the mediatically connective. The modes of performance of theory tell us something about the theories themselves, and, we argue, require us to rethink the very status of media theory today. Put differently, accounting for the materiality of media theory opens the space for rethinking the materiality of media.

We might paraphrase Kittler, then: situation determines our media theory. Or perhaps more accurately: the situation of more or less temporally and spatially bounded media cultures and ecologies determines or informs media theory. This gives us the opportunity to, on the one hand, test the ways canonical media theories from Europe and North America have fared in different climes, and, on the other, also see how existing philosophical or critical movements in Japan can be read differently when looked at from the angle of media and mediation. The importance of the situation does not simply mean we need to gather more empirical facts about local media theories; it also means that the very contours of what we call media theorization must be tested, and reexamined. Situation informs, or transforms, theorization.

Media Theory in Japan, then, presumes that different media-cultures give rise to distinct forms of media theorization, and also require that thinkers of media reexamine what they mean by "media theory." Rather than starting with a restrictive or prescriptive sense of what media theorization is or should be, our contributors approach the contours of media theory in an exploratory manner. As always, what is included in the category of theory is a political question that often brings understandings of media encrusted from years of living with the existing canon. Without wishing to completely relativize the term, the essays here nonetheless provoke a sense of questioning around what habitually is called "theory." This means that on the one hand, writers in the European and American context should understand their work as conditioned by historical circumstance, and on the other, that they use this as a basis for understanding other contexts as something more than a variation on a universal theme. It also means that writers in Japan or other non-Euro-American contexts understand their discourses as something other than "local." Our hope is that the diverse modes of media theorization or media studies in Japan (and elsewhere) potentially highlight the presuppositions of "media theory" as it is practiced and articulated today, in a predominantly European and American media studies context.

Hence this book does not walk the narrow path of an intellectual history, nor does it offer an account of pure ideas that stands in for the ahistorical aura of high theory. Instead it holds on to the premise that the conditions of knowledge production work back on the knowledge produced. It also aims to build on existing channels that create the institutional conditions for multichannel exchange. By building on existing projects such as *Traces, Inter-Asia Cultural Studies*, and *Mechademia*, which aim to create new series of "interreferences"—to borrow Kuan-Hsing Chen's felicitous term—that translate and generate dialogues in, around, and outside Asia, as well as projects that aim to translate and make available film and cultural theory in English, this volume participates in the questioning and unsettling of the unidirectional translation of Western sources into local target languages.[17]

In *Kittler and the Media*, Geoffrey Winthrop-Young addresses the manner in which non-Anglo-American media theories are marked from the outset:

> The overwhelming presence of the Anglo-American academic industry in media and communication studies is such that many Anglophone practitioners no longer consider it necessary to situate their work by using national adjectives, yet contributions that originate elsewhere need to be labeled "French," "German," or "Japanese." These appellations do not refer to anything specific to France, Germany, or Japan, but merely serve to indicate that the work in question is *not* English. Nonetheless, the label *German* can and should be applied to Kittler.[18]

The question we engage here is a similar one: To what degree is Japan not merely an appellation designating something that is *not* Anglo-American? How might "in Japan" designate a set of qualities or conditions that orient the work of media analysis, and mark the modes of circulation of media theory? How might attention to the situation force us to pause, and rethink our assumption—held particularly strongly in North American institutions— that the default setting for media theory is America; for a philosophy of media, France; and for media philosophy, Germany?

Zeronendai—Thought from the Aughts

Perhaps this point would be best made by referring to the situation from which this project emerged. In medias res, as it were, in the midst of an effervescence of media theorization in Japan: the 2000s. This is a moment when an increasingly large group of writers—collectively referred to in Japan as *zeronendai no shisō*, or "thought of the aughts"—took to analyzing Japan's vibrant popular media formations from the vantage point of an engagement with critical theory. The result was a critical mass of multigenerational writers bending themselves to the task of engaging critically with the spread of mobile phones, the rise of the Internet, the increasing cultural prominence of console and computer games, and especially the transformations of fan cultures that were read as the frontlines of changes in Japan's media-cultures. It was also a moment when such theorization produced best sellers, fueling a high-velocity rhythm of zeronendai publications. Examining the particularities of this moment will allow us to demonstrate the complexities of the situation of media theory.

Starting in the early 1990s practitioner-critics such as Nakajima Azusa and Ōtsuka Eiji began to write complex analyses of the intersection of fandom and the popular media culture around manga and anime, often as an indicator of broader sociopolitical developments. From the mid- to late 1990s, writers such as the psychoanalyst Saitō Tamaki, the sociologist Miyadai Shinji, the sociologically inflected writer Kotani Mari, and a young critic trained in Russian literature and Derridean philosophy called Azuma Hiroki turned toward the crucial intersection of anime-manga-games-light novels and the cultural transformations they saw as attending the rise of digital media. Azuma in particular began actively fostering an even younger clique of writers who took on various aspects of (generally male-oriented) *otaku*, or geek media forms, though the discourse was by this point largely dominated by young male voices. This very male clique points to a longer history of exclusion of female voices from Japanese media writing, which in turn suggests the need to look elsewhere to sites where female writers *could* do media theoretical work, from manga writing and criticism—where important work on queer (media) theory has developed—to art historical writing. The centrality of zeronendai critics was due in part to their creation of multiple platforms for their work, among which was the prominent if short-lived journal *Shisō chizu* (Thought map), which Azuma cofounded and coedited with sociologist and media theorist Akihiro Kitada.[19] This and other platforms gave the sense of a coherent discursive space in which these writers could develop critical analyses of aspects of Japanese media culture. Most engaging was the way the writers combined an attention to techno-cultural transformations that were under way with a close attention to fan media forms.

Azuma's *Otaku: Japan's Database Animals*, originally serialized in 2001 and published as a paperback volume in the same year as *Dōbutsuka suru posutomodan* (*Animalizing the Postmodern*), became a best seller and one of the main markers of this development, performing a function similar to Lev Manovich's landmark *The Language of New Media*, published the very same year in English. Azuma focuses on animation, theorizes the database as a principal construct for the interpretation of post-Internet culture, and examines new media artifacts such as fan-produced video games—all topics that resonate with Manovich's work. Where they differ is that for Azuma the representative structuring force of new media and contemporary Japanese society (what Azuma calls the "postmodern," extending the life of a term by then in the decline) is to be found in Japan's fan culture and the figure of the otaku. In short, it is an analysis of new media through the prism of the geek.[20] Instead of a study of new media anchored in discussions of the filmic and net.art avant-gardes (Manovich), the central anchor for new media studies in Japan becomes the lowbrow, avant-pop, subcultural forms of anime, manga, and dating simulation games.

As a result, the grounds for new media theorization of the 2000s in Japan were less what Geert Lovink calls "vapor theory" and Jeffrey Sconce calls "vapor studies"—speculative and questionable studies of new media from the angle of future technologies to come (albeit there was some of this too).[21] Rather, the grounds for zeronendai thought tended to be the actually existing, concrete, if equally masculinist studies of male fans' productions of and interactions with dating sims, often down to the level of programming code. Fan cultures were placed at the center of this media writing, albeit removed from the complexities of reception studies normally associated with the study of fans from a cultural studies perspective. To put it polemically, imagine if 4chan (a clone of the Japanese Futaba channel, which is itself a clone of the 2chan), not net.art or virtual reality, were at the analytical core of new media studies in North America, and one will get the sense of the object parameters of Japanese new media theorization.

The interest the zeronendai writers generated both inside and outside of Japan—Azuma is widely read in South Korea, for example—in many ways made this volume's project of writing a history of media theory in Japan thinkable. As a network of theorization that is both proximate and distant, the zeronendai work became, for us, a useful point of departure.[22] For one thing, an encounter with zeronendai work also necessitates a recalibration of what we mean by "theory"; the works produced by the zeronendai writers draw on but do not usually read as high theory. It also is not Theory in the capital T sense that is figured in Terry Eagleton's suggestion that "theory means a reasonably systematic reflection on our guiding assumptions," or, as he puts it later in his book *After Theory*, in speaking of "critical self-reflection which we know as theory": "Theory of this kind comes about when we are forced into a new self-consciousness about what we are doing."[23] While theory may indeed be defined as a kind of self-reflexive practice, it is also something more. It has another angle that we might term the *cultures of theory*—cultures here including languages, disciplines, institutions, publishing venues, politics of knowledge mobilization, bookstore display patterns, and local cartographies of theoretical production and consumption. The cultures of theory must also include the geopolitical situation in which this theorizing takes place: print capitalism, the Cold War, the structure of knowledge transfer that mirrors the very special relationship of the United States and Japan during the postwar period, and so on. This "something more" to theory becomes exceedingly clear when we look at the zeronendai group, which never unfolded its debates through academic journals, and only rarely through conferences. Nor was it neatly the kind of popular theory or vernacular strategies of fans adopting or "poaching" theory, as suggested by Matt Hills—that is, a kind of theorization from below, by fans.[24] That said, it is clear that the writers associated with zeronendai often themselves explicitly self-identify as fans, and even more interestingly, self-identify as *fans of theoretical practice itself*. Azuma's operation of theory camps, or *dojo*, and the theory competitions modeled on the GEISAI amateur art festivals deployed and exploited by artist-provocateur Murakami Takashi to find new artistic talent, actively harnessed this amateur-theory-fan nexus.

The conception of the cultures of theory we posit here finds resonance in what Françoise Lionnet and Shu-mei Shih envision in their call to "creolize" theory. "Creolization," they write, "indexes flexibility, welcomes the test of reality, and is a mode of theorizing that is integral to the living practices of being and knowing." It denotes a mode of theory that "is not the 'Theory' most familiar to, and at times most vilified by, scholars in the United

States."[25] This unfamiliar theory, which nonetheless must be accepted as theorization, interests us most here.

Defining Media Theory

We have perhaps come to a point where we can better address the questions that the title of our volume raises, and that we flagged in the opening of this introduction: What are media? What is media theory? What is media theory *in* Japan? Here we would like to move from a general definition of the terms to a consideration of the disciplinary locus of media theorization, first in the Anglo-American academies—where traditions of media studies have been particularly strong—and then in Japan.

Following Mitchell and Hansen, we would assert, "What is to be understood [in media studies] is not media in the plural, but media in the singular; and it is by understanding media in the singular—which is to say, by reconceptualizing understanding from the perspective of media—that we will discover ways to characterize the impact of media in the plural" (*Critical Terms*, xxii). Media should not simply be understood as a collection of individual mediums—books, newspapers, radio, television, Internet, computer, and so on. Media are not simply "a plurality of mediums, an empirical accumulation of things" (*Critical Terms*, xxi); they are also the experience of media in the singular-plural, and the theorization of media that arises from this experience. Thus understood media are also (significantly for any media society but maybe especially so for Japan) an emergent system with its own set of dynamics and semiautonomous rules. As Galloway, Thacker, and Wark formulate in their introduction to *Excommunication,* "Media force us to think less about things like senders and receivers, and more about questions of channels and protocols. Less about encoding and decoding, and more about context and environment" (2). That is, media make us think about more than classically conceived modes of communication—they force us to examine the context and environment in which they not only operate but also cocreate. Hence media theory cannot be reduced to communication theory.

There are many possible accounts for the development of media studies. John Guillory has recently offered an insightful genealogy of the genesis of the concept of media, arguing that ultimately it is only in the context of the plurality of media forms that we can come upon something like the concept of medium.[26] In other words, the specificity of a given medium—as much as the set of general properties of a category usefully termed "medium"—is only revealed upon the emergence of another, newer medium with which it can be compared, and through which it is remediated. Akihiro Kitada in this volume quotes Mizukoshi Shin, who argues similarly that "tremors in media can awaken media theory"—that is, transformations in the media give rise to something like media theory. This is certainly something we find borne out in the various essays of this volume; moments of new media are often moments of new developments in media theory.

What we would call media theory in the European and North American context finds its origins in a particular institutional lineage of media studies.[27] A brief overview of this lineage would trace: (1) early research on communications technologies, as it curves through (2) the Marshall McLuhan moment—arguably the first figure to articulate a research agenda around the development of media theory—into (3) the rise of film studies in the French, British, and particularly American academy during the 1970s, inspired by a particular conjuncture of formal analysis allied with Marxist and feminist theories of the filmic image, to (4) the simultaneous impact of television studies and UK cultural studies on the landscape of film studies, shifting to another, more quotidian medium—the television—at the same time as more empirical forms of analysis are introduced, to (5) the rise of "new media" in the 1990s, which saw a revival of earlier media theories (notably McLuhan's) and the embrace of wider-ranging theories of media to make sense of the sometimes novel media forms (Wendy Chun, Jay Bolter and Richard Grusin, Lev Manovich, Geert Lovink, Mark Hansen, and Lisa Nakamura), to (6) the more recent dropping of the term "new" to brand a kind of *media studies* that nonetheless is indebted to the epistemological frameworks and questions of power that emerge through the particular lineage sketched here (shifting to analyses of formats, platforms, media objects, and materialities: Lisa Gitelman, Jonathan Sterne, Alexander Galloway, and Jussi Parikka). This is largely an outline filtered by the engagement with media in institutionalized, academic contexts. There exists of course an entire body of theorization outside of this specific form of institutionalization. And, as we know from the abundant self-referentiality within film, comics, and television, media auto-theorize. At yet another level, as John Caldwell has effectively shown, "industrial cultural theorizing," or middle-level theorization, also happens at the level of media producers themselves.[28]

We call "media theory" any sustained engagement with media such that it produces new ways of knowing this media. This engagement could be of a theoretical, reflective kind of the sort imagined by Eagleton in his definition of theory cited above. But it must also make room for a kind of vernacular theorization, or a theorization that happens in the performance of the media condition, rather than in a reflection on these conditions. Distinct from communication theory, this is a theory of media that is produced from within media; from media lived as context, and as ecology.

Media Studies in Japan

Nonetheless, theory located in and produced from within university structures plays a decisive role in shaping the course of other locations of theorizing. It is therefore important to acknowledge the institutional history of media theory in Japan as well. There is a difference implied in the terms *theorization of media* and *media theory*. The latter tends to point to an academic institutionalized setting. It is difficult to claim that this was the dominant force in determining the course(s) of the theorization of media in Japan, and indeed media theory/theorization in Japan may provide an important occasion for complicating the relation between theory and Theory. Yet the work done from within the university has provided important affordances for, and exerted considerable influence on, nonacademic contexts as well. Though the institutional history of the study of media in Japan appears in the coming chapters in fits and starts, it is useful to give a rough account of it here. Before doing so, it is important to note that the following institutional account neglects the important noninstitutional history of media theory that includes particularly female voices such as Osaki Midori, whose work on cinema is often cited as an important moment within film theory in Japan, or the TV criticism of Nancy Seki, whose combination of written text and metatheoretical "eraser prints" is the subject of Ryoko Misono's essay in this volume.[29]

Meiji era thinkers such as Fukuzawa Yukichi have already discussed the importance of print, electric transmission, and postal services for "modern civilization." With the presupposition that media theory is closely connected to the development of mass media and tends to ask questions about the interconnection of textual content and issues of circulation, reception, and the resulting system, the study of media from within academia arguably makes one tentative start in Japan in the 1910s with sociologist Gonda Yasunosuke's investigations into film (although Gonda did not have a full university position at the time but rather worked at a school teaching German). However, the initiative for creating a legitimate site for the study of media took hold in the 1920s, when Ono Hideo promoted *shinbungaku* (literally "newspaper science"). The term was directly translated from the German *Zeitungswissenschaft*, and Ono's theoretical approaches were strongly oriented toward the German model, a fact that became a common point of criticism by figures such as philosopher Tosaka Jun. Ono, set on establishing an institutional home for shinbungaku in Japan, travelled in 1923 to various institutions in Germany, Britain, and the United States. After an initial attempt to establish a research institute for newspaper studies at Tokyo Imperial University (currently University of Tokyo) in 1927 failed (it was deemed too practitioner-oriented), a proposal for a newspaper research seminar (*shinbun kenkyūshitsu*) was approved in 1929. This seminar quickly developed a sociological bent—another legacy of German influence via Karl Bücher—and would exert considerable influence over the course of media theory in Japan until today.[30]

The Second World War exerted an inhibiting influence on the study of media, while in the immediate postwar period the US occupation actively encouraged establishing shinbungaku departments, for example at Waseda University in 1946. Media studies received its next big push in the 1950s when the introduction of television in 1953 created an awareness of the need to shift away from a purely print-based model of media research. Yet for several decades, media theory would not take place in specialized departments but rather in departments for literature, psychology, and, to a significant degree, sociology. The sociologist Katō Hidetoshi developed an influential approach to television in the late 1950s, and indeed it was one of Katō's teachers, Minami Hiroshi, who would become the first chairman of the Japan Society of Image Arts and Sciences (Nihon Eizō Gakkai; JASIAS) in 1974. This was to become one of the main venues for research on film, television, and other aspects of moving-image media. Both Katō and Minami had studied at American universities (Katō at Harvard, Chicago, and Stanford; Minami at Cornell), and the influence of American social science on their work was considerable.

The Society for Cinema and Media Studies in the United States originally focused on film (or rather cinema) and only added "media" to its name in 2002. The term *eizō* as used by the JASIAS provided a similar but somewhat different bent on accommodating a larger perspective on media. The term can loosely be translated as "moving image," but Yuriko Furuhata has argued that in the debates around the term in the 1960s it most basically suggested a mediated image, be it still or moving.[31] Such an attempt to avoid a medium-specific orientation is also visible in the founding of the Department for the Study of Culture and Representation (Hyōshō Bunkarongakka) by film critic and literature theorist Hasumi Shigehiko, theater director Watanabe Moriaki, and others at Tokyo University, where the influential Interfaculty

Initiative in Information Studies was later founded in 2000. The Association for the Study of Culture and Representation, which grew out of the Department for the Study of Culture and Representation, was founded in 2006 and takes a high-theory approach toward what one might call media studies. Specialized societies for the study of a particular medium came later; the Japan Society for Cinema Studies (Nihon Eiga Gakkai) and the Japan Society for Animation Studies (Nihon Animēshon Gakkai) were founded in 2005 and 1998, respectively.[32]

Issues of institutional power have played a significant role in the development of media studies in Japan. While much of the media theoretical work of the 1950s to 1980s straddled the line between academic work and *hihyō* (criticism) and was formulated in a wider space of discourse across many institutions, media theory as it developed from the 1990s onward was heavily influenced by the sociological model developed at Tokyo University. (For the decisive role of the specific genre of hihyō criticism in both theorizing and negotiating the possibilities of theoretical language caught up in postcolonial tensions, see Keisuke Kitano's chapter in this volume). In part due to shinbungaku's role as forerunner at the university, and also due to the university's cultural capital and its financial power to institute new departments, the University of Tokyo's sociological model of media studies has spread widely and can be sensed in the work of prominent theorists such as Yoshimi Shunya, Miyadai Shinji, Mizukoshi Shin, Akihiro Kitada, and Azuma Hiroki. From this brief institutional history we can see that general questions around media have superseded investigations of a particular medium.

As we discuss in more detail below, the individual chapters in this volume similarly range across media—from photography to film to television to architecture to fashion and the Internet—in an attempt to account for the diversity of sites around which the theorization of media takes place, and where discussions of media are concentrated at particular moments in time. Yet this approach also sometimes puts this volume at odds with the institutional history of media studies within Japan. Above we stress the importance of a critical approach to media theorization in Europe and North America, and its marginalization of other modes of theorization; in this volume our contributors similarly take up different moments in the development of media theory, some from within the halls of academic institutions, and some from within the structures of the mass media themselves. The rejection of familiar modes of legitimation is key to (re)narrating the history of media theory. Nonetheless, there are institutional dynamics of field and discipline that this volume has to work with while working around them. The contributors to this volume predominantly write from within either a film and media studies or an area studies context. While disciplinary affiliation by no means determines approach, it does have an impact on how the scholars here treat media theorization—whether as part of an institutional or cultural formation, or as part of a philosophical inquiry. That said, we believe that each contribution here does some of the work of chiseling away at the traditional complicity of the divide between history (or culture) and theory. Each chapter embarks on an account of media theorization that is historically nuanced and aware of the geopolitics of Theory.

Volume Structure

Does the materiality of the book form of necessity support a "brutal" conception of history, that is to say a chronologically determinist one? Does a printed volume on media theory necessarily bias its investigations toward the allegiances of print capitalism—modernity and nationally organized, linear history? These are decisive questions for a volume concerned with how theorists of media in Japan negotiated these concerns and how they dealt with narratives of "the West" and temporally skewed hierarchies.

This volume does not track the history of media theory in Japan via a simple line drawn from the 1920s to today.[33] This is due in part to a refusal to subsume a markedly diverse series of encounters to a linear history and the overly simplistic trajectory it implies. In part this is also due to our sense that contributions to this volume broach different topics, and take different tacks. Some essays are more accurately described as cultural histories of an encounter with media theory; others trace the engagement of different theorists around common questions, such as technology. Others still dig deep into the philosophical questions around mediation such that they encourage us to think media theory more precisely as mediation theory. Some deal with particular media forms, others with a multiplicity of media, others still with the problem of mediation as such. The organization of this volume reflects this diversity of approaches.

The volume opens with a section titled "Communication Technologies," which groups together a series of inquiries into how media technologies were thought, be it as materials, as environments, or as orchestrators of consumption. At times their theorization unfolded as a forgotten return, as they were framed much like previous media were, without an explicit awareness of the prior debates. Tracing such a development, Aaron Gerow turns our attention to tensions arising around the strangely familiar theorization of the new kid on the media block in the 1950s: television. Television first began broadcasting in 1953, and gained much theoretical and critical attention during its first decade of existence. But, as Gerow informs us, theoretical accounts of the medium began appearing as early as the 1930s, a point in time when the medium was still in its experimental phase. Moreover, these accounts recall earlier theorizations of film and its specificity in the 1910s and 1920s. Against this historical backdrop, Gerow examines debates around television during the 1950s, suggesting, "Early television theory was as much about the possibility of media theory in a changing society, as it was about the medium and its effects." He poses the question of why many discussions around early film returned, accompanied by a sense of (strategic?) amnesia in the late 1950s. Television is associated, as most material and immaterial technologies are, with a certain spatial practice that has strong connotations of class, gender, and a certain temporality—in this case, newness. Gerow disentangles these associations and how they interact with "TV theory," which becomes a major impetus for the development of an explicit theory of media.

Yuriko Furuhata's contribution moves from the wartime period through Expo '70, focusing our attention on the site of a redefinition of technologies of mediation: the field of architecture. Furuhata's essay sheds light on the role of the renowned architect Isozaki Arata as an intercessor between avant-garde visual artists and architects, suggesting the importance of architectural discourse as a site of media theory. Furuhata's essay sheds light on what she calls the "cybernetic turn" of Japanese architectural theory as a historical precursor to contemporary attempts to rethink media's relationship to the environment. Focusing on the formative role of Tange Lab and the work of associated architects Tange Kenzo and Isozaki Arata, Furuhata suggests how the postwar articulation of the cybernetic model of the information city both inherited the legacy of colonial urban planning, and responded to the postwar governmental push for postindustrialization and the experimental practices of building multimedia environments. Furuhata hence examines the intersection of architectural practice with communications theory, discourses around cybernetics and the information society, and media theory.

Takeshi Kadobayashi traces a very different model of environment and mediation in the work of Azuma Hiroki, one of the most influential young theorists of the 2000s and a major figure of the zeronendai group. Azuma wrote his first work in the pages of the journal *Hihyō kūkan* (Critical space)—

the main platform for criticism in the 1990s, established by Nyū Aka (New Academism) veterans Asada Akira and Karatani Kōjin—and the new media journal *InterCommunication* (a journal that is the focus of Marilyn Ivy's contribution). Kadobayashi sees Azuma's *InterCommunication* article series "Why Is the Cyberspace Called Such?" as a transitional phase for Azuma. It was this moment that led Azuma from his role as young apprentice to the older generation to what he is known as today: the preeminent theorist of popular media culture in Japan. It is here too that Kadobayashi discovers Azuma's incipient—and partially abandoned—media theory.

Marilyn Ivy examines a form of missed or mis-communication through the history of the pathbreaking *InterCommunication* journal in the 1990s and 2000s. Sponsored by one of the largest telecommunication companies in the world and edited by some of the major intellectual figures of the time, the journal was planned to provide a passageway to the global intellectual sphere and heavily featured translations and, at least initially, English sections. Ivy interrogates the different functions of this journal, positioned in the interstices of exchange and insulation; traces the utopian bent the journal followed with regard to technologies of communication in particular; and gives an outline of some of the decisive debates of 1990s media theory in Japan. Insofar as these debates lay the ground for the central media theorists of the 2000s, Ivy's essay provides a picture of an often-overlooked transition point between the Nyū Aka movement of the 1980s, and the zeronendai no shisō (thought of the aughts) generation that emerges in the 2000s, of which Azuma was a central figure.

The next section, "Practical Theory," assembles six contributions that look at the practice of media theorization as performative acts, or, put differently, how acts such as creating advertising campaigns, translating theories (and performing that translation), or even performing a media persona have in Japan functioned as implicit and sometimes explicit theorizations of media. Marc Steinberg details one of the most prominent cases of performing theory, which took place around the translation and interpretation of one of the ur-texts of media theory in North America and (Western) Europe, Marshall McLuhan's *Understanding Media*. As Steinberg details, McLuhan's work also possesses this status in Japan, where the term *media-ron* (media theory) emerges around the introduction of the Canadian media theorist's work. This introduction was channeled by a kind of doppelgänger theorist who both mirrors and redirects McLuhan's very flexible body of work: Takemura Ken'ichi, a man deeply embedded in the advertising world. Steinberg outlines the contours of the lively public debates around McLuhan's work in the late 1960s. These debates—which often revolve around how well McLuhan can be used in advertising practice—suggest the important ties between media theory and commercial practice that inform media theorization in Japan to this day, and highlight the key institutional role advertising agencies played in introducing and popularizing media theoretical work, as "actionable theory." They also shed light on the politics of influence and translation on the reception of theory, and even on the conception of theory itself.

Miryam Sas explores the contentious discussion, aggravated by mistranslations, at a symposium organized in connection with the visit of German poet and (at the time) media theorist Hans Magnus Enzensberger. Sas lucidly analyzes the reactions of a number of key leftist intellectual figures of the 1970s to the direct encounter with Enzensberger. The chapter is also very much an account of the attempt to salvage and defend the model of ideological critique within media theory at a moment when the depoliticization of the public sphere in Japan already loomed on the horizon. Highlighting this site of interdisciplinary encounter between artists and media critics, Miryam Sas uses Enzensberger's visit to Japan as a vantage point from which to examine how networks of media theory operate along transnational axes. In so doing, she reopens the question of nation and how it functioned at what was a highly performative event, in which almost all participants were aware of the intersections of geopolitical power relations that undergirded their conversation. Here Sas points to the importance of placing Marxist media theory in a transnational context, with the arrival of Enzensberger providing a chance to reveal a vibrant cross section of Marxist media theory in Japan and beyond. The Enzensberger moment also sheds light on an increasing preoccupation of intellectuals and writers of the time: the growing prominence of the cultural industries, the shifts occurring within the cultural industries, and the transformation of political society under their influence.

It is to this transformation of the cultural industries that Tomiko Yoda turns, focusing on the manner in which market segmentation and industry practice created the identificatory figure of the young girl and placed her at the center of a consumer culture conceived of as both utopian and egalitarian. Dubbing this the "girlscape," Yoda investigates the medial practice of defining this new consumer as situated on a plane of free choice that is apparently removed from the pressures and power relations that structured society in Japan. Mapping the visual and verbal strategies that accompanied the rise of the girlscape, she relates this development to the highly political "landscape theory" developed in Japan in the late 1960s and early 1970s—a prominent discussion of how power structures life in a rapidly transforming country. The cultural industries developed their own theory of media at the time, one that was fundamentally dependent on the (en)gendering of consumers, and the incorporation of these consumers into the girlscape.

Alexander Zahlten's chapter probes the coincidence of the rise of the academic media celebrity in early 1980s figures such as Asada Akira and Nakazawa Shinichi with a ten-year winter of media theory. Zahlten tracks the appearance of the so-called Nyū Aka theorists and the discourse around these massively popular best-selling authors, who were in such high demand in print, TV, and radio of the 1980s. He argues that while in a transitional moment—the effects of which are still felt today—Nyū Aka seemingly never formulated a theory of media, and that the reason for this is to be found in the manner in which the group changed the mode of theorizing itself: Nyū Aka performed a media theory rather than formulating one. A central aspect of this practice as media theory is the concept of irony as it was employed by Asada and fellow Nyū Aka writer Karatani Kōjin. Irony, by softening up the relation between content and form, allowed this group to play with the semantics of theory while actually enacting a theory of media in practice.

Ryoko Misono focuses on the body of work of the popular media figure, TV critic, and eraser-stamp artist Nancy Seki. An enormously prolific author writing about TV at exactly the moment its primacy in the media ecology of Japan began to wane, Seki developed a complex reservoir of self-reflexive tactics that included artistic practices that reference Warhol and deploy a sharp humor. Misono sees the late Seki as *enacting* a media theory that made heavy use of the tools of popular culture itself. As Misono outlines in her essay, Seki's tools were threefold: critical text; an "eraser print" illustration of a TV celebrity's face, based on a carving into the medium of the rubber eraser; and a short tagline included below the illustration. The three elements worked together to offer an immanent critique of television itself, circulated in the form of a weekly or monthly page-long magazine column. A singular figure within popular culture, Seki understood her work as dealing with media when there is no longer an outside to media. Misono examines Seki's concern with the question of what shape the public sphere takes in a mediatized society, and how to operate within media flows, all the while critiquing them.

Finally, Anne McKnight looks at how art practices in the 2010s are developing alternative modes of reflection on media. Focusing on the example of the artist Rokudenashiko, who was arrested for obscenity, McKnight specifically looks at ways in which Rokudenashiko circumvented the male-dominated space in which theorization has largely taken place in Japan—the space of hihyō that Keisuke Kitano outlines in his contribution to this volume. By using humor to work through issues of the commodified female body and the restrictive national role assigned to it, Rokudenashiko hit a nerve that provoked a state reaction. While Nancy Seki attempted to ironically reflect on the media system while deliberately positioning herself at its center, Rokudenashiko operates at its fringes, using its shrapnel to construct an alternative space. Referencing McKenzie Wark's concept of "low theory," McKnight maps one attempt to connect reflections on media models and gender roles to everydayness in ways that appear whimsical but are decidedly oppositional.

The final section, "Mediation and Media Theory," brings together four contributions that each engage with the fundamental questions of what mediation is and how to deal with it theoretically. What is a medium, and what are media? How can they be configured between materiality and metaphysics, between social reality and geopolitical power relations? The section begins with a contribution by one of the foremost Japanese media theorists today, Akihiro Kitada, a central figure of the "thought of the aughts" generation. Kitada's chapter offers a close and unique reading of the media theory of Nakai Masakazu, a leftist theorist with some connections to the Kyoto school (a philosophical movement of the 1930s and 1940s), and later head of the National Diet Library. Nakai draws on German philosophy to create a highly corporeal theory of cinematic spectatorship, a sophisticated communal model of how we make sense of filmic media that stands in productive tension with today's phenomenological and embodied approaches to film. Nakai is often considered the Walter Benjamin of Japan—for reasons that will be made apparent in Kitada's essay. He was fascinated by the new medium of the cinema, and deeply involved in thinking through the kind of political potential this medium could have. Kitada's essay on Nakai points to the latter's development of the German concept of the *Mittel*, which becomes the basis for an embodied theory of media effects. For Nakai, the disjunctures of meaning that media create are bridged by audiences/users, who intuitively and physically adjust to the common experience of media. Kitada goes on to outline how Nakai both prefigures important developments in Euro-American media theory by decades, and can at the same time still function as an important stimulus for thinking about media today.

Fabian Schäfer's chapter reenvisions the philosophy of the Kyoto school—which for many has problematically become a metonym of philosophy in

Japan—as a philosophy of mediation, or what in German is called *Medi-enphilosophie*, which we may provisionally translate as "media philosophy." Schäfer provides an overview of early debates on mediation and distills many of the conceptual stakes of media theory that philosophers in 1930s Japan prepared, addressing the work of central figures such as Nishida Kitarō, Tanabe Hajime, Tosaka Jun, and Nakai Masakazu, as well as that of the sometimes marginalized figures of Watsuji Tetsurō and Kimura Bin—most of whose work dates to the prewar and wartime eras. In this very unusual perspective, Schäfer suggests that these thinkers' work on mediation and in-betweenness is in fact a full-fledged theory of mediation that in turn forms the basis for a media philosophy (with a strong allusion to the term "media philosophy" in the German context). This novel rereading of the central figures of the Kyoto school suggests that their work should be reevaluated as central to the media theory that came after it.

Kitano Keisuke then focuses our attention on the literary sphere, in order to explore how questions of media theorization were framed. It is to the key figure of the mid-twentieth-century critic Kobayashi Hideo that Kitano turns to investigate the status of a particular kind of media critique in the 1950s, focusing on Kobayashi's approach to media such as photography and cinema through the genre of criticism known as hihyō. Hihyō and its conventions have defined the larger part of public intellectual discourse in Japan since the 1930s, and inevitably shaped most of the discussions of media presented in this volume. Taking place mostly in magazines and journals and situated somewhere between criticism and academic theory, hihyō was tailored to the needs and speeds of a massively productive print culture. As conceived of by Kobayashi, it deals fundamentally with the question of how to use language and thought that is always-already-hybrid in order to consider the specific location of modern Japan. Put differently, Kobayashi grapples with the complex question of how to talk about media in Japan when the technology/medium of language and theory already operates with gears and screws that are not entirely "made in Japan." Kitano thereby shifts our attention from the sphere of high philosophy to that of literary critique and the attempts of public intellectuals from the literary establishment to find another site of media theorization—albeit a more vernacular one.

Thomas Looser closes the section with a review of media theory from the 1980s to the 2010s, and a return to a consideration of theories of mediation—this time in the contemporary moment, and in relation to questions of social change. Looser considers how media theory and the possibilities it offers has in Japan always been tied to a crisis in thinking about possible social orders and subjectivity. Focusing on the "lost decades" and the sense of crisis that began in the 1990s and gained a new sense of urgency with the meltdown at the Fukushima Daiichi reactor, he follows especially the work of Azuma Hiroki. Looser detects shifts in the way Azuma and his group deal with the problem of mediation and suggests that these shifts are closely tied to the manner in which media technology and social change are thought together. At the same time, Looser tracks the role of media theory as an indicator of social change, demonstrating how the presuppositions underlying media theory have transformed from the economic boom time of the 1980s to recessionary, post-Fukushima Japan. In so doing, Looser brings to the surface the (otherwise implicit) theories of mediation that structure the work of contemporary media theorists such as Azuma, Kitada, and others.

This volume concludes with an afterword by Mark Hansen, whose work on media theory has been germane to and inspirational for this volume. Hansen acutely engages with the essays in this volume by rethinking their organization and the possibilities this reorganization offers. Beginning with the significant tension between the intra- and transcultural he finds underlying the volume's stress on media theory *in Japan*, Hansen rearranges the contributions into three "modes": "Remediating the West," "Mediatizing Japan," and "Inter-izing (beyond) Japan." By doing so he draws out possibilities of speaking to specificity of media and media theorization while taking the movement across contexts into account. It is in this negotiation, which he distills out of a careful rereading or rather additive reading of this volume's contributions, that he locates ways to consider the concrete manifestations of the "continuum of life in the age of global media."

To close this outline of the volume's contributions, we end with its opening, or rather, the preface, written by Akira Mizuta Lippit, whose work has consistently operated as theory at the borders and interstices of Japanese and North American academies. Like Hansen, Lippit emphasizes the many valences and crisscrossing passageways the "in" Japan indicates. Far from proposing a closed national boundary, Lippit underlines how he sees the project of the volume pointing to an out, or rather "an inside-out as much as an outside-in." This spatial dynamic, according to Lippit, plays out on the background not only of media and their theorization from different times but also of the different temporalities they respectively are charged with: "The task then may lie in finding the temporality that allows the incommensurate temporalities that define the media to interface, to encounter one another in a temporality other than one's own." It is an encounter that is in Lippit's view both necessarily overdue and timely.

Conclusion

These, then, are the parameters of this volume, one that attempts to be capacious in its coverage of time period and eras, but also focused in its concern for key debates within media theory in Japan. However inclusive we may have aspired to be, we cannot claim adequate *coverage*. Indeed, a mere list of what is left out would itself take a dedicated chapter. Or two. It would include, for instance, a discussion of the interaction of media theorization with Japanese colonialism or a more sustained engagement with the influential postwar *Shisō no kagaku* movement of the 1950s (which both Gerow and Furuhata touch upon in the course of their essays); the encounter of free radio, radical Marxist media theory, and Deleuzoguattarian thought in the persons of Kogawa Tetsuo and Ueno Toshiya; a close examination of the feminist media work of Ueno Chizuko in the 1980s and 1990s; theories arising from authors/fans/theorists such as Ozaki Midori (in the 1930s) and Nakajima Azusa (in the 1980s/1990s); the move toward dialogues around media within Asia in the 1990s and 2000s via the Inter-Asia Cultural Studies collective, with key figures such as Yoshimi Shunya, Chen Kuan-Hsing, and Chua Beng Huat, or, later, Kim So-Young with the TransAsia Screen Culture project, moving discussions of media beyond the nation-state and to questions of the regional—and this is just to scratch the surface. All of these specific moments will in turn provide intersections with larger developments and spheres of study. Many of the above cases would allow for a much-needed foray into the exploration of the role of sound, for example—from the role of music on the street to avant-garde music's role within 1960s experimental media cultures in Jikken Kobo and at the Sogetsu Art Center to the central role of popular music in the media mix, and from sound demonstrations to ambient sound design to contemporary idol culture. This volume tendentially weighs itself toward discourses in and through print and visual culture primarily to provide a focused point of departure (in several senses) for such investigations in the near future.[34]

This also brings us to the issue of media forms covered in this volume. As we noted earlier, this volume opts for thinking media as more than (to quote Mitchell and Hansen again) "a plurality of mediums, an empirical accumulation of things" (*Critical Terms*, xxi). As such, the essays in this volume do not treat individual media as a set of channels or technologies to be covered each in turn. The reader will not find a procession of media commodities or institutions, from woodblock prints to newspaper to film to radio to film to video, and so on, each afforded a distinct chapter. That said, despite being thought of as always-already-relational, the contributions in this volume do provide a plurality of media forms to be considered, from television through architecture and the medium of a journal. Insofar as the particular materiality of a given medium lends greatly to the manner in which it is theorized, a consideration of multiple distinct media forms (and their effects on the manner of their theorization) *is* nonetheless fruitful, if provisional. A particularly underrepresented medium that has been subject to vibrant theorization is film itself; we omit a close discussion of film because there has been such impressive work on it already, and additional work being prepared.[35] The body of work existing and forthcoming on film in particular reduces the urgency for this volume to focus on the question of the theorization of film, even if it does play a large role in the background.

The chapters within this volume both introduce key moments of media theorization in Japan and pose questions relevant to media theory in general (that is, media theory both in Japan and outside of it). This work is a beginning, and the issues, movements, and events within Japanese media theory that we have not been able to discuss will, we hope, be the subject of subsequent study that further expands what we understand by media theory in Japan, and what we include as media theory in this volume. We hope that this volume both initiates and continues a move toward a more nuanced and less geopolitically centered conception of media theory. It hopefully stands alongside other emerging nationally, regionally, or transnationally conceived accounts of media theory that will write not only the history of media theory more or less known to media studies in North America and Europe but also those histories that are not yet known, thereby transforming once again our established understanding of what media theory is. But "discovery" is not the impetus that can drive such a project. Rather it is the expectation of increased engagement, interaction, and ultimately intra-action (to abuse Karen Barad's term) between contexts of theorization. Together the essays here represent, we hope, a moment on the road to developing an organic or useable definition of globally situated media theorization. Geographically situated but constantly intra-acting media infrastructures, after all, determine our situation. And media theories that respond to this situation remain one of our central tools for describing, critiquing, and transforming it.

NOTES

1. For an exemplary text in this regard, see Alexander R. Galloway, Eugene Thacker, and McKenzie Wark, *Excommunication: Three Inquiries in Media and Mediation* (Chicago: University of Chicago Press, 2014).

2. Think of the fruitful influence of a materialist strain of media theory that initially entered English-language scholarship through the reception of Friedrich Kittler's work, and the further interaction of that line of media theory with more recent work often subsumed under New Materialism, such as Jussi Parikka, *A Geology of Media* (Minneapolis: University of Minnesota Press, 2015).

3. The opposition—and complicity—between theory and history that Yoshimoto isolates in his earlier critique in "The Difficulty of Being Radical" (251–52) is rearticulated as the distinction between Western *theory* and non-Western ("Japanese, Taiwanese or Indonesian") *text* in his extension of this important work in *Kurosawa: Film Studies and Japanese Cinema*, 36–37. For the original essay, see Mitsuhiro Yoshimoto, "The Difficulty of Being Radical," *boundary 2* 18, no. 3 (fall 1991): 242–57; and for its extension, see Mitsuhiro Yoshimoto, *Kurosawa: Film Studies and Japanese Cinema* (Durham, NC: Duke University Press, 2000).

4. Aaron Gerow, "Introduction: The Theory Complex," *Review of Japanese Culture and Society* 22 (December 2010): 2.

5. Umesao Tadao established the term in *Jōhō Sangyō-ron* [The theory of the information industry, 1963], and was possibly influenced by Fritz Machlup's *The Production and Distribution of Knowledge in the United States* (Princeton, NJ: Princeton University Press, 1962). The expression "information society" (*jōhō shakai*) gained currency in articles from 1967 onwards, and especially in Masuda Yoneji's *Jōhō shakai nyūmon: Konpyūta wa ningen shakai wo kaeru* [Introduction to information society: Computers transform human society] (Tokyo: Pelican, 1968), while "informationalizing society" became an important term from Hayashi Yūjirō's *Jōhōka shakai: Hādo na shakai kara sofuto na shakai e* [Information society: From hard society to soft society] (Tokyo: Kōdansha Gendai Shinsho, 1969) onward. See also Tessa Morris-Suzuki, *Beyond Computopia: Information, Automation, and Democracy in Japan* (New York: Kegan Paul, 1988).

6. Galloway, Thacker, and Wark, *Excommunication*, 5.

7. Unsurprisingly, important work in these areas is emerging. See, for instance, Weihong Bao, *Fiery Cinema: The Emergence of an Affective Medium in China* (Minneapolis: University of Minnesota Press, 2015); Victor Fan, *Cinema Approaching Reality* (Minneapolis: University of Minnesota Press, 2015); Bhaskar Sarkar, *Mourning the Nation: Indian Cinema in the Wake of Partition* (Durham, NC: Duke University Press, 2009); and Kay Dickinson, *Arab Cinema Travels: Syria, Palestine, Dubai, and Beyond* (London: British Film Institute, 2016). While not engaging media theory per se, an important challenge to rethinking the boundaries of theory comes in the way of Françoise Lionnet and Shu-mei Shih's edited collection, *The Creolization of Theory* (Durham: Duke University Press, 2011).

8. Johannes Fabian, *Time and Its Other: How Anthropology Makes Its Object* (New York: Columbia University Press, 1983).

9. This reason for the lag in translation for the Manovich book was suggested to us by Kadobayashi Takeshi.

10. David Rodowick, *Elegy for Theory* (Cambridge, MA: Harvard University Press, 2014), 3.

11. Lev Manovich, "Postmedia Aesthetics," in *Transmedia Frictions: The Digital, the Arts, and the Humanities*, ed. Marsha Kinder and Tara McPherson (Oakland: University of California Press, 2014), 34–44.

12. W. J. T. Mitchell and Mark B. N. Hansen, *Critical Terms for Media Studies* (Chicago: University of Chicago Press, 2010), xiii.

13. Friedrich Kittler, *Gramophone, Film, Typewriter,* trans. Geoffrey Winthrop-Young (Stanford, CA: Stanford University Press, 1999), xxxix; quoted in Mitchell and Hansen, *Critical Terms,* vii.

14. Mitchell and Hansen, *Critical Terms,* xxii.

15. The exception to this slant is found in David Graeber's and Lydia H. Liu's contributions, which, while evoking a wider geography, refer to these places in relation to their past (in the history of exchange in Graeber's case, and the history of writing in Liu's). This unfortunately reproduces the sense of West as present, and Rest as past.

16. For an early, incisive critique on the consumption of theory as a commodity in Japan, see Marilyn Ivy, "Critical Texts, Mass Artifacts: The Consumption of Knowledge in Postmodern Japan," in *Postmodernism and Japan*, ed. Masao Miyoshi and Harry D. Harootunian (Durham, NC: Duke University Press, 1989).

17. Kuan-Hsing Chen, *Asia as Method* (Durham, NC: Duke University Press, 2010), 211–55. This volume is directly influenced by the growing number of books in the field of Japanese cinema that put the theoretical into the history of the discipline, such as Thomas Lamarre, *Shadows on the Screen: Tanizaki Jun'ichirō on Cinema and "Oriental" Aesthetics* (Ann Arbor: University of Michigan, 2005); Markus Nornes, *Cinema Babel: Translating Global Cinema* (Minneapolis: University of Minnesota Press, 2007); Aaron Gerow, ed., "Decentering Theory: Reconsidering the History of Japanese Film Theory," special issue, *Review of Japanese Culture and Society* 22 (December 2010); Yuriko Furuhata, *Cinema of Actuality: Japanese Avant-Garde Filmmaking in the Season of Image Politics* (Durham, NC: Duke University Press, 2013). This project began to take on its current form at the Histories of Film Theories in East Asia conference organized by Nornes and held at the University of Michigan, Ann Arbor, September 27–30, 2012.

18. Geoffrey Winthrop-Young, *Kittler and the Media* (Cambridge, UK: Polity Press, 2011), 2.

19. The journal had a five-volume run, and was published biannually from 2008 until 2010, when Kitada split off from the project and Azuma continued the journal under the name *Shisō chizu β*.

20. This approach has been adopted more recently in relation to North American geek or hacker culture. See in this regard Christopher Kelty, *Two Bits: The Cultural Significance of Free Software* (Durham, NC: Duke University Press, 2008); and Gabriella Coleman, *Coding Freedom: The Ethics and Aesthetics of Hacking* (Princeton, NJ: Princeton University Press, 2013).

21. Geert Lovink, interview by Peter Lunenfeld, "Enemy of Nostalgia: Victim of the Present, Critic of the Future: Interview with Geert Lovink," *PAJ: A Journal of Performance and Art 70* 24, no. 1 (January 2002): 8; Jeffrey Sconce, *Haunted Media: Electronic Presence from Telegraphy to Television* (Durham, NC: Duke University Press, 2000), 181.

22. Yet even as the zeronendai functioned as an initial motivating factor for this project, it also continues to work as a cautionary tale against setting up this recent effervescence of media theory in Japan as the end point in the narrative here.

23. Terry Eagleton, *After Theory* (New York: Basic Books, 2003), 2, 17.

24. Matt Hills, "Strategies, Tactics and the Question of *Un Lieu Propre*: What/Where Is 'Media Theory'?" in *Social Semiotics* 14, no. 2 (2004): 133–49.

25. Françoise Lionnet and Shu-mei Shih, "Introduction: The Creolization of Theory," in Françoise Lionnet and Shu-mei Shih, ed. *The Creolization of Theory* (Durham: Duke University Press, 2011).

26. See John Guillory, "Genesis of the Media Concept," *Critical Inquiry* 36, no. 2 (winter 2010): 321–62.

27. Nick Couldry offers a useful synopsis of the institutional history of media studies in "Theorizing Media as Practice," *Social Semiotics* 14, no. 2 (2004): 116.

28. John Caldwell, *Production Culture: Industrial Reflexivity and Critical Practice in Film and Television* (Durham, NC: Duke University Press, 2008), 9.

29. For a consideration of Ozaki's work, see Livia Monnet, "Montage, Cinematic Subjectivity and Feminism in Ozaki Midori's *Drifting in the World of the Seventh Sense*," *Japan Forum* 11, no. 1 (1999): 57–82.

30. For an excellent overview of the debates around shinbungaku, see Fabian Schäfer, *Tosaka Jun: Ideologie, Medien, Alltag* (Leipzig, Ger.: Leipziger Universitätsverlag, 2011).

31. For a thorough outline of the discourses around the term *eizō*, see Furuhata, *Cinema of Actuality*.

32. Dudley Andrew offers a brief overview of the history of film studies in Japan in "The Core and the Flow of Film Studies," *Critical Inquiry* 35 (summer 2009): 885–87.

33. The reader may, of course, choose to read it that way, in which case we would advise reading in the following order: Akihiro Kitada, Fabian Schäfer, Keisuke Kitano, Aaron Gerow, Marc Steinberg, Yuriko Furuhata, Miryam Sas, Tomiko Yoda, Alexander Zahlten, Ryoko Misono, Marilyn Ivy, Takeshi Kadobayashi, Tom Looser, and Anne McKnight.

34. Moreover, a large body of work on sound and music exists for such explorations to draw on; research by such scholars as Hosokawa Shūhei, Michael Bourdaghs, Mori Yasutaka, David Novak, Sasaki Atsushi, and others already provides an immensely fertile ground for future work.

35. The special issue on film theory in Japan in the *Review of Japanese Culture and Society* (December 2010), guest edited by Aaron Gerow, stands as an immensely important intervention that explores the question of what theory means in the context of Japan as much as how it manifests vis-à-vis film. The forthcoming edited collection on film theory in Japan by Markus Nornes and Aaron Gerow will add even further to the discussion of film and its theorization.

I. COMMUNICATION TECHNOLOGIES

1. FROM FILM TO TELEVISION

Early Theories of Television in Japan

AARON GEROW

Repeating Theory

Lev Manovich has already speculated in *The Language of New Media* about the parallels between the historical development of new media and that of older media such as cinema,[1] but I would like to explore possible parallels between the histories of theories of a new media, here television in Japan, and those of a previous media, the motion pictures. New media are new to the degree that they are accompanied by a theoretical apparatus that stakes out their claims to newness, but just as Wendy Hui Kyong Chun has underlined, the meaning of "new" itself often "contains within itself repetition," as something is *re*-newed only after it has become old in a cycle that manifests itself through planned obsolescence and endless upgrades.[2] Theories too may replicate this repeated newness when they name the new, but likely again in a cycle of theory becoming—or being—outdated and then novel.[3] Peter Krapp suggests as much when he argues that claims made about new modes such as hypertextuality either forget precomputer hypertextual modes such as the card index, or seem to recall the past as a confirmation of the digital present: "Recollection becomes oblivion, the interface-principle WYSIWYG becomes WYSIWYF: what you see is what you (for)get."[4]

One can see similar repetitions in Japanese film theory and Japanese television theory in their early stages, even when the latter was contrasted with the "old" as a "new" media. Not only were there analogous efforts at arguing media specificity, comparing the new to the old, particularly through the issue of the relation of image to spectator, but also claims about the specificity of the new that, it was forgotten, were already made of the old. Such parallels, I would argue, not only problematize arguments about the new and about medium specificity, but they can also, through close analysis, show how claims about new media can serve to mask larger continuities in the struggles over media in industrial capitalism. In Japan in particular, theories of film and television were deeply imbricated with historically specific but long-standing conflicts over problems of class, mass society, the everyday (*nichijō*), theory, and the place of the intellectual.

Shisō and Shimizu Ikutarō on Television

As was also the case with film, discourses about television preceded the existence of the medium as a real presence. As Jayson Makoto Chun has summarized, prewar writings about television emphasized its ability to establish connections with the West, and bring the outside into the domestic sphere. Its utility for education and for national or imperial unity was also stressed, as well as its importance as a gauge of national progress.[5] These were all arguments made for cinema in its first decades as well.[6] What was different was television's potential for live simultaneity, but that was a claim already made about radio. Chun argues that discussions of radio actually laid the foundations of prewar television discourse, even as prewar discussions of television then established the basis for postwar television theory.

Writings on television increased after the war, especially after broadcasting truly began in 1953. Journalistic discourse concerning the medium was in many ways epitomized by Ōya Sōichi's expression of frustration in 1957 that through television Japan would become a nation of "100 million idiots" (*ichioku sōhakuchika*)[7]—a phrase that became such common currency that it even appears in Ozu Yasujirō's *Good Morning* (*Ohayō*, 1959), a film that centers on two boys who start a protest to get a TV set. Other scholarly writings would be less alarmist, even as they attempted to specify what was particularly new or problematic about the medium. Arguably, the first major milestone in television theory was the November 1958 issue of *Shisō* (Thought)—perhaps the premier intellectual journal at the time—an issue that declared itself the start of television studies and which, as Yoshimi Shun'ya claims, proved "a major influence on subsequent television research."[8] Authors included not only such established sociologists, psychologists, and culture critics as Shimizu Ikutarō, Hidaka Rokurō, Hatano Kanji, and Min-ami Hiroshi, but also names such as Katō Hidetoshi, Arase Yutaka, and Inaba Michio that would later dominate mass communication research in Japan. The variety of writers included the film critic Uryū Tadao, the film and liter-ary critic Sasaki Kiichi, and even literary giants Nakamura Mitsuo and Abe Kōbō.

Shimizu's essay "Terebijon jidai" (The Television Age), which appeared as the leadoff batter in the issue, was in many ways seminal; *Shisō* even re-printed the piece in its 2003 issue commemorating the semicentennial of television broadcasting. Analyzing it, along with some of Shimizu's other television essays ("Terebi no honshitsu" [The Essence of Television], an *Asahi shinbun* essay from 1957; and "Terebi bunmeiron" [On TV Civilization], pub-lished a few months before his "Terebijon jidai" piece in *Kinema junpō*), I will consider how Shimizu's focus on medium specificity, audience behavior, and the everyday is emblematic of early approaches to television, while also being oblivious to how early texts of film theory treated the same issues.

Shimizu was a prominent leftist sociologist who was active from before the war in such organizations as the Yuibutsuron Kenkyūkai (Materialism Study Group). In such books as *Ryūgen higo* (*Rumors*, 1937), he had already voiced his concerns about the interactions between official and unofficial communication. Investigating the phenomenon of rumors after such events as the 1923 Kantō earthquake, Shimizu considered how breaks in official news information could be filled by unofficial flows of information among the masses, ones that could be both resistive and reactionary. While rumors were by definition without basis in fact, they could serve as social modes of belief that functioned as an alternative to inadequate official announce-ments. Shimizu thus distinguished between rumors born from the masses in crisis and those purposely created to foment unrest, even as he described how rumors could be manipulated or controlled through information.

Shimizu did not see television's flow of communication as either estab-lishing the rule of facts or enabling horizontal modes of social belief. He primarily considered television in contrast to printed media. Both may be mass media, but Shimizu saw a fundamental difference between reading and viewing. Reading, he argued, requires energy and concentration because the book does not provide the reality beforehand: the reader must construct it. Television viewing however, "starts from the image that appears at the end of the act of reading," leaving the viewer "excused from the hard work involved in creating and supporting reality by oneself."[9] A reader can stop reading in order to avoid being overwhelmed by the reality of the book, meaning "one can desire only the degree of reality that fits one's capacity." That is why Shimizu thought that the pressure to reform or reconstruct one's sense of self (*jiko no kaizō*) rarely occurs with reading, since there is always a critical space for the reader to negotiate such forces.[10] Television, however, is "forceful," refusing to allow a critical space for negotiation; instead, "the entire person is absorbed" and possibly reconstructed.[11] The book remains in hand, available for critical reflection, while "the television program only exists on a metaphysical level," leaving no evidence behind after viewing that can be used for critique. To Shimizu, this indicates that "the transition from the age of printing to the age of images is the transition from an era where we possess the evidence to one where evidence is taken from us."[12] He associates this with the rise of monopoly capitalism. While he recognizes the potential of television, given its forcefulness, to deeply penetrate the viewer if and when it did actually engage in critique of the current situation, he believes neither commercial television nor Nihon Hōsō Kyōkai (Japan Broadcasting Corporation) (NHK) would allow that.[13] Given the capital involved, "the more advanced a media is, the easier it is for its content to become conservative or reactionary."[14]

To Shimizu, television is the culmination of capitalistic mass communication. Earlier commentators on television, such as Kamimura Shin'ichi, had argued that the new medium represented the revival of the family, as fathers supposedly ceased seeking entertainment outside the home in bars or at the movies, and returned to the bosom of their family.[15] To such theorists, argues Shimizu, mass communication is what removes the individual from the home and melds them into the mass. The motion pictures are purportedly the epitome of this, but to Shimizu, cinema actually represents an inadequate development of mass communication. If the history of the movies were likened to that of soap, cinema would be like women going to the village center to wash clothes together, and television would be like mass-produced soap, which everyone can bring home to use.[16] People come home because television has succeeded in the true mass production and distribution of symbols. Quoting Günther Anders, Shimizu says turning on the TV is like "turning on a cultural faucet," making television equivalent to modern utilities.[17] To Anders, this had profound implications: "If the world comes to us instead of we to it, then we are no longer in the world. Instead we are merely spoiled consumers in the world. . . . If the world comes to us as an image, then it is partially present and partially absent, thus a phantom or illusion."[18] Shimizu does not go as far as Anders—concluding that through television humanity loses the world through a form of idealism—in part because he wants to maintain a space for individuated reading. Still, the critique resembles Anders's. The problem is that the return to the home does not entail a new life for the family: under the power of the image, "they have come closer spatially, but they do not face or talk to each other.... People have not returned home from the movie theater; the relationship between screen and audience has instead occupied the inside of the home."[19]

To the sociologist Shimizu, this constitutes a problem. Resonating with what Jürgen Habermas was writing about at the same time regarding media and the public sphere, Shimizu saw the home as ideally a space free of society, where the individual could become "zero." "Human beings can restore their selves for the first time at the moment they become zero to society,"[20] gaining the time and freedom to complain about society. While he does not, like Habermas, theorize a space of discourse between the private and the public that can serve to mediate and check the two, Shimizu does share Habermas's worries that new media dissolve the boundaries between public and private, facilitating both the invasion of the private by the public, as well as the publicization of a reduced form of the private.[21] Television to Shimizu now structures that once-free time, leaving little opportunity for people to develop critical perspectives. "The human being that had become zero is now again absorbed through the television set in what is external to the home." For Shimizu, a socialist, "Television cannot permit the conditions that foster the roots of revolution."[22]

Before considering what Shimizu may propose as a solution to these problems, let us dissect whatever distinction he might make between the new and old media of film and television, focusing first on his contention that "people have not returned home from the movie theater; the relationship between screen and audience has instead occupied the inside of the home." Despite asserting that the need to collectively watch images in a dark theater was a mark of the underdevelopment of cinema as mass communication, Shimizu essentially contends that the relationship of image to viewer does not change when the screen enters the home. This does not mean he finds no difference between film and television. While admitting he was not much of a moviegoer, he said that the confusion he experienced emerging from the dark symbolic space of cinema into the real world did not last long. Television, however, is on all the time one is not at work or sleeping, making unclear what is fiction and what is reality. This is even more the case with the realistic world of color television: "The vibrant world of television itself becomes reality, and the faded world that contradicts that becomes fiction. We will live under the rule of appearances."[23]

For Shimizu, then, the difference between film and television is primarily a matter of location and frequency. If film consumed as much time in the day as television, viewers would presumably experience the same rule of appearances. The real difference between film and television viewing lies less in the nature of the medium than in its space; the fact that television is, unlike film, viewed in quotidian space makes frequent viewing more likely, a condition that ultimately undermines the distinction between the image and everyday life. The everydayness of television, from its location to its repetitiveness, was to Shimizu more central in defining the medium than its technology.

The Everyday in Film and Television

Not all of Shimizu's contemporaries concurred with his assertion that there was an essential similarity between film and television. The majority were engaged in a medium-specific argument about the apparatus of television, even as they, like Shimizu, could argue that the effect of television can vary depending on how it was received. Most did echo Shimizu's focus on the everyday and contended that television's form of reception was fundamentally different. Katō Hidetoshi, who published his own book, *Terebi jidai* (*The Television Age*, 1958), the same year, argued that if all popular arts up until then were arts of the crowd (*gunshū geijutsu*), television involved the small group.[24] This could disrupt the absorption in the image Shimizu presumed was equal between film and television. Sasaki Kiichi contended that the multiple viewers in the home put a brake on one-way communication, in the sense that, even if family members did not always talk together as they watched, there was a kind of "unconscious communication" between viewers, forming a distance that could enable greater control of television and occasional critique.[25] Minami Hiroshi went so far as to argue that this was precisely the problem with television from the standpoint of developmental psychology. If identification is crucial to the process of subject formation, then television viewing thwarts this by occurring in a place where identification is often disrupted by the disturbances of family members and domestic activities. Minami even suggested having a television for each family member as a way to prevent this.[26]

Conceptions of the effects of television viewing on quotidian life may have differed, but most agreed on the central relation between the new medium and the everyday. Katō in particular defined television through the everyday—not only its content and place, but even its form of reception, he argued, is that of everyday life. Focusing on the relationship between the performer and the spectator, Katō argues that television renders spectating, which in the age of the massification of spectatorship still necessitated proactively going to see something, into an activity that requires no special effort: one just remains at home and watches TV "because it's there." "The unique characteristic of television as a form of entertainment," he writes, "can be found in its rendering spectatorship everyday."[27] Its relationship with quotidian life is both the danger and potential of television. To Katō, its ability to penetrate everyday existence provides it with considerable power, and could lead to the establishment of fascism in a time of peace. But its allegiance with an everyday that is not planned or scripted—evident in both documentary and sports programming—makes television a medium centered on realism, in contrast to the printing press, which developed out of fiction.[28]

Whether writers see this relation to the everyday as positive or negative, they usually use the everyday to contrast television with cinema. Shimizu aligns cinema and television as image media against print media, but then consigns cinema to incompleteness because it has not penetrated the everyday world on a massive scale. Katō sees cinema spectators entering a fictional world in such a way that they are incapable of relating it to an everyday context.[29] And to Minami, television, unlike film, "does not leave the fiction world to be as it is, but rather crams fiction into the quotidian world and makes it recognized as part of the everyday."[30]

Reading these accounts, one encounters early formations of many of the ideas that would dominate later accounts of television, but it is important to stress their historical contingency. First, the association of television with the everyday and the home was based on an ideologically refracted view of the contemporary situation. In 1958, a major sector of the Japanese population did not view television in the home but at television sets located in public spaces such as train stations or cafés. As Yoshimi Shun'ya argues, the association of television with the home is a historical construction that involved forgetting television's history of being viewed by anonymous crowds outside the home.[31] This selective view of the historical context was in part class-based. When Katō argues that the content of television is the everyday, he does so by claiming that viewers recognize a certain reality in its content, seeing in home dramas, for instance, "the same furniture or dishes" or finding "little separation between the conversation of a mother and daughter sitting there and that found in a real home."[32] Yet in November 1958, still only 8.2 percent of Japanese households had a television set: it was still a luxury that even the middle class could not yet acquire.[33] In television theory, however, we already see the construction of both the television audience and the Japanese as uniformly middle class, at the cost of ignoring significant sectors of the populace. Furthermore, considering that in 1958 a major portion of television programming was foreign, the claim that Japanese would see themselves in *Father Knows Best* makes sense only if one adopted a deterministic vision of the televisual apparatus that in practically imperial fashion ignored geopolitical difference.

This vision in part resulted from the fact that many Japanese scholars of television, like Katō, were schooled in American communication studies.[34] Shimizu was often ambivalent, both criticizing the capitalist Cold War geopolitics of the United States—sometimes through the lens of Marxism and European critical theory—while also using American sociology and Deweyan pragmatism as the basis on which he built his arguments.[35] Other authors in the *Shisō* issue, however, repeatedly cite some of the major contemporary American academic research of mass media and society, such as that of Paul Lazarsfeld, Bernard Berelson, David Riesman, Reuel Denney, and Leo Bogart. Although Japanese social scientists had closer ties to Marxism than their American counterparts, they also, like the Americans, seemed to have shifted the object of media research from propaganda to mass communications, a concept that, especially under the limited effects model, considered the mass to be less a broad and long-term social phenomena than an accumulation of levels of personal influence and short-term minimal effects. Several of the writers in the *Shisō* issue, including Katō, Minami, and Hidaka Rokurō, were members of Shisō no Kagaku (Institute of Science of Thought), a long-lasting postwar research group that, while eclectic in politics and methodology, largely focused on "studying the philosophy of the common man"—that is, the ideas borne by the average Japanese.[36] Even though they could often produce bottom-up conceptions of cultural production, and use these to promote the reform of Japanese society—a reform-mindedness that Katō thought distinguished Japanese communication studies from those of America[37]—this reform was usually modeled on a modernization thesis grounded in American social science.

It may not be easy to claim of Japanese scholars that they were, as Timothy Glander and others have charged of American media researchers, shifting from propaganda to mass communications research in order to protect television—and the media corporations they had financial ties to—from criticism as propaganda, thereby providing cover for more precise manipulations of media by Cold War industries and governments.[38] Some, like

Minami, were supported by sectors of the media industry, however.[39] As a whole, Japanese television researchers were operating in a space in which Japanese television was deeply imbricated in Cold War politics, as recent research on the relations between Matsutarō Shoriki (the head of the Yomiuri media conglomerate and founder of NTV (Nippon Television Network), the first commercial television broadcaster) and the CIA shows.[40] While their positions do not neatly map onto the American debates over media effects—"limited effects" versus the "hypodermic" model—their writings could reflect how the contingency of American TV studies came to claim the essence of television theory, and thus how much Japanese television theory, as with the Japanese TV industry, was shaped by Cold War visions.

Forgetting Theory

Japanese researchers seem not only to be wearing the blinkers of American theory, they also appear to be forgetting Japanese prewar media theory as well. Katō's history of communication research in Japan, written in 1959, declares that "the study of communication did not develop" before the war because of the lack of free speech and an obsession with foreign theory.[41] The line thus drawn at 1945 helps valorize postwar media research as democratic and homegrown, but effaces continuities and the fact that, in this case, many early television commentators echoed statements originally made about cinema. Minami Hiroshi's arguments about identification, for instance, while cloaked in the discourse of developmental psychology, essentially replicate the efforts of the Pure Film Movement in the 1910s to create a mode of film-spectator relations that would allow for deep interactions with the image, in part through attempts to eliminate distractions in the theater (such as the benshi, or noisy spectators). Shimada Atsushi's arguments about television as art, while posing an intriguing thesis that it is the montage less of shots than of TV programs in the flow of the programming day that makes television artistic,[42] heavily depend on film theory and echo the position of such early aestheticians as Shimizu Hikaru that only montage enabled cinema to escape the mechanical reproduction of reality that Konrad Lange defined as antithetical to art.[43] Further, Yoshimura Tōru's argument that televisual signs are inadequate for transmitting concrete thought, and thus that print media should leave description to television while keeping the job of "forming consciousness" to itself, although based on a general argument about "image symbols" (eizō shinboru) that can include film, essentially replicates the claims made by Murayama Tomoyoshi and others over twenty years earlier about the "limitation" of cinema: film was too rooted in the visual and the bodily to depict psychology and complex ideas.[44]

What I would like to concentrate on here is how claims about television and the everyday tend to forget how theorists argued decades before for an essential relationship between cinema and the everyday. Gonda Yasunosuke was one of the first. *The Principles and Applications of the Moving Pictures* (*Katsudō shashin no genri oyobi ōyō*), published in 1914, described in cinema a cultural mode that not only aligns with the practical methods of understanding used by lower-class audiences but also creates "the value of everyday life," first, by enabling its audiences to become the subject of culture; second, by taking art (if not also scholarship) away from the halls of the elite, where in the Kantian dictum it was defined as "purposiveness without a purpose," and reinserting it in the world of practical value; and third, by bringing the everyday world into art (through photographic recording) and simultaneously allowing spectators to insert their everyday emotions and ideas into the film.[45] Unlike Shimizu Ikutarō's claims about the image, Gonda argued that viewing cinema required effort, as it was the spectator who supplied the silent film with sound, color, and three-dimensionality, "an unconscious but difficult task" that resulted in the viewer inserting not only their subjectivity but also, in contrast to Katō's claim, their everyday life into the film.[46]

Harry Harootunian has already described a number of prewar Japanese thinkers, from Kon Wajirō and Gonda Yasunosuke to Hirabayashi Hatsunosuke and Tosaka Jun, who looked to the category of everyday life as both a means of understanding modernity and an enabling concept for constructing a better present and future.[47] Against those who, like Yanagita Kunio and Watsuji Tetsurō, turned to an atemporal folk culture for an alternative to a modern everyday that temporalized everything, rendering all aspects of life in the present, these thinkers sought the possibilities entailed by newness, by a modern life that was novel because it was embodied by the manifestation of newness in everyday existence. The modern opened up novel personal worlds of experience, challenged existing social identities and relationships, and promised new realities that would be experienced in new ways. While this may seem to be a celebration of capitalism and commodity culture, to Harootunian, many of these thinkers believed that the difference between the abstract present of the commodity and the lived now of the everyday could enable a "revolution [that] came from *within* modernity" that could break the commodity form and resolve alienation.[48] I see a similar use of the everyday with film. Most of those thinking about the everyday wrote about film precisely because they saw it both as embodying the infusion of the modern into the everyday and as the primary means of expressing the novel forms of living found in the new everyday.

Gonda, for example, responded to efforts to forcibly locate cinema in districts (such as Asakusa) or in peripheral class cultures, first by reversing these spatial hierarchies, rendering the periphery the center, and second by then looking to the modern undermining of divisions of space, especially as enabled by capitalism, as a force breaking up even those hierarchies. Cinema became less an issue of space and territory than a question of time (the now), of experience, and of culture. Gonda was attempting to bring cinema back to the real world not by arguing for a realist style, or even for a realist aesthetic philosophy, but instead by arguing for an experiential realism, in which what mattered was less the ontological than the existential relation of film to reality. Cinema was conjoined with everyday reality more through the mediating actions of spectators making film part of their everyday existence than through textual style or technological indexicality. Cinema not only ceased to be confined to the realm of disinterested art, but it would also undermine all such art, and diffuse it throughout lived experience. Art itself would then cease to have a proper location but simply become part of life. Gonda, who had been trained in aesthetics at the University of Tokyo, wrote "about popular matters in a popular mode" in his first book in an attempt to also relocate theory.[49] If film entertainment returned culture to the everyday, his film study would take theory out of the ivory tower and bring it back to the realm of popular discourse.

Gonda was not alone in exploring the political possibilities of cinema's relation to the everyday. Modernists such as Hirabayashi Hatsunosuke, for instance, saw the machine art of cinema as less the domination of space than a means of eliminating the alienation between work and life, and of better presenting on-screen a more mechanized modern life through mechanical means.[50] Nakai Masakazu, whom Akihiro Kitada discusses in this volume, contemplated forms of "unmediated mediation" in which the masses' practically bodily interaction with cinema enabled them to fill in the gaps in such media with their world historical experience. The Marxist philosopher Tosaka Jun, who is the subject of Fabian Schäfer's chapter, offered probably the most suggestive ideas about epistemology and the cinema of everyday life. As Naoki Yamamoto has described them, Tosaka's essays on film treated motion pictures as an essentially epistemological problem,[51] and his concern was elucidating how cinema had its own means of presenting thought.[52] These means, Yamamoto argued, fundamentally revolved around everyday life, or *fūzoku*, as Tosaka called it. In the first place, cinema had a unique ability to inform people of their everyday life: "The screen," he wrote, "teaches humans about the *goodness of materiality*, the delight of the movement of matters in this world. These are the things we usually see in our daily life, but we haven't recognized their virtues until they appear on the screen."[53] It can do that precisely because cinema is the art of the everyday, presenting society in a sensual, not necessarily intellectual fashion, in such a way that society becomes visible in a concrete manner.[54] There is something reminiscent of André Bazin in Tosaka, especially when he focuses on cinema's unique ability to approximate everyday modes of perception: for him, "film's particular realism lies in where the actual reality of the real world becomes the aesthetic reality of the medium as it is . . . . Particular attractions of film are thus derived from a simple fact that on the screen we are able to see the world in the same manner as we observe it in reality."[55] With Tosaka, however, the manner in which we observe things in reality is not a natural mode of perception but rather one that is shaped by *fūzoku*, the manners and mores of everyday life particular to historical relations of production. Cinema does not just approximate modes of perceiving reality, it embodies a society's—to Tosaka, mostly the masses'—ways of both thinking and confirming itself, of articulating and knowing itself in a social fashion. Watching film is then a means of experiencing, embodying, and eventually knowing the social formulation of everyday life. This is not solipsistic idealism, but one fundamentally based on material modes of thinking, which is why Tosaka connects cinema to science. While Tosaka could not develop this idea before he was arrested (he eventually died in prison), others, such as Imamura Taihei, contemplated the possibility of cinema actually being a material mode of thinking that uses everyday things themselves as elements of thought.[56] This is one of the reasons that Imamura, the prominent theorist of documentary, was attracted to animation as a form: it enabled everyday objects in the world to expressively embody thought about the world.

A number of important early film theorists thus believed that the relation between cinema and the everyday was a fulcrum for overcoming alienation and rethinking art and epistemology. Why then did early television theorists forget these precedents, and then actually assert the opposite about cinema, relating the everyday to television instead? First, we must understand that this forgetting is not uncommon: as I have noted elsewhere, the history of Japanese film theory is plagued by such amnesia, especially as part of a "theory complex" that is crisscrossed by neocolonial anxieties and political ambivalences, in which Japanese theory is conceived as subordinate to that of the West, and thus not sufficiently theoretical to be included in the historical narratives of film theory.[57] Second, the conception of the relation of the image (*eizō*) to the everyday might also have changed over time, especially considering the claims made in the "eizō debates" of the late 1950s, in which some participants, such as Okada Susumu and Hani Susumu, argued that a new reality necessitated a new image, thus rewriting the image/everyday axis.[58] Similarly, and third, one could argue that the content and meaning of the "everyday" had also changed after the war. Gonda and Tosaka are primarily discussing a social phenomenon, seeing in the new mass and public forms of interaction a novel form of quotidian life that represented a transformative modernity. The everyday of Shimizu and Katō is largely the middle-class home, defined by its privacy and atomism. Postwar theorists were facing a bourgeois consumer culture on a scale quite different from what it had been before the war.

Fourth, this is the foundation for the everyday having taken on a more negative political valence. Shimizu prizes the sphere of intellectual reading, and sees in the mundane space of daily repetition an antithesis that television comes to represent. Sasaki warns that the flow of a speedy and efficient modernity has entered the mind through television. While hoping that developing new expressive forms based on nonwritten communication may help viewers "digest" television, he declares that it is "impossible for television in its current state to provide viewers with an experience of artistic stimulation." To him, even if "television is a need [*hitsuyōhin*] in everyday life, it is not a need for building a true human life."[59] Sasaki thus clearly distinguished between "real human life" and "everyday life," with contemporary television satisfying only the latter. One could find in postwar artistic intellectuals an increased suspicion of the everyday, fueled by anxiety about the spread of consumer mass culture, Cold War image politics, and disillusionment with the artistically conservative old Left. The promotion of avant-garde, experimental, or surrealist expressive forms by Haneda Kiyoteru or Matsumoto Toshio was aligned with the project of undermining conventionalized modes of seeing that had become quotidian.[60] Later on in television, Tahara Sōichirō's stance on documentary similarly sought to battle against the everyday, but from within, making the goal "to make a non-everyday space or way of life not outside the everyday but inside it. To drop out inside everyday life."[61] In these accounts, overcoming the everyday, not recuperating it, was the means of overcoming alienation.

This did not mean that the everyday was always a negative object. The end of the 1960s saw several attempts to reappropriate the everyday as a radical realm. The television director Wada Ben in his book *Engi to ningen* (*Acting and the Human*) theorized television as that which is severed from both cinema and history: the everyday flow of expression that is resistant to thought.[62] The founders of TV Man Union—Hagimoto Haruhiko, Muraki Yoshihiko, and Konno Tsutomu—concluded their famous TV manifesto, *Omae wa tada no genzai ni suginai* (*You Are Nothing but the Present*), with eighteen precepts, one of which touched on the everyday: "Television is the everyday [ke/nichijō]: Life itself—to both the senders and the receivers. The mundane [zoku]. The massive details up until the encounter with the divine. Drama with a date attached."[63] It was by being everyday that television could, to them, be a radical non-art, one defined by the present, the fluid, and the physical—by a kind of jazz. Miryam Sas, in this volume, discusses Konno's effort to seek out modes of thought within the "concrete, everyday labor process," a project that aligns with other attempts she describes to enact bodily modes of thinking and return to the physical everyday. One could argue, however, that this later reevaluation of the everyday is involved with yet another politics than that of 1950s television theory, one more closely associated with a late 1960s questioning of language and representation, particularly the attempts to rethink the relation of the individual to media she notes in Matsuda Masao and others. Given the shift from a positive to a more negative approach to media, the everyday was neither transformative modernity nor bourgeois torpidity but perhaps a last-ditch, positive, less mediated site for questioning the modern regimes of time and narrative.

Class and Everydayness of Theory

It is important to acknowledge these debates over and transformations in the use of the concept of the everyday. As Chun suggests, there is repetition in each of these attempts to fashion a new politics vis-à-vis media. What I want to stress here is that each repetition involves a forgetting that at the same time also enables the repetition. The assumptions in early television theory that television was uniquely associated with the everyday, made at the cost of ignoring the history of cinema's relations with the mundane, functioned in part to repress the historical politics of the everyday, or, more specifically, the history of media's relationship with the everyday. To a certain extent this was a factor of the forgetting common to claims about a new media, as the assertion that a media is new often involves claims of medium specificity that assert too-clear binaries between media such as film and television or, as earlier, between film and theater.

I would also argue, however, that this forgetting is also a means of avoiding the problems underlying the project of the media theorist. Shimizu's groundbreaking essay ends not with a conclusion about television but with a call for printed media to combat the feared dictatorship of the televisual image. This core text about a new medium was then really about a supposedly old medium. Shimizu's turn to the printed medium was intimately related to what became his solution to the problem of television: theory, or *shisō*, as Yoshimi Shun'ya summarizes it. While Shimizu often placed himself on the side of the people (*shomin*) against intellectuals,[64] his stance was in the end often that of the scholar enlightening the masses.[65] The threat to intellectual thought posed by television had to be dealt with through intellectual thought and only in the medium conducive to it: the printed word. But not only does this solution reproduce the hierarchies between the intellectual and the viewer (who is often of a lower socioeconomic class than the scholar), it ultimately argues that new media is inimical to theory, or that, in a corollary, theory's role is to control such threatening media.

Here again, early television theory is repeating early film theory. From the days of Nakagawa Shigeaki, who wrote the first philosophical account of cinema in Japan in 1911—only to reject film as an art—the resistance of many intellectuals to cinema was deep rooted, and, as is evident in the Pure Film Movement, could often manifest itself in film practice by only creating hierarchies between word and image, intellectual and spectator, modernism and modernity. Television theory of the 1950s was largely in continuity with these structures of power, effectively reconstituting them not by recalling that history but rather by obfuscating it, by stressing the difference of new media in its relation to the everyday. New media theory then served to mask continuities in the sociopolitical conflicts over media in modern capitalism.

Early TV theory also forgot Gonda. Although Katō cites Gonda, he does so in the wrong field. What Gonda was ultimately stressing by focusing on the relationship between cinema and the everyday was not simply the new lived geography of media, but the problem of theory as well. The debate over the everyday was not just about which media was closer to the everyday or what constituted the mediated everyday, but also about the relation of theory to the everyday—the everydayness of theory. Hidaka also suggests this at the end of his contribution to the *Shisō* issue, when he declares that it would be purely illusory to study "100 million becoming idiots" without considering why there were no labor unions in the Japanese broadcast industry—that is, how capital operated on the everyday bodies of TV workers and spectators.[66] A new media demanded not only a new theory but also a new way of doing theory, one that itself had to confront the problems of the intellectual, modernity, capital, labor, and medium through considering its own everydayness. Otherwise, it would simply repeat the theory of an older media.

NOTES

1. Lev Manovich, *The Language of New Media* (Cambridge, MA: MIT Press, 2001).

2. Wendy Hui Kyong Chun, "Introduction: Did Somebody Say New Media?," in *New Media, Old Media: A History and Theory Reader*, ed. Wendy Hui Kyong Chun and Thomas W. Keenan (New York: Routledge, 2006), 3.

3. Others have found and explained such repetitions in various ways. Ellen Wartella and Byron Reeves, who found similarities in early research of film and television's effects on children, blame such repetitions on basic assumptions in American social sciences; "Historical Trends in Research on Children and the Media: 1900–1960," *Journal of Communication* 35, no. 2 (June 1985): 118–33. Jan Simons argues that many theories of new media end up repeating an insufficiently questioned "folk theory" of media; "New Media as Old Media: Cinema," in *The New Media Book*, ed. Dan Harries (London: BFI, 2002), 231–41. And William Uricchio even suggests that the repetition may be reversed: "television . . . can be argued to have established the horizon of expectations for film itself some ten to 15 years before the Lumières' first 1895 projection"; "Old Media as New Media: Television," in Harries, *New Media Book*, 223.

4. Peter Krapp, "Hypertext *Avant La Lettre*," in Chun and Keenan, *New Media, Old Media*, 361.

5. Jayson Makoto Chun, *"A Nation of a Hundred Million Idiots"?: A Social History of Japanese Television, 1953–1973* (New York: Routledge, 2007), 25–29.

6. See my *Visions of Japanese Modernity: Articulations of Cinema, Nation, and Spectatorship, 1895–1925* (Berkeley: University of California Press, 2010).

7. Ōya first used the phrase in January 1957 in the *Tokyo shinbun*, but later softened his stance. See Ōya Sōichi, "'Ichioku sōhakuchika' meimei shimatsuki," in *Ōya Sōichi zenshū* (Tokyo: Eichōsha, 1975), 339–48.

8. See Yoshimi Shun'ya's introduction to the reprint of Shimizu Ikutarō's "Terebijon jidai" [The television age]: "'Terebijon jidai' kaidai'" *Shisō* 956 (December 2003): 7–10.

9. Shimizu Ikutarō, "Terebijon jidai," *Shisō* 413 (November 1958): 6.

10. Shimizu, "Terebijon jidai," 11.

11. Shimizu, "Terebijon jidai," 11–12.

12. Shimizu, "Terebijon jidai," 12–13.

13. Shimizu Ikutarō, "Terebi no honshitsu" [The essence of television], *Asahi shinbun*, May 2, 1957 (morning ed.), 5. Nihon Hōsō Kyōkai is Japan's national public broadcasting organization.

14. Shimizu, "Terebijon jidai," 8.

15. See J. M. Chun, 47–48.

16. Shimizu Ikutarō, "Terebi bunmeiron" [On TV civilization], in *Besuto obu Kinema junpō* (Best of Kinema junpō) (Tokyo: Kinema Junpōsha, 1994), 1:709.

17. Shimizu, "Terebijon jidai," 15.

18. Günther Anders, *Die Antiquiertheit des Meschen* (Munich: C. H. Beck, 1980), 1:111; quoted in Paul van Dijk, *Anthropology in the Age of Technology: The Philosophical Contributions of Günther Anders* (Amsterdam: Rodopi, 2000), 47. Shimizu is working with the original 1956 edition.

19. Shimizu, "Terebijon jidai," 16.

20. Shimizu, "Terebijon jidai," 16.

21. Habermas said this of television and radio: "They draw the eyes and ears of the public under their spell but at the same time, by taking away its distance, place it under 'tutelage,' which is to say they deprive it of the opportunity to say something and to disagree." Jurgen Habermas, *The Structural Transformation of the Public Sphere: An Inquiry into a Category of Bourgeois Society*, trans. Thomas Burger (Cambridge, MA: MIT Press, 1991), 171.

22. Shimizu, "Terebijon jidai," 17.

23. Shimizu, "Terebi bunmeiron," 708.

24. Katō Hidetoshi, "Terebijon to goraku," *Shisō* 413 (November 1958): 43–47.

25. Sasaki Kiichi, "Terebi bunka to wa nanika," *Shisō* 413 (November 1958): 227–28.

26. Minami Hiroshi, "Terebi to ningen," in *Kōza gendai masu komyunikēshon 2: Terebi jidai*, ed. Minami Hiroshi (Tokyo: Kawade Shobō Shinsha, 1960), 7–16. In the *Shisō* issue, Minami argues that television, because it cannot be reviewed due to its continual flow, demands concentration. Since that is a burden on viewers, however, they have to resort to such tactics as personalization, viewing everyone on television as if they are "like" someone in the neighborhood, in order to bring the image closer and make it easier to consume. See Minami Hiroshi, "Terebijon to ukete no seikatsu," *Shisō* 413 (November 1958): 105.

27. Katō, "Terebijon to goraku," 43.

28. Katō, "Terebijon to goraku," 52.

29. Katō, "Terebijon to goraku," 46.

30. Minami, "Terebijon to ukete no seikatsu," 106.

31. Yoshimi Shun'ya, "Terebi ga ie ni yatte kita," *Shisō* 956 (December 2003): 26–47.

32. Katō, "Terebijon to goraku," 50.

33. *NHK Nenkan: 1962* (Tokyo: Rajio Sābisu Sentā, 1962), 8. The rate of ownership would increase dramatically in the next few years, but significant regional differences would remain. In March 1962, for instance, 68.6 percent of Osaka households would have a TV (compared to the national average of 49.5 percent), but only 17.4 percent of Kagoshima homes would (see *NHK Nenkan*, 10). The TV middle class was even then not uniformly national.

34. Katō himself studied at Harvard and the University of Chicago in the mid-1950s and was a student of David Rietman. See Yoneyama Toshinao, "Katō Hidetoshi," *Gendai jinbutsu jiten* (Tokyo: Asahi Shinbun, 1977), 335.

35. See, for instance, Amano Yasukazu, *Kiki no ideorōgu: Shimizu Ikutarō hihan* (Tokyo: Hihyōsha, 1970), 193–205.

36. Hidetoshi Kato, "The Development of Communication Research in Japan," in *Japanese Popular Culture*, ed. Hidetoshi Kato (Rutland, VT: Charles Tuttle, 1959), 35.

37. Kato, "Communication Research in Japan," 41–43.

38. See Timothy Glander, *Origins of Mass Communications Research during the American Cold War* (Mahwah, NJ: Lawrence Erlbaum Associates, 2000).

39. Kato, "Communication Research in Japan," 38.

40. See Arima Tetsuo, *Nihon terebi to CIA* (Tokyo: Shinchōsha, 2006).

41. Kato, "Communication Research in Japan," 34.

42. Shimada Atsushi, "Terebi geijutsu no kiso," *Shisō* 413 (November 1958): 232–39.

43. See Shimizu Hikaru, *Eiga to bunka* (Kyoto: Kyōiku Tosho, 1941), especially 3–22.

44. See Murayama Tomoyoshi, "Eiga no genkaisei," *Kinema Junpō* 507 (June 1, 1934): 67–68.

45. See Gonda Yasunosuke, *Katsudō shashin no genri oyobi ōyō* [The principles and applications of the moving pictures] (Tokyo: Uchida Rōkakuho, 1914); or my translation of sections of that book, "The Principles and Applications of the Moving Pictures (Excerpts)," *Review of Japanese Culture and Society* 22 (2010): 24–36.

46. Gonda, "Moving Pictures," 26.

47. Harry Harootunian, *Overcome by Modernity* (Princeton, NJ: Princeton University Press, 2001), 95–101.

48. Harootunian, *Overcome by Modernity*, 101.

49. Gonda, *Katsudō shashin no genri*, 441. For more on his attempts to relocate theory, see also my discussions of Gonda in my *Visions of Japanese Modernity*; and "The Process of Theory: Reading Gonda Yasunosuke and Early Film Theory," *Review of Japanese Culture and Society* 22 (2010): 37–43.

50. See Harootunian, *Overcome by Modernity*, 106–18.

51. Naoki Yamamoto, "Realities That Matter: The Development of Realist Film Theory and Practice in Japan, 1895–1945" (PhD diss., Yale University, 2012), 163–81.

52. Tosaka Jun, "Eiga no ninshikironteki kachi to fūzoku byōsha," *Nihon eiga* 2, no. 6 (June 1937): 13–19.

53. Tosaka Jun, "Eiga no shajitsuteki tokusei to fūzokusei oyobi taishūsei," in *Tosaka Jun zenshū* (Tokyo: Keisō Shobō, 1966–67), 4:285–86, quoted in Yamamoto, "Realities That Matter," 170.

54. Tosaka, "Eiga no ninshikironteki kachi," 17.

55. Tosaka, "Eiga no shajitsuteki tokusei," 289; quoted in Yamamoto, "Realities that Matter," 171–72.

56. See, for instance, Imamura Taihei's "Geijutsu keishiki to shite no eiga," in *Eiga geijutsu no keishiki* (Tokyo: Ōshio Shoin, 1938), 129–62. One can accept Yamamoto's argument that "Imamura was different from Tosaka in his tendency to define cinematic cognition not as the process but as the result of someone's cognitive activity" (Yamamoto, "Realities That Matter," 206), but even then, it is a result that involves a process of rendering thought concrete.

57. Aaron Gerow, "Introduction: The Theory Complex," *Review of Japanese Culture and Society* 22 (December 2010): 1–13.

58. See, for instance, Hani Susumu and Okada Susumu, "Eiga ni okeru henkakuki to wa nanika," in *Besuto obu Kinema junpō* (Tokyo: Kinema Junpōsha, 1994), 1:882–85. For

more on the debates, see Yuriko Furuhata, *Cinema of Actuality: Japanese Avant-Garde Filmmaking in the Season of Image Politics* (Durham, NC: Duke University Press, 2013).

59. Sasaki, "Terebi bunka to wa nanika," 774–75.

60. See, for instance, Matsumoto Toshio, "A Theory of Avant-Garde Documentary," trans. Michael Raine, *Cinema Journal* 51, no. 4 (2012): 148–54.

61. Tahara Sōichirō, "Nichijō kara no tonsō," *Tenbō* (October 1971): 78; quoted in Niwa Yoshiyuki, "Dokyumentarī seishun jidai no shūen," *Terebi da yo! Zen'in shūgō*, ed. Hase Masato and Ōta Shōichi (Tokyo: Seikyūsha, 2007).

62. Wada Ben, *Engi to ningen* (Tokyo: Mainichi Shinbunsha, 1970), 2–10.

63. Hagimoto Haruhiko, Muraki Yoshihiko, and Konno Tsutomu, *Omae wa tada no genzai ni suginai: Terebi ni nani ga kanō ka* [You are nothing but the present: What is possible for television?] (Tokyo: Tabata Shoten, 1969), 367.

64. See Oguma Eiji, *Shimizu Ikutarō* (Tokyo: Ochanomizu Shobō, 2003), 38–45.

65. According to Takeuchi Yō, Shimizu "used the people as a means of confronting intellectuals, but when confronting the people, could say they 'needed to listen to the research and opinions of scholars.'" See Takeuchi Yō, *Media to chishikijin: Shimizu Ikutarō no haken to bōkyaku* (Tokyo: Chūō Kōronsha, 2012), 331.

66. Hidaka Rokurō, "Terebijon kenkyū no hitotsu no zentei," *Shisō* 413 (November 1958): 29.

2. ARCHITECTURE AS ATMOSPHERIC MEDIA

Tange Lab and Cybernetics

YURIKO FURUHATA

Much of the current debate and critical approaches to media ecology and ubiquitous computing echoes architectural discourse on the media-saturated urban environment from the 1960s. It was then that the rapid growth of telecommunication networks and the intensification of data traffic prompted architects to consider urban space in relation to technical media. For these architects, thinking about urban design became inseparable from thinking about communication and information technologies, and architectural criticism became contiguous with media theory. While an echo from the past is only part of the conversation in the present, the reverberations between Japanese architectural theory from the 1960s and current media theory are worth considering, if only to contextualize the historical specificity of the former and to gain a comparative perspective on the latter.

The current discussion of technical media in North America is increasingly inflected by ecological and environmental factors. Mark Hansen, for instance, has argued that twenty-first-century media—from social media to data mining to microsensor technologies that imperceptibly shape our social milieu—is more "elemental" or "atmospheric" than twentieth-century media, whose temporal vectors are directed toward the past and the present while directly addressing human users. Characterized by the anticipatory temporality of the future, and embedded in computational processes that operate below the thresholds of human perceptual experience, twenty-first-century media, in contrast, offer new sensory affordances that radically reconfigure the relationship between humans and their environments. "Human experience is currently undergoing a fundamental transformation caused by the complex entanglement of humans within networks of media technologies that operate predominantly, if not almost entirely, outside the scope of human modes of awareness (consciousness, attention, sense perception, etc.)," argues Hansen.[1]

What he calls the constitutive doubleness of these networked media thus derives from their dual capacity to mediate our sensory access to the world, and to affect this access by becoming constitutive of the very sensory data of the world. One of the most provocative points Hansen makes in this reformulation of media lies precisely in his characterization of media as atmospheric. Media has become our atmosphere, seamlessly blending into our surroundings, like the air that we breathe and that envelops us.

Although operating from a different perspective, John Durham Peters makes a similar observation in his recent book, *The Marvelous Cloud*. The ubiquity of digital devices, argues Peters, "invite[s] us to think of media as environmental, as part of the habitat."[2] Contemporary technical media are again conceived as atmospheric and elemental, actively blurring the boundary between artificial and biological environments. Taking this observation as a point of departure, Peters calls attention to the conceptual affinity between medium and milieu: "*Medium* has always meant an element, environment, or vehicle in the middle of things." Tracing the etymological root of the term "media" back to the ancient notion of natural environment, he then demonstrates how the instrumental understanding of an intermediate agent, articulated by eighteenth-century philosophy, paved the way for the modern understanding of media as man-made channels and processes of human communication: "The concepts of *medium* and *milieu* have long orbited each other, as twin offspring of Aristotelian material and the Latin word *medius*, middle."[3]

Returning to this older connotation of media allows Peters to conceive of environments—from natural elements such as water and fire to cultural artifacts and infrastructures—as media, that is to say, as means and processes of communication not only for humans but also for nonhuman agents. While Hansen's and Peters's theoretical premises are different, they share a common ground: to rethink media as atmospheric, as an immediate given.

One discipline in which much thought has gone into this presupposed connection between media and milieu is architecture. Although the current discourse on atmospheric media in North America complicates our understanding of the ubiquity of electronic media through the framework of the environmental given, the Japanese architectural discourse of the 1960s sheds a different light on this situation. It allows us to see how specific economic, political, and epistemic conditions contributed to this environmental understanding of media in the first place. The Japanese situation, in other words, shows that the connection between media and milieu is a historical construct.

This chapter will examine the historical connection between media and milieu articulated by Japanese architects at a time when the cybernetic concepts of communication, control, and feedback first entered architectural criticism. The aim here is to trace what might be called "the cybernetic turn" of Japanese architecture during the 1960s in order to tease out its relevance to the current discussion of atmospheric media. This moment unfolded in relation to several historical factors, including postwar high economic growth and governmental investment in the reconstruction of communication infrastructures devastated by the war.

At the center of this cybernetic turn was a group of architects who boldly reimagined urban space: Tange Kenzō and his students who worked in and graduated from Tange Lab at the University of Tokyo. Tange Lab was a birthplace of visionary architects, including those who called themselves Metabolist. Politically, it also functioned as an informal think tank that conducted government-commissioned research on the economic and social optimization of urban design and national land planning since the late 1940s. While technofuturistic images of Metabolist projects (such as Kurokawa's capsule housing) tend to obscure the complex activities of Tange Lab and its participation in the rebuilding of Japan, the political importance of Tange Lab cannot be measured by its futurism alone. Rather, as architect and critic Yatsuka Hajime sharply argues, the legacy of Tange Lab is inseparable from the grand project of nation building, a project that harkens back to the imperial days of colonial urban planning.[4] If that is the case, then, we need to take a nuanced look at Tange Lab's cybernetic turn in the 1960s.

In the sections that follow, I will first sketch the general context surrounding Tange's turn to cybernetics ("The Cybernetic Turn") and his inheritance of the biopolitical vision of colonial urban planning ("The Biopolitical Vision of Colonial Urban Planning"). Next, I will explore the specific contexts within which architects at Tange Lab and their associates responded to cybernetics through the managerial discourse on the postindustrial information society and logistics ("The Information Revolution"). I will then address the postwar importation of communication theory and the artistic uptake of interactivity, which informs the work of Isozaki Arata, a graduate of Tange Lab and architect whose vision of the responsive cybernetic environment anticipates the contemporary debate on atmospheric media ("The Cybernetic Environment"), before concluding with some thoughts on the relevance of this history to contemporary media theory.

The Cybernetic Turn

Among others, Marshall McLuhan's idea that housing is a medium of communication best captures the mid-twentieth-century vision of atmospheric media.[5] McLuhan famously defined media as a technological extension of the human body, whose historical impact is measurable through its capacity to alter our sensory perceptions. "For the 'message' of any medium of technology is the change of scale or pace or pattern that it introduces into human affairs."[6] The railroad, for instance, accelerated the scale of movement and transport. In so doing, it reshaped the contours of modern cities. Becoming an indispensable part of housing, the electric light also reconfigured living and working spaces by abolishing "the divisions of night and day, of inner and outer, and of the subterranean and the terrestrial."[7] Electric lighting was not, however, the only technological invention that altered our perception of the habitable environment: electronic media and information technologies had radically changed the way architects envisioned it.

As Mark Wigley notes, architects gave serious consideration to information networks accelerated by the proliferation of electronic media in the 1950s and 1960s. It is not an overstatement to say that architecture was at the core of media theory's turn to information networks. Even McLuhan's idea of electronic media as a prosthetic extension of the human nervous system owes to his encounter with architects.[8] By the mid-1960s, architects and urban planners across continents were collectively developing a new paradigm of urban design based on insights gleaned from cybernetics and communication theory. Architects Constantinos Doxiadis and Jaqueline Tyrwhitt, for instance, gathered an interdisciplinary and international group of scholars— from Margaret Mead to Marshall McLuhan—in order to analyze urban planning in relation to information flow and communication networks. It was then that the very idea of the network became integral to architecture, and the Japanese architect Tange Kenzō was among those who partook in this international effort to rethink urban design through the lens of cybernetics.

According to Wigley, "Tange drew on cybernetics to discuss the influence of all the contemporary systems of communications—arguing, in McLuhanesque fashion, that there has been a second industrial revolution, an information revolution that prosthetically extends the nervous system in the same way that the first one physically extended the body."[9] Popularized by the work of Norbert Wiener, cybernetics draws parallels between the information-processing machine and the human nervous system. Wiener did not simply draw a comparison between social organization and biological organization; he collapsed the two by redefining both through their internal communicative capacities to fight entropy or disorder through feedback loops.[10] This structural parallel between the communicative capacities of the city and those of the living organism appeared frequently in Tange's own writing in the 1960s.

Tange shared his vision of the city as a living organism endowed with its own nervous system at the Delos symposium organized by Doxiadis in 1966. His vision seems to have struck a chord with many who attended the meeting. This was partly because his idea had already been introduced to an international audience through the architectural journal *Ekistics* as early as 1961.[11] Having taught at MIT in 1959 and participated in various architectural symposia, Tange was familiar with the impact cybernetics had had on architecture, though it would be remiss to simply conclude that his vision of the city as a sentient organism was a direct result of his experience abroad. As we will see shortly, Tange's appropriation of cybernetic metaphors was, in part, also a logical extension of the biopolitical discourse on colonial architecture and urban planning.[12]

Well before his participation in the Delos symposium, Tange frequently used the biological metaphors of blood circulation and the central nervous system to articulate his vision.[13] In order to grow and maintain its healthy metabolic cycle, the city, in his view, required the constant circulation of energy and information to facilitate efficient communication among its organic parts. Tange set this biological analogy of energy and information circuits at the center of his urban planning.

For instance, Tange's well-known but unrealized urban project, Plan for Tokyo 1960, hinges on the reconfiguration of transportation networks. These networks are organized along "the spinal axis" stretched across Tokyo Bay. This axis functions as the "central nervous system" of the city, as if to emulate the anatomical structure of the vertebrate animal.[14] Similarly, in his essay "The Future of the Japanese Archipelago: The Formation of Tōkaidō Megalopolis" (1965), Tange presents a biological metaphor of the Japanese archipelago as a vertebrate animal that grows along the central urban "spinal" axis that links and networks several metropolises.

In the course of the 1960s, Tange updated this biological model of the city as a complex living organism—his favorite example was the vertebrate animal— to a cybernetic model of the city, adding the communicative elements of feedback and control to the static infrastructure of circulation. But if he did so, it is because the models of organism and communication provided by cellular biology and cybernetics were compatible. For Tange, urban planning was all about organizing space in order to maintain an effective communication or circulation of elements within the organism called city.[15] Following Wiener, he argued that an organism strives toward organization through the communicative processes of information management and feedback. Tange applied this logic to his theory of urban design by highlighting the centrality of traffic, energy, and information networks.[16]

This thematization of circulation—of air, vehicles, and pedestrians—was not new. Rather, it was a central tenet of modern architecture and urbanism. In the late 1920s, designing efficient networks of transportation became one of the main objectives of modern architecture and urbanism. The idea was first promoted by the Congrès internationaux d'architecture moderne (International Congresses of Modern Architecture), an international association of architects founded by leading European figures such as Walter Gropius and Sigfried Giedion.[17] This modernist idea of efficient circulation clearly influenced Tange, but he read it through the newly acquired lens of cybernetics and its organizational logic of feedback. He writes: "Organization is neither a perfect container for freedom nor a despotic mold. Rather, it is a living organism that voluntarily controls the process of feedback between freedom and order. I believe that a modern society is a highly developed form of a living organism. Its growth resembles an evolutionary process of development from plant to animal, to human, as it has developed its own nervous system within social organizations, and started to engage in brain activities."[18] The modernist discourse on urbanism had long relied on organic, cellular, and evolutionary metaphors of the city.[19] But Tange's organicist view of the city also has a more specific origin, namely the biopolitical vision of colonial urban planning.

The Biopolitical Vision of Colonial Urban Planning

While the cybernetic paradigm of organization brought a new way of imagining the environment, the political function of postwar Japanese architecture, especially that of Tange Lab, cannot be dissociated from the imperial project of expanding Japan's "living sphere" (*Lebensraum*) through colonial urban planning. As Yatsuka suggests, the Metabolist and Tange's organicist vision of the city in the postwar period clearly inherits the earlier biopolitical vision of the colonial administrators and urban planners such as Gotō Shinpei.[20]

Gotō, who served as the colonial administrator in Taiwan and Manchuria and oversaw a number of urban projects in the colonies as well as on the mainland, is often credited as the founding father of Japanese urban planning.[21] In addition to serving in high-ranking positions, such as director-general of the Manchurian Railway Company, a linchpin of Japan's settler colonialist expansion in Northeast China, Gotō also served as the communications minister, the first chairman of the Urban Studies Association, and even the mayor of Tokyo. He is also known as an infamous proponent of the scientific management of colonies based on "biological principles" combined with biopolitical structures of governance such as centralized medical police. It is his experiments in colonial administration and city planning that Yatsuka highlights as an important precursor to Tange's and Metabolists' postwar urban projects of expanding Japan's "living sphere" after the loss of all of the overseas colonies. Even the seemingly technofuturistic projects of megastructures suspended in the sky and floating over the sea fit within the purview of this imperial paradigm of literally expanding the territory and its habitable environment.[22]

Echoing Yatsuka's historical repositioning of Tange and Metabolism as direct heirs to colonial architecture and urban planning, Isozaki Arata and Sawaragi Noi have also noted that the wartime discourse on "the environment" (kankyō) was an important precursor to the postwar popularization of the term by Asada Takashi, another affiliate of Tange Lab.[23] Among other graduates of Tange Lab, Isozaki held the most critical stance toward Tange's commitment to nation building and his collaboration with the wartime regime, though, as we will see later, he too came to embrace the organizational logic of cybernetics.

When we look closely at the writings of Gotō and his biopolitical vision of the colonial administration, we begin to see how much Tange's postwar vision of the city as a living organism echoes an earlier Japanese discourse on urban planning and nation building. After all, Tange was not the first to deploy the metaphors of the "vertebrate animal" and the "central nervous system" to describe the organization of the city. Gotō had done so in his discussion of optimizing the communicative capacities of the administrative apparatuses of the empire during the 1910s, using the same metaphors of the vertebrate animal and the nervous system in his discussion of the governance of Manchuria.[24]

As if to anticipate Tange's postwar call for the self-regulating growth of the living city along the spinal axis of the centralized transportation network, Gotō argued for the organized growth of the empire through communication networks. "The current state of colonial Manchuria in the empire is characterized by its disunity, which is comparable to the de-centralized nerve ganglia of a lower form of animal life," writes Gotō. In his view, if the office of the Kwantung governor-general in Manchuria were to function as the "brain" of Japan's imperialist expansion in Asia, it had to unify its judiciary, police, civil engineering, and telecommunications apparatuses. Only then could these administrative apparatuses properly function as the "central nervous system" of the empire. And the Japanese empire, in his view, was analogous to the intelligent "vertebrate animal."[25]

Given Tange's wartime contribution to the expansionist ideology of the empire—as demonstrated by his design for the Commemorative Building Project for the Construction of Greater East Asia (or the Greater East Asia Co-Prosperity Sphere Monument) of 1942—it is not surprising to find this similarity between his and Gotō's organicist visions.[26] While Tange spoke nothing of the empire—or his wartime involvement—his ambition to rebuild the city of Tokyo and to restructure the entire Japanese archipelago through the cybernetic paradigm of communication and control betrays a residual trace of the biopolitical rhetoric of governance that colonial administrators such as Gotō espoused and passed down to later generations of architects and urban planners.

That being said, however, I do not mean that Tange's view of urban design did not change from the wartime to the postwar period. Rather, I would argue that it mutated in a timely response to the infrastructural and discursive changes taking place around the conceptualization of the environment in the postwar years. His embrace of cybernetics was part of this timely response to these changes.

The Information Revolution

The cybernetic metaphor of the city so favored by Tange, in other words, did not simply follow the colonial discourse on urban planning but was prompted by the postwar debates on the information society, postindustrialization, and the logistics revolution. Promoted by a group of sociologists, economists, architects, and policy makers (some of whom had a direct link to Tange Lab), the Japanese discourse on the information society (*jōhōka shakai* or *jōhō shakai*) applied the cybernetic logics of feedback and control to business, and saw logistics and automation as essential to the optimization of the economic productivity of the nation. This discourse critically inflected the way in which architects such as Tange interpreted cybernetics.

One of the characteristics of information society discourse, like its contemporary American counterpart, is an overtly optimistic outlook on computerization. For instance, according to Masuda Yoneji, a bureaucrat, futurologist, and the founder of the Institute for the Information Society, computer technology signaled the dawn of "computopia" (or computer-based utopia) and the arrival of "the information époque." For Masuda, the information society is characterized by the rise of intellectual labor, economic synergy across industries, automation, and participatory democracy in which citizens actively engage in policy decision making through networked systems of communication feedback. He contends, "As the 21st century approaches . . . the possibilities of a universally opulent society being realized have appeared in the sense that [Adam] Smith envisioned it, and the information society (futurization society) that will emerge from the computer communications revolution will be a society that actually moves toward a universal society of plenty."[27] Masuda's optimism is echoed in much of the Japanese information society discourse of the 1970s.

In hindsight, we can see that the Japanese discourse on the information society was part of the governmental and corporate push toward postindustrialization. But in the early 1960s, when the idea of the information society first began to circulate, there was no definitive understanding of what the term meant. As Tessa Morris-Suzuki argues, "The term 'information society' is one which is more often used than defined."[28] Even though the term circulated widely through a myriad of publications, the meaning of the term itself was not always clear to its users. For instance, in the book *Information Society: From Hard Society to Soft Society* (1969), Hayashi Yūjirō—an advisor to the influential Economic Planning Agency and the person who is often credited for the popularization of the term "information society"—lists a series of heterogeneous definitions of "information" excerpted from the work of prominent academics such as Umesao Tadao (an intellectual known for developing the idea of the information society in Japan), Miyagawa Tadao, and Fritz Machlup. Ultimately, however, he admits that there is no precise definition of "information society." Referring to an international symposium organized by the Japan Techno-Economics Society (Kagaku Gijutsu to Keizai no Kai) and held in 1968, Hayashi explains that the conclusion he drew from the symposium was that the definition of "information society" remained ambiguous to both Japanese and American academics.[29]

Similarly, in the opening chapter of the *Japan's Information Society: Its Vision and Challenges* (*Nihon no jōhōka shakai: Sono bijon to kadai,* 1969), edited by the Information Committee for the Economic Council (Keizai shingikai jōhō kenkyū iinkai, an advisory board for the prime minister composed of corporate and governmental representatives), the meaning of the keyword "informatization" (*jōhōka*) is ultimately left undefined: "The word *informatization* became popularly used in the past few years, but as is usual with a trendy neologism its meaning remains vague. . . . Certainly, the term *informatization* is often equated with computers but they are not the same thing."[30]

In spite of its vagueness concerning the key concept of informatization, the book nonetheless covers a wide range of topics, including the rise of the information industry (*jōhō sangyō*), the computerization of banking systems, strategies of business management, the impact of automation on the labor market, and the introduction of computers into educational institutions, as well as transformations in logistics and the distribution of commodities. And it is this last topic—logistics—that deserves special attention, as it holds a direct relevance to the research activities of Tange Lab.

Broadly defined, "logistics" concerns the management of movement, and the coordinated flow of both things and military operations. The term derives from military usage, but it has come to be associated with the post-Fordist capitalist mode of production and distribution through the expansion of the business logistics of the 1960s and 1970s. Business logistics also focuses on supply chain management, a field that grew rapidly amid the introduction of computers and operations research, the innovation of the containership and the corresponding reconfiguration of transport infrastructures, and the application of cybernetics to the manufacture and distribution of goods.

In Japan, this way of thinking about logistics began to circulate in the early 1960s, in popular books such as economist Hayashi Shūji's *A Revolution in Distribution* (*Ryūtsū kakumei*).[31] Indeed, the 1960s was the time when operations research, systems theory, and the technocratic discourse of the information society all converged around a set of related issues: logistics, computerization, and the transportation and communication infrastructures of urban space. All of this left an indelible mark on Japanese architectural criticism and informed its embrace of cybernetics.[32]

Moreover, if cybernetics can be broadly defined as "the field concerned with information flows *in all media*,"[33] architecture was cybernetic even before architectural criticism embraced its vocabulary. In this regard, Tange Lab's systematic studies of information and energy flows in the 1950s and early 1960s warrant attention. For instance, in 1963 Tange Lab conducted a comprehensive analysis of "the connections between the more than 100 departments and bureaus of the government and the movement of 10,000 workers" inside the Tokyo Metropolitan Government Building.[34] Throughout the 1960s, Tange's interest in the coordinated management of the flow of things as a key component of architecture and urban design coincided with the economic rationality of the information society discourse, and dovetailed with governmental investment in the studies of information traffic.

Given the close institutional ties between the postwar Japanese government and Tange Lab, it is not surprising to find this resonance between Tange's theorization of urban design and information society discourse. For instance, two architects trained at Tange Lab—Shimokōbe Atsushi and Obayashi Jun'ichirō—went on to become powerful bureaucrats who worked for the Economic Planning Agency, the Ministry of Construction, and the National Land Agency. Shimokōbe's and Obayashi's research on industrial productivity had a direct impact on the Comprehensive National Development Plan (Zenkoku Sōgō Kaihatsu Keikaku) launched by the Economic Planning Agency in 1962, around the same time that Umesao Tadao's essay on the information industry and Hayashi Shūji's book on the logistics revolution were published.[35]

Under the aegis of Shimokōbe, one of the masterminds behind the Comprehensive National Development Plan, several members of Tange Lab also participated in government-sponsored research activities on the impact of information technologies on urban space. In 1967, for instance, Shimokōbe appointed Kurokawa Kishō, a graduate of Tange Lab and a prominent member of the Metabolist group, to take part in an information network research group. In 1970, Shimokōbe edited and published a book, *Dialogues with Information Society: Information Networks for Future Japan,* and presented the outcome of a research project commissioned by the Economic Planning Agency (see fig. 2.1). We find Kurokawa's name yet again listed among the participants of this research group, which included both government officials and corporate representatives from the telecommunications industry, such as the Nippon Telegraph and Telephone Public Corporation (NTT), Japan Broadcasting Corporation (NHK), and Dentsū.[36] In 1972, Kurokawa published

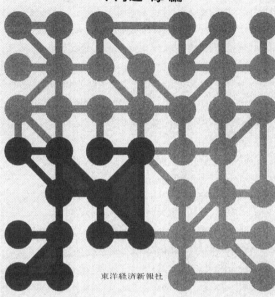

情報化社会との対話

未来日本の情報ネットワーク

下河辺 淳 編

東洋経済新報社

[FIG. 2.1] The cover
of Shimokōbe Atsushi,
*Jōhōshakai to no
taiwa: Mirai Nihon
no jōhō nettowāku*
[Dialogues with
information society:
Information networks
for future Japan]
(Tokyo: Tōyō Keizai
Shinhōsha, 1970).

The Future of Information Archipelago Japan, a book that echoed the title
of Tange's 1965 essay "The Future of the Japanese Archipelago."[37] Kurokawa was also a participant of the futurology division of the Japan Techno-
Economics Society, which published an official report titled *Developing a
Super-Technological Society: Humans in Information Systems* in 1969. The
book was edited by none other than Hayashi Yūjirō.[38]

Tange Lab thus had close ties to the proponents of the information society and their government-sponsored research activities at a time when
Japan was undergoing massive infrastructural transformations. The aforementioned essay by Tange ("The Future of the Japanese Archipelago") was
also a direct result of Tange's lecture delivered at the Japan Center for Area
Development Research, a foundation established and administered by the
Ministry of Construction.[39] Throughout the 1950s and 1960s, Tange Lab
carried out a number of similar statistical and theoretical research projects,

analyzing issues ranging from population density, the distribution of industrial resources, and transportation infrastructures to urban reconstruction and development. It is reasonable to assume that Tange Lab's emphasis on communication, information flow, and cybernetics directly paralleled the Japanese government and telecommunication industry's investment in the processes of informatization.[40] Tange's interest in cybernetics and electronic media, and his biological metaphors of the city as a living organism endowed with a central nervous system, develop different implications once we situate them within the historically specific context of Japan's postwar land development, economic reform, and logistics revolution. The futuristic vision of the Japanese archipelago as a self-organizing organism extending its tentacles of information networks did not simply emerge out of the discipline of architecture. Nor was it simply a continuation of the wartime discourse on colonial urban planning; rather, it was fostered within the expanded sphere of information society discourse.

As Tange and his students clearly understood, the logistics revolution in Japan went hand in glove with the proliferation of electronic media, and with it the connotation of communication infrastructure shifted from the visible networks of transportation to the invisible networks of information. This paradigmatic shift in their understanding of networks critically inflected the way in which these architects also understood the relationship between architecture and media. They frequently turned their attention to the ephemeral presence of wireless signals and invisible flows of data traffic crisscrossing urban space. To design the urban environment meant to pay attention not only to "hard" transportation networks but also to "soft" information pathways. In short, milieu became contiguous with media.

It is not surprising, then, to find frequent discussions of media in relation to urban design in the writings of architects associated with Tange Lab. Everything from community cable television to facsimile and computers, electronic media, and their environmental nature are mentioned repeatedly as being part of the challenges facing architects working in the age of the information society. Kurokawa, for instance, attributes his interest in the biological system of data processing to the architect's need to respond to the demand of the time: "I became interested in the vital mechanism, especially in the living organism's information systems since I predicted that the informational soft component of the human environment—namely, communication, transportation, and energy—rather than its hard component would become more prominent in the future."[41]

The work of Isozaki Arata, a graduate of Tange Lab who kept a critical distance from the Metabolist group but who also shared their interest in a biotechnical conception of the city, participated in this paradigm shift.[42] Isozaki's theorization of the "cybernetic environment" and his exploration of the semiotic dimension of information networks suggest another important aspect of the cybernetic turn of Japanese architecture. In the last section, I will explore how Isozaki's work paralleled the postwar reception of communication theory in addition to cybernetics, and how he inflected both through the notions of interactivity or responsiveness, notions that were gaining traction within the avant-garde art world.

The Cybernetic Environment

Isozaki worked for Tange on several key projects, such as the Plan for Tokyo 1960 and Expo '70, the first world's fair held in Japan. If Shimokōbe, Obayashi, and Kurokawa represent the bureaucratic face of Tange Lab as a research institution, then Isozaki represents its artistic face. He was closely involved in the art world,[43] and was close to avant-garde artists such as Yamaguchi Katsuhiro, Yasumura Masunobu, Shinohara Ushio, and Arakawa Shūsaku.[44] He produced artworks and was interested in "happenings" and action painting. Isozaki was a member of the artist collective Group Environment (Enbairamento no Kai), which organized the landmark exhibition "From Space to Environment" (Kūkan kara kankyō e ten) in 1966. With Yamaguchi, he also founded the company Environmental Planning as he prepared to design the multimedia setup of the Festival Plaza at Expo '70.[45] He called this main attraction site a prototype of the cybernetic environment, one that relied on computer-programmed operations of multimedia devices and built-in sensor technologies.

Describing the Festival Plaza as a type of "soft architecture" or responsive environment, Isozaki designed it with the man-machine interface in mind.[46] Its multimedia setup included two giant robots that allegedly formed a feedback circuit with the mainframe computer placed inside the central control room. The ambitious plan for the Festival Plaza aimed to wire the robots with sensors that collected ambient data on changing sounds, light, and movement. This data was then supposed to be sent back to the control room computer, which would modulate the multimedia devices accordingly.[47] Although the Festival Plaza fell short of actualizing a fully interactive system modulated by the ambient data of the physical environment, it was still

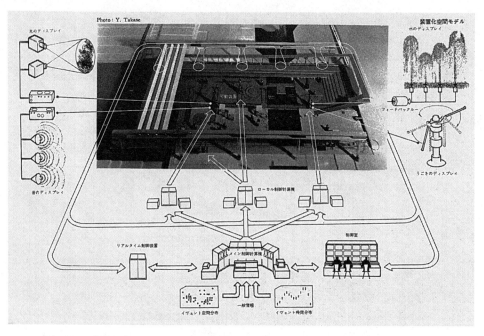

[FIG. 2.2] The diagram of the Festival Plaza from *Kenchiku bunka* (January 1970).
Courtesy of Isozaki Arata.

visionary,[48] and one could read its architectural design as a precursor to our contemporary atmospheric media, which incessantly collect ambient data and modulate our environment.

The plan for the Festival Plaza, which was developed over two years, from 1967 to 1969, emphasized the elements of communicative interactivity and feedback. Isozaki and Tsukio Yoshio, an architect and computer programmer who helped design the plaza, envisioned this computer-controlled space as a type of "environment as a responsive field" (*ōtōba to shite no kankyō*, see fig. 2.2). Bridging the disciplines of architecture and computer science, the multimedia setup of the plaza fits the description of a responsive environment defined by computer artist Myron Krueger: an environment "in which a computer perceives the actions of those who enter and responds intelligently through complex visual and auditory displays."[49] Isozaki's design thus paralleled and, in part, anticipated the theorization of responsive, intelligent architecture equipped with artificial intelligence by architects such as Nicholas Negroponte.[50] Isozaki and Tsukio originally envisioned this responsive, cybernetic environment of the Festival Plaza as modulating its output according to the self-learning process of its main computer, though this ambitious plan of having a fully operative artificial intelligence ultimately failed due to technical and economic limitations. Regardless of its practicality, however, what is crucial is the fact that the Festival Plaza signaled a new phase in the cybernetic turn of Japanese architecture. Here, architectural design literally merged with electronic media, creating a communication feedback loop between human participants and computers.

Indeed, in Japan in the 1960s, communication itself was a frequent focus of boundary-crossing artistic experiments—from multimedia installations to expanded cinema and video art. Arguably, buzzwords such as "information," "feedback," "participation," "interactivity," and "communication" that characterize Japanese art criticism of this decade all belong to the same cybernetic paradigm. Postwar Japanese avant-garde art's investment in the notion of the environment, in particular, hinged on the desire to transform passive viewers into "active receivers of the message" sent by the artwork.[51] It is here that we see an interesting twist in the postwar iteration of the concept of the environment, which played an important role in prewar and wartime architectural discourse and its articulation of the biopolitical management of the empire and its occupants. The term "environment" (kankyō) gained popularity in postwar Japan partly through the impact of avant-garde art movements such as Fluxus and the rise of intermedia and environmental art practices. Yet, to separate the architectural context of thinking about the environment from its avant-garde art context would be to miss a historical convergence of these two contexts around Tange Lab, and more specifically around Isozaki, who frequently collaborated with avant-garde artists such as Yamaguchi Katsuhiro.[52]

As we saw earlier, even Tange Lab's approach to the environment shifted from its biological understanding of the milieu to a cybernetic understanding of the communicative field. When transposed to the context of art, the communicative process of feedback also gained the added connotation of interactivity, resonating with the leftist critique of the unidirectionality of mass media.[53] Throughout the 1960s, the construction of multimedia installations and environmental artworks that allowed interactive and participatory experiences through feedback loops thus became the locus of experimentation among artists as well as architects in Japan.[54]

Crucial to this collective investment in interactivity and participation was the postwar reception of communication theory. As media scholar Matsui Shigeru suggests, the loan word komyunikeeshon (communication) gained currency in Japan in the immediate postwar period, when scholars associated with the Institute for the Science of Thought (Shisō no Kagaku

Kenkyūkai) began introducing communication theory from the United States.[55] The institute, led by liberal intellectuals such as Tsurumi Shunsuke and Minami Hiroshi, was instrumental in popularizing the term and establishing the disciplines of communication studies and social psychology in Japan.[56] The Cold War political climate heavily conditioned this institutionalization of communication studies during the occupation era and after.

According to Tamura Norio, a communication studies scholar associated with the Institute for the Science of Thought, the journal *Shisō no kagaku* published a special issue, titled "Studies of Communication," in 1948. Tamura also credits the work of Inokuchi Ichirō for the establishment of the "new" newspaper studies and communication science (*komyunikeeshon kagaku*) in Japan,[57] the latter based as it was on the American style of communications studies.[58] Noting UNESCO's first General Conference (1946) and its promotion of communication research, Inokuchi contended that communication science could contribute to the maintenance of peace in the nuclear age.[59] In short, the timing of the Japanese reception of communication theory perfectly coincided with the Cold War campaign by the United States to promote mass communication research, a campaign couched in the rhetoric of liberal democracy. Tsurumi, for his part, argues that the English terms "communication" and "mass communication" were introduced to Japan around 1947.[60]

By the early 1970s, however, the Institute for the Science of Thought tried to tackle this Cold War provenance of communication research. Tsurumi, for instance, cautioned against the danger of subordinating academic research to the interests of the military-industrial complex. Tsurumi writes, "In the midst of the superpowers' arms race, research on communication history could easily be used for studying and testing the optimal communication methods within the military."[61] In order to steer the nascent discipline of communication studies away from Cold War military science, Tsurumi called for a more holistic framework for understanding communication, which went beyond the history of technical media. Referencing the work of Jacques Ellul, Aldous Huxley, Claude Lévi-Strauss, and Johan Huizinga, he argued that communication studies scholars must not let their research become "a technique that benefits the oppressor."[62]

The ideologically ambivalent position occupied by the Institute for the Science of Thought in the postwar Japanese period mirrors the political ambivalence Isozaki recognized in his own application of cybernetics to the Festival Plaza. In both cases, the emancipatory potential of communication is haunted by its ghostly provenance in military operations research.

Isozaki's turn to cybernetics was, moreover, underscored by a critique of architectural modernism. It is on this point that he went a step further than Tange. While both architects helped initiate the cybernetic turn of Japanese architecture, Isozaki's vision was more in tune with the avant-garde art context, and perhaps more representative of the new generation of architects who actively sought to expand the conceptual horizon of architecture through their engagement with technical media. Isozaki articulated his practice of urban design as a deconstructive gesture, an act of dismantling "architecture" that is akin to boundary-crossing approaches of the avant-garde art movement of the 1960s. When we place Isozaki's articulation of the cybernetic environment within this context, we also find nuanced differences in Tange's and Isozaki's cybernetic approaches to urban space. To better understand these differences, let us examine Isozaki's writings on cybernetics and urban design.

In his essay "Methods of Urban Design" (Toshi dezain no hōhō, 1963), for instance, Isozaki articulates the main difference between Tange's vision of urban planning and his own. The difference is suggestive insofar as it indicates how the cybernetic paradigm embraced by Isozaki ultimately shifted the focus of urban design away from the hardware of transportation and communication infrastructures toward the software of responsive environments.

In this essay, Isozaki divides the history of urban design into four stages: the substantial, the functional, the structural, and the symbolic. His own practice belongs to the symbolic stage, and Tange's practice belongs to the structural stage. Isozaki cites Tange's conception of the "urban axis" in the Plan for Tokyo 1960 as an example. The notion of the urban axis reflects Tange's structural perspective, which privileges physical or visual "patterns" of the city.[63] By contrast, Isozaki argues that his approach to urban design is based on a simulated *model* instead of an existing *pattern* of the city. In short, the symbolic stage of architecture based on the cybernetic logic of simulation is distinct from and opposed to the structural stage of architecture based on the mechanical logic of coordination. Put differently, the structural approach extracts a pattern from the already existing city, while the symbolic approach generates a model conceived in and through technical media.

The idea of coordination was central to industrial modernity. From Le Corbusier to Bruno Taut, modernist architects and urban planners operated within the twin logics of coordination and organization. This mechanical model of urban design "concentrated entirely on the organization and coordination of elements or on the discovery of a structure to serve as an assembly theory."[64] What the modernist practice of urbanism lacked, in Isozaki's view, was a model of feedback. Tange tried to incorporate the insight of cybernetics into his urban design, but his priority was still on structural organization and coordination, although filtered through a newer engagement with logistics and information society discourse. By contrast, Isozaki takes ephemeral networks of information to be the central element of urban design.

Isozaki's interest in the ephemeral or informational dimension of the city is also evident in his earlier essay, "Space of Darkness" (Yami no kūkan, 1964), in which he discusses the importance of the man-machine interface that mediates our experience of the city. He uses the example of a pilot who flies an airplane at night. Because of the darkness, the pilot cannot trust his own vision and thus "must rely solely on signals received by flight instruments" in order to navigate the aircraft.[65] Isozaki extends this metaphor of the pilot to the daily experience of the contemporary city that is heavily networked with information and communication signals.[66] Inversely, the task of contemporary architects becomes how to design urban space without losing sight of these virtual networks of information and communication signals. For Isozaki, architecture's turn toward cybernetics and methods of computer simulation comes naturally out of this understanding of the city as primarily an information environment.

Arguably, Isozaki's emphasis on computer-generated models as the new basis of urban design is indicative of the historical moment within which he was writing. Simulation, as historian of science and technology Paul Edwards reminds us, was the reigning cultural logic of the Cold War era.[67] The era of simulation also signaled for Jean Baudrillard the end of the modernist order of mechanical reproduction. Writing around the same time as Isozaki, Baudrillard argued that the simulation of models—rather than serial products, which belonged to the second order of simulacra—ushered in the third order of simulacra that corresponded to the proliferation of codes.[68] Isozaki's vision of urban design that privileged codes, signs, and simulated models is reflective of the time when cybernetics and information science changed the ways in which the relation between technical media and reality was understood in various fields.

Isozaki's interest in the primacy of codes is best articulated in his essay "The Invisible City" (Mienai toshi, 1967), which also provides a theoretical framework for his design of the cybernetic environment of the Festival Plaza.[69] The essay begins by addressing the inadequacy of using the existing concept of urban space to understand cities such as Los Angeles and Tokyo.[70] The chaotic layout and sprawl of these cities prevents him from seeing their structure in a systematic manner. Lacking grid patterns and land-mark structures, the urban space of the contemporary city is no longer representable through spatial coordinates. Instead of landmarks and grids, the city is grasped relationally, that is, by gauging constantly shifting "relations between objects."[71] Precisely because the experience of space is no longer connected to physical elements, however, the city becomes intelligible only when one pays attention to "an aggregate of various invisible signs and codes; flickering lights, acoustic sounds, telecommunications, traffic, activities, and trajectories of moving objects." In place of measurements, these ephemeral signs, codes, and signals generate haptic sensations. The city dislodged from measurable space thus becomes subjective, relative, and environmental.[72] Isozaki calls this "invisible city" composed of invisible networks of ephemeral signs, codes, and signals a "virtual structure."[73]

The term "invisible city" used in this essay seems to evoke Lewis Mumford's theorization of urban space. Tracing a history of the reorganization of cities in the early 1960s, Mumford argues that invisible networks of communication and information systems represent and condition contemporary urban space: "The electric grid, not the stone age container, provides the new image of the invisible city and the many processes it serves and furthers. It is not merely the pattern of the city itself, but every institution, organization, and association composing the city, that will be transformed by this development."[74] Taking a cue from Mumford's observation of the invisible infrastructure of communication, Friedrich Kittler has also suggested that the modern city has long served as a model of media. "Ever since it had become impossible to survey cities from a cathedral tower or a castle, and ever since walls and fortifications have ceased to contain them, cities have been traversed and connected by a network of innumerable networks." In a typically axiomatic tone, Kittler contends that "no matter whether these networks convey information or energy—that is, whether they are called 'telephone,' 'radio,' and 'television,' or 'water supply,' 'electricity,' and 'highway'—they all are information (if only because every modern stream of energy needs a parallel control network)."[75] For Kittler, media is what stores, transmits, and processes information. In this broad definition of media, "media include old-fashioned things like books, familiar ones like cities, and new ones like computers."[76] Isozaki would agree with Kittler, given how he too conceives of urban space as first and foremost networks of information.

Of course, to simply state that Isozaki and Kittler share the idea of the city as a medium of communication would be to overlook manifold historical factors that affected postwar Japanese architectural criticism and practice, which I have traced in depth in this chapter. Nonetheless, a theoretical affinity between their approaches to architecture through the lens of media theory is worth noting, because the conflation of the city and media has become reality, or at least, so it appears in today's debates around ubiquitous computing and atmospheric media. As I noted at the beginning of this essay, the connection between milieu and media is a historical construct, yet this historicity gets lost if one takes this analogy between media and the city as a point of departure, as Kittler does. To graft a history of architecture onto the history of media theory is all the more necessary today, as the discipline of media studies increasingly directs its attention to the atmospheric, elemental, and ecological dimensions of media, and takes the environment as an ahistorical given.

Conclusion

In hindsight, Japanese architects' theorization of urban design through the conceptual frameworks of information networks, cybernetics, and communication theory points to an incipient theory of the city environment as atmospheric media. Like the critical stance video and multimedia installation artists took to go beyond the modernist adherence to medium specificity, the cybernetic model of communication embraced by these architects was meant to dismantle the modernist ideal of architecture. Cybernetics and its concomitant logic of feedback in particular played an enabling role by allowing young architects such as Isozaki to shift the weight of urban design away from the monumental permanence and the functionality of built structures toward the ephemerality of information flows and semiotic systems of codes and signs.

While there is no space in this chapter to elaborate, it is worth mentioning that this cybernetic turn in Japanese architecture paved the way for the subsequent, separate reception of French critical theory—in particular the structural semiotics that brought attention to the systematic understanding of signs and codes—in the 1970s and 1980s. In recent years, scholars have outlined the significant impact cybernetics and information theory had on the development of structuralism and semiotics.[77] Isozaki, for instance, became closely involved with the so-called New Academic circle, most notably through his collaboration with Asada Akira in the international *Any* conference series, along with architects and philosophers such as Peter Eisenman and Jacques Derrida.[78] The early stages of the Japanese reception of structuralism and poststructuralism might thus be found in the cybernetic turn of architecture in the 1960s.

The cybernetic turn of Japanese architecture also points to the fact that the theorization of media, including architecture, is heavily determined by the political and technological conditions of the time in which it is produced. Theory, as we know, is never value-free or conflict-free. If what we mean by "media theory" implies a systematic way of thinking about mediation (not only technological, but also political, economic, and social), as well as the geneses of various apparatuses of communication, and the interrelations between these different media forms, then Japanese architectural discourse of the 1960s offers a productive site to rethink these issues. This was the moment when architectural discourse thought seriously about the atmospheric and environmental nature of electronic media, and reconceptualized urban space through networks of information and communication.

Historically, architecture has held close affinities with the notion of a system. Its propensity toward organization and unity—architectonics—has, for instance, made it a privileged metaphor of rational and systemic thinking in philosophy.[79] Japanese architectural criticism of the 1960s complicates the architectonic aspect of architectural design by introducing a new kind of systematicity based on cybernetics. Architecture changed from a practice of constructing buildings to a practice of designing a communication environment through information technologies. At that point, architecture became part of the communication network, or what Gregory Bateson once called "media ecology."[80] It is here that we find a clear link between contemporary theories of atmospheric media and Japanese architectural criticism. Moreover, these early theorizations of architecture as media environment could provide some inspiration—or at the very least further contextualization—for contemporary scholars turning to the environment as the basis for their theorization of media.

NOTES

Acknowledgments: This essay greatly benefited from the intellectually stimulating conversations I had with the participants of two workshops: "Media Theory in Japan," organized by the editors of this volume, Marc Steinberg and Alex Zahlten, at Harvard University in 2013; and "Media Crossings," organized by Thomas Lamarre and Alanna Thain, at McGill University in 2014. In addition, I want to thank Yatsuka Hajime for his generous and thoughtful engagement with my research, as well as Matsui Shigeru and

Orit Halpern for their comments on this essay. Special thanks go to Isozaki Arata for allowing me to reproduce the diagram of the Festival Plaza.

1. Mark B. N. Hansen, *Feed-Forward: On the Future of Twenty-First-Century Media* (Chicago: University of Chicago Press, 2015), 5.

2. John Durham Peters, *The Marvelous Clouds: Toward a Philosophy of Elemental Media* (Chicago: University of Chicago Press, 2015), 4.

3. Peters, *Marvelous Clouds*, 34.

4. Yatsuka Hajime, " 'Metaborizumu Nekusasu' to iu 'kindai no chōkoku' " [The overcoming modernity called Metabolism Nexus], in *Metaborizumu no mirai toshi* [Metabolism: The city of the future] (Tokyo: Mori Bijutsukan, 2011), 11. See also Yatsuka Hajime, *Metaborizumu Nekusasu* [Metabolism Nexus] (Tokyo: Ohmsha, 2011).

5. Marshall McLuhan, *Understanding Media: The Extensions of Man* (Cambridge, MA: MIT Press, 1994), 127.

6. McLuhan, *Understanding Media*, 8.

7. McLuhan, *Understanding Media*, 126.

8. Mark Wigley, "Network Fever," in *New Media, Old Media: A History and Theory Reader*, ed. Wendy Hui Kyong Chun and Thomas Keenan (New York: Routledge, 2006), 377.

9. Wigley, "Network Fever," 387.

10. Reinhold Martin, *The Organizational Complex: Architecture, Media, and Corporate Space* (Cambridge, MA: MIT Press, 2003), 21.

11. Wigley, "Network Fever," 388. Wigley writes, "Doxiadis's idea of network form had itself been informed by the earlier work of Tange."

12. Following Michel Foucault, I use the term *biopolitics* to mean a modern regime of governance and regulatory techniques applied to control and manage the biological processes of the human population, or "man-as-species." For more on this concept of biopolitics, see Michel Foucault, *"Society Must Be Defended": Lectures at the Collège de France, 1975–1976*, ed. Mauro Bertani and Alessandro Fontana, trans. David Macey (New York: Picador, 2003); Michel Foucault, *Security, Territory, Population: Lectures at the Collège de France, 1977–1978*, ed. Michel Senellart, trans. Graham Burchell (New York: Palgrave Macmillan, 2007).

13. Tange Kenzō, *Nihon rettō no shrōraizō: 21 seiki e no kenchiku* [The future of the Japanese archipelago: The formation of Tōkaidō megalopolis] (Tokyo: Kōdansha, 1966), 32.

14. Tange Kenzō, *Kenchiku to toshi: Dezain oboegaki* [City as architecture: Notes on design] (Tokyo: Sekai Bunkusha, 1975; repr., Tokyo: Shōkokusha, 2011), 87.

15. Tange's cybernetic turn can be seen as part of the epistemic paradigm, which Reinhold Martin has called the "organizational complex."

16. Tange, *Nihon rettō no shrōraizō*, 34–35.

17. Eric Paul Mumford, *The CIAM Discourse on Urbanism, 1928–1960* (Cambridge, MA: MIT Press, 2000), 25.

18. Tange, *Nihon rettō no shōraizō*, 42.

19. Martin, *Organizational Complex*, 57–61.

20. Yatsuka, *Metaborizumu nekusasu*, 19.

21. Kobayashi Hideo, *"Manshū" no rekishi* (Tokyo: Kōdansha Gendai Shinsho, 2008), 41–42. On the activities of the South Manchuria Railway Company's research department, see also Kobayashi Hideo, *Mantetsu chōsabu: "Ganso shinku tanku" no tanjō to hōkai* (Tokyo: Heibonsha, 2005).

22. Yatsuka, *Metaborizumu nekusasu*, 19; and Yatsuka, "Metaborizumu," 13.

23. See Sawaragi Noi, *Sensō to banpaku* (Tokyo: Bijutsu Shuppansha, 2005); Isozaki Arata, "Tange Kenzō no 'kenchiku=toshi=kokka' kyōdōtai to shite no Nihon," in *Sanshutsu sareta modanizumu: "Nihon" to iu mondai kikō* (Tokyo: Iwanami Shoten, 2005), 173–202. It is worth noting that Yatsuka studied with Tange and worked with Isozaki. For more on the relation between the postwar notion of the environment and architecture, see Yuriko Furuhata, "Multimedia Environments and Security Operations: Expo '70 as a Laboratory of Governance," *Grey Room* 54 (winter 2014): 56–79.

24. Gotō Shinpei, *Seiden: Gotō Shinpei, Mantetsu jidai, 1906–1908* (Tokyo: Fujiwara Shoten, 2005), 4:149.

25. Gotō, *Seiden*, 4:149.

26. This was an unrealized project, though some of its elements are preserved in his postwar design of the Hiroshima Peace Memorial Park. On the connection between these two projects, see Lisa Yoneyama, *Hiroshima Traces: Time, Space, and the Dialectics of Memory* (Berkeley: University of California Press, 1999); and Hyunjung Cho, "Hiroshima Peace Memorial Park and the Making of Japanese Postwar Architecture," *Journal of Architectural Education* 66, no. 1 (2012): 72–83.

27. Masuda Yoneji, *The Information Society as Post-Industrial Society* (Tokyo: Institute for the Information Society, 1980), 147.

28. Tessa Morris-Suzuki, *Beyond Computopia: Information, Automation, and Democracy in Japan* (London: Kegan Paul, 1988), 8.

29. Hayashi Yūjirō, *Jōhōka shakai: Haado na shakai kara sofuto na shaka e* [Information society: From hard society to soft society] (Tokyo: Kōdansha Gendai Shinsho, 1969), 49.

30. Keizai shingikai jōhō kenkyū iinkai, *Nihon no Jōhōka shakai: Sono bijon to kadai* [Japan's information society: Its vision and challenges] (Tokyo: Daiyamondo Sha, 1969), 5.

31. Hayashu Shūji, *Ryūtsū kakumei: Seihin, keiro, oyobi shōhisha* [A revolution in distribution: Products, pathways, and consumers] (Tokyo: Chūō Kōron Shinsho, 1962).

32. For more on this, see Morris-Suzuki, *Beyond Computopia*, chapters 4–6.

33. Katherine Hayles, "Cybernetics," in *Critical Terms for Media Studies*, ed. W. J. T. Mitchell and Mark B. N. Hansen (Chicago: University of Chicago Press, 2010), 145; italics in source.

34. Toyokawa Saikaku, "The Core System and Social Scale: Design Methodology at the Tange Laboratory," trans. Watanabe Hiroshi, in *Kenzō Tange: Architecture for the World*, ed. Seng Kuan and Yukio Lippit (Zürich: Lars Müler Publishers and the President and Fellows of Harvard College, 2012), 25.

35. Toyokawa Saikaku, *Gunzō to shite no Tange Kenkyūshitsu: Sengo Nihon kenchiku toshi shi no meinsutoriimu* [The Tange Lab as a group: The mainstream of postwar Japanese architecture and the history of urban design] (Tokyo: Ohmsha, 2012), 44. On

Tange Lab's impact on social and economic policies, see also Toyokawa, "Core System and Social Scale," 15–28.

36. Shimokōbe Atsushi, ed., *Jōhōshakai to no taiwa: Mirai Nihon no jōhō nettowaaku* [Dialogues with information society: Information networks for future Japan] (Tokyo: Tōyō Keizai Shinhōsha, 1970), iii. See also Rem Koolhaas and Hans Ulrich Obrist, eds., *Project Japan: Metabolism Talks . . .* (Cologne, Ger.: Taschen, 2011), 638.

37. Kurokawa Kishō, *Jōhō rettō Nihon no shōrai* [The future of information archipelago Japan] (Tokyo: Dai San Bunmei Sha, 1972), 1–2. Kurokawa argues that he became first interested in the concept of information around 1958, when he began to formulate the "metabolic" conception of the city as a living organism.

38. See Hayashi Yūjirō and Kagaku Gijutsu to Keizai no Kai, eds., *Chō gijutsu shakai e no tenkai: Jōhōka shisutemu no ningen* [Developing a supertechnological society: Humans in the information system] (Tokyo: Daiyamondo Sha, 1969).

39. Yatsuka, *Metaborizumu nekusasu*, 320.

40. Toyokawa, *Gunzō to shite no Tange kenkyūshitsu*, 314.

41. Kurokawa, *Jōhō rettō Nihon no shōrai*, 2.

42. Isozaki often describes the difference between his view of urban design and that of the Metabolist group as a difference between the image of "ruin" and the image of utopia. On his discussion of the future city as a ruin, see Isozaki Arata, "Haikyo ron," in *Kigō no umi ni ukabu "shima"* [Islands in the sea of signs] (Tokyo: Iwanami Shoten, 2013), 24–40.

43. Isozaki participated in landmark art exhibitions, including *Shikisai to kūkan ten* [Color and space, 1966]; *Kūkan kara kankyō e ten* (From space to environment, 1966); and the Fourteenth Milan Triennale (1968). He also worked as an exhibition space designer for *Okamoto Tarō ten* (Okamoto Tarō exhibition, 1964).

44. Isozaki Arata, "Aatisuto-Aakitekuto no jidai: Osaka banpaku nosōzōryoku o hokan shita aato shin" [The era of an artist-architect: Art scenes that supplemented the imagination of the world's fair in Osaka], interview with Arata Isozaki, by Yasuko Imura, Yuriko Furuhata, and Shigeru Matsui, *Tokyo Geijutsu Daigaku Eizōkenkyū Kiyō* (October 2012): 36–80.

45. Isozaki notes that they established this company in order to receive public funding. Isozaki Arata, in discussion with the author, June 2013.

46. In his essay "Sofuto aakitekuchua," published in *Kenchiku bunka* in 1970, Isozaki described the computer-programmed cybernetic environment of the Festival Plaza as "soft architecture," a phrase he borrowed from Warren Brodey's work. See Warren M. Brodey, "The Design of Intelligent Environment: Soft Architecture," *Landscape* 17, no. 1 (autumn 1967): 8–12.

47. Isozaki Atelier, "Sofuto aakitekuchua: Ōtōba to shite no kankyō," *Kenchiku bunka* 279 (January 1970): 73. Moreover, the model for this tightly networked two-way communication environment was the mission control center at NASA, which he had visited in 1967. See Isozaki Arata and Hino Naohiko, "Taaningu pointo: Kūkan kara kankyō e," *10+1* 48 (2007): 203.

48. While the published materials of the Festival Plaza, such as the article "Sofuto aakitekuchua" in *Kenchiku bunka* (1970), indicate that the robots were responsive, Tsukio Yoshio notes that the plaza's computerized system of control was imperfect and

did not actualize the original plan of creating a fully interactive environment. Tsukio Yoshio in discussion with the author and Matsui Shigeru on November 12, 2015.

49. Myron W. Krueger, "Responsive Environments," in *The New Media Reader*, ed. Noah Wardrip-Fruin and Nick Montfort (Cambridge, MA: MIT Press, 2003), 379.

50. For more information on Negroponte's and Krueger's work, see Nicholas Negroponte, *Soft Architecture Machines* (Cambridge, MA: MIT Press, 1976); Krueger, "Responsive Environments," 379–89.

51. Isozaki Arata and Tōno Yoshiaki, "'Kankyō' ni tsuite," in "Kūkan kara kankyō e," special issue, *Bijutsu techō* [Art notebook] 275 (November 1966): 100.

52. Isozaki and Yamaguchi set up a company called Kakyō Keikaku (Environmental Planning) during their participation in Expo '70. See Isozaki and Hino, "Taaning pointo", *10+1* 48 (2007): 197.

53. For more on this, see Miryam Sas's contribution to this volume.

54. The use of video was particularly important for creating feedback loops. See David Joselit, *Feedback: Television against Democracy* (Cambridge, MA: MIT Press, 2007); and on multiscreen environments, see Fred Turner, *The Democratic Surround: Multimedia and American Liberalism from World War II to the Psychedelic Sixties* (Berkeley: University of California Press, 2014). On intermedia and environmental art experiments in Japan, see also Miryam Sas, "By Other Hands: Environment and Apparatus in 1960s Intermedia," in *The Oxford Handbook of Japanese Cinema*, ed. Miyao Daisuke (Oxford: Oxford University Press, 2014), 383–415.

55. Matsui Shigeru, "Fukusei gijutsu no tenkai to media geijutsu no seiritsu: 1950 nendai no Nihon ni okeru terebi, shakai shinrigaku, gendai geijutsu no sougo shintō" [The development of reproduction technology and the establishment of media arts: Interpenetrations among television, social psychology, and contemporary art of the 1950s], *Eizō media gaku: Tokyo geijutsu daigaku daigakuin eizō kenkyūka kiyō* 2 (March 2012): 46.

56. Andrew E. Barshay, "Postwar Social and Political Thought, 1945–90," in *Modern Japanese Thought*, ed. Bob Tadashi Wakabayashi (Cambridge: Cambridge University Press, 1998), 305.

57. Tamura Norio, "'Atarashii Shinbungaku' no tanjō to 'Masu komi' ron no eikyō: Inokuchi Ichirō ni hajimaru sengo no 'Amerikashu' kenkyū no inyū" [The birth of "new newspaper science" and the impact of mass communication theory: The postwar introduction of the "American" style of research that began with Inokuchi Ichirō], *Komyunikeeshon kagaku* 35 (2012): 123–33.

58. Inokuchi Ichirō, *Masu komyunikēshon: Dono youni taishū e hataraki kakeru ka* [Mass communication: How to influence the masses] (Tokyo: Kōbunsha, 1951), 26.

59. Inokuchi, *Masu komyunikēshon*, 30–31. As evidenced in Inokuchi's implication of a nuclear threat, discourse surrounding the emergent discipline of communications studies in Japan clearly belonged to the Cold War context.

60. Tsurumi Shunsuke, "Komyunikēshon shi e no oboegaki" [Notes on the history of communication], in *Komyunikēshon shi: Kōza komyunikēshon* [The history of communication: A course on communication], ed. Etō Fumio, Tsurumi Shunsuke, Yamamoto Akira (Tokyo: Kenkyūsha, 1973), 2:17. See also Matsui, "Fukusei gijutsu no tenkai," 47;

and Ann Sherif, *Japan's Cold War: Media, Literature, and the Law* (New York: Columbia University Press, 2009), 44.

61. Tsurumi, "Komyunikēshon shi e no oboegaki," 19.

62. Tsurumi, "Komyunikēshon shi e no oboegaki," 19.

63. Isozaki, "Toshi dezain no hōhō" [Methods of urban design], in *Kūkan e* [To space] (Tokyo: Kajima Shuppankai, 1997), 106.

64. Isozaki Arata, "Invisible City," in *Architecture Culture, 1943–1968: A Documentary Anthology*, ed. Joan Ockman (New York: Columbia Books of Architecture, 1993), 405.

65. Isozaki Arata, "Yami no kūkan," in *Kūkan e* [To space] (Tokyo: Kajimashuppankai, 1997), 151.

66. Isozaki, "Yami no kūkan," 151.

67. Paul N. Edwards, *The Closed World: Computers and the Politics of Discourse in Cold War America* (Cambridge, MA: MIT Press, 1996), 14.

68. Jean Baudrillard, *Symbolic Exchange and Death* (London: Sage Publication, 1993), 56.

69. Isozaki Arata and Hino Naohiko, "*Kūkan e*, Omatsuri Hiroba, *Nihon no toshi kūkan*: 1960 nen dai ni okeru toshiron no hōhō o megutte," *10+1* 45 (2006): 187–97.

70. Isozaki Arata, "Mienai toshi" [The invisible city], in *Kūkan e* [To space] (Tokyo: Kajima Shuppankai, 1997), 374. My translation. This first section of the essay has not been translated into English, though the second half of the essay has been translated under the same title, "Invisible City." See Isozaki, "Invisible City," 403–97.

71. Isozaki, "Mienai toshi," 378.

72. Isozaki, "Mienai toshi," 381.

73. Isozaki revisits this notion of the city as the invisible information environment in "Konpō sareta kankyō" [Packaged environments], in *Kūkan e* [To space] (Tokyo: Kajimashuppankai, 1997), 421.

74. Lewis Mumford, *The City in History* (New York: Harcourt, 1961), 567.

75. Friedrich Kittler, *The Truth of the Technological World: Essays on the Genealogy of Presence*, trans. Erik Butler (Stanford, CA: Stanford University Press, 2013), 139. Kittler's point, however, is that these information networks also existed in the past, well before modernity.

76. Kittler, *Technological World*, 144.

77. As Bernard Dionysius Geoghegan notes in his careful research on Roman Jakobson's and Lévi-Strauss's investments in information theory and cybernetics and their ties to the Rockefeller Foundation, MIT, and Harvard, French structuralism and semiotics are rooted in the mathematical theories of communication. See Bernard Dionysius Geoghegan, "From Information Theory to French Theory: Jakobson, Lévi-Strauss, and the Cybernetic Apparatus," *Critical Inquiry* 38 (autumn 2011): 96–126.

78. Isozaki and Asada were regular participants in the *Any* series of international conferences on architecture and philosophy, which Isozaki initiated with Peter Eisenman in 1999. For more on the *Any* conference series, see Isozaki Arata and Asada Akira, eds., *Any Kenchiku to tetsugaku o meguru sesshon, 1991–2008* [*Any*: Sessions on architecture and philosophy, 1991–2008], (Tokyo: Kajima Shuppan, 2010).

79. Jacques Derrida, "Architecture Where the Desire May Live," in *Rethinking Architecture: A Reader in Cultural Theory*, ed. Neil Leach (London: Routledge, 1997), 319.

See also Karatani Kōjin, *Inyu to shite no kenchiku* [Architecture as metaphor] (Tokyo: Kōdansha, 1989), a book translated into English as *Architecture as Metaphor: Language, Number, Money,* ed. Michael Speaks, trans. Sabu Kohso (Cambridge, MA: MIT, 1995). On Isozaki's interest in poststructuralism and deconstruction, see his conversation with Derrida, "*Anywhere*: Dikonsutorakushon to wa nanika" [*Anywhere*: What is deconstruction?], in *Any: Kenchiku to tetsugaku o meguru sesshon, 1991–2008* (Tokyo: Kajima Shuppan, 2010), 81–100.

80. Tracing the genealogy of the term *media ecology* (which has garnered much attention in recent years) through the work of the British social scientist and cyberneticist Gregory Bateson and the video art magazine *Radical Software,* William Kaizen has argued that media ecology is deeply intertwined with the cybernetic discourse of communication, and in particular with Bateson's theory of communication. See William Kaizen, "Steps to an Ecology of Communication: *Radical Software,* Dan Graham, and the Legacy of Gregory Bateson," *Art Journal* 67, no. 3 (fall 2008): 91.

3. THE MEDIA THEORY AND MEDIA STRATEGY OF AZUMA HIROKI, 1997–2003

TAKESHI KADOBAYASHI

Since the turn of the twenty-first century, Azuma Hiroki has been one of the most influential public intellectuals in Japan. As a critic he works mainly in the field of *otaku* culture, although his recent writings cover various issues, from the possible revision of the Constitution of Japan to the aftermath of the accident in the Fukushima Daiichi Nuclear Power Station, and he has even written novels and anime scenarios. In what is up to now his most important work, *Dōbutsuka suru postomodan: Otaku kara mita nihon shakai* (*Otaku: Japan's Database Animals*), published in 2001, he analyzed various fields of otaku culture, such as anime, video games, trading cards, and light novels through the key concept of the "database animal," placing these in the broader context of the societal transition from modernity to postmodernity. According to Azuma, the media mix strategy and derivative amateur works have become the norm in otaku culture since the 1990s, in which the otaku's consumptive activities are oriented toward the database-like grand nonnarrative (*ōkina himonogatari*) behind individual works, exemplifying the broader social phenomena of postmodernity after the collapse of modernity's grand narratives (*ōkina monogatari*). To this day the book remains one of the most influential works in the study of subcultures in Japan, and it offers insights into the new media environment that appeared with the development of information technology. Indeed, it would be impossible to think of postmillennium media theory in Japan as a whole without acknowledging Azuma's work.

In spite of this, Azuma Hiroki is not necessarily regarded as a "media theorist" in Japan. This probably has something to do with the trajectory of his career as a critic. He debuted in 1993 with a paper published in the highly influential critical theory journal *Hihyō kūkan* (Critical space), "Solzhenitsyn shiron: Kakuritsu no tezawari" (An essay on Solzhenitsyn: The feel of probability), which he wrote while still an undergraduate student. He then began to publish studies on Jacques Derrida in the same journal, and this culminated in his first book in 1998, *Sonzairon teki, yūbin teki: Jacques Derrida ni tsuite* (*Ontological, Postal: On Jacques Derrida*). In the 1990s Azuma Hiroki was thus a promising young critic who used sophisticated philosophical language to develop highly abstract arguments.

In a different vein, Azuma began publishing articles on subculture in the late 1990s, and since the publication of *Otaku* in 2001, he has been active regularly as a critic of otaku culture. In the so-called *zero nendai* (the first decade of the 2000s), critical discourse on otaku culture such as anime, manga, light novels, idols, and video games blossomed in Japan and drew wider social attention. As a result, and also because of the increasing international visibility of otaku culture and the Japanese governmental policy toward it ("Cool Japan"), the negative implications the word "otaku" formerly possessed were swept away. Azuma, who had turned from the high-blown discourse of contemporary philosophy and critical theory to subcultural criticism, played a significant role in this shift, and his influence in this regard is hard to overestimate.

The image we have of Azuma is thus somewhat overdetermined by these two careers, and there is a certain sense of incongruity, at least in the Japanese context, to insert between them a different moment of Azuma as a media theorist.[1] Nevertheless, Azuma's career so far abounds with thoughts on media and information technology. In addition to *Otaku*, which dealt with otaku culture using the terminology of information technology, Azuma also hosted, for example, an interdisciplinary roundtable series on the information society at the International University of Japan's Global Communication Center from 2004 to 2005, later published as a massive two-volume book: *Ised: Jōhō shakai no rinri to sekkei* (*Ised: Ethics and Design of the Information Society*, 2010). One of his most recent books, *Ippan ishi 2.0: Rousseau, Freud, Google* (*General Will 2.0: Rousseau, Freud, and Google*, 2011), is an attempt to visualize the possible shape of government in the age of the Internet.

Furthermore, Azuma wrote two serial articles that explicitly addressed the subject of media theory in the context of the information society around the time of the publication of *Otaku*: "Cyberspace wa naze sō yobareru ka" (Why Is Cyberspace Called Such?), serialized in *InterCommunication* (1997–2000), and "Jōhō jiyū ron: Data no kenryoku, angō no rinri" (On Information and Freedom: The Power of Data, the Ethics of Code), serialized in *Chūō kōron* (2002–3). According to Azuma's own recollection, he intended to assemble these two series of articles with another series of articles, "Kashiteki na mono tachi" (The Overvisibles) in *Eureka* (2001)—which is in fact an earlier version of *Otaku*—and publish them all as "a book that contains something like a comprehensive theory of the postmodern."[2] As I will argue later, given that postmodernity, for Azuma, is a historical condition that cannot be separated from the social penetration of information technology, it is reasonable to regard this trilogy as a blueprint for his grand theory of media in the postmodern age.

Ultimately, this conception of a book that offered "a comprehensive theory of the postmodern" was not realized. Azuma quickly published the second installment of "The Overvisibles" independently as *Otaku* after a thoroughgoing rewrite, even before he began the subsequent serial "On Information and Freedom."[3] Considering the attention he had already gained from critical circles and journalists in Japan, we can assume that it would have been possible, and even desirable, for him to publish "Why Is Cyberspace Called Such?" and "On Information and Freedom" in book form without extensive rewrites—yet Azuma opted not to. Indeed, Azuma's decision to instead publish a book about otaku culture has come to have a definitive effect not only on his career but also on the whole discursive space of the zero nendai in Japan. These circumstances seem to partly explain why he has not been read as a media theorist to this date, at least in Japan, despite his extensive interest in issues of media and information technology.

This chapter seeks to explore Azuma's work from 1997 to 2003 to trace the possible shape of his abandoned media theory. My purpose will be to reconstruct the implicit theory he envisioned in this period, and at the same time, through a close reading of the texts themselves, expose the reason why it failed to bear fruit. In addition to uncovering a neglected aspect of Azuma as a media theorist, this reading will also offer an account of his change in attitude as a critic (and its corollary, a change in his media strategy). In so doing, I hope to cast light on the break that divides the 1990s and the zero nendai, not only within the career of Azuma Hiroki but also within the discourse on media in Japan more broadly.

Cyberspace as Metaphor, Postmodern as Condition

The idea of cyberspace first appeared in William Gibson's cyberpunk novel *Neuromancer* (1984). In it, Gibson bestows upon the near-future city of Chiba in which the story takes place an Asian or techno-orientalist character, and at the same time creates a space in which the consciousness of the characters appears within their electronic bodies—that is, a space called "cyberspace," which is distinguished from physical space. According to Azuma's first serial "Why Is Cyberspace Called Such?," these two imaginary spaces—the near-future "Oriental" urban space and the electronic space detached from the real world—function in the same manner. That is, both of them are needed to localize the "*uncanny (unheimlich)* elements" manifest in the information technologies within a space divorced from the (Occidental) real world in order to "exorcise" (*akuma barai*) them.[4] Therefore, the metaphor of cyberspace in *Neuromancer* is an ideological apparatus used to project toward the other the heterogeneous elements within oneself, that is, the products of "techno-orientalism."[5]

For Azuma, these "*uncanny* elements" are "the sense of the division of the 'here and now' of the characters and the duplication of their consciousness, themselves mediated by electronic media, and the resulting spectrality of the electronic self" (WC1, 164). In other words, introducing the stage of "cyberspace" as a location separate from real space and then confining the electronic self within it, *Neuromancer* excludes the possibility that the consciousness of the characters in the "here and now" of real space are haunted by electronic selves that serve as their doubles.

According to Azuma, this notion of cyberspace appeared alongside the social transformation from the modern to the postmodern, although, crucially, it was still a modern idea in denial of the postmodern, given that it appealed to a spatial metaphor (WC10, 173–75). In other words, the metaphor of cyberspace was a modern idea that was deployed to repress the postmodern conditions that already characterized contemporary society. To understand how the arguments in "Why Is Cyberspace Called Such?" proceed toward such a conclusion and its implications, we need to first evaluate the contours and background of Azuma's theory of the postmodern, which goes beyond an interpretation of the metaphor of cyberspace as it appears in *Neuromancer*.

In the serialization of "Why Is Cyberspace Called Such?," the terms "postmodern" and "postmodernism" are introduced in the fifth article (August 1998) in relation to Slavoj Žižek's discussions of cyberspace. In the two articles that Azuma cites, Žižek criticizes the studies of Sherry Turkle and Allucquére Rosanne Stone—who both suggest that the splitting of identity is caused by computer-mediated communication—using Lacan's model of subjectivity.[6] In "Why Is Cyberspace Called Such?" Azuma limits his discussion to Žižek's criticism of Turkle, and, in the course of summarizing the issue, theorizes postmodern subjectivity by sublating and synthesizing their standpoints, defining this new subjectivity as "interfacial" (WC5, 165).

According to Azuma's summary, Žižek's critique of Turkle proceeds as follows. Turkle argues that virtual communications such as IRC (Internet Relay Chat) and MUD (Multi-User Dungeon) create a split in the user's identity that she characterizes with the term "taking things at interface value."[7] That is, the user takes information appearing on the interface of the screen *at face value*, constructing his or her self through imaginary identification with it, so that the user comes to have plural, disintegrated identities that correspond to the plural virtual communications on screen. However, for Žižek, this is a crude argument that fails to grasp the dimension of symbolic identification, as outlined in Lacanian theory: following the latter's conception of subjectivity, the virtual subject that arises from this "at interface value" attitude on each occasion is in fact only an effect of the imaginary identification with the *objet petit a*, and human subjectivity completes itself by symbolic identification with the big Other that unifies these imaginary identifications. Therefore, Žižek argues, the imaginary splitting of identity that Turkle points out never threatens the Lacanian concept of subjectivity.

Following this argument, Žižek discusses the decline of the symbolic order in contemporary society in general, concluding that the metaphor of cyberspace is desired as a supplement to the loss of the symbolic order. Azuma, in turn, prompted by this view, argues that Turkle's theory, in the first place, is structured in a way that reflects the decline of the symbolic order. In other words, he hypothesizes that the "at interface value" attitude Turkle argues for is an attitude that is inevitably required, because the invisible big Other behind the visible world of the screen suffers a malfunction; it substitutes symbolic identification with imaginary simulation. Azuma calls such a formation of subjectivity "interfacial subjectivity." For him, this new subjectivity presents a radical break from the modern idea of subjectivity, and therefore is inherently a postmodern conception of subjectivity.

For Azuma, the modern idea of subjectivity has been constructed alongside the metaphor of the eye, and is organized by the dialectic of the visible and the invisible (WC6, 158–65). For example, the Lacanian concept of subjectivity, to which Žižek refers, is constructed by the duality in which the imaginary identification with the visible *objet petit a* is sustained by the symbolic identification with the invisible big Other. According to Azuma, however, postmodern conditions are those that render impossible such a modern conception of subjectivity based on the distinction between the visible and the invisible. Such conditions appeared in the 1970s and saturated the 1990s in the following two moments:

1   The decline of the symbolic order, or the "grand narrative" that gives order to the visible world presented to the subject, though remains invisible itself. Referring to the theories of Jean-François Lyotard and Fredric Jameson, Azuma in "Why Is Cyberspace Called Such?" summarizes the emergence of postmodern conditions in the 1970s, an epoch characterized by the gradual collapse of "the world view and the political vision (grand narrative) that sustained the counterculture of the 1960s" (WC5, 165). His subsequent writings then begin to argue that this situation reached a saturation point in the 1990s: if the fall of the Berlin Wall in 1989 and the following disintegration of the Communist bloc was a crucial moment in the decline of the grand narrative in world history, then the terrorist attack by the Aum Shinrikyo cult in 1995 can be considered an equivalent historical moment in Japan.

2   The invention of the GUI (Graphical User Interface) in the 1970s and its social saturation in the 1990s. GUI technology leaves the user unaware of the invisible behind the screen—the binary data running inside the integrated circuit. As a result, there appears an interfacial subjectivity that causes the user to take the visible on the screen at face value (the "at interface value" attitude) without considering the existence of the invisible behind.

Azuma then proposes to offer a distinction between postmodernism as a philosophical standpoint and the postmodern as a historical situation. That is, he argues that postmodernism as a philosophical standpoint, which appeared in the 1970s in the West and was represented particularly by New Academism in the 1980s in Japan, should rather be understood as a resistance to the historical tendency toward the postmodern. Azuma offers an intricate explanation of this view in the ninth article of "Why Is Cyberspace Called Such?" and in another independent article titled "Postmodern saikō" (Rethinking the Postmodern), which can be schematically summarized as follows.[8] While the postmodernists insisted on the decline of the invisible symbolic order that made possible the distinction between the visible and the invisible, when it came to the tendency toward an information society, they followed the preceding discourses of the 1960s and the 1970s, such as Daniel Bell's "post-industrial society" and Alvin Toffler's "third wave," often summed up under the umbrella term "futurology" (*miraigaku*) in Japan. The ideology of futurology, however, is inherently in opposition to postmodernism's insistence upon the impossibility of grand narratives, in that it foresaw the next stage of capitalism as coterminous with the rise of information technologies, and thus it newly reconstructed the grand narrative. And yet, independent of the macroscopic view futurologists took toward the coming information society, there proceeded the development of GUI technology, which nullified the distinction between the visible and the invisible at a microscopic level, and brought forward the new "interfacial subjectivity." Postmodernism as a philosophical standpoint could not foresee the advent of this new subjectivity radically disconnected from the modern idea of the subject, and thus it paradoxically functioned as an ideology that constituted the newer narrative of "the end of the modern," resisting the historical tendency toward the postmodern. That is, the discourse of postmodernism "appeared in order to acknowledge postmodern reality, and at the same time deny it" (*WC*10, 173). In this sense, Azuma argues, postmodernism as a philosophical movement is modern thought par excellence.

In this way, the postmodern condition, for Azuma, is a social phenomenon that began taking shape in the 1970s, and then, after its denial by the philosophical movement of postmodernism in the 1980s, reappeared in full force in the 1990s, constituting at this moment a clear break from modernity. Now, how can the idea of "cyberspace" be situated within this gradual, multitier transition from the modern to the postmodern? As I have already noted, the conclusion in "Why Is Cyberspace Called Such?" is that cyberspace is a modern idea in denial of the postmodern in that it still appeals to a spatial metaphor. Accordingly, in Azuma's argument, the idea of cyberspace shares the same position as postmodernism distinguished from the postmodern in that they both "acknowledge postmodern reality, and at the same time deny it"—in other words, "deny" (*verleugnen*) in the sense of a psychoanalytic defense mechanism.

This conclusion, however, derives from Azuma's somewhat illogical identification of the spatial metaphor with the visual one (spatial metaphors are not, of course, necessarily limited to visuality, as, for example, in Marshall McLuhan's appeal to the metaphor of "acoustic space" in describing the nature of electric media). That is, for Azuma, the idea of cyberspace provides a spatial, and therefore visual, metaphor of postmodern conditions, in which there is no longer a distinction between the visible and the invisible, thereby functioning as an exorcism of uncanny elements. According to him, cyberpunk "is a movement in which the sci-fi imagination, having lost the totality of the modern world in 1968—and as a result, the validity of the modern non-world such as the universe (space) or the future (time), too—attempted to revive itself by compensating this loss with the introduction of the new image of 'cyberspace'" (WC7, 146).

However, during the course toward the postmodern, interfacial subjectivity has appeared, a phenomenon that cannot be analyzed by the visual metaphor founded on the antithesis between the visible and the invisible, since everything is totally visible on the surface. This new subjectivity without depth, argues Azuma, therefore requires a new theoretical metaphor. However, there was not to be a substantial theoretical push toward this new task within this serial, and Azuma's next serial article, "The Overvisibles" (which formed the basis of *Otaku*) should have been the place where his argument developed in full. As indicated by the title, however, the theoretical metaphor Azuma introduced there was more thoroughly visual. In addition, the division of the visible and the invisible, which he had rejected as a modern theoretical framework, seemed to reappear in a different form.

From Cyberspace to Database

According to the formulation in "Why Is Cyberspace Called Such?," the postmodern age, in which the distinction between the visible on the surface and the invisible in depth has lost its effect, is a result of the collapse of the symbolic order that had sustained modernity. Interfacial subjectivity, for Azuma, is a new form of subjectivity in which everything is visible on the surface and therefore cannot be analyzed by visual-spatial metaphors. In contrast, "The Overvisibles" abandons the idea of total superficiality, introducing the "database" as "the new depth of the postmodern" at the beginning of its first article, as if it were already established previously in "Why Is Cyberspace Called Such?"[9] However, "Why Is Cyberspace Called Such?" barely uses the term "database," and certainly does not construct it as a key concept. Accordingly, we can assume that Azuma, upon assembling these serial articles as a book, planned to reconstruct the discussions in "Why Is Cyberspace Called Such?" with "database" as its central concept. Since such a work has not been realized, and since our purpose here is to reconstruct the media theory being conceptualized at this moment, we must thus speculate on how "Why Is Cyberspace Called Such?" could have been rewritten, referring to the arguments concerning the database in "The Overvisibles" and in *Otaku* as clues.

Let us begin this task by reintroducing the theoretical framework of *Otaku*. In this work, Azuma theorizes what he calls "database consumption," taking examples from collectible stickers (*bikkuriman* stickers), characters in anime (Ayanami Rei from *Evangelion*), the genre of young adult novels which would later be called "light novels" in Japan (the works of Seiryoin Ryūsui), dating sims (*Kizuato*, *Yu-No*, etc.), and so on. Especially exemplary among these is the case of Di Gi Charat, an image character of Gamers, a retail store group that sells anime and game-related goods.

Di Gi Charat is said to have appeared around 1997 or 1998, originally only as a graphic design, and without a narrative world behind it. However, it gradually gained attention, and anime, novels, and games with the character as a protagonist were later produced. In the process, the narrative world around the character (the story, other characters, the personalities of the characters, etc.) came to be formed anonymously and collectively. Thus, in Di Gi Charat, the normal order in which the narrative world of a certain work is followed by its character goods is reversed, and its narrative is only one subordinate element within the whole strategy of the media mix.

In addition, the visual appearance of Di Gi Charat is composed of design elements favored by otaku (Azuma calls them "*moe*-elements"), such as cat ears, hair sticking up like antennae, and maid costumes, "as if to downplay the authorship of the designer as much as possible" (OV2, 202). According to Azuma, "We should grasp what is currently called 'character' rather as a kind of output generated from preregistered elements and combined according to the program of each work" (OV2, 202), and Di Gi Charat is exemplary in this regard.

Therefore, in otaku culture, according to Azuma, each individual work that appears at a surface level can be understood as an expression of a database-like depth in the following two ways. On the one hand, each narrative-based work is a subordinate element of a media mix strategy without coherent order. On the other, each character is an "output" of a latent database of "*moe*-elements" accumulated within the whole otaku culture. By consuming each individual work or good, the otaku consumes this database-like deep structure behind it, which is an accumulation of random and incidental data without any order or hierarchy. Azuma thus calls this deep structure the grand nonnarrative, distinct from the grand narrative that sustained modernity as a symbolic order. In this manner, the theory of database consumption retrieves an invisible depth behind the interfacial subjectivity that is entirely visible on the surface.

To find the appropriate place of this database-like depth within the theoretical framework of "Why Is Cyberspace Called Such?," we might be able to interpret it as the uncanny elements exorcised by cyberspace. Azuma in "Why Is Cyberspace Called Such?" argued that the two spaces described in *Neuromancer*, cyberspace and Chiba city, are needed to localize the uncanny elements manifest in information technologies. What if these two imaginary spaces reflect the surface/depth double structure of postmodern subjectivity? In other words, what if the image of cyberspace in this novel provides a figuration of the place in which interfacial subjectivity appears, while the disordered Oriental urban space cluttered with various gadgets is an image of the uncanny elements behind it? For this to be the case, the new database-like depth inserted within postmodern subjectivity would require substantial modification to the place of *Neuromancer*—and cyberspace as a general idea—within the transition from the modern to the postmodern in "Why Is Cyberspace Called Such?"

However, we must remember that Azuma figures GUI technology as an exemplar of interfacial subjectivity. If we follow his argument in "Why Is Cyberspace Called Such?" that interfacial subjectivity—exemplified by GUI technology—takes what appears on the surface "at face value" without any assumption of the invisible behind the screen, then the database-like depth of the postmodern corresponds precisely to the innumerable data and programs behind such superficiality. In fact, Azuma's argument concerning the postmodern in "Why Is Cyberspace Called Such?" might become a theory that accounts strongly for the Internet environments that came to the fore after the 2000s, if postmodern subjectivity is reformulated as a double structure with interfacial surface and database-like depth (this idea was partly developed in "On Information and Freedom").[10] However, the stance of "Why Is Cyberspace Called Such?," which emphasizes the superficiality of the postmodern discursive space—Azuma shared this view with the postmodernists he criticized in this work—could not adequately describe the rapid transformation of the situation as it stood.

It would be too simplistic to suggest that Azuma's abandonment of this early media-theoretical project came only as a result of theoretical discrepancies and the rapid transformation of information environments behind them. It is also bound up with a dramatic shift in Azuma's writing style—in other words, a change in strategy in which he addresses his thoughts to his readers, a remarkable shift when we compare "The Overvisibles" with *Otaku*. "The Overvisibles," written as a follow-up to "Why Is Cyberspace Called Such?" and originally intended to be included in a voluminous book on the postmodern, shares by and large the same style as Azuma's previous work: it prioritizes the clarity of abstract arguments, and uses the terminology and idiolect of contemporary philosophy and critical theory. Discussions on this level are largely omitted in *Otaku*, which is oriented more toward a nonacademic prose that dispenses with the technical terms of critical theory (this shift of course also reflects certain considerations for publishing the work as a paperback book for a general audience).

In line with such a stylistic change, there is also a significant shift in Azuma's critical position towards otaku culture. Around the opening of the first article of "The Overvisibles," he makes it clear that his arguments concerning otaku culture are useful insofar as they represent exemplary cases in understanding the larger issue of postmodern society (OV1, 226). In sharp contrast to this scholarly attitude, Azuma concludes *Otaku* by announcing his will to engage in a struggle of values in defense of otaku culture: "This book was written to create a moment in which great works such as this [a dating sim titled *Yu-no*] can be freely analyzed and critiqued, without distinctions such as high culture versus subculture, academism versus otaku, for adults versus for children, and art versus entertainment. The development from this point is left to each reader."[11]

As a result of this change in his stance as a critic—one might paraphrase this as a change in media strategy—Azuma's theoretical book on the postmodern was destined to reach a deadlock at the moment *Otaku* was published, even before Azuma started his next serial article, "On Information and Freedom." Conflicts on the level of theory due to a long span of serialized articles were coupled with a break in his strategy. For our purpose of describing the media theory he conceived at this period in its totality, however, we should ascertain how "On Information and Freedom" can be positioned within the whole program, and *how it cannot be.*

On Information, Freedom, and Animals

"On Information and Freedom" is an attempt to consider how the idea of "freedom" can be reconstructed in a society in which social engineering via informational management has started to control the privacy and security of the individual in a hitherto unimaginable way. Accordingly, this article orients itself toward the dimension of political power, and the dimension of ethics that the subject can or should secure, while taking over the analysis of postmodern subjectivity from the preceding two series. As one of the major theoretical frameworks for such a task Azuma refers to a late short essay by

Gilles Deleuze, "Postscript on the Societies of Control" (1990), in which Deleuze famously suggested the possibility that a new form of power, different from the disciplinary power Michel Foucault articulated, had been taking shape. As exemplified by Jeremy Bentham's panopticon model of surveillance, the Foucauldian modern subject is formed by the internalization of power by discipline. In contrast to this, Deleuze conceives of a new power that does not require such internalization, using the term "societies of control." Deleuze offers an image of such power through his description of a system that controls the entrance and exit of a certain building or block by certification with an electronic identification card.[12] In this case, the power resides in the information network and database that decide if a certain person is legitimate or not, without the need for the subjective internalization of norms. Azuma labels this "environmental control power" (*kankyō kanri gata kenryoku*). The transition from disciplinary power to environmental control power, for Azuma, signals the end of the modern subject formed by the internalization of the external gaze, and thus corresponds to the broader social context of the transition from the modern to the postmodern.

To paraphrase these arguments in "On Information and Freedom" in line with the terminology of Azuma's prior work, we can say that the symbolic order that determines the subject from within at a deep invisible level has collapsed, and instead, the database-like depth, no longer located within the interiority of the subject, comes to exercise a determining power on the subject. In this way, "On Information and Freedom" shares many things in common with *Otaku*. However, there is also a barely reconcilable difference between their attitudes toward postmodern subjectivity. Media theorist Hamano Satoshi gives an account of this, referring to the (apparently unofficial) statement by Azuma himself that "['On Information and Freedom'] drew too much on the motif of left wing criticism of surveillance society."[13] In other words, the point of conflict lies in whether postmodern subjectivity is regarded affirmatively as an emancipation from the troubles that the modern idea of the subject implies, or negatively as a crisis of the subject *per se* (the same ambiguity that characterized preceding postmodernist discourse, as Azuma himself points out; WC9, 160–68).

Azuma accords an important role to the metaphor of the "animal" in explaining this ambivalent state of postmodern subjectivity in both *Otaku* and "On Information and Freedom," albeit in different ways. The abovementioned point of conflict manifests itself most clearly in this metaphor. We can largely divide the origin of the figure of the "animal" in Azuma's discussions into the following three sources:

1. The ontology of the animal and the problem of anthropocentrism in Heidegger. In *The Fundamental Concepts of Metaphysics* (1929–30), Heidegger states that the stone is worldless (*weltlos*) and the man is world-forming (*weltbildend*), while the animal is world-poor (*weltarm*).[14] In an article preceding "The Overvisibles" serial "Sōzōkai to dōbutsuteki tsūro" (The Imaginary and the Animal Route), Azuma outlines the theoretical path in which Heidegger's statement above paradoxically leads to anthropocentrism by referring to its deconstructive reading by Derrida.[15] According to Derrida-Azuma, Heidegger formalizes the distinction between the thing and man as an ontological difference between the objective presence (*Vorhandensein*) and Dasein so that he can do away with the essentialist definition of man, and thus rejects anthropocentrism. However, the intermediate state of the "world-poor" animal inserted between the "worldless" thing and the "world-forming" man unsettles the sharp formal distinction made between the thing and man, reducing it to a difference in degree. This loss of formalism again brings about an essentialist definition of what determines man, thus leading to a return to anthropocentrism, and even to ethnocentrism (the racist ideology of National Socialism). The figure of the "animal" plays an ambivalent role in this reading. On the one hand, it unsettles the formal distinction between the thing and man, secretly introducing "the animal route" in between, but, on the other hand, it is precisely this "animal route" that makes anthropocentrism return to the philosophy of Heidegger, which should ostensibly have rejected a naïve humanism.

2. Alexandre Kojève's arguments on "return to animality" and "Japanese snobbery." In a long footnote added to the second edition of *Introduction to the Reading of Hegel* (1962), Kojève mentions two modes of life that remain after the end of History in the Hegelian sense: "man's return to animality" as a result of the "American way of life," and "Japanese snobbery," a condition nurtured by experiences following the end of History that had continued for around three centuries (since the Edo period).[16] For Kojève, the society of consumption in postwar America has brought about "the *definitive annihilation* of Man *properly so-called*" (Kojève, *Introduction*, 160), and people there live an animal life in which they satisfy their wants by conditioned reflexes. Contrary to this, Japanese snobbery barely makes a man human by living "according to totally *formalized* values" (162).

Azuma, in turn, relates Kojève's ideas to the arguments concerning the end of modernity—that is, the postmodern—in "The Overvisibles" and *Otaku*, and discusses them as follows. The mode of snobbery, in which people live according to pure form without content (history), corresponds to the intermediary phase from the modern to the postmodern, in which one had to "believe in *the semblance that life is meaningful*" (OV3, 223) by fabricating the grand narrative in spite of it having already been lost. Contrary to this, in the more complete phase of the postmodern after the 1990s, the otaku does not need even false narratives to fulfill the meaning of life anymore, as (s)he has become an animal whose mode of existence is closed within the "want-satisfaction circuit," consuming *moe*-elements in order to pursue instant satisfaction.

3. Hannah Arendt's idea of *animal laborans*. In *The Human Condition* (1958), Arendt classifies human activities into three categories: labor, work, and action. According to her, labor "is the activity which corresponds to the biological process of the human body," and thus she calls this mode of being *animal laborans*.[17] Conversely, work and action are activities that belong to and form the human world in opposition to nature. Following Azuma's reformulation, work is an activity that forms the world of artifacts, though its subject remains anonymous, while action is an activity to appear in the world with a proper name, and he proposes the term "onymous" (*kenmei*) as opposed to "anonymous" (*tokumei*) in order to consider this domain of activity called action.[18]

Arendt considers labor as an activity coupled with consumption, and warns against the state in which, with the advent of the society of consumption, labor encroaches on the domain of work and action, thus depriving us of humanity. Following this argument, in "On Information and Freedom," Azuma points out that the social saturation of information networks exemplified by RFID (radio-frequency identification) technology instead deprives us of anonymity in the animal layer of our living, that is, labor-consumption. For him, the new form of environmental control power deprives us of modern subjectivity by making onymous our animal activities, which in turn gain more and more weight in our social life. In order to theorize the right for freedom anew in such a situation, Azuma reconstructs the dichotomy of anonymous/onymous in a more complicated way, and foregrounds the right to reject the passive onymity that is put into effect in the animal layer, in other words, "the right not to be connected to networks" (IF11, 286–95; IF12, 264–73).

Now, is it possible to reconcile these three distinct genealogies of animal metaphor within the development of Azuma's theory at this particular moment? His comments about this matter are limited to a short footnote in "On Information and Freedom" that points out the similarity between Kojève and Arendt (IF10, 289n102). Indeed, their texts, written around the same period, share a line of argumentation that recognizes in the kind of lifestyle that has become conspicuous in postwar America a negative moment—a retreat from humanity—and they describe it through the metaphor of the animal. What about, then, the two animalities Azuma himself has developed from these two genealogies respectively? For this purpose, let us consider the position of the first genealogy (Heidegger-Derrida) within the whole argument Azuma made about animality. According to his argument in "The Imaginary and the Animal Route," the intermediary state of the world-poor animal makes the formalization of ontology in Heidegger incomplete, piercing it to open a "route" that short-circuits and confuses different categories of being. Is it possible to open an "animal route" in the divide between man and animal in Kojève and Arendt by such a deconstructive procedure? Azuma after *Otaku* ceased to make such arguments through abstract conceptual operations at the formal level. The conception, however, of the coexistence of animality and humanity within the same subject, which is shared by *Otaku* and "On Information and Freedom," can be seen as executing at different levels a conceptual operation that is analogical to the short-circuiting of different categories via the "animal route."

In "On Information and Freedom," Azuma questions the necessity to "subjectify" oneself again as Man in order to overcome the tendency of the information network to make onymous the animal level of our being. For him, "we cannot be a full-time man. . . . Our starting point should not be the dialectical image of man that overcomes inner animality and is elevated into a total man, but rather the fragmented postmodern image of man in which part-time actions are stranded in a lazy animal life of consumption" (IF11, 293). Analogically speaking, his task here is to partially open a "human route" within the general tendency toward animality by breaking up an exclusive antinomy between man and animal. At its most modest, Azuma's argument proposed "the right not to be connected to networks," that is, to momentarily or partially recede from animal onymity.

In *Otaku*, on the other hand, Azuma acknowledges a counterargument to the assertion that the otaku's animality is closed within the "want-satisfaction circuit" of database consumption—that is, that they exhibit a strange sociality in the information exchange about such databases—and says: "Corresponding to the double-layer structure of the database world, the postmodern subjectivity is also divided into double-layers. This subjectivity is motivated by 'the need for small narratives' at the level of simulacra and 'the desire for a grand nonnarrative' at the level of database; while it is animalized in the former, it maintains a virtual, emptied-out humanity in the latter" (*Otaku*, 95).

However, according to Azuma, this humanity that coexists with animality within postmodern subjectivity always reserves the freedom "to drop out" (*Otaku*, 93), contrary to modern subjectivity, which was accompanied by responsibility. To quote a sentence from "The Overvisibles" that is omitted in *Otaku*, "The postmodernized otaku in the 1990s never allows for ethics that support the whole society, thinking that they can always cut off uncomfortable social circuits insofar as they do not threaten their own small narratives" (ov3, 234). For the otaku subject, the "human route" is nothing but a route that opens insofar as it can be cut off at any time.

Around the conclusion of the "On Information and Freedom" series of articles, Azuma states, "There is no freedom without the spirit of tolerance towards alterity, that is, the other" (IF14, 332). Azuma had hopes for the possibility of securing the domain of anonymity as a space in which such alterity could appear within the total onymity environmental control power had brought about. From this point of view, the "human route" must always be open, however fragile it may be, and the sociality of the otaku that reserves the possibility to be cut off would never be desirable. At a different level, however, one could make the argument that the spirit of tolerance toward the other has to be extended also toward the otaku, the database animal. Openness to alterity, that is, should also include openness to the otaku. As we have noted, in the course of the revision of "The Overvisibles" into *Otaku*, Azuma steered his critical strategy in the direction of the latter. As a result, "On Information and Freedom," which continued to be written after *Otaku* as a part of tripartite works on the postmodern, could not find a proper place within Azuma's activities as a critic.[19]

Conclusion

This chapter has analyzed three serialized articles that Azuma Hiroki published from 1997 to 2003, examining how his theory and strategy of media have developed intertwiningly. During this process, Azuma gradually transformed from a young critic who wrote with highly philosophical terminology into a more mature critic who provided a clear-cut perspective on otaku culture. In this period, the transformation of the cultural environment around the Internet had gradually taken shape, the completed form of which would later be called Web 2.0.[20] Internet culture in the 1990s was fostered by a DIY atmosphere, and possessed somewhat of a countercultural appeal. At least a certain amount of knowledge of programming language was necessary to actively participate in this culture. Such sharp distinctions between the sender and receiver of this culture have been gradually dissolved, first by the popularity of blogs, and then by the saturation of social networks. At the same time, Google and commercial services such as Amazon have reabsorbed such a culture into the mainstream capitalist economy.

We can characterize the media theory of Azuma at this period—informed by the key terms of interfacial subjectivity, database-like depth, and the animal—as pioneering work that quickly responded to such transformations of information culture, providing a plausible theoretical framework with which to understand them. Though "Why Is Cyberspace Called Such?" was published in *InterCommunication*, which at that time was one of the vehicles that represented earlier, critical Internet culture, this serial clearly intended to distance itself from the 1990s discursive space on media by critically examining one of its central concepts: cyberspace. Azuma's intention gained more tangible theoretical results in his following two series of articles, especially through the discussions of environmental control power in "On Information and Freedom." This meant, however, that in order to respond to the transformation of the information environment that occurred during the six years of his writing, each serial necessitated substantial modifications to his theory.

The conversion of Azuma's stance as a critic and the ongoing transformation of the information environment at the same moment necessitated the almost constant remodification of Azuma's thought: the former urged a change in his media strategy, and the latter forced a change in his media theory. These two factors, which prevented Azuma's three serial articles from bearing fruit as a unified grand theory in spite of their abundant theoretical possibilities, no doubt possess an inseparable correlation. As I cannot fully demonstrate this in this chapter, I instead wish to conclude by citing a sort of primal scene that illustrates the intricate relation between Azuma's strategy and his theory.

On January 9, 1999, when Azuma had already started the serial article "Why Is Cyberspace Called Such?," a symposium titled "Ima hihyō no basho wa doko ni aru noka" (Where is the place of criticism now?) was held at Kinokuniya Hall in Tokyo. The participants included Karatani Kōjin and Asada Akira, who edited *Hihyō kūkan*; the conservative literary critic Fukuda Kazuya; and two young critics associated with *Hihyō kūkan*, Azuma Hiroki and Kamata Tetsuya.[21] Azuma began the symposium with a keynote speech, in which he outlined his dissatisfaction with what was then a common criticism of his recently published work *Ontological, Postal.* According to him, a reviewer had misunderstood the concept of "postal text," an idea that Azuma proposed by deconstructing the dichotomy of "constative" (the meaning of a certain text) and "performative" (the effect achieved by a certain text).[22] For Azuma, the postality of text is its possibility of misdelivery or its unpredictability, but this is never related to linguistic style per se. Though we cannot introduce his argument in detail, in the context of the symposium, such ideas lead to the strategy to make text postal.

> I am engaged in something which might look like a "selling activity," though my understanding of the current situation is that criticism cannot come into existence today without such selling activities. . . . Even if you made up a text at a high level, I think it would be so unpostal if it were only read among thousands of fixed readers. In this sense, there is no distinction between the constative and the performative— these two are entangled with each other. My book is as it is including this selling activity. ("Ima hihyō no . . . ," 11)

By reducing the idea of postality to having as many readers as possible, it might appear that this statement undermines this very idea, that is, the condition of the text to reach various addressees (sometimes in spite of the author's intent). Karatani disregarded Azuma's comments as being "too self-conscious" ("Ima hihyō no . . . ," 17), while Asada repeatedly insisted to Azuma that to write a text is after all akin to throwing a message in a bottle from a desert island: one cannot control its performative effects. However, Azuma's statement that "selling activity" (eigyō katsudō) was necessary for a text to be postal uncannily predicted the discursive space in Japan in the late 2000s and 2010s—after he had abandoned his project of media theory. It is simply commonplace today that critics and other writers make use of Twitter or Facebook to enhance the postality of their texts—in the sense of reaching a wider audience—and Azuma is one of the critics who uses such a strategy most skillfully.

At the aforementioned symposium, Azuma proposed, "A new strategy is needed that weaves the constative and the performative together" ("Ima hihyō no . . . ," 27). How about, then, understanding the media theory and media strategy he developed from 1997 to 2003 as a trial leading toward this "new strategy"? In other words, what if we can understand these serial articles on media as Azuma ceaselessly altering his own media theory (constative), while interweaving a newer media strategy (performative) within it? Of course, this is only an analogy based on a crude interpretation of the elaborated reading of Derrida by the early Azuma. It seems, however, to help us understand this unfinished project, much like Azuma's paraphrasing of postality as a "selling activity." To pursue this analogy with postality further, can we not say that as a media theory in the postmodern age, Azuma's tripartite project was, in fact, misdelivered? Perhaps we should rather say that Azuma sealed part of a letter conceived as media theory, wrote "otaku culture studies" on the envelope, and posted it.

NOTES

1. In addition to the reason discussed above, this sense of incongruity also has to do with the fact that the term "media theory," or *media-riron*, is not particularly common in Japan. In Japan, *media-ron* ("arguments on media" or simply "on media") is a more commonly used term, and accordingly, discourses on media tend to be constructed loosely.

2. Azuma Hiroki, "90 nendai o furikaeru: Atogaki ni kaete 2" [Looking back at the '90s: In place of postscript], in *Cyberspace wa naze sō yobareru ka+: Azuma Hiroki archives 2* [Why is cyberspace called such?+: Azuma Hiroki archives] (Tokyo: Kawade bunko, 2011), 453.

3. "Why Is Cyberspace Called Such?" and "On Information and Freedom" were later published as *Jōhō kankyō ronshū: Azuma Hiroki Collection S* [Papers on information and environment: Azuma Hiroki collection S] (Tokyo: Kōdansha, 2007) with slight modifications. The former was subsequently published with other essays as *Cyberspace wa naze. . . .*

4. Azuma Hiroki, "Cyberspace wa naze sō yobareru ka" [Why is cyberspace called such?], ten articles in *InterCommunication,* nos. 22–30 and 32 (1997–2000), 1:163 (hereafter cited as *wc*, with serial part number followed by page numbers as they appeared in the original article). Azuma makes it explicit that his term *akuma barai* (literally "devil expulsion") derives from Jacques Derrida's terminology of "conjuration," explaining in a footnote that it is "a function of ideology" (*wc*1, 165n12), though without further elaboration. In the following, I use "exorcise" or "exorcism" as a straightforward translation of *akuma barai*, avoiding the intricate implications of the Derridean term "conjuration," one meaning of which is equivalent to "exorcism" in English. See Jacques Derrida, *Specters of Marx: The State of the Debt, the Work of Mourning, and the New International,* trans. Peggy Kamuf (New York: Routledge, 1994).

5. Azuma refers to Ueno Toshiya's article "Techno-orientalism to Japanimation" [Techno-orientalism and Japanimation], *InterCommunication* no. 16 (1996): 84–89. See also David Morley and Kevin Robins, *Spaces of Identity: Global Media, Electronic Landscapes, and Cultural Boundaries* (London: Routledge, 1995).

6. Slavoj Žižek, "Cyberspace, or, the Unbearable Closure of Being," in *The Plague of Fantasies* (London: Verso, 1997), 161–213; "Cyberspace, or How to Traverse the Fantasy in the Age of the Retreat of the Big Other," *Public Culture,* 10, no. 3 (1998): 483–513. Žižek refers to the following two studies: Sherry Turkle, *Life on the Screen: Identity in the Age*

of the Internet (New York: Simon and Schuster, 1995); Allucquére Rosanne Stone, *The War of Desire and Technology at the Close of the Mechanical Age* (Cambridge, MA: MIT Press, 1996).

7. Turkle, *Life on the Screen*.

8. Azuma Hiroki, "Postmodern saikō: 'Gendai sisō' o, hitotsu no ideology toshite saiseiri suru tame ni" [Rethinking the postmodern: In order to rearrange "contemporary thought" as an ideology], *Asteion* no. 54 (2000): 203–17.

9. The full sentence reads as follows: "We have confirmed in the previous chapters that the new depth of the postmodern can be understood as a database, and the predominant model of the new subjectivity there is in part necessarily multiple personality (plurality by the combination of memories)." Azuma Hiroki, "Kashiteki na mono tachi" [The over-visibles], four articles in *Eureka*, vol. 33, issue nos. 3, 4, 6, and 8 (2001), 1:226 (hereafter cited as OV, with serial part number followed by page numbers as they appeared in the original article).

10. In this sense, it is remarkable that Azuma wrote "Why Is Cyberspace Called Such?" around the same time that Lev Manovich published his groundbreaking work *The Language of New Media* (Cambridge, MA: MIT Press, 2001), in which Manovich argued that the database is a symbolic form in the era of new media. For further developments in this direction, see, for example, Lev Manovich, *Software Takes Command* (New York: Bloomsbury, 2013); Wendy Hui Kyong Chun, *Programmed Visions: Software and Memory* (Cambridge, MA: MIT Press, 2011).

11. Azuma Hiroki, *Otaku: Japan's Database Animals*, trans. Jonathan E. Abel and Shion Kono (Minneapolis: University of Minnesota Press, 2009), 116.

12. Gilles Deleuze, "Postscript on the Societies of Control," *October* 59 (1992): 7.

13. Hamano Satoshi, "Kaisetsu: Azuma Hiroki no jōhōronteki tenkai ni tsuite," [Introduction: On Azuma Hiroki's development of information theory], in Azuma, *Cyberspace ha naze . . .* , 470.

14. Martin Heidegger, *The Fundamental Concepts of Metaphysics: World, Finitude, Solitude*, trans. William McNeill and Nicholas Walker (Bloomington: Indiana University Press, 2001).

15. Azuma Hiroki, "Sōzōkai to dōbutsuteki tsūro: Keishikika no Derrida-teki sho-mondai" [The imaginary and the animal route: Derridean problems of formalization], in *Hyōshō: Kōzō to dekigoto* [Representation: Structure and event], ed. Kobayashi Yasuo and Matsuura Hisaki (Tokyo: University of Tokyo Press, 2000), reprinted in Azuma, *Cyberspace ha naze . . .* , 232–60.

16. Alexandre Kojève, *Introduction to the Reading of Hegel: Lectures on the Phenomenology of Spirit*, ed. Alan Bloom, trans. James H. Nichols, Jr. (Ithaca, NY: Cornell University Press, 1980), 159–62.

17. Hannah Arendt, *The Human Condition* (Chicago: University of Chicago Press, 1998), 7.

18. Azuma Hiroki, "Jōhō jiyū ron: Data no kenryoku, angō no rinri" [On information and freedom: The power of data, the ethics of code], fourteen articles in *Chūō kōron*, vol. 117, issue nos. 7–12, vol. 118, issue nos. 1, 3–7, 9, and 10 (2002–3), 9:306–7, 10:285–86 (hereafter cited as IF, with serial part number followed by page numbers as they appeared in the original article).

19. As noted in the last article of "On Information and Freedom," the publisher of *Chūō kōron* planned to publish this serial as a book. However, Azuma abandoned the rewriting work and instead published the original articles on his website, Hajō-genron, in 2005, in response to requests for easy access (it was later republished in *Jōhō kankyō ronshū: Azuma Hiroki Collection S* in 2007). On this web page, Azuma mentions "the change in his philosophy" as a background to the abandonment of its publication as a book, requesting that readers take note of this on the occasion of citation or reference. According to this web page, Azuma's plan for a book on the postmodern around the beginning of the 2000s was to "treat the theoretical issues of the postmodern in the first chapter, its developments in the information society in the second chapter, and its developments in subculture in the last chapter." In this plan, "The Overvisibles" and "On Information and Freedom" correspond to the third and second chapter, respectively, and thus were written in the reverse order. See *Jōhō jiyū ron: HTML Version Index* [On information and freedom: HTML version index], 2005, http://www.hajou.org/infoliberalism/.

20. Tim O'Reilly, "What Is Web 2.0: Design Patterns and Business Models for the Next Generation of Software," O'Reilly, September 30, 2005, http://www.oreilly.com /pub/a/web2/archive/what-is-web-20.html.

21. Karatani Kōjin, Asada Akira, Fukuda Kazuya, Kamata Tetsuya, and Azuma Hiroki, "Ima hihyō no basho wa doko ni aru no ka" [Where is the place of criticism now?], *Hihyō kūkan* II-21 (1999): 6–32.

22. Azuma Hiroki, *Sonzairon teki, yūbin teki: Jacques Derrida ni tsuite* [Ontological, postal: On Jacques Derrida] (Tokyo: Shinchōsha, 1998). On the idea of "performative" in speech act theory and its deconstructive reading, see also, for example, J. L. Austin, *How to Do Things with Words*, ed. J. O. Urmson and Marina Sbisá (Cambridge, MA: Harvard University Press, 1962); and Jacques Derrida, *Limited Inc.*, trans. Samuel Weber and Jeffrey Mehlman (Evanston, IL: Northwestern University Press, 1988).

4. THE *INTERCOMMUNICATION* PROJECT

Theorizing Media in Japan's Lost Decades

MARILYN IVY

They're bound in sunflower-gold covers, when not in dull olive or darkened burgundy or plain black: the back journals, that is, stored in the libraries of Columbia University. One can check out bound journals for two weeks at a time and renew them online eight times before having to return them to the library to reboot the process. In a first in my academic career, I checked out the entire run of a journal: *InterCommunication: New Contexts of the Post-Digital World*, a landmark Japanese journal of media and communication theory, digital technology, and art, which first appeared in 1992 and ran for sixteen years and sixty-five issues. I had to roll two substantial suitcases to the Starr East Asian Library to transport them to my office, not including the three volumes shelved at Columbia's industrial-park offsite storage facility, which it shares with Princeton University and the New York Public Library. The journals are nothing if not heavy—extraordinarily heavy (it's the hard covers).

It would be temptingly dramatic to say that I was the first person at Columbia University ever to check out *InterCommunication* (*Intākomyunikeishon*, in romanized Japanese). I wasn't. In 2005 someone checked out one volume. But I was, indeed, the first person ever to have checked out any of the other twenty-odd volumes. That is not to say that students and scholars of Japan did not peruse issues of *InterCommunication* as they languished on the periodical shelves of the Starr East Asian Library reading room. But once bound and shelved, the journals have more or less remained archivally incommunicado. True, it is possible that a curious Japanologist has pulled one of the volumes (NT 72.T4 Z58) from the shelves on occasion. And I must recognize here the lone Japanese-language reader in 2005 with enough interest to borrow and haul one of these heavy tomes (issue nos. 47–50) from the sub-basement depths of the Starr East Asian Library to the street level of Morningside Heights. But substantially, for twenty-one years, these volumes of *InterCommunication* were simply not in communication.

Thus I begin with the melancholy instance of a Japanese journal about communication, about *inter*communication, a journal titled *InterCommunication*, interred, out of communication, in the depths of an American university library. It signals an intercommunication that has been *inter*-rupted, ruptured between the two poles of its ostensible sending and receiving: in this case, one in Japan, the other, here in the United States. It is the place of the "inter" that ruptures and reveals the broken redundancy of the very idea of "intercommunication" itself. Indeed, when is a communication *not* an *inter*communication? For *inter* means "between or among." The OED tells us that it can also mean "mutually" and "reciprocally." Tellingly, *communication*, in English, comes from the Latin word *communicare*, "to share." To share means there must be more than one, an overlap, an exchange of some sort. Can there be a *one-way* communication? Isn't communication *inter*communication, always already? But what is the (inter)communication of a journal rarely opened, seldom read?

This allegory of a media and communications journal virtually out of communication is one that gestures, perhaps paradoxically, to the status of media theory in Japan and the communications/media/information complex that is disaggregated with increasing difficulty in the contemporary post-digital moment. What is media? What is media theory? And not least: what is Japan? All these questions must come to the fore in an English-language work, published in the United States, on media theory in Japan. Perhaps the archival discommunication of this journal implies an indictment of the state of Japanese studies at American universities today. Perhaps it is an indication of the difficult nature of the journal itself, the understandable reluctance to read too much translated European theory rendered in Japanese, the lack of directed study of contemporary theory in East Asian studies, or simply the decline of Japan as an object of intensive scholarly engagement in the wake of the recessionary years and the dominance of China. Or perhaps it equally indicates the receding fortunes of print in general, and in particular those of back issues of print journals, which even in the best of times were often destined to repose for years in suspended animation.

I want to consider the significance of this notable arts, culture, and technology journal for the theorization of media in post-1990 Japan, the decades after the deflation of the bubble economy. I aim concurrently to reflect on the destinies of the trope of "communication" (*komyunikeishon*) itself during this period as it both discursively formed the theoretical surround of the journal and as it moved through the pages of *InterCommunication*—that trope that so often is complexly enfolded within the ambit of "media" and "mediation," often without remainder. One has only to look, for example, at the "communication" entry in the authoritative *Critical Terms for Media Studies* (or the introduction to the volume) to get a sense of the theoretical difficulties of separating the notions of "media," "communication," and "information."[1] Lev Manovich's now-canonical distinction—between *communication* as entailing a notion of real-time contact, disclosed by the ubiquitous use of the Greek preface *tele-* (telegraph, television, telephone), in opposition to the archiving, memorializing function of the term *media*, which highlights the mediatic object itself (film, CDs, video) rather than the temporality of transmission—sought to maintain a workable division between the two terms. While there might be instances when *communication* does theoretical work that *media* cannot (and the reverse), new digital technologies and diverse aesthetic and experimental theorizations in their wake have thrown into question the real efficacy of the distinction. Nowhere would that distinction lose its force more so than in the complexly cosmopolitan and intellectually rich terrain of Japanese media/communications theory in the decades around the turn of the millennium.

Even given this abundance, however, *InterCommunication* had an unusually overdetermined relationship to the communication trope in media studies (although its actual content was not limited to anything that could be imagined narrowly as "communication studies": contributions ranged ambitiously and promiscuously over the entire globalized terrain of technology, media theory, arts, and culture) because it was founded and financed by Nippon Telegraph and Telephone—commonly known as NTT (Nippon Denshin Denwa Kabushikigaisha)—the massive corporation, originally a state-run "public corporation" (originally known as Nippon Denshin Denwa Kōsha, founded in 1952) that monopolized telecommunications in the Japanese postwar period: think AT&T in overdrive. Nippon Telegraph and Telephone was still dominant in 1992, the inaugural year of *InterCommunication*, even after its then-recent privatization. Part of an ambitious arts and technology initiative developed by NTT in the early 1990s, the journal was imagined as an avant-garde house organ in anticipation of the establishment of the performance, gallery, and documentation space called ICC, the InterCommunication Center, opened in 1997. Both these enterprises vividly disclosed NTT's aspirations to develop cutting-edge cultural theory and to sponsor performances that would reveal the utopian, fabulously novel dimensions of the emergent digital universe and its capital importance for (tele)communications.

The print journal ceased publication in 2008, but the InterCommunication Center itself flourishes even now in western Shinjuku, on the fourth and fifth floors of the Tokyo Opera City Tower, one of the highest skyscrapers in Tokyo (with fifty-four floors, the seventh-highest skyscraper in Tokyo, a global city of multiple towering megabuildings). Construction on Tokyo Opera City began in 1992, the same year as NTT started the publication of *InterCommunication*, and was completed in 1997, when NTT East (NTT became a holding company divided into NTT East and NTT West) moved into its newly completed quarters at the Tokyo Opera City Tower, along with none other than Microsoft and Apple (and the New National Theater, on the lower levels).

Disseminating globally sourced writings on communication, technology, and media; showcasing a staggering number of intellectuals, performers, artists, and writers from around the world (heavy on Europe) in performances and lectures; and featuring Japan's own homegrown theorists and practitioners in almost endless roundtables, symposia, exhibitions, and conversations, ICC and the journal (and website) *InterCommunication* (all funded by the original mother ship of NTT and then NTT East, when NTT was broken up into independent regional corporations)—the *InterCommunication* project, I'll call it—played pivotal curatorial roles in delineating and expanding the parameters of media theory and technoart in Japan at the turn of the millennium and beyond. In close conversation with its linked sister-journal *Critical Space* (*Hihyō kūkan*), and along with other high-powered technology and arts publications, perhaps most important the architecture-focused journal *10+1*,[2] the journal *InterCommunication* committed itself to extensive labors of translation: translating EuroAmerican works on media into Japanese; providing interpreters from (mostly) European languages for the many non-Japanese artists, scientists, and theorists ICC brought to Japan; and publishing select translations of articles from Japanese into English, a number of which are archived on its still-functioning website.

The 1990s milieu of intensifying globalization, Japanese recession, expanding privatization, and dramatically ramifying digital communications and media technologies coalesced into an official and also popular discourse of "internationalization" (*kokusaika*). *Kokusaika* provided an overarching rubric for efforts to think theory and media beyond the Japanese frame, efforts that ever and always entailed the necessity of translation. The project of *InterCommunication* was a large-scale experiment in what one of its editorial founders, the noted theoretician, postmodern critic, and scholar Asada Akira called an attempt at "dialogue"—a model of communication based on an exchange of speech—between technoscience and art. At the same time, the project unfolded within a translational economy that was aimed precisely at overcoming the conditions of something called "Japanese media theory," such that the place of what one could confidently call "Japanese theory," "Japanese media," "Japanese media theory," or "media theory" *in Japanese* was ceaselessly destabilized. The journal was thus as much about translation, one could argue, as anything else.

Yet its splendid efforts at interlinguistic and international intercommunication ran up against the ever-recurring limitations of translation itself, the forlorn textual evidence of those limitations archivally remaindered in the stacks, in this instance, of an American university library. It was perhaps in the aftermath of the inevitable limitations of interlinguistic intercommunication that the digital arts—particularly the visual and sonic arts—came to occupy an increasingly valuable place of mediatic communication-without-remainder: non-Japanese-speaking people could still revel in a language-free performance by Ikeda Ryōji (recently performing at MoMA, for example), virtual reality demonstrations, or an exhibition of oneiric architecture—works that could stand alone and "communicate" internationally, without the undue mediations of the translations that the journal project required. Media arts, digital arts, and communication arts (and, crucially, architecture) held out promises of transcending the impasses of mutually unintelligible languages, of the hard labor of translation in a globalizing world. When we speak of "media theory in Japan," then, we have to remind ourselves repeatedly of the global (inter)translational economy of which Japan is, and was, a part, and that fatefully determines much of what becomes legible outside the intra-Japanese surround.

The journal *InterCommunication,* or IC, thus rode the sequential waves of the extraordinary digital *tsunami* that overtook Japan and the rest of the world in the 1990s and beyond, translating and theorizing, recording, and—indeed—archiving the transformations as they were occurring in technology and the arts on a global scale. Funded as the journal was by a corporation originally founded as the sole provider of telephone and telegraph service throughout Japan, IC was commercially framed within the well-worn logics of telephonic communication. By the 1990s, the fundamental ideological presuppositions of that logic—the transmission of information, messages, and affect across a material sonic connection, connected by voice itself— were in the midst of a shake-up of seismic proportions. The digital upheavals in communications and media prompted NTT to turn to the premier media, art, and cultural critics in Japan to establish a cutting-edge technoarts and theory journal and center, a complex that could help NTT divine the cultural future of the digital telecommunications revolution. The positioning of IC revealed that the journal was tied, however loosely, to a vision of communicative technologies as unifying, domesticating, and humanizing forces within a late capitalist, globalized economy. As the *InterCommunication* project spanned the unfolding recessionary "lost decades," the decades of Japan in the 1990s and 2000s (which some recent scholarship now claims were not as lost as we had thought), it revealed tenuous, yet tangible, lines of connection between the recessionary and neoliberalizing movements of capital during this period.[3] The project's admirable efforts to harness the fading afterlife of corporate largesse in the name of cultural reflection, technoaesthetic experimentation, and media theoretical explorations were, of necessity, linked to NTT's neoliberalizing strategies, which evolved as the recession was unfolding.

The founding editorial figures and powers, committed to what we might imagine as a high (post)modernist take on what was still a bubble-enabled cosmopolitanism, defined the project's extraordinarily ambitious, even utopian, energies. These figures were important cultural-intellectual presences of the 1980s, 1990s, and beyond, most prominently Asada Akira, who was also coeditor with Karatani Kōjin of the journal *Hihyō kūkan* (Critical Space), itself a massive enterprise in the translation of high theory from European languages. The trajectory of *InterCommunication* thus expressed a commitment to media and arts theory at the ever-receding edge of postmodernism. The Asada touch is evident, which meant that recognizably international Japanese figures from architecture (Isozaki Arata), music (Takemitsu Tōru and Sakamoto Ryūichi), performance art (Dumb Type), computer art, and beyond regularly contributed to the journal, supported by a veritable army of translators and interpreters, mobilized for the plethora of art events and symposia featuring artists and performers from outside Japan (William Forsythe, Bill Viola, and Laurie Anderson, among many others). The online archive of

these performances, lectures, and exhibitions—along with numerous videotaped interviews, assiduously translated for Japanese viewers—forms a
remarkable repository of media arts and theory over a span of some twenty
years.

What were the ramifications of one of the largest telecommunications
companies in the world providing the resources for *InterCommunication*?
As noted, NTT had been a public corporation, but by the early 1990s it was
in the endgame of its thoroughgoing privatization. At the time, it was the
largest privatization of a national telecommunications agency in history, one
that was seen to be a model for the developing world's communications industries. As Timothy E. Nulty, a senior economist at the World Bank, stated
at the time:

> The privatization (or partial privatization) of NTT stands as the single
> largest effort of its kind in history and for that reason alone merits care
> ful attention. But there are more reasons:
>
> The telecommunications sector is, and is likely to remain for some
> time, on the cusp between wholly private and wholly public activities.
> Further, it is one of the most rapidly growing and technologically
> dynamic of all sectors. Thus, the "privatization" of the telecom sec
> tor (or "transformation," or "reform"—whatever term one finds most
> sympathetic) presents some of the most difficult issues currently faced
> anywhere in the field of microeconomic policy making. The pressure
> to move the sector out of its traditional public utility monopoly status
> into something new—more liberal, more competitive, more private—
> is being felt everywhere in the world and is ultimately irresistible.[4]

Thousands of employees were laid off in NTT's privatization (as many as
169,000) in one of the most explicit demonstrations of the neoliberalizing
costs of the lost decades.[5] It was precisely at this moment that the *InterCommunication* project was initiated as a high-profile revelation of NTT's investment in the future, as the promise of a better digital tomorrow shimmered
on the distant horizon of the deepening Japanese recession. Yet this optimism, of course, was tightly entwined with a palpable nostalgia for earlier
moments of capitalism when then-novel forms of technology indicated a
brighter, more expansive future—a nostalgia, indeed, for the telephone itself: NTT founded *InterCommunication* at least in part to commemorate and
celebrate the one-hundredth anniversary of the start of telephone service in
Japan in 1890. This appeal to the origins of the telephone firmly placed the
InterCommunication project in a retrospective mode, a retrospection that,

again, secured the departure point for another communications revolution, this time digitally underwritten.

The promise of so-called information capitalism was palpable in the 1990s. From Tessa Morris-Suzuki's prescient book *Beyond Computopia: Information, Automation, and Democracy in Japan* (published in 1988, right before the Japanese boom went bust), we know that the dream of "information capitalism" and the technocommunicative innovations it entailed were increasingly promoted as a way out of late twentieth-century economic impasses.[6] The fantasy of unbridled and unencumbered telepresent labor took off from the imperatives of capitalism to revolutionize productive technologies, at any and all costs. In this narrative, NTT (along with other communication and transportation bureaucracies and industries) played a crucial role. Only with the burgeoning promises of Internetted communication pathways, along with the computer and media technologies that facilitated them, could the fantasy of telecommuters in decentralized, utopic work zones take on real force. It is not evident in the early 1990s issues of *InterCommunication* that the radical implications of mobile cellular phone technologies had really come into sharp relief. The Internet, however, and VR technologies vividly figured as salvational technological fixes for what would come to be the increasingly obvious woes of Japanese (and global) capital.

Yet a stable telephonic logic installed at the journal's origins worked to keep the metaphor of communication (and transmission and education) overarching the radical mediatic projects generated at ICC. Models of contact and transmission basic to the telephonic paradigm were an important part of the *InterCommunication* project; metaphors of contact, communication, connection, and conversation all point to the at-least residual structuring of the experimental spaces of "dialogue" between art and technology (itself an opposition that bespeaks a necessarily instrumentalized relationship to the sphere of business and publicity). A still-regnant "capitalism of the voice" (and the fact that voice figured centrally in the telephonic regime, what we might call *televoice*) would continue to shape NTT's strategies even within the exploding communicative regimes of email, texting, and messaging.[7]

To look at these back issues of *InterCommunication* in all of their graphic splendor (Japanese book and journal design of this period went far beyond the standard American fare) is to be struck by the markers of techno-temporalities past. To look at advertisements in old journals is to wonder at superseded fantasies, both unfulfilled and fulfilled, as prophetic precursors of the present. In opening 1992's issue number 0 (yes, zero), the first image one sees is IBM's then-newest word processor, now impossibly retro. The ad emphasizes the computer's lightness and the fact that it is bilingual in Japanese and English; it is able to be used throughout the world and is therefore global. Turning the page, the next ad, for the *Mainichi Shinbun* (Mainichi newspaper) contains the headline "Shinbun kakumei shinkōchū" (In the midst of the progress of the newspaper revolution). Here we can see, in 1992, the unfolding of the revolutionary implications of the "digital revolution" that was overtaking newspapers and, indeed, all print-based communication. In Virilian fashion, this revolution was about speed. The headlines continue: "You can understand the news in 19 minutes and 30 seconds" is emblazoned above a newly redesigned front page dated December 5, 1991 (one wonders at the exactitude of nineteen minutes and thirty seconds). New colors, flags, indices, and graphics: simple to use, easy to understand, clearer type, big color pictures—in short, approaching, approximating the layout, the aesthetic of the screen. In its invocation of an *atarashii jidai* (new age), *Mainichi Shinbun* recognized the writing on the wall, or the page, as the case may be: the drive to consume the "necessary news" (*hitsuyō nyūsu*) in a short period of time (*mijikai jikan de*). Little did *Mainichi Shinbun* know how short that time would become with the acceleration of digitalized temporality, but the newspaper nevertheless anticipated it in its now-poignant attempt to retain the primacy of print by making the page look like a screen.

There are a few other ads: for high-end French timepieces, phone cards (yes, phone cards), and *Pia Magazine*, with its assertion of being "Japan's first real cultural event data service." *Pia*'s "Cultural Event Data File," too, was a print "file," but imagined, and presented, in the language of digital storage. There are no telephone ads from NTT, strangely enough, but Japan's international phone company, for international calls, KDD (as it was called then; it is KDDI now) placed an advertisement instructing callers to use *zero zero wandafuru* (zero, zero, wonderful)—that is, 0-0-1—to make their phone calls, followed by an example of a call to New York in what must have been a novel bit of information for at least some of the readers of *InterCommunication* (how to make an international phone call to New York?). And in what was really an almost ad-free issue, there are two final solicitations at the back: a modest one-page ad for NTT Publishing (the publisher of *InterCommunication*) and, finally, unexpectedly, an ad for Key Coffee, one of the most ubiquitous brands in Japan (hardly high-end), with a two-page spread on the cost effectiveness and value of coffee from Toraja, Indonesia, as opposed to the more famous and widely distributed Blue Mountain coffee.

Telephones, newspapers, computers, and coffee: such are the communication resources the journal featured in 1992. The advertisements, of course, were part of the layout of the entire quarterly, committed to print, as it would be for sixteen years, alongside an ever-burgeoning web presence. They operate consistently in *InterCommunication* as virtual framing devices. One might say that magazine advertisements always have an ambiguous relationship to the "real" work, nowhere more so than in contemporary fashion and design magazines, where one is sometimes hard-pressed to know where commercial solicitation begins and the ostensibly noncommercial spreads end. But in a journal of high theory, translation, and technoartistic experimentation—and one sustained by corporate sponsorship—the place of advertising was marginalized, reduced to a near-zero degree. As discreet parerga, the ads appear to be both inside and outside the primary body of the work at hand.

The parergonal advertisements of NTT East had shifted, of course, over the years. In 1996, just a few years after the journal debuted, the corporation ran two innovative ads in *IC*, both featuring a dapper, bespectacled man, an aesthete from the 1920s, perhaps (a time of intense cultural intercommunication and what is sometimes called "borrowing" from Europe). In the first ad, the bourgeois gentleman (in a three-piece suit) is seated on a tatami mat floor, *zazen* style, with floating images of the iconic rock garden of the Zen temple Ryōanji emerging from the floor and repeated on Japanese screens in the background (see fig. 4.1). He muses on media and communication—as the copy reveals:

Ah, so humans *are* multimedia!
The human heart is indomitable. On the other side of what we can see, we always sense a truth that is concealed. On the other side of a beautiful melody, we imagine an unknown landscape. People are tied together by images. Really, humans *are* multimedia. We can communicate more. We can understand each other more. Telecommunication [*jōhō tsūshin*] is getting more interesting. . . .

The bottom of the ad reads "Anata ni, jōhō no chikara [To you, the power of information]," brought to you by the corporate sponsor, in this case identified as the NTT Group [NTT Gurūpu].[8]

Here we see an evolution toward the explicit promise of "information"—*jōhō*—and away from the simple wonders of making a long-distance telephone call to New York, featured just four years earlier. These NTT Group ads—probably the most textually and visually sophisticated within the long run of NTT's *InterCommunication* sponsorship—feature a lone man, an educated

[FIG. 4.1] NTT ad in *InterCommunication* (winter 1996).

and alert modernist at a technological turning point, mirroring the opportunities offered by the intensifying digital revolution of the 1990s. An intercommunicating aesthetic fusing East and West and a cosmopolitan humanist vision suffuse the technological excitement that NTT seeks to convey. In the following ad in this sequence, our cosmopolitan man is standing, arms folded, with neat bow tie, in front of a multitude of framed depictions of Giverny, with Monet's lily pads escaping their frames and flowing into what becomes a lush Western (French?) drawing room, complete with yellow roses on a table (see fig. 4.2). West meets East again, ineluctably. The revolution in the sensory depiction of the world that impressionism disclosed becomes the backdrop for the digital transformation:

> Within me, multimedia is starting to move. . . .
>
> Humans live by connecting emotional impressions. We feel sounds in light, sense colors in sounds, and we try to transmit all the dynamism that is found there as a single image. What we really want to describe are the vicissitudes of time. What we really want to convey are the quiverings of our hearts. Becoming the shape of those feelings . . . multimedia *are* the technologies of the human heart.
>
> To you—the power of information.

[FIG. 4.2] NTT ad in *InterCommunication* (summer 1996).

In succeeding years, as new cable, optical fiber, and broadband technologies advanced, NTT East held out hopeful promises of an ever-expanding future, now couched increasingly—perhaps as IC's core readership aged—in the less-exalted terms of convenience, practicality, enjoyment, and connection. The lone philosopher-entrepreneur embodying the best of East and West gave way to images of single young women, telecommunicatively surrounded by family and friends. The overdetermined term *kizuna*, indicating the emotional "bonds" of relationship, rather than the sheer possibilities of "information," emerged as key, at the same time that new broadband telecommunications technologies promised to bring the far near, to bridge what distance separated, all with the familiar possibilities and logic of telepresence. Yet NTT's repeating and abiding theme through the years was still that of *anata ni*: "to you." In a final variation on that theme published in the last year of *InterCommunication*'s publication, NTT East revealed a good deal of exactitude when it stated that what it was communicatively conveying "to you" was not only the power of information and the words and feelings of those bonded to you, but also ultimately light itself (*hikari*): "Hikari wa anata e" (Light—to you). In an unambiguous allusion to the laying of fiber optic cables throughout the archipelago, in its "next generation network"

(NGN), NTT East suggested that light is now not only the medium of transmission but also the very stuff of mediation, simultaneously the luminous conveyance and the spiritualized essence of (tele)communication itself.

The advertising strategies used by NTT and NTT East in the pages of *InterCommunication* indicate the technological and subjective transformations of the communication paradigms that coincided with the journal's run. We are not able, however, to draw unmediated lines of influence from NTT's advertising strategies and *InterCommunication*'s editorial vision. In an online interview in 1998 with the Polish media theorist and journalist Krystian Woznicki, Asada Akira answered his interlocutor's pointed queries about the dilemmas created for a radical media journal when it is funded by a megacorporation such as NTT:

> WOZNICKI: Does the fact that the financial basis for this magazine (as well as for the entire ICC project) is provided by the biggest telephone company [NTT] in Japan affect the editorial agenda?
>
> ASADA: Well, of course it is very hard to persuade people at NTT, first to make the ICC and then to provide resources for research activities or publications. Until now we have somehow succeeded. But I am not really sure. Now that they are having a center. . . . As soon as you have hardware it is very easily institutionalized and bureaucratized. Therefore I am not sure if we can go on as we have been doing. But at least until now there has been only little influence or pressure from the company.
>
> WOZNICKI: I wonder what it means to do research for a telephone company that has naturally also its own plans to go into multimedia and the Internet.
>
> ASADA: In fact NTT is a huge bureaucracy and they do not have a unified agenda. There are many people and no unification, no unified strategy. They are speaking about corporate Japan and it's a myth. It's a very ineffective huge bureaucracy. Everyone has something to say and nobody is ready to take responsibility. The same thing accounts for NTT. There are a lot of institutes: such as the institute for human interface, basic research, etc. but no unified planning. We are basically taking advantage of the situation. . . . In a sense the ICC project is regarded as . . . independent of NTT's business, as an activity to cleanse their hands. In that way we have been somehow independent. At least from my personal point of view *Critical Space* and *InterCommunication* are both sides of the strategy. . . . With *InterCommunication* we

are trying to open up new horizons and to stimulate a dialogue of what has been called culture and technoscience. For the time being I think that they are, if not complementary to each other, then some vague sides of a unified project.[9]

Here Asada makes no bones about it: the IC project was designed to take radical advantage of the situation, to use the massive telecommunications and technology capacities of NTT (and their support) to further a freewheeling, experimentalist set of endeavors exploring the interfaces of art, technology, and media. In this context, Asada remarks upon the dense interconnections between *Critical Space* and *InterCommunication*. While *Critical Space* even now is viewed (at least in the United States) as an academic or para-academic journal, *InterCommunication* was tied more directly to corporate sponsorship, as it were, as well as to the innovative art and media projects of the ICC itself. *Critical Space*, like IC, is immediately attached to the name of Asada Akira, yet even more so to the name of Karatani Kōjin, perhaps Japan's most esteemed literary and cultural theorist. Karatani was, however, not as prominent in the *InterCommunication* project.

We might take the inaugural issue of the journal as a special revelation of the theoretical, aesthetic, and political choices of *InterCommunication*, ones that did not necessarily accord in any simple, or even complex way, with NTT's commercial fantasies. And, after all, shouldn't the first issue give some indications of the aims, ambitions, and predilections of the editors? If we look then at the first essay in *InterCommunication*'s opening issue, issue number 0 (again, zero), we see that it was a translation from an essay by the French technology and media theorist Paul Virilio, "The Revolution in Speed" (Sokudo kakumei), followed by a review of Virilio's related exhibition in Paris. Virilio's work thus marks the initial issue, and his work becomes a touchstone and point of return in later issues as well. The Virilio essay and the exhibition review exemplify the entirely impressive translation work and international interests that occupy much of the journal. Virilio and Derrida, Baudrillard and Kittler: these theorists provided the governing Franco-Germano communication and media theory armature for the quarterly. In the mix were also essays by eminent computer theorists, virtual reality scientists, science fiction writers, and industrial designers—foreign and domestic—as well as uncounted *taidan*, or roundtable discussions, with Japanese artists and intellectuals, architects and performers.

Subtitled on the cover as a "journal exploring the frontiers of art and technology" (different from Columbia University's catalogue subtitle: "new contexts of the postdigital world") IC no. 0 featured a special section titled "The Contemporary Moment of Communication" (Komyunikeishon no genzai), with a further section titled "Frontiers of Communication."[10] In this first issue, then, the emphasis fell on the trope of *communication,* and indeed, *inter*communication. We see the straining toward the evidence of translation, and translatability, throughout, with the careful English-language translations of all headings, subheadings, and article titles. By the end of the journal's run in 2008, this labor of translation had been effectively abandoned (and we see the same thing on the website; after the year 2000, it appears that no, or few, new English-language translations of article titles appear online). It is as if, by then, the dream of (inter)communication across languages had been given up and the inevitability of the native language had reasserted itself in a kind of exhaustion of the effort to intercommunicate. Never in the journal's history was there any attempt to provide translations into any language *other* than English, although there were translators of other European languages for the visiting foreign artists, scientists, and creators (French, German, Polish . . .).

Nevertheless, the inaugurating issue no. 0 presented the hope of intercommunication across two languages: Japanese and English (with the hidden languages of French and German constituting the source languages for much of the theory to be translated). The non-Japanese-reading reader could find some limited solace in the titles and headings, giving a sense, at least, of what was at stake, some ability to grasp the import of the meandering density of the journal, with its head-spinning mash-up of topics, themes, images, and essays. Graphically and theoretically, the journal attempted to communicate, if you will, as much as possible in its densely overwritten pages. The reiteration of the *inter* itself structured the format with sections titled (in English only): "InterDialogue," "InterCity," "InterTechnology," "InterCritique," "InterForum," "InterProject," and "InterCreation." Throughout, the printed evidence of the desire to find that mediate place between, that *inter,* that would allow communication to take place, in-between cities, technologies, critiques, dialogues—all become substitutable, metaphorized in the interspace of intercommunication. It is as if in this movement of the in-between, the *inter-,* a Japanese media theory might be found. In the discursive space of the journal, it is as if a theory of media, mediation, and communication became possible only in the intercommunicative interspace *between* theoretical formations and possibilities. While Asada called for a dialogue between technoscience and art (and *dialogue* implies that the poles of the conversation are already constituted in advance), the journal itself

seemed to embody what would be more appropriately imagined as a rhizo-
matic structure, marked by an immensity and diversity of information, with
theoretical and topical nodes communicating metonymically, horizontally,
and often unexpectedly. Dialogue, however, in its explicit form was never
excluded, and the familiar Japanese format of the roundtable discussion, or
taidan, in addition to numerous interviews, symposia, and conferences, takes
its place throughout.

What is arguably the most original translation project of the journal,
however, and one that has particular import for thinking about media
theory in Japan in the post-bubble decades, was the first installment of a section of Jacques Derrida's 1980 *La Carte postale* (The Post Card), (the translation of the entire work did not come out until 2007, uncharacteristically late
for a Japanese translation of Derrida).[11]

While it might have operated on some levels as a mere signifier of French
theory and its relevance to all things intellectual, *The Post Card* nevertheless
marked a milestone in media/communication theory. Following Virilio's
rethinking of speed and velocity, here was a Japanese translation of Derrida's interrogation of communication as always-already conditioned by the
condition of its *miss*, with its governing metaphor the postcard that always
might not arrive at its destination, a *might not* that determines the possibility of any communicative destination and arrival whatsoever. *The Post
Card* also wrote of the signature that could possibly move across media to
motivate a transportation—a translation?—of the force of the writer, of the
destination and always-assumed arrival that secures both the poster and the
postee of a self-same identity: sender and receiver.

This postal logic, this normative postal logic, could be said to be of a similar
order to telephonic logic, the logic of the telephone that would undergird
NTT in its place, at least in 1992, as the dominant carrier of electronic communications in Japan. It is a logic that would assume that a message sent
out from the sender, here, should reach, would reach a receiver, and that
the receiver, there, would pick up the phone. Of course, the phone might be
busy (this was pre–call-waiting, after all), or the intended receiver might not
be present to answer the call. The "call," of which Avital Ronell makes so
much, could be missed, even refused. The differences between postal logic
and telephonic logic are, however, not inconsequential, turning on the destination and destiny of the voice as opposed to the problematic of writing and
the authority of the signature foregrounded in *The Post Card*.[12]

This question of postal logic and the place of Derrida is not unimpor-
tant, for Derridean deconstruction was the theoretical work that perhaps

more than any other defined the turn to poststructuralism and, indeed, to postmodernism in 1980s Japan. And it was Asada Akira, more than any other Japanese intellectual figure of that period, who popularized the array of theories subsumed by the term "poststructuralism" with his 1983 *Kōzō to chikara* (Structure and power).[13] In the 1990s, *InterCommunication* and *Critical Space*—with Asada figuring prominently as energetic force and editorial presence—became public discursive spaces for large collaborative projects involving architects, artists, translators, computer technologists, scientists, virtual reality experts, musicians, media theorists, composers, and writers (and more). An entire generational world of high theory and culture was drawn together into the curatorial space of these two intertwined journals.

So it should come as no surprise that *IC*, with Asada as one of its editorial founders, should begin its publication life with selections translated from the French icons of communication theory in the late-twentieth century: Virilio and Baudrillard, who immediately come to mind as media theorists, if not more-than-media theorists. Yet it might not be as obvious (or acceptable) to many in university media or communications programs, say, that Jacques Derrida should be considered a signal media or communication theorist. By translating *La carte postale* into Japanese, *IC* signaled that Derrida was a foundational thinker for the theorization of the intersection of new communication technologies, new media, and the arts (in a journal funded by NTT).

What is striking, even in the midst of the fabulous abundance of theories, events, fantasies, and possibilities purveyed by the *InterCommunication* project, is how closely it hewed to a demanding standard of what might be called, not ironically, a late-modern international style (following the journal's inspirations from the icons of postwar modernist Japanese architecture), artistic endeavor, and reflection. This was not primarily a journal about the media effects generated by mass culture or popular culture, nor did it regularly feature critical writings that crossed over into pop terrain, stylistically. Although every potential permutation of the technoarts and creative new media was pursued, work about anime, mass mediation, manga, and the minutiae of everyday Japanese mass culture tended not to be foregrounded. Moreover, one searches the journal in vain for even passing references to the defining political or economic crises of the day. In the issues for 1995 (or even 1996), for example, I found no articles or discussions about Aum Shinrikyō, the religious group that carried out the infamous poison gas attacks in Tokyo's subways in 1995. Nor did I encounter any essays dedicated to the Kōbe earthquake of 1995, the recession, or the so-called Shōnen A (youth A) incident of 1997, in which a high-school student carried out a decapitation of another student. That is to say, the quarterly resolutely kept to its primary mandate to explore new technology and art—to theorize media, communication, and culture (although that is not to say that contemporary political issues were not discussed in any of the numerous roundtables and dialogues that IC published). It was this intercommunication, this exchange, between technology and art—and perhaps with the emphasis on the powers of art—that seemed to provide a way out of the deepening crises of the recessionary period. With its late (if not post) modernist notion of the resistant powers of art and theory to harness technological powers, *InterCommunication* kept a certain distance from the more ubiquitous products of the culture industry, as well as from the vicissitudes of natural, social, and political disasters.

Much of the 1990s constituted a period before the global fame of art superstar Murakami Takashi and the international reach of his "Superflat" concept, even if, alternatively, anime auteur Miyazaki Hayao was becoming a household name in Euro-America. The decisive lamination of high cultural theory with the stuff of Japan's everyday mass-mediated digital worlds did not occur conclusively until what we might call the Azuma Hiroki intervention.

It is therefore telling to trace Azuma's rise to prominence through his writings in *Critical Space*, but also, revealingly, in *InterCommunication*. His first contribution to the journal was a book review, published in 1995 (issue no. 14) titled "Sore ni shitemo mediaron wa naze konnani konnan nano ka?" (Why is it that media theory is so difficult?), in which he reviewed three then-recent books about media theory.[14] One of the books he reviewed was Ohsawa Masachi's *Denshi mediaron* (Theories of electronic media), a book consisting of articles about media written by Ohsawa in the pages of *Inter-Communication*, starting with issue number 0.[15] Azuma starts the review by stating that there are no good Japanese books on media theory, critiquing Ohsawa's essays by asserting that he (Ohsawa) does not understand the place of the "other" (seeing the other as only a projection from an internal split), does not problematize the very notion of media, and that—in fact—much of his book has nothing to do with media. Azuma ends his short review with a toss-off recommendation: take some hints from Derrida's newly published *Mal d'Archive* (*Arushiivu no aku*) to get away from the present situation that is so poor in media theory (*mediaron no mazushii genjō o nogareru*). Azuma thus promoted Derrida as a peerlessly deep media theorist, a theorist who could rescue *mediaron* from its impoverished circumstances.

Azuma was already theorizing anime in the mid-1990s, including one article in *InterCommunication* in 1996, so anime was not completely excluded from the journal. He also wrote a series of articles on cyberspace for *InterCommunication* in succeeding years (he was publishing in *Critical Space* during this time as well). But I linger on the Derrida connection through *InterCommunication* because Azuma consolidated his place as a Japanese intellectual superstar with his 1998 book *Sonzaironteki yūbinteki: Jakku Derrida ni tsuite* (Ontological, postal: On Jacques Derrida).[16] Yet by 2000, at least, and certainly by the publication of his *Dōbutsuka suru posutomodan* (The animalized postmodern) in 2001, Azuma had performed a renunciation of his Derrida fixation, which was no doubt entangled with Asada's and Karatani's suspicions of Azuma's *otaku* theorizations and with his increasingly direct denunciations of the Asada-Karatani approach to critical work.[17]

InterCommunication, therefore, did not accompany Azuma into his future, a future that established "Japanese media theory" today as finding its exemplary objects in anime and the complex *inter*netted media mixes constituting everyday electronic culture, enabled by the communication devices and services that NTT (East and West), among others, provides. Nor did IC go the Superflat route, while Azuma's collaborations with Murakami Takashi became globally celebrated.[18] Instead, the journal and the center continued to invest in the Euro-style critical fusions of art, theory, and new media technology with which it started. Projects have included, for example, a collaborative 2007 installation titled *Life—Fluid Invisible Inaudible* by Sakamoto Ryūichi and visual artist Takatani Shirō, a core member of the renowned performance group Dumb Type. This project is exemplary of the kind of installations, projects, and exhibitions that might be found at the Centre Pompidou in Paris, or at any of the innovative exhibition spaces in Amsterdam, Berlin, Milan, Oslo, or New York, for that matter—at Eyebeam, Performance Space 122, the Park Avenue Armory (where the sonic and visual artist Ikeda Ryōji had a mega-event titled the *Transfinite* in 2011), or perhaps even MoMA. Performance art, installations, exhibitions: the place of visual or sound art becomes the site for staging the internationalized intercommunication that is particularly vibrant in Euro-American *avant*-classical spaces. It is arguable that these performative stagings of the aesthetic possibilities of digital technologies and telemediatic arts constitute the most powerful internationalized, intercommunicative legacy of the *InterCommunication* project.

InterCommunication ceased print publication in the annus horribilis 2008 (the same year as the journal *10+1*). Its final issue (no. 65) ended with a short note to its readers:

With this issue, *InterCommunication* will suspend publication. The magazine has been the house bulletin of NTT's Intercommunication Center, established in 1997, and which it preceded by its initial publication in February 1992. Since that time, *InterCommunication* has continued publication, making its editorial objective the illumination of current issues with a focus on art and science, media technology, and information environments, as well as music, film, architecture, sociology, philosophy, and more—the vast territory of contemporary culture.

However, during the sixteen years since our initial publication, huge transformations have occurred in society, in media, and also in the publishing world. At this time, our company has decided to suspend publication of *InterCommunication*, with our determination to end its role in the medium of a magazine [*zasshi media*]. Thank you for reading *InterCommunication*.

NTT Publishing Corporation
InterCommunication Editorial Staff[19]

By this time, Asada Akira and the original editorial group were no longer directly involved in the publication (although Asada still takes part in live events at ICC). In retrospect, one might be amazed that the journal continued for as long as it did through the dramatic digital transformations that it so presciently publicized, theorized, critiqued, and celebrated. *InterCommunication*'s archive migrated to the website of the ICC, where it lives a selective afterlife: some articles are available for perusal, some are not; some are translated into English, most are not. There was never any effort, it appears, to reach Asian readers or constituencies: to my knowledge, no Chinese, no Korean translations. Japanese has become more default than ever. Yet the InterCommunication Center continues to operate as an ongoing site for new media explorations, including its gallery, Open Space; its website archive, called the "Hive," and its still-numerous live performances and symposia.[20]

In 2013, five years after the cessation of *InterCommunication*, I visited the InterCommunication Center in the Tokyo Opera City Tower, with its bookstore, interactive displays, and galleries (where entry was free, as it had always been). The facilities are not grand, but they are respectable (the original vision of the center was compressed for financial considerations, post-bubble). Upstairs, on the fifth floor, is the Open Space gallery, with its signature sunken timeline, a glass-covered trench in which is embedded—in chronological order—a curation of artifacts from information ages past:

first editions of McLuhan's works, Beatles albums, artifacts of obsolete communications technologies (telephones), and newspaper articles from each period documenting the important events of the day (strange how the fragile reality of newspapers becomes the perduring last guarantee of temporal authenticity, even now).

Open Space has exhibitions of long duration, possibly because of ongoing financial constraints (again, entry is free). The permanent works are largely interactive, with hands-on computer activities, projections with digital cameras, remote sensing games. The bona fide art installations in the fifth-floor galleries are meant to dramatize the mandate of the "dialogue between art and technoscience" that Asada Akira first articulated. Like the journal itself, however, ICC's installations continue to theorize and stage the complexities of communication far beyond the humanistic model that NTT would explicitly want to purvey in its own commercially driven enterprises.

ICC—like the journal—is not only a site for the new, which was always one of the objects of *InterCommunication*, but also for retrospection, even nostalgia. Surmounted technologies are not left out. The intercommunication between art and technology staged in the journal and the center is an inter-ruptured one, a broken dialogue perhaps, at times staged with tangible force. Here remain palpable the investments in the performance, or the staging, of the aporias of new and not-so-new and old media technologies and their communicative possibilities.

Technoartist Hachiya Kazuhiko's mid-recessionary installation *Seeing Is Believing* (Miru koto wa shinjiru koto, 1996) was restaged at Open Space in the summer of 2013, explicitly reopening the emergent aporia of communications in the 1990s to the space of public legibility. In 1995, in the still-early stages of email and Internet communication, Hachiya solicited contributions from a global range of emailers, asking them to send him "diary" entries on the Internet, as he assembled an early archive of Internet messages. The translated English-language web page on ICC Online states, "The artist refers to his dream of a library collecting diaries written by people around the world as the catalyst that inspired him to launch the project. In a way it may be considered as a realization of the dreamed library in times saturated with web services such as blogs and Twitter."[21]

But Hachiya did not simply post the messages in his installation (or online, or anywhere else). When one entered the darkened chamber of his installation at ICC, a ceaselessly moving array of digital lights randomly streamed over the electronic signboards that covered the gallery's walls, a random constellation—no transmission of messages, no language, no reception of

communication. Only by taking up what appeared to be a species of stereoscopic device (called a *hitsuji*, or "sheep") and peering through it could
one see that the streaming lights were in fact the LED-articulated messages
of innumerable people, the Internetted archive of the diaries of Hachiya's
informants. The lights became legible, readable; the title of the installation
might well have been *Miru koto wa yomu koto* (Seeing is *reading*). The
sublimity of the virtually inexhaustible relay of text, now readable, through
the intimate prosthesis of the *hitsuji*; the action of *peering* through the device, reminded one of nothing more than the fascination of the stereoscopic
View-Master devices of childhood, with their frozen revelations of unknown
landscapes, arrested in uncanny 3-D relief. At Hachiya's installation, the
hitsuji allowed the digital stream to resolve itself into characters, into sentences, into the messages of emailed communications, now rendered legible
and believable—because visible?—for the solitary viewer, positioned as the
now-authorized reader of private communications, made public—yet only
for those with the proper technoprosthesis, looking back from 2013 to the
moment of 1996.

The Library of Babel, the Borgesian dream of the complete archive, is reimagined here in the partial, streaming terms of the digitally hidden emailed
communications of the most intimately quotidian variety. Anticipating all
the technical and aesthetic labors and wonders that would increasingly pre-
occupy the InterCommunication Center (not yet in place when the installation was first produced in 1996), and which would eventually displace the
paper-based work of the print journal *InterCommunication*, *Seeing Is Believing* staged the obscure dream of a technology of revelatory translation,
rendering visibility into belief itself (see fig. 4.3).

The aporia of the technologies of communication, the interruptions that
consolidate it, the broken temporalities and technological doublings that enable it at the same time as they disable it, have structured many of the critical technoaesthetic projects at the InterCommunication Center, works that
travel to and from Japan, works that originate within and outside of Japan.
Hachiya has another interactive work dating from 1993 that was restaged in
New York in 2004 at Eyebeam, one of the premier media arts centers in the
United States. This work technoperformatively theatricalized the ways that
intercommunication is founded on a fundamental impasse and a foundational instability of terms, in an undoing of the transparency of communication that seemed to be commenting, uncannily, on the theoretical aporia
structuring the journal *InterCommunication* itself—most vividly in its Derridean encounters (see fig. 4.4).[22] To quote from Eyebeam's website:

[FIG. 4.3] Hachiya Kazuhiko, "Seeing Is Believing,"
(Miri koto wa shinjuru koto) 1996. Image courtesy of the artist.

Kazuhiko Hachiya's *Inter Dis-Communication Machine*, composed of
a video camera, transmitters, head-mounted displays, batteries, and
feathers is a communication system aimed at transmitting and receiving sensual experiences.

Used by two people wearing head-mounted displays, the "machine"
projects one wearer's sight and sound perception of the environment
into the other one's display, thus confusing the borders between the
identities of "you" and "me."

The Inter Dis-Communication Machine allows its wearers to "enter"
each other's body and perception without being able to influence it.[23]

Hachiya's potently playful virtual reality piece, complete with two pairs of
angel wings (one pair black, one white), produces exactly what *Eyebeam*
describes: the "trading places" of the perceptual apparatus of one subject
for the other, a sensual intercommunication confused, willingly (Hachiya
titled the piece in Japanese *Shichōkaku kōkan mashin* [Audiovisual exchange
machine]). Disorientation ensues in the midst of the interrupted "inter,"
a between that allows an exchange. The space *between* is the space of

[FIG. 4.4] Hachiya Kazuhiko, *The Inter Dis-Communication Machine*, (Shichōkaku kōkan mashin) 1993. Image courtesy of the artist.

miscommunication, even *dis*-(inter)communication, allowing the possibility of contact in the very gap opened up. Hachiya's interdiscommunicated (if not excommunicated) angels, along with his invisible email archive made visible, linger on, virtually, in spaces already prepared by the labors of the *InterCommunication* project. That he would title his work (in English) "The Inter Dis-Communication Machine" reveals a pointedly amusing, yet uncanny, recognition of the paradoxes of communication and a barely coded reference to the *InterCommunication* project itself (another exhibition by Hachiya was one of the last exhibitions at the center while the journal was still in operation).

We can take Hachiya's work as an allegory of angelic intercorporealization, an instantiation of the transformative powers of vr art, when the other virtually becomes one's self. Perhaps this is the dream of intercommunication, one we saw imagined in the discursive space of the journal, shifted into a theatrical, technoperformative domain that stages "trading places" through an audiovisual exchange machine: an exchange that technologically embodies the dream of perfect intercommunication in its very impossibility (and, thus, an exchange of angels: angels as impossible beings). It enacts a post-utopian moment of translation's beyond, a communico-mediatic theory made palpably, technologically corporeal.

This allegory of inter dis-communication taken to its extreme is a potently wry commentary on the end, indeed, of the kinds of translation endeavor that deeply anchored the *InterCommunication* project. Yet to return to the status of Japanese media theory—or media theory in Japan, or of Japan—the question of translation cannot help but be ceaselessly reiterated. Within Hachiya's New York performance at Eyebeam, where is Japan located? And what is a media theory that could be located within something called Japan? The *InterCommunication* project was an unprecedented experiment in theorizing technocultural futures in Japan, in all their mediatic and communicative possibilities—both via the journal itself and through the ongoing performative and exhibitionary spaces of the ICC—where novel mediatic and aesthetic possibilities were publicized. While providing artistic cover to a neoliberalizing NTT, the experiments that took place, both theoretical and otherwise, far outstripped the gigantic telecommunication corporation's capacity to contain them. At the same time, they did not accede to a kind of post-Azuma take on media theory as primarily linked to youth culture and to a distinctly Japanese sensibility ranged under the now-omnibus heading of *otaku* culture. Instead, the *InterCommunication* project embraced an older cosmopolitanism refunctioned for the recessionary decades of neoliberalization and globalization, along with a stubborn experimentalism in which aesthetic practice and performance were bound up with theory itself and the critical necessity of translation work. The IC project held open, even in the recessionary period, the ongoing promises of internationalist high-theory and avant-gardist technocultural work. As such, it played a critical role in ensuring that media theory in recessionary Japan was not located simply within Japan, and that a beleaguered, cosmopolitan intercommunication was not inevitably reduced to the containments of an exclusively Japanese *intra*communication.

My bound volumes of *InterCommunication* will go back to the Columbia University stacks soon enough. When disinterred from their library burial—and perused—they reveal the wild proliferation of media thought in Japan's rapidly receding lost decades. They signal, perhaps first and foremost, the foundations of mediatic thinking in theories of transmission, translation, and (inter)communication. At the same time, they perdure as material-textual reminders of a singular institutional project, one that articulated corporate sponsorship and the passions of avant-garde media theory and practice. Even in its uninterrupted archival slumber the journal continues to disclose the *InterCommunication* project's critical centrality to our reflections on what we could possibly mean by media theory in Japan, today.

NOTES

1. See Bruce Clarke, "Communication," in *Critical Terms for Media Studies*, ed. W. J. T. Mitchell and Mark B. N. Hansen (Chicago: University of Chicago Press, 2010), 131–44.

2. The journal *10+1* began publication in 1995, three years after *InterCommunication*. It ended publication in 2008, the same year as *IC*. As of 2014, the association of architects that founded the journal maintains a vibrantly useful website, as well as an accurate subsite that lists the back issues of *10+1*, including English-translated titles of special issues and articles. See LIXIL, "10+1," accessed July 9, 2014, http://10plus1.jp/.

3. See Eamonn Fingleton, "The Myth of Japan's Failure," *New York Times*, January 6, 2012.

4. Timothy E. Nulty, "Introductory Note," in Yoshiro Takano, *Nippon Telegraph and Telephone Privatization Study: Experience of Japan and Lessons for Developing Countries*, World Bank Discussion Paper 179 (1992), vii.

5. See Thomas Thummel and Max Thummel, "Privatization of Telecommunications in Japan," in *Limits to Privatization: How to Avoid Too Much of a Good Thing*, ed. Ernst Ulrich von Weizsäcker, Oran R. Young, and Matthias Finger (London: Earthscan, 2005), 77.

6. Tessa Morris-Suzuki, *Beyond Computopia: Information, Automation, and Democracy in Japan* (London: Routledge, 1988).

7. See Yoshimi Shunya's Kittler-inspired *"Koe" no shihonshugi: Denwa rajio chikuonki* (Tokyo: Kōdansha, 1995).

8. This ad was repeated in *InterCommunication* twice during 1996, both in issue no. 15 (winter 1996) and issue no. 16 (spring 1996). Translations mine.

9. Asada Akira, interview by Krystian Woznicki, *Nettime Mailing Lists*, accessed July 9, 2014, http://www.nettime.org/Lists-Archives/nettime-l-9802/msg00100.html.

10. *InterCommunication*, no. 0 (spring 1992).

11. Published as "Hagaki yori," [From *The Post Card*], *InterCommunication*, no. 0 (spring 1992): 34–39. See Jacques Derrida, *The Post Card: From Socrates to Freud and Beyond*, trans. Alan Bass (Chicago: University of Chicago Press, 1987).

12. See Avital Ronell's unclassifiable work *The Telephone Book: Technology, Schizophrenia, Electric Speech* (Lincoln: University of Nebraska Press, 1989) for a wildly inventive performance of the radical potentiality opened up by telephonic logic.

13. Asada Akira, *Kōzō to chikara: Kigōron o koete* [Structure and power: Beyond Semiotics] (Tokyo: Keisō Shobō, 1983).

14. Hiroki Azuma, "Sore ni shitemo mediaron wa naze konnani konnan nano ka?" [Why is it that media theory is so difficult?], *InterCommunication*, no. 14 (1995); see footnote.

15. Ohsawa Masachi, *Denshi mediaron* [Theories of electronic media] (Tokyo: Shinyōsha, 1995).

16. Jonathan Abel has provided an overview of Azuma's relationship with Asada and Karatani as custodians of a determined high cultural ambiance in the journals they edited. See Jonathan Abel, translator's introduction to *Otaku: Japan's Database Animals*, by Hiroki Azuma (Minneapolis: University of Minnesota Press, 2009), xxii–xxvi.

17. Azuma, *Otaku*, 120–21. See Abel's notes.

18. Azuma has been closely and collaboratively involved with Murakami Takashi's work; he is perhaps Murakami's most important critic. See, for example, Azuma's important essay "Superflat Speculation" in *Superflat*, ed. Murakami Takashi (Tokyo: Madra, 2000).

19. *InterCommunication* 65 (summer 2008): 151. Translation mine.

20. Please see the center's remarkable website: NTT, "NTT Intercommunication Center," accessed July 9, 2014, http://www.ntticc.or.jp/index_e.html.

21. Both Japanese and English-language descriptions exist for his installation: NTT, "Seeing Is Believing," accessed July 9, 2014, http://www.ntticc.or.jp/Exhibition/2013/Openspace2013/Works/Seeing_Is_Believing.html.

22. Eyebeam, "About Eyebeam," accessed March 7, 2016, http://eyebeam.org/about. Eyebeam explains its project thus: "Founded in 1997, Eyebeam was conceived as a nonprofit art and technology center dedicated to exposing broad and diverse audiences to emerging artistic practice critically engaged with new technology, while simultaneously acting as an educator of technology's potential for creativity."

23. Eyebeam, "Inter-Discommunication Machine," accessed March 7, 2016, http://eyebeam.org/projects/inter-discommunication-machine. A video of the devices in use was uploaded by Hachiya to YouTube: Kazuhiko Hachiya, "Inter Dis-Communication Machine (1993)," YouTube, accessed March 7, 2016, http://www.youtube.com/watch?v=JOzVzcmKoVU.

II. PRACTICAL THEORY

5. McLUHAN AS PRESCRIPTION DRUG
Actionable Theory and Advertising Industries
MARC STEINBERG

One of the turning points in the history of Japanese media theorization *as media theory* was the influx of Marshall McLuhan's work into Japan in the years 1966–68, and the "McLuhan boom" that ensued. McLuhan likely needs no introduction: he was a Canadian theorist of media famous for his aphoristic one-liners such as "The medium is the message" and "The content of one medium is another medium." He is known for his polarizing distinctions between hot and cool media and between literate and oral cultures. Hot media, such as the radio, are information-dense and prone to firing up emotions. Cool media, such as the low-res television image of the pre-HDTV years, require a good deal of viewer participation and involvement (the latter being another key term in his vocabulary). Retribalization and the reemergence of the synthetic, multisensory, oral "man" was McLuhan's vision for humanity under conditions of electr(on)ic media. He was duly famous for his technological determinism, or at least his deterministic view of media forms—it doesn't matter what a train car is carrying, what matters is that train tracks connect one city to another. Content is irrelevant, and to focus on it would mislead the analyst; only the social effects of media matter, and those effects follow from their mediatic form. In shifting the object of analysis from message to channel, and in understanding channel with an eye to its environmental and social effects, McLuhan often claims the distinction of being one of the first theorists of media as such.

Being a figure who read into technological transformations the rise of a social formation based around total awareness and the reunification of the senses, and made grandiose claims about global retribalization—following in the wake of the specialization and separation of the faculties brought about in the West under print technologies—McLuhan was unsurprisingly divisive. Tempers flared, and there were some very hot reactions to his supposedly systematic, cool approach. Not only was McLuhan seen as *divisive*, he was also seen as *divided*. For evidence of this we can turn to the introduction of one of the first collections of critical essays around the media theorist's work: *McLuhan: Hot and Cool*. There editor Gerald Emanuel Stearn writes, "It is fashionable to suggest that there are two Marshall McLuhans: one, a rather donnish, slightly eccentric professor, working away in the sheltered, musty precincts of the academy on trivial literary exercises; the other, a wild idiosyncratic Popster who is on to a good thing—media analysis, a subject badly in need of exploration."[1] Ultimately Stearn suggests that this image of two McLuhans is misguided, as there are real continuities across the figure's work. Yet the image of a divided McLuhan is perhaps nowhere more tangible than in Japan in the 1960s, where on the one hand he was painted as the savior of the business world, a made-for-advertising guru, and on the other as a potentially influential media theorist who was badly misread.

The Japanese reception of McLuhan seems to repeat some of the familiar debates found in his Anglo-American reception. Yet it also has significant local inflections that stem from the sites and institutions that mediated this introduction, and this, in turn, influenced the manner in which he was presented. Concretely, McLuhan's reception in Japan was colored by the fact that he was introduced by figures closely associated with television broadcasters and ad agencies, and thus he was read as a management guru by white collar "salarymen," media workers, and business moguls alike. In Japan perhaps more than anywhere else, McLuhan was regarded as a prophetic figure who spoke directly to ad executives and the managerial class. To be sure, elements of this reception by business and marketing people exist elsewhere in the world; McLuhan was famously taken up as the darling of Madison Avenue and lectured at major corporations in North America in the mid-1960s and early 1970s. The image of McLuhan as an oracle for executives had currency for contemporary commentators, many of whom touch on this in their assessments of the writer.

Nonetheless, an examination of the McLuhan boom in Japan reveals that there, more than anywhere else, the writer was received first and foremost as a marketing guru. In a 1967 article, Kadoyama Nobu outlines three peculiarities of this reception: (1) McLuhan's works had yet to be translated into Japanese (and hence those who did not read the English original were wholly reliant on his local interpreters); (2) in Japan people assume that McLuhan gave birth to a revolutionary change in marketing, and also assume that this is the reason for his popularity in the United States; and (3) McLuhan is not being introduced as a theorist but rather as a prophet.[2] As this chapter will argue, McLuhanite media theory was seen as marketing theory, or what I will call *actionable theory*—theory that promises to provide concrete results to its users (with the caveat that with theory the promise is more important than whether results are in fact provided).[3]

The perception of McLuhan as a marketing guru is in large part due to the man most responsible for his introduction: Takemura Ken'ichi, a figure as reviled for bastardizing McLuhan as he is recognized for his popularization of the man. In fact, one might better describe Takemura as someone who *channeled* McLuhan, more than popularized him. Takemura *was* the Japanese McLuhan. Indeed, contemporaries of Takemura, such as Seijō University professor Ishikawa Hiroyoshi, dub the late 1960s media theory craze the "Takemura/McLuhan boom," putting distinct emphasis on the Takemura side of the equation.[4] McLuhan's work was so marked by his most vocal proponent in Japan that the two were collectively known as "Takemura McLuhan."[5] The verb "channel" is not chosen arbitrarily: Takemura often says that he "understands McLuhan *in his whole body*."[6] He functioned as something of a local spiritual medium for the Canadian media theorist, producing something else in the process. Here I dub this thing produced *TakeMcLuhanism*.

Not surprisingly, Takemura also came to stand in for everything intellectuals and writers in Japan and around the world hated about McLuhan. So, rather than writers treating McLuhan as a false prophet, they tended to treat Takemura as one, and this had the effect of immunizing McLuhan against the type of attacks he was subject to in North America and Europe. Indeed, some of the fiercest critics of Takemura were in fact those who claimed to find theoretical value in McLuhan. As I will demonstrate here, the reception of McLuhan through Takemura—TakeMcLuhanism—points to the institutional importance of the advertising industries in enabling and channeling the adoption of media theory in Japan.[7]

Takemura is a particularly fascinating figure because he stands at the intersection of media theory, the advertising industries, and advertising practice. To many in Japan, Takemura may be best known for his long career as a television *tarento*, or celebrity performer, a commentator on contemporary affairs who hosted his own television programs on the major national networks during the 1970s and 1980s.[8] Yet Takemura has at least two other claims to fame, both germane to the topic at hand: first and foremost, he is known as the person who popularized McLuhan in 1960s Japan; and second, he was an advocate for *mōretsu*, or "intense," as a principle of advertising practice in the mid- to late 1960s. "Mōretsu" became a buzzword in the world of advertising and television commercials especially, and Takemura was known as one of its strongest proponents as a principle of advertising.[9] While this article will not be able to cover the brief intersection of McLuhanism and mōretsu, this close relationship does presage the bond between media theory and advertising practice that informs later instances of theoretical work analyzed in this volume. Insofar as the introduction of McLuhan launched Takemura's television career—as of 1968 Takemura became an embodiment of McLuhanism as a kind of media practice—this episode also points to the peculiar yet fundamental role that ad agencies and media practices have played in the history of media theory in Japan.

Media Theory Put to Work

There are three reasons in particular why we should consider the McLuhan boom (and TakeMcLuhanism) to be a key moment or inflection point in the history of media theory in Japan. First, and perhaps most significantly for a volume on the history of media theory in Japan, the very term for *media theory—mediaron* or, alternatively, *media riron*—was coined around the time of the influx of McLuhan's writing into Japan.[10] Hence, though the lifespan of the McLuhan boom may have been brief, it marked a shift in the terminological terrain of media theory. In a recent essay on McLuhan, Tsuno Kaitarō suggests that it was only in the late 1960s that "media" became a stand-alone word in Japan. Previously the term had always been coupled with the qualifier "mass," as in "mass media," and even then, the term appeared only in the early 1950s. This coincides with the introduction of the term "mass communications" (*masu komyunikēshon*) into Japan in the late 1940s and early 1950s by UNESCO, with the contraction *masu komi* and its variation *masu media* popularized by journalists in 1954, just in time for the emergence of the newest of mass media, television.[11] The first use of the term "media" as a stand-alone entity coincides, Tsuno suggests, with the 1960s McLuhan boom in Japan. Confirming McLuhan's key role in the reception of media theory, Akihiro Kitada suggests that the term itself was most firmly established in the Japanese language when a new 1987 translation of *Understanding Media* rendered McLuhan's famous work as *Mediaron*.[12] Hence the very term "media" and the concept of "media theory" (*mediaron*) are both firmly associated with the reception of McLuhan.

A second reason for this chapter's emphasis on the McLuhan boom is its effects on adjacent fields, such as art history and architectural theory. Yuriko Furuhata's contribution in this volume notes his influence on architectural discourse, but it also made inroads to the field of art criticism in Japan: it featured prominently in the writings of critics such as Hyuga Akiko and Tōno Yoshiaki, among others, and the art journal *Bijutsu Techō* dedicated a special issue to McLuhan's work in January 1967, at the height of his popularity.

The third and perhaps most important reason for examining the Mc-Luhan boom is that it makes visible the central role Japanese television broadcasters and ad agencies have played in the introduction and filtering of theory in general. Ad agencies would later become hubs of critical theory—particularly its French variety, from Baudrillard to Derrida to Deleuze and Guattari—in the late 1970s through the 1990s. As Marilyn Ivy points out in her seminal work on the consumption of theory in the bubble era, the poststructuralist emphasis on difference and play gelled well with the principles of market segmentation and the production of identity-through-consumption, inspiring ad practice in the 1980s in particular.[13] At this time ad agencies functioned as zones of contact between academics (Asada Akira and Nakazawa Shin'ichi), independent and affiliated sociologists and critics who wrote for marketing journals or ad agencies (Miyadai Shinji, Kayama Rika, and Ōtsuka Eiji), and copywriters who circulated among critical theorists (Itoi Shigesato and Fujioka Wakao).

The embrace of McLuhan in the late 1960s was an early instance of the translation of theory into commercial practice, a translation that involved the production of actionable theory that resulted in the transformation of existing models of consumer society as well as the literal creation of television commercials. Takemura congratulates himself for starting a trend whereby books by "intellectuals" became best sellers in Japan, writing, "This [McLuhan boom] was the first time an intellectual became a hot topic in the Japanese publishing world. After that intellectual books like [Peter] Drucker's works, Alvin Toffler's *Future Shock*, and [Edwardo] de Bono's *Lateral Thinking* [*New Think*] became bestsellers or booms, but the start of all of this was *McLuhan's World*."[14] This narrative is clearly self-serving, and omits the earlier adoption of other non-Japanese intellectuals before McLuhan, but it does contain a kernel of truth: this was the first of a series of best sellers that walked the fine line between futurology (*miraigaku*)—a discipline popular in Japan from the early 1960s—management theory, and media studies.[15] In this context

McLuhan's thesis concerning the epochal shift from print-oriented, and thereby linear "man" defined by a focus on a single sense organ (the eye), to a sound-oriented, multisensory man defined by total field awareness provides the explanatory framework for the success of ad campaigns. The Mustang brand was popular, according to Takemura, because it acknowledged the "birth of tactile man."[16] It also provides the basis for understanding changes in production technique and product design: Takemura praises Honda for understanding that they needed to cater to the "age of variety" and personalization, and personally takes credit for Toyota's important shift to product diversification and small-batch production.[17] McLuhan's work—as Takemura presents it—is a handbook for the creation of successful ad campaigns.

Nowhere was the impact of the practical McLuhan more strongly debated than in the fields of television, advertising, and management theory. It is to this reception that I now turn.

Two Pillars of the McLuhan Boom

The McLuhan boom in Japan was brief but intense: it began in late 1966, and had all but died out by mid-1968.[18] Takemura Ken'ichi, who takes credit for this boom, was at the time a little-known media researcher and jack-of-all-trades writer who had spent some time in the United States. By the early 1960s he was writing a column in *Hōsō Asahi* (Asahi broadcasting), a journal published by the television network and newspaper publisher Asahi. One of these columns was rather fittingly titled "Buraunkan no kage ni," or "In the Shadow of the Television Screen." Takemura remained in the shadows of television until his debut as a McLuhan popularizer in the August 1966 edition of *Hōsō Asahi*. This introduction provoked a groundswell of interest in the media theorist and his popularizer. According to Takemura's meticulous bibliographical accounts, by January 1968 at least eighty-one newspaper, magazine, and journal articles and eight books had been published on McLuhan, the bulk of which were released in 1967.[19] This gives a sense of the magnitude of the McLuhanacy whirlwind sweeping through Japan in the late 1960s.

Takemura's introductory article and its institutional context are worth examining, since both shape what was to come. *Hōsō Asahi* was a widely circulated PR journal published by the Osaka Asahi Broadcasting Corporation.[20] The journal featured relatively highbrow debates around issues key to the emergent information society discourse, and television culture in particular. It was a mixture of an in-house research journal, a promotional magazine, and a forum for debate among public intellectuals who worked in the field of moving-image culture.[21] It was also the launching pad for a group of future studies scholars who would have a large impact on the conceptualization of Expo '70, as well as the development of information society discourse. Indeed, prior to Takemura's introduction to McLuhan, *Hōsō Asahi* had been running a multiyear series of specials titled "Theory of Information Industries" led by Umesao Tadao and novelist Komatsu Sakyō, among others. It was here that Umesao first coined the term "information industries" (*jōhō sangyō*) in 1961 in an article on the figure of the "broadcaster" (*hōsōjin*)—the human component of the radio and television industries. It was also here that he published his programmatic essay "A Theory of the Information Industries" in January 1963, an article that launched the discourse on information industries and information society in Japan.[22] *Hōsō Asahi* followed up on this by running numerous articles and hosting roundtables on the information industries through 1963, and formalized the growing body of work into an official series in its November 1964 issue, under the title "Towards the Development of the 'Theory of the Information Industries.'"

In August 1966, Takemura's essay on McLuhan inaugurated a new series titled "Eizō bunka ron," or "Theories of Image Culture,"[23] that followed closely on the heels of the "Information Industries" series and included many of its contributors in subsequent issues. Given McLuhan's own debt to cybernetics and emerging accounts of postindustrial capitalism, it is appropriate that he should be introduced following a series on the information industries, as Takemura himself remarks in his introductory article.[24] Moreover, Umesao treated the "communication industries" of television, radio, and so on *as* information industries, and the editors of *Hōsō Asahi* followed him in this equation. Hence theorizing the image would be seen as a natural extension of theorizing information industries.[25]

In fact, Takemura was not alone in introducing McLuhan in this issue of *Hōsō Asahi*. There was another article by a certain Gotō Kazuhiko, who was at the time a researcher affiliated with the Broadcasting Research Department of NHK, the national public broadcaster in Japan.[26] If Takemura represented one side of the McLuhan boom in Japan, then Gotō, his principal detractor and occasional nemesis, was the other. Takemura was described as a critic; his article for *Hōsō Asahi* was titled "Marshall McLuhan, the Prophet of the Television Age" and was accompanied by the subtitle, "Introduction to the Person." Gotō's contribution is the more academically titled "The Medium Is the Message: Introduction to the Theory." The difference between these two inaugural articles sets up the two poles of McLuhan's reception in

Japan: Takemura was the popularizer, Gotō the academic; Takemura went for spirit and application, Gotō for fidelity and theory. Takemura's McLuhan was all personality, style, and performance, while Gotō's McLuhan was a serious academic, the understanding of whose work required laborious reading. The difference in institutional affiliation is also telling: Takemura was giving biweekly courses on McLuhanism at the planning division of the Ōsaka office of Dentsū, the largest ad firm in Japan, under the title "McLuhan's Theory and Its Application for Broadcast Programming."[27] Gotō, as well as working as a researcher on broadcasting in the government-funded NHK research lab, wrote for leftist magazines as often as broadcasting journals. Both were attracted to McLuhan as a communications theorist, but Gotō claims to have first heard of the man as a graduate student in the United States in the 1950s, well before the North American McLuhan craze (a friend introduced him to McLuhan's 1951 work *The Mechanical Bride*). Takemura first encountered McLuhan's work in 1966 when he visited New York City and was introduced to the media theorist's oeuvre by friends who worked on Madison Avenue during the height of the McLuhan craze there.[28] The differences in their encounters with McLuhan are sharp, and profoundly shape their readings of him.

Takemura was from the start firmly entrenched in the advertising world, and this is the perspective from which he introduced McLuhan to Japan. In fact, a *Shūkan sankei* article from September 1967 on the McLuhan boom insinuates that Dentsū itself was the sponsor of this boom, and claims the ad firm saw McLuhan as a means of snagging more advertising contracts.[29] The article also claims that Dentsū funded Takemura's trips to the United States and Canada, where he would learn more about the McLuhan phenomenon. Takemura's version of the story is that he was working for the US Department of Education as a Japanese-language consultant in Minneapolis from September 1967 to 1968, during which time he did indeed contact McLuhan, arranging a meeting with him that formed both the basis of a thirty-minute TV special broadcast on Mainichi television, and a later book titled *Makurūhan to no taiwa* (Conversations with McLuhan).[30] What makes the *Shūkan sankei* article interesting is how it voices the perception that the McLuhan boom was manufactured by an ad firm. And indeed this is not so far from the truth: Takemura acknowledges that it was Dentsū's Osaka office planning director, Irie Yūzō, who suggested that he study McLuhan, based on Irie's intuition that McLuhan would be big.[31] Gotō himself also suggests that the McLuhan whirlwind was produced by ad agencies.[32]

Several months after his *Hōsō Asahi* article, Takemura published his 1967 book *Makurūhan no sekai* (McLuhan's world), a work of applied McLuhanism that sold 200,000 copies, ten times more than the eventually translated *Understanding Media*, making it up to eighth on the best-seller list of 1967.[33] *McLuhan's World* was the *Understanding Media* for Japanese audiences. What marked Takemura's work was its appeal to the general reader, and its presentation of McLuhan as the prophet of the electronic age, best read by business people, salaried workers, television industry heads, and marketing executives. He subsequently published a number of other books, all combining introductions to McLuhan with his own prophecies of things to come. Takemura channeled a very specific McLuhan for Japanese readers: McLuhan the business visionary, the adman, the prophet of media industries and their transformations—and, perhaps most importantly, a McLuhan localized for the Japanese context, complete with references to Japanese popular culture, ads, and politics, with predictions about the coming transformations of society and commerce thrown in to boot. McLuhan's focus on television as a tactile medium meshed with then current journalistic discussions about TV kids as the "skin tribe"; television was presented as a "happening" medium, a conceptual link invented by Takemura (albeit loosely based on McLuhan's own interest in happenings) that influenced both TV producers and advertising directors; Toyota came in for praise for properly grasping the current age as one of variety, market segmentation, and post–mass production, and so on.[34]

It is for this tendentious reading of McLuhan that Takemura's work was derided by scholars such as Ōmae Masaomi, Tōno Yoshiaki, and Gotō Kazuhiko, who published their own articles and books on McLuhan. Gotō, as we've already seen, was particularly active, publishing in ad journals, leftist periodicals, and newspapers, as well as authoring books. For a time he was everywhere, preaching a reasoned approach to McLuhan that was decisively *not* the applied McLuhanism Takemura practiced. Yet Gotō's work perhaps unwittingly reads as defensive, written against what is clearly the dominant Takemura-esque understanding of McLuhan as adman. Even his translation of *Understanding Media* did not help rectify the dominant positioning of McLuhan as a prophet of the information age. Takemura implicitly references Gotō and these other writers, suggesting that they were at "the forefront of anti-McLuhanism" in Japan, in a 1968 letter to McLuhan (a letter that also includes an apology for having "sensationalized" the media theorist's work, resulting in sales of "320,000 copies" of *McLuhan's World*).[35] It would, however, be more accurate to say that they were anti-TakeMcLuhanism.

Gotō presented himself as the rational assessor of the merits and limitations of McLuhan's work. The dust jacket of the book Gotō, Tōno, and others cowrote loudly proclaims that the book is "the first genuine introduction" to McLuhan, a clear dig at Takemura's earlier *McLuhan's World*. In the conclusion to his section of the book, Gotō remarks that he hopes the reader has now come to a better understanding of McLuhan's thinking and concepts. His remarks encapsulate the divide between his camp and Takemura's:

> The reader will likely find their impression of McLuhan [as explained here] to be very different from the image of McLuhan that has spread throughout our nation. The image of McLuhan that has been spread here is that of an extremely applicable McLuhan. It is a McLuhan that can be used like a prescription drug for management, advertising, marketing and store window displays. It is true that even in the US we can find this kind of reception here and there. However, if we were to think through McLuhan himself directly, there is no way one would arrive at this image.[36]

Against this "prescription drug" model of an applicable McLuhan who provides actionable theory and immediate results for the ad industries, Gotō's aim was to get to the real meat of the man's thought, treating it as "objectively" and academically as possible.[37]

Yet fight as Gotō would against this practical McLuhan that promises to work like a prescription drug, it is precisely this latter variation of McLuhanism that most marks his reception in Japan. Takemura was lambasted by Gotō and others who saw in him a snake charmer who distorted media theory into advertising practice. Takemura unabashedly presents McLuhanism as a "weapon for businessmen and admen" and argues for its usefulness in management practice.[38] Yet despite the common use of Takemura as an intellectual punching bag, his influence cannot be underestimated—he truly did shape the McLuhan boom in Japan. There is no better measure of the effect of Takemura's McLuhan than to look at the multitude of reviews, both negative and positive, of McLuhan's work. Ultimately many of the articles within magazine special issues titled "Advertising and McLuhan" or "Commercials and McLuhan" came to the same conclusion: the drug didn't work as promised. A common complaint about the way McLuhan was introduced was that he promised an easy road to commercial application, a road that was either false (Gotō et al.) or misleading (writers griping that McLuhan is harder to read than initially expected, has little immediate applicability, does not talk all that much about advertising after all, etc.). This sentiment was expressed in many of the specials on McLuhan and the advertising or man-agement worlds at the time.[39] Yet this very framing of McLuhan in terms of functionality or applicability is an index of Takemura's enduring influ-ence, and a clear indication of the pervasiveness of this image of the media theorist as marketing guru. TakeMcLuhanism framed the manner in which McLuhan was understood in Japan, with *McLuhan's World* displacing *Un-derstanding Media* as the must-read text.[40]

In part this displacement is due to the physical absence of McLuhan him-self; the author did not make an appearance in Japan during these years, apart from a short TV program, despite appeals by Takemura and corpora-tions for him to visit and stay in the country. The result of this displacement was that Takemura became the target for any and all the criticism about McLuhan as adman. Gotō, for his part, came off looking like the serious academic. Takemura adopts the performative dimension of McLuhan, pres-ent in both his writings and his media presence in North America; and Gotō takes up only the constative dimension of McLuhan, focusing solely on what McLuhan objectively *meant*.[41] In playing the performative to the hilt (and instrumentalizing it in the process), Takemura adopted the most divisive elements of McLuhanism, thereby becoming the object of criticism in McLuhan's place. The end result is that he immunized McLuhan from the outright denunciations we find in his Anglo-American reception.

Media Times, Media Institutions, Media Consulting

Let us take a moment to consider the issue of the performative translation of theory in Takemura's time and our own. For all of the fascination of seeing McLuhan played to the hilt within the iconoclastic TakeMcLuhanist project, the performativity of Takemura's McLuhanism occasionally comes off as a bit unidimensional. McLuhan's performativity refers to his tendency to enact his theory of media through language itself. Takemura tends to translate this performativity into mere performance, a repetition of the gestures of McLu-han. Nothing is more striking than Takemura's easy way of denouncing nay-sayers: he claims they are stuck in an earlier media age, and an old way of thinking. This is vintage McLuhan as mannerism; anyone who didn't follow McLuhan was easily dismissed as a "print person"—stuck in a linear mode of thinking that just did not fit the new electric media era, with its focus on integral thinking and total field awareness. Rational, step-by-step argumen-tation was past its best-before date, a relic of a bygone era in which the lin-earity of print dominated both thought and critical discourse. Takemura all too readily adopts this dismissive attitude toward critics. Total media change is a useful tool for dismissing critics as being merely behind the new media times.

Yet this very formalization of the gesture of media-determined dismissal does raise a series of useful questions around the relation between media technologies and media theory. Do new media conditions require new modes of critique, that is to say, new forms or temporalities of criticism? Can new media conditions *produce* new ways of thinking or writing about these conditions? To what degree are theories of media affected—in content or in form—by the media they describe? Do new media forms require new forms of media theory? These questions reassert themselves at various moments in media history. In recent years they reappeared in debates around whether the "real time" temporality and heightened speed of Internet-enabled communication required a new mode of criticism that would adopt the speed and tactical strategies of the Internet and its users. Outlining the contours of this debate, Wendy Chun notes that some argue that the "time of theory itself needs to change," with certain theorists such as McKenzie Wark and Geert Lovink advocating a form of theory that would "take on the same temporality or speed as digital media, refusing to stand outside their mode of dissemination."[42] Chun herself ultimately rejects this approach, arguing that "we need to think beyond speed,"[43] implicitly upholding a purist model of theory.

Jodi Dean similarly finds problem with what she sees as the immediacy of electronic media, praising the slower temporality of print as an enabler for thought. Dean sees the lag inherent in print as a positive form of slowdown that contrasts with the libidinally driven immediacy of blog posting and re-posting, which she describes as "react and forward, but don't by any means think."[44] Dean hence finds something redemptive in the very temporality of print, suggesting that "critical media theory is possible in book form. . . . The book mobilizes the gap of mediacy so as to stimulate thought."[45] Internet-fueled "react and forward" media networks do not create the mediacy necessary for critical thought, but the book form in its slower temporality and its medial gap does. If Dean discovers resistance to the affective dynamics of the web in the inertial pull of print, Geert Lovink searches rather for a new form of Internet criticism adequate to the age, interrogating existing terms such as *network, community, blog, friends,* and *link,* as well as developing his own conceptual paradigms such as *network cultures.*[46] Where Lovink and Dean agree is in the way in which they reflexively grapple with the problem of how to write in an older medium (print) or in an older form (criticism) under new media conditions.

This dilemma recalls McLuhan's own transformation of writing under the pressure of the televisual image and the new logic of culture he believed it generated. McLuhan's aphoristic, fragmented style was presumably not merely a result of the influence of the modernist writers he admired; it was an active, formal response to the electronic media conditions that saw fragmentation, reading across gaps, total field awareness, and so on emerge as defining elements in a new media environment. McLuhan's to some merely unintelligible writing style and illogical mode of argumentation can be more charitably read as the writer's attempt to develop a style of writing and argumentation adequate to the new electric media era. Where McLuhan differs from Dean and Lovink is that he attempts to perform the media effects within the print medium. This attempt later led him to collaborate with Jerome Agel and Quentin Fiore, who took this principle to its logical conclusion in their creation of what scholars Jeffrey T. Schnapp and Adam Michaels have smartly called *The Electric Information Age Book*.[47]

Returning to the reception of McLuhan in Japan, we may ask: Did Takemura also innovate in print or prose in accordance with the pressures of the electric (im)age? Do Takemura's writings perform the new media conditions in their form? Are Takemura's works the appropriate form of response to the televisual era, in a way that Gotō's are not? While Takemura operates far more in the spirit of McLuhan than does Gotō, he did not perform new media in the fragmented manner of McLuhan. Takemura's writing is easy in a way that McLuhan's is not; his slide toward application is not an immediate consequence of media transformation per se but rather a consequence of the commercial institution of corporate broadcasting and advertisers' drive toward sloganeering. Takemura may have understood McLuhan in his entire body and performed a kind of McLuhanite media prophet in his writings and in his subsequent career as a TV personality. However, his performance of McLuhanism as prophesy-making for ad agencies stands as a reminder that we need to examine the institutional conditions and economic auspices under which media change happens. Under the right conditions, media theory is channeled into media prophesy. Or, to use a slightly more modern term for the latter, media consulting.

Examining the McLuhan boom in Japan, we can discern three conditions for the channeling of media theory into consulting practice: the source material (Marshall McLuhan), the institutional conditions (ad agencies' need for actionable knowledge), and the medium (Takemura Ken'ichi) who could transform the first into a body of work fit for the second, and thereby produce TakeMcLuhanism.

Takemura's performance of media theory registers a very real complicity between his own style and McLuhan's; it exposes the ease with which the latter's work slides from analysis to futurological prediction. McLuhan's aphoristic sound bites were easily translated into ad speak and management theory; the fragmented abstraction of McLuhan's high modernism as media theory becomes the language of ad copy. This *works* in part because embedded within both McLuhan and *Understanding Media* is a certain complicity with the existing order. Consider McLuhan's easy dismissal of the entire critical tradition of Marxism, his tendency to write from the point of view of the capitalist affirmation of novelty (not to mention the seemingly inexorable march of the spirit of innovation), and a propensity to throw in free advice for media masters and corporate heads with whom he seemed to identify in his writing. Consider too the stated goal of *Understanding Media*, to "bring [media] into orderly service," and his later, rather governmental vision of using media to "program a reasonable and orderly future for any human community."[48] Consider all of this, and it is no surprise that McLuhan was sometimes seen as a prophet for a decidedly apolitical but business-oriented elite.

On this count Hans Magnus Enzensberger's rather unkind assessment of McLuhan as "an author who admittedly lacks any analytical categories for the understanding of social processes, but whose confused books serve as a quarry of undigested observations for the media industry" nowhere rings more true than in Japan.[49] The abstraction of McLuhan's style and the binaries and ad-copy-ready catchphrases found therein are also what enabled his work to be channeled through the person of Takemura. Takemura, in turn, further filtered this writing through the existing needs of the advertising industry and management discourse, both of which necessitated the translation of McLuhan into media practice or *actionable theory*. TakeMcLuhanism, that is, highlights an aspect of McLuhan that must not be forgotten in the more recent moves in Japan and elsewhere to reclaim him as a media theorist.

The figure of Takemura is also important as a reminder of the key role *media institutions* play in the brokering and adoption of media theory, particularly but by no means exclusively in Japan. Theoretical activity can never be divorced from its medial and institutional conditions, and Takemura's career as a McLuhanist both in print and on television reminds us of the formative role ad agencies and broadcasters had in the generation of Japan's first McLuhan boom. Whether or not Dentsū created the McLuhan boom or funded Takemura's travels, it was Dentsū and the massive Asahi group where the McLuhan whirlwind first touched down. These institutions evince a thirst for knowledge and managerial direction found first in McLuhan, and later in the other bestselling foreign authors with whom Takemura puts his own *McLuhan's World* on a continuum: management guru Peter Drucker, and futurologists and consultants Edward de Bono and Alvin Toffler.

Today, this role is increasingly played by a professional class known as management consultants. Consultants hail from such globally operating firms as the Boston Consulting Group and McKinsey and Company—which established offices in Japan in 1966 and 1971, respectively, just as the Japanese corporate model seemed to be eclipsing the American one.[50] Consultants operate as agents of knowledge transfer. As Christopher McKenna argues, "Consultants acted as the transmitters—or as technological historian Hugh Aitken called them, the 'translators'—of managerial ideas developed in other organizational settings."[51] Former McKinsey and Company Tokyo office consultant Obara Kazuhiro describes consultants in similar terms, as agents who transmit knowledge from other contexts—in Obara's case mainly what was going on in US companies during the 1990s—and who operate at a faster pace than magazines or the popular press. Consultants' reports have, in his words, "a time machine-like value."[52]

Takemura operated as a protoconsultant for Dentsū. Translator, time machine, and medium, Takemura provided actionable theory for the media industries, McLuhanism as prescription drug. As such he anticipated the effect of consulting practice in years to come, as well as the continuing search on the part of ad industries for new theories from which to learn new models of practice. By the time the McLuhan whirlwind of the mid- to late 1960s started to lose momentum, Takemura had parlayed his initial fame as a channel for the media theorist into a successful television career, even as he continued to write digestible sound bites about media for popular consumption. Takemura may well have been the first television celebrity (*tarento*) whose inspiration, spiritual guidance, and road to fame were born of a media theorist. But he was certainly not the last. Takemura's embodied performance and translation of McLuhan anticipates later engagements with media by theorists—such as Asada Akira, as is argued by Alexander Zahlten in this volume—who deepen this performative mode of theory. TakeMcLuhanism may have been a short-lived phenomenon, but its influence persists to this day in the continuing dependency of ad agencies on the transformative translation of media theory into commercial practice.

Beyond the particular situation of Japan, TakeMcLuhanism also provides a useful lesson of the manner in which theory is always instrumentalized in some manner, and is always already on a continuum with action, no matter the end, putting the sanctity of "Theory" in question. Academic practitioners of the arcane art of Theory would likely identify with Gotō's defense of an objective approach to McLuhan, neglecting thereby the economic, institutional, and medial conditions of theory itself, and by the same token also delimiting what can and cannot be inducted into the cannon of theoretical work. Takemura may be an extreme case of the rendering-actionable of theory. But he is also much more than a symptom of a particular cultural milieu in which theory is made actionable; his is, rather, an extreme case that makes legible the actionability at the heart of theory everywhere. As such it is also a directive to expand the very bounds of what we call theory. A useful drug indeed.

NOTES

1. Gerald Emanuel Stearn, introduction to *McLuhan: Hot and Cool*, ed. Gerald Emanuel Stearn (New York: Signet Books, 1967), xv.

2. Kadoyama Nobu, "Māketingu kihon genri ni arazu" [These are not the basic principles of marketing] *Kindai keiei* [Modern management] (September 1967): 60.

3. Actionable theory is proposed as a variant on the military and business buzzword "actionable intelligence." The US military defines the latter term as "intelligence information that is directly useful to customers for immediate exploitation without having to go through the full intelligence production process." "Department of Defense Dictionary of Military and Associated Terms," November 8, 2010 (amended February 15, 2016), http://www.dtic.mil/doctrine/new_pubs/jp1_02.pdf, 1. Actionable theory would hence imply a theory that could be immediately implemented for (in this context) commercial results. The actual economic value of theory interests me less here than the perception of the theory as valuable, or actionable.

4. Ishikawa Hiroyoshi, "Bijinesuman dokusho hakusho" [White paper on the businessman's reading], *Eguzekutibu* [Executive] (December 1967): 7.

5. Takemura Ken'ichi, *Nijū shikō no ōyō to tenkai* [The application and development of twofold thought] (Tokyo: Daiwa Shobo, 1970), 30. Takemura emphasizes his feelings of shared sensibility with McLuhan, and writes of using the latter's mouth to speak his thoughts. See Takemura Ken'ichi, *Takemura Ken'ichi jisenshū: Makurūhan no sekai: Gendai bunmei no taishitsu to sono miraizō* [Takemura Ken'ichi's self-selected works: McLuhan's world: The constitution of contemporary civilization and its future] (Tokyo: Tokuma Shoten, 1980), originally published as *Makurūhan no sekai: Gendai bunmei no taishitsu to sono miraizō* [McLuhan's world: The constitution of contemporary civilization and its future] (Tokyo: Kodansha, 1967), 2.

6. Takemura Ken'ichi, *Media no karuwazashi tachi: Makurūhan de yomitoku gendai shakai* [Media acrobats: Reading contemporary society through McLuhan] (Tokyo: Bijinesu Sha, 2002), 7; italics mine.

7. I would like to take this opportunity to acknowledge the important work of Gary Genosko on the reception of McLuhan in France as a precursor and inspiration to the

work done here. Among his opening remarks to his *McLuhan and Baudrillard: Masters of Implosion*, is the following statement: "Further work needs to [be] done on his influence in Japan, for instance, with special attention given to the debates over the relevance of the 'cult of McLuhanism' in the Tokyo press recounted to McLuhan in unpublished correspondence with Kenichi Takemura." It is precisely this suggestion that forms the starting point for this article, as well as a similar, verbal suggestion by Ueno Toshiya that Takemura is a key figure in both McLuhanite theory and advertising practice in the 1960s. See Gary Genosko, *McLuhan and Baudrillard: Masters of Implosion* (London: Routledge, 1999), 1. Thanks go to both Genosko and Ueno for their encouragement to pursue this line of research.

8. Here I use Patrick W. Galbraith and Jason G. Karlin's translation of the term *tarento*. Galbraith and Karlin, "Introduction: The Mirror of Idols and Celebrity," in *Idols and Celebrity in Japanese Media Culture*, ed. Galbraith and Karlin (Basingstoke, UK: Palgrave Macmillan, 2012), 6.

9. Takemura acknowledges his advocacy for *mōretsu* in several places, among them a dialogue in which he describes himself (if self-mockingly) as the "ancestor" of the popular catch term *mōretsu*. See Takemura Ken'ichi, "Ima wadai no TV komāsharu wo saiten suru" [Rating the most talked about current TV commercials], in *CM Gurafiti, Terebi 25nen no kiroku*, ed. Yamamoto Kōji (Tokyo: Sebundō Shinkōsha, 1970), 2:24. Fujioka Wakao, one of the most important copywriters of the 1970s, similarly credits Takemura with being "the trendsetter for the *mōretsu* boom" and the man who "fanned the flames of the *mōretsu* boom in magazines like *Shūkan Posuto* and *Shūkan Genzai*." See Fujioka Wakao, *Mōretsu kara biutifuru e* [From intense to beautiful], vol. 2 of *Fujioka Wakao zen purodūsu* [Fujioka Wakao's complete production] (Tokyo: PHP, 1988), 29. Takemura first introduced the keyword *mōretsu* in his 1967 book on American entrepreneurs such as Hugh Hefner titled *Gonin no mōretsu na Amerikajin* [Five intense Americans] (Tokyo: Kodansha, 1967).

10. Dennitza Gabrakova has recently, albeit in a different context, noted the ambiguity of the suffix *ron*: "Now, the Japanese suffix *ron* . . . requires an attention and indeed a theory of its own. *Ron* is an expression that is relatively easily attached to common and personal names and could mean anything from an opinion to a view to a doctrine." See Dennitza Gabrakova, "Archipelagic Thought and Theory's Other: Traveling Theory in Japan," *positions* 22, no. 2 (spring 2014): 473–74. Hence *mediaron* could as readily be translated as "on media" as "media theory." It is this ambiguity that this volume on media theory in Japan investigates—writings around media, about media and theories of media. McLuhan's work is alternatively framed as *mediaron* and *media riron*, the latter being unambiguously "media theory," the former being—more in keeping with the problematic of this volume—"theory of media" or, perhaps more simply, "writing on media."

11. Saitō Ryōsuke suggests that the term *masu komi* was first introduced in 1951. Saitō Ryōsuke, *Omocha hakubutsushi* [A natural history of toys] (Tokyo: Sōjinsha, 1989), 160–61.

12. Kitada Akihiro, *"Imi" e no aragai: Mediētion no bunka seijigaku* [An assault on "meaning": The cultural politics of mediation] (Tokyo: Serika Shobō, 2004), 7.

13. Marilyn Ivy, "Critical Texts, Mass Artifacts: The Consumption of Knowledge in Postmodern Japan," in *Postmodernism and Japan*, ed. Masao Miyoshi and H. D. Harootunian (Durham, NC: Duke University Press, 1989), 21–46; and Ivy, *Discourses of the Vanishing: Modernity, Phantasm, Japan* (Chicago: University of Chicago Press, 1995).

14. Takemura, *Makurūhan no sekai*, 14.

15. On Japanese futurology or future studies, see William O. Gardner, "The 1970 Osaka Expo and/as Science Fiction," *Review of Japanese Culture and Society* (December 2011): 26–43.

16. Takemura, *Makurūhan no sekai*, 100.

17. Takemura Ken'ichi, *Makurūhan no riron no tenkai to ōyō* [The development and application of McLuhan's theory] (Tokyo: Kodansha, 1967), 97, 115–7; on Toyota, see the 1980 discussion in the republished edition of *Makurūhan no sekai*, 24.

18. The adjectives used most often to describe this phenomenon are McLuhan "boom" (*būmu*) and "whirlwind" (*senpū*).

19. Takemura Ken'ichi, *Makurūhan to no taiwa: Nihon bunka to Makurūhannizumu* [Conversations with McLuhan: McLuhanism and Japanese culture] (Tokyo: Kodansha, 1968), 212–22.

20. Gardner, "1970 Osaka Expo," 29.

21. In a retrospective glance at the era, Gotō Kazuhiko introduces *Hōsō Asahi* as an Asahi PR journal from Osaka. See Gotō Kazuhiko, "Makurūhan to Nihon no media" [McLuhan and the Japanese media] *Chishiki* (April 1981): 190. Umesao Tadao, one of its most significant contributors, describes *Hōsō Asahi* as a PR magazine created by the recently established Asahi Hōsō company, but one that featured dense quality content and "the vision of a high quality magazine." See Umesao Tadao, *Jōhō no bunmeigaku* [A civilization study of information] (Tokyo: Chūō Bunko, 1999), 16.

22. The latter essay was subsequently republished in *Chūō Kōron* in March 1963, and both essays are collected in Umesao, *Jōhō no bunmeigaku*, 37–63.

23. While the shift from "information industries" to "theories of image cultures" had already been planned, Takemura claims credit for suggesting the special on McLuhan, having mentioned the recent *Life* magazine special on the media theorist to the editor of *Hōsō Asahi*, Igarashi Michiko, who asked him to write his introductory article on McLuhan. Takemura, *Makurūhan no sekai*, 239. For an overview of and intervention into debates around the eizō, see Yuriko Furuhata, *Cinema of Actuality: Japanese Avant-Garde Filmmaking in the Season of Image Politics* (Durham, NC: Duke University Press, 2013).

24. Takemura Ken'ichi, "Terebi jidai no yogensha M. Makkurūhan: Jinbutsu shōkai" [M. McLuhan, the prophet of the television age: An introduction to his personality], in *Makurūhan: Tanjō 100nen media (ron) no kanōsei wo tou* (Tokyo: Kawade, 2011), 160.

25. See the "Kaisetsu" in the second installment of the special section "Towards the Development of a Theory of the Information Industries," *Hōsō Asahi* (December 1964): 10.

26. By 1967 he is described as the section chief of the NHK General Broadcasting Research Center, Broadcasting Research Department. See his biography in Masaomi Ōmae, *Makurūhan: Sono hito to riron* [McLuhan: The man and his theories] (Tokyo: Daikosha, 1967), 282.

27. Takemura, *Makurūhan no sekai*, 23, 240.

28. Takemura, "Terebi jidai no yogensha," 161.

29. "Mōi no Makurūhan senpū" [The raging McLuhan whirlwind], *Shūkan sankei* 16, no. 40 (September 1967): 98.

30. Takemura discusses arranging this meeting in *Media no karuwazashi tachi*, 82–85; he discusses the Mainichi TV program in a letter to McLuhan dated May 24, 1971, held in the National Archives of Canada, MP 38/30. Takemura wrote and published *Makurūhan to no taiwa: Nihon bunka to Makurūhanizumu* [Conversations with McLuhan: McLuhanism and Japanese culture] (Tokyo: Kodansha, 1968) while in Minneapolis, subsequent to meeting with McLuhan at the beginning of November 1967.

31. Takemura Ken'ichi, "Uchū wo nomu hitotsu me" [One eye that swallows the universe], *Hōsō Asahi* (June 1967): 9.

32. Gotō Kazuhiko, "Makurūhan no unda gensō" [The illusion produced by McLuhan], *Asahi jyānaru* 9, no. 42 (October 8, 1967): 19.

33. Media Rebyū, ed., *Za messeeji: McLuhan ikō no media kankyō* (Tokyo: Heibon Sha, 1982), 56.

34. Takemura discusses the "skin tribe" in *Makurūhan no sekai*, 73; television as a happening media is found in *Makurūhan no sekai*, 182; and his praise of Toyota and Honda are most developed in *Makurūhan no riron no tenkai to ōyō*, 97, 115.

35. Letter to McLuhan dated January 9, 1968, held in the National Archives of Canada, MP 38/30.

36. Ōmae, *Makurūhan*, 72.

37. Ōmae, *Makurūhan*, 11. Takemura's response to the call for an objective reading of McLuhan came soon after: if read objectively—and as *typographic* people—McLuhanism would die. See *Makurūhan no riron*, 3. This restages the all-too-familiar back and forth between those who would embrace the spirit of McLuhan and those who would hold the author and his supporters accountable for their words.

38. Takemura, *Makurūhan no riron*, 248.

39. Such specials include marketing journal *Brain*'s "Makurūhanizumu to kōkoku" [McLuhanism and advertising], special issue, 42, no. 10 (October 1967); management journal *Kindai keiei*'s special McLuhan issue (September 1967); and Dentsū's ad journal *Māketingu to kōkoku*'s special McLuhan issue (October 1967).

40. The significance of the very frame of understanding of McLuhan—in terms of use for marketing—and Takemura's influence on it is suggested by Ishikara Hiroyoshi (who considers this framing a misunderstanding), within the "McLuhanism and Advertising" special issue of *Brain* 42, no. 10 (October 1967): 35.

41. Here I draw on a very useful distinction Kadobayashi Takeshi makes within McLuhan's own work. See *Whatcha Doin, Marshall McLuhan? An Aesthetics of Media* (Tokyo: NTT Shuppan, 2009), 24–25.

42. Wendy Hui Kyong Chun, "The Enduring Ephemeral, or The Future Is a Memory," in *Media Archaeology: Approaches, Applications, and Implications*, ed. Erkki Huhtamo and Jussi Parikka (Berkeley: University of California Press, 2011), 186–87.

43. W. Chun, "Enduring Ephemeral," 187.

44. Jodi Dean, *Blog Theory: Feedback and Capture in the Circuits of Drive* (Cambridge, UK: Polity Press, 2010), 3.

45. Dean, *Blog Theory*, 3.

46. Geert Lovink, *Networks without a Cause: A Critique of Social Media* (Cambridge, UK: Polity Press, 2011), 69–70.

47. Jeffrey T. Schnapp and Adam Michaels describe this McLuhan/Agel/Fiore collaboration on *The Medium Is the Message* and *The Global Village* in their brilliant *The Electric Information Age Book: McLuhan/Agel/Fiore and the Experimental Paperback* (New York: Princeton Architectural Press, 2012).

48. See Marshall McLuhan, *Understanding Media: The Extensions of Man* (New York: McGraw-Hill, 1964), 6; McLuhan, "The Relation of Environment to Anti-Environment," in *Marshall McLuhan Unbound*, ed. Eric McLuhan and W. Terrence Gordon (Corte Madera, CA: Ginko Press, 2005), 19.

49. Hans Magnus Enzensberger, "Constituents of a Theory of the Media," in *The New Media Reader*, ed. Nick Montfort and Noah Wardrip-Fruin (Cambridge, MA: MIT Press, 2003), 271.

50. Christopher D. McKenna, *The World's Newest Profession: Management Consulting in the Twentieth Century* (Cambridge: Cambridge University Press, 2006), 189.

51. McKenna, *World's Newest Profession*, 53. McKenna (277n11) describes the concept of translators within Aitken's work as "those individuals who transfer a critical piece of information from one network to another," referring the reader to Hugh G. J. Aitken, *The Continuous Wave: Technology and American Radio, 1900–1932* (Princeton, NJ: Princeton, 1985).

52. Obara Kazuhiro, *IT bijinesu no genri* [The principles of IT business] (Tokyo: NHK Shuppan, 2014), 26.

6. THE CULTURE INDUSTRIES AND
MEDIA THEORY IN JAPAN

MIRYAM SAS

Transnational, Media, Theory

The term "transnational" has gained broad currency in film and media studies since the late 1980s as a way of tracking an intermediate scale of analysis—neither "local" or "national" nor "world/global." Some have argued persuasively that the theories of the transnational arising out of Miriam Hansen's writings on vernacular modernism tend to underplay the unequal power relations that condition transnational relations and can lead to an elision of the specificity of local contexts; nonetheless, she articulated a useful aspect of that transnational scale in which the "local" is inherently imbricated with various world systems.[1] The editors of a recent volume on transnational cinemas similarly argue that the transnational, because it "operates 'above the level of the national' but below the level of the global," can represent an emergent mode of analysis, one that "acknowledges the persistent agency of the state" and yet takes into account unevenness, mobility, and shifting social relations.[2] Transnational, they claim, replaced "international" in critical discourse where the prefix "inter-" seemed to imply parity, and "global" pressed toward a picture of increasing homogenization. In such an open and mobile vein, then, this essay aims to analyze a key moment within a broader shift in leftist discourses that we might say was mediated at such a "transnational" scale—understanding locally embedded articulations (already replete with intertextuality) alongside this broader network of (unequal) relationships.[3]

If globalization, for many critics, marked a direction of homogenization and an infrastructurally conditioned reduction of specificity/difference, the well-known *fūkeiron* (landscape theory) discourse developed in Japan was a trenchant critique of this overriding vector toward flatness and uniformity and a careful analysis of infrastructural manifestations of power. The critics around fūkeiron were important media theorists who played a crucial role in the 1970s culture industry debates that are the subject of this essay. Matsuda Masao, born in 1933, was a key theorist of fūkeiron, a set of discourses that emerged out of and in conjunction with the work of filmmakers such as Adachi Masao and Ōshima Nagisa,[4] as well as in the essays and photographic practices of Nakahira Takuma. The work of Matsuda and Nakahira around 1970 form part of a web of leftist thought and artistic work that encompassed the pioneering, provocative theories of Tsumura Takashi, known for his work on (internalized) discrimination, and critic Taki Kōji, who was a member of the groundbreaking photography collective that founded the photo journal *Provoke*. These thinkers can be understood as part of a much wider network of leftist artists/intellectuals who first participated in the late 1960s protest movements and, at the moment that such protests were seen to be "over," catalyzed the shifting modes of critique in the early 1970s. Deeply engaged with the new theorizations of the "third world" and emergent postcolonial thought, they were part of a historic critical shift in strategies and tactics of the Left in the wake of the perceived failure of the violent confrontations of the protest movements. Each in his own way was engaged at a deep level in a form of activism and media practice (art, organizing, photography, filmmaking) that informed and responded to the pressing theoretical articulations of the day; each held a profound commitment to the question of the relation between language (critical writing, theory) and other forms of making or acting in the sphere of "media."[5]

Suga Hidemi describes the situation in Japan around 1970, when the strategies of protest were seen to have failed, in the following terms:

> Prior to [1970], Japan's "1968" movement was caught up in a kind of "resolution-ism" [determinism, *ketsudan-shugi*: wanting to escalate violence to achieve a decisive result]. With the "defeat" of January 18– 19, 1969 at Tokyo University's Yasuda Auditorium,[6] the New Leftists were driven into a corner, realizing that there was nothing more that could be done with staves, thrown rocks, and fire bottles. In such a

context, there began to be talk in the Bund [Communist Party alliance, established in 1958 among New Left groups] about the establishment of an "army," and the Red Army came on the scene. . . . Each party began escalating their armed fights on the streets. There were already visions of fights with bombs as well. This impetus, today, is critically reflected on as a [problematic] "weaponism" (唯武器主義) that dreams about revolution by means of escalated armament.[7]

Many leftists both in Japan and internationally argued that the struggle had to be pushed further in the direction of radical violence. Others felt that the struggle should be shifted to a more symbolic level, fought more in terms of cultural values and discursive power structures, with particular focus on immigration control, discrimination, and minority issues. A crucial intertext for these articulations was Gramsci's reading of Machiavelli's *Art of War*. Following Machiavelli,[8] Gramsci outlined an opposition between a "war of maneuver" (*kidōsen* in Japanese, a mobile war)—the war of "staves, thrown rocks, and fire bottles" mentioned above, or of even more explosive arms— and a "war of position" (*jinchisen*, a positional war, war of encampment) or "protracted war" (*jikyūsen*, a contest of endurance) to be fought on the terrain of culture, thought, law, and power.

My argument maps how, along with these shifting strategies, new critical understandings emerge of both "media" and "theory," in their relation and nonrelation, as depicted by practitioners who had a deep stake in both terms. These thinkers' work reflects a highly dense notion of the relation between theory and practice, an investment that conditions their writings on media and theory. They ask: Is "media" always already complicit with capital? How can theory "mobilize"? In ways that partially parallel Baudrillard in his "Requiem for the Media" (1971), these critics in 1973 Japan called for a deep deconstruction of the systems and structures of media as currently constituted, and in the process a rethinking and restructuring of theory as a critical act as well.

Media Theory, Culture Industries, and the Enzensberger Moment

Hans Magnus Enzensberger (1929–) was (and is) a prominent media theorist, part of a network of leftist intellectuals in Europe that includes Jürgen Habermas (also born in 1929), following in the lineage of Walter Benjamin, Herbert Marcuse, Siegfried Kracauer, Ernst Bloch, and to some extent Georg Lukács and Bertolt Brecht, among others. Enzensberger's "Constituents of a Theory of Media" made a splash when it was published in Japanese in August 1971 in

Bungei journal.[9] Media theorists and artists gathered in force when the German Cultural Center and the publisher Film-Art Company (Firumu-āto-sha) invited him to appear in a two-day symposium at Asahi Hall in Tokyo on January 22–23, 1973. It was an event filled with promise: two days of conversation bringing together the most prominent artists and critics of the day.

The leading filmmaker Kawanaka Nobuhiro, known for spearheading the "personal film" movement, staged the event as a producer, using monitors in two lines that extended out through the rows of seats of the auditorium so that it was reflexively "mediated/mediatized" in its very moment of occurrence.[10] On the first day, the symposium included Tōno Yoshiaki, one of the "Big Three" art critics of the day who also wrote critical essays on television and had done his own closed-circuit television performances; Terayama Shūji, the theater director, filmmaker, and writer who was also active in radio and television; Sasaki Mamoru, the TV/radio/film scenario writer and editor of *Kiroku eiga* (Documentary film), producer, and activist; the architect Hara Hiroshi; and, as moderator, the television producer, writer, and activist Konno Tsutomu, who founded the first independent TV production company (*terebiman yunion*). On the second day, the symposium featured the art critic Hariu Ichirō, another of the "Big Three"; the photographer/theorist Nakahira Takuma; and the radical Left critic Tsumura Takashi. In various publications, a flurry of reflections and responses, reactions and—as we shall see—passionate rejections ensued.

Why was it necessary to rethink media and its relation to capitalism at this particular moment? Or one might ask why invite Enzensberger—clearly a media star in his own right—to stand at the center of this Japanese debate? Enzensberger and many other American and European theorists had been read and translated extensively throughout the 1960s and early 1970s, and in the end the Japanese theorists would both draw on and push against the model he provided. Enzensberger's essay is by no means univocal in its optimism, but his essay is usually cited for its "linking of media critique with a systematic plan for alternative production, together placed in the service of cultural empowerment."[11] Indeed, the essay functions—among its many caveats and reservations—as a "call to arms" for alternative modes of production, as his closing sentence signals. In the process of "bringing the liberating factors in the media . . . to fruition," Enzensberger closes, the author/artist must "work as an agent of the masses. He can lose himself in them only when they themselves become authors, the authors of history."[12]

Enzensberger himself articulated one of the most persuasive summaries of the contradictions involved in such a process and the many false forms of "feedback"—meaningless or empty participation—that can be constructed in the media, he ultimately lands on an argument for an inherent power and potentiality of the media as a participatory and mobilizing force. Such an argument, J. T. Caldwell rightly notes, "prefigures digi-speak." In the end, both Enzensberger and Jean Baudrillard in his famous retort to Enzensberger, "Requiem for the Media," agree that the media need a fundamental destructuring and reorganization in order to realize whatever potentiality they may have.[13] Both agree that there are many false directions and impasses. Yet the emphasis of Baudrillard in his retort to Enzensberger is part of a deeper doubt about the way the superstructure (within which we find semiosis, discourse, representation) should be understood in relation to infrastructure (base, economic production)—a strong critique of the Marxist tendency to read both as responding to the same dialectical progression. Baudrillard accuses Marxists of homogenizing: thinking infrastructure and superstructure as if they were part of the same substance that could be thought in the same forms. He claims that, for now, the "dialectic lies in ashes," and "it is necessary to toll the requiem of the infra- and super-structure."[14]

It is worth considering this Enzensberger-Baudrillard debate here in some detail as part of the backdrop for a wider—transnational—scale of leftist discourse in which Matsuda most strikingly but also Taki, Nakahira, and Tsumura Takashi are key participants. If our critical viewpoint excludes these contributions, we miss a highly nuanced and center-shifting (or decentering) piece of the story, and the opportunity to understand this mobile and antihomogenizing critique in a manner that itself performs a movement against the flattening of perception and debate.

Today, when we read Enzensberger's "Constituents of a Theory of Media," it is striking how many aspects of his writing still resonate for contemporary discussions of electronic media. We may note the very speed of circulation of these theoretical works, along with the speed and ease of circulation of persons (with the rise of affordable airline tickets), as well as the powerful extensiveness of what Enzensberger was calling "new media" in 1970. Among the prior twenty years of "new media" he referred to in 1970, he included news satellites, color television, cable relay television, videotape recorders, videophones, stereophony, laser techniques, electrostatic reproduction processes (copy machines), electronic high-speed printing, time-sharing computers, and data banks.[15] The issue of telephone tapping that he discusses and the impossibility of monitoring all phone lines (which he claims is unfeasible because it would require a monitoring system larger than the entire telephone network) resonate with today's questions around corporate use of search result algorithms and the monitoring of email (Matsuda, like Baudrillard, points out that sampling can work wonders: as Matsuda says, "*my phone is tapped*"). Enzensberger's analysis of the situation of media and empowerment draws on Fanon, Lefebvre, Benjamin, Lissitzky, and Adorno—all of whom were available to Japanese media theorists to differing degrees in translation or through citation by other Japanese media theorists—and also includes critiques of Lukács and a trenchant dismissal especially of McLuhan, the latter having just a few years earlier enjoyed great influence in Japanese art-critical circles.[16]

The affective dimension of this encounter, brought on by the layers of identification and (mirroring) investment in the figure of Enzensberger, turned out to be a telling component of the dialogue with Japanese media critics. Enzensberger himself famously characterized the symposium during day one as "four pessimists and one optimist." Nagai Kiyohiko attempted to explain this by pointing out differences in the situation of West Germany and Japan: "In general, the very fact that Enzensberger, a 'dangerous person' with revolution on his lips, can be sent into Japan by a public institution/organization from West Germany, eloquently expresses the difference from the current situation in Japan."[17] Nagai argues that the overall positive support of work such as Enzensberger's by TV and radio—some of it was sponsored by state-owned West German television, for example, though it was also restricted from some print media—might have contributed to his alleged optimism about these media. By contrast, within the symposium, Nakahira refers to the anti-NHK war and affirms the need to destroy rather than reform the bureaucratic media structure.[18]

Enzensberger's theoretical writings relentlessly look for spaces of what he calls "leakiness"—the "leaky nexus of the media"—and yet he also advocates "utilizing" the contradictions within media while remaining aware of the propensity for absorption of contradictory opinions within the liberal/reformist frame. In "Constituents for a Theory of Media," his "optimism" consists especially in a critique of the leftist sense of impotence and the oversimplifying oppositional logic that views the media as pure manipulation of the masses, a view he links to the 1960s New Left.

Matsuda's Critique: A New Axis for Media Theory

Matsuda opens his *Bijutsu Techō* article of May 1973 in full (negative) critical mode. He compares Enzensberger's statement that "television, like the telephone before it, should come to be used effectively, free of the 'oppressive uses of media'" with Kropotkin's writing in *The Conquest of Bread* that the railroad network was an example of a "free agreement" that foreshadowed the dying away of the state.[19] Matsuda explains the sleight of hand that allows Enzensberger to misperceive TV as mobility and therefore potential freedom: "The first concrete example that Kropotkin raised of his free agreement was none other than the *railroad network*. In other words (not to sound too much like Tsumura Takashi, but) every problem of power must actually begin with a problem of communication."[20] Enzensberger accounts for many of the possible counterarguments to his theses in his own writings, and does so compellingly. Matsuda thus mobilizes the critic's own language to attack his "unbearable" optimism, citing Enzensberger's *The Consciousness Industry* to diagnose such thinking as a form of false consciousness: "What is abolished," writes Enzensberger/Matsuda, "is therefore not exploitation but the consciousness of exploitation. . . . I should declare that precisely on account of the existence of the 'free agreement,' the cunning [kōchi] of history has enabled the state to maintain its full force"; Matsuda, "Media kakumei," 53–54.

Matsuda thus criticizes the panelists *and* Enzensberger, not for their pursuit of incommensurability, or the delving into chaos at its deepest level (as Kobayashi Hideo might put it), but for the fact that they establish and end up standing too much on common ground, Enzensberger and Sasaki resembling each other, Matsuda says, "like two acorns." Both hold either absolute or relativized oppositions between a "we" and a "they," "our media" and "their media." The commonality *establishes the use of binary oppositional axes*—they/we or theirs/mine ('*yatsura' to 'ore*') or in other cases plays itself out in a dichotomy between idealist/conceptualist (Terayama) versus realist (Enzensberger).

Matsuda argues that it is necessary to shift the ground from such a series of binary oppositions, framed in the symposium around the issue of "access," to another directionality or vector ("axis"):

> Today, what media theory needs is to rotate fundamentally what appears as an existing given, the axis between "them" and "us" or of "them" and "me" [ore]. Instead of debates about access [akusesu], what is needed is to reset the axis [akushisu] itself. . . . [To say it in Enzensberger's words,] "It would be impossible without the self-organization (institutionalization) of the participants. This is itself the political crux of the problem of media." Exactly so: the axis for media revolution should be set in a direction, to speak metaphorically, where the question is by what circuits (paths) the lonely "I" [ore] before the television set will

organize himself toward a "we," and only in this direction. (Matsuda, "Media kakumei," 56)

Here Matsuda once again speaks alongside Enzensberger. His citational performance takes on without mirroring Enzensberger's meaning, or takes it farther, in a sense performing the redirecting axis shift that he is advocating: he reorganizes an altered collectivizing theoretical mode that figures a version of the lonely "I" redirecting itself toward a "we." Matsuda effectively asks: How can discourses—say, media theory—themselves dependent on the media for circulation, catalyze a reorganization of the relation of the individual to media? Through what forms of movement can the individual pass (circulate, circuit) in order to be organized as part of a collective of some kind, and what kind of collectivity?

Matsuda's statement about this shift in relation is highly striking because issues of communication or commensurability, and of comparability or correspondence, are themselves key problems for Marxist media theory as a whole, where at stake is precisely the relation that should obtain between the "vanguard" thinkers and the "masses," as well as between thought and movement. In Matsuda's own past essays, he had written in terms of a "spontaneous harmony" between intellectuals and the masses, a kind of unmediated direct access, but in this essay he criticizes his own earlier position—and here he shows the *ore* (I) itself as multiply constituted over time by its own language and transmission, such that the issue of the external network has to relate also to an "internal network" discussed by some symposium panelists, especially Terayama and Nakahira.[21]

Matsuda realizes that he had depended on an idea of one unconscious or subconscious directly and instantly connecting to (another)—a kind of "correspondence replacing communication" (as Léopold Sédar Senghor had put it), *kōkan* (empathy) instead of *dentatsu* (transmission).[22] Here again he uses furigana for *corespandansu* (correspondence, or, more deeply, the Baudelairian *correspondances*) to double the physical feeling, the affective experience of kōkan, empathy showing correspondence as an affective mode, to replace the more media-based transmission of information=dentatsu as communication, but at that time he had still been within a frame of binary thinking, what he calls the "demon of dichotomy" (*nibunhō no oni*). Like Baudrillard, Matsuda had earlier framed the communication model of dentatsu, the transmission of a message from producer to receiver, as a model that needed to be transcended and ruptured in order to give way to a more direct, unmediated relation. However, here repudiating his Senghorian framework (as many came to do), he instead articulates a new and alternative view of mobility and mobilization, and of gestures, one by which he reframes the whole question of media theory, saying, "The only thing that could organize the frenzied heat of the overwhelming majority of the 'masses' was the media/mediation of the unconscious power that spurted out (*funshutsu*) all at once (instantaneously) from within the 'masses', in other words, 'what was not words/language'" (Matsuda, "Media kakumei," 59).

Matsuda's writing in this moment thus traces a shift between "media" and "mediation" (*baitai,* 媒体), where the word *baitai* has the katakana furigana reading "media" filled in. Media here is seen not as something external but as something that has a bodily quality, something like blood, that spurts out all in an instant not from an individual body but from a collective, "the masses," not in the form of language but in the form of an unconscious power that has the capacity precisely to organize passion, affect, and frenzied heat into a *soshiki* (an institution, formation, or organization). In this formulation, media is not itself the system or organization, but media is the *mediating* force that has the power to organize the unconscious power of the masses. The member of the masses, "only by performing revolution in this way, was able to transform himself into one of the innumerable nameless people who slashed open history, so that he could mobilize [*dōin*] himself in the true sense of the word, like a dancer, a football player, a guerilla . . . " (Matsuda, "Media kakumei," 59).[23] It is in this way that Matsuda argues for directing the vector (or axis) of media theory toward the question of how the individual comes to relate to the broader organization, and how the person can "mobilize himself" not via language but via a corporeal movement (in some sense beyond consciousness or language). At the same time, he inhabits Enzensberger's language of mobility, moves within Enzensberger's theory and redirects it toward this spurting, this tearing, this organization of affect, the mobilization of an organization that emerges in an instant, the "media"/mediation of the power of the masses' emergent unconscious.

Matsuda then concludes, "The Kropotkian inversion (*tentō*/overturning) extends far beyond the 'symposium with Enzensberger' to cover (conceal/hang over) not only the theory of violence but also the entire sphere of the theory of media" (Matsuda, "Media kakumei," 60). Theory of violence, theory of media: for Matsuda, these whole realms contain the problem he had named with Kropotkin—the sense of a "freedom" or "free will" that conceals an infrastructural network underlying and conditioning them. The unconscious gesture and the affective mood become crucial pathways and potentialities within Matsuda's concluding call to continue to "dig ever deeper" (into what he ironically calls the "unconsciousness industry").

Paradigm Shift of the New Left

To more fully understand the significance of Matsuda's intervention in cultural media theory, it is worth taking a moment to understand the ideas of voice/parole and the complex assertions about mediation made by other theorists at the time. In the postscript to the republication in 2012 of the writings of prominent leftist critic Tsumura Takashi, Suga Hidemi suggestively situates Tsumura as perhaps *the* pivotal player in the "paradigm shift of the new left" in the late 1960s to early 1970s discussed above. Tsumura, who in the early 1980s abandoned this form of political writing to launch a career as a new age qigong practitioner and writer about Asian health practices, had been a prolific critic and journalist on topics including antinuclear power theory, ecology, "third world" issues, and urban space. He was known as an activist protest organizer around immigration issues and Koreans and Chinese living in Japan, and his "discrimination theory" (*sabetsuron*) made him a central player in the important Kaseitō Kokuhatsu incident.

At a meeting commemorating the thirty-third anniversary of the Marco Polo Bridge (Rokōkyō) incident known as a trigger for the launch of the Sino-Japanese War, on July 7, 1970, a group known as the "Overseas Chinese Youth Strike Committee" (Kaseitō Kokuhatsu) accused Japanese new leftists of harboring nationalism/narcissism in their thought and policies. The group was protesting Japan's immigration control policy; Suga argues that this episode, in which Tsumura's writings on discrimination played a key role, "can easily be considered one of the most important events in postwar ideology." "To date," Suga writes, "we are not able to free ourselves completely from the paradigm which this event created."[24]

Far ahead of the cultural studies and postcolonialism debates, Tsumura (along with Matsuda, Taki, and Nakahira) gave us a piercing analysis of the intersecting constructs of race, class, and (to a lesser extent) gender. Suga contends that Tsumura's arguments have a concreteness and practicality often missing in what Suga sees as the "politically correct" consensus of some later versions of postcolonial critique, cultural studies, and feminist thought as received in Japan's academic world.[25] In the more subtle "war of positions" that emerged at this time, struggles turned to questions of *buraku* (social minorities traditionally considered as outcasts), feminism, race, immigration, nuclear power, rural residents' struggles, and the "minorities as a potential subject of revolution."[26]

Photographer Nakahira Takuma in the late 1960s to early 1970s wrote trenchant leftist theoretical critiques—part of the discursive "war of positions"—while pursuing a correspondingly innovative and rigorous photographic practice. For example, in 1971 Nakahira Takuma had contributed his photography project *Circulation: Date, Place, Event* to the Seventh Paris Biennale, an event whose theme was *Interactions* (along the continuum of concerns about response and interactivity contemporaneously addressed by Enzensberger, Baudrillard, Matsuda, and Taki). Nakahira had spent each day of his time at the exhibition running around Paris taking photographs/documents, developing and printing them on that same day in the darkroom, and he had then allowed those fragments, or what art critic Yasumi Akihito calls "remnants," to intervene back into the landscape of Paris in the space of the biennale—rumpled, tacked up, piled on the floor, barely dry, including some photos of the exhibition itself among them. Although Nakahira was extremely critical or even dismissive of the biennale event and encountered many difficulties in the process of participation, Yasumi has argued nonetheless for the importance of Nakahira's contribution, writing that *Circulation: Date, Place, Event* functioned to "cut up the continually moving world and its homogeneous flow of time: a history is buried within this cutting process itself, like a time bomb."[27]

Nakahira's roughly contemporaneous writings on the homogenization of landscape (*fūkeiron*), developed alongside Matsuda's, bring the power regulation of landscape and infrastructure as well as image and perception into the realm of media critique. Not only, as Nakahira claims in his response to Enzensberger, is it the "political role" of media such as television to "enforce a certain rhythm throughout everything, a rhythm of pre-established harmony so the world can continue as it is,"[28] and not only do the dominant media, as he wrote in the same essay, "squeeze our senses into molds and regulate our senses on a daily basis," a factor that he calls "the only and biggest political role of existing media," in essence flattening time (alongside landscape), but also, beyond those roles of media, the problem is that the landscapes both of Japan and of the rest of the world have come to seem flattened, frozen, immutable—not only within images or representations but within our own perceptions or ability to apprehend. "Like the flattened 'landscape' of Japan . . . " argues Nakahira, "the worldwide relationships between exploiter-exploited, oppressor-oppressed have been snugly enveloped within a landscape like a beautiful picture postcard, a landscape which to me appears to lack even a single crack, or a single indication that perhaps the beauty and stability of this landscape will one day be overturned."[29] Addressing the complicity of the individual subject within these larger systems was the key goal of *Circulation*: as Nakahira put it in his writing on the project, "From the midst of everyday existence I took up the camera as a means of immediately recording and then discarding the bias arising from the process of continually eroding, transforming, and violating my self by subjecting it to the world."[30]

The key problem of *langue* versus *parole* (structured system versus intervention of a momentary instance selected from within it) structures Nakahira's response to Enzensberger, as it does Baudrillard's. Nakahira calls for a "kinetics," and it is in this way that his search for speech/voice/parole (*nikusei*) parallels Matsuda's interest in gesture and mobility. In order, shall we say, to "claim expression," or to "respond" at all, to "take on the role of the manipulator" (in Enzensberger's words), it would be necessary from Nakahira's point of view first of all to invent a new way to *be* in/amidst media, to be a photographing/media-involved subject. In his writing on Enzensberger and media theory, then, Nakahira evokes the voice (*parole/nikusei*) as a collective: "What exactly is our voice? It is something which has rather nothing to convey—it is just our silence directed towards the dismantlement of all existing things: this is what our paradoxical language is."[31] In relation to a hegemonic and engulfing homogenization, as well as the futility and battering of the world, it is his own "silence," then—his time bomb—as another side of parole, that Nakahira feels goes unnoticed in all this hypersaturated discourse on culture industries and media.

Inverted Eyes

For *Provoke* cofounder Taki Kōji, Nakahira's paradoxical parole joins with questions of postcoloniality, the "third world," and the gaze in photography. For Taki, too, media takes the form of a hegemonic system/force, a veritable "monument." His response to Enzensberger takes the occasion of the "death of *Life*" (*Life* magazine had temporarily ceased publication in 1972) to reflect on the gaze constructed by this monolithic and homogenizing media structure. The emergence of parole (*nikusei*, moment of speech, raw voice) would involve an overturning of the intensely homogenizing logic of media.

For Taki, *Life* magazine's "visual logic" requires analysis because this media "gaze" *is* the "productive force of media itself."[32] He argues that *Life*'s journalism—FSA photographers such as Walker Evans, Margaret Bourke-White, Dorothea Lange—had participated in the spirit of the New Deal by making "objective reports" that were also aesthetic and emotional in their effects. In his view, with the Vietnam War there was a shift from the reporting that had happened earlier in *Life* on the New Deal and US foreign policies in the Spanish Civil War, World War II, and the Korean War, a shift that concerned the structure of the "public" (*taishū*). In the *Life* version of a document, he tells us, what is photographed becomes an exhibition or exemplary display (*chinretsu*, Taki writes, following Lefebvre) and monument (following Foucault). "*Life*, while making every document into a monument, has also come to confirm itself as a new monument, or in other words, as media," writes Taki (Taki, "Aru media no bohimei," 47).

To understand what needs to change (and is changing), Taki cites Ortega, who in the 1930s wrote of the masses as an "image" that emerged precisely with reproductive media but is "a group/mass that has neither a specific culture nor its own voice [*nikusei*]." What is needed is "to look into technological media from the other side of words [*kotoba no acchi*], through inverted eyes [*sakasa no me*]" ("Aru media no bohimei," 48). For Taki, the "eyes of America" represent an ethnocentric gaze historically based in European imperiality, capital, and metaphysics. He identifies the beginning of the postcolonial era as the moment when the unified myth that he calls in quotation marks the "eyes of America," and the concept of document or record that was *Life* magazine, comes to be exposed to the danger of dissolution because "the eyes looking back from the third world [which he also calls the "historical eye of the oppressed"] began to be understood by part of the U.S. public" (44), although those "eyes of America" continue to have a disconcerting resilience. For Taki, there is nonetheless a gap opened by the (ultimately momentary) death of *Life*: "At the same time that *Life* brought to the surface an image of the masses, it absorbed the consciousness of the masses, and made them one part of its own story. The fact that *Life* was abandoned (*haihinka*, made junk) as a medium is political, and this happened [this junk media/abandonment was born, as it were] when the masses began to have their own voice. . . . This potential for the acquisition of a voice is precisely what is indicated, as a photographic negative, in *Life*'s death (49)." Taki hovers intriguingly between the metaphors of voice/parole and those of the photographic logic of the negative, just as above he conceptualized the *other side of* words alongside the *inverted* eyes. In another mixed metaphor, like Matsuda with a figure of burrowing, he envisions the conditions of possibility for "digging out the voice."

As Benjamin and other Frankfurt school theorists also argued, it is through mass media and technological reproducibility that the idea of the "mass" comes into its own, even as it is, in some fundamental way, objectified or managed through these same media. Taki writes,

> Until very recently there was a deep-rooted perception of the masses as a floating thing that was easy to manipulate as a whole. However, whether it has a voice or not, whether this is only internal or external, individual or collective, cannot be decided. On both of these sides, both of these faces, [the problem of speech/parole] is correlated with "freedom," and moreover, concrete and real freedom itself can have a metaphysical meaning. For as long as they are split by class, neither the exclusive and internal intellectual bourgeoisie nor the regulated masses has a voice. *Freedom* itself is (just) a *word*, but no one yet has this *word*. (Taki, "Aru media no bohimei," 48)

The subtlety of Taki's point emerges in his attempts to transcend the "demon of binary" that haunts the very language and analysis of freedom and voice. Metaphysics and materiality meld; there is an "ambivalence of media" in that it holds to a place of having and not having a voice, "opening up and closing down" possibility. Taki goes so far as to *suspend* temporarily the question of having or not having a voice (*parole*): this in itself is only an opportunity proposed that depends for its realization on the transcendence of class divisions, the division between individual and collective, materiality and metaphysics.

Examining the paradigm shift of the New Left at this (transnational) scale, we see how, as with Baudrillard, the concept of parole takes on a central role: it opens a promise for imagining (mediated) immediacy, response, interaction, overturning, or breaking through the homogenizing structures of time and space. Though the theory of the last thirty years has taught us to find even-tempered calls for immediacy suspect, we can nonetheless respond to these articulations of a movement that would aim to be both practical and theoretical at once—a dismantling and trenchant analysis of critical impasses offered by these theorists for problems that extend only deeper in today's new media theory and utopian/antiutopian dialectics of digispeak.[33] For Taki, the ambivalence of the media is that it "opens up and closes down political possibilities" at each stage of advancement. Nakahira (quoting Georges Sorel on the disheartened optimist) says that a "pessimist's glory" is to "stay in this reality and to crush it," representing his own kind of positive negativity (Taki, "Aru media no bohimei," 97). Each media theorist carefully evades the naïve optimism of unqualified "agency" or "subjectivity," as well as a reified or essentialized notion of embodiment, focusing instead on the ideas of movement, of liminality and affective irruptions, trying to frame a critique that will allow for a "grasp" or a "handhold" on the pervasive system of media that of course will come to absorb/redeem, by turning into a media-event both Enzensberger and their own responses to his ideas.

The Future of Media

The moderator of the Enzensberger symposium, Konno Tsutomu (Ben) insightfully summarizes the problems and approaches to media that emerged from the culture industry debates at the time with an eye toward the increased prominence of electronic media and future changes in the media system. Konno, known for forming the first independent television production company, "TV Man Union," in 1970, along with his colleagues Hagimoto Haruhiko and Muraki Yoshihiko, proposes a mode of thought from within the "concrete, everyday labor process" of working in television production, as a "broadcast laborer" (hōsō rōdōsha).[34] Some critics in Japan, like film scholar Hirasawa Gō, would point out that there should be a **very dark line** drawn between theorists such as Matsuda Masao, Tsumura Takashi, and Nakahira Takuma | (there it is) and Konno Ben and his TV Man Union group. Matsuda, with his entirely unflinching critique of capitalist structures, was expelled from France on suspicion of plotting guerilla activities with Japan's Red Army and continued to support escalated armed resistance from within Japan. People like Konno were, from Hirasawa's perspective, entirely aligned, or (depending on your stance) absorbed, brought to collude, or at the very least believed it was possible to work from within the established TV system.[35] The problem, then, according to Konno (citing Tsumura), is how the "two attitudes and two battle fronts"—the critical spirit of the radical militant Left and the "proposals of the possible" that work within the media production process like his own—can "be mediated synthetically (strategically)."[36] In their book published in 1969, Konno and his colleagues had attempted a praxis-based theory of television:

> If "power" is that which has the right to restructure time politically as a matter of course and then present it as "history," then the existence of television, which tries to present the "present" [genzai] **as it is** would be something difficult for power to allow. If "art" is that which selects and internalizes "time" and presents it as a "work," then television,

only by *pursuing time and thus trying to possess its own specific expression*, will lack the essence of art in its primary sense. Not desiring to be restructured either by power or by art, but only by *creating/developing the present* can television determine its own future. And that which can do so is of course not the functionality of television itself but the new expressive person who has taken part in television: the TV man.[37]

There is more to say about the idea of capturing the present as it is (Konno and his colleagues write the words in English as well as paraphrasing them *aru ga mama*), and its resonances with theories of photography and document in the same period, like those of the (dark line separated) Nakahira in his *Circulation* project, who "cuts up the flow of time" and "buries history within it . . . like a time bomb." Konno understands that it is easy to mistake a theory of media for a "theory of the future"—a superficial optimism and opportunism. Konno begins his discussion of the Enzensberger symposium with his group's manifesto from the book in order to attempt to aggregate the more possibility-inclined position (although he refutes the position of optimist for himself and Kawanaka Nobuhiro, as producers of the event in its media form) with the more purely negatively dialectical critical stance of leftist theorists who, like Matsuda, find themselves "dumbfounded and taken aback" by Enzensberger's position. Like Matsuda attempting to move beyond the binary, Konno tries to envision—and he again turns to the framework of mediation, a term worth further inquiry here—some way to mediate and/or synthesize these seemingly opposed frames, and hence to come to a kind of "organization" that would be strategic. Thus he returns to the problems of mobilization that Matsuda also left us with, but with a very different tactical approach.

Konno thus allows us to see clearly one wing of a transition that was taking place in this historical moment, from approaches to photography and document with their theories of matter/materiality to thought of electronic media/television (he calls it *chūkei no shisō*—relay-thought?) as a site of radical media theory. The disparate media theorists who gathered to engage in these culture industry debates give us a fuller picture of the possibilities and contradictions that opened in this key era of the development of electronic media, problems that persist unresolved and in many ways remain caught in similar impasses in today's critical writings on capitalism, globalization, and digital media.

How, that is, can one mobilize in a world where so many things are already (and increasingly) mobile without really changing? What does it mean to move (affectively)? Nakahira, Matsuda, and Tsumura offer highly incisive analyses of the media system within the rubric of a "total media" (*sōgō media*) and a broad comprehension of urban media geographies.[38] Taki sees reason for a qualified hope in the death of *Life* and the activated return of the gaze of the "third world." Tsumura (and Konno) ask in different ways how to mediate between the two seemingly opposed strategies or, more pertinently, to transcend (shift their axis) of opposition. Tsumura quotes his own statement from the end of the symposium to open precisely this question:

> It *is real* to say that there is nothing to be done except struggle persistently within the system, however unstylish that position may be; and it *is real* to say that the only way to proceed is by complete personal refusal. Each approach grounds itself on one side of the extreme polarity of bourgeois society which continues its "flight toward the future." Neither approach can therefore smash through its own *limits*—which are the limits of this society. The problem, then, is none other than this: how is it possible to *mediate* [*baikai*] synthetically (strategically) these two attitudes, these two battle fronts, one that is the display of the possible, the other that is leftist criticism?[39]

Tsumura goes on to develop his concept and practice of "limit criticism" (*genkai hihyō*) as a response to his own question. Reflections on media, that is, require a larger grasp of "dominant urban media" as environment within a broader biopolitics—what Tsumura calls "super-media."[40] Rereading media critique and culture industry debates of the 1970s thus takes us to a moment when globalization was imminent and perceptible, 1968 was vivid in recent memory, and a new "battle of position"—the slower battle of significations—was taking a new form. An understanding of urban infrastructure and social forms as a part of the media system opened leftist thought to new critiques of gender, class, and racial power. Yet the feeling of a pressing need for present action, combined with a profound sense of theory's necessary relation to daily practices, found one of its most compelling transnational articulations here in a way it has seldom since touched again.

NOTES

1. Hansen challenges "the fixation of the vernacular on the side of the local—for instance, through ahistorical notions of indigenous identity—and [she] allows us to see vernacular practices as part of the very processes of translocal interactions that produce the local as much as the global." Miriam Hansen, "Vernacular Modernism: Tracking Cinema on a Global Scale," in *World Cinemas, Transnational Perspectives,* ed. Nataša Ďurovičová and Kathleen Newman (New York: Routledge, 2010), 297.

2. See Nataša Ďurovičová and Kathleen Newman, *World Cinemas, Transnational Perspectives* (New York: Routledge, 2010), 10, x. While the editors of that volume generally see the term "globalization" as marking homogenization, they and others acknowledge the decentered and potentially decentering practices of late capitalism. For Arjun Appadurai, the term "globalization" can be paired with "grassroots" ("grassroots globalization") to give it a more fragmenting nuance that more closely aligns it with Ďurovičová and Newman's sense of the transnational. See Arjun Appadurai, *Globalization,* ed. Arjun Appadurai (Durham, NC: Duke University Press, 2001).

3. I am indebted to Maiko Morimoto Tomita and Takako Fukasawa for their excellent research assistance during the development of this essay.

4. For an excellent discussion of fūkeiron, see Yuriko Furuhata, *Cinema of Actuality: Japanese Avant-Garde Filmmaking in the Season of Image Politics* (Durham, NC: Duke University Press, 2013), especially chapter 4.

5. It is interesting that each of the four main theorists considered here subsequently ran aground in some part of their media and political practices. Nakahira famously suffered an attack of illness and aphasia in 1977 and stopped writing and photographing for many years, only picking up his photography practice again quite recently. Tsumura shifted to a qigong practice and ceased explicit leftist political journalism in the early 1980s (again until quite recently). Matsuda lived in France in 1973 but was detained and deported from France in 1974 on suspicion of planning international guerilla activities with Japan's Red Army, and after that was confined to Japan (though he continues to write and support Red Army activities and the East Asia Anti-Japan Armed Front, and continues to work on films off and on). Taki's work as a practicing photographer was confined to the groundbreaking *Provoke* journal, though he went on to be a celebrated critic of photography, painting, and architecture, and was posthumously awarded the lifetime achievement award for criticism from the Photographic Society of Japan. All but Taki are still living at the time of this writing.

6. Students occupied the nine-story clock tower at Tokyo University and over the course of two days in January 1969, thousands of police in riot gear with tear gas and high-pressure water broke down the student barricades. Students retaliated with Molotov cocktails, threw flagstones, and used the famous *geba-bō*, Gewalt (violence) sticks or pointed wooden sticks. Many were injured on both sides. Neither side used firearms.

7. Suga Hidemi, "'1968-nen' to 3.11 ikō o tsunagu shikō" [Thought that links 1968 to the aftermath of 3.11], in *Tsumura Takashi seisen hyōronshū: 1968-nen igo,* ed. Suga Hidemi (Tokyo: Ronsōsha, 2012), 388.

8. Note Barbara Spackman's excellent essay on Machiavelli's resistance to firepower and his advocacy of a warfare of "brute semiosis." Spackman, "Politics on the Warpath: Machiavelli's *Art of War*" in *Machiavelli and the Discourse of Literatur,* ed. Vicky Kahn and Albert Ascoli (Ithaca, NY: Cornell University Press, 1993), 179–93. See also Antonio Gramsci, *Prison Notebooks, Volume 3* (New York: Columbia University Press, 2010).

9. The work was originally published in German in the opposition and student movement journal *Kursbuch 20* in 1970 (*Baukasten zu einer Theorie der Medien*), in *New Left Review* in English also in 1970, and in Japanese in August 1971 in *Bungei.*

10. Kawanaka, born in 1941, is an experimental filmmaker, founder of Japan Film-makers Cooperative, founding member of Image Forum, and a central member of Video Hiroba.

11. John Thornton Caldwell, "Introduction: Theorizing the Digital Landrush," in *Electronic Media and Technoculture*, ed. J. T. Caldwell (New Brunswick, NJ: Rutgers University Press, 2000), 18.

12. Hans Magnus Enzensberger, "Constituents of a Theory of the Media," *New Left Review* 64 (November/December 1970): 36.

13. Jean Baudrillard, "Requiem for the Media," trans. Charles Levin, in *For a Critique of the Political Economy of the Sign*, ed. Charles Levin (Saint Louis, MO: Telos Press, 1981): 164–84.

14. Baudrillard, "Requiem for the media," 166, 169.

15. "News satellites, color television, cable relay television, cassettes, videotape, videotape recorders, video-phones, stereophony, laser techniques, electrostatic re-production processes, electronic high-speed printing, composing and learning ma-chines, microfiches with electronic access, printing by radio, time-sharing computers, data banks. All these new forms of media are constantly forming new connections both with each other and with older media like printing, radio, film, television, telephone, teletype, radar and so on." Enzensberger, "Constituents," 13–14.

16. See Marc Steinberg's work in this volume on the presentation/dissemination of McLuhan in Japan for advertising executives as a "practical" and applicable work on how to do things with media; see also Kadobayashi Takeshi's writings on the reception of McLuhan, including "Umesao Tadao's Theory of Information Industry and 1960s Japanese Media Theory," presented at Histories of Film Theories in East Asia confer-ence, University of Michigan, September 29, 2012.

17. Nagai writes of the quieting down of student movements in both Germany and Japan, and of how, around 1972, Enzensberger "was still as cheerful and optimistic in his viewpoint [as he had been in 1968]. . . . Perhaps it has something to do with his being from south Germany. An ordinary German, affable and vivacious [yōki] in a way that one can hardly imagine in a radical left fighter." Nagai Kiyohiko, "Kaikaku to handō to—Entsensuberugā no rainichi o megutte," *Sekai* (May 1973): 228, 231. The image of the "south" seems to figure in Nagai's identification of/with Enzensberger to place him in a more flexible and marginal position in relation to the power of German culture as a whole. (He too is "other," Nagai seems to say—like us—and at the same time he is ideal-ized as someone who performs this role as a confident, optimistic leader.)

18. The anti-NHK war was a movement against NHK led by Maeda Yoshinori, who was famous for his authoritarian management style and his ties to conservative politics and the prime minister, Satō Eisaku. The anti-NHK war involved the labor union and more general public components; for example, Honda Katsuichi published a book, *The Logic of NHK Payment Refusal*, in 1971.

19. Petr Alekseevich Kropotkin, *The Conquest of Bread and Other Writings*, ed. Mar-shall Shatz (Cambridge: Cambridge University Press, 1995).

20. Matsuda Masao, "Media kakumei no tame no akushisu" [The axis of media revo-lution], *Bijutsu techō* (May 1973): 53; italics in original.

21. For a discussion of the ideal of direct access or nonmediation in Terayama and others, see Miryam Sas, *Experimental Arts in Postwar Japan: Moments of Encounter, Engagement, and Imagined Return* (Cambridge, MA: Harvard University Asian Centre, 2011). Baudrillard in his "Requiem for the Media" also ends up advocating for an immediacy of response and interaction to transcend or rupture the semiotic models of transmitter-message-receiver, even as a two-way street: he favors a model of reciprocity and "immediate communication process" (182), a contestatory ambivalence of meaning. ("Speech must be able to exchange, give, and repay itself, as is occasionally the case with looks and smiles"; 170.) Without giving a full account of Baudrillard and the intellectual trajectory he launches into—toward literary deconstruction, Kristéva's *Révolution du langage poétique*, and alongside Foucault's reading of power—we can note that his emphasis on *speech* (*parole*) as intervention parallels that of Taki and Nakahira discussed below.

22. It is notable here that Matsuda had been drawing on the work of Senghor, president of independent Sénégal from 1960 to 1980, who was widely criticized for his essentialist version of the idea of *négritude* and had a Bergsonian view of "vitalism" that informed his ideas of African culture. It is notable that the emphasis on the affective dimension thus can rhyme with other racially inflected vitalist views, and that Matsuda later discredits or disavows these earlier affiliations even while sustaining his interest in the affective and embodied dimension.

23. Here Matsuda uses Enzensberger's image: "like a dancer, like a football player, like a guerilla." Discussion of Matsuda's appropriations of Yamaguchi Masao's (and theater historian René Fülöp-Miller's) ideas of gesture remains for another time; this, too, is an example of the generation of movement at an unconscious communicative level, and leads him to the formulation cited above. Matsuda uses *butōka* as the word for dancer, as the translation for Enzensberger's dancer, which to my ears has a very specific local ring (think Hijikata).

24. Suga summarizes the Overseas Chinese Youth Strike Committee and describes Tsumura's role and others' responses to it in his postscript to Tsumura's work. Suga, " '1968-nen' to 3.11 ikō," 381.

25. For an interesting analysis of this problem of political correctness as a *détournement* of critical feminist and race theory, see the writings of Barbara Johnson, for example in the recent collected volume of her essays, *The Barbara Johnson Reader: The Surprise of Otherness*, ed. Melissa Feuerstein, Bill Johnson González, Lili Porten, Keja L. Valens (Durham, NC: Duke University Press, 2014).

26. Suga Hidemi, " '1968-nen' to 3.11 ikō," 381; 388. Tsumura commented on the limitations of this last position and the "rationalization" it implied.

27. The photographs from the *Circulation* project have been published in a photography book, along with Yasumi's essays and three essays by Nakahira related to the event. Yasumi Akihiro, "Optical Remnants: Paris, 1971, Takuma Nakahira," in Nakahira Takuma, *Sākyurēshon: Hizuke, basho, kōi = Circulation: Date, Place, Events*, trans. Franz Prichard (Tokyo: Oshirisu, 2012), 316.

28. Nakahira Takuma, "Nikusei no kakutoku wa kanô ka: Media-ron hihan e mukete" [Is it possible to capture the voice (*nikusei*)?: Toward a critique of media theory], *Nihon dokusho shinbun*, March 19, 1973, 97.

29. Nakahira, *Circulation*, 53.

30. Nakahira, *Circulation*, 45.

31. Nakahira Takuma, "Nikusei no kakutoku wa kanô ka: Media-ron hihan e mukete," 97.

32. Taki Kōji, "Aru media no bohimei," *Bijutsu techō* (May 1973): 38–50, 40.

33. From Arlie Hochschild's analysis of emotion work and deep capitalism to Eva Illouz's understanding of the structures of everyday intimacy, the analysis of embodied articulations of capitalist forms and media proceeds in many directions. See Arlie Hochschild, *The Managed Heart: The Commercialization of Human Feeling* (Berkeley: University of California Press, 1973) and Eva Illouz, *Consuming the Romantic Utopia: Love and the Cultural Contradictions of Capitalism* (Berkeley: University of California Press, 1997).

34. For a fuller elaboration of their theory and practice, see Hagimoto Haruhiko, Muraki Yoshihiko, and Konno Tsutomu, *Omae wa tada no genzai ni suginai: Terebi ni nani ga kanō ka* [You are nothing but the present: What is possible for television?] (Tokyo: Tabata Shoten, 1969).

35. Hagimoto Haruhiko had already been deeply involved in experiments in formally provocative *and* entertaining television broadcasts, such as his collaboration with Terayama Shūji in the sixties. For example, in the latter half of the decade, they produced "Anata wa . . . ?" at TBS. (By contrast, the constraints of commercial viability, as Enzensberger also discussed, limited the formal radicality of independent/subcontracted productions such those of TV man union. On this show and the development of TV in the 1960s, see the writings of Matsui Shigeru. Such programming is precisely what Nakahira was referring to when he discusses radical programming as still, in spite of its radicality, self-consciously or unwittingly reinforcing television's dominating rhythm.)

36. As we saw above, Tsumura rejected the stance of radical negativity of the Japanese leftist intellectuals, and urged them to move toward thinking "what is possible," or at the least to explicate the base and conditions of the existing contradictions. Yet Matsuda and Nakahira also emerged into their own forms of radical practice and continually rethought their relation to the larger media systems.

37. Konno Tsutomu (Ben), "Kanōsei no teiji ni mukatte" [Toward the presentation of possibility], *Geijutsu kurabu* [Art Club journal] (July 1973): 91.

38. Tsumura, for example, writes in 1971, "When the computer line and television are combined, and albeit a somewhat radical hypothesis, if NHK and Nippon Telegraph and Telephone Public Corporation were to merge, this net will perhaps possess power equivalent to the former imperial state [*kokutai*] system." From Tsumura Takashi's comment on the Enzensberger symposium in Tsumura "Toshi=soshikiron to shite no mediaron o kaku to suru jōhō kankyō-gaku e no kōsatsu" [Thoughts toward information-environment studies centered on urban=organizational theory], *Hōsō hihyō*, no. 4 (1973): 38. The essay was reedited and included in Tsumura's *Media no seiji* [The politics of media] in 1974.

39. Tsumura, "Toshi=soshikiron," 36; italics mine.

40. Tsumura is citing a work by Marxist economist Inomata Tsunao (1889–1942), "The Contemporary Phase of the Urban and the Rural," in which Inomata elaborates

a theory of "the media of dominant authority" (i.e., hegemonic media) and "city as media." Tsumura writes, "What Inomata calls 'The Contemporary Phase of the Urban' is a *super-media* encompassing the distribution system of information + trust (credit) + logistics [the physical distribution of objects]. . . . Only from this perspective can the labor unions, farmers unions and consumer unions be understood as *urban media* of varying types, and it becomes possible to reconsider scientifically both the urban media of dominant authority and these movements as their strategic and objective complement." "Toshi=soshikiron," 37.

7. GIRLSCAPE

The Marketing of Mediatic Ambience in Japan

TOMIKO YODA

In discussing contemporary conditions, distinctions among terms such as "media culture," "material culture," and "consumer culture" are difficult to parse out, not only because market forces seem to affect all forms of cultural production, but also because of changing modalities of object, media, and media environment. Jean Baudrillard famously argued in his analysis of consumer society that modern objects are marketed not so much for their utility, sociosymbolic meaning, or the economic (exchange) value attributed to *discrete* products but rather are sold in relation to other objects.[1] While Baudrillard characterized this system of objects as semiotization (organized under a signifying system akin to language), Adam Arvidsson, in his study of modern brands and brand marketing, discusses the "mediatization" of objects in a more open-ended manner. He examines how modern objects have become interconnected with each other through diverse social and technological arrangements—that is, networks of meanings, symbols, images, discourses, and information diffused by media such as television, magazines, film, radio, and the Internet.[2] Thereby, objects have come to be swathed, as it were, in "mediatic ambience," blurring the distinction between the manufactured product itself and its distribution and promotion.[3]

One of the major concerns of contemporary marketing, then, is how to manage this mediatic ambience of things—to associate commodities with a more or less consistent set of affects, sensibilities, and intensity—which can be extended onto the diverse reaches of the mediascape, and translated across multiple media platforms. Themed environments of consumption, transmedia marketing (or *media mix*, as it is known in Japan), and perhaps most importantly, branding, are some of the overlapping means of marketing mediatic ambience. Scott Lash and Celia Lury, while covering similar ground to Arvidsson, also emphasize the concurrent "thingification of media." On the one hand, not only material objects but also physical infrastructures of consumption such as dining, retail, and resort facilities are mediatized, injected with themes, icons, characters, and narrative. On the other hand, blockbuster films, popular television dramas, and lifestyle magazines serve as material links in the relay of commodities. Their signifying function as media texts seems secondary to their capacity to channel consumers' attention to itself and other objects, encouraging operational and navigational rather than interpretive engagement. Lash and Lury suggest that the media environment today is a meeting ground between things and media, matters and images, constituting the continual flux of things becoming media and media becoming things.[4]

Relatedly, the conceptualization of consumption has also undergone significant transformations. As Marx has pointed out, classical liberal economics tended to define consumption as the terminal point in the social processes (of production, exchange, and distribution) wherein objects move from the domain of economic relations into the private sphere of reproduction.[5] By contrast, marketing discourses today increasingly cast consumption as an expressive, experiential, and generative endeavor. The productivity of consumers has been at the center of debates over the explosive spread of social media and the plethora of user-generated content on the web. Moreover, contemporary marketing and advertising foreground the consumer's "creative" relation to oneself and others. Many of the most celebrated advertising campaigns—from the "Think small" slogan of a Volkswagen Beetle ad in the 1960s (launched in 1959) to Apple's "Think different" in the late 1990s— have associated brands and products with consumers' ability to craft their sense of self and relation to others in *differentiation* from existing sociocultural identities and norms. In other words, the mediatic ambience of commodities serves as the milieu for continual experimentation with and the performance of one's personality or connectedness to social groups.

If, as Michael Hardt and Antonio Negri have argued, the dominant form of contemporary production is "biopolitical"—generating "immaterial goods" such as ideas, knowledge, communication, social relationships, and forms of life[6]—marketing also appears to have taken a biopolitical turn. It seeks to extract value from consumers' capacities to produce lifestyles, sub-jectivities, and social relations through their engagement with commercial goods and services.[7] For such biopolitical marketing, consumer behaviors are to be governed not through prescription or prohibition but "by provid-ing an ambience in which freedom is likely to evolve in particular ways."[8] Put differently, the biopolitical turn of marketing points to the broader ten-dencies of contemporary capitalist enterprise as discussed by Maurizio Laz-zarato, which endeavors to generate less the object than the "world" in which both objects and subjects exist.[9] In the face of the massive proliferation of commercially designed and managed ambiences, serving as platforms for our action and experience in everyday lives,[10] a key question for the critical study of contemporary media culture is how to conceptualize the disjunc-ture immanent to such media ecological conditions.

The Mediatization of Consumption and 1980s Japan

In Japan, the mediatization of commodities drew heightened attention among culture-industry professionals, critics, and scholars during the 1980s, a decade remembered for the rise of the speculative bubble economy and the heady excesses of conspicuous consumption. Mediatization was discussed largely in terms of the postindustrial and postmodern changes in marketing and advertising techniques that foregrounded the informational and semi-otic values of objects.[11] These processes were also understood to reflect a large-scale shift in Japanese consumers, epitomized by the rising generation of youths dubbed by the media as the "new breed" or "new human" (shin-jinrui). Coming of age after the youth rebellion and experimentation of the 1960s, these post–baby boomer children of affluent Japan were profiled as self-absorbed and cheerfully complacent with regard to the status quo. It was said that they sought their self-realization through the selective consumption and manipulation of commodities and mass-mediated information, form-ing fragmented lifestyle tribes and subcultural groups. They were deemed to be exemplary subjects of the post-, meta- and segmented-mass society announced in marketing literature.[12]

The mediatized consumer culture and the new breeds' adaptation to it were discussed in highly expansive terms—that not only objects but physi-cal environments, bodies, identities, and social relations were absorbed into webs of sign-objects. Akihiro Kitada suggests that these totalizing discourses grew out of the close interworking between commercial practices and popu-larized brands of high theory (in particular, Baudrillard's theory of consumer society and cultural semiotics). On the one hand, these theories were disseminated and given credence through marketing and advertising practices, which already drew on them. On the other, the theories announced the power of marketing and advertising (to turn everything into images and signs), underwriting the industries' privileged status in 1980s Japan. Kitada suggests that in this "discourse network of the 1980s," even the critique of consumer society often seemed to echo ad and marketing speak, reinforcing the image of Japan as a postmodern, simulacral world without an outside.[13] The discussion of the new breed and the excesses of semiotic consumption fell out of fashion as the bubble economy went bust and Japan entered a long-term economic downturn and stagnation. Nevertheless, the narrative of mediatized consumer culture in Japan—that it took shape in accordance with 1980s advertising and marketing discourses and was buoyed by the activities of depoliticized Japanese youth—remains largely unchallenged. How might we address contemporary media-cultural transformations, grappling with their novelty, without reproducing the claims of marketing literature as its putative vanguard?

In this chapter, I would like to offer an alternative account of the history of mediatized consumer culture in Japan. My discussion will focus not on the 1980s but on conditions roughly a decade earlier, when the mediatization of consumption was just crossing over the threshold of recognition. Early forays into marketing the ambient milieu of consumption often involved practitioners who saw themselves as critics of postwar capitalist order and the mass society it generated. These projects—which germinated in zones of contact between the commercial and the avant-garde, such as advertising, graphic design, fashion, and photography—sought to mobilize youth, drawing on countercultural ideas and tactics popularized in the late 1960s. Their experimental fervor and utopianism complicate the received narrative that draws a simple contrast between the politically charged turbulence of 1968 and the hyperconsumerism of the subsequent decades.

Moreover, the new marketing trend addressed not just baby boomer youths (a generation of Japanese as a whole) but *female* youths (high teens and young adults) in particular, evoking what I refer to as "girlscape."[14] Girlscape refers not so much to the actual sites of shopping, recreation, and leisure designed for young female consumers. Rather, it is a mediatic milieu, disseminated via a variety of media channels, linking feminine bodies, affects, objects, and environment. It was promoted as the setting of female pleasure and self-fashioning, autonomous of institutions of production and social reproduction, such as the family, the workplace, and school. In analyzing the emergence of girlscape in late 1960s to early 1970s Japan, I will foreground the multiplicity of forces at work, as well as unanticipated reverberations and accidental mobilizations. At the end of the chapter, I will consider how attention to these contingencies, often missing from global accounts of mediatized consumer culture as well as from more localized discussion in and on Japan, may clear some ground for the feminist and micropolitical analysis of contemporary media culture.

Post–Mass Consumption and Market Segmentation

The years between the late 1960s and the early 1970s in Japan marked the end of an era characterized by massive postwar economic expansion, the surge of radical oppositional movements, the reorganization of everyday life under the spread of electronic technologies into homes, and the establishment of mass consumer society. Advertising and marketing discourses at the time expected the decade of the 1970s to see the deceleration of high-speed economic growth, inaugurating more differentiated modes of consumption. As mentioned earlier, the notion of the mass market displaced by fragmented niche markets and lifestyle groups is a marketing and managerial discourse that came into vogue in Japan in the 1980s, but its initial iterations date back to the early 1970s.

A number of media brands appeared roughly simultaneously, becoming high-profile responses to this anticipated change of tide. Here, I would like to focus on two in particular. First, in 1969, Parco began its operation as a developer of "fashion building" (*fasshon biru*), a form of shopping center that brings together as its tenants various fashion-related specialty stores. Parco was influential not only for pioneering this new model of trendy fashion retail (fashion buildings proliferated in Japan during the 1970s and 1980s) but also for its advertising and multipronged marketing campaigns, which incorporated bold visual advertising, event marketing, and urban development. Second, in 1970, an advertising agency, Dentsū, launched the Discover Japan (DJ) campaign, a massive multiplatform campaign for Japanese National Railways. The campaign promoted individuated domestic travel as opposed to organized, group tourism and the massive traffic of people traveling from cities to hometowns during traditional holidays. Operating on a scale unprecedented in the history of advertising in Japan, it became a major reference point not only for advertising, tourism, and corporate PR, but also for 1970s popular culture in general. Consequently, it also became a significant object through which Left critics tackled the shifting politics of image and media in the early 1970s. Girlscape, then, exploded into visibility not so much by the design of a particular industry or corporation but through reinforcements among discrete projects pursued by multiple actors.

A key strategy shared by Parco and the DJ campaign was a form of market segmentation that targeted youth. Here, I will draw on *Campaign of Parco: Parco's Advertising Strategy* (*Kyanpēn obu Paruko: Paruko no senden senryaku*), a dense exegesis of Parco's advertising, marketing, and organizational techniques, published by the editorial department of its in-house marketing research journal, *Across*. This book explains that market segmentation was typically used in the past as a means to sell existing products more cost-effectively, by dividing the market into smaller units rather than taking on the mass market all at once. By contrast, Parco coordinated its products to meet the latent demands of a specific market segment: "A campaign cannot have a strong impact unless it sets off a chain of explosions—consumers detonating other consumers—eventually blowing up everything around them . . . we designed campaigns that set off domino effects, starting with the powerful baby boomers, affecting other generations."[15] The passage is a striking example of the hyperbolic rhetorical style favored by Masuda Tsūji, the maverick manager who directed the launch of Parco and later became its president (he is credited as *Campaign of Parco*'s editorial supervisor). It also highlights the demographic target of Parco's market segmentation: baby boomers who were reaching their late teens and young adulthood in 1969, when the company opened its first store in Ikebukuro. Not only that, Parco's campaign expected the boomers to draw other generations into the force field of its campaign. Masuda discusses advertising as an instigator of "movement," agitating the youth to become sympathizers and sect members, relying on their energy to influence other generations.[16] Parco's advertising and marketing strategy, therefore, was to be fundamentally different from those that addressed the "masses" indiscriminately.[17]

The notable rise of youth marketing was a global trend in industrialized societies during the 1960s and 1970s. What was more locally specific to the new marketing current in Japan was the degree to which it was gendered, focusing on single women in their early twenties as the model consumer. For instance, Parco's initial marketing target was "21-years old, single, office worker."[18] We need to keep in mind that until the late 1960s, a large-scale marketing campaign that concentrated on young female consumers was an underexplored venture in Japan. Needless to say, the image of young women—valorized for their aesthetic appeal and often serving as a symbol

[FIG. 7.1] The image of fashionable young women in Parco's poster advertising the opening of the Ikebukuro store in 1969.

of modernity—has been a staple in Japanese advertising art since the early twentieth century. But paradigmatic female consumers in Japanese advertising during the 1960s were middle-class housewives who controlled spending on mass-produced and mass-marketed consumer durables.[19] In fashion retail, large department stores, which had traditionally catered to married women as their prime customers, were just starting to have fashion sales events for youth. Parco, by comparison, took youth-oriented fashion retail to a new scale: the first Parco in Ikebukuro assembled around 170 specialty stores as its tenants, and the company went on to open a series of fashion buildings in Tokyo and other cities.[20] Feminist scholar Ueno Chizuko underscores the risk that Parco took in setting its demographic focus, when she explains that it "literally ventured or gambled when it created a market of powerful female consumers that had not yet existed."[21]

Female Youth Marketing and the Critique of Mass Society

How should we understand the rise of speculative investment in the gendered youth market in Japan in the late 1960s and early 1970s? A recollection by Fujioka Wakao, the account executive at Dentsū who led the DJ project team, is highly suggestive. Fujioka was tasked with developing advertising and marketing strategies for Japanese National Railways to counter the expected downturn of domestic tourism after the half-year run of Expo '70 held in Osaka (a megaevent that attracted over sixty-four million visitors). Fujioka recounts that it was not on the basis of careful market research that the team decided that their campaign should target young women.

When the project team began discussing the campaign, they quickly realized that their own experience of leisure travel was limited to harried overnight golfing trips or special-occasion honeymoon trips. Fujioka observes that the men on his team, and salarymen in general, are members of "administered society" (*kanri shakai*), and therefore assume that their lives should revolve around their professional commitments and ambitions, even when they are away from their offices. Spending time otherwise—on hobbies, family, or travel—would stigmatize them as "social dropouts" (*shakai no rakugosha*). He admits that the team could have explored these issues further, but this was not where the discussion went: "Before these questions bounced back on each of us and cast a chill in the room, we arrived at a mutual understanding. Our close-knit team reached an agreement that travel is for young women."[22] Fujioka writes as though the team (presumably all men) reached the consensus to target young women as a way to avoid confronting their social conformity head-on.

Fujioka rationalizes this decision by pointing to the different ways in which the pressures of administered society bear down on women and men. While men, even rebellious student radicals, will submit to social strictures and the logic of their corporate employers sooner or later, women never have to be a part of rule-bound society. Even after marriage, Fujioka mused, younger generations of wives were given free rein because husbands, exhausted from the grind at work, simply sought safe haven at home.[23] This greater latitude of freedom enjoyed by women predisposed them to new values and consciousness. As a result, Dentsū's campaign addressed women as an "entry point" (*iriguchi*) through which they could influence other demographic groups into adopting new forms of individuated leisure travel.[24]

Fujioka came to the DJ project on the heels of developing an acclaimed ad campaign for the Fuji Xerox, known as a manufacturer of photocopiers.

The Xerox campaign's first TV commercial aired in 1970, featuring Katō Kazuhiko of Folk Crusaders, the most commercially successful band to emerge from the underground folk-music scene in the late 1960s Japan. In the commercial, Katō, sporting longish hair, strolls leisurely through a crowded street in Ginza, holding flowers and a handwritten sign in English: "BEAUTIFUL." At the end of the segment, the frame freezes and copy runs across it: "From gung ho to beautiful" (*mōretsu kara byūtifuru e*). Only in the final shot does the ad refer to its sponsor—a Xerox logo briefly appears against a blank background. Instead of an explicit "sales pitch," the ad brands the corporate image through the countercultural celebration of a hip, romantic, and individuated lifestyle.

Fujioka recalls that in 1970, the waves of radical student movements had already receded, but the focus of public attention had yet to turn to environmental pollution. He was deeply irritated by the "gung-hoism" (*mōretsu shugi*) saturating the Japanese mass media, epitomized by the fevered, anticipatory drumroll to the opening of Expo '70—a gargantuan paean to Japanese postwar economic expansion and prosperity.[25] Fujioka sought to work against this national zeitgeist by promoting *post-* or *de*-advertising (*datsu kōkoku*). Reminiscent of the term *datsu kōgyōka* (postindustrialization) popular at the time, the notion of de-advertising envisaged advertising stripped of its primary function: selling products. Fujioka suggests that to the extent that advertising is becoming a ubiquitous environment and a form of expressive culture in its own right, it needs to take its social effects and ethical responsibility more seriously.[26] Both in terms of message and form, he saw his Xerox and DJ campaigns as exercises in de-advertising.

Fujioka's notion of de-advertising echoes the iconoclastic gestures that thrived in the US advertising industry of the 1960s, referred to as "anti-advertising" by Thomas Frank in his book *The Conquest of Cool*. Frank points out that during the decade of the "creative revolution," Madison Avenue loved to hate the mass society of the 1950s—a social order defined by soul-numbing conformism, technocracy, and rigid hierarchy. Moreover, it rebelled against the dominance of scientific marketing and propagandist techniques, concurring with growing public criticism against its own industry, aroused by books such as Vance Packard's bestselling *Hidden Persuaders*. Frank argues that in the course of the 1960s, the advertising industry celebrated and even at times anticipated tendencies of counterculture as an embodiment of creativity and youthful attitudes, turning "hip" into a central way in which American capitalism understood and explained itself in public.[27]

Promoters of youth marketing in early 1970s Japan also had their fingers on the pulse of domestic countercultural and underground movements. In 1970, Fujioka's team recruited two leading troupes of underground theater movements, Tenjō Sajiki and Jōkyō Theater (led by Terayama Shūji and Kara Jūrō, respectively), for a three-month run of performances at Fuji Xerox's showroom located in the upscale Sony Building in Ginza.[28] Parco's Masuda, a theater buff (and a left-leaning teacher at a vocational high school until he became a department employee in the early 1960s), also kept a close watch on figures such as Terayama and Kara, noting the way the underground theater scene won the hearts and minds of youth audiences.[29] In Japan as elsewhere, the contemporary advent of youth marketing arose not simply to sell products to young consumers.[30] Hamano Yasuhiro, an influential fashion marketer and a lifestyle producer, writes in his dizzyingly oracular marketing tract published in 1970, "In fashionized society, in the society of flux, in order to prognosticate triggers of change, one needs to focus on youth. Hence all products will youthify . . . and the mass of 'young at heart' will evolve, youthifying the whole society."[31] Thus, young female consumers evoked in the new marketing trend were less an actually existing, coherent body of the population than a lifestyle group, called forth by the very marketing of *young thinking* and *young feeling* (or, more specifically, *girl thinking* and *girl feeling*). In other words, the female youth market was not just segmented in terms of scale; it incarnated a new mode of conceptualizing consumers.

The City as a Medium

The "environment" was a pivotal notion in the strategy for cultivating such consumers, defined by their shared aesthetics, affects, attitudes, and bodily comportments. With the opening of its flagship Shibuya store in 1973, Parco began to systematically market "scenes" constituted of people, goods, events, and the urban milieu. In this regard, it saw the city as a medium of segmentation, an apparatus that gathers, directs, and intensifies the sympathy and participatory energy of its vanguard consumers.[32] Parco's flagship store was built in an area more than five hundred meters away (and partly uphill) from Shibuya station, a site considered to be relatively ill-suited for a retail location. *Campaign of Parco* discusses how the firm turned this geographic disadvantage into an asset. The slope leading to its store, drably known as "District Ward Office Street" (*kuyakusho dōri*) was renamed "Park Street" (*kōen dōri; parco* is "park" in Italian). For the opening campaign, the street was lined with old-fashioned street lamps, "Via Parco" street signs, and a traditional horse and carriage offered a ride between Shibuya Parco and trendy Harajuku. A catch copy of its opening campaign reads like a haiku of fleeting exchanges among urban strollers: "Beautiful people . . . glancing back . . . Shibuya Park Street" (*furikaeru hito ga utsukushii, Shibuya Kōen Dōri*). Parco sought to brand Park Street (and thus itself) as a milieu, drawing on the bodily movement, sociality, and aesthetic appeal of consumers themselves.

In the course of the 1970s and 1980s, Shibuya Parco continually launched a diverse range of campaigns that spilled out into its urban neighborhood not only to attract customers to the cluster of fashion buildings it operated (by 1981, Parco Part 2 and Part 3 were opened in Shibuya) but also to stimulate and steer the circulation of people in the surrounding streets. Parco is often credited for transforming Shibuya from a busy but staid urban hub of commuting traffic to a shopping and entertainment zone teeming with youths. At the same time, the firm drew criticism for enacting the corporate takeover of urban space. In an influential study published in 1987, Yoshimi Shun'ya characterizes the changing cultural geography of Tokyo during the 1970s as a transition from "Shinjuku-esque" (*Shinjuku teki*) to "Shibuya-esque" (*Shibuya teki*). Shinjuku was arguably the densest urban center in Tokyo in the late 1960s, well known for a high concentration of intimate bars and entertainment facilities, and attracting people from all walks of life, both mainstream and marginal. Toward the end of the decade, in particular, it was a highly charged locus of repeated (and some very large-scale and violent) political demonstrations, youth street culture, and underground (*angura*) experimental theater, film, and performance.

Yoshimi describes Shinjuku in the 1960s as a disorderly place that absorbed a high volume of youths moving from rural to urban areas, a space where a shared sense of dislocation brought solitary migrants into contact with each other.[33] He contrasts this with what began taking shape in Shibuya in the 1970s and crystallized in the 1980s—an insular and controlled urban environment shaped by corporate design, inhospitable to those who did not meet the standards of youth, trendiness, hygiene, or "cuteness." He analyzes the Shibuya-esque as a trend supported by an increasingly urban- and suburban-raised youth population and their ebullient and depoliticized postmodern culture of consumption (i.e., new breeds). Moreover, Yoshimi argues that under the guise of freedom and creativity, it turned urban interactions into an alibi for narcissistic self-performance played out against ready-made scripts, backdrops, and props.[34]

Miura Atsushi, a marketer who worked under Masuda in the 1980s, objects to such characterization of Parco's urban strategy. Rather than seeing Parco as exemplifying 1980s postmodern consumer culture, he argues that the firm's orientation (at least in its heyday between the 1970s and the early 1980s) was powerfully shaped by Masuda's sensibility, which was closely in tune with the hippy counterculture and street culture of the 1960s.[35] Indeed, Masuda's expressed taste in urban aesthetics was hardly aseptic: he favored streets that accommodated the homeless and urban locations that hinted at their underside of sewer systems and vermin scurrying in the shadows.[36] Masuda, like Fujioka, saw himself as a nonconformist, challenging the modus operandi of his industry and the bureaucratic order of mass society. A long-term Parco employer characterizes his management style as antiauthoritarian and nondogmatic, centering on "staff work" that promoted open debates and creative collaboration among employees, regardless of their seniority or gender.[37] Masuda also recalls favoring talented female employees, who tended to care less about their corporate standing than the quality of their work: "I am a combative type who disobeys rules. So I liked working with combative women, who wouldn't let me hide behind my corporate authority."[38]

What both Miura and Yoshimi overlook is the more slippery status of Parco, straddling between the cultural and aesthetic experimentation of the late 1960s and new sets of commercial and managerial strategies that became increasingly normalized in subsequent decades. Parco and other early promoters of youth marketing prefigured the system of capitalist accumulation and government we have come to know as neoliberalism, precisely by harboring critical attitudes toward the postwar capitalist order (which also made them sympathetic toward counterculture)—celebrating creativity, experimental openness, individuated lifestyles, self-organization, flexibility, the removal of rigid hierarchy, and schemes to extract values from cultural volatility. Drawing on the postoperaist thought of Paolo Virno, Gerald Raunig suggests that while Adorno and Horkheimer described the culture industry as a latecomer to Fordism, the contemporary culture industry anticipated the post-Fordist transition ahead of the curve.[39] What is crucial for our discussion, however, is less the point that contemporary marketing (or advertising) may have functioned as the leading edge of post-Fordism or neoliberalism. Rather, we need to address the challenges of analyzing media culture and culture industries in relation to the unstable and constantly mutating capitalist socius, in which multiple regimes of control and capture (as well as lines of flight) coexist.

DJ Posters and Radical Media Criticism

The DJ campaign operated across a variety of media platforms, including television commercials, a tie-up television travel program, print ads, and so on. But it is most remembered for a series of advertising posters that appeared on the walls of train stations and inside train carts around the country in large numbers. These posters powerfully linked the DJ campaign to a broader constellation of new images and discourses of feminized travel at the time. Of particular importance was the campaign's synergy with the new generation of fashion and lifestyle magazines such as *An·an* and *Non·no* that targeted young, unmarried female readers (launched in 1970 and 1971, respectively). These magazines were unprecedented in many respects, utilizing the latest printing technology to pioneer large-sized all-gravure-printed "glossy" magazines in Japan. Emphasizing visual appeal through their ample use of color photography and innovative layout design, they promoted fashion as a matrix of lifestyle, covering a wide variety of goods, services and leisure activities, including travel. Although women's magazines of the 1960s occasionally ran fashion photos taken at well-known touristic destinations, *An·an* and *Non·no* wedded fashion and travel with much greater frequency and intensity. Their articles on travel typically featured photographs of fashionably dressed models shot on location, striking casual but dynamic poses. The photos also frequently played with the cultural/ethnic association of places and the models, using tall white models to offset traditional Japanese settings or staging the comical mismatch of city girls in rustic settings (see figure 7.2).

The signature motif of early DJ posters echoed the visual composition of *An·an* and *Non·no* travel photographs—fashionable young women either alone or in pairs against unnamed scenic or atmospheric backgrounds such as natural landscapes, traditional storefronts, and temple hall interiors (see figure 7.3). Instead of promoting particular touristic destinations, they foregrounded the ambience heightened by the unexpected chemistry between the women and their surroundings. One of the first DJ posters featured a photograph of a young woman bending over the ground to rake fallen leafs at an unspecified outdoor location (without even the fine print identifying the place; see fig. 7.4). The image is so heavily blurred that we cannot make out the model's expression. We just see the uneven outline of her body and

[FIG. 7.2] Photograph from a fashion and travel feature, "Happy New Year at 'Shinshū,'" *An·an* (January 5, 1971).

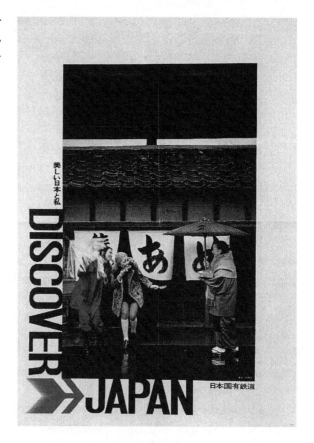

[FIG. 7.3] Discover Japan poster no. 4, January 1971.

[FIG. 7.4] Discover
Japan poster no. 2,
November 1970.

clothing bleeding into the ruffled texture of the autumn light and colors that surround her.

The massive circulation of DJ posters, using cutting-edge advertising art to promote the financially beleaguered and state-owned national railways, did not go unnoticed by writers on the Left. Nakahira Takuma, a critic and a leading proponent of radicalizing Japanese photography, recalls that when the DJ posters were first released, a friend teased him that *Provoke* (a short-lived [1968–70] but influential coterie photography journal of which he was a founding member) had become so big, even the Japanese National Railways was doing the blur.[40] *Provoke* was known for featuring photographs using the so-called *are, bure, boke* (grainy, blurred, and out-of-focus) effects. The journal was an experimental project seeking to negate the dominant mode of photography, "which clings to meaning, begins with meaning and ends up in meaning—photography as an illustration of pre-articulated words."[41] Moreover, Nakahira describes *Provoke*'s impulse to challenge the dominant regime of vision using the photographer's "corporeal voice" (*nikusei*, glossed in French as *parole*).[42] Yet he ponders whether the true lesson of *Provoke,* which the DJ posters brought home, might have been something more chilling: "Though we dared to believe in *are bure* as techniques that resulted from our raw experience of life, from the direct encounter with the world, they were instantly transformed into a design (*ishō*). Our rebellious stance and its image were tolerated and embraced as rebellious mood and rebellious feeling."[43]

Fujioka, for his part, claims that among the various advertising media that his team used, the posters were most critical because they conveyed the DJ campaign's inner theme, which was not only "discovering Japan" but also "discovering myself."[44] He explains that the association of travel with self-discovery was inspired by interviews he conducted with women about their travel experiences. Interviewees spoke about their trips rapturously, as if describing scenes from movies in which they were the heroines. What seemed to matter to these women was that travel offered them a setting in which they could become someone other than their ordinary selves at home or at the workplace.[45] Fujioka then turned this observation into the idea that the essence of travel lies in the longing that everyone has to break free of administered society and find another, more authentic self. If that was the case, the DJ campaign should arouse consumers' desire to travel in order to discover not a nature, a landscape, or a people but *oneself.*[46]

Hence, DJ posters were designed to negate the referentiality of landscape photography used in conventional tourism ads.[47] Moreover, the DJ project team agonized over the question of how to convey the journey of self-discovery—the sensual experience of contact (and missed contact)—without drawing too much attention to female models.[48] In other words, they sought to highlight the subjective *experience* but not the subject represented. Thus, although there are clear formal differences between the colored blur of DJ posters and the grainy urban images of Nakahira's monochrome photographs from the *Provoke* era, we may detect certain strategic resonances between them. Nakahira himself hints that the DJ campaign did not simply mimic his technique but corroded the rapport between theory and praxis by neutralizing the political relevance he had invested in an experimental approach.[49]

Furthermore, by 1972, the DJ posters seem to have become indicative for Nakahira of the changing modality of power that the Left needed to contend with—from the heavy-handed state suppression of dissent and insurgency to the more dispersive and intimate effects of urbanization and the saturation of everyday life by mass media and commercial objects. Correspondingly, Nakahira's concern about the politics of image began moving away from the problem of representation/signification to that of simulation. One of his main theoretical sources on this issue appears to be a text that he does not cite explicitly but evokes obliquely by referring to "the age of illusion/image" (gen'ei/imēji no jidai).[50] This is the Japanese title of Daniel J. Boorstin's *The Image; Or, What Happened to the American Dream* (1962; published in Japanese in 1964).[51] In *The Image*, Boorstin argues that our experience of reality has been fundamentally altered under three major historical developments since the nineteenth century: (1) the "graphic revolution"—that is, the explosive development of technologies to reproduce, transmit, and disseminate visual and acoustic images; (2) the exponential growth of mass media and advertising; and (3) the growing reliance on manufactured events (staged "pseudoevents") in journalism, politics, and all forms of public relations. "Image," Boorstin writes, "more interesting than its original, has itself become the original. The shadow has become the substance. Advertising men, industrial designers, and packaging engineers are not deceivers of the public. . . . They elaborate image, not only because the image sells, but also because the image is what people want to buy."[52]

For Nakahira, too, the "age of image" marks the prevalence of the simulative process in which the image appears "more real" than reality and reality begins to model itself on the image.[53] Moreover, this predominance of the image has triggered a perverse chain reaction, in which the medium becomes more fetishized than the mediated content. Thus, Nakahira argues that the image, which used to be a copy of reality, becomes autonomous, constituting a second reality.[54] Boorstin saw the proliferation of the image and of pseudoevents as a deviation that unwittingly crept into American society. By contrast, Nakahira identified a system of control at work. We may draw a parallel between Nakahira and the French situationist Guy Debord, who drew on Boorstin while rejecting his conservative idealization of the past.[55]

In the early phases of the DJ campaign, some voiced suspicion that the posters served as state propaganda, falsely romanticizing the rural, the natural, and the native. Nakahira cautions such critics that "authentic" nature, rural life, and the reservoir of premodern traditions have already been effaced from Japan. Regardless of the superficial appearance of differences, the whole archipelago has become urbanized.[56] Moreover, he argues that such an ideological critique is ultimately ineffective because the DJ posters are not conventional mediums of propaganda, delivering false representations of reality. Instead, they draw viewers into the image or design, which no longer represents and embellishes a message but is itself a message.[57] In a sense, Nakahira seems to agree with Fujioka's claim that the DJ posters are less about discovering Japan than about discovering "myself." Yet, instead of the utopic authenticity of the experiential subject (the true theme of the DJ posters according to Fujioka), he detects a form of capture: "The image ultimately systematizes life itself. We are now living ourselves as image."[58] For Nakahira, the autoreferential system of advertising neutralizes the revolutionary potential in the desire of the oppressed mass, arresting it in fascination with an image of the "nature" and "freedom."[59]

The Micropolitics of Girlscape

The female youth market that the advertisers and marketers speculated on seems to have swiftly found a highly visible incarnation. By 1973, the mainstream media were issuing reports on young women alone or in small groups, crowding travel destinations (and urban shopping districts) promoted by An·an and Non·no, carrying these magazines in their arms, and dressed up in the youthful, hip fashion styles promoted by these titles. The "An-non tribe" (an-non zoku) was described as a perplexing but harmless outburst of feminine consumerist exuberance, more an object of mockery than moral panic. However, in retrospect, some have observed that the media at the time underestimated the significance of the event at play—that is, the mastery over information on travel and many other fields of lifestyle consumption switching from men to (young) women.[60] Even though the An-non tribe was relatively short-lived (diffusing into an exploding diversity of youth fashion and means of consumption by the late 1970s), it inaugurated a continual series of girl and girly personae spotted on the streets and touted in the media as the embodiments of latest consumer lifestyles.

The biopolitical effectiveness of girlscape, which aroused feminine passion for consumption, activating their bodies, and spawning a new form of life (or at least a lifestyle), may conjure up the specter of a gendered cliché—feminine and feminized consumers as easy prey to media deception/manipulation. Yet, if as Nakahira suggests, the force of the DJ posters bypasses the conventional problematics of representation and the modern, liberal ethics of communication (concern for truth value, reason, relevance, and so on), the very question of whether female consumers were duped by them would be moot. It did not matter whether or not young women, either individually or in groups, interpreted the DJ posters as the representation of gender, youth, or nation—what was more important for the marketing of girlscape was that spontaneous and yet identifiable patterns of action by a large number of young women materialized the scene. Or, perhaps more accurately, girlscape became operational as a mediatized milieu not only because of the fortuitous reverberations among commercial media brands but also because of the intensity that female youth supplied. If advertising and media campaigns helped project an environment of consumption and self-fashioning, feminine bodies appeared to serve as the medium that relayed and amplified its effects.

At the same time, this account of the emergence of girlscape may seem too proximate to the very kind of marketing discourses that began to circulate in the 1970s, which claimed to harness the dynamics of trends and booms, profiting from these fluxes. If we follow Nakahira's suggestion that the paradigm of representation is no longer an adequate tool for analyzing the politics of media, should we also heed his caution that even if the DJ poster does not *deceive*, it still operates as an insidious form of postideological control? Moreover, even if the concern over media deception and gullible feminine consumers turns out to be a "false question," how should feminism approach girlscape and its implications for our present—that is, the media mobilization of feminine bodies and affects that does not seem to hinge on the construction of norms and meanings?

To begin responding to these questions, I want to turn to a different set of scenes, those that preceded the appearance of girlscape. By so doing, I hope to foreground the forces at work in the emergence of girlscape, unnoticed by cutting-edge marketers or by radical media critics at the time. In January 1968, *Sōen*, a leading fashion (and dressmaking) magazine, ran a special feature on travel. Together with a travel guide to a well-known touristic destination, there are articles that list, in excruciating detail, the things one needs to pack and all of the advanced planning to be done before taking off. One of the articles enumerates various maxims to keep in mind while traveling, and concludes by cautioning the readers that common inns are hostile to women traveling by themselves: "If they see you smiling by yourself, they will think that you are mentally unhinged. If you are quiet, they will worry that you are about to kill yourself."[61] *Sōen*'s tedious advice and fussy injunctions give us a glimpse into the many forms of discipline expected of young women that were taken for granted in the mass media of the time.

Writing in 1981, Tsumura Takashi traces the past decade back to two seemingly unrelated events: on the one hand, the opposition against the resigning of the US-Japan Security Treaty in 1970, and on the other hand, the launch of the DJ campaign and *An·an*. Tsumura characterizes the former, centered on student movements, as a radicalism aimed not only at social but also subjective transformation—the metamorphosis of the subject (*henshin*). The latter, however, demonstrated how capitalism stole this idea and ran with it, especially by appealing to women, offering commercial and pre-emptive self-transformation: "It was women more than youths who urgently craved self-transformation at the time, trapped in the cage of middle-class domesticity, isolated and stifled. If only the student radicals' theme of subjective transformation could have been conveyed to women in terms accessible to them, something truly momentous could have happened."[62] During the 1970s, Tsumura was a leading left activist/theorist of minoritarian causes and a significant media critic. Anticipating the displacement of class politics by semiotic consumption,[63] he paid close attention to pop culture, advertising (including the DJ campaign), and the early discourses of lifestyle marketing. While Nakahira was blind to the gender-modulated address of the DJ posters, Tsumura, perhaps with the benefit of hindsight, identified the question of women looming over the media-cultural shift that the campaign took part in. Nevertheless, his lament over the missed opportunity for student radicals to politicize feminine yearnings for self-transformation seems misplaced, if not outright patronizing.

As many have testified, the constraints and expectations that followed women to leisure travel in the late 1960s had also stalked them to the very sites where established order was being radically challenged. At campus barricades and street clashes between students and riot police, female activists were told to stay away from the frontlines, to crack pavements into pellets for male comrades to throw, to take care of the injured, and to serve in the "rice-ball brigade" (*onigiri tai*) so as to feed others. The new generation of radical feminists appeared in Japan in the early 1970s, voicing their rage over the gender division of labor, sexism, and sexual exploitation that female activists encountered in New Left movements.[64] Recent scholarship has also directed our attention to the limits imposed on female participation in radical artistic experimentations of the 1960s. Noting the absence of female directors in small theater movements in Japan until the latter part of the 1970s, Nishidō Kōjin points out the patriarchal and homosocial tendencies of underground (*angura*) theater in the 1960s.[65] Citing Nishidō, Kuroda Raiji comments on the homosociality and masculinism of "anti-art" performers and performance groups of the 1960s, such as Zero Jigen. Kuroda observes a pervasive failure to question patriarchal/heteronormative violence and oppression not only in works by these outliers of the art world but also in more broadly recognized avant-garde performances by male artists at the time.[66]

If Shinjuku was an urban refuge for migrant youths as Yoshimi has suggested, perhaps it was not equally so for girls who had left their homes. Fukasaku Mitsutada's urban ethnography in late 1960s Shinjuku hints at the gender pecking order operating in an informal sociality of street youths, loosely held together by their common disdain for middle-class domesticity.[67] When the mass media clamored to report on the "loitering" (*fūten*) youths hanging out by Shinjuku station in the summer of 1967, Fukasaku saw that the boys glowed under media attention—showing up in hippie-style hair and attention-grabbing attire, responding to the barrage of reporters' questions with idiosyncratic eloquence. Girls by contrast, he writes, remained hemmed in by conventions, looking drab, sullen, and lacking in opinions of their own.[68] A documentary film on Japanese youth made in 1968, *Nippon Year Zero* (*Nippon zeronen*), features Kyōko, who might have been one of the *fūten* girls that Fukasaku studied.[69] Not shy about speaking her mind when prodded by an interviewer, she says she left home because she could not stand the confinement of "familial relationships" and has been hanging out in Shinjuku for about a year. Asked what she would like to do most, she answers that she wants to go travelling and visit Kanazawa (a quaint, historical city that the An-non tribe will flock to in a few years), so she can be alone and gaze into herself. Though she had fled "the cage of domesticity" for a life on the street, she appears ill at ease and restless, speaking repeatedly about wanting to find herself, by any means possible, but she doesn't know how to.

THE DJ CAMPAIGN targeted young women as the social group least encumbered by the strictures of administered society, and thus they presented the path of least resistance for promoting a hip, individuated lifestyle. Yet, as I have sketched out above, not only in conventional disciplinary enclosures such as the home, school, and workplace but also in leisure travel, oppositional political activism, and even loitering on the streets, female youths seem to have had more of a limited space to negotiate than their male counterparts. If DJ and other media campaigns of the early 1970s helped excite the new mobility of traveling feminine bodies, it was in spite of the industries' misrecognition of the multiple layers of constraints imposed on young women.

This is to say that the emergence of girlscape was a release of potential, which was under blockage even in oppositional discourses and practices, and in sites marginal to the mainstream. At the same time, we need to note that this release was almost immediately recaptured as a form of new lifestyle consumption and segmented mass, quickly normalized as the habitus of feminized youth as consumers. The currents that decode femininity, unmooring it from the relative fixity of social identity in a disciplinary regime of mass society, also recode it as a more fluid set of qualities and personalities animating the mediatized milieu of consumption and biopolitical production. Nevertheless, the gap between "before" and "after" the appearance of girlscape is an important aperture for the feminist study of media culture. Through this narrow fissure we can probe the forces pushing back against the limited room for mobility afforded to young women, creating pathways that cannot be reduced to preexisting social conditions, or to new advertising and marketing techniques. Fujioka himself admits that the mobilization of the An-non tribe was something unexpected (he appears untroubled by the irony of having built his career as an advertising guru on the promise to control and repeat such unintended consequences).[70]

Thus, I would like to argue that the rapid proliferation of girlscape was a political event, however minor, or precisely politics in a minor register, conditioned on "missing the people"—that is, prearticulated forms of sociopolitical identities and collective justification.[71] It was not a contestation against the capitalist state's exploitation of the mass, an opposition to the patriarchal subjugation specifically exercised on women, nor a generational rebellion against the adult establishment. Instead, it was an assemblage of maneuvers against the concrete, local, and yet broadly spread forms of constriction traversing the ordinary lives of young women. I should hasten to add that my intention is not to valorize the An-non tribe and their consumer lifestyle as agents wresting "small victories" from the hegemonic—along the lines of arguments often made in popular cultural studies of the 1980s and 1990s. For one, the An-non tribe did not constitute but was constituted in the milieu that I have referred to as girlscape. Moreover, traveling, shopping, and dressing up are not, in themselves, subversive to modern patriarchal norms and clichés of "femininity." Yet, as girlscape came into visibility, these quotidian and dissipating practices, steeped in commercial media culture, exerted tactical effects, jiggling loose new passages, enabling a new distribution and mobility of feminine bodies in physical spaces and mediascape. And, in that process, these practices marked something heterogeneous to the design, operation, and logic of marketing. As I suggested at the beginning of this chapter, the marketing of mediatic ambience has been theorized as an indication that contemporary capitalism increasingly encompasses social life as a whole, foreclosing any exteriority. The history of girlscape challenges us to map the difference not against but immanent to this field, dilating as it does out of minor figures and their micropolitics. It draws our attention to media-cultural transformation in Japan in the late 1960s and early 1970s, as a contentious and contingent event that involved radical practices and theorization, competing strategies within culture industries, speculations made on misguided assumptions, and feminine bodies, desires, and imaginations pressing against the power holding them in tight spaces.

NOTES

1. Baudrillard discusses this notion both in his *System of Objects* [1968] and in *The Consumer Society: Myths and Structures* [1970]. See Jean Baudrillard, *The System of Objects*, trans. James Benedict (London: Verso, 1996); Jean Baudrillard, *Consumer Society: Myths and Structures*, trans. Chris Turner (London: Sage, 1998).

2. Adam Arvidsson, *Brand: Meaning and Value in Media Culture* (London: Routledge, 2006), 36.

3. Arvidsson, *Brand*, 77.

4. Scott Lash and Celia Lury, *Global Culture Industry: The Mediatization of Things* (Cambridge: Polity Press, 2007), 9.

5. Karl Marx, *Grundrisse*, trans. Martin Nicolaus (London: Penguin Books, 1973), 89. On the complexity of Marx's own views on consumption and its relation to production, distribution, and exchange, see Jason Read, *The Micro-politics of Capital: Marx and the Prehistory of the Present* (Albany: State University of New York Press, 2003), especially 48–60.

6. Michael Hardt and Antonio Negri, *Multitude: War and Democracy in the Age of Empire* (New York: Penguin Press, 2004), 94.

7. Zwick Detleve and Julien Cayla, eds., *Inside Marketing Practices, Ideologies, Devices* (Oxford: Oxford University Press, 2012), 236–37.

8. Arvidsson, *Brand*, 74.

9. Maurizo Lazzarato, "Struggle, Event, Media," republicart, accessed June 2015, www.republicart.net/disc/representations/lazzarato01_en.htm.

10. Celia Lury, *Brands: The Logos of the Global Economy* (London: Routlege, 2004), 6.

11. Kido Hiroyuki, "Shōhi kigōron to wa nandatta no ka?" [What was the theory of consumer semiotics?], in *Wakamono ron o yomu*, ed. Kotani Satoshi (Kyoto: Sekai Shisōsha, 1993), 86–109.

12. Some of the representative pronouncements from mid-1980s on the displacement of the mass market by the segmented mass include *Across* Henshūshitsu, ed., *Ima, chōtaishū no jidai: shin shōhin-kankyōron* [Now, is the age of the meta-mass: the new theory of product environment] (Tokyo: Parco Shuppan, 1985); Hakuhōdō Sōgō Seikatsu Kenkyūjo ed., *Bunshū no tanjō: nyū pīpuru o tsukamu shijō senryaku to wa* [The age of segmented mass: what is the market strategy for capturing the new people?] (Tokyo: Nihon Keizai Shinbunsha, 1985); and Fujioka Wakao, *Sayonara taishū: kansei jidai o dō yomuka* [Goodbye mass: how to read the age of sensibility] (Tokyo: PHP Bunko, 1987).

13. Akihiro Kitada, *Kōkokutoshi Tokyo: Sono tanjō to shi* [Advertising city, Tokyo: Its birth and death] (Tokyo: Kōsaidō, 2002), 93–94.

14. I would like to acknowledge Vera Mackie's use of "girlscape" as a term conveying a peculiar "place of young girl (*shōjo*) in Japanese culture." In a nuanced study of the contemporary subcultural figure of "Lolita" in Japan, Mackie unpacks its relation to the longer genealogy of discourses on shōjo, stretching back at least to the early twentieth century. See Vera C. Mackie, "Reading Lolita in Japan," in *Girl Reading Girl in Japan*, eds. Tomoko Aoyama and Barbara Hartley (New York: Routledge, 2010). While I adopt the term "girlscape" in this chapter, my use of "girl" in "girlscape" is not meant to be a translation of shōjo. Instead, it refers to the new conceptualization of feminine youth emerging out of the media-cultural transformations in the late 1960s and early 1970s Japan. Moreover, although I did not have the space to elaborate on this issue here, I initially coined the term "girlscape" to work off and against the "landscape" (*fūkei*) debated by filmmakers and critics who sought to theorize the nonrepressive forms of control permeating the urbanized, commodified, and technologically mediated quotidian (*nichijō*) in post-1968 Japan. While leftist critics such as Nakahira Takuma (whom I will discuss later in this chapter) and Matsuda Masao identified the landscape as an apparatus of the capitalist state, I propose to approach girlscape as a milieu of creation *and* capture, tactical resistance *and* modulated control. Moreover, while Nakahira and Matsuda were invested in positing the autonomy of political subject that "tears up" (*kirisaku*) the landscape of seductive lure, inauthentic image, and regressive, mock utopia (mobilizing a whole host of predictable gender binaries in the process), I discuss the politics of girlscape in relation to the new distribution and mobility of feminine bodies it afforded. On the association of "landscape" with an ironic citation of maternal fantasy (the utopic desire to return to the womb), see Matsuda Masao, *Fūkei no shimetsu* [The extinction of landscape] (Tokyo: Kōshisha, 2013), especially 7–20 and 141–50. For a sophisticated discussion of landscape theory and its critical innovation, see Yuriko Furuhata, *Cinema of Actuality: Japanese Avant-Garde Filmmaking of the Season of Image Politics* (Durham, NC: Duke University Press, 2013).

15. Gekkan *Across* Henshūshitsu, ed. *Kyanpēn obu Paruko: Paruko no senden senryaku* [Campaign of Parco: Parco's advertising strategy] (Tokyo: Parco Shuppan, 1984), 40.

16. Masuda Tsūji, "Sōzōteki Paruko kyōwakoku: Sono kyōkan konseputo" [Republic of creative Parco:Its concept of sympathy], *Senden kaigi* (November 1976): 12.

17. Gekkan *Across* Henshūshitsu, *Paruko no senden senryaku*, 31.

18. The target of sales for Ikebukuro Parco was somewhat broader: nineteen- to twenty-nine-year-old single women. See Gekkan *Across* Henshūshitsu, *Paruko no senden senryaku*, 58.

19. Yoshimi Shun'ya, " 'Made in Japan': The Cultural Politics of 'Home Electrification' in Postwar Japan," *Media, Culture, and Society* 21, no. 2 (1999): 158–60.

20. Gekkan *Across* Henshūshitsu, *Paruko no senden senryaku*, 182–83.

21. Ueno Chizuko, "Onna to iu shisō" [A theory called woman], in *Onna no nanajūnendai, 1969–1986: Paruko posutā ten*, ed. Masuda Tsūji (Tokyo: Disuku Emu, 2001), 28

22. Fujioka Wakao, *Karei naru shuppatsu: Disukabā Japan* [A splendid departure: Discover Japan] (Tokyo: Asahi Shuppan, 1972), 29–30.

23. Fujioka, *Karei naru shuppatsu*, 32.

24. Fujioka, *Karei naru shuppatsu*, 30.

25. Fujioka Wakao, *Mōretsu kara byūtifuru e* [From gung-ho to beautiful] (Tokyo: Dentsū Shuppan, 1991), 17.

26. Fujioka Wakao et al., "Zadankai: Disukabā Japan kyanpēn uraomote" [Roundtable discussion: Front and back of Discover Japan campaign], *Senden kaigi* (January 1972): 18. See also Fujioka, *Mōretsu kara byūtifuru e*, 92.

27. Thomas Frank, *The Conquest of Cool: Business Culture, Counterculture, and the Rise of Hip Consumerism* (Chicago: University of Chicago Press, 1997), 26.

28. They performed *kamishibai*, or "paper theater"—a street theater for children popular before the war and during the early postwar era. It tells stories through narration and by showing a series of illustrated boards.

29. Masuda Tsūji, *Kaimaku beru wa natta: Masuda shiatā e yōkoso* [The opening bell has rung: Welcome to Masuda theater] (Tokyo: Tokyo Shinbun, 2005), 110–12.

30. Adam Arvidsson, *Marketing Modernity: Italian Advertising from Fascism to Postmodernity* (London: Routledge, 2003), 112–19. Also see Frank, *Conquest of Cool*, 119–21.

31. Hamano Yasuhiro, *Fasshonka shakai: Ryūdōka shakai, fasshon bijinesu, kyōkan bunka* [Fashionizing society: Society in flux, fashion business, and the culture of sympathy] (Tokyo: Bijinesusha, 1970), 74.

32. Gekkan *Across* Henshūshitsu, *Paruko no senden senryaku*, 134–36.

33. Yoshimi Shun'ya, *Toshi no doramaturugī: Tokyo sakariba no shakaishi* [Dramaturgy of the city: The social history of Tokyo and entertainment districts] (Tokyo: Kōbundo, 1987), 296.

34. Yoshimi, *Toshi no doramaturugī*, 320–21.

35. Miura Atsushi, *Jiyū no jidai no fuan na jibun: Shōhi shakai no datsu shinwa* [The anxious self in the age of freedom: Demythologizing consumer society] (Tokyo: Shōbunsha, 2006), 125.

36. Masuda Tsūji, "Shibuya: Machi wa butai da" [Shibuya: City is a theater], parts 1–4, *Asahi Shinbun*, morning edition, October 7, 1986; October 8, 1986; October 9, 1986; October 10, 1986.

37. Masuda, *Kaimaku beru wa natta*, 113.

38. Masuda, *Kaimaku beru wa natta*, 107.

39. Gerald Raunig, Gene Ray, and Ulf Wuggenig, eds., *Critique of Creativity: Precarity, Subjectivity, and Resistance in the "Creative Industries"* (London: Mayfly, 2011), 197; and Paolo Virno, *The Grammar of the Multitude: For an Analysis of Contemporary Forms of Life*, trans. Isabella Bertoletti, James Cacaito, and Andrea Casson (Los Angeles: Semiotext(e), 2004), 58–59.

40. Nakahira Takuma, *Mitsuzukeru hate ni hi ga* [Fire on the shore of continual looking] (Tokyo: Orisis, 2007), 234.

41. Nakahira, *Mitsuzukeru hate ni hi ga*, 231.

42. Nakahira, *Mitsuzukeru hate ni hi ga*, 233. For a more extensive discussion of this concept, see Miryam Sas's chapter in this volume.

43. Nakahira, *Mitsuzukeru hate ni hi ga*, 233–34.

44. Fujioka, *Karei naru shuppatsu*, 111.

45. Fujioka, *Karei naru shuppatsu*, 40.

46. Fujioka, *Karei naru shuppatsu*, 48. We need not take Fujioka's account of how the campaign theme evolved at face value, especially given the fact that (as many have pointed out) DJ's copy bears more than a passing resemblance to the "Discover America" tourism campaign in the United States that began in 1967. Moreover, Fujioka's slippery rhetoric, which begins with observations on feminine theatricality and moves on to associate travel with the authentic masculine yearning for emancipation, or how the journey of self-discovery becomes translated into the campaign title advocating the discovery of Japan, raises many questions. For a series of penetrating analyses on these issues, see Marilyn Ivy, *Discourses of the Vanishing: Modernity, Phantasm, Japan* (Chicago: University of Chicago, 1997).

47. Fujioka, *Karei naru shuppatsu*, 104.

48. Fujioka, *Karei naru shuppatsu*, 106.

49. Nakahira, *Mitsuzukeru hate ni hi ga*, 234.

50. Nakahira, *Mitsuzukeru hate ni hi ga*, 215; Nakahira Takuma, *Naze shokubutsu zukan ka: Nakahira Takuma hihyō seishū, 1965–1977* [Why an illustrated botanical dictionary: Nakahira Takuma's critical writings, 1965–1977] (Tokyo: Chikuma Shobō, 2007), 281.

51. The Japanese translation of Boorstin's book is, *Gen'ei no Jidai: Masukomi ga seizō suru jijitsu* [The age of illusion: The manufactured reality by mass media], trans. Gotō Kazuhiko and Hoshino Ikumi (Tokyo: Gensōsha, 1964); on the book cover, the Japanese word "gen'ei" (illusion) in the title is glossed in English as *image*.

52. Daniel Boorstin, *The Image: A Guide to Pseudo-Events in America* (New York: Vintage Books, 1992), 204.

53. Although Nakahira did not use the term "simulation," his writings from the 1970s repeatedly allude to the problem of the growing autonomy/disassociation of "copy" vis-à-vis its original, "design" vis-à-vis its content, or "image" vis-à-vis its supposed referent, sometimes using the term "graphism" to discuss this condition (see for example, his essay "Gurafizumu gensōron" [Theory of graphism as an illusion], in *Mitsuzukeru hate ni hi ga,* 114–26).

54. Nakahira Takuma, *Mitsuzukeru hate ni hi ga*, 215.

55. Guy Debord, *The Society of Spectacle,* trans. Donald Nicholson-Smith (New York: Zone Books, 1994), 199.

56. Nakahira, *Naze shokubutsu zukan ka*, 279.

57. Nakahira, *Naze shokubutsu zukan ka*, 282–83.

58. Nakahira, *Naze shokubutsu zukan ka*, 281.

59. Nakahira, *Naze shokubutsu zukan ka*, 282–84.

60. Mabuchi Kōsuke, *Zokutachi no sengoshi* [A postwar history of tribes] (Tokyo: Sanseidō, 1989), 223–32.

61. "Tabi no kokoroe jukkajō" [Ten maxims for travelling], *Sōen* (January 1968): 63.

62. Tsumura Takashi, "An·an kara no jūnen" [Ten years since *An·an*], *Waseda bungaku* (August 1981): 28.

63. Tsumura Takashi, "70nen bunka kakumei to 'hōkōtenkan' no shomondai" [The cultural revolution of the 70s and the problems of "changing course"], *Shin nihon bungaku* (May 1972): 159.

64. I make this point while acknowledging Setsu Shigematsu's warning not to reduce the complex relations between the New Left movements and the rise of radical feminism in Japan to the issue of feminist outrage against the former's sexism. See Setsu Shigematsu, *Scream from the Shadows: The Women's Liberation Movement in Japan* (Minneapolis: University of Minnesota Press, 2012), 55–62.

65. Nishidō Kōjin, "Enshutsuka no shigoto" [The work of the director], in *Enshutsuka no shigoto: 6onendai, angura, engeki kakumei*, eds. Nihon Enshutsusha Kyōkai and Nishidō Kōjin (Tokyo: Renga Shobō Shinsha, 2006), 60–61.

66. Kuroda Raiji, *Nikutai no anākizumu: 1960nendai nihon bijutsu ni okeru pafōmansu no chika suimyaku* [Anarchy of the body: Undercurrents of performance art in 1960s Japan] (Tokyo: Grambooks, 2010), 408.

67. Fukasaku Mitsutada, *Shinjuku kōgengaku* [Shinjuku modernology] (Tokyo: Kadokawa Shuppan, 1968), 128.

68. Fukasaku, *Shinjuku kōgengaku*, 147–48.

69. There are many uncertainties about the history of this film, which began as a collaborative documentary project organized by Ōtsuka Kano, a producer at the Nikkatsu film studio. The segments on Kyōko and other fūten youths were apparently composed of documentary footage taken by Kawabe Kazuo. *Nippon Zeronen* [Nippon Year Zero], dir. Kazuo Kawabe and Shigeya Fujitam (Tokyo: Paionia LDC), DVD.

70. Fujioka Wakao, ed. *Disukabā Japan 40nen kinen katarogu* [Discover Japan fortieth anniversary commemorative catalogue] (Tokyo: PHP Kenkyūsha, 2010), 119.

71. Gilles Deleuze, *Cinema 2*, trans. Hugh Tomlinson and Robert Galeta (Minneapolis: University of Minnesota Press, 1989), 216.

8. 1980S *NYŪ AKA*

(Non)Media Theory as Romantic Performance

ALEXANDER ZAHLTEN

Oboccha-man Asada Akira (roughly "man-child Asada Akira") is the title of an article written by Ura Tatsuya for the journal *Ushio* in 1984.[1] The essay is a commentary on the notorious and until then unthinkable success of Asada's book *Structure and Power* (Kōzō to chikara: Kigōron o koete) and the immense media presence that followed.[2] Observers at the time were stunned by the fact that a book on poststructuralist theory could become a massive best seller. Asada and a slew of young academic celebrities that appeared at this time were branded as belonging to "New Academism" (*Nyū Akademizumu* or *Nyū Aka*) and became the center of an intense public interest that they reacted to with astonishing media savvy. Yet in the previously unimaginable near-omnipresence of these pop stars, speaking in the language of French high theory in print, on the radio, and on prime time TV, there is one conspicuous and surprising absence: The arguably most intense diffusion of "theory" in popular media—in fact, theory's synchronization with the rhythms of popular culture—takes place without a formulated media theory.

This fact is all the more remarkable seeing as media theory had been building up to a critical mass in Japan since the mid-1960s.[3] It was the diffusion of TV that had initially raised the question of media specificity and led to attempts to modify what had previously been an almost entirely print-focused area of inquiry. Katō Hidetoshi's "The age of television" (Terebi jidai, 1958), and especially his "From spectacle shows to television" (Misemono kara terebi e, 1965), opened up new lines of questioning at a time when media and communications studies were still largely conducted under the umbrella of *shinbungaku* (newspaper studies). Publications such as manga superstar Ishinomori Shōtarō's "Introduction to manga artistry" (Manga-ka nyūmon, 1965) stake out an aesthetic specificity for manga, and the first introduction to Marshall McLuhan appears in 1967 (see Marc Steinberg's chapter in this volume). The subsequent McLuhan boom is also a sign of a heightened sensitivity to media as a larger formation.

In discourse on film throughout the late 1950s and 1960s, the attempt to negotiate medium specificity vis-à-vis the increasing interconnectedness of media gravitated around the term *eizō*, roughly translatable as "technically mediated (moving) images."[4] According to Kitada Akihiro, in the 1970s such approaches to non-text-based media platforms exerted influence back onto literary theory, with Maeda Ai's seminal "The creation of the modern reader" (Kindai dokusha no seiritsu, 1973) becoming a particularly central work. At the same time publications on *jōhō shakai* / "information society" and *jōhō kankyō* / "information environment" were gaining currency throughout the 1970s and taking a wider perspective on media interactions.[5] It seemed as if the time of media theory was arriving.

Why then did the appearance in the early 1980s of the first generation of scholars to surf the entire breadth of the mediascape with apparent ease also press the pause button on the broad discussion of theoretical approaches to media? Arguably, this happened at exactly the same moment that the media ecology in Japan transitions into a quantitatively and qualitatively new degree of intensity. Yet not until the petering out of New Aca discourse in the late 1980s to early 1990s would this line of inquiry resume, with books such as "Telephone as media " (Media toshite no denwa) in 1992.[6] How can we explain this strange state of affairs?

This question, however, may rely on a false premise. This chapter will explore what one might call the implicit media theory of Nyū Aka discourse and especially the "man-child" Asada Akira. It will map a grand and partially failed experiment in redefining the practice of "theory" itself, which plays out exactly as a *performed* media theory. Put differently, it is in the practice of highly self-reflexive, playful, and ironic performance—all in the context of the high time of consumer culture and the "high-image" society (Yoshimoto Takaaki) in Japan—that a media theory is formulated.[7] Various voices have claimed a seminal break in the practice of *shisō* (theory/thought) in the early 1980s.[8] This chapter will attempt to map some aspects of the transformations of that time through the implicit media theory it developed.

When in 2008 cultural critic Kayama Rika asked Nakazawa Shinichi if he and the other stars of New Aca discourse at the time assumed that their readers understood their arguments or theoretical frameworks, he simply laughed and replied, "Most definitely no."[9] And yet their writings achieved a commercial success that was regarded as a sensation at the time. It has become customary to point out that when *Structure and Power*, an introduction to poststructuralist thought, was published in September 1983, certainly no one expected it to sell 150,000 copies and become a major best seller. Nakazawa published his similarly successful *Tel-Quel* and Kristeva-infused "Mozart in Tibet" (*Chibetto no mōtsuaruto*) in 1983, and only half a year after his first book Asada published "A theory of escape" (*Tōsōron*), which became another best seller. On January 23, 1984, an article in the *Asahi Shimbun* newspaper identified a group of emerging young theorists as part of Nyū Akademizumu (New Academism). They quickly became the center of a publishing boom and, in a way, their own transmedia franchise. This loose grouping was seen to center mostly on young graduates of Tokyo University or Kyoto University, such as Asada, Nakazawa, Yomota Inuhiko, and—one of the few female "members"—Ueno Chizuko. However, the group also came to include more senior names, such as Karatani Kōjin, Hasumi Shigehiko, and Kurimoto Shinichirō, who had written works that in many ways prepared the performative mode of theorization that came into full force after *Structure and Power*.

While the intense media presence of the group associated with the Nyū Aka label was founded in print culture—a connection we will return to shortly—these theorists were common guests on radio and television. No one was more present than Asada Akira, who became the main representative of the diffuse Nyū Aka designation. He could be found on television presenting his thoughts on fractals, cellular automata, or the Menger sponge. For a pop-cultural moment he was seen as cool, and carrying his books was a fashion statement. While it is almost a tradition among those writing about Nyū Aka discourse to announce the suspicion that virtually no one read Asada's volumes beyond the front page and some of the graphs, a number of buzzwords from the books immediately entered into circulation. Among these were two contemporary archetypes Asada sets up with some inspiration taken from Deleuze: the paranoiacs and the schizo-kids. Despite understanding New Aca's role as a performative (media) practice and not as a group with a coherent theory, it is nonetheless useful to consider some of the conceptual ground that Asada covers.

Paranoiacs were essentially conceived as a personification of the modern. Functioning along a logic of accumulation and control, the paranoiac searches out information only for the purpose of integrating it into a larger, cohesive structure—differently put, a grand narrative. In contrast, the schizo-kids are nomadic, rejoicing in the fragmentary and an excess of information. To explain these strategies Asada sets up two further terms, *shirake* (to be left cold) and *nori* (to get on board). *Shirake* describes the feeling of being unimpressed, maybe even cynical about a situation, which Asada saw as one of the attributes of information-saturated, depoliticized and mediatized youth culture. *Nori* is a straight-faced adherence to and passion for something, which is by implication associated with the student movement of the 1950s and 1960s. However, the schizo-kids do not commit themselves to either, as this would represent an acceptance of grand-narrative type consistency. Rather they oscillate between the two, dipping their toes into commitment and then returning to the opposite pole of disinterest. This movement is what Asada describes as *asobi*, or play.

The schizo-kids were in some ways the intellectualized and idealized version of the early 1980s subcultural category of the moment, the New Humans (*shinjinrui*). The New Humans were conceived and promoted by a new alliance of academic writing and fashion and lifestyle magazines and referred to the generation that graduated from university in the late 1970s and early 1980s. They were defined by a specific relation to labor that distinguished them from the previous prototype of the salaryman. Working primarily in "creative" jobs and in the media, they were seen as stylish free agents existing in an economic sphere parallel to that of corporate office workers. An amalgamation of popular fantasies and actual shifts toward less long-term contractual work relations, shinjinrui was a category made possible by the intensification of consumer culture, and indeed Asada makes this connection for his loftier schizo kids. At the center of the schizo-kids' existence is not only a nomadic mode of navigating information but the performativity involved in handling it.

One of the most visible examples of the New Human phenomenon was Itoi Shigesato, in some sense the advertising industry counterpart to Asada: a near-omnipresent media personality of the early 1980s and something of a prototype for the shinjinrui category.[10] Itoi also personified the supposed switch from political activism to an intensified, self-reflexive consumer culture. Initially active in the student movement, Itoi became famous for designing the postmodern advertising campaigns for the fashionable department store chain Parco. His highly successful activities eventually ranged from designing calendars to writing books, developing video games and conducting interviews for magazines with public figures and intellectuals. It is with figures such as Itoi or Asada that one of the decisive strategies of the early 1980s comes into relief. As one writer claims, "When regarding Itoi Shigesato and what one might call his constantly changing associations, one realizes that more than what we conventionally call a medium—such as TV, magazines or newspapers—Itoi the person himself is the medium."[11]

Such a Copernican turn to the human as medium is in fact an increasingly common theme from the late 1970s onward, and is deeply embedded in New Aca practice. It is an important element of the econo-cultural current that Asada in particular picks up on, and that leaves few of the New Aca associates untouched. This is also one of the reasons that New Aca is today often evaluated as the moment of the commodification of theory in Japan. The acceleration of discovering ever-new subcultural groups, such as the New Humans, to write about is then only one symptom of this consumer-oriented approach to theorization.[12] Indeed, Karatani Kōjin, with his strong background in Marxist theory, felt uneasy with New Aca—and certainly with being grouped in it—almost as soon as it appeared. Karatani felt that the postmodern/poststructuralist approaches New Aca developed and marketed were too closely synchronized with accelerating consumption cycles—in this case the consumption of knowledge.[13] An increasing turn to tentatively explicit leftist politics of critique and resistance in the late 1980s and especially the run-up to the first Iraq war were seen as marking the end of Nyū Aka (ニュー・アカ), or rather the turn toward, as Sasaki Atsushi puts it, the homophonic Nyū Aka ("New Red" / ニュー・赤).[14]

This somewhat simple narrative of repoliticization needs to be complicated if we are to understand what New Aca's strategies in the 1980s were designed for. As Asada himself claims several years later, he was following an accelerationist master plan that "attempted to drive consumption towards the extreme point when it becomes apparent that it is 'game over.'"[15] This point, of course, never arrived—despite the burst of the assets bubble and the onset of recession in the early 1990s—and Asada would later take recourse to his model of infantile capitalism to find a longer-term explanation for the resilience of the system.[16]

New Aca as a set of practices without doubt took a highly participatory stance toward capitalist commodification and market-oriented performativity. However, as a practice it also widened the scope of how theory functions. New Aca discourse shifted the performance itself into the practice of theorization, made the theorist into the medium of the performed discourse,

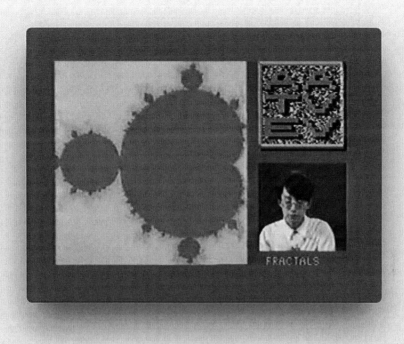

[FIG. 8.1] Screenshot from "Asada Akira TV."

and blurred the lines between content and form. It integrated the lessons of Marshall McLuhan and his reception in Japan into the idea of the public intellectual: the medium is the message is the celebrity academic. In terms of mediation, New Aca enthusiastically participated in the dissolution of borders between theory and theorizing practice, between transmission and performance, mediated and mediating. Along this line it is not surprising that Asada Akira's almost only explicit treatment of a media platform—the computer and its synthetic, postmedium, virtual qualities—was itself designed as a TV series called "Asada Akira TV," with Asada essentially becoming television (see fig. 8.1). Such a complex strategy necessitated a significant shift in the mode of delivery, both in terms of media practice and in terms of what we might diffusely call (performed) sensibility. Irony—in its definition as radical undecidability—in particular was a central part of the New Aca project, and it is one that is extensively discussed by the New Aca associates.[17]

This ironic strategy is, historically speaking, high context. It forms as a reaction to very specific developments in both academia and society in Japan in the 1960s and 1970s, about which more in a moment, and its effects on theories of media can still be felt today. But irony also presents a link for an indirect historical connection—that between early German Romanticism and New Aca—that this chapter will touch upon briefly. First, however, a brief look at the direct prehistory of New Aca discourse will offer some insights into the role of play and performance.

Transitioning to New Aca

For the volume "Film: Ecriture of seduction" (Eiga: Yūwaku no ekurichūru), Hasumi Shigehiko designed the format of the book and of the text to conform to the 35-millimeter film ratio of 1.33 to 1, which Asada saw as one sign of Hasumi transforming words into film. This dissolution of formal borderlines between media platforms may seem to run counter to the ideas of medium specificity that Hasumi seems to uphold when he valorizes film (and the analog) over TV (and the digital). Asada however interprets such an argument as simply an ironic, self-consciously "snobbish" gesture.[18] Hasumi and Kurimoto Shinichirō were the figureheads of a beginning shift in criticism/theory in the 1970s that embraced form as a central channel of communication. It was a shift that struck a nerve, especially with the generation that had been born in the mid- to late 1950s.

Hasumi was originally known for translations of French literature (Flaubert) and theory (Deleuze). In the late 1970s, he began to publish extensively on film, poststructuralist theory, and questions of criticism. Hasumi's writings quickly gained a reputation for near esoteric, unusually long sentences—one of his books famously begins with a sentence stretching one and a half pages—and almost deliberately oblique arguments.[19] Yet Hasumi acquired a small but dedicated following among university students, though less for his introductions to poststructuralist theory than for his writings on film. Director Kurosawa Kiyoshi, a student of Hasumi's at Rikkyo University, remembers that Hasumi's focus on film as an aesthetic formation to be played with, and not as necessarily representative of an explicit political stance, was perceived as liberating by a young generation increasingly phobic and wary of direct and programmatic political expression (and indeed, tawamure, or jest/play, was one of Hasumi's central concepts).[20] For the same reason, it was also eyed suspiciously by an older generation of intellectuals. In a discussion between Hasumi and Yoshimoto Takaaki, who in some ways was a transitional figure between traditional politicized public intellectuals and New Aca discourse, Yoshimoto admits to harboring doubts whether Hasumi is serious. Hasumi replies that when writing, he is confused, and in turn the reader is confused as well; however, "if both are confused anyway then playing [*tawamurete*] with that confusion is one way to go."[21]

The reasons for this shift from a transmission model of theory (and politics) to a formalistic, performative one are multiple, but two appear particularly plausible. Firstly, the readers of the early 1980s were the first generation that had grown up in an everyday suffused by an overabundance of visual, textual, and aural media. Moving image media now seamlessly permeated both private and public space, and were not just situated in the anti-quotidian spectacle of cinema or street corner television. This provided a perspective on media that went beyond a mere transmission model that understands media as merely transporting "content." It is a perspective that intuitively recognizes media materiality and the forms that it helps produce as constitutive of the meaning it produces.

Secondly, the emergence of media-aesthetic form as a principal force in communication, as opposed (as far as this can be separated) to the level of content, was accompanied by a decrease in at least very explicit political stances in media texts. The much repeated idea that a general disillusionment with explicitly formulated (leftist) politics and political action set in after the discovery of the horrific internal violence within the United Red Army in 1971 and 1972 is in definite need of reassessment. In its rough outline, however, it adequately describes a very real and much-registered depoliticization of public discourse that was concomitant with the rejection of—not only political—blunt communication.

Kurimoto Shinichirō was more aggressive than Hasumi in abandoning the humanist stance of earlier public intellectuals. It was Kurimoto that is often purported to have coined—or at least popularized—the term "shinjinrui," and even more than Hasumi he became a common presence in magazines and on TV. In his writings, Hasumi (who was originally an economist) picked up on the (French) intellectual trends of the 1970s—such as Bataille's ideas on an economy of expenditure based on the tradition of potlatch—and quickly morphed them into more general theories of society. Kurimoto was less willfully perplexing in his writing style than Hasumi, yet much more performatively provocative and antihumanist, with one of his best-known books on human society being "Apes in pants" (Pantsu o haitta saru, 1981). It is no doubt significant that the two intellectuals to most visibly begin redefining academic discourse in the public sphere were an economist and a cinephile who cared increasingly less about the boundaries of their disciplines, and who were both subject to a strong influence by French poststructuralist theory.[22]

Hasumi and Kurimoto were becoming part of the mainstream of intellectual practice with their shift from explanatory criticism, or *hihyō*, to style and performance (for an analysis of the significance of hihyō to intellectual discourse in Japan, see the chapter by Kitano Keisuke in this volume). However, this breaking down of borders between realms of expertise and both modes and platforms of expression was taking place in the Japanese media more generally. Structurally speaking, a negotiation between respective media set in, one that experimented with the overlapping and the coordination of media channels. Such intensified interaction between theater, film, literature, and the graphic arts was perhaps most prominently practiced in the 1960s by Terayama Shuji, but it affected nearly all artistic practice of the younger generation, often under the umbrella term "intermedia" (*intāmedia*). Even in the realm of highly commercial "pink film" production, the combination of stage performances and pink film screenings became commonplace in the late 1960s.[23] The mid-1970s then saw the introduction of the systematic *media mikkusu* (media mix) as a mainstream business strategy, most confrontationally and—again, significantly—performatively practiced by the publishing company Kadokawa and its flamboyant president, Kadokawa Haruki.[24]

Kadokawa entered the film industry in 1976 and began to coordinate marketing efforts for novels, films based on novels, and film soundtracks to immense success. The company and the man were reviled by film critics because of Kadokawa's heavy reliance on advertising, media spectacle, and what they termed a "superficial image culture." Kadokawa also marketed the concept of the media mix itself as part of the Kadokawa brand, introducing a new level of self-reflexivity that is one of the most significant aspects of late 1970s and early 1980s media culture in Japan. Additionally, he introduced a new kind of talent in the *Kadokawa sannin musume* ("three Kadokawa girls"), most successfully with the actresses Yakushimaru Hiroko and Harada Tomoyo, whom he used to tie together the films, music, magazines, and other products he sold while carefully avoiding providing them with a fixed public image. To remain semiotically flexible and mobile across media platforms, the actresses had to remain as empty and, in a sense, as unreal as possible.

At the same time, new formats in established media platforms were working hard to establish and commodify a culture of amalgamation. The magazine *Yū* (Play), which was published from 1971 to 1982, is one of the most intriguing examples. Conceived and edited by Matsuoka Seigō, who later became the chairman of NTT's Information Culture Research Forum (see Marilyn Ivy's essay in this volume for more on NTT's activities), *Play* was an eccentrically designed wild fusion of topics (from design to academia to criticism to art and media) that unapologetically announced its roaming attitude toward knowledge and synthetic playfulness in its fragmented, no-holds-barred design and cover subtitles: "[Moving] from Higher Learning to Play Learning," "Logic Is Fashionable," "Stealing Isn't Scary if We All Do It Together," and, referencing the publication's self-reflexive and ironic spin, "Yū Is an Important Magazine That Will Show You the Forest *and* the Trees."[25] *Play*, previously mentioned as a central term for Hasumi as well, was becoming a kind of cultural paradigm, preparing the way for the "man-child" Asada Akira's explosive entrance.

Enter the New Aca: Tropes and Themes

The perception of a generational divide became central to the rhetoric that suffused New Aca's reception, again, often with a focus on Asada Akira. The idea of youth as dangerously disruptive is of course common anywhere, and had gone through recent cycles in Japan as well. As a media manifestation, it most prominently featured in the postwar *taiyōzoku* ("sun tribe") films of the 1950s and in periodic sensational crimes committed by young adults. But this time it seemed that youth was beginning to be perceived less as a problematic phase than as both an essential alterity and an optional state. The term "shinjinrui" and its career in lifestyle magazines is a testament to this.

This shift had been brewing for quite some time. By the mid-1970s, terms such as *naikō sedai* (inward-looking generation) and *mijuku* (unripe/immature) were in common use by cultural critics, and the bestselling book "The age of the moratorium human" (Moratoriamu ningen no jidai, 1978) by psychoanalyst Okonogi Keigo announced the inability to mature as a national problem.[26] In the early 1980s, this trope began to be used in a more ambiguous sense, sometimes with scorn and at times as valorization. It became intricately tied to the public image of New Aca discourse.

Especially in the first years after Asada entered the public media sphere, it became almost mandatory to allude to his youthful appearance and the young age at which he had achieved his extraordinary prominence. Miyamoto Mitsugu, in an article titled "The Complete Mystery of This Terribly Difficult Book's Sales," in a special on the "Asada phenomenon" in the *Asahi Journal* in 1984, only refers to him as the "boy Asada" (*shōnen* Asada), connecting him to the "internationally virulent" Peter Pan syndrome. Ura Tatsuya of NHK (Japan Broadcasting Corporation) is much more positive about Asada, while retaining the association of adolescence in his above-mentioned "man-child Asada Akira." He compares Asada to a *shitamachi no kodomo* (downtown kid) as well as an "alien from the near future," and supposes that his propensity for play gives him a "psychological age of five." Ura quite explicitly, and affirmatively, ties the childhood theme in with the other tropes and concepts often connected to New Aca: play, boundlessness, and an ahistoric "absence of trauma."[27] Youth seemed to suggest both a frightening and an attractive state of free-floating suspension, not tied down by a problematic national history or, increasingly, even the present. Again, this discourse permeates multiple spheres in Japan and is not only a hermetic intellectual concern. The 1970s is also the time when youth becomes a major theme for pop idols, whose age dropped significantly—Minami Saori's 1971 hit "17 Sai" (Seventeen years old) can be seen as a starting point for this development.

Asada and others embraced these tropes of unboundedness and integrated disciplinary promiscuity into their intellectual projects. Prepared already by *Yū*'s ironic promotion and the increasing disciplinary border crossing of Yamaguchi, Hasumi, Kurimoto, and others, Asada Akira, Yomota Inhuhiko, and Itō Toshiharu edited the legendary magazine/journal GS, short for *Gay Science*, or *Gai Savoir*, which achieved such high sales that it merited an article in the *Nihon Keizai Shinbun* financial newspaper.[28] A well-known section from the editors' statement in the inaugural issue is worth quoting: "Speed, unfaithfulness, humor. Until recently 'fun knowledge [*chi*]' has been forbidden within the solemn expression of knowledge, and we will now don it like the magic cloak of a pagan religion. Neither the initiation chant of an esoteric sect nor the efficient writing of enlightenment, we ask you to keep an open eye out for this frivolous and radical plot of perverse knowledge." Again, this refusal to be bound by specialization and the joy of freely indulging in different territories of knowledge and practice was seen as a common cultural practice of the young generation, including not only academic figures such as Asada, Nakazawa and Yomota, but also copywriter Itoi Shigesato, TV commercial director Kawasaki Tōru, film director Morita Yoshimitsu, playwright Noda Hideki, and novelist Shimada Masahiko. It also enabled the increasing commodification of knowledge/discourse and essentially turned New Aca discourse into a form of knowledge curation. Asada's waxing philosophic about the connection of schizo-kids and gambling in a horse-racing magazine did not endear him to critics of the breadth of topics, themes, and media channels that New Aca participated in, and was seen as symptomatic of a lack in focus, depth, and seriousness.[29] New Aca discourse was formed and promoted in lockstep with developments in popular media and the structure of the media industry itself. Indeed, it can be argued that it deliberately modeled its practices on the media industry, thus making itself into a radicalized reflector of emerging media practice.

Synchronization and Performativity

Criticism leveled against both the superficiality and the obscurity of New Aca discourse may then be founded in a misinterpretation of New Aca's project as one based on a transmission model of media. Play as a central concept of New Aca was closely tied to questions of performativity and re-flexivity, both of them popular topics of cultural critique in the early 1980s. This is a sign of New Aca's deliberate synchronization with themes and strategies in contemporary popular culture.[30] On the structural side, how-ever, it is both an indication of the intensified synchronization of intellectual discourse with the publishing cycles of print capitalism in Japan (founded in hihyō; again, see the chapter by Kitano Keisuke in this volume) and the in-creasing interlocking of print capitalism with other media systems. The New Aca practice's drive for a dissolution of media borders, and for a departure from a transmission model of media even for intellectual discourse, was no doubt centered on print, and indeed, Nakazawa Shinichi has named several journal and magazine editors he regards as central to creating and sustain-ing the New Aca boom. However, it also almost directly overlaps with the establishing of media mix strategies as a default media industry strategy by companies such as Kadokawa.

Performativity was such a prominent topic at this time that the *Asahi Journal* organized a large conference on it and devoted a three-issue spe-cial to the transcripts of the discussions. Asada Akira was part of the third and final panel, and asked to give a first conclusion concerning the discus-sions. He proposed two general tendencies as apparent in current cultural production that made performativity such a prominent topic: that the work (*sakuhin*) itself was being deemphasized vis-à-vis the process of producing a work, and that individual subjectivity was being deemphasized vis-à-vis the external relations that help produce the work. The root of this development, according to Asada, was a developing distrust of the idea of a finished work as a representation of the coherent subjectivity of the producer.

The way it is phrased, Asada's analysis can relate to artistic production as much as to academic production. Fundamentally it points to shifting ideas of mediation: a simple transmission model, operating on the assumption of a clear sender and receiver mediated by a decodable, bounded work and evaluated according to its truth value is not feasible anymore. In terms of strategies for coping with such a situation, Asada might as well be talking specifically about New Aca. Works such as Hasumi's "Declaration of surface criticism" (Hyōsō hihyō sengen) or Asada's *Tōsōron* function less on the basis of transmitting an easily decipherable set of ideas than on *performing* a discourse of play and, self-reflexively, of performance.[31] The process of play becomes more relevant than the straightforward formulation of a message, and consequently this academic discourse and hihyō shift toward formalism.

Politics?

What, then, did (media) politics mean for the New Aca discourse? Its shift toward a more formalist model embraced the blurring of the mode of enunciation, the content of the enunciation, and the channel it was transported with—and deconstructed such a simple model of transmission along the way. New Aca discourse's performativity was an attempt to recalibrate the handling of information and mediation, not to condemn it. As Asada famously punned, *"beta yori meta,"* or, roughly, "meta-perspectives rather than sticky seriousness." Such a directive met with considerable ambivalence on the side of academia and mainstream cultural criticism. A stream of articles trailed the success of *Structure and Power* and *Escape Theory* in attacking Asada's mode of scholarship. While these attacks often enough announced themselves as such interventions, they essentially participated in the "Asada Akira phenomenon" while criticizing it, as for example in an article by Ozeki Shūji from 1984 subtitled "Criticizing the Asada Akira Group's 'Fashionable Thought.'"[32] The ease with which Asada and others seemed to discard any attempt at resistance-based political conversation like an out-of-fashion pair of shoes was difficult to swallow for the only slightly older generation of scholars that had come of age in the milieu of student activism and Marxist debates.

Yet at the same time, New Aca discourse was immensely popular, especially among young academics and students. The popular press, as well as advertising trade magazines such as *Hōkoku Hihyō* (where Asada had a series of articles that would later be collected in *Escape Theory*) and more intellectually inclined magazines and journals such as *Gendai Shisō, Gunzō,* and *Chūo Kōron* wanted in on the theory/practice that had obviously captured the public imagination (and immense sales numbers). Nonetheless, Asada's initial exposure came in the *Asahi Shimbun*, on the pages of which the label "New Aca" was first proposed, and the *Asahi Journal* was one of the most active facilitators of New Aca discourse (it also featured Kurimoto Shinichirō's column on the New Humans). That these left-leaning media outlets essentially facilitated if not enabled the boom of this aestheticized discourse is significant and points to the way in which political discourse had already gone through a deep transformation.

How, then, can this development of "depoliticization" be described without resorting to problematic concepts of historical rupture, without simply following the announcement of New Aca as "new"? One avenue is that of searching for trajectories connecting 1960s politics and 1980s consumer culture rather than seeing them as radically separate or even opposed. Kitada Akihirō, for example, has traced a continuity of reflexivity in popular culture in Japan. According to Kitada, the spiral of reflexivity developed its first level of intensity within the Japanese left of the 1950s and 1960s, with its culture of *hansei* (reflection) and *sōkatsu* (roughly "self-summary"), institutionalized as self-criticism. This reached its radical apex in the lynchings within the United Red Army in the winter of 1971–72, which were largely committed for the supposedly insufficient (tellingly) performance of *hansei/sōkatsu*.[33] What the 1970s brought, according to Kitada, was not a traumatic rupture between leftist activism and frivolous consumer culture but a migration of practices of reflexivity. Essentially, the famously self-aware catch-copies of former student activist Itoi Shigesato for the Seibu department store chain, the rise of reflexivity on TV in the form of shows that observe media personalities as they observe other media personalities (now the bread and butter of Japanese television), and the explicit performativity of New Aca all fit into this general shift.[34]

The mixed feelings over the perception of a depoliticized New Aca practice erupted at several points in the 1980s. The author Haniya Yūtaka and the philosopher and critic Yoshimoto Takaaki's famous spat over a photo shoot for the fashion magazine *Anan* is a many-layered example. Yoshimoto, one of the heroes of the Japanese New Left of the 1960s, was featured in an *Anan* article for which he posed in clothes designed by Kawakubo Rei of the fashion label Comme des Garçons in 1984 (with the price for each piece of clothing conveniently displayed beneath the picture). Haniya, a figure of the Old Left, harshly criticized Yoshimoto for the excursion into high fashion in his "Final Letter to Yoshimoto Takaaki," in which he accused Yoshimoto of collaborating with the violent powers of capitalism. In a sense a belated and displaced falling out between two senior figures of the intellectual scene (neither of which was directly associated with New Aca discourse), this incident nonetheless demonstrated how intellectual discourse was moving into the proximity of consumption practice—or, indeed, was significantly overlapping with it.

While the deterritorializing impetus of New Aca discourse was immensely successful in generating attention and media presence, it was much less successful in the institutionalized setting of the university, which was largely built on the territorial logic of disciplines. Even the arguably central figure of New Aca discourse, Asada Akira, had some trouble finding a university position, and the "Nakazawa Shinichi incident" of 1988 was a case in point. Nakazawa, who was phenomenally successful in terms of book sales, was one of the most experimental thinkers that appeared in the early 1980s and was perceived as one of the most obscure in terms of his writing. The attempt to provide him with a faculty position at Tokyo University was eventually voted down in what became a very public controversy, in which it was widely assumed that older faculty had rebelled against the appointment, illustrating the generational rift and the fantasies surrounding it.

Irony, Humor, Theory, and Romantic Mediation

What then, in terms of a theory of both media and mediation, sets New Aca discourse apart from Marshall McLuhan's model of performative, aestheticized theory? Was McLuhan's claim that the medium is the message simply internalized and localized by New Aca practice? The initial path that McLuhan's introduction in Japan took via advertising theory (described in Marc Steinberg's contribution to this volume), in combination with the closeness of New Aca discourse to advertising, offers one way of detecting continuity. However, there is another important line of discourse embedded here, one that allows the detection of somewhat unexpected parallels: that of irony.

The concept of irony first became central to modern thought via early German Romantics such as Friedrich Schlegel. In its initial usage by Schlegel, irony represented primarily radical indeterminacy. For the Romantics, irony was interesting because it does not supply us with a closed and static structure of meaning, with a secure knowledge about what is being said. Rather it opens up possibilities and keeps them open, at its best creating constant oscillation, restless movement. For the Romantics and for New Aca discourse, irony is thus connected to basically the same central vocabulary: it is both tool and representation of total relativity (*relativität/sōtai-sei*), of fragmentation and differentiation (*zersplitterung/sai-ka*), and it reveals a focus on the aesthetics of play (*spiel/asobi*)—and there are an astonishing number of additional examples.

The working principle of irony is constant movement. Sasaki Atsushi, reflecting on discursive practice in theory/criticism (*shisō*) in Japan since the early 1980s, proposes a seesaw model in which there is no directionality to shisō anymore, only a constant performative and aestheticized action-reaction swing. These positions—or poses—elicit counterreactions, which again lead to counterreactions, all with the sole purpose of generating movement.[35] Ruth Sonderegger, in her analysis of Schlegel's romanticist aesthetic strategy, finds a similar pattern. Sonderegger frames Schlegel's proposed perspective as a back-and-forth movement between hermeneutic and deconstructive practice, with a clear commitment to neither or both, with the emphasis lying on the eternal movement this swinging motion generates. This of course bears a strong resemblance to Asada's model of oscillation between *shirake* and *nori*, which results in a movement he terms play/*asobi*. It is thus motion and play itself that becomes the center of a new epistemology, not a transmittable message or theory. Accordingly, it is media practice that becomes linked to such a model, not a theory of media. An additional ingredient in this genealogy is the Japanese Romantic movement of the 1930s, most centrally Yasuda Yojūrō. Yasuda famously (and true to romantic tenants, with a strong nationalist bent) framed Japan itself as quintessentially ironic, as oscillating between production and destruction. Without being able to treat this aspect exhaustively, there are considerable unacknowledged parallels between discourses surrounding New Aca and the Japanese Romantics, from the emphasis on the centrality of the ahistoric "poems of youth" (Yasuda) to "Japan as irony" and an eventual turn toward culturalism along the lines of *nihinjinron* theories (theories of the Japanese) that were so popular in the 1980s.[36]

Humor played a role in New Aca's project, though more as an object of study than one of practice. Unsurprisingly for the inherently reflexive strategy of irony as the main tool for performative mediation, both the Romantics and New Aca discourse theorized extensively about the role of irony, and through it arrived at humor. In a roundtable reprinted in *Escape Theory*, Asada and Karatani discuss the difference between humor and wit (referring to the German terms *Humor* and *Witz*). Marx and Freud, so their opinion goes, followed a model of humor that is explained by Freud himself. Humor here is an in-between position that allows for making a statement but knowing of its relativity, a kind of doublethink that is both "situated in a certain position" but "at the same time stands on the meta-level." Again, the similarities to Yū's media-reflexive proposition of showing "both the forest and the trees" are clear. This distinguishes *Humor*—which only a select group can understand—from *Witz*, which has no metalevel or awareness of its own relativity. Asada sees the tendency toward *Humor* in Marx as his nomadic (=Deleuzian) side. *Humor,* Asada claims, has the distinct advantage of creating endless movement, while serious (*majime*) commitment exhausts itself at some point.[37] Both Karatani and Asada come back to this point, and the question of irony itself, in various later texts.[38]

As described above, such a valorization of the noncommital elicited pushback. The criticism that met New Aca discourse also mirrors that directed at the Romantics. Carl Schmitt's harsh treatment of the German Romantics in his *Political Romanticism* reads almost as if it were directly targeting the styles of Asada, Hasumi, and Nakazawa. Schmitt derides Romanticism as "anti-categorical" and as an "expansion of the aesthetic": "In romanticism the subject treats the world as occasion and opportunity for its romantic productivity." He sees the valorization of irony only as a kind of flight from actual engagement with the world: it is obsessed with retaining the widest thinkable range of potentiality and therefore decides to do nothing. "The romantic, in the organic passivity that belongs to his occasionalist structure, wants to be productive without being active."[39]

These are correspondences that open intriguing avenues, and there are more: the nationalism of the Romantics and the increasing focus on *nihonjinron* (theories of Japanese specificity) of New Aca discourse in the late 1980s is but one example. While such similarities are not usefully framed as simple repetition, it is interesting to think about the parallels in the perceived situation in which these two elite groups of (over)educated young men found themselves: the fall of grand narratives (the church, feudalism, Marxism), the full bloom of a media revolution and an explosion of available knowledge (intensified print culture, intensified media society), and accelerated globalization viewed from a decidedly national vantage point.

New Aca discourse is usually seen to have petered out in the early 1990s, just after the burst of the assets bubble and as the first Gulf War introduced a tentative repoliticization to intellectual discourse. Karatani, always by far the most unhappy with the New Aca label and his association with it, repurposes the theory of irony in his antiwar activities, although this time with different valences.[40] In a discussion with Takahashi Genichirō in May 1992, he identifies different positions toward the Iraq war. Deleuze, who protested the war, is associated with humor; his is a positive attitude toward the other with no ulterior motive.[41] Baudrillard, however, with his famous statement that the Iraq War never actually took place, is associated with irony—seen here as a perspective that interprets everything external as stemming from oneself, an eminently Romantic position. There is no question that Karatani aligns himself squarely with Deleuze.[42]

After the New Aca fever had receded, Asada and Karatani published the journal *Hihyō Kūkan* throughout the 1990s, and it became one of the central platforms for theory in Japan. In terms of wider cultural influence, it was also a relatively marginal journal, far from the public hysteria of the New Aca boom. Asada, Nakazawa, Karatani, Yomota, and others stayed prominent figures in intellectual discourse but never again achieved the kind of media presence they almost magically attracted in the early 1980s. Nonetheless, the legacy of New Aca discourse is profound, and can be traced without much trouble in the *zeronendai* (thought of the aughts) theorists of the early 2000s. In a symposium organized by Azuma Hiroki for the Azuma co-published journal *Shisō Chizu*, Asada Akira states that nothing he heard from zeronen- dai representatives such as Azuma, Uno Tsunehiro, or Hamano Satoshi seems new, and that all of these ideas were already discussed in the 1980s. While this is undoubtedly true, it is this time Asada who may have misunderstood the mode of theorization at play, indeed employing a different model of play. While *Structure and Power* appeared in the same year as Nintendo's Fami- com gaming system (called NES, or Nintendo Entertainment System in the United States), it was the zeronendai theorists that grew up with it and inter- nalized a different perspective on play, both in theory and in practice. This, however, is a topic for a different occasion.

NOTES

1. Tatsuya Ura, "Oboccha-man Asada Akira" [Man-child Asada Akira], *Ushio* 304 (August 1984): 106–14.

2. Akira Asada, *Kōzō to chikara: Kigōron o koete* [Structure and power: Beyond semi- otics] (Tokyo: Keisō Shibō, 1983).

3. See the introduction to this volume on the discourse of media as a "singular-plural."

4. For an excellent overview of the debates around *eizō*, see Yuriko Furuhata, *Cinema of Actuality: Japanese Avant-Garde Filmmaking in the Season of Image Politics* (Durham, NC: Duke University Press, 2013).

5. See, for example, Hidetoshi Katō, *Jōhō shakai kara no chōsen* [The challenge issued by the information society] (Tokyo: Tōyō Keizai Shinpō-sha, 1971). Also see Uchikawa

Yoshimi et al., eds., *Jōhō shakai* [Information society] (Tokyo: Tokyo Daigaku Shuppan-kai, 1974). The term "information society" was introduced by Umesao Tadao.

6. Shunya Yoshimi, Mikio Wakabayashi, and Shin Mizukoshi, *Media toshite no denwa* [Telephone as media] (Tokyo: Kobundō, 1992).

7. Takaaki Yoshimoto, *Hai imēji-ron* [High-image theory] (Tokyo: Fukutake Shoten, 1989).

8. For an early example, see Akira Kōzu, *Bunka no keikō to taisaku* [The tendencies and countermeasures of culture] (Tokyo: Chijin Kan, 1984). For a more current example, see Atsushi Sasaki, *Nippon no shisō* [Japanese thought] (Tokyo: Kodansha Gendai Shinsho, 2009).

9. Rika Kayama, *Poketto no naka 80 nendai ga ippai* [My pockets are filled with the 1980s] (Tokyo: Bajiriko, 2008).

10. For an excellent account of the connection between New Aca discourse and the logic of the advertising industry, see Marilyn Ivy, "Critical Texts, Mass Artifacts: The Consumption of Knowledge in Postmodern Japan," in *Postmodernism and Japan*, ed. Masao Miyoshi and Harry Harootunian (Durham, NC: Duke University Press, 1989), 21–46.

11. Across Henshū-shitsu, ed., *Ima, chō-taishū no jidai* [Now, the age of the super-popular] (Tokyo: Parco Shuppan, 1985), 179.

12. An opinion voiced by Marilyn Ivy and many others, though most recently in Sasaki, *Nippon no shisō*.

13. See Kojin Karatani, *Hihyō to posutomodan* [Criticism and the postmodern] (Tokyo: Fukutake Shoten, 1989).

14. Sasaki, *Nippon no shisō*.

15. Quoted in Sasaki, *Nippon no shisō*, 147.

16. For more on infantile capitalism, see Akira Asada, "Infantile Capitalism and Japan's Postmodernism: A Fairy Tale," in *Postmodernism and Japan*, ed. Harry Harootunian and Masao Miyoshi (Durham, NC: Duke University Press, 1989), 273–78.

17. See, for example, Kōjin Karatani, *Hyūmoa to yuibutsu-ron* [Humor and materialism] (Tokyo: Kodansha Geijutsu Bunko, 1999).

18. Akira Asada, *Tōsōron: Sukizo kizzu no bōken* [Escape theory: The adventure of the schizo kids] (Tokyo: Chikuma Bunko, 1986), 289.

19. Shigehiko Hasumi, *Hyōsō hihyō sengen* [Announcement of a critique of surface layers] (Tokyo: Chikuma Bunko, 1985).

20. Kiyoshi Kurosawa (film director), in discussion with the author, March 2004.

21. Shigehiko Hasumi and Takaaki Yoshimoto, "Hihyō ni totte sakuhin to wa nani ka" [According to criticism, what is a work?], *Umi* 12, no. 7 (1980): 236–66. The concepts of *tawamure* and *asobi* used by Hasumi and Asada are most probably both influenced by Derrida's concept of free play / freeplay. See Jacques Derrida, "Structure, Sign, and Play in the Discourse of the Human Sciences," in *Writing and Difference* (Chicago: University of Chicago Press, 1978).

22. There are, of course, a number of other precursors to New Aca discourse; Maeda Ai, Maruyama Keizaburō, and especially anthropologist Yamaguchi Masao are often named as examples.

23. Combinations of stage performance with film screenings had been common in the form of *rensageki* in the early phase of cinema in Japan, but had disappeared by the 1930s.

24. For more on the highly self-reflexive business strategies of Kadokawa Haruki, see Alexander Zahlten, "The Role of Genre in Film from Japan. Transformations, 1960s–2000s" (PhD diss., UMI, 2009).

25. See *Yū* volume 11 (1980) and volume 12 (1981).

26. Keigo Okonogi, *Moratoriamu ningen no jidai* [The age of the moratorium human] (Tokyo: Chūo Kōron Shinsha, 1978). Etō Jun was an important figure in establishing the idea that maturation had become problematic in the postwar Japanese climate. See, for example, Jun Etō, *Seijuku to Sōshitsu* [Maturity and loss] (Tokyo: Kawade Shobo Shinsha, 1967).

27. Mitsugu Miyamoto, "Kono chō-nankai-sho ga ureru makafushigi" [The complete mystery of this terribly difficult book's sales], *Asahi Journal* 26, no. 15 (June 1984): 11–13. See also Tatsuya Ura, "Oboccha-man Asada Akira." The disc, discussion of adolescence, especially of the male, has a long and complicated history in the Japanese context that, especially in the postwar period, became strongly connected to questions of the nation, a discourse picked up on by Etō Jun, among others. Aaron Gerow has claimed that the *manzai* comedy boom of the early 1980s was an attempt to stake out a gendered space for the immature male. See Aaron Gerow, *Kitano Takeshi* (London: British Film Institute, 2008). Taking Tomiko Yoda's thesis of the development of a "girlscape" in 1970s Japan into account (see her essay in this volume), it is also possible to interpret New Aca practice, despite the presence of Ueno Chizuko, as strategically gendered. It is worth noting that Ueno attempted to gender New Aca themes such as play as female in several of her books. See Chizuko Ueno, *Onna asobi* [Women's play] (Tokyo: Gakuyō, 1988); and *Watashi sagashi gêmu* [Search-myself game] (Tokyo: Chikuma Shobo, 1987).

28. "Wadai no Zasshi 'GS,'" *Nihon Keizai Shimbun* (Tokyo), June 29, 1984.

29. Miyamoto, "Kono chō-Nankai-sho ga Ureru Makafushigi."

30. For more information on the spirals of reflexivity and performativity intensifying throughout the 1980s, especially in terms of TV culture, see Akihiro Kitada, *Warau Nihon no nashonarizumu* [A sneering Japan's "nationalism"] (Tokyo: NHK Books, 2005).

31. It is no surprise, then, that Hasumi would, in 1980, participate in the aforementioned discussion with Yoshimoto Takaaki titled "For Criticism, What Is a Work?" See Hasumi Shigehiko and Yoshimoto Takaaki, "Hihyō ni totte sakuhin to wa nani ka" [What is a work according to hihyō?], *Umi* 12, no. 7 (1980): 236–67. Also Hasumi, *Hyōsō hihyō sengen.*

32. Ozeki Shūji, "Gendai no ningenkan o tō: Asada Akira-ra no 'ryūkō shisō' o hihan suru," [Inquiry into the contemporary idea of the human: Criticizing the Asada Akira group's "fashionable thought"], *Bunka Hyōron* 279 (June 1984): 28–57.

33. Kitada Akihirō, *Warau nihon no nashonarizumu* [A sneering Japan's "nationalism"] (Tokyo: NHK Books, 2005), 27–64.

34. It is interesting to note that Itoi himself had a history within the student movement, and in many ways embodies exactly this shift.

35. Sasaki, *Nippon no shisō*, 19–23.

36. See, for example, Kevin Michael Doak, *Dreams of Difference. The Japanese Romantic School and the Crisis of Modernity* (Berkeley: University of California Press, 1994).

37. Akira Asada, Katsuhito Iwai, and Kōjin Karatani, "Marukus, kahei, gengo" [Marx, currency, language], in *Tōsō-ron: Sukizo kizzu no bōken*, by Akira Asada (Tokyo: Chikuma Bunko, 1986), 151–239. It is worth noting that the Japanese transliteration of "irony," when used by Asada and Karatani, in the 1980s begins with *ironī*, which transliterates the German pronunciation that probably goes back to Yasuda, and in the early 1990s becomes *aironī*, the English pronunciation that is probably more influenced by the translation of Richard Rorty's work.

38. See, for example, Karatani, *Yūmoa toshite no yuibutsu-ron*.

39. My translation of Carl Schmitt, *Politische Romantik* [Political Romanticism] (Berlin: Duncker & Humblot, 1998), 18, 65. In an interesting turn, Uno Tsunehiro, one of the main figures of the *zeronendai* discourse of the 2000s, made Schmitt's concept of decisionism one of the cornerstones of his analysis of contemporary popular culture in Japan.

40. Karatani voiced explicit criticism of New Aca discourse as early as 1984, but generally continued to be seen as associated with it. See, for example, Karatani, *Hihyō to posutomodân*.

41. In the transliteration of humor into Japanese, we find a shift from Karatani's earlier usage, which used the German pronunciation, to the English translation being used here.

42. Kōjin Karatani and Genichirō Takahashi, "Gendai bungaku o tatakau," *Gunzō* 47, no. 6 (May 1992): 6–50.

9. CRITICAL MEDIA IMAGINATION
Nancy Seki's TV Criticism and
the Media Space of the 1980s and 1990s

RYOKO MISONO

Translation by Ryoko Misono,
Edmond Ernest dit Alban, and Marc Steinberg

Famous entertainers have the right to tell their own stories, be it about their personal lives, their "philosophy," "aesthetics," or even trivial subjects like "my dog and me." Open any magazine and you'll find somebody telling their story about something. These stories accumulate in the media, whether in the form of the "extended interview" or the "exclusive confession," never to be corrected, refuted, or mocked. TV talk shows also have this function. But the efficacy of TV as a transmission medium is reduced by the inclusion of the talk show host's unnecessary commentary and reactions. Sure, in magazine interviews there's always an interviewer asking the questions, too, but in most cases, the personality of those interviewers doesn't come to the fore in the text. In the case of the magazine interview made to highlight a specific celebrity, the personality of the interviewer is no more than an intrusion, a mere means of increasing the intensity of the interview (even if the interviewer shares just a little in the narcissism of the celebrity). However, as talk shows follow the principle of TV as medium, a certain balance must be struck between the host and the celebrity, sometimes allowing the host's personality to take priority.

NANCY SEKI, " 'Wain de dekiteiru' Kawashima Naomi wo rikai dekiru ka" (Made of Wine: Can We Understand Kawashima Naomi?), in *Shūkan Bunshūn*, 1997

Nancy Seki, Eraser Print Critic

The above is a passage from an analysis of "the story" told by an actress in her late thirties, Kawashima Naomi, during a short TV interview program. The resemblance of this text to the academic study of television is striking.

This media critique here grasps the political implications of the complete absence of political analysis that should exist between "sender" and "receiver," all the while attacking the uncritical nature of the producers and performers behind TV, magazines, and other information media.

This incisive gaze that cuts through the irrationality of the information business resembles that of media studies scholars. But, in fact, this text was written by Nancy Seki (born Seki Naomi), the most energetic and edgy female columnist and illustrator Japan has known, who was active from the 1980s through the 1990s. Holding the unique title of "eraser print artist," she was the author of numerous columns, and made TV criticism the core of her writing activities. She had more than ten serial columns in monthly and weekly magazines when she died at the young age of thirty-nine in 2002, in the midst of her most productive period as a writer and illustrator. Nevertheless, even now her popularity has not waned, and the incisiveness of her criticism has not gone dull. What factors make her TV criticism so compelling? While playfully debating key concepts of media theory, she was gifted with the talent of managing the circulation of her written texts and printed images as commodities within the market of the publishing industry. What are the historical, environmental, and cultural factors that generated the critical imagination and unique vocabulary of this outstanding media performer who lived in the media network herself? Before undertaking to answer this question through an analysis of her work, I will first present the particular characteristics of Nancy Seki's TV criticism.

Nancy Seki began her career as an "eraser print" illustrator, for which reason her early works were mostly illustrations, though she also undertook interviews and reportages. That said, her representative work was undoubtedly her TV criticism serialized in two major weekly magazines, and it was there that her basic style was established. Her columns were in principle one page long, and within this short page she would develop her criticism of TV personalities and celebrities (*tarento*). Next to the text in each column would be an engraved likeness of the celebrity discussed, made by Nancy Seki using her unique medium or technique of the eraser print—a print made from an eraser carving—and accompanied with a poignant one-line comment. Within this particular format, composed of a short text and an image with a sharp catchphrase published together in the temporally immediate medium of the weekly magazine, we can, I would argue, find the most basic style of TV criticism for which Nancy Seki is known.

Nancy Seki's TV criticism was satirical and ironical, to be sure, but it also never forsook its nature as a form of entertainment. It was a bracing read,

but also an amusing one. The main reason for this was Nancy Seki's special talent for comical phrasing, and her ability to perfectly verbalize what
people were thinking in the depth of their minds. Her sharp analysis would
at times be gentler, at times more abrasive, but this textual analysis was always paired with the rough lines unique to the eraser print technique of her
portrait, lines that revealed her deep understanding of the person discussed
in the article, and lines that returned the reader to the world of visual representation from which that person came. What she did was slow down the
immediacy and quickness of the televisual medium through the medium
of text, at the same time as she returned the reader back to the realm of
the image, albeit as a new kind of image. This interaction between text and
image was in turn put back into circulation using the fast-moving medium
of the weekly magazine, where readers would consume it. Nancy Seki's television criticism can therefore be defined as a cyclical system that has three
distinct moments: (1) the reception of televised images and information;
(2) the conversion of these images into critical written analysis combined
with the primitive eraser print image; and (3) the subsequent recirculation
of analysis and eraser print image in the form of print media such as the
weekly magazine.

To be sure, we cannot overlook the moment of the reader's active decoding of Nancy Seki's texts. Nancy Seki's fans (including many who did not
really watch TV) often say that *she wrote what they were thinking*. But in fact
this shows that her real talent was precisely to put into words, give simple expression to, and make comprehensible what people could plainly see but not
articulate. Her talent was to say what people thought but could not themselves express. She had the ability to find, name, and express the universal
truths found within the secular microcosm of popular television. This sort
of cathartic revelation of the truths about TV, fused with her comical writing
style, was at the core of her appeal.

However, the period during which Nancy Seki was most active as a
critic—from the late 1980s to 1990s—is known in Japanese media history as
a time of decline for the television industry. It is said that during the 1980s,
TV culture reached its apex and saturation point. This, combined with the
collapse of the bubble economy in the early 1990s, accelerated the decline
of television as an image-based information industry which leads us to ask:
Why would Nancy Seki put TV criticism at the center of her critical activities
in an age of decline for TV as a medium? What were her intentions in doing
so? And how did her TV criticism grapple with the general degeneration of
TV culture?

As the citation at the opening of this essay suggests, Nancy Seki was endowed with a theoretical perspective on media that enabled her to develop metalevel analyses of the very structure of media. She had an ability to critically read the information emitted from a medium to decipher a hidden signification different from the "official" meaning intended by the sender, and then offer it to her readers as an alternative reading. As a part of a period when the images and information transmitted on TV were no longer part of a monolithically constituted entity but rather, were troubled by complex gaps of meaning and dissonances, I would argue that her TV criticism played an ethical and indeed pedagogical role as an alternative form of media literacy aimed at the general public.

That said, we also have to acknowledge that, filled as it is with proper names, Nancy's TV criticism can be very difficult to grasp for those who were not part of her media environment. Moreover—and perhaps related to this—there has been little theoretical analysis of the way her TV criticism was fostered by the dynamics of multiple media crossovers during the late 1970s and 1980s, and little engagement with the crucial relationship between her written text and her unique eraser print images, which she never gave up, even after she was recognized for her prose. In this article, I will explain the conditions for the emergence, development, and consumption of Nancy Seki's unique talent. I will examine the power of her critical imagination as well as its limitations, and, finally, I will ask whether there is a means of going beyond these limitations.

Television as a Media Public Sphere

By the end of the 1950s, television had become the medium with the greatest influence for many Japanese. Before the creation of personal computers, our lives were filled with newspapers, radio, magazines, films, records, and so on, but television unquestionably occupied a central place within mass media. Even today, watching television is the activity Japanese people spend the most amount of time doing at home, aside from sleeping. Of course, this is not unique to Japan; television has had a powerful influence all over the world since World War II. But the influence of television is especially strong in Japan, where it occupies a symbolically key place in people's consciousness. For instance, while cinema was at the center of the media ecology in postwar America, in Japan the television in the living room was the centerpiece of its media sphere. But how did television come to occupy such a central place in Japan?

From the 1950s to 1960s, in the United States and in European countries, as well as in Japan, television became a mass medium almost simultaneously. After the 1960s, it permeated everyday life in many countries, exerting an influence greater than cinema, radio, or even newspapers. In the case of Japan, two symbolic factors for the popularization of the TV were "street-corner television" (*gaitō terebi*) and the broadcasting of the marriage parade of Crown Prince Akihito. These were also two defining moments for the connection between television and the public sphere in Japan.

The first defining moment, street-corner television, was born in 1953 as a marketing strategy for Nihon Terebi (NTV), a private broadcaster that emerged almost simultaneously with the national broadcaster Nihon Hōsō Kyōkai (NHK). As a strategy for generating an audience and a consumer base for television at a time when TV sets were prohibitively expensive, NTV's street-corner television set gave the masses a feel for television, even as NTV profited from the advertising revenues it received for the expanded audience. More than 220 large-sized television sets were put around the Tokyo metropolitan area and its surrounding prefectures, located mostly near train stations and high-traffic entertainment quarters. Television in this incarnation was first and foremost a public medium.

The other defining moment, the crown prince's marriage in 1959, was a decisive opportunity for the television industry to expand the locations of TV sets from the street corners on which they had started to the homes of individual viewers. The number of television sets in Japanese homes had surpassed the one million mark in May 1958, but after the announcement of the engagement of Prince Akihito and Shoda Michiko later that year, and of the marriage procession that was going to be televised, the number of television sets sold exploded, reaching two million sets by April 1959, and then three million by October 1959. Amid this sudden diffusion of television sets into homes, the live coverage of the April 1959 marriage parade became the first national media event on Japanese television.

This event symbolizes the birth of a *media public sphere*, a communication space made accessible through the mediation of television as a medium and as a technology. However, this space was at the very same moment limited by the publicness of another rival public space: the nation. We can indeed call this the *national public sphere*. Any person who is part of this public sphere could freely communicate within it by using its language. However, the media public sphere created by the television network was built on the outlines of the nation, and was therefore trapped inside the national space. I would like to try to propose a definition of this national public sphere as it is mediated by television. For this is a form of public sphere that ironically inverts the original meaning of the concept "public sphere." And, in my view, Nancy Seki's discourse is closely tied to the establishment of this televisually mediated national public sphere.

Jürgen Habermas, the leading thinker of the concept of "public sphere," defined "civic publicness" as follows in his *Structural Transformation of the Public Sphere*: "The bourgeois public sphere may be conceived above all as the sphere of private people come together as a public; they soon claimed the public sphere regulated from above against the public authorities themselves, to engage them in a debate over the general rules governing relations in the basically privatized but publicly relevant sphere of commodity exchange and social labor. The medium of this political confrontation was peculiar and without historical precedent: people's public use of their reason."[1] The private sphere has the intrinsic potential to resist "public power" (represented by the state or an aristocratic society), operating through commerce, clubs, newspapers, and even the "city" as the space where heterogeneous forms of exchange take place, all of which form a parallel network of information and a space of free discussion distinct from public power. It goes without saying that this definition illustrates Habermas's idealist model of the media space, and we should add that this very model has often been criticized for this very idealism. Nevertheless, from the perspective of the media history of television in postwar Japan, engaging with Habermas's work may be useful. There is a double-sidedness to this usefulness, which relates directly to the definitions of the terms "citizen" (*shimin*) and "publicness." To anticipate my conclusion, television in postwar Japan succeeded in definitively connecting the private sphere to the network of the public sphere. In a sense, this was a kind of "opening."

The magical box of the TV had within itself, or, perhaps more accurately, *through* itself, the power to make possible the sharing of information, becoming the basis for reciprocal communication. Moreover, there was one such magic box for each and every household, and each magic box was placed in the center of the family living room. Television clearly opened the private space of the family living room onto the public communication network.

However, regardless of the fact that postwar Japan's television network started with the two-tiered system of the NHK public channels and private broadcasting channels, because of its deep ties to the advertisement industry and ultimately to the economic and industrial worlds, TV ended up as a medium of "national unification." In other words, the originally open TV network was quickly bound to the confines of the nation, and with it, citizens became national subjects, and publicness became national community. The manner in which public space emerges from the actions of independent citizens is from the start antithetical to the logic of blood that binds together private space and nation. As this communicational space emerging from the private sphere changes into a public one, their intimate relationship evolves into an equation between the private and the national. Hannah Arendt firmly denounces the merging of the private and the public, seeing their confusion as having brought about the worst tragedies of the twentieth century.

Nevertheless, even as Habermas quotes Arendt in the citation that follows, he modifies her argument to suggest that the convergence of the two spheres is inevitable, and that they are in fact difficult to separate in the first place: "Hannah Arendt refers to this *private sphere of society that has become publicly relevant* when she characterizes the modern (in contrast to the ancient) relationship of the public sphere to the private in terms of the rise of the 'social.'"[2] Here, Habermas clearly, and perhaps intentionally, transforms Arendt's conceptualization of the relationship between the public and the private spheres. What Arendt calls "the 'social'" is the contaminating element within public space that signifies the decay of publicness itself. (As Arendt writes, in a passage cited by Habermas, "Society is the form in which the fact of mutual dependence for the sake of life and nothing else assumes public significance, and where the activities connected with sheer survival are permitted to appear in public."[3])

Recalling that Arendt's concept of the public space is based on the model of the ancient Greek polis, we must of course be generally wary of the Eurocentrism and elitism of her views on "publicness." Nevertheless, what I would like to do here is to examine the manner in which the peculiar relationship between *nation* and *publicness*—terms that are normally mutually exclusive—gains a paradoxical if concealed compatibility within the space created by postwar Japanese televisual media.

Nancy Seki's National TV Criticism

Nancy Seki was born in Aomori prefecture the same year the very first national media event aired on TV—the wedding parade noted above. She herself has explained how she was not very close to the medium of TV in her childhood, but despite this, we can say that her own growth and development was synchronized with the establishment of TV as a national media network. Along with the diffusion of the TV network, the 1960s saw the start of the collapse of the original television broadcasting system wherein NHK was responsible for national broadcasting, and commercial broadcasting was in principle fragmented between different local stations. While there are many reasons for the expansion and consolidation of commercial broadcasters into national networks, a few of these include the limited social role of small, local broadcasters; the inability of local stations to compete on the programming end with TV shows produced and aired by metropolitan broadcasters; and the attempt by these metropolitan stations to augment advertising revenues. Private broadcasting companies also increasingly strengthened their stations, with a particular focus on news. By the second half of the 1970s, the five major commercial TV stations had established business affiliations with the five national newspapers. In particular, the national newspapers and the Tokyo-based flagship commercial networks (known as key stations, or *kiikyoku*) increasingly deployed their shared capital and human resources to make the best use of their commercial alliances.

Following national broadcaster NHK's example, the five central Tokyo flagship networks and their regional affiliates developed on a national scale. At this point, wherever people were in Japan, they would be able to watch NHK as well as a number of local affiliates of the five major commercial networks. For this reason, Nancy Seki, who was raised at the northmost tip of Honshū Island in Aomori prefecture, could, at least in principle, watch the same programs as children raised in the massive metropolises of Tokyo or Osaka, or for that matter, as children raised in regions equally far removed from these cities. They were all connected by the fact of living in a shared media public sphere called "television." All of them could know the same TV celebrities, could watch the same programs, and could speak the same language. Indeed, I would argue that it is the certainty of this capacity to communicate with a large number of unknown people through the same experience of the televisual media public sphere that lies at the very core of Nancy Seki's TV criticism.

We have to understand that Nancy Seki's critical strategy of using TV celebrities' nicknames without any explanation, making in-jokes about celebrities, assuming the public's general knowledge of the significance of these names and their televisual referents, and so forth, could not work without a certain prerequisite: her readers' participation in a common media network. As much as Nancy Seki's rise as a TV critic was based on her ability to assume a common knowledge of this media network, her decline was also tied to the collapse of this common network starting in the 1990s. As a preliminary hypothesis, then, we can say that Nancy Seki's TV criticism was born within and intimately connected to this particular televisual public sphere.

Yet we cannot forget that this media public sphere within which she operated was national at the same time as it was public. This public sphere was bounded and enclosed, forming an insular and homogeneous community. If Nancy Seki's criticism had limitations, they are to be found in the way the borders of the nation and the national media sphere strengthen the basis of her critical language yet also prevent her work from crossing these borders. Her words and the images she made with her eraser carvings seemingly cannot cross national boundaries. These limitations follow from her choice of the national public sphere formed by TV as her workplace.

Nancy Seki liked to write about famous personalities. Consider Hagimoto Kinichi, Nakamori Akina, and Maeda Chūmei, for example. These three names will be familiar to anyone of any generation within the national public sphere of Japanese television. But outside of Japan, are there any who would know who these people were, what jobs they held, or the television programs in which they appeared? Hagimoto is a comedian in his sixties; Nakamori is a former idol (*aidoru*) in her thirties; and Maeda is a famous entertainment news reporter in his fifties. The core technique of Nancy Seki's criticism was to capture and satirically poke fun at the moments when the public image of celebrities such as these broke down. For instance, she did not fail to point to the moment when Hagimoto failed to act like a proper show business entertainer (*geinōjin*) at the closing ceremonies of the Olympics. She pointed out the inability of Nakamori to get back her formerly wholesome image after her failed suicide attempt. And when Maeda, who publicly boasted about being the number one reporter in the entertainment world, failed to get the scoop on the wedding of his closest friend and idol—this, too, Nancy Seki would not let slide. However, as I will argue here, Nancy Seki's deep understanding of television's information transmission system also allowed her criticism to dislocate and denaturalize it. What she offered, then, was not a simple caricatured portrait of celebrities but rather, something closer to a metalevel, media theoretical analysis of the phenomenon of TV.

It is difficult to crack the code of these TV personalities as mediatic signs without a deep familiarity with Japan's television culture. Moreover, given that this media network was circumscribed by national boundaries and enclosed within a public space, and given that the signs to which Nancy Seki referred could be consumed only within this space, the power of her critical discourse was also trapped within her country's national boundaries. Nevertheless, is this really a decisive limitation of her criticism? Does it also circumscribe the reach and applicability of the meta-level reflections and the media theory that she develops through her criticism? To respond to these questions, we must first look at the origins of her critical imagination, which, unsurprisingly, are not to be found solely in the national medium of TV. Then we must examine the factors at work in her transformation from Seki Naomi, a female university student from the countryside, into Nancy Seki, the nationally famous eraser print artist, TV critic, and columnist.

Media Crossover City: Tokyo

Nancy Seki failed at her first attempt to pass her university entrance exams and moved to Tokyo in 1981 to attend preparatory school and then retake the exams the following year. It is said that she was seduced by the attractions of the Seibu Department Store in Ikebukuro—which was along the route to her preparatory school—and began going there regularly. To understand why we should not regard this merely as an example of her attempt to satisfy her desires as a consumer requires that we acknowledge the specific social meaning and indeed vibrancy possessed by the Ikebukuro Seibu Department Store in the 1980s. In doing so, we must also touch on the role that the parent company, Seibu Saison, and its particular "Seibu Saison culture," played in creating this vibrancy, as well as the meaning it possesses within the history of urban culture.

The Seibu Saison Group, which was responsible for creating Seibu Saison culture, is, to more precisely define it, "a distribution enterprise that had at its nuclei Credit Saison, Seiyū and Seibu Department Stores."[4] The Seibu Saison Group was in turn divided into Seibu Railway and Seibu Department Stores (its retail distribution unit), each managed by one of the two brothers of the Tsutsumi industrialist family. Tsutsumi Seiji, the older of the two brothers, managed the retail distribution unit, while the younger brother, Tsutsumi Yoshiaki, was responsible for overseeing Seibu Railway. It was Tsutsumi Seiji who planned and developed Seibu Saison culture. Although Yoshiaki was the better industrial manager, Seiji was something of a literary figure who also published many novels and poems under the pseudonym Tsujī Takashi. The two faces of Tsutsumi Seiji—the manager and the artist—were reflected in the development of Seibu Saison culture. During the 1980s and 1990s, the Seibu Saison Group was widely known for supporting artists and organizing different cultural activities.

The Seibu Department Store of Ikebukuro, where Nancy Seki was a regular, included the Seibu Museum within the space of the department store. The museum mostly presented art thought to represent the international artistic avant-garde of the twentieth century, and took on many projects in cooperation with Tokyo's National Museum of Modern Art. In addition to the museum, the Ikebukuro Seibu also had a multifunctional live music venue on its eighth floor, called Studio 2000, which became a center of cultural activities, including film, drama, and dance. Seibu Saison culture also included a variety of establishments, including the edgy record shop WAVE (found in Roppongi, Shibuya, and Ikebukuro), the film theatre Cine Vivant Roppongi, the Ikebukuro bookstore LIBRO, and others too numerous to name. All of these were incredibly influential sources of information on urban and cutting-edge arts. Going to a department store, and particularly to the Seibu Department Store, as Nancy Seki did, was not, therefore, merely an act of satisfying one's desires for commodities; it was rather a means of basking in the shower of information found there. In this department store, Nancy Seki, a newcomer to Tokyo, was exposed to a complex multimedia apparatus creating and diffusing information about the semiotic matrix of urban culture in which she now dwelled.

The information relayed by the Seibu Saison culture was the result of what we might call the crossover of multiple kinds of media. Of course, even before this time, the department store already functioned as a complex and composed cultural medium, but its life as media node was further crystallized by its encounter with the advertising industry. It was the ad industry that remade the department store into an image that could be circulated even further. Central to this transformation was, not surprisingly, the celebrity copywriter Itoi Shigesato, whose fresh sensibility allowed him to leave a permanent mark on the history of Japanese advertising. By 1980, Itoi was in charge of the Seibu Department Store ad copy. In 1981, he came up with the copy "Strange, I love it" (Fushigi, daisuki), and in 1982, he offered up what was later recognized as the number one ad copy in the history of postwar Japanese advertising: "Delicious living" (Oishii seikatsu). These phrases transcended their roles as catchphrases for a department store to become expressions that symbolized an era. They also launched the copywriter boom of the 1980s, during which the advertisement industry came to occupy the center stage of urban culture. During this time, Itoi Shigesato went from being a simple copywriter to becoming a kind of nexus who linked multiple media forms.

In 1980, Itoi took charge of the readers' letters section of the subculture magazine *Bikkuri House*. This section—humorously titled "Good Little Perverts Newspaper" (Hentai yoiko shinbun)—gained passionate young fans; Nancy Seki herself was an enthusiastic reader from her high school days onward, and often sent in letters. It is also at this period that Itoi began associating himself with artists and musicians, often collaborating on lyrics. He became even more renowned between 1982 and 1985, when he hosted YOU, the NHK program for youngsters. Itoi became the vessel for transmitting cutting-edge information even as he actively crossed over multiple media, from advertising to publishing to music and television. One of the representative media celebrities of the 1980s, this copywriter connected music, fashion, theatre, and publishing, dynamizing them all and becoming the very embodiment of Tokyo's vibrant culture at the time.

Let us step back and imagine for a moment the figure of Nancy Seki walking in Ikebukuro Station in 1981. The Seibu Department Store she often visited was directly connected to the station, and the walls and pillars of the station were covered with posters animated by Itoi Shigesato catchphrases. Station kiosks sold magazines and newspapers filled with information. In the museum, she could see art; in the record store, she could catch up on the latest music; and in the bookstore, she could look for the latest publications—all depending on her mood. Riding the train, she could easily get to other cultural hubs in the city, such as Shinjuku, Shibuya, and Roppongi. "Now, I stand at the crossroads of media"—this is likely how Nancy Seki felt in her very body.

Nevertheless, compared to the high-speed movement of the information network in Tokyo, Nancy Seki herself was a "stationary person" (*ugokanai hito*). After a year of studious preparation for the entrance exams, she finally passed them and entered Hosei University. But after a short period in classes, she suddenly stopped going to school, instead staying at home reading books and watching TV. Soon after entering Hosei she left it, choosing instead to go to the vocational school Kokoku Gakkō (literally Advertising Academy). This was a school aimed at training copywriters, run by the magazine *Kōkoku hihyō* (Advertising criticism). The very metamedia existence of a magazine such as *Kokoku hihyo*, which aimed to offer a space for the criticism of advertising, a medium initially meant to simply transmit information, is a testament to the highly developed media environment of 1980s Japan. That said, the Kokoku Gakkō advertising academy, while riding on the popularity of copywriting at the time, can hardly be considered a serious training ground for copywriters given its short length (three months) and the absence of any clear path toward careers. According to Nancy Seki's own recollections, she was not particularly attracted to copywriters or their profession (indeed, she is said to have had a very critical opinion of Itoi Shigesato's catchphrases), and once the program ended, she quickly returned to her lazy life. But the experience at Kokoku Gakkō in fact led to her job as columnist and illustrator.

A friend she met at Kokoku Gakko fell in love with both her eraser print art and her rhetorical abilities, and introduced Nancy to her boyfriend, who was working as a freelancer for magazines. Nancy Seki, an amateur still using her given name (Seki Naomi), took some of her eraser prints to a meeting with her friend's boyfriend, who immediately recognized the originality and unique sensibility of her work, and granted her membership in Shuwac-chi, the freelance writers group he was part of. This was in 1985. From there, Nancy Seki quickly made her name in the publishing industry.

She debuted as an eraser print illustrator in a male fashion and culture magazine called *Hotdog Press*, eventually taking on a series of written columns too. With the help of a number of young writers and editors that she collaborated with, Seki turned out one ambitious and original work after another. From 1988 to 1991 she was the official cover illustrator for the well-established *Music Magazine* (significant because before Nancy Seki, only artists with long illustrious careers had this honor), and from there, she gained societal renown as both a professional artist and a columnist. A girl from the far north of Japan who in 1980, arrived at the intersection of media in Ikebukuro's Seibu Department Store and experienced firsthand the dynamism of Tokyo's multiple media crossovers, Nancy Seki now found herself on the path to the very center of this media environment.

However, it is said that Nancy Seki herself, as well as her close friends who were writers and editors, did not have the sense that her work would continue indefinitely. The very name Nancy Seki was the on-the-spot invention of an editor of *Hotdog Press*, Itō Seikō (who later became a novelist and a celebrity), and Nancy Seki never really got used to it. The whole process of her career, therefore, seemed a mere extension of the playful activities of an amateur young woman looking to do something interesting. Her eraser prints and her very name, Nancy Seki, reflected how Seki was playing the role of a young woman trying to make it big, as if it were a game. This feeling of *play* and the temporal consciousness of *living for the moment* is very closely tied to the general sentiment of 1980s Japan, an atmosphere sustained by economic prosperity and the delicate premonition of life within an economic bubble, with crisis on the horizon. Indeed, at that time the publishing industry was experiencing an era of unprecedented economic vitality, and was in a constant search for young talent. When Nancy Seki began her career as writer and illustrator in 1985, the annual income of the print market was ¥1.7 trillion; it would continue rising until its peak at ¥2.6 trillion in 1996. The scale of the market at the time is clearly different from that of the present, in which the publishing industry has been in a recession for a long time. In this sense, we can say that Nancy Seki timed the start of her career well. The 1980s seemed like a time when anyone who dreamed of making it onto media's shining stage could do so, and Nancy Seki was one of the many people who realized this dream.

Nancy Seki at the Crossroads of Media

Of course, the reality was that things were not that simple; not just anyone could ascend to the media stage, and luck alone was not sufficient to get you there. Nancy Seki had the precious ability to survive the exalted and rapidly changing dynamics of a diverse media environment. But what kind of media environment was Nancy Seki raised in, in which her talents ultimately bore fruit in the form of her television criticism? In this section, I would like to emphasize the fact that even though Seki ended up working in the medium of TV, TV itself was not the only source of her critical imagination. She was raised and lived at the crossroads of media that included radio, magazines, and music, in addition to the medium of television, around which she ultimately focused her critical talents.

Nancy Seki often repeated the story that one of the greatest influences on her was the legendary midnight radio program "Beat Takeshi's All-Night Nippon." Kitano Takeshi is now internationally recognized as a film director, but he got his start as a *manzai* comic actor under the name of Beat Takeshi as part of the two-man manzai team Two Beat.[5] Although Beat Takeshi started in show business's underground, he quickly gained renown as a talented entertainer with devastatingly sharp jokes and a quick delivery style.

"Beat Takeshi's All-Night Nippon" debuted at midnight on New Year's Day in 1981 and aired each Friday from 1 AM to 3 AM. Although today Kitano Takeshi is extremely popular and a key figure on national television, the comedian Beat Takeshi was just starting to gain renown when his radio program kicked off in 1981, riding on the manzai boom of the time. Subsequently, Beat Takeshi's TV appearances also grew more frequent. The radio program continued airing until 1990, during which time it influenced many young creators and gave birth to successors. Nancy Seki was still in high school in Aomori at the time the program started and became a passionate fan. She never missed an episode, and recorded each and every one on tape, continuing this practice even after she became a busy columnist.

Beat Takeshi's assistant host on the show, Takada Fumio, recalls, "'All-Night Nippon' was the radio show that marked a complete transformation of Japanese humor."[6] Through the nationally syndicated but somehow still seemingly underground format of midnight radio, Beat Takeshi developed a unique style of rhythm and humor that diverged from Japan's existing system of repetitive comedy, and thereby extended his influence to all youth in Japan, carving his unique intensity into their hearts. Around that time, increasingly large numbers of regular men started emulating Takeshi's manner of speaking. As for Nancy Seki, her prose exuded Takeshi's influence, and possessed a strange cadence, with colloquialisms suddenly interrupting her text, and sudden bursts of self-criticism, such as "or maybe not" inserted at the end of a long, reasoned argument. Nancy Seki's prose possessed an oral quality that clearly distinguished it from a more academic style of prose; in this aspect alone, we can sense the influence of "Beat Takeshi's All-Night Nippon." Fellow columnist Odajima Takashi recounts his surprise at Nancy Seki's manner of speaking—that she spoke as if raised in downtown Tokyo, just like Kitano Takeshi, rather than in the dialect of her native Aomori.[7] Much like television, the medium of radio reinforced the homogeneity of the Japanese nation with its countrywide network, making it possible for people from Japan's remotest areas to its major city centers to share the same information and the same sense of an era. In this sense, we can say that Nancy Seki's writing style and even her sense of humor were born from the medium of late-night radio as a form of national public sphere.

Another factor that developed Nancy Seki's alternative media sensibility was the proliferation of subcultural magazines on art and culture that emerged at the end of the 1970s. When, in magazine interviews, Nancy Seki was asked what kind of magazines she had read as a high school student, she responded with titles such as *Bikkuri House, Omoshiro hanbun, Goku, Kōkoku hihyō, Studio Voice, Takarajima,* and *Yasō.* These magazines have by now mostly ceased publication, or have downsized, but in the 1980s, they were representative of the subculture boom, and indeed were part of the fringes of the New Academism or Nyū Aka movement (on Nyū Aka, see Alexander Zahlten's essay in this volume). One element common to all of these magazines was their active exclusion of political discourse. From the 1960s through the beginning of the 1970s, the arts influencing youth culture (such as film, theatre, art, and music) were inevitably colored by leftist ideology or leanings; their most commonly shared values can be summed up by the attitude that "to rebel against the established order is cool." However, after the 1973 hostage taking by the Japanese Red Army, known as the Asama Sansō incident (which, incidentally, is remembered as a televisually mediated media event), the social influence of leftist ideology went into a quick and sudden decline. What took its place was an intellectual culture industry—Nyū Aka—and a relatively apolitical subculture, both of which arose against the background of economic prosperity.

In a sense, the cultural industries that were the very basis of the bubble economy's extravagant consumer culture were themselves made possible by the widespread change in values among youth, wherein "being intellectual," "being urban," and "having a mastery over all things media" became the new cool. Of course, by the late 1970s, the number of youth who shared these values was still limited to those cutting-edge young people who were particularly sensitive to these media changes. Nancy Seki recalls that in her hometown, the only person reading these magazines, aside from her, was her best friend. But what should amaze us is that these art and subculture magazines were sold in local bookstores in the countryside, even despite such a limited readership. This fact speaks to the publishing industry's high level of maturity, but also to the delicate weave of a media network capable of distributing even such niche magazines all across Japan. Nevertheless, what we also must conclude from this is that the media apparatus itself was still very much focused on Tokyo, with the concordant centralization of power that this implies. As the epicenter of the diffusion of such information, the publishing industry and media intellectuals located in Tokyo sustained and indeed heightened the mythic representations of Tokyo as an information city. Therefore, moving to Tokyo was a completely natural decision for girls in high school with a highly developed media sensibility, such as Nancy Seki and her friend. They innocently dreamt of going to Tokyo to bathe in the glow of the latest information, to penetrate the media network, and to themselves become the senders and disseminators of information.

In addition to the impact of "Beat Takeshi's All-Night Nippon" and the proliferation of subcultural magazines on art and culture, a third major factor that brought Nancy Seki into this network of media subcultures was music. A particularly strong influence on her in this respect was the electronic music group Yellow Magic Orchestra, or YMO. While the legendary YMO lasted only from 1978 to 1983, in these five years of activity it became a central group in techno and new wave movements at the beginning of the 1980s. One could say that the group's rise constituted a major cultural event that transcended music, fashion, speech, and media. Moreover, it represent an exception in Japanese music as YMO's CDs were released abroad and the group even undertook worldwide tours. YMO was a pioneer in its deliberate crossing of national borders. Even after the group disbanded, the members continued to influence Japanese popular music by creating music for international films or songs for national idols at the height of their careers.

But how did Nancy Seki come upon this cutting-edge music? We get a glimpse in her recollection of how she spent her time after school let out: "During high school my behavior was pretty much determined. First thing after school ended, I went to a bookstore with my friends. After two hours spent there we went to the nearest electronic shop, sat on bicycle seats and watched videos of YMO concerts. Then after that we'd go to a record shop, but couldn't buy anything 'cause we didn't have any money."[8]

With this testimony, we can see the media environment in which Nancy Seki was ingesting information before her move to Tokyo. She was always going to places that were part of a public space with access to the national media network, such as bookstores, electronic shops, TV and record shops, and so on. From the different information and signs lined up as commodities before her, she chose the most subcultural and cutting-edge elements, and burned them into her eyes and ears, even without buying them. This practice of absorbing information—quite similar to hunting—allowed her to transform even such mainstream devices as the television set into a transmitter of subcultural signs such as YMO. Could the sharpening of her ability to dissect and absorb semiotic information have been the educational process that ultimately trained her eyes to see the truth of TV that everyone can see but no one actually notices?

Here I want to highlight again the fact that, although Nancy Seki made her worksite the national TV network that united Japan as a nation, her manner of absorbing information allowed her to feed on underground or alternative media. The information she collected was far from the mainstream of so-called national culture. This ability to "read obliquely" no doubt allowed her to develop her highly perceptive media sensibility. Nevertheless, we can also see that within the media environment of the 1970s and 1980s, this cutting-edge subcultural information was itself part of the national media network, and was concentrated in the privileged center called Tokyo. Perhaps, then, Nancy Seki's true talent as a television critic was to put herself at the crossroads of multiple media. From this place, she resisted the power of mainstream media to unify the nation, and from within the high volume flow of information and signs, she found for herself a uniquely contrarian and nondominant perspective.

Furthermore, given that Nancy Seki was one of the rare women who had succeeded in establishing her position as a "female critic" in a male-dominated, masculinist discursive space, there is a need to consider her identity from the point of view of gender theory. In many senses, Seki was not a person who could easily be characterized as an "ordinary woman." Perhaps what most made her a rather exceptional woman in Japan at the time was her large figure, which became the basis of her public image. Although she was of average weight as a young child, in her fourth year of elementary school, she suddenly gained a considerable amount of weight. As a precaution, she was checked by the hospital, but was diagnosed as healthy, albeit heavyset. While obesity could have been a sensitive problem for a girl during adolescence, Seki was not bullied at school. That said, I do think that her physical size did have a significant impact on the formation of her personality.

In a three-way conversation published in 2000 in the gay magazine *Queer Japan* (*Kuia Japan*) that included editor Fushimi Noriaki and Matsuko Deluxe (now an immensely popular female cross-dressing TV personality known for her cynical manner of speaking, who was, at that time, the editor of another gay magazine), Nancy Seki rather surprisingly discussed her own physique and sexuality.[9] The apparent reason she was asked to participate in the dialogue was that Fushimi was under the misconception that she was bisexual—a label Nancy Seki dismissed. Nevertheless, Fushimi persisted; he sensed something "queer" about her style, to which Seki responded that from her childhood on, she had always considered herself a "nonstandard" person, someone who did not make the same choices as other girls (who always wanted to have the same hairstyle as pop stars or idols). This was not because she was troubled, she emphasized, but simply because she positioned herself differently. In fact, one might suggest that Nancy Seki's consciousness of herself as "nonstandard" in relation to the majority of girls may have been the basis from which she developed her critical wherewithal for deciphering media from an oblique point of view. When this nonconformist attitude is thought from within the frame of sexuality, "queer" may indeed be the most suitable category to describe her.

Indeed, Nancy Seki's critical texts and logically constructed thinking present some nonbinary or genderqueer elements. According to numerous testimonies, many of Seki's readers thought that she was a man because of her style. Of course, this very reception reflects the gendered categorization of discourse itself, wherein well-structured texts and critical thinking are labeled as "masculine" in style. But as a persona, Nancy Seki was not described as a scornful masculine figure, but rather as a delicate and thoughtful woman, or even as an intimate older sister. Even as she maneuvered within the gender stereotypes of queer or masculine styles of speech at the discursive level, Nancy Seki cannot be inserted into the heteronormative dichotomy of male or female. In other words, Nancy Seki was a woman who, unlike other women, did not need to participate in the heterosexual model of gender politics, nor did she feel that becoming the object of male sexual desire was the necessary condition for the formation of her gender identity. While fleeing from the pressure of compulsory heterosexuality, she nonetheless maintained her "femininity." This rather exceptional, antiestablishment gender identity (within the context of Japanese media) enabled her to have a panoramic view of the decadent media market, and of TV in particular, where the commodification of sex was on full display. By developing her unorthodox "sexuality," Nancy Seki was in turn able to see sexuality objectively as a sign that is culturally constructed by power.

Facial Supremacism and the Elements of Nancy Seki's Critical Practice

We can trace the origins of Nancy Seki's turn to TV as an object of criticism to her series of columns in the magazine *Uwasa no shinsō* (The truth about rumors), which debuted in the May 1990 issue and continued until her death. Nancy Seki's column started as a short text, without the eraser print illustrations, but ended up as one of the most emblematic and widely read columns in the magazine. *Uwasa no shinsō* was a scandal magazine that published articles about celebrities without regard for their truth or falsity. Yet it was also a magazine put together by an anarchic and antiauthoritarian editorial team that was unique in the publishing industry. This extremely subcultural magazine matched perfectly with Nancy's bold and sharp style of criticism. A year and a half after its start, Nancy Seki's column was renamed "Meikyū no hanasono" (The flower garden labyrinth), becoming a full page in length and featuring an eraser print image. The reason for the expansion of Nancy Seki's column was the release of her first book and the serialization of some of her works in other major magazines. In other words, she started to become famous.

A year later, the title of Nancy Seki's popular column changed again, this time to "Ganmen shijōshugi" (Facial supremacism), and remained in this form for the next ten years or so. Seki would later explain the meaning of the peculiar title—which she claimed expressed her basic stance on TV itself—in the following terms: "Facial Supremacism is based around the motto that 'the human is the face,' and centered on the principle that humans can be judged on their face alone." "You can only see what is to be seen," she continued. "But if you look close enough, you can break through to their inner truth. That is Facial Supremacism."[10] Seki refuses the conventional attitude of the TV viewer who decodes the information or meaning inside or beneath the television image. Instead, she focuses her attention squarely on the image alone, seeking to discover a meaning other than the official one. In other words, she relates to the TV not as a preconstructed viewer or receiver (*ukete*) but rather as a critical reader (*yomite*). This was the crux of Seki's TV criticism, and for this reason I would like to highlight the merits of her focus on the surface of images transmitted through the TV set.

The face is the extreme condensation of a person, the very proof of existence. To find the distortions and gaps, the conflicts and excesses in the face (which acts as the ostensible guarantee of the self-sameness of the person), is to look beyond the semantic meaning transmitted by the medium of television, and to expose the failures in the structure of signification itself. This is an extremely risky activity. But Seki put her work decoding the surface of the image into practice in the form of her eraser print illustrations of the facial images of the TV personalities who were the objects of her criticism. In these illustrations of faces that she reconstructed through the filter of her critical eye, she revealed what "everything anyone could see but failed to notice." In 1993, in recognition of her penetrating criticism, Seki was given two new series of TV columns and became a nationally famous columnist. The first column was "Komimi ni hasamō" (Let's overhear it), for the major weekly *Shūkan Asahi*, and the second was "Nancy Seki no terebi shōtō jikan" (Nancy Seki's TV curfew time) in another national weekly magazine, *Shūkan Bunshun*. These serial columns were her first weekly column series, and she would not miss a submission until her death in 2002.

Many people tend to elevate Nancy Seki's prose criticism over her eraser prints that accompanied it. However, this article takes the opposite stance. Of course, her texts were of fine quality both as sharp social criticism and as entertaining reads. However, it was her adoption of the unique eraser print form that was most indispensable; it was these prints that allowed her work to transcend the status of a mere cultural commodity circulating within the publishing industry and become the true scalpel for taking apart and analyzing the TV medium. Nancy Seki used her unique eraser prints as a knife blade to extract and put on display alternative interpretations of an original image that appeared within the real-time flow of images that is television (ostensibly a medium for transmitting information and meaning via images). Below, I would like to examine the most notable features of Nancy Seki's criticism, focusing especially on her unique combination of text with eraser print image.

The first notable feature of Nancy Seki's criticism that she herself emphasized is the fact that almost all of the images of TV personalities engraved in her eraser prints are of faces. As I've already noted, her TV criticism was in principle the *criticism of TV personalities*, and is hence full of personal names difficult to decode without sharing the same contemporaneous media environment. In the case of the TV medium, TV personalities are all given a sort of semantic meaning as an image and are asked to play their role in accordance with this meaning. Personalities are reduced to a sign designating a proper name that slowly takes the place of their real identities. In the case of the structure of television as a medium, the corporeality of TV personalities is reduced to the mere image of their face, appearing on the screen. There the very proof of existence of a personality is found in their proper name, and its image equivalent, a face. However, Nancy Seki takes this proof of the existence of the television personality—their face—and transforms it into the reproducible medium of the eraser print.

The face of public personalities as altered by the clunky lines of the cheap medium of the eraser print revealed that their televisual images were merely commodities of mass consumption operated on and reproduced by TV, far removed from that personality's material existence. Moreover, this medium into which their faces were recoded and carved is the rubber eraser—the very instrument made to *erase* images and words. Here we should recall that Nancy Seki referred to her eraser print engravings as her *hanko* or "seal." In Japan, one's *hanko* seal is used in place of one's signature, as the proof of the very existence of a person, proxies of a being who leaves no handwritten trace. Indeed, even the artisanal technique of grinding ink to stone in preparation for the creation of a print is absented from the *hanko* seal process, which uses an industrially produced ink-pad instead.

The method whereby Nancy Seki replaces the image of a TV personality with a reproducible printed image which in turn becomes a commodity consumed on the market has much in common with the method of pop art. In fact, for her 1996 exhibition, "Ganmen Hyakkaten" (Department Store of Faces), she displayed several plastic works which are reminiscent of pop art practice. For example, she recovered a Lichtenstein-like picture of a blonde beauty with the face of the B-level celebrity Mickey Yasukawa, made an upper body print of TV personality and musician Ono Yasushi and covered the entire door of a white refrigerator with it, printed a white wedding dress with a pattern made from the face of *enka* singer Suizenji Kiyoko, and so on. On the one hand, these works disclose the fact that the existence of a TV personality is reduced to his or her face and, as such, is quite similar to ready-made commodities that are merely reproduced and consumed. On the other hand, we can also see how close to pop art she was as she disrupted the meaning of those images as commodities by breaking the direct relationship between face and proper name. That said, making artwork was never the main focus of Nancy Seki's practice. For her, even the most subversive pop art creation ended up becoming a form of authority and commodity at the moment it was endowed with artistic value—thereby becoming the butt of her jokes and criticism. Most damningly, the moment artworks became art *objects* they fell off the stage of the present-tense media environment that was her real object of interest.

Nancy Seki was, then, not a capital "A" "Artist," but rather something of a *performer* who participated in the media network herself, functioning as an agent for sending and receiving information within this system. She pinpointed the real essence of TV personalities as a *semiotic commodity of the TV medium* and grasped the reproduction of their existence in the equation "face=proper noun." But rather than stopping there—or perhaps producing stand-alone artworks based on that formula—she re-imaged these celebrities through the ironic reproductive technique of the eraser print, and circulated these revised images in the high-speed medium of the weekly magazine. This method demonstrates her highly attuned media sensibility and literacy.

The second major feature of Nancy Seki's criticism is to be found in the critical attitude she manifests in her very reproduction of faces through her eraser print technique. The delicately if purposefully deformed traits of the face capture the moment of a semantic gap or rupture within a TV personality's public persona, effectively introducing a contradiction between public image and eraser print image. In addition, the short line appended to the image of the face discloses that the image is not merely a reproduction of the existence of the person her/himself, but rather its reconstruction from a critical perspective. As an example of this, let us look at her treatment of Guts Ishimatsu (born Suzuki Yūji), the legendary professional boxer who became a TV personality, and later a congressman.

The face of Guts Ishimatsu is depicted in a small square frame, with the face just a little too big for the frame. With only a small gap separating the image and text, we find the line: "Congressman Guts" (Gattsu daigishi). The accompanying prose text functions as a sort of comical commentary destroying the strong image of the face: "Guts Ishimatsu—there are no other 'idiots' for whom so many people have such high expectations." After succeeding as a professional boxer, Guts Ishimatsu achieved public notoriety with his unique, comedic speech and behavior, graduating to a career as a TV personality. For the media, his semantic meaning was "a strong person who isn't so smart, but who does and says funny things." Yet, this very person who was semantically marked as an idiot on TV became a congressman in the political field. Of course, this move into politics was not fully his idea; this career development was nothing but a political strategy to use his popularity. However, Nancy did not leave this paradox unseen. Her illustration of the face of Guts Ishimatsu drew on his persona on television as strong but familiar, recalling the image of him as an "interesting man lacking common sense." Against this common image of his televisual personality she juxtaposed his nominal identity: "Congressman Guts." The gaps and contradictions raised by this juxtaposition lead to multiple questions: Why would a known unintelligent character like Guts Ishimatsu take on the serious job of being a congressman? Is the combination of the name "Guts" with the occupation "congressman" itself nothing more than an antinomy (though of course an antinomy that would no doubt draw laughs from people)? In the face of this antinomy, Nancy combines a humorous text with the image, easing the anxiety caused by this apparent incongruity, and finding the truth within this contradiction—even as she sublimates criticism into entertainment. In other words, she did not directly mock Guts Ishimatsu's entry into politics, but rather showed that what general audiences still expected from him was not a political program, but rather the televisually habituated semantic meaning of Guts as the unintelligent TV personality. In the succinct yet humorous lines of the text, she also shows her discomfort and critical consciousness about the political exploitation of a TV personality in this manner.

Nancy Seki's TV criticism is hence composed of three distinct yet co-constituting elements: the image made with her eraser print technique, the brief one-liner engraved below the print, and the critical text on the personality. Her criticism demands that her readers move back and forth between the three elements; as such, it operates as a lesson that teaches readers the media literacy required to analyze the medium of TV, allowing them to interrupt for a moment the present-tense and unilateral flow of televisual images. Moreover, her engagement with both image and text equally in turn highlights the materiality of language itself—a materiality normally obscured in the supposedly transparent transmission of information in the medium of the magazine. To summarize, Nancy Seki's TV criticism on the one hand was a media practice based on the evaluation of TV personalities. On the other hand, her criticism interrogated the mediality of words and images themselves; it disrupted the natural power difference between words and images, and gestured at the materiality of both words and images that was normally hidden under the expectation of the transparent transmission of information or meaning.

The third feature of Nancy Seki's TV criticism was her humorous manner of revealing the TV personality as a commodity, and of deconstructing TV as a media market informed by the logic of capitalism. The short lines inscribed either alongside the face of a TV personality on the eraser print, or as the title of the column that week, were arresting in their amusing phrasing and the condensed meanings hidden within. In this sense, these one-liners recall the advertising copy writing practices that are the symbol of consumer culture, and the origins of Nancy Seki's career as a writer. But in the case of her eraser print one-liners, they do not function to illuminate the TV personality as a commodity (as an ad copy would). On the contrary, the one-liners strip away the aura attached to the popular facial image, and uncover the true nature of the TV personality as a media commodity concealed under a smooth and decorated appearance. Let us take a look at the following line as an example: "Male nipples also earn money; the true equality of the sexes is close."[11]

This cheeky line is the title of the July 1997 edition of her serial column "TV Curfew Time" for *Shūkan Bunshun*. Few people could guess the topic of this column from its peculiar title. By borrowing the vocabulary of orthodox feminism ("the true equality of the sexes"), Nancy Seki sarcastically demonstrates the extent of the market's commodification of sexuality with the unexpected twist that "male nipples" too earn money, inverting ordinary male/female gender roles. The line is remarkable for its rhetorical ability to surprise readers even as it brings smiles to their faces. In fact, this particular column happens to be about the TV drama *Beach Boys* (*Bīchi bōizu*), which featured two popular male actors in the leading roles. The commodity value of this drama as a TV program was surely the sexual attractiveness of the two main actors, as well as the fashionable setting and subject. The "Monday 9 PM" slot of the Fuji TV station is known even now as the slot with the potentially highest ratings, in which celebrities at the height of their renown appear. Seki took the male nipple element from this prestigious Monday 9 PM drama and introduced it into a classical feminist frame of reference, destroying the image of the TV drama, which was supposed to be consumed for its "stylishness," and exposing instead how it was simply being sold as a sexual commodity created by a media market selling signs of male sexiness.

The eraser print put alongside this critical text was not of the two main actors but of a young male assistant of the nationally popular variety program *Waratte iitomo!* (It's okay to laugh!). Seki described this famously incompetent young assistant—known for his inability to perform his job—as "revolutionary," suggesting that he was "a man operating within the same patterns as a woman."[12] Before this young assistant's appearance, only female celebrities existed on air solely because of their value as sexual objects in the media commodity market. The rise of this man who was clearly "incapable of doing anything" was for Seki a signal that now men, too, had become sexual commodities. Hence, she treated the image of the incompetent assistant for *Waratte iitomo!* as the effective equivalent of the popular male actors playing the leading roles in the mainstream TV drama *Beach Boys*, heightening the irony by adding her catchy tag line, "Male nipples also earn money; the true equality of the sexes is close." By adopting this ironical critical strategy in her column, which then itself circulated as a commodity through the medium of the magazine, Nancy Seki inverted the commodity flow of the TV medium and adopted a critical method that satirically commented on the commodification of sex within media capitalism. In other words, she deployed "parody" as a critical method against the logic of media capitalism.

The fourth feature of Nancy Seki's TV criticism is what we might call her ethical attitude toward the TV medium. For Seki, TV personalities existed as "signs" within a semantic network generated by the TV medium; their labor was to play the roles assigned to them by their semiotic markers, and this in turn was the basis on which they received their wages and compensation. Nancy Seki presented these facts as self-evident truths within a TV medium manipulated by the system of capitalism (that the foundation of the TV industry was its cozy relationship with big business had become apparent to all by the late 1980s), and she herself operated with an awareness of this in mind:

> To me the term "show business" [*geinōkai*] is almost synonymous with TV itself. For me, TV is my lens to look at entertainment. But the major difference between TV and show business lies in the fact that no one could survive only by their work in show business (we often hear people calling themselves entertainers [*geinōjin*], but in fact only a handful can survive as entertainers alone). Most entertainers can only put food on the table by being on TV. The moment the entertainer appears on television, no matter what they may be doing, they are in fact laboring; this is what they look like when they are "making money." Of course,

the cost of their performances differs greatly from one entertainer to another and it is hard to say how much they can actually "live" on this activity. What we can say for sure is as soon as they appear on TV they are making money.[13]

This passage is taken from an article in which Seki discusses a volleyball player become TV personality, Kawai Shun'ichi. Kawai was given the semantic meaning of "someone who can't do anything" or simply "a uselessly tall person" on TV. However, while Kawai is not doing anything to merit the term "labor" in its traditional sense, Seki uses this column to think more broadly about what she terms "Kawai Shun'ichi–style labor."[14] To analyze this further, she chooses to focus on a scene that occurred during a midnight talk show program. There, Kawai, who had just returned from his honeymoon, introduced his bride and handed over a Gucci bag as a souvenir to the talk show host Wada Akiko, who had a higher position than Kawai within show business and in the semantic arrangement of the TV medium. In return, Wada surprised him with a wedding-cake-cutting ceremony during the show. Nancy Seki opines, "This scene between a powerful figure of the industry and a person living under her umbrella should be a private scene. It is only an everyday life situation."[15]

Nancy Seki was outraged by the fact that TV had either abandoned its original mission of creating entertainment, or had lost its power to do so. This scene was proof that the barrier that was supposed to exist between the entertainment industry and everyday life—and that *should* have existed— had fully collapsed, and that exposing everyday life had itself become a form of "labor." As a side note, we might recall that this scene comes at a particular moment within the history of Japanese TV sketched above. After its popularization (or nationalization) in the 1960s, its maturation in the 1970s as a self-referential medium, and its saturation in the 1980s, by the 1990s, with the end of the bubble economy, Japanese TV had already passed its peak. It goes without saying that it was during this moment of contraction, when TV no longer possessed its former power of attraction, that Seki was writing her TV criticism. And yet, even in this period of stagnation, Nancy Seki continued to develop her critical attitude toward TV as a medium. The eraser print next to the text was a portrait of Kawai Shun'ichi: an average man, an everyman, without any special characteristics. And yet, without doubt, it also resembled Kawai. Instead of emphasizing Kawai's uniqueness, then, this eraser print image emphasized "mediocrity" as the most prominent feature of Kawai as a TV personality, demonstrating the vagueness of the sign called

"Kawai Shun'ichi." Moreover, when this vague image is put alongside the critical column that interrogates the ambiguity of the contours of Kawai as a sign, the eraser print image becomes like a knife blade that cuts through the increasing laziness and corruption of the TV medium. Beside Kawai's portrait we can read the short phrase "Akko-saaan (the nickname of Wada Akiko)," recalling Kawai's spoiled tone of voice. Tagline, eraser print image, and critical text together offer a bracing and clear critique of the unethical stance of the TV industry that so easily and cheaply commodifies and circulates the everyday life of its celebrities.

Conclusion

In this article, I have attempted to present and analyze the activities of the eraser print artist, TV critic, and columnist Nancy Seki, outlining the unique and novel perspective she developed principally in her work as a magazine columnist. Early on, Seki made the national medium of TV the focus of her critical work. The effectivity and reach of Seki's criticism was arguably circumscribed by the enclosure of Japanese television within its national boundaries, constituting as it did a very *national* public sphere. Nancy Seki's work, as we have seen above, overflows with proper names and signs that are arguably understood only within the Japanese context. But was Seki really just limited to the medium of TV? When we examine the process that led to her becoming a critic, or indeed the process of her identity formation before she arrived in the media city of Tokyo, we see clearly that she herself was not enclosed by the centralizing medium of television. Rather, she fostered and sharpened her unique media sensibility at something of a media crossroads that included music and radio, magazines and department stores. More important still, the media Nancy Seki fed on in her adolescence was anything but mainstream; rather, she grew up on alternative and subcultural media forms. On the one hand, her ability to access this subcultural media without regard for whether she was in the metropolis or in the countryside was a testament to the maturity of Japan's media network; on the other, we can also see that this network had the political effects of homogenizing national media space and centralizing power.

Within the transformative moment of this media space, around the years 1979 to 1980, Seki put herself at the center of its increasingly rapid stream of information, and started to distinguish herself as an illustrator and, later, as a columnist. The main battlefield, which she ultimately made her own, was, of course, television criticism. That said, her finely sharpened style of prose, combined with her unique eraser print images, allowed her to avoid being subsumed by the national medium of TV. Instead, Nancy Seki was able to see through the semiotic meanings of the people who appeared on TV, to reverse and make inoperative the information and meanings transmitted by television, and ultimately to critique the very nature of television as a medium. In so doing, the proper names and the facial images that were the objects of her criticism became mere signs cut off from the physical existence of the real TV celebrities themselves, and Nancy Seki analyzed them from within the perspective of the media network. In other words, despite appearing to take proper names and people as her objects, Seki's TV criticism in fact cut the singularity out of proper names, showing how they operated as signs within the medium of television, and thereby exposing the truth of media as an information market. For this reason, in answer to the question as to whether Nancy Seki's TV criticism was by definition limited to the TV media space as a national public sphere, I believe this essay has shown it is not. The object of Seki's criticism was not the singularity of the names of individual TV personalities, but rather the very structure of the media as an information network. For this reason, regardless of whether or not one was an avid TV viewer, one could find pleasure in Nancy Seki's TV criticism—at least so long as one is interested in the politics and principles behind the media network and the information circulated within it. Conversely, when this manner of critical reception became increasingly required during the decade of the 1990s, we can say that Nancy Seki's criticism performed a pedagogical function by showing the possibility of "unorthodox" readings. In a word, her critical texts were lessons in how to look at and read things from another perspective.

Nancy Seki's good friend and interlocutor, the ethnographer Ōtsuki Takahiro, put it best when he said, "Always keep Nancy in one's heart."[16] This phrase asks us to relativize our own thoughts and to develop our capacity to critique—our self-reflexivity—all the while keeping ourselves in the middle of the maelstrom of information flowing through the media network. Indeed, Nancy Seki was the driving force behind the type of critical imagination that everyone needs in this media society. We have yet to see another critic of her stature.

NOTES

1. Jürgen Habermas, *The Structural Transformation of the Public Sphere: An Inquiry into a Category of Bourgeois Society*, trans. Thomas Burger with Frederick Lawrence (Cambridge, MA: MIT Press, 1991), 27.

2. Habermas, *Structural Transformation*, 19.

3. Hannah Arendt, *Human Condition*, 46.

4. "Saison Gurupu," *Wikipedia*, accessed July 16, 2016.

5. *Manzai* is a type of Japanese stand-up comedy, usually involving two comics having a humorous conversation.

6. Yokoda Masuo, *Hyōden Nancy Seki: "Kokoro ni hitori no Nancy wo"* [A critical biography of Nancy Seki: "Always keep Nancy in one's heart"] (Tokyo: Asahi Bunko, 2014), 102.

7. Yokoda, *Hyōden Nancy Seki,* 102.

8. Nancy Seki and Ōtsuki Takahiro, *Jigoku de Hotoke* [Like meeting my saviour in Hell] (Tokyo: Asahi Bunko, 1999), 209.

9. "Kuia Japan, tokushū: Miwaku no busu," in "Alluringly Ugly," special issue, *Kuia Japan* [Queer Japan] 3 (October 2000).

10. Nancy Seki, *Nani wo ima sara* [What do you want now?] (Tokyo: Kadokawa Bunko, 1999), 26.

11. Nancy Seki, "Otoko no chikubi ga kane ni natte, shin no danjo byōdō wa chikai" [Male nipples also earn money; the true equality of the sexes is close], *Shūkan Bunshūn*, July 1997; reprinted in Nancy Seki, *Terebi shōtō jikan 2* (Tokyo: Bunshu Bunko, 2000), 24–27.

12. Seki, *Terebi shōtō jikan 2*, 25.

13. Nancy Seki, "Kawai Shun'ichi wa ikiteiru koto ga sunawachi rōdō de aru" [Kawai Shun'ichi's very act of being alive is labor], in *Terebi shōtō jikan 2*, 2000), 53.

14. Seki, *Terebi shōtō jikan 2*, 54.

15. Seki, *Terebi shōtō jikan 2*, 55.

16. Seki and Ōtsuki, *Jigoku de Hotoke*, 310.

10. AT THE SOURCE (CODE)

Obscenity and Modularity in
Rokudenashiko's Media Activism

ANNE MCKNIGHT

Timeline

June 30, 2012	*Decoman* manga published
June 18, 2013	Crowd-funding campaign for "man-boat" begins; ends September 6
July 12, 2014	First arrest
July 18, 2014	Released on bail
March 2014	Launch of "man-boat"
December 3, 2014	Second arrest
December 26, 2014	Released on bail
April 3, 2015	*What Is Obscenity?* (ワイセツって何ですか？) published
April 14, 2015	Trial begins in Tokyo District Court
May 20, 2015	*My Body Is Obscene?!: Why Is Only My Lady Part Taboo?* (私の体がワイセツ？女のそこだけなぜタブー) published

| February 1, 2016 | Prosecutor states intent to seek fine of eight hundred thousand yen but no prison term |
| May 8, 2016 | Tokyo District Court hands down mixed verdict. A four hundred thousand-yen fine is imposed for distributing 3-D printer data over the Internet, but Rokudenashiko is acquitted on charges from the July 2014 gallery arrest of "displaying obscene materials publicly." Rokudenashiko and her team vow to appeal |

The Source of Activism

On a fine spring day in March 2014, the artist Rokudenashiko, known legally as Igarashi Megumi, set sail on a voyage down the Tamagawa River, a major waterway that empties into Tokyo Bay, where it connects to the open seas.[1] The boat was featured in later news reports not only for its cute rubber-ducky look and handcrafted aesthetic; more notoriously, Rokudenashiko's voyage down the Tamagawa River ultimately landed her in jail and on trial for obscenity. This innocuous-looking boat and other works of DIY sculpture provoked two arrests at the same time that the media splash over the artist's works, many of which were confiscated by police along with her computer, launched Rokudenashiko into coverage in the news, in flagship journals of music and art criticism, and even in mainstream women's magazines and blogs, where response has been even more supportive outside Japan than inside.

While Rokudenashiko's works provoked outsized reactions in Japan, at the same time, awareness of her trial plugged her into a global cohort of artists that includes iconic Chinese dissident Ai Weiwei. Following Rokudenashiko's June 2015 visit to Beijing to meet Ai, an exhibition of her work took place in Hong Kong in the fall of 2015 with the aim of "thinking feminism via the works of artists from Japan and Hong Kong."[2] The show featured contributions from the internationally known contemporary artists Aida Makoto and Sputniko!. News of Rokudenashiko's arrest and trial has been the subject of a documentary feature on *Vice* magazine's new women-geared channel Broadly, and the technorati blog *Boing Boing* posted its related story, written by editor in chief Mark Frauenfelder, under the tags "art," "censorship," "hypocrisy," and "war on women."[3]

Rokudenashiko's arrest conferred on her the honor of being the first woman in Japanese history tried on grounds of obscenity as spelled out in

[FIG. 10.1] Rokudenashiko stands by her "man-boat" kayak, whose top attachment was modeled on her vulva, on the banks of the Tamagawa River. Photograph by Taishiro Sakurai.

Article 175 of the Criminal Code of Japan.[4] The trial began in April 2015 and served as a venue for Rokudenashiko to challenge a double standard that judges the representation of women's bodies in starkly different terms than that of male bodies.[5] Rokudenashiko's works link to existing lines of feminist art that employ new media, challenge the sexual politics of the art world in their crafting of digital cultural forms, and create a persona for activism based on humor and the customization of mass cultural forms via craft.

In the following sections, I map the legal case against Rokudenashiko as Megumi Igarashi. Then I turn to explore the formal composition of two types of works, figures and dioramas, and the processes of their making as prototypes of modular aesthetics. Finally, I situate Rokudenashiko's work in the broader context of cute aesthetics and show how she uses modular forms to engage with processes of everyday life, not only suggesting critique but modeling alternatives to the fantastically plastic ways that women's bodies are imagined under Abenomics. This set of policies typically presented as a salve to a national crisis of degrowth imagines women to be available for any and all jobs at hand, from care giving for the elderly, to child rearing, to upward climbs through the glass ceiling of corporate life.[6]

This chapter argues that the aesthetic of Rokudenashiko's DIY projects—which I call modular aesthetics—is a powerful case of speculative design with resonance in Japan as well as in transnational fields of digital and craft-based art. Though her media—which include sculpture, dioramas, and figures—replicate parts of the body that are often sexualized, the works themselves are not about eroticizing those body parts. Bawdy, meticulously crafted, and funny, Rokudenashiko's sculpture work draws on the traditionally low tones of art found in craft to offer media theory an invitation to "low theory." "Low theory," in McKenzie Wark's turn of phrase, is an attempt to connect ideas with life processes using what he calls "the labor point of view," with an eye to the infrastructures and collaborations that connect the art work to the cultural work.[7] In this case, the lowness comes in the common or mass-produced materials as well as the perceived vulgarity of subject matter. The kayak is made of a customized insert attached to a mass-produced base; the dioramas are meticulously handcrafted with art materials and found objects on top of an alginate cast; and the figures are cast from plastic. Rokudenashiko's low-theory use of new media forms in the digital age poses questions about how material (usually female) bodies might be meaningful beyond ways they are conventionally morcellized and sexualized in a commodity-based market of images.

Rokudenashiko's use of her own body as a raw material for dematerialized art making is a call for a return to experience, to grasping how one's own body can be understood in the same terms as other media—specifically other plastic media. The question of how a body might be a medium and its experiences revalued in a better future is characteristic of the field of speculative design, a field that according to Anthony Dunne and Fiona Raby is guided by

> the idea of possible futures and using them as tools to better understand the present and to discuss the kind of future people want, and, of course, ones people do not want. The[se projects] usually take the form of scenarios, often starting with a what-if question, and are intended to open up spaces of debate and discussion; therefore, they are by necessity provocative, intentionally simplified, and fictional. Their fictional nature requires viewers to suspend their disbelief and allow their imaginations to wander, to momentarily forget how things are now, and wonder about how things could be.[8]

In both small plastic sculptures and digitally produced 3-D-printed objects, Rokudenashiko's body is presented as just such a "necessity provocative, intentionally simplified, and fictional" prototype that imagines such better futures beyond the tired tits-and-eyes images, pixelated genitals, and fetishized body elements seen in commercial representations of the female body that overvalue parts (breasts, genitals, etc.) at the expense of not only a whole but of any other context or value. In the words of the digital historians Alan Galey and Stan Ruecker, one goal of the prototype designer "has been deliberately to carry out an interpretive act in the course of producing an artifact."[9] In this case, interpretation comes from the speculative questions that arise from interpreting the artifact of the female body as something resignifiable, whose meaning may shift into new narratives—not guaranteed to be better in terms of female power, but at least different, with potential. What if your body were just another surface or backdrop—like a rolling lawn, the moon, or a golf course? Would you disappear into the background like camouflage? Or would you be framed into another narrative? Or made meaningful as a stand-alone entity in another way entirely?

Rokudenashiko calls her works *manko*—named for the vulgar word for "vulva," or, more generally, the ensemble of her external genital nether areas (the word in Japanese is pronounced MAHN-ko). Her "man-boat" (see fig. 10.1), is thus a kayak with one part modeled on a representation of her vulva (her English translator translates this word as "pussy," perhaps in tribute to the feminist art activist group Pussy Riot, or perhaps simply to claim ownership of the "dirty" word). Rokudenashiko claims this boat is a work of art rather than a pornographic image, a creative object that interprets but departs from reality because it lacks realist details such as hair, and not a reproduction that can be judged obscene on the basis of verisimilitude. The term "art" is important in a legal sense because realism is typically judged as being closer to obscenity. Still, the word "manko" itself is controversial and has the signifying power of undiluted reality despite its rather blurry, personal, and idiosyncratic definition for each person. The word is rarely printed in Japanese without *fuseji*, marks that block out characters to obscure their meaning.

While print censorship literally blocks out parts that represent the female body, Rokudenashiko's art has drawn attention to the fixation on defining sexuality via one body part by developing an entire aesthetic out of the modular unit of the manko and its plastic boundaries. She uses the manko as a surface, ground, and platform for plastic arts and reconnects this blurrily defined body part to other processes by which women's bodies are valued. Rokudenashiko makes the process of prototyping the centerpiece of both her creative work and the basis of her representation of the legal system in her manga and a range of other media forms. By challenging the idea that a woman's body is a medium for promoting national economic growth using artistic forms that rely on digital materialities, she extends the feminist critiques of women's relation to property that began in the 1970s.

Contexts: Materials and Fighting Words

Rokudenashiko was indicted for three separate counts of violating Article 175 of the criminal code, the main basis for regulating obscenity in postwar Japan. Her boat is a product of the most exuberant element of her art—modeling parts of her sculptures on her own vulva. Rokudenashiko makes art in character, sculptures that are accompanied by extensive textual apparatuses that contextualize modular elements of the story. For example, the manko theme reappears in her manga, as well as in her figures and stickers. Her aim is to not only critique but defamiliarize or render impossible the fetishization of women's bodies that both reduces the freedom of their own expression and which accrues a different value than, in contrast, fetishized male organs and the powers they underwrite. While visitors flock to phallus festivals celebrated by city fathers and judged as "tradition" and "folkloric tradition," bringing sought-after tourist dollars to rural areas, the art lovers who seek out Rokudenashiko's work are testimony of its "social danger," which is prosecutable under Article 175.[10] A two-part exhibition of *shunga*, Edo-period erotic art, was held at the Eisei Bunko Museum in 2015. Many male and female bodies were ravished and lavished with erotic attention and graphically drawn sexual organs that are arguably more provocative than the vulva of Rokudenashiko's art.

The provocation and ultimately the cultural work of this project lies in Rokudenashiko's treatment of her own body as a digital prototype that can be dematerialized into a mass of code, exchanged, transformed, and customized in myriad open-ended directions by users in their own time, in their own place. Rokudenashiko's works—whether 3-D kayak, figure, handheld sculpture, or sticker—are all portable and available to be customized in their possessor's settings. While Rokudenashiko labors, she does not present herself as a "worker." She appears publicly in character; it is only newspaper scolds and law enforcement officers who use her legal name to define her as a public figure. She wears a wig, uses the "pen name," and has a militantly cheerful attitude. We can read Rokudenashiko's use of the manko and her whimsical character persona as a meditation on what it means to take the female body out of an economy and reshape it to meet more personal (or even irrelevant or whimsical) needs with the same materials available to policy makers, who use them for productivity and nationalism.

Rokudenashiko first established herself as a manga artist and then as a peripheral member of the art scene. Sculptures whose making she documented in her first published stand-alone manga in 2012 attracted the ire of law enforcement and made her a major figure in the media. Her plastic sculptures have served as a lightning rod for discussions of media representation of female sexuality far beyond the world of art and craft. Her contribution to media theory comes most forcefully through practice. It is self-authorized through experience rather than anchored in the almost exclusively male pantheon of conceptually oriented media critics who work in the category of "criticism" (*hihyō*) historicized in Kitano Keisuke's essay in this volume. Rather than analyzing the approach in which a subject stands outside a system (such as modernity, Frenchness, the self) and analyzes it as a set of externalities, Rokudenashiko is planted firmly in that system as it moves dynamically around and through her, giving her the very means to make things. Her works reference less these groundings and more the possibility of generating new works, new readings, and, accordingly, new articulations of social formations.

Rokudenashiko's media persona depends on her work and her character being taken lightly, an approach that staves off automatic resistance by appearing benignly humorous or playful as opposed to agonistic. Early in the legal struggle, she distanced herself both from mass politics and, ironically, from feminism, when she put the anger of the age of protests behind her. As we see in the manga *What Is Obscenity?*, this anger also manifests itself in angry men who lash out at the Rokudenashiko character for daring to take artistic license with "their" object of sexual desire. However personally fuelled by anger to turn the tables Rokudenashiko may be, in terms of artistic process she says, "I see myself as an artist who turns anger into smiles through manga and art. I'm often called a feminist, but the word doesn't really capture me. . . . I don't intend to fight anger through demonstrations or rallies, I'd rather express myself through art and make people smile" (にこにこする *niko niko suru*).[11]

These "demonstrations or rallies" are shorthand for a series of sometimes violent protests that took place in the 1960s and 1970s contesting US military presence, the reversion of Okinawa, and the eminent domain takeover of farmland for the Narita airport, among other struggles. Those uninformed about Japanese media history of the last ten years may interpret Rokudenashiko's statement as an insouciant step away from such mass politics into a glib realm of kitsch that, like many Cool Japan products, seems out of touch with lived reality or the kind of cultural work that art can do. These people would be wrong. While Rokudenashiko may disavow the term "feminism," or give it more fluid definitions than is customary among academics, we should note that she uses the word "smile" strategically with awareness of its media context and its gendering. She is able to remain on point with her messaging and at the same time appear playfully nonallied to a party in her quest for a level playing field for the female body.

Rokudenashiko's rhetoric taps into interfaces with immense popular appeal and stands apart from the angry male revolutionary figure whose exhaustion has prompted many to seek alternate emotional grounds for galvanizing popular movements. The verb for smiling, *niko niko suru*, is a homonym for the name of one of the most popular media platforms in millennial Japan.[12] *Nico nico dōga* (ニコニコ動画 smiling moving images) allows users to upload their comments to video files so that they can be played back simultaneously while additional users comment in real time on the right. Rokudenashiko introduced her "man-boat" project on this platform, much to the amusement of its users. Most commenters giggled and made liberal use of *x*, a mock-fuseji letter, and *w*, indicating laughter, making fun of the practice of censorship while delighting in using the word "manko."[13]

Naming her mission in terms of a "smile" does not refer to happiness or hospitality ("Have a Coke and a smile!") but instead locates Rokudenashiko within a style of media performance that emphasizes user-generated content and draws attention to the user-object relation as it exists in a process of making, including value making. Niko Niko is also the name of a tech/IT think tank, the Niko Niko Beta Working Group (学会 *gakkai*). Niko Niko Beta sponsors large symposia at which members present their gadgets and new tech experiments, many in "beta" mode, not fully formed and still in the process of modeling, testing, and troubleshooting. 110,000 people attended the first conference in 2012.[14] The working group is composed of academics, fringe intellectuals, tech researchers, and entrepreneurs. All of its projects rely on user-generated research.[15] Given this connection to high tech, Rokudenashiko's citation of "smile" when describing her mandate situates her in the thick of maker culture: DIY culture that emphasizes experiments in technology that occur in irreverent ways.[16]

As a freelancer who has hustled at multiple part-time jobs while making art as a hobby (趣味 shumi), Rokudenashiko is part of this class of user-creators. What makes her work distinct from many Niko Niko Beta projects is the close link it retains to her body as its source; differentiating her is her use of amateur craft styles as well as high-tech tools while the market role of the work's prototype is untested.[17] Many forms of applied knowledge prototyped at Niko Niko Beta, including the "man-boat," fall into the category of what I call "modular aesthetics." "Modular aesthetics" is a term with broad application that encompasses a tendency in Japanese cultural forms. "Modular objects"—which we can call "modular aesthetics" when they work as art objects—refers broadly to media objects that follow a tendency in Japanese cultural forms to serialize (as in the case of modern fiction), link (in the case of video games or manga), or translate across media platforms (in the case of media mix products) such that story or object parts can recombine, reproduce, or innovate story worlds while extending their reach and interconnections.[18] The other feature of modularity is its ability to detach and reattach, due to a set of standards that are technical as distinct from textual: like light bulbs that work in all sockets with the same wattage, modular aesthetics plug and play in any media environment with the same standards. Use of modular aesthetics in general proliferated with mass production (tracks on a record), amplified with figures and personal electronics (like the Walkman), and overflowed in the digital era (software plug-ins).

Modularity

Modularity as a design discourse was coined by architect Arthur Bemis in the 1930s and appeared in the fields of architecture and the construction of electronic computers in the 1950s and 1960s, according to information historian Andrew J. Russell—but it really took off in the 1970s. In the architectural field, modular practice sprung up "within the mid-century American housing and building industries."[19] The idea of modular replaceable elements featured similarly in the design and construction of projects by Metabolist architects active in Japan from about 1960. Modularity was especially strong in the works of Kikutake Kiyonori (1928–2011) and Kurokawa Kishō (1934–2007). Kikutake saw wooden buildings as exemplary because their structural system allowed the "possibility of dismantling and reassembling" standard components to compose a "system of replaceability" that could be adapted to various scales throughout a city.[20] Kurokawa, in turn, was the pioneer of the affordable capsule hotel as well as more avant-garde buildings such as the Nakagin Capsule Tower, built in Tokyo in 1972. In the computer field, modularity helped to equilibrate traffic to make networks transmit information smoothly and evenly, and in the industrial literature, modularity is associated with order and control. But when we transfer the concept of distribution to Rokudenashiko's sphere of speculative design and social formations, the equilibrium that is operationalized here aims to level beliefs, practices, and desires vis-à-vis the sexualized body.

Rokudenashiko's works all stress a connection to processes of "making" in the realm of modular materiality and use both retro forms such as dioramas and hand drawing as well as postdigital forms such as 3-D printing and scanning. While modularity is by no means restricted to Japanese cultural forms, Japanese makers, from auto makers to craft makers, tend to think about design objects as well as narrative arcs and make plugging, playing, and translating conceptual issues important over and above technical issues. Characters also exist in modular form, as with artist Murakami Takashi's DOB character. Dubbed Murakami's most "ubiquitous and enduring character" by WIRED magazine, DOB appears in paintings and installations in many iterations of color, size, and, especially, setting.[21] Rokudenashiko's keen focus on the content of her "module," however, singles her out from the pack of analysts who treat technical or infrastructure elements, or create characters but deprioritize the substance of their content.

Modular aesthetics can be operationalized by using media machines as common as any convenience store copy machine. In the summer of 2015, a series of visible protests against modifying the constitution used the network of these ubiquitous stores to distribute a prominent antiwar poster. A *Japan Times* article notes, "The poster features characters originally written in a calligraphic style by haiku poet Kaneko Tota. It can be printed from multifunction photocopiers with Internet connections at convenience stores nationwide. To access the data, copier users need a code distributed by activists on websites, Twitter and Facebook."[22] There is nothing technologically determined about the use of modularity in design; in fact, using that means of production in similarly distributed ways has allowed makers to use industrial standards to challenge and customize cultural and political norms. Customizing, in the case of Rokudenashiko's kayak, follows through the process of speculative design to register an awareness of the "standards" of gender norms at the same time as it distributes a customized and transformed vision of prototyped bodies that build but depart from those norms.

The 3-D printer, to whose wonders Niko Niko Beta introduced Rokudenashiko, is modular in many ways. It is modular at the level of the data that it uses (it dematerializes a given design into component parts of 1's and 0's).[23] Then, it is modular because it makes parts that have to be assembled with other parts to make the object. And finally, it is modular because the same set of coding standards ensures that however personal Rokudenashiko's body was, it can be scanned, designed, and printed so that it becomes part of multiple and innumerable kayaks that fit the same design standards. In other words, the vulva attachment could hypothetically fit any of a number of ready-made store-bought kayaks. The link to property is especially key to the third category of modular design: Rokudenashiko retains the "original" mold, so while it may be technically possible to reverse engineer the kayak part, retaining the mold and the data allows Rokudenashiko to technically allow reproducibility while also prioritizing access to the information to those who have donated to her cause. As in many fan cultures, a tacit trust is assumed between the artist and the funder/fan who will customize the data in his/her own form.

Niko Niko Beta provided Rokudenashiko's modular aesthetics with a bridge to out-of-reach R&D resources such as the printer.[24] The artist credits Niko Niko Beta with changing her aesthetic, which had had an "ero-guro" look, an aesthetic deriving from the pulp press in prewar Japan and known for its erotic, perverse, and decadent genre stories.[25] When Rokudenashiko states that the 3-D printer was a conduit to something more "pop" and "high-tech," she retains the link to mass culture through which pop art takes its materials but empties it of its perversity. I take "high-tech" to mean made with costly electronic machines with high-level software. With this move, Rokudenashiko both takes the manko out of the field of a recognized genre of erotics and estranges it so that we see it as just another set of potential materials. We should thus think of her cheerful "smile" as less an act of feminine hospitality and, like her manko itself, more a plug into the world of high-tech maker culture with a feminist twist.

Indiscreet Rules

One of the mainstays of the women's lib movement (in Japanese, *ūman ribu*, typically known as *ribu*) that emerged in the 1970s was a sustained critique of how not only laws but also labor, domestic, and erotic practices collaborated to situate women as objects in a system of property relations that transferred women as assets between men, while using their labor as a conduit to affirm these relationships of patriarchy.[26] Mass media and the culture industry were not exempt from this critique. Rokudenashiko's works draw on parts of this history, such as personal liberation, and making life experience the grounds for liberation. This section analyzes the story of Rokudenashiko's first full-length manga to show how it provided a basis for two key aspects of her work: modularity and process.

The story of how the "man-boat" set sail is rooted in the aesthetics and industry of manga. After graduating from college in Tokyo, Rokudenashiko's career in the manga industry began in the genre of "experiential reportage" (体験ルポ *taiken rupo*), or reality manga. In 1998, she won a new artist award from big-three publisher Kōdansha's women's manga *Kiss*. The story was a love comedy about a "sort of stalker-like" character modeled on the artist herself who worked in a real estate agency. Despite the initial fast-track entrance into the industry, Rokudenashiko found that the prize only meant an entrée to further competitions, and even when a work finally was selected, if it did not get good results in reader surveys, it would be pulled. The momentum faltered, and Rokudenashiko sought work at a publisher that specialized in experiential reportage. In this stint, which provided the basis for Rokudenashiko's sculptural work, life experience became a source material for work.

Reportage in general is a genre that emerged in the proletarian literature movement and refers still to fact-finding missions that reveal obscure or hidden information to a larger public. Experiential reportage mixes the fact-finding mandate of earlier reportage with the expressive rhetorics of first-person fiction—"literally putting real experiences into manga," as

[FIG. 10.2] The cover for *Decoman*, Rokudenashiko's first stand-alone manga,
published in 2012. The style draws on the introspection, iconography,
and color palette of the suspended princess story that is a staple of *shōjo* manga.
© Rokudenashiko/Bunka-sha [ろくでなし子／株式会社ぶんか社].

Rokudenashiko puts it.[27] The sub-genre of experiential reportage emerged in the late 1970s as fieldwork-oriented reporting by devotees, as opposed to scholars published in manga or para-academic paperbacks called *shinsho* (new books). Early examples of the genre featured life experiences of labor, while more recent examples focus on how people have navigated the systems of life such as elder care ("Social Welfare and Elder Care in Japan") or more frequently gambling and the sexual underworld ("Sex with Women from Fifty-One Countries: Diary of a Man Who 'Conquered' 5000!").[28] Experiential reportage is documentary in its depiction of real events, but focalizes the story through a writer's eyes, body, and pen, and is often organized in modular case-study form. In Rokudenashiko's case, the first-person voice compounds the fact-finding impulse of reportage with the highly interpretive visual and story conventions of *shōjo* manga. The result is a first-person story buttressed by empirical details that contribute a truth effect to the highly personal vision and track a process while the outcome often remains suspended.

The processing of modular elements frames this tale conceptually because shōjo are frequently represented in mainstream media as raw materials that will ultimately be brought into a sexual marketplace after a phase of consumerist polishing. This pending state was described in a 1982 article by literary historian Honda Masuko, who was among the first to establish "girls' culture" as an independent field of study. Her essay used the key metaphor of the cocoon to explain the ontology of the shōjo: "There comes a day when a girl realizes she is a shōjo, a day she also learns she can never be a boy, a *shōnen*. From that time it is as if she spins a small cocoon around herself wherein to slumber and dream as a pupa, consciously separating herself from the outer world. Here, she lives life to her own time, a time that can never be lost."[29] This cocoon-like ability to put reality on pause and develop a vivid interior life is the hallmark of shōjo manga, one that Rokudenashiko puts to different ends than either opting out of the system or entering the marketplace leading to marriage.

Rokudenashiko's big break came with a manga that mixed these two genres by putting life on "pause" to figure out her alienated and vexing relationship with her own sexual body. *Decoman* (2012) (see fig. 10.2) is an ambitious tale of experiential reportage that is structured as seven fairy tales, modular chapters, in the mode of shōjo manga. Processing is also an important alternative to both the technocracy that disadvantages female cultural producers and to the act of revolution and conflagration pursued by male revolutionaries. These modular aesthetics work to shift and show the shift of relations between women-as-things and the world of things in general. While shōjo texts often introduce technological processes into the everyday through subplots that involve magic, these projects articulate processes that are replicable in the nontextual world. They are geared toward questions about feminine invisibility and how to disrupt that invisibility.

Decoman pursues the question of visibility as a kind of *kunstler*-manga. It documents Rokudenashiko's artistic formation vis-à-vis a series of anxieties she represents about her own body and what she thought of as its abnormalities, sparked by a beautiful older sister, a too-blunt family and a series of careless lovers and eager surgeons. (In her later manga *What Is Obscenity?* the Rokudenashiko character explains that her editor at the time encouraged her, in order to ramp up sales, to depict feelings of inadequacy that inspired her to get plastic surgery on her labia. The frame story in the later manga distances Rokudenashiko from feelings of inadequacy and plastic surgery-related "complex" to cast the art as less sensational and more speculative.) In *Decoman's* story of artistic formation, the Rokudenashiko character comes to the conclusion that many other women labor under the same internalized anxieties, and starts making art and giving art workshops on making decorated manko art (see fig. 10.3).

"Deco" is an abbreviation of "decoration," where decorating the objects is a demonstration of its attachment to your person, and a sense of intimacy. A related, and equally gendered, example is the *deco-tora*—a trailer truck whose macho driver spruces it up with the flair of paintings, horns, and interior design that in total plays the part of an eighteen-wheeled low-rider. Rokudenashiko advocates a kind of manko relativism, while chronicling the process of those discoveries for herself and others. The story closes in a metamoment, as Rokudenashiko closes a scrapbook—the materials of this comic itself—and congratulates herself for having survived and thrived. The phrase she uses, *jiko-man* means "self-satisfaction," and includes the first syllable in the word for vulva, *man*. After living through this series of trials, the syllable "man" becomes Rokudenashiko's modular key to finding and rejoicing in anything "man"-related she comes across.

The sculptural form Rokudenashiko returns to is the decorated manko, or "decoman" diorama, of which there are two kinds. The "deco" part is a process that involves Rokudenashiko taking an impression of her vulva on a disposable sushi tray with the same kind of alginate molding that dentists use to make casts for false teeth and pouring a cast of the mold (see fig. 10.4). Then the solidified object serves as a surface for various miniature decorations. The result is that the manko becomes the setting for a world, like a little landscape dollhouse with people caught in motion.[30]

[FIG. 10.3] The technical information of experiential reportage comes through as a plastic surgeon explains how he will reconstruct the character's labia after a botched attempt at another clinic. The big bold type and skeleton face indicate the intensity of horror felt by the narrator as she realizes the mistake in process.
© Rokudenashiko/Bunka-sha [ろくでなし子／株式会社ぶんか社].

[FIG. 10.4] A decoman diorama depicts a pastoral scene outside of a girls' school.
Credit: Shinjuku Gankarō Gallery.

Let us look briefly at two kinds of diorama. The first is more traditional, derived from the nineteenth-century genre of landscape scenes, in which the ground of landscape for each diorama is the cast of Rokudenashiko's own vulva. With this kind of diorama, the key formal property is verisimilitude. Trees look like trees, and the scale of distance from the church to the grassy knoll is proportionate to real life. Each scene features a group of people in a mass setting, oblivious to the ground on which they walk. The second kind of diorama is purely decorative and nonrepresentational. In this mode, Rokudenashiko's work is reminiscent of "craft" in its individual miniature scale. Her workshop recalls the cottage industries such as the transistor radios that were put together by deft feminine hands to propel Japan's economic success in the late 1950s (see fig. 10.5).[31]

In a slightly different vein of craft, one US journalist (in the *Daily Beast*) called Rokudenashiko the Norman Rockwell of manko art. I take this to refer to the homemade look and the sense of generic tableau in art objects

[FIG. 10.5] Rokudenashiko at her home workshop, full of craft materials.
Photograph by Christina Sjögren.

distributed in a mass cultural form. Other decorative objects include lamp-shades, tissue covers, and the delightful category "et cetera" (など nado). This strikes me as a wonderful characterization of modular manko art—that as a medium it could be anything, and it could turn into anything or serve as the ground for anything. The object featured in the *Decoman* manga, the manko itself, gradually eclipsed the medium of the manga as the star of the show. Initial works were process-oriented in three ways: their production required carefully sequenced and reflexive steps; they engaged the viewer in a sense of play in tandem with literal reorientations of sight; and their paratexts linked them to the world in ways that speculated on changes that the world, too, might start processing.

In addition to the dioramas depicted in *Decoman*, Rokudenashiko began to devise new formats for her manko art, of which two are most key: figures and the man-boat.

Character-based figures such as these *manko-chan* often spin off from known franchises, but here it is the emotion that is key—there is no "larger" arc or world (see fig. 10.6). These examples look perhaps shocked (almost as

[FIG. 10.6] An array of *manko-chan* figurines, each of which features a clitoral third eye. Photograph by Christina Sjögren.

if screaming "Help!"), and their facial expressions and arms akimbo are a bit at odds with the bright pink and plastic-toy aesthetic. They are palm-sized, small in scale; Rokudenashiko often appears with them in photos. These images are for sale on the Shinjuku Ophthalmologist Gallery website.[32] They are very affordable, and you can buy one at a time; there is no push to proliferate characters or to "collect them all." The whole point is that they are modular—they are all variations on a theme. This is a further way of evacuating the aura that applies both to the work of art and to the manko itself at the same time that Rokudenashiko also uses modularity to build a "brand" and garner support. Manko-chan images, character figures modeled on a cute personified manko, are modular in that they appear on her newsletter, in the autographed pictures she gives out at book signings, and in a stamp set for supporters—character "goods" for people who go to her events and donate to her campaign.

In summer of 2015, the kayak, despite its modular programming, distribution, and possible reproduction, was beached—confiscated and held as evidence. Its existence as data and as boat begs the question of how processing affects the legal status of an object: what is the status of a set of manipulable data? An *Asahi shinbun* article from July 15 notes that Rokudenashiko was charged with sending a thirty-year-old male company employee in Kagawa prefecture the data from her "female sexual organ/s" (女性器) that he could reproduce (復元) as a third object.[33] As a later *Asahi* article pointed out, data has a materiality that does not restrict it to "reproducing" something.[34] For example, a faculty member of Tokyo University of the Arts used data compiled from weather info collected in Tokyo in one day in 2014 and formed it into the shape of a big, squat vase. He demonstrated that the processed product bears no resemblance to its place of origin or its processing software, nor is it supposed to.

Traversing media with the special 3-D software demonstrates how, as Johanna Drucker notes, "the stripping away of material information when a document is stored in binary form" of zeros and ones "is not a move from material to immaterial form, but from one material condition to another."[35] Rokudenashiko's claim hinges on this point: that data from her body can represent it but are not it as such. To think of data as a medium that requires processes and shaping to become an object is a very empowering thing. What the kayak enables via digital materiality it loses in authenticity. No longer does the kayak retain an indexical link to Rokudenashiko's body. As of 2016, although the manipulation of data into a new material form would seem to anchor it in the realm of "art," the legal status of data is undecided, as is the status of a work of art in a digital process.

Despite the manifest cuteness, the emotion that overwhelmingly appears in Rokudenashiko's descriptions of reactions to her art—very modestly displayed in small galleries at prices that even small collectors could find reasonable—is rage. The story of this little woman in a boat leapt off the page and into everyday life in 2014. On June 18, 2013, Rokudenashiko started a campaign on the crowd-funding site Campfire to seek funding to build an attachment to a kayak modeled on her vulva. The campaign reached 194 percent of its goal—a total of one hundred million yen—on September 6, with contributions from 125 people. In July 2014, at 9:00 on a holiday morning, Rokudenashiko was arrested for an alleged violation of Article 175 of the criminal code for distributing obscene data (ワイセツ電磁記録媒体頒布罪) in March of the same year. Rokudenashiko had emailed a link to the 3-D scanner data of her vulva to people who had supported her campaign at the level of three thousand yen and above (sixty-five people were eligible), and gave a CD-ROM with the data to seventeen others.[36] Rokudenashiko was released after a week, after an online petition at Change.org registered more than 21,000 signatures. "I turned the whole ordeal into a manga satirizing the police. That hurt their pride, so they trumped up some charges and arrested me in December."[37]

After this first arrest, the press portrayed Rokudenashiko as angry, and something of an imposter as a "so-called artist" (自称芸術作家), a label she embraced proudly in her 2015 manga *What Is Obscenity?* by using it as the subhead for the eighteen chapters that narrate both her artistic formation and her run-ins with police. The initial press followed the line of police press releases closely.[38] And indeed, as we saw above, Rokudenashiko's early manga show her as angry, taken aback, frustrated, and outraged. In this, her affect coincides with a classic oppositional mode of protest, often gendered male in Japanese leftist politics. After the student movement dwindled in the late 1960s, many male activists suffered melancholia or political fatigue.[39] Following that portrayal, Rokudenashiko made a change in her camera demeanor and in her writing to use emotional directness less, and emotional processing more. She began to use humor in a way that did not stress the absurdity—although her target, the law and the state, could be made to seem absurd, and therefore belonging to a dimension apart from reality. She became militantly cute, an approach I explore later in this section.

On December 3, 2014 Rokudenashiko was arrested for a second time at an exhibition of her works—a collection of dioramas—in the window of a gallery in a sex shop owned by Kitahara Minori.[40] This arrest became the subject of Rokudenashiko's second book, *What Is Obscenity?*, a memoir of her time in jail.[41] *What Is Obscenity?* ditches the shōjo narrative structure to narrate the experience leading to Rokudenashiko's arrest, confinement, and continued activities after her release. The period of confined waiting often featured in shōjo stories must have seemed difficult to maintain as a fantasy after being handcuffed in a locked room with five other people over an eight-hour period in mid-July while waiting for trial. The book features a number of stand-alone essays and *taidans* with male leftists, and made way for a slightly new version of the character.

Cute Strategies, Close Readings

After Rokudenashiko's media baptism, her new camera demeanor and conspicuous use of humor had two prongs: cuteness and ubiquity. Rokudenashiko's strategy of cuteness differs almost 180 degrees from the typical revolutionary's method of leadership standing outside of the masses or taking an avant-garde role that precedes them. Her stance indeed draws on outrage: a classic emotion that sparks a narrative of wrong, critique, and redress to announce a position of strength and conviction typically based on ideals or reason. At the same time, her stance rings supremely cute, an aesthetic that solicits protection but

[FIG. 10.7] An official photo from Rokudenashiko's blog captures her candidly, in a girlish color palette, modestly dressed and smiling. Courtesy of Rokudenashiko.

can also engender aggression, and exists in a commodity-based world of exchange. It calls on intimacy, feelings of belonging and play that follow from the attachment to personal-sized modular objects. Cute, writes Sianne Ngai, taps into a "spectrum of feelings, ranging from tenderness to aggression, that we harbor toward ostensibly subordinate and unthreatening commodities."[42] This spectrum is evident in users' reactions, which range from the devoted standing in line to solicit her autograph to the outsized police reaction of confiscating works of art that any art lover actually has to make a great deal of effort to track down (see fig. 10.7).

Rokudenashiko's cheerful insistence on the word "manko" embodies this dual tone of supplication and aggression. The tactic might be mistaken for shock art that provokes or shames by confronting the viewer with something uncomfortable. But Rokudenashiko's mandate is quite the opposite of shock. Her strategy is stressing the ubiquity of this foregrounded object, the manko, draining the dreaded syllable of its impact and redirecting it by showing how it is already present, and we already converse with it in daily life.[43] The familiarity of "cute" allows users to realize that they already fully integrate this word and the body part it refers to into daily life; the effect is to deprive it of its aura, and it even loses its frisson of eroticism (and shame) as "just a part of a woman's body."[44]

At this point it is worth setting Rokudenashiko's affect and stance in context of the women's liberation movement indigenous to Japan known as *ūman ribu* (women's liberation, usually known as *ribu*). Ribu activists who emerged in the waning days of the student movement critiqued the fact that women were legally framed as objects, not subjects, by the family system (家制度 *ie seido*) that regulated structures of inheritance. But the critique went beyond literal realms of inheritance to touch on social and cultural forms that underwrote women's status as object. Sexuality was included in this equation; activists opposed the default of marriage and railed against the cult of virginity.[45] Ideas and debates were often spelled out in *mini-komi* (mini-communications or small-circulation periodicals, alternative print and image media production-distribution systems in contrast to large-circulation *masu-komi* media) communicators. Writing in retrospect about the student movement, the ribu activists and writers who published in ribu journals and mini-komi provided critiques of the way in which sexual and gender politics were sidestepped as mass protest escalated in violence. Mini-komi emerged to confront this system of property relations and to enable liberation through critique and the creative acts of other alternatives as personal life was imagined to empty into politics. Although it is based in digital materiality and plastic arts rather than print culture, Rokudenashiko's use of modular aesthetics allows for the distribution of information that facilitates building social movements in ways that recall the cultural work of mini-komi.

Setsu Shigematsu summarizes Iijima Akiko's well-known position paper from 1970, one that "cleared a politico-theoretical space for *ribu*" as an indictment of the fact that "the 'laboring class,' 'labor unions,' and 'theory' were men's domains," and went so far as to declare that "theory was a man."[46] While this claim is easy to discard as hyperbolic if taken literally, it is readily understood to mean that theory has worked in myriad ways to reinforce rather than dismantle patriarchal structures. The same is true of critics, practitioners of theory in commercial, academic, and para-academic areas of the culture industry. One venue that included the culture industries and saw creators as critics was the journal *Onna erosu* (Woman/eros). *Onna erosu* began publication in 1973. Its first issues featured lacerating critiques of patriarchal systems, one of which was media institutions, up to and including independent film productions. For instance, one contributor penned an essay about her disappointment with the heroine of a successful porno movie series called *The Young Wife: Confessions* (幼妻: 告白 *Osana dzuma: kokuhaku*) directed by Nishimura Shōgorō and starring Katagiri Yūko. The series depicts the heroine as "embracing [!] the dream of marriage," but she is raped by the older brother of her fiancé. Initially protesting, she gives way.

The older brother gives her some money, and she says resignedly, "I knew that things would end up this way." The *Onna erosu* writer, in a column called "The Female Sharpshooter" (女狙撃兵 "Onna sogeki-hei"), writes that the film disappoints because it does not offer a reality other than the patriarchal one that currently exists, but rather affirms it while posing as progressive:

> Film is supposed to have the quality of transporting the spectator to "another reality." It is a medium where it is possible to present reality, anticipating it, and anticipate what might come of it. Among which, "porno" is able to be so far ahead of its time that it causes scandals in court. But because only this kind of "pitiful woman" is the only one featured, in the end porno film is not able to set foot out of its dark little self-satisfied castle and fly the flag of progressivism.[47]

At the time porno movies were embattled with censors. There were obscenity trials, but directors and staff also reveled in an antiestablishment antiauthoritarian stance. Kishida ends her article in disbelief. About the disconnect between *roman porno*'s bout for legitimacy in the courts and the conventional passive fate of this movie's heroine: "You call that a struggle?!?" (闘争 tōsō). Kishida's main objection is that, in the film, the heroine is "cast upon the flow of fate," both sacrificed and numbly meek about her fate, whereas many women in this era actually "make fate and move forward."

Like the ūman ribu activists, Rokudenashiko's stance of militant cheer and "making" is an alternative to the sacrificial maiden role to which women were frequently consigned in 1960s mass movements.[48] In the end, both Rokudenashiko and ribu activists refuse to delink the female body from other systems. But unlike ribu activists, Rokudenashiko does not look directly to the erotic dimension of sexuality as her domain, although one could certainly introduce the manko into a new discourse of sex, once its fetish value has been leveled. Nor does Rokudenashiko demonize particular men or male characters. Rather than raising the ideal of freedom via sex, she chooses to deflate a word that represents something so ideal as to be talismanic: manko. This effort resembles the precision of ribu activists when they shifted the word for woman from *fujin* (wife) or *josei* (woman) to another slightly more salacious and lower-class-sounding term, *onna*, as a marker of departure from conventional gender norms. But Rokudenashiko's strategy inverts this: the very syllable of the word destigmatized is actually built in everywhere. Of course, the words are standing for the body part that, if it is not exactly everywhere, is one among many parts of half the world's population.

The Japanese syllable *man* can be found everywhere, in every walk of life, from *man*-boat, and *man*hole, to one-man (ワンマン運転) driven train, *man*-dala, even *man*ga.[49] When you consider how the syllable *man* is built into the Japanese language, it quickly becomes clear that language as a whole would be poorer without it. But at the same time, the arbitrariness of judging *man*ko as obscene while *man*dala are revered clarifies how much human projection is committed to fetishizing this one modular organ. These strategies of ubiquity and cuteness embrace if not celebrate contemporary consumer capitalism, within which Rokudenashiko is very much located. If in consumer culture and its close relative, media culture, we are saturated at all times with overflows of information, Rokudenashiko's strategy is to cheerfully and polemically point out that "man" is a syllable that has always been with us and whose absence would cause significant semiotic damage not only to that syllable but to others attached to it. At a roundtable and book signing in May 2015, Rokudenashiko laughed gleefully at the way the translator at the Foreign Correspondents' Club mispronounced her signature work as "man," adding a second-language opinion to her claim of ubiquitous male privilege. "Man" is present, it is ubiquitous, and by deleting it, we delete significant parts of reality while making it a source of abjection consigned to its secret, shameful, and hidden place.

Angry Reactions

An acrimonious Twitter exchange in July 2015 saw Rokudenashiko being castigated for incorrect use of the label "feminist." The discussion between Rokudenashiko's more freewheeling use of the term and her critics' literal criteria is ongoing. We might wonder why police officials as well as some feminists react so strongly. We could guess at reasons, both art historical and political. On the art-historical front, these dioramas seem to be sui generis— self-authorized. In early works before the arrests, Rokudenashiko rarely made reference to earlier artists.[50] This tendency distinguished her from the ribu generation as well as from its academic allies. Sociologist and critic of feminine wartime collaboration Ueno Chizuko's stand-alone first essay collection, for instance, *Women at Play* (女遊び, Onna asobi), used modular elements from Judy Chicago's *The Dinner Party* in its book design and in its structure.[51] Chicago's installation is epic in scale and in labor. It is a work of media archeology that retrieves underknown women's biographies, concretizes a design form for each, and places them in a stylized communal setting as a metaphor for a convivial conversation between women across spaces and times. *Dinner Party* incorporates rather than proliferates its model and variations, as does Rokudenashiko's work. Because of this sui generis presentation, the interpretive weight of Rokudenashiko's work was likely placed fully on her. What is compelling about her works is that they do not attempt to hide their source, but they do not flaunt it either: they use it as just another material—unlike Ueno and ribu, Rokudenashiko's work directly refers to no past, and sees the manko as another substance, not an ideal; but like Ueno and ribu, it seeks to use this modular body part to create the ground for a better, or more potential-filled, future.

Rather than monuments, Rokudenashiko's works are miniature. The handheld dioramas invite intimacy, and their small size demands close scrutiny to read the arrangement in any way; the figures and dioramas are cryptic in the emotions they invite. Interrupting with the body of the artist seems important in the way people interpret Rokudenashiko's work. Realizing that the mass-produced object is indexically related to a specific body causes shock and repulsion—or amusement. That these fantasies should be made concrete in a kitsch form, and not very well groomed, goes against the disciplinary rules of cosmetics and grooming culture that regulate many women's relations to their bodies and that surface in Rokudenashiko's early manga.[52] The nonchalance with which soldiers lie in wait for the enemy in foxholes dotting a manko battlefield, or the schoolgirls romp up a manko hill to chapel might strike someone as inappropriate, if they were interested in female bodies as either pure functionality, or pure erotic fetish "belonging" to them. Far from being erotic (the subject of sexualized fetishism never surfaces, Rokudenashiko's works are very much seen as killjoys), they are a kind of medium.[53]

Coda

Rokudenashiko joins other manga artists who are technically too old to be shōjo yet use the received conventions of suspended time and interior expression to dilate on a particular issue. A sense of personal time detached from chronological time lends itself to the genre of the fairy tale. These formal dimensions reinforce a set of story conventions that privilege yet suspend the happy ending—a temporal dynamic of suspension I return to vis-à-vis Abenomics in the coda to this essay.

In 2016, the role of women in a national context is driven by Abenomics— the policy directives of prime minister Abe Shinzō's administration that aim to stabilize the economy as well as increase the birth rate. Forty percent of the Japanese work force does contract labor, and frugality and craft have surged in popularity. The labor situation for women is asymmetrically bleak, with female workers occupying disproportionately low-paying or temporary jobs with yet less chance for advancement or security than male workers. Abenomics is a grey area whose policy ideals have been articulated, even if the concrete results are new or not in place. In the interim, women have started to press for equal wages, but without using the label "feminist." These women are of the generation that grew up with the narrative of the shōjo manga, whose key metaphor was the cocoon and whose key climax was the happy ending. Rokudenashiko is one of these women who grew up with suspended creation as an ideal, but used that cocoon moment in her work to dream and make rather than to sleep.

Rokudenashiko's navigation down the Tamagawa River, avoiding the rocky shoals of obscenity and delivering its content to its destination, resembles nothing less than the voyage of Norbert Wiener's storied cybernaut.[54] In Wiener's account of cybernetics, the system requires a steersman who is responsible for the self-reflexive check on communication processes and who ensures that the system continues to function while incorporating input from outside the system, and at the same time stays on course ethically. Rokudenashiko channels and updates the critique of property by claiming her body as an object that she steers and navigates in a dynamic world that the river is, stands for, and connects. Who is to govern sexual representation is precisely the question at stake.

This river, like many ecological objects, including media ecologies, is no longer a closed system that can be isolated in analysis or lived experience from a larger ecology and the human effects on it. While Rokudenashiko reconnects the art object to a prominent natural location, she does not connect it to wild feminine nature. Her boat launch suggests a bawdy and unabashedly suburban version of Gaia in which a human-object encounter ends up taking the artist back to a primal source of life, water, at the same time that it connects her to the thoroughfares of the nation and world, not to mention mass-produced products and digital communications. The works challenge and redraw ideas of ownership and property—typical concerns of ūman ribu, Japan's 1970s feminist liberation movement.[55] They do so by anticipating and rerouting what consumers, male or female, expect to receive when they purchase a small and affordable, even cheap, art piece. Rokudenashiko's work is celebratory not because it builds a canon, or even because it sees knowledge as enlightenment—though it definitely has its pedagogical side. These enthusiasts merely reinforce the point Rokudenashiko's manko art brings home over and over again about this vessel: it is already there, it is a free channel, its boundaries are fluid, and as a taxpayer (or owner), it already belongs to you. Own it.

Thanks to Jean-François Blanchette, Phil Brown, Kirsten Cather, Laura Forlano, Ian Lynam, Namiko Kunimoto, Lisa Onaga, and the editors of this volume.

1. The Tamagawa River boat launch draws on histories of freedom, expression, and resourcefulness that characterize riverbanks as a space. Like many such spaces in Japan, the Tamagawa's banks have a rich tradition of serving as a public space for physical and artistic activities. Sports teams have playing fields there, while the grassy open spaces also offer a refuge for musicians and others who cannot make their noise at home. Historically, rivers were home to social outcasts called *kawaramono*, river dwellers who later specialized in garden design and became artistic advisors to the ruling government.

2. See "Gender, Genitor, Genitalia—Rokudenashiko sapōto-ten," Campfire, accessed July 12, 2015, http://camp-fire.jp/projects/view/2809.

3. Mark Frauenfelder, "Japanese Artist Goes on Trial over 'Vagina Selfies,'" *Boing Boing*, July 28, 2015, http://boingboing.net/2015/07/28/japanese-artist-goes-on-trial.html; "Who's Afraid of Vagina Art?," *Broadly*, accessed March 1, 2016, https://broadly.vice.com/en_us/topic/rokudenashiko. Rokudenashiko's name itself is a definite step away from a feminism of virtue that stands outside a system and judges. Rokudenashiko—meaning a "no good" but ultimately harmless woman who is a known or familiar character—comes from the pen name the artist used when writing an experiential reportage about cheating on her husband. The "no good" was clearly a parodic knock on the artist's own everyday life, and contributes to the rhetoric of honesty about conventional morality that affirms the "true story" quality of her chosen genre.

4. Jonathan E. Abel, *Redacted: The Archives of Censorship in Transwar Japan* (Berkeley: University of California Press, 2012). Kirsten Cather, *The Art of Censorship in Postwar Japan* (Honolulu: University of Hawai'i Press, 2012). There was one earlier case of public obscenity that featured a woman. Ichijō Sayuri was a celebrated stripper from Osaka who also appeared in Kumashirō Tatsumi's roman porno films, including one in which she plays herself doing strip shows and is arrested by the police. Though Ichijō's media were crime and live performance, like Rokudenashiko, her crime was exposing her genitals. Ichijō was arrested under Article 174, public indecency, and served six months in prison. See Kirsten Cather, "The Politics and Pleasures of Historiographic Porn," *positions: east asia cultures critique* 22, no. 4 (2014): 753.

5. Two examples from different generations of creators are photographer Araki Nobuyoshi's celebrated nudes, which strengthen the indexical relation to reality via their personal tie to the photographer himself, and Murakami Takashi's 2015–16 exhibition at the Mori Art Museum, *The 500 Arhats*, which features a drawing of an elephant inspired by Edo-period aesthetics in which the elephant's fantastical "third eye" is an aestheticized vulva.

AT THE SOURCE (CODE) [277]

6. Helen Macnaughtan, "Womenomics for Japan: Is the Abe Policy for Gendered Employment Viable in an Era of Precarity?," *Asia-Pacific Journal: Japan Focus*, April 5, 2015, http://apjjf.org/2015/13/12/Helen-Macnaughtan/4302.html.

7. McKenzie Wark, *Molecular Red: Theory for the Anthropocene* (London: Verso, 2015).

8. Anthony Dunne and Fiona Raby, *Speculative Everything: Design, Fiction, and Social Dreaming* (Cambridge, MA: MIT Press, 2013), 2–3.

9. Alan Galey and Stan Ruecker, "How a Prototype Argues," *Literary and Linguistic Computing* 25, no. 4 (2010): 406.

10. "Seiki katadotta sakuhin geijutsu ka waisetsu ka" [Is a decorated sex organ art or obscenity?], *Asahi shinbun*, December 17, 2014, chōkan edition.

11. Samantha Allen, "Japan's 'Vagina Kayak' Artist Fights Back against Obscenity Charges—and Misogyny," *Daily Beast*, January 13, 2015, http://www.thedailybeast.com /articles/2015/01/13/japan-s-vagina-kayak-artist-fights-back-against-obscenity-charges -and-misogyny.html.

12. Although the spelling differs, the pronunciation of *nico* and *niko* is the same. The spelling *nico* is part of the branding of the online commenting platform and is favored by its users; *niko* is the standard favored by linguists and dictionaries; and Niko is the preferred spelling of the name of the working group.

13. "Rokudenashiko 'Decoman,'" *Niconico dōga*, accessed June 30, 2015, http://www .nicovideo.jp/watch/sm24004330.

14. Kōichirō Eto, *Niko Niko Gakkai Beta wo kenkyūshite mita* [I went and studied Niko Niko Beta working group] (Tokyo: Kawade Shobō Shinsha, 2012).

15. While affiliated with research universities and corporate think tanks, Niko Niko Beta's organizers are less concerned with institutional authority than the think tanks analyzed in Marilyn Ivy's chapter in this volume. And while the extrainstitutional spirit of New Aca is echoed, Niko Niko Beta is less about epistemology's role in producing a "gay science" than about experimenting irreverently with forms of applied knowledge.

16. Niko Niko Beta partnered with Maker Faire to hold a conference in Singapore in 2015.

17. *Megumi Igarashi (Rokudenashiko): Art and Obscenity: Did the Japanese Police Go Too Far with Her?* (Tokyo: Foreign Correspondents' Club, Tokyo, 2014), https://www .youtube.com/watch?v=u35rEg_nTV8.

18. For a discussion of the "media mix" and pop culture commodity forms, see Marc Steinberg, *Anime's Media Mix: Franchising Toys and Characters in Japan* (Minneapolis: University of Minnesota Press, 2012).

19. Andrew L. Russell, "Modularity: An Interdiscplinary History of an Ordering Concept," *Information and Culture* 47, no. 3 (2012): 259. For a discussion of how Arthur Bemis's idea was transposed into Japanese architecture after 1945, see Izumi Kuroishi, "Mathematics for/from Society: The Role of the Module in Modernizing Japanese Architectural Production," *Nexus Network Journal: Architecture and Mathematics* 11, no. 2 (2009): 201–16.

20. Zhongjie Lin, *Kenzo Tange and the Metabolist Movement: Urban Utopias of Modern Japan* (New York: Routledge, 2010), 102.

21. Jeff Howe, "The Two Faces of Takashi Murakami," *WIRED*, November 1, 2003, http://www.wired.com/2003/11/artist/. Thanks to Namiko Kunimoto for noting the Murakami exhibition.

22. "United in Outrage, Protesters Printing Anti-Abe Posters in a Nationwide Campaign of Dissent," *Japan Times*, accessed February 16, 2016, http://www.japantimes .co.jp/news/2015/07/19/national/politics-diplomacy/anti-abe-posters-raised-across -nation-protesters-rally-security-bills/#. Published July 19, 2015.

23. The 3-D printer has changed design processes not only in architectural offices but also in artistic practice. Workspaces such as Fab Café in Tokyo's Shibuya neighborhood offer the use of facilities and machines such as 3-D printers for hire that struggling artists cannot afford on their own.

24. Rokudenashiko, *Watashi no karada ga waisetsu?!: Onna no soko dake naze tabū* [My body is obscene?!: Why is only my lady part taboo?] (Tokyo: Chikuma Shobō, 2015).

25. Mark Driscoll, *Absolute Erotic, Absolute Grotesque: The Living, Dead, and Undead in Japan's Imperialism, 1895–1945* (Durham, NC: Duke University Press, 2010). A comparably vulgar scene of the pink film is explored in *The Pink Book*, an anthology of writings on the "ero-duction" that is very much of this era—grungy, low budget, embedded (enseated?) in its viewing context, and slowly disappearing. Kimata Kimihiko's essay taps into an ancestral strand of parody and irreverence whose tributary may be found in Rokudenashiko's work. Essays by Roland Domenig and Kirsten Cather focus in particular on censorship issues, where Cather also points out that "obscenity" was a positive marketing term for pink films because it referred to a sub-genre. Sharon Hayashi's essay in the same volume notes Wakamatsu Koji licensed his staff to shoot "anything as long as it was anti-authoritarian and anti-establishment" (Sharon Hayashi, "Marquis de Sade Goes to Tokyo," 284). Markus Nornes, ed., *The Pink Book: The Japanese Eroduction and Its Contexts* (Ann Arbor, MI: Kinema Club, 2014).

26. Much crucial work has been done on the intellectual, social, and movement histories and discourses of ribu. In English, see Setsu Shigematsu, *Scream from the Shadows: The Women's Liberation Movement in Japan* (Minneapolis: University of Minnesota Press, 2012); and Vera C. Mackie, *Feminism in Modern Japan: Citizenship, Embodiment, and Sexuality* (Cambridge: Cambridge University Press, 2003). Curious readers interested in media are referred to a three-volume set of documents, Mizoguchi Akiyo, Saeki Yōko, and Miki Sōko, eds., *Shiryō Nihon ūman ribu-shi* (Tokyo: Shōkadō, 1992). Work on documentary film treats women in new left contexts; see Markus Nornes, *Forest of Pressure: Ogawa Shinsuke and Postwar Japanese Documentary* (Minneapolis: University of Minnesota Press, 2007). Many recent feminist studies of early twentieth-century social and art movements have recently appeared, forming a protohistory of ribu as seen in shōjo and revolutionary cultures, but a synoptic media history of ribu is still a work to come.

27. Rokudenashiko, *Watashi no karada ga waisetsu?!*, 117.

28. Yamai Kazunori and Saitō Yayoi, *Taiken rupo: Nihon no kōrei-sha fukushi* (Tokyo: Iwanami Shoten, 1994). Demachi Ryūji, *Taiken rupo: Zainichi gaikokujin josei no sekkusu 51-ka kuni: 5000-nin o "seiha" shita otoko no nikki* (Tokyo: Kōbunsha, 2011).

29. Masuko Honda, "The Genealogy of Hirahira: Liminality and the Girl," in *Girl Reading Girl in Japan*, ed. Tomoko Aoyama and Barbara Hartley (Oxford: Routledge, 2010), 19–37. Media artist Sputniko's work, based at the MIT Media Lab, has also used the cocoon as a metaphor for *shōjo* culture. See her 2015 installation, "Tranceflora: Amy's Glowing Silk," *Sputniko! Official Website*, accessed February 22, 2016, http://sputniko.com/2015/04/amyglowingsilk/.

30. Unlike other recent uses of the term "world," the decoman sculptures are not part of a larger narrative structure, nor are they translations of or exports to other national discourses. For the former approach, see Ōtsuka Eiji, *Teihon monogatari shōhi-ron* [Authoritative edition: On monogatari consumption] (Tokyo: Kadokawa Shoten, 2001). For the latter, see Pascale Casanova, *The World Republic of Letters*, trans. M. B. DeBevoise (Cambridge, MA: Harvard University Press, 2004).

31. See Simon Partner, *Assembled in Japan: Electrical Goods and the Making of the Japanese Consumer* (Berkeley: University of California Press, 2001).

32. Shinjuku Ophthalmologist Gallery website. See http://www.gankagarou.com/shop.html.

33. "3-D purintā yō dēta 'waisetsu-butsu' hanpu no utagai: Jishō geijutsu-ka taiho, yōgi hinin" [3-D printer data charged with "distribution of obscene item": Self-professed artist arrested, denies charges], *Asahi shinbun*, July 15, 2014, chōkan edition.

34. Ōnishi Wakato, "Āto to waisetsu—hasama de" [Between art and obscenity], *Asahi shinbun*, July 23, 2014, chōkan edition.

35. Cited in J.-F Blanchette, "A Material History of Bits," *Journal of the American Society for Information Science and Technology* 62, no. 6 (2011): 1042–57.

36. Campfire is restricted to people with Japanese addresses and bank accounts.

37. Samantha Allen, "Japan's 'Vagina Kayak' Artist Fights Back against Obscenity Charges—and Misogyny," *Daily Beast*, January 13, 2015, http://www.thedailybeast.com/articles/2015/01/13/japan-s-vagina-kayak-artist-fights-back-against-obscenity-charges-and-misogyny.html. That manga was called *Waisetsu-tte nan desuka?* and was published by Kinyōbi (for whom Rokudenashiko has written some articles) on April 3, 2015.

38. Shibuya Tomomi, "Sekai no shio: Rokudenashiko taiho ga aburidasu shakai no jinken kankaku" [Winds of the world: Rokudenashiko's arrest shakes up the perception of human rights], *Sekai*, no. 860 (2014): 38.

39. See Miryam Sas's essay in this volume about the afterlives of male revolutionaries.

40. Love Piece Club is open once a week by appointment, and does not allow male visitors. Kitahara is not only a small-business owner, but a visible public intellectual and writer. Her recent published *taidans* include dialogues with novelist Takahashi Gen'ichirō and academic feminist Ueno Chizoku. Along with sex toys, swimsuits and horoscopes, the store's website also blogs regularly on issues of concern to women, work, and sex with a focus on the sexual double standard that parallels Rokudenashiko's.

41. Rokudenashiko, *Waisetsu tte nan desu ka?* [What is obscenity?] (Tokyo: Kinyōbi, 2015).

42. "Zany, Cute, Interesting: Sianne Ngai on Our Aesthetic Categories," *Asian American Writers' Workshop*, accessed June 8, 2015, http://aaww.org/our-aesthetic-categories-zany-cute-interesting/.

43. As testimony to how powerful a re-alignment this is, I will note that her supporters in English have insisted in translating her work as "vagina" art. It's not, it's about the vulva, or the pussy, or—but the word "vagina" has come to be a part of public discourse in much more acceptable ways in the last twenty years due to Eve Ensler's play *The Vagina Monologues*. The play was produced both in English and Japanese beginning in 2004, when a Filipina theatre troupe did the first production.

44. *Support MK Boat Project! The World's First 3-D Scanned Peach on the Beach*, accessed June 9, 2015, https://www.youtube.com/watch?v=A5qq4cXoR9w.

45. For a representative manifesto, see Tanaka Mitsu, "Benjo kara no kaihō" [Liberation from the toilet], *Onna erosu*, no. 2 (1973): 178–90.

46. Shigematsu, *Scream from the Shadows*.

47. Kishida Masao, "Porno eiga no heroinu wa naze furui onna ka?" [Why is the porn movie heroine so old-fashioned?], in "Onna sogeki-hei" [The woman sniper], *Onna erosu*, no. 1 (1973): 170.

48. Kanba Michiko was the most frequently cited and mourned of these students. See Chelsea Szendi Schieder, "Two, Three, Many 1960s," *Monthly Review*, June 10, 2015, http://mrzine.monthlyreview.org/2010/schieder150610.html.

49. *Man* doesn't necessarily recall the English word referring to maleness, but it cannot be completely ruled out. A recent movement to encourage men to take a greater role in child raising is called the *ikumen* movement, from the words for raising children (*ikuji*) and the English "men." And the cartoon character Anpanman is, after all, an indeterminately aged male figure with a head made of delicious *anpan* (bean paste–filled bread).

50. As the trial dragged on, however, Rokudenashiko and her legal team began to use more examples of internationally-known artists such as Valie Export, Shigeko Kubota and Judy Chicago to point out the double standard at work.

51. Ueno Chizuko, *Onna asobi* [Women's play] (Tokyo: Gakuyō Shobō, 1988). I should note that Ueno's book—a New Aca edition—also uses the word "manko" without fuseji. Modular book design took off in the 1980s when the style of New Aca writing started to depend on data points of knowledge to which it linked in footnoted summaries and bibliographies. This mode of citation is linked to broader trends in data visualization, such as the chart (of intellectual movements, tendencies, and relations), and DTP design aesthetics allowed for multiple layers of print and page units without the labor of typesetting.

52. Article 175 has been especially active in policing "hair nude" or full-frontal nude photography where pubic hair but not genitals is captured. Enforcement of a block on photographing pubic hair started to relax in the 1980s and 1990s, with Shinoyama Kishin's 1991 *Water Fruit* a benchmark.

53. In this Rokudenashiko is like the photographer Takano Ryūdai, who had an exhibition at the Aichi Prefecture Art Museum from August through September 2014. The photos featured naked and mostly male bodies, and were censored; instead of taking the photos down, the photographer displayed them with the odd-looking curtains.

54. Norbert Wiener, *Cybernetics; Or, Control and Communication in the Animal and the Machine* (New York: J. Wiley, 1948).

55. Setsu Shigematsu, "The Japanese Women's Liberation Movement and the United Red Army," *Feminist Media Studies* 12, no. 2 (June 1, 2012): 163–79.

III. MEDIATION AND MEDIA THEORY

11. AN ASSAULT ON "MEANING"

On Nakai Masakazu's Concept of "Mediation"

AKIHIRO KITADA

Translated by Alex Zahlten

The sociologist Inaba Michio once complained that "the state of 'newspaper studies' is such that while there is a profusion of talk about whether the newspaper constitutes a medium or a mass medium, the theoretical meaning of the argument that a newspaper is a medium or a mass medium is not explored at all."[1] In the pages of the *Japanese Journalism Review* (*Shinbungaku hyōron*) Inaba proposed, as a remedy to this "state," a discussion of Nakai Masakazu's theory of mediation—despite the fact that Nakai had been known until then primarily for his philosophy of aesthetics.[2] The relevance of Inaba's acute formulation of the problem—"Media researchers disregard the question of 'What constitutes media?'"—as well as his attempt at opening interdisciplinary avenues through a link with Nakai's theory of aesthetics, has not faded in the thirty years since.

However, it seems difficult to dispute that Inaba's attempt to unearth the range of Nakai's work on aesthetics has been insufficiently pursued by subsequent "media researchers." Of course Nakai himself—the heretic theorist of aesthetics within the Kyoto school of philosophy—was not engaged in direct intellectual exchange with the "media research" specialists of his time such as Ono Hideo and Koyama Eizō.[3] Yet one can assume that Nakai, precisely by being situated outside of the institutionalized system of journalism studies, was paradoxically able to develop a penetrating logic regarding the problems of "What are media?" and "What kind of act is mediation"? The first two sections of this article will target the various approaches and answers Nakai's theories of technology and mediation offer to the basic question "What are media?" The last section will then proceed to ascertain the relevance of Nakai for contemporary media studies, especially the central fields of the theory of reception and theory of the public media sphere. The aim is to pursue and further develop the questions that Inaba raised thirty years ago within the present context.[4]

What Are Media and Technology? The Thinking of Unmediatedness and the Thinking of Common Labor

Any attempt to comprehend Nakai's discussion of medium and media (*baitai/media*) must naturally begin with a consideration of the early literature on Kant's third critique.[5] However, in light of the amount of space available here, this article will take a detour and first identify Nakai's deliberately assumed distance from the media technology discourses of his time, tracing his arguments by way of this contrast.

The cultural situation of the 1920s and 1930s saw the entertainment media of radio, sound film, and records permeating urban space. The metadiscourse turning these media technologies into objects of study can roughly be divided into two basic patterns. Nakai described the first pattern as focusing on the "living and romantic beauty of the machine," "detecting something alive, a combustion-inducing adoration, in the pathos-like passion of the machine, loving the great profile it discovers in the blueprint for steel and concrete."[6] This includes the views of machines held by American romantics such as Walt Whitman just as much as those by the futurists. The second pattern puts forth "a thinking that despises machinization and massification as the mortal enemy of culture," "imagining machinization, or the materialist machine, and its cold steel and toothed wheels cruelly wringing out the blood of humanity."[7] In other words, it theorizes the masses and machines from the perspective of alienation. Acutely contrasting these discursive spaces, Nakai then proceeds to discuss both of them critically.

First, he condemns the "machine romanticism" that stretches from Marinetti to Léger and cubism as being "not a legitimate push [toward the problem], but a temporary, fanatic gust, nothing more than an interested glimpse passing by in the accelerating fashion of street consumerism."[8] It seems legitimate to say that the foundations for this line of argument basically lie in Nakai's unique theory of technology that originates in Kant. According to Nakai, the "new perspective" that combines cause and effect phenomena subordinate to the natural order—such as falling water—with an intentional-ist "human order," expressed through such terms as "in order to," is part of "the meaning of technology as dialectical mediation."[9] In other words, the essence of technology's mediating character is not "mediation by epistemo-logical categories" (*ninshiki hanchūteki baikai*), which separates the human (the subjective / *shukan*) and the world (the objective / *kyakkan*) and thereby enables the former to consciously observe the latter. Rather, the essence of technology's mediating character is "mediation by existential categories" (*son-zai hanchūteki baikai*).[10] Like acquiring skills in sports, "humans can make mistakes, and based firmly on these mistakes turn the actions of the self into an object for the self, and through this mediation be able to create new actions by themselves."[11] Technology as mediator is then not an abstract phase, such as a school of thought and systematic principles, mediating human thought and consciousness; it is rather a (physical) thing that initiates the trial-and-error process of interaction between the human and nature, as well as, within this process, the transformation of its own functions/abilities. Technology is not a tool enabling the human manipulation of nature but rather a medium that enforces both reflection on and renewal of the very relationship of hu-manity and nature.

Such a perspective on technology must be critical of the romanticism that pulls the machine from the context of concrete usage—"abstract isola-tion rather than real existence"—and detects in the machine a possibility of overcoming the human. It is a romanticism that suppresses the original dynamic mediatory nature of technology while covering up the dynamism of the trial-and-error process with abstract theory.[12]

Next, when Nakai discusses alienation discourse, he does not treat it as a constative discourse but rather as a discursive effect brought on by the inse-curity of intellectuals unable to comprehend the historicity and the mediating nature of technology.[13] Thus, according to Nakai's diagnosis, when intellec-tuals attempt to comprehend the form of communication made possible by machines/technology through "existential category-based mediation" via the frameworks of modern individualism (where the subjective and objec-tive become epistemologically opposed) or romanticism (where the genius grasps the world's culture ironically), the result is "the philosophers' harsh criticism of machine culture."[14] But what exactly does this mean?

As just described, technology, neither affirming nor negating, enforces reflection on the relationship between humanity and nature. Put differ-ently, technology points out the fact that the *Etwas* called "self" is deprived of its privileged position as epistemological subject (*Subjekt*) in the world, and is relativized as a term (*kō*) in a function (*kino/kansū*) that is itself only one of many in the series of human–nature relationships.[15] That is to say, the individual and the self are nothing more than terms in the trial-and-error process mediated by technology. It follows that since the individual has become a term in a function, consequently "its expression as well as sensual reception exceeds the realm of individual consciousness, and is instead formed on the grounds of a collectively structured sociality" when it enters the territory of the machine/technology.[16] Now, when this historical state of the "functional relativization of the individual" and the "turn to a collective principle of expression and sensual reception" is judged from the emphatically modern frameworks of individualism or romanticism, the results are the contemporary notions of "alienation of human beings through technology" or "contempt for the masses." Nakai criticizes the intellectuals that so lament the "machinification and massification" in the following way: "A certain class of intellectuals commonly refers to machines, jazz, or the talkies when discussing their fears of the modern aesthetic. They endlessly bemoan these as unavoidable nuisances. However, at the heart of this lament lies a cruel contempt for humanity that these intellectuals themselves are perennially unaware of."[17] When reality, prompted by the mediation of the machine/technology, probes a new relationship between human beings and nature, intellectuals attack this as "human alienation" in their discourse. Such an enlightenment discourse, harboring a "cruel contempt for humanity," is much like Minerva's owl in always being too late to begin its flight, missing its opportunity.

Now, what form exactly does this concept of technology as a "medium" take, one that enables Nakai to criticize the futurist celebration of the machine as well as, one might say, the "cultural industry" approach of alienation theory? Here, the well-known distinction Nakai makes between *Mittel* (*baikai*) and *Medium* (*baizai*) is highly relevant.[18] We will try to grasp this distinction by using (1) the aspect of the relationship between medium and human, and (2) the aspect of the communication between humans (which is itself connected to the first aspect) as the two axes of investigation. The example of a boating competition, which Nakai himself employs, will make it comparatively easy to understand.

(1) First of all, let us think about the way that the tool/technology of the oar and the human body that employs it are involved with each other. As one can say of every sport, "mastering" a sport does not involve "understanding" the technique and rules of the sport by way of speculative thinking but

rather learning by experience on the level of corporeal knowledge, in the sense of "getting the hang of it," the respective connection between body—tool (oar)—nature (water).

> When the, so to say, structural *Funktion* of the water and the bodily structure's *Funktion* become deeply intertwined in a continuous and unobstructed relationship, it is exactly here that one finds a developing *Form*, a model of the living body.[19] This reduces the coach's countless admonitions to mere complications; this *Form* is basic and not conveyable with words but only as something that falls into place, or in other words, it is something only labor itself can convey.[20]

This "getting the hang of it" is obtained by "not leaving out a single beat of the oar, without deception, it is not something that must be said but rather something that must be tasted by the muscles." In other words, the distinction between the subjective and the objective becomes idle in the sense that "subjectivity is muscular, just as objectivity is muscular." Here, there is no room for the "conscious" theory and thought presented by the coach's directives that "must be spoken." Nonetheless, it is not as if the attainment of corporeal knowledge is achieved without any reflection. Certainly, reflection using abstract theory or thought as its Medium does not take place; however, in the continually ongoing negotiation/trial-and-error process between nature (water) and human (oarsman), an "Ah, that was it!" post factum kind of reflection is continually demanded of the oarsman.[21] Hence, what can unearth the opportunity for moving the subject toward direct and unmediated reflection is not "the mediation of the *Medium* on the conscious level" brought about by theory and thought (*shisō*), but the concrete reality of beating the oar.[22] Nakai refers to this "unmediated mediation," as one should call it, this paradoxical kind of mediation, as the *Mittel*, and clearly distinguishes it from the term he uses as representative of systematic thought, Medium.[23]

Keeping Walter Benjamin's theory of technology in mind, I would like to call the character of Nakai's concept of the Mittel a thinking of *Unmittelbarkeit*.[24] According to Nakai, the Mittel is not an apparatus for transmitting intentions/messages/meaning/information in the sense of "through or *durch*," but rather a site where humanity progressively renews/reestablishes/renegotiates the relationship with nature in the sense of "*amid* or *in*."[25] As the next section will show, this incorporation of the concept of the Mittel into Nakai's theory of film allows him to sharply contrast it with a discourse that simply posits film as a message-transmission device.

(2) Now this mediated—in the sense of a Mittel—boating competition will not only affect the individual relations of competitor—oar—water, it also effects a displacement of the communication between the athletes. This is to say: "every individual self follows the specific functions and positions of each of the other seats and only has a meaningful existence as a mutually collaborative existence."[26] Especially in terms of sports, it is "that mutual collaboration" that is the main point, "rather than a tool entrusted [*futaku-sei*] with considering the collective."[27] Of course, the type of cooperation discussed here is not one in which unity (*Einheit*) is guaranteed in advance through thought or concepts; rather it must be called a dynamic "common labor," based on the faith that "this is going well," which continually and mutually adjusts the basic state of dis-communication.[28] Individuals are not connected by transcendent ideas as in a social contract (as in a Medium-type mediation), but rather each individual relativizes itself as a term in a function. It is the "peculiar spatial character" of sports that creates the opportunity for reflecting on the relationship of one's function to others.[29]

I will call this intellectual perspective of Nakai's, one that stakes itself on a group structured by Mittel-type concrete action, "*Ko-operation* based thought." Nakai himself refers to this kind of common labor as possessing a "social collective character," and it can be thought of as sharply opposed to the concept of an (interpretative) community that is integrated by abstract "meaning."[30] The communication space made possible amid/in technology always already obstructs the all too easy pre-assumption of a homogenous identity.

Here it becomes clear that Nakai conceives the reproductive technologies of film and radio as shattering the (pre-machine-technological culture) aesthetics based on contemplation and individual reception through the medium of thought. He proposes viewing reproductive technologies affirmatively, as an opportunity for a space of unmediated coexistence between human beings and nature; here a common labor is realized that does not tolerate conceptual or individualist self-sufficiency. When modern individualism attempts to comprehend this opportunity, it simultaneously invites two discourses that actually stem from the same root: a romanticism that turns the machine into an object of contemplation, and an alienation theory that laments the burying of individualism under larger forms of organization. Yet, it is precisely Nakai's highly original theory of the medium, connoting the "thinking of direct, unmediated thought" and "thinking of common labor," that enables us to keep a distance from the binary options of both extreme optimism and extreme pessimism regarding machine/technological culture.

Severing the Space of Meaning: The Cinematic Theory of the "Lack of the Copula"

Nakai set his sights on film, the most popular medium of his time, as the space where "the thinking of directness / the thinking of unmediatedness" and the "thinking of common labor" were most completely realized. In the following I will focus on Nakai's fairly well-known theory of the "lack of the copula" to investigate his theory of film and media, all the while confirming the unique quality of his approach in the context of his time.

The copula possesses a syntactical function, essentially allowing the speaker (or writer) to present a judgment, such as "is" or "is not" (*de aru* and *de nai* in Japanese), regarding the content of a proposition, enabling easy comprehension by the listener (or reader). The copula can thus be thought of as an indicator that clarifies the intention of the speaker on a metalevel, in the sense of an instruction to "understand it in this way." Generally, in symbolic actions such as theater and literature, the continuity of meaning is controlled (to a degree) in advance by the sender by way of the copula. According to Nakai, film is characterized by the lack of such a copula: "Literature possesses 'is' / 'is not,' the copula that connects one representation to another. The sequentiality of film lacks this. What this means is that the filmmaker's subjectivity cannot attach conditions to an editing cut. It is the heart of the viewing public that establishes continuity between shots."[31] Of course, there is no question that filmmakers keep this fact in mind when working.[32] However, "even if the filmmakers intend to create a continuity of meaning from this 'cutting off' [*setsudan*], it is not possible for them to demand of the audience an explanatory account based on the copula in the manner of literature or novels."[33] In other words, film spectators go beyond the original intentions of filmmakers by reading an unanticipated continuity (a meaning-based connection of shot to shot); in film, any attempt to exert control via "meaning" is, in the end, futile.

Here it is important to keep in mind that the audience implied in the theory of the "lack of the copula" is not of the same kind as the hermeneutic reader of reception aesthetics, one that tries to fill a vacuum or fill in any kind of "meaning" that might be useful for interpretation.[34] Rather, presented amid or in film/media, this audience is able to transparently view (*durchsehen*) the new arrangement of the relation of nature-humanity itself.

For example, writing on the film *The Power of Plants* (*Kraftleistung der Pflanzen*, dir. Wolfram Junghans, 1934), Nakai praised the fact that this film, "by shooting the sprouting of a bud with dropped frames over a long period of time, and reproducing it in a talkie of 24 frames per second," creates an intersection between "plant time" and "human time," "placing the essential structure of the plant before the essential structure of the human, as if they can be converted into equivalents."[35] If a novel (*Roman*) were to attempt to express the same thing, it would necessarily "mediate it via psychological subjectivity" in the sense of "like a sprouting bud." In contrast, film does not mediate via the eminently human Medium of psychological subjectivism but rather allows the spectator to immediately/unmediatedly construct a "way of looking" at (or a way to read the transparency/*Durchsichtigkeit* of) this new nature. When the human connects with water via the medium of the oar, the opposition of human/subject to nature/object becomes invalid; in film, the human is able to see a state of nature and an immediate negotiative relationship that was previously inaccessible—the mediated marriage (*bai-kai kekkon*) of human judgment and physical order.[36] In other words, film is an opportunity to make manifest the "thinking of directness/unmediated-ness." Accordingly, the audience is not mediated by the human-born contemplative Medium of "consciousness" and "subjectivity," but rather it "sees through" an "unexpected order" or functional connection.[37] The "lack of the copula" is not compensated via human intentionality or "meaning/*Sinn*," but is gradually supplemented through an always ongoing projection/*Entwurf* by an audience that "within differential categorical structures discovers a projected and relational equivalence of the *modi* of concern [*Sorge*]."[38] This is not an audience that strings together a story or meaning in the sense of a hermeneutical subject but rather must be called a naked corporeal (*kinetic*) subject that, physically situated within the film-receptive space (*in*), creates an *Entwurf*.

This also means that, according to Nakai, the speech-based copula presented through dialogue in sound film or through subtitles and intertitles—facilitating control of the audience via the language-based meaning implemented by the filmmaking side—should not be viewed uncritically, much less affirmatively.[39] Certainly, as the sociologist Sugiyama Mitsunobu has pointed out, Nakai does not exhibit the same definite sense of crisis as Benjamin about the introduction of sound and how it turns film into a mere device that transmits "meaning."[40] He was, however, very clear that film-specific "cinematic sentences" and "cinematic sound" are entirely different from the language-based meaning of sub- and intertitles and cannot be reduced to linguistic meaning.[41] Nakai saw the "visual vocabulary" that is unique to film, and which creates a different horizon than the "spoken word," "written word," and "printed word,"[42] as overcoming the limits of conventional language-based meaning. It places stake in the opportunity to construct the new relationship between the human being and nature that the "thinking of directness/unmediatedness" dreams of, where "meaning" and "intention," which result in the continuity of comprehension, are ceaselessly deconstructed. Film is not a tool for transmitting messages or meaning in the sense of passing "through/*durch*." The person positioned "*in*" film, which severs the self-evident meaning-space of the everyday, relativizes his/her existence as a "term" in a function, or as "a body that completely becomes nature," and never ceases perceiving the continuously new arrangement of "human-nature" (or of connected functions).[43]

Just as in the case of sports, the film audience that projects a plan (=creates an *Entwurf*) into the "lack of the copula" is not solely situated in the relation of "individual (spectator)–technology (film)–nature" but also participates through common labor with others. Of course, it is the "individual" that is the point of reception for a film; yet, since the filmmaker cannot present a consistent recipe for "how to fill the lack" in a film, the spectator must constantly confirm his/her own "way of filling the lack" via his/her relationship with other spectators.[44] "Together the characters of the lens, film, and vacuum tubes possess a particular, collective character. This is not only in the sense that they possess a relational atmosphere as contemplative objects. Rather, it has to be stressed that they intrude into the senses themselves. They are, so to speak, the very nerve tissue of the social collective character."[45]

Take the example of a montage in which the timelines of various events are portrayed simultaneously, or in which a flashback summons past events into the temporal plane of the present. This evokes a temporality completely different from the quotidian sense of time, yet this filmic sense of time is by no means something that can be obtained individually. Rather, it is experientially acquired first through image-based conventions that are constructed socially or collectively: "The individual cannot accept this given light without passing through this new social collective atmosphere."[46] A "training" that takes place through common labor is necessary to experience the new sense (the new relation of human—nature) that the technology of film offers. Of course, it is not possible to completely share this sense with others through such training; yet if the exchange with others is abandoned, the "lack" cannot be filled, and it becomes impossible to see a film.[47] As long as a "way of viewing" based on a univocal "meaning" cannot be guaranteed, the audience must endure this endless process of common labor with others as a "viewing existence."[48]

For us, as a contemporary audience that naturally understands such "techniques" as the flashback, Nakai's arguments may seem exaggerated. However, we must remember that the 1920s and 1930s, when Nakai began his speculations on film, were without question a transitional period in which such conventions as described above were still in the process of becoming systematized and self-evident. A "memo" by Suzuki Shigesaburō illustrates this transitional aspect quite well:

> When visiting a third-run theater I saw there was a poster advertising the following week's screening, *Blood Splattered Takadanobaba* [*Chikemuri Takadanobaba*], and next to it a poster twice the size presenting a "warning" as follows: "In this film there are scenes that proceed very quickly. This is not a mistake of the projection, but a new method of shooting." It seems that if one goes to the theaters in the city outskirts that it is not uncommon to hear jeering when a flashback, which is currently very popular, appears: "Projectionist, get your act together!" ... It made me think that running a film theater is truly a tough job.[49]

Until the 1930s, in Japan the film narrator, or *benshi*, in communication with both the audience and the projectionist, played a central role by spinning out stories in an *occasional* sense. When Suzuki describes a jeering audience unable to understand the function of the "technique" of the flashback, it shows the "confusion" of bodies acclimatized to the reception style of benshi culture (which was centered around *jidaigeki*, or period films) coming into contact with foreign films that had fully internalized the unique "grammar" of film (while jidaigeki were basically copying theater, and the "lack of the copula" was somewhat weak). In the context of the twisting and turning of transitional spectatorship within the urban space, Nakai, rather than retreating to "stage-theatrical-like film" (which would have meant the submission of film to theater), or depending on the language-based meaning made possible by subtitles, intertitles, and the like (which would have indicated the defeat of film by literature), turned his thoughts to the possibilities of films that used a film-specific "visual vocabulary" that cultivated the common labor of the audience as a "viewing subject."

However, Nakai's views on the common labor of the audience are less restricted to the "audience" than reliant on his excellent discussion of the "collective." In an unpublished early text from 1930 titled "Collective Aesthetics" (Shūdanbi), he writes the following: "Public [kōshū] language is inflected with the sense of 'the multitude as chaos' and is related to a single center. But a collective's [shūdan] language implies the idea of 'the multitude as order,' an order in which everything, functions and compounds, are elements of the collective, and which derives from the mutual regulation of those elements. There is no center. Rather, the individual is a connective formation that has always already completely penetrated the whole."[50] Nakai's "collective" is characterized not by a public as "chaos," or as supported by a center/Medium, but rather by an autopoietic order, a multitude in which order emerges as a result of mutual regulation. Therefore, this must be understood as completely removed from the notion of the homogeneous community whose unity is (or should be) secured through some kind of idea/Medium, as was the case with the "proletariat that must be enlightened," the stance that [the 1920s/1930s leftist film organization] Prokino assumed, or with the "state citizen" that national policy films (kokusaku eiga) aimed for.[51] Rather, while retaining an excess that resists assimilating with the community, common labor is given the name "collective"—in contrast with the "public"—precisely due to this very continuous relationality itself. For Nakai film is not a device "through which" (durch), the ideological or hermeneutic space of the public was enlightened but rather a topos "amid which" (in) the public characterized by "multitude as chaos" was trained to move toward a "multitude as order."

To our contemporary eyes, Nakai's film and media-theoretical conception of film certainly seems excessively optimistic, with its idea of film as a training equipment, constantly presenting a new relationship of humanity and nature, and of the space of film reception as a locus where links with others, which resist the assimilation into a meaning-based community, can be born. However, in the discursive situation of the 1930s and 1940s, not only the national policy films supervised by the renovationist bureaucracy but also those produced by the leftist camp shared a view of film focused solely on appropriating cinema as a tool for the transmission of messages. Thus, Nakai's attempt to liberate film from a perspective that positions cinema as a device for the transmission of meaning must be regarded as exceptional.

Nakai is frequently remembered as the "progressive" coeditor of journals such as Beauty/Criticism (Bi Hihyō) and World Culture (Sekai Bunka), an "oppositional scholar of aesthetics" who organized resistance together with students during the Takigawa incident at Kyoto University and was later victimized under the Peace Preservation Law.[52] However, rather than reductively considering him an ideological dissenter, we should view him as a radical critic and materialist scholar of humanities who rejected the meaning-centered doctrine of modernism.[53] He should be regarded as a radical who saw through the—to this day inescapable—"disease of meaning."

The Current Relevance of Nakai Masakazu

Up to this point I have considered Nakai Masakazu's film theory together with an outline of his theory of technology and the medium. As a final point, I will now discuss the topicality of Nakai's ideas in the context of contemporary media research, especially the currently central themes of reception theory and media network theory.

First, by basing his theory of media technology on the "thinking of direct-ness/unmediatedness," Nakai brings to the surface the problems inherent in treating media as a simple transmission device for meaning/messages. The communication model of "sender—code—receiver" shared—if one abstracts the finer differences—by Claude Shannon and Warren Weaver's information theory, by semiotics in the vein of Umberto Eco and Roland Barthes, or by Stuart Hall's encoding/decoding model, all treat media as a device for transmitting meaning and information "through/*durch*."[54] It is difficult to say that these in any way suitably consider the status of the recipient with a concrete body "amidst/*in*" media who is constantly projecting herself. Of course, there is no need to deny the importance of ideology-focused readings, or of the critique of the content of transmissions and messages. However, is it not true that when analyzing, for example, manga, soap operas, or films, we inadvertently omit questions such as "Why manga?" or "Why television?" and thereby leave out the specific historical context of the respective media, simply extracting—truly in the sense of a Medium-type medium—an abstracted ideology? Drawing on Inaba's criticism from the beginning of this article, we can say that the question "What are media?" is overlooked in favor of a focus on the (highly modern) hermeneutical theme "What is the message?" and "How is it interpreted?"

Media technology is not merely an accessory "tool" to the mediation of thought and consciousness in the sense of a Medium. With Nakai's "think-ing of directness/unmediatedness," we are able to reassess the—one might say media-theoretical—state of the receiver: the human (the receiver) is a subject in the sense of an existential category (*Wie-sein*) that is amidst (*in*) media in a direct/unmediated way, and throws its body into the receptive space. It is not a hermeneutical subject (*Was-sein*) that limits itself to the interpretation of meaning.

Second, from the "thinking of common labor," which rejects the kind of community guaranteed by "meaning," our attention is emphatically turned to the heterogenous confusion of the "public sphere / *Öffentlichkeit*" made possible by media. Media do not simply expand communication in space and time but rather are a space where the discommunication with another person is exposed: the state of being in a double bind that is always already laden with the gap between "what is said / the message" and "what is connoted / the meta-message," in which the "failure" of transmitting an intention cannot be synchronously repaired via a direct meeting.[55] They are a field of confrontation that seems to repeatedly demand common labor for its continuity. For example, the recently much-discussed internet community should not just be seen as an information exchange system or an expansion of the time-space continuum of community; rather, we should give attention to the state of discommunication seen in the appearance of "flaming" and cyber-crimes. That is to say, we must not only abandon treating media as an information transmission apparatus but also relativize the dream that media will produce community in the sense of Marshall McLuhan's "global village."[56]

Nakai's penetrating thought does not regard film as a device for implementing community but as a locality for enduring the anxiety of common labor with that which is qualitatively Other. Of course, it goes without saying that the dominance of classical Hollywood (narrative) films had systematized film as a meaning device by the 1940s, and that, as various cinematic apparatus theories have pointed out, it had been conditioned into an ideological/subject-establishing device (apparatus).[57] However, as current developments in media technology have made diverse forms of reception possible, the problem of the corporeal character of reception through the audience, irrecoverable by the narrow communal interpretation of meaning, has to be addressed once again.

If one were, very simply, to position Nakai's theory of the medium within the coordinates of contemporary film studies and media research, it would look something like this:

The range inherent in Nakai's theory of film can be described as follows: First, it shares with the Antonio Gramsci / Hall schools of "hegemony / theory of articulation" (1) an awareness of how psychoanalytic theories of the subject-establishing apparatus (3) may have grasped the political nature of media but have simplified the spectator and disregarded the diversity/

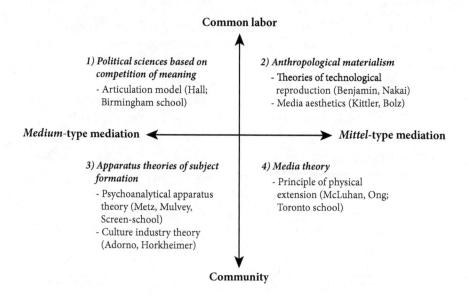

Common labor

1) Political sciences based on competition of meaning
- Articulation model (Hall; Birmingham school)

2) Anthropological materialism
- Theories of technological reproduction (Benjamin, Nakai)
- Media aesthetics (Kittler, Bolz)

Medium-type mediation ←——————→ *Mittel*-type mediation

3) Apparatus theories of subject formation
- Psychoanalytical apparatus theory (Metz, Mulvey, Screen-school)
- Culture industry theory (Adorno, Horkheimer)

4) Media theory
- Principle of physical extension (McLuhan, Ong; Toronto school)

Community

confusion of the multilayered interpretative space. Second, it does not focus on the struggle over the simple interpretation of meaning "through" media but rather prioritizes the status of the possibilities "*in*" media for the corporeal projection of the spectator (in a different sense than the technological determinism of [4]). Of course, Nakai's "theory" cannot lead to a framework for direct, experiential research in the sense of, for example, the encoding/decoding model. The question of how to inherit and translate Nakai's acute theoretical framework regarding media into effective, concrete research will test our "sociological imagination."

If it is true that, as media theorist Mizukoshi Shin has said, "tremors in media can awaken media theory," then Nakai's texts, just like Benjamin's, will be called upon again and again when society goes astray amidst the dynamics of the media environment.[58] Just as Inaba did when a flood of TV and weekly magazines rose before his eyes, we must once again "discover" Nakai at a time when rumors spread of the "decline of mass media."

NOTES

Originally published as Akihiro Kitada, "<Imi> e no aragai: Nakai Masakazu no 'bai-kai' gainen o megutte," in Akihiro Kitada, *<Imi> e no aragai: Mediēshon no bunkasei-jigaku* (Tokyo: Serika Shobō, 1994), 47–73. The translator would like to specially thank Patrick Noonan, Aaron Gerow, and Miya Elise Mizuta for their very helpful comments on the translation.

Nakai Masakazu (1900–1952) was a philosopher, critic, librarian, and social activist often seen as loosely connected—and sometimes placed in opposition to—the Kyoto School of philosophy. After graduating from Kyoto Imperial University in aesthetics and philosophy in 1925, he taught there until resigning in protest after the Takigawa incident (see footnote 52 for details). He was active as one of the chief editors of the leftist intellectual magazines "Beauty/Criticism" (Bi Hihyō) and later "World Culture" (Sekai Bunka) as well as the newspaper "Saturday" (Doyōbi), which relied largely on anonymous article contributions. Arrested in 1938, Nakai went on to become first vice librarian at the National Diet Library after the war. Today Nakai is best known for his theory of aesthetics, which has recently attracted renewed attention among a new generation of media scholars in Japan.

1. Translator's note: The sociologist Inaba Michio (1927–2002) was a prominent figure in Tokyo University's Newspaper Research Department (Tokyo Daigaku Shinbun Kenkyūjo) in the 1960s and 1970s, and served as department head from 1980 to 1984.

2. Inaba Michio, "Nakai Masakazu no 'baikai'-ron shōkai," Shinbunkagu hyōron 18 (1989): 112. Translator's note: The Japanese Journalism Review was published by the Japan Society for Studies in Journalism and Mass Media Communication from 1952 to 1992.

3. Translator's note: The journalist Ono Hideo (1885–1977) was instrumental in introducing newspaper studies (shinbungaku) in Japan. Partially due to his background in German philology, and partially for reasons of institutional legitimization, he chose the theoretically oriented German Zeitungswissenschaften (which also translates as "newspaper studies") as a model over the more pragmatically oriented American journalism studies. He also wrote the first monograph on the history of newspapers in Japan and later became the first director of the University of Tokyo's Newspaper Research Department. Koyama Eizō (1899–1983), a disciple of Ono's, was active in researching print media and advertising at various universities, introducing sociological approaches to the study of the press and its effects. For an excellent overview of the historical roles of Ono and Koyama, see Fabian Schäfer, "Public Opinion and the Press: Transnational Contexts of Early Media and Communication Studies in Prewar Japan, 1918–1937," Social Science Japan Journal, advance access, published June 28, 2010, doi: 10.1093/ssjj/jyqo30.

4. Nakai's quotes, unless otherwise noted, will be taken from the four-volume Nakai Masakazu zenshū, ed. Kuno Osamu (Tokyo: Bijutsu Shuppansha, 1964–81).

5. Sugiyama Mitsunobu, Sengo keimō to shakaikagaku no shisō (Tokyo: Shinyōsha, 1983).

6. Nakai, Nakai Masakazu zenshū, 3:251.

7. Nakai, Nakai Masakazu zenshū, 2:44.

8. Nakai, Nakai Masakazu zenshū, 2:74.

9. Nakai, Nakai Masakazu zenshū, 2:127.

10. Nakai, Nakai Masakazu zenshū, 2:124.

11. Nakai, Nakai Masakazu zenshū, 2:128.

12. Nakai, Nakai Masakazu zenshū, 2:74.

13. Translator's note: The term Nakai uses in Japanese and that has here been translated as "alienation discourse" is sogaironteki gensetsu, which actually carries a dual

meaning. First of all, it denotes a discourse on alienation, but it also hints at the fact that the discourse itself possesses aspects of alienation, or better, possesses an alienated quality.

14. Nakai, *Nakai Masakazu zenshū*, 2:45.

15. Nakai, *Nakai Masakazu zenshū*, 1:191. Translator's note: Here the double meaning of "function" in English comes into play, as Kitada uses both the words *kinō* and *kansū*, both of which can be translated as "function" in English. *Kinō* means "function" in the sense of ability or practical function, while *kansū* denotes a mathematical function (as in "a trigonometric function"). The word *kō* denotes a term in a mathematical function.

16. Nakai, *Nakai Masakazu zenshū*, 1:194.

17. Nakai, *Nakai Masakazu zenshū*, 2:78.

18. Nakai, *Nakai Masakazu zenshū*, 3:171. Translator's note: *Baikai* can be translated as "mediator" or "mediation," while *baizai* refers to a mediating material. Nakai himself uses the German terms.

19. Translator's note: Here Nakai uses the German words *Funktion* and *Form*. This pair was frequently discussed by Hegel and Kant, both major influences on Nakai's work.

20. Nakai, *Nakai Masakazu zenshū*, 2:419–20.

21. Nakai, *Nakai Masakazu zenshū*, 2:132.

22. Nakai, *Nakai Masakazu zenshū*, 2:136.

23. Walter Benjamin, "Gengo ippan oyobi ningen no kotoba ni tsuite," in *Benjamin korekushon I*, trans. Asai Kenjirō (Tokyo: Chikuma Gakugei Bunkō, 1995), 13. Also Imai Yasuo, *Benjamin no kyōiku shisō* (Tokyo: Seori Shobō, 1998), 62–64. Translator's note: Nakai himself uses the German terms *Mittel* and *Medium*. Aaron Moore translates the term as "middle" in his essay "Para-Existential Forces of Invention: Nakai Masakazu's Theory of Technology and Critique of Capitalism," *positions* 17, no. 1 (2009): 125–57. However, I choose to let the German term stand just as Nakai did (and Kitada does); the translation of *Mittel* as "middle" makes the term easily understandable but erases the philosophical reference to the Hegelian term *Vermittlung* just as much as the more quotidian meaning of "means to an end," both of which the heavily Hegel-influenced and German-reading Nakai was well aware of.

24. Translator's note: In German *Unmittelbarkeit* denotes immediacy, and literally means "unmediatedness."

25. This *Mittel*-type mediation can be understood as a *geworfener Entwurf*. See Inaba, "Nakai Masakazu no 'baikai'-ron shōkai," 112. Translator's note: The Heideggerian term *geworfener Entwurf* is usually translated as "thrown projection" or "thrown project" in English. For more on the term *Entwurf*, see footnote 38.

26. Nakai, *Nakai Masakazu zenshū*, 1:398.

27. Nakai, *Nakai Masakazu zenshū*, 1:399.

28. However, the workings of common labor (*kyōdō*) are, for those involved, grounded in the reliance on community (*kyōdōsei*), and it is exactly the failure of community that sets common labor in motion. Therefore, it is important to emphasize that the gap between common labor and community does not point to a distinction between two different patterns of communication. Translator's note: Nakai here contrasts two homophonic words, both pronounced *kyōdō*, that are written with different Chinese

characters and have a similar meaning but subtly different connotations. The more commonplace 共同 usually refers to cooperation or collaboration, while the less often used 協働 also denotes cooperation, but the characters emphasize the aspect of common labor and activity. This translation will follow these connotations in distinguishing the terms.

29. Nakai, *Nakai Masakazu zenshū*, 1:398.

30. Translator's note: Here I will follow Aaron Moore's translation of the term *shakai-teki shūdan-teki seikaku* as "social collective character"; literally, it connotes a combination of the concepts of society and community, which in turn relies on the distinction of *Gesellschaft* and *Gemeinschaft* proposed by Ferdinand Tönnies at the end of the nineteenth century, which again Nakai would have been aware of.

31. Nakai, *Nakai Masakazu zenshū*, 3:192. Translator's note: Nakai here uses the word *hyōshō*, which is usually translated as "representation" in English. He is thereby using the Japanese translation of the German *Vorstellung*, which is also commonly translated into English as "representation" (and is a very central term for both Kant and Heidegger). This translation has recently received some criticism, as it very much narrows down the meaning and implications of the German term, which is actually somewhat closer to "presentation," especially in its Kantian usage. Nakai will no doubt have been aware of that usage, so the word "representation"—used here for the sake of consistency—should be regarded with some caution.

32. Translator's note: Here the term *seisakusha* is translated as "filmmaker." The Japanese term can be written in two ways, and Nakai chooses one that is diffuse enough to encompass both directors and producers.

33. Nakai, *Nakai Masakazu zenshū*, 3:77.

34. Translator's note: Reception aesthetics is a school of literary criticism introduced primarily by Hans Robert Jauss and Wolfgang Iser.

35. Nakai, *Nakai Masakazu zenshū*, 1:171. Translator's note: In the original Nakai here uses the Japanese title of the film, *Moe dezuru chikara*. The one-reel film was directed by Wolfram Junghans for the largest German studio, UFA (Universal Film AG).

36. Nakai, *Nakai Masakazu zenshū*, 3:169.

37. Nakai, *Nakai Masakazu zenshū*, 3:253.

38. Nakai, *Nakai Masakazu zenshū*, 2:28. Translator's note: A few words on the nomenclature that Nakai employs: *Entwurf* is a Heideggerian term translated in Japanese as 投企 (*tōki*), and in English often as "project" or "plan"; however, to convey Nakai's usage of it, the Japanese term will here be translated as "projection," literally meaning a plan/project that is of a tentative, temporary nature (the Chinese characters used literally mean "thrown plan," and parallel the Heideggerian expression of a "*geworfener Entwurf*." In German *Entwurf* also means "draft, sketch," although the Heideggerian usage emphasizes the literal connotation of *Wurf*=throw; it is this physical connotation that Nakai also is undoubtedly aware of.

Sorge is Heidegger's term for the being of the being-there (*Sein des Daseins*). It is basically an existential-ontological term that refers to the complete structure of existence, although in German it literally means "care" or "concern," and that connotation carries over into Heidegger's theory as well; we are always already concerned / in care, as we are always already inside being.

39. Nakai, *Nakai Masakazu zenshū*, 3:196.

40. Sugiyama, *Sengo keimō to shakaikagaku no shisō*. Translator's note: Sugiyama Mitsunobu is currently professor on the faculty of literature at Meiji University. He has worked widely on the thought of postwar Japan and on the theory of journalism.

41. Nakai, *Nakai Masakazu zenshū*, 3:149. Nakai felt a need to examine this specific "language" of film, and actually produced an experimental film together with Tsujibe Seitarō, a fellow collaborator on the magazine *Bi hihyō* (Beauty/Criticism). Nakai Masakazu, "Shikisai eiga no omoide," in Nakai, *Nakai Masakazu zenshū*, 3:232–35. Also Iwamoto Kenji, ed., *Nihon eiga to modanizumu, 1920–1930* (Tokyo: Ribropōto, 1991), 205–9. Translator's note: Nakai himself referred to *Kinosatz* and *Kinoton*, and while Kitada quotes the Japanized terms *eigago* (映画語, literally "cinema language") and *eigaon* (映画音, literally "cinema sound"), the translation orients itself toward the nuance of the German terms.

42. Nakai, *Nakai Masakazu zenshū*, 3:150.

43. Nakai, *Nakai Masakazu zenshū*, 2:196.

44. Nakai, *Nakai Masakazu zenshū*, 3:160.

45. Nakai, *Nakai Masakazu zenshū*, 3:159–60. Translator's note: This quote takes hints from Aaron Moore's translation of the same passage, which can be found in Moore, "Para-Existential Forces of Invention," 144.

46. Nakai, *Nakai Masakazu zenshū*, 3:160.

47. Nakai emphasizes not an "enlightenment" via thought but rather a physical discipline that evokes "training, practice, getting used to" (Nakai, *Nakai Masakazu zenshū*, 1:415). In terms of film, his thinking here shares common ground with Benjamin, who argues that film was the "most adequate tool for training," a reception in the sense of distraction/*Zerstreuung*. Walter Benjamin, "Fukusei gijutsu jidai no geijutsu sakuhin," in *Benjamin korekushon I*, trans. Asai Kenjirō (Tokyo: Chikuma Gakugei Bunkō, 1995), 626.

48. Nakai, *Nakai Masakazu zenshū*, 3:310. Asada Akira's statement that "Nakai Masakazu [while denying that] a return to the old form of subjectivity was impossible, was, I think, trying to theorize a process in which the subjectivities do not stay bound to a single place but are connected transversally, opened up to the outside" encapsulates the point of Nakai's communication theory; Asada Akira, Karatani Kōjin, and Kuno Osamu, "Kyōtō gakuha to sanjū-nendai no shisō," *Hihyō kūkan* II, no. 4 (1995): 25. Also to be taken into consideration is Tsurumi Shunsuke's view that the relation of Nakai's concepts of organization (*soshiki*) and collective (*shūdan*) are like that of Japan to the "Japanese Soviet," one that differs from both the "individual" of modernist literature and from the "collective" of the Soviet or Chinese type. Tsurumi Shunsuke et al., "Zadankai: Nakai Masakazu to wareware no jidai," *Shisō no kagaku* 14 (1983): 84. See also Suzuki Tadashi's argument for similarities between Nakai's *Iinkai no ronri* [The logic of committee]; and Mao Zedong's *Jitsuroron* [On practice], in Suzuki Tadashi, *Nihon no gōri-ron: Kanō Kōkichi to Nakai Masakazu* (Tokyo: Gendai Shichōsha, 1961). See also Ueyama Shunpei, "Nakai Masakazu no 'Iinkai no ronri,'" *Shisō no kagaku* 23 (1960): 55–60.

49. Suzuki Shigesaburō, "Zakkan," *Eiga ōrai* (April 1928): 60.

50. Nakai, *Nakai Masakazu zenshū*, 2:184.

51. Translator's note: Prokino was the Nihon Puroretaria Eiga Dōmei (Proletarian Film League of Japan). Officially formed in 1929, Prokino was a left-wing organization with many prominent members from the film industry and film criticism, and was active in filming and screening of events such as labor day parades or demonstrations. It additionally published magazines such as *Shinkō Eiga* and *Puroretaria Eiga*, and produced educational animation. Coming under increased pressure from the government in the early 1930s, it was officially disbanded in 1934. For a detailed account of Prokino's activities in English, see: Markus Nornes, *Japanese Documentary Film: The Meiji Era through Hiroshima* (Minneapolis: University of Minnesota Press: 2003).

52. See, for example, Yamada Munemutsu, "'Bi hihyō,' 'Sekai bunka,'" *Shisō* 470 (1963): 101–14. Also see Hirabayashi Ichi, "'Bi—hihyō' 'Sekai bunka' to 'Doyōbi,'" in *Senjika teikō no kenkyū I* (Tokyo: Misuzu Shobō, 1968), 239–75. However, Kinoshita Nagahiro objects to the 1960s-style characterization of Nakai as an "oppositional person" by focusing on Nakai's "conversion" (*tenkō*) to the topic of "Japanese beauty." See Kinoshita Nagahiro, *Nakai Masakazu—Atarashii "bigaku" no kokoromi* (Tokyo: Riburopōto, 1995). While I am in agreement with Kinoshita's insight that Nakai's aesthetics contain elements that can be articulated within the discursive space of "overcoming the modern," I would, however, like to direct attention to the fact that Nakai's theory of technology/mediation has the fundamental potential of dislocating the very premise of a meaning-centered ideological critique. Translator's note: The "Takigawa incident" unfolded in 1933, when the minister of education, Hatoyama Ichirō (grandfather of the recent prime minister Hatoyama Yukio), forced the resignation of Kyoto Imperial University professor of law Takigawa Yukitoki due to supposedly Marxist thought. This led to the resignation of the thirty-nine remaining members of the faculty as well as organized protests by the students. The incident is referenced in Kurosawa Akira's film *No Regrets for Our Youth* [*Waga seishun ni nikui nashi*, 1946]. The Peace Preservation Law mentioned here refers to the Peace Preservation Law of 1925 (there were several previous such laws passed) that was in force until the end of the war in 1945. Introduced to provide the government with increased legal leeway for suppressing particularly leftist political activities, it essentially made any kind of political opposition potentially illegal.

53. Walter Benjamin, "Shururearizumu," in *Benjamin korekushon I*, trans. Asai Kenjirō (Tokyo: Chikuma Gakugei Bunkō, 1995).

54. Translator's note: The model of communication developed by Claude Shannon and Warren Weaver postulates a linear chain of information transmission. This chain consists of an information source, a transmitter that encodes the message, a channel through which it is transmitted, noise as an entropic factor that distorts the message, a receiver that decodes the message, and a destination at which it arrives. While Shannon was an employee at Bell Telephone Labs when they developed the theory, it proved immensely influential for the social sciences, although it has often been criticized for being applied to human communication in an overly simplified way.

55. I have elaborated on this kind of discommunication concept and its media-theoretical connotations in Kitada Akihiro, "'Kansatsusha' toshite no ukete," in *Masu komyunikēshon kenkyū* 53 (1993): 83–96. Further, for the distinction between "things

one is told" and "things that are connoted," see Paul Grice, *Studies in the Way of Words* (Cambridge, MA: Harvard University Press, 1989).

56. Katsura Eishi, "Automaton Kompurekkusu," in *20 seiki no media 3 maruchimedia no shosō to media porichikkusu*, ed. Katsura Eishi (Tokyo: Jasuto Shisutemu, 1996).

57. For the conditioning via film, see Nakamura Hideyuki, "Tobichitta gareki no naka o," in *Jōhō shakai no bunka 2: Imēji no naka no shakai*, ed. Uchida Ryūzō (Tokyo: Tokyo Daigaku Shuppankai, 1988).

58. Mizukoshi Shin, *Media no seisei* (Tokyo: Dōbunkan, 1993). Translator's note: Mizukoshi Shin is associate professor of the Interfaculty Initative of Information Studies at the University of Tokyo.

12. MUCH ADO ABOUT "NOTHING"

The Kyōto School as "Media Philosophy"

FABIAN SCHÄFER

Prelude: What Is "Media Philosophy"?

The term "media philosophy" (*Medienphilosophie*) is not particularly common in either Japan or the United States. Thus, I suggest beginning this article by explaining the term. Most philosophers of media agree that "media philosophy" does not deal with single media ontologies in particular but with the concept of "medium" itself. According to Stefan Münker, "It is the affair of media philosophy to reflect upon conceptual problems caused by the manipulation and utilization of electronic and digital media."[1] In addition to Münker, who considers media philosophy to have become particularly necessary in the digital age, Alexander Roesler defines media philosophy as "the contemplation on . . . the concept of the 'medium'" in general, namely "the apprehension of what this concept could mean and everything related to it." It is thus "the contemplation on the theoretical ramifications this concept has for other concepts, and on the status of theories built around this concept."[2]

In everyday language, the term "media," or "*the* media," is most commonly used interchangeably with "mass media," and thus functions as an umbrella term for different types of information or entertainment media, such as radio and television broadcasting, the press, or film. From an etymological perspective, however, the Latin term *medium*, as well as its Sino-Japanese counterparts *baikai* and *chūkai*, refer to the "middle" or "middle ground" (*medius*). Moreover, as something situated "in-between" (*metaxy* in Greek), the medium "mediates" (namely constitutes *and* separates) the things that lie on either side of it—it is the mediation of things mediated in a medium. Accordingly, "in-betweenness" and "mediation" might thus be considered the two most fundamental philosophical meanings of the concept "medium." German philosopher Georg Christoph Tholen describes this pair as the philosophically "strong" conceptual meaning of the term, arguing that it was with the Enlightenment and Romanticism that "[an idea of the] self-referentiality of language-induced understanding assumed shape, which didn't consider the medium as a passive tool or instrument, but as the constitutive activity of 'in-betweenness.' "[3] Whereas the focus lay exclusively on the role of language in the Idealistic and Romanticist media philosophy of Hegel or Schleiermacher, its contemporary counterpart "assumes a universal concept of the medium, which enables us to understand language as merely one specific and prominent medium amongst others."[4] Hence, philosophical investigations into the concept of the medium, according to Sybille Krämer, refer to the "study of the constitutional power of the medium" within the epistemological process of cognition and apperception in general.[5]

With that said, what I will attempt to do in the subsequent part of this chapter is to reread the Kyōto School, Japan's most prominent strand of modern Japanese philosophy, as a Japanese version of a media philosophy in the aforementioned sense. This is of the utmost importance, since the Kyōto School has been repeatedly and exclusively labeled as a "philosophy of nothingness." Scholars in Japan who contributed to this opinion were assisted by scholars of Japanese religions in Europe and the United States, who considered the proponents of the school as creators of an original Japanese or "Eastern" spiritual mysticism or Buddhist theology based on nothingness, which they could exoticize and oppose to certain dogmatic religions or rationalistic philosophies in the "West." Moreover, the sole critique of this affirmative view of the school was in fact just as ideological, since it was mostly Marxist or leftist scholars who, since the postwar period, criticized certain proponents of the school for their unprompted hypostatization and essentialization of the term "nothingness" in the 1930s and 1940s, so that it would match with the official propaganda of the Japanese ultranationalist wartime regime.

If one shifts attention away from the concept of nothingness and instead toward the concepts of "dialectic" (*benshōhō*) and/or "mediation" (*baikai*)—dialectics understood here as one form, or rather method, of mediation—

one is able to observe at least one further conceptual constancy in the 1930s among the school's core members. Accordingly, I will argue that—borrowing and slightly modifying the title of James Heisig's landmark study of the thought of the Kyōto School, *Philosophers of Nothingness*—one might also consider the members of the school as *philosophers of mediation* and, thus, the Kyōto School as a school of "media philosophy."[6] Considering mediation and in-betweenness instead of nothingness as common conceptual denominators reveals a very different picture regarding possible membership of the school. Not only would Watsuji Tetsurō's concept of in-betweenness (*aidagara*) or Kimura Bin's concept of in-between (*aida*)—which I unfortunately do not have the space to touch upon in this chapter—fit perfectly in this regard, but so do thinkers not typically associated with the school, most notably its "left wing," namely Tosaka Jun, Nakai Masakazu, and Miki Kiyoshi.

Rereading the Kyōto School as media philosophy, however, is also significant in that it broadens our understanding of the prewar discourse on media in Japan in general, which was at that time dominated by single media theories of the press, emerging from the then new academic discipline of *shinbungaku* (newspaper studies).[7] In fact, until as recently as 1989 sociologist Inaba Michio could still complain that newspaper studies, based on its own disciplinary boundaries, did not produce a more universal theory of the medium.[8] To remedy this theoretical desideratum, Inaba himself introduced Nakai Masakazu's media philosophy of the 1930s (see also Kitada Akihiro's chapter in this book) in which he, together with Tosaka Jun, engaged in an intellectual debate on the philosophical meaning of film. The aim of this chapter, however, is to take a further step back in time and inquire into the various ways the first generation of thinkers of the Kyōto School dealt with the concepts of medium and mediation, which has to be understood as the intellectual background against which Nakai could develop his thought.

Nishida and Tanabe: "Unmediated" and "Absolute" Mediation

Generally, Nishida's thought is divided into at least three, though sometimes five, phases, characterized by the terminology he used predominantly at each particular stage of his thought. Nevertheless, one can argue that the foundation of his thought was already included in his first important book, *An Inquiry into the Good*, (*Zen no kenkyū*), published in 1911.[9] Here Nishida defines "pure existence" as the nondivided "Chora"—in a Derridean sense, so to speak—prior to any epistemological or ontological division into subject and object, being and nonbeing, or spirit and matter:

By pure I am referring to the state of experience just as it is without the least addition of deliberative discrimination. The moment of seeing a color or hearing a sound, for example, is prior not only to the thought that the color or sound is the activity of an external object or that one is sensing it, but also to the judgment of what color or sound might be. In this regard, pure experience is identical with direct experience. When one directly experiences one's own state of consciousness, there is not yet a subject or an object, and knowing and its object are completely unified.[10]

The phrase "direct [*chokusetsu*] consciousness," by which Nishida refers to this precognitive condition in which subject and object cannot yet be thought of as distinct entities, is replaced by various other terms in the subsequent phases of his intellectual development. Starting with *Jikaku ni okeru chokkan to hansei* (Intuition and reflection in Jikaku, 1917), the term *jikaku* replaces Nishida's often-misunderstood notion of pure consciousness, and has since then found a permanent place in his thought. Commonly mistranslated as "self-consciousness," the compound consisting of the two characters *ji* (self) and *kaku* (aware) is perhaps best translated as "self-awareness." In Nishida's own words, *jikaku* needed to be understood as "a self, reflecting itself in itself."[11] It is therefore not the conscious self-reflection of the Cartesian ego and does not refer to a perceiving or knowing Kantian subject (self), but in fact means a completely unmediated spontaneity (*Von-sich-selbst*).

Heralding the beginning of the third phase of his thought, Nishida, in another anthology published in 1927, *Hatarakumono-kara mirumono-e* (From acting to seeing), for the first time employed the original term *basho* (place, or, perhaps more accurately, field) of "absolute nothingness" (*zettai mu no basho*) to explain, and slightly modify, the function of pure experience or *jikaku*. Nishida's nothingness is an absolute nothingness because it is different from relative nothingness in the sense of "nonbeing." Nevertheless, absolute nothingness is not the same as "absolute negativity," as Nishida pointed out, since within the field of absolute nothingness affirmation and negation reciprocally self-reflect each other eternally; it is a field engendering (*umareru*) and extinguishing (*kie*) all contradictions, which at the same time lets "these contradictions retain in themselves."[12]

Since the end of the 1920s, which was considered to be the beginning of phases four and five of Nishida's intellectual development, Nishida started to use the term "dialectic" to describe the nature of the preontological and preepistemological field of nothingness. He found the concept of dialectics so useful in relation to his own thought because he considered it a prelogical concept—something he (mis)understood through his reading of Marx and Hegel—that integrates all contradictions. In his understanding, dialectic was the "absolute contradictory self-identity" of the subject and object in particular, and of the universal and the individual in general. Nishida explicitly differentiated, in his terms, this "true" understanding of dialectic (*shin no benshōhō*) in the sense of an all-embracing "dialectical space" of nothingness, encompassing all possible contradictions, from any form of Hegelian or Marxian "procedural" (*katei-teki*) dialectics.[13] Despite the fact that Nishida began to use the term "mediation" (*baikai*, denoting it "M") almost synonymously with the term "dialectic" in his thought in a further attempt to conceptualize nothingness as the mutual interrelation and interpenetration of all things, since around the beginning of the 1930s, nothingness in fact remained something unmediated and absolute:

> True dialectical determination needs to be thought of as the mutual determination of at least three things: A relates to B in the same way as to C, and B to A and C in the same way as C to A and B. . . . To think of the mutual determination of these three things in such a way means the same as to think of it as the interrelation among innumerable individuals. It is only in this way that the mutual determination of truly independent things, i.e., the mutual determination of individuals, can be conceived. . . . The medium M between individuals signifies a placial/-field-like determination. This is the reason why I define dialectics as the self-determination of the dialectical universal, and why I ground it not on procedural determination, but on placial/-field-like determination. My notion of one [universal] qua many [individuals; *ichi soku ta*], of many qua one, also signifies this placial/-field-like determination. . . . The idea of an internal link fails here, and ideas of the linear and the procedural must be negated. Otherwise, we remain bound to the standpoint of the idealistic dialectic.[14]

This is not concrete mediation but rather the *sum of all possible mediations* between innumerable individuals. It should be apparent already that Nishida's philosophy of nothingness, particularly his nondialectical understanding of dialectics, in fact represents a philosophy of nonmediation rather than one of mediation, and as such, is fairly remote from what I have called "media philosophy." For Nishida, dialectics in fact meant the self-contradictory "unmediated mediation" (*mu-baikai-teki baikai*) of any possible ontological or epistemological opposition within the place/field of absolute nothingness.[15]

Nishida understood dialectics not in the Hegelian sense as the triangular movement of thesis, antithesis, and synthesis (or a mediating tertium, something in-between A and C), but instead used it as yet another name to denote the field of absolute nothingness, in/from which any contradiction or conceptual opposition collapses and arises. Nevertheless, it was his "misappropriation" of the term that gave cause for critical debate on the meaning of the concept of "mediation" within the Kyōto School at large.

In the first instance, it was Nishida's colleague Tanabe who accused Nishida of absolutizing and hypostasizing nothingness, because to him, Nishida's unmediated or transdialectic absolute nothingness must be considered an "ultimate and static-transhistorical thing" (*chorekishi zettai-teki naru mono*) and thus the complete opposite of something dialectically mediated. To Tanabe, any assumed dynamic inherent to absolute nothingness which could trigger a process of distinction into subjects and objects, or into the particular and the universal, could thus be merely described as emanationist (*hasshutsuron-teki*). To him, Nishida's philosophy was nothing but a permutation of idealistic Fichtean identity philosophy—and hence a monistic philosophical theory rejecting any ultimate bifurcation into spirit and nature or subject and object, finding fundamental unity only in the absolute:

> If one turns absolute nothingness into the underground or background of the dialectical world and considers this as the place where all beings are situated . . . , absolute nothingness is fixated into an immediate being and at the same time actually forfeits its meaning as nonbeing. Thus, despite all other beings that are negatively mediated [*baikai*] as dialectical unity of negation and affirmation [*hitei soku kotei*] and become being within nothingness, the place of mediation itself, which lets them be beings within nothingness, is nondialectically and immediately affirmed. Thereby absolute nothingness forfeits its meaning as being as well as nothing and inevitably turns into an immediate being.[16]

In Nishida's thought, absolute nothingness is not mediated, either in the sense that it is a middle, or mediation, or in-betweenness. According to Tanabe, for nothingness to be truly dynamic and dialectical, its nature cannot possibly lie in an unmediated annulment of all contradictions and oppositions but rather has to sustain the mediated tension between them. Put differently, Nishida's monistic and static understanding of dialectics as unity-despite-duality stands against Tanabe's dialectical and procedural duality-despite-unity. In opposition to Nishida, Tanabe understood dialectics as the "universal mediation of any particular through the universal," and not as the reciprocal annulment of both within the field of nothingness. In this regard, Tanabe's critique resembles Horkheimer and Adorno's severe repudiation of any kind of sociological or philosophical thought based on the nondialectical and total identification of the universal and the particular, which "nullifie[s] . . . the absence of tension between the poles: the extremes which touch have become a murky identity in which the general can replace the particular and vice versa.[17]

Any dialectical mediation, to be a true mediation (and not some philosophically nonsensical and superficial application of the rather specific term "mediation" as "unmediated mediation") has to be thought of as procedural. In fact, Nishida's interchangeable usage of the static-transhistorical absolute nothingness and terms such as "mediation" and "dialectics" must be considered a categorical mistake, because the latter cannot, by terminological definition, encompass an idea of a superordinate and ultimate truth, even if this ultimate "truth" is considered as "absolute nothingness."

Refusing to succumb to the pitfalls of identity philosophy as Nishida had done, Tanabe asserted that, for an absolute mediation between the particular (individual) and the universal (genus) to be truly dialectical, the species (*shu*) is necessary as a mediating third term (which from here on I will call the *tertium mediationis* of mediation), in the sense of something lying in-between, reciprocally mediating the things mediated. Generally speaking, and this is important, Tanabe's inclusion of the third term into the process of mediation (what other than a "process" would mediation be?) must not only be considered an intellectually innovative attempt to convert Nishida's identity-philosophical perspective into a genuine media-philosophical perspective, but also an intellectual intervention into underlying post-Kantian "correlationism," itself based on the Cartesian dualism of subject and object that forms the basis of most philosophies in the West.[18]

Hence, it is arguable that it was not until Tanabe's substantial critique of Nishida's paradoxical idea of the nonmediatedness of nothingness that the members of the Kyōto School improved theoretically by performing a turn toward a true media philosophy. This turn, however, would remain unnoticed by Western scholarship, because of the aforementioned labeling of the Kyōto School as an "Eastern" philosophy of "nothingness." Beginning with Tanabe's critique of Nishida, it was, in particular, the disciples of the two with a strong inclination toward Materialist dialectics, most significantly

Tosaka Jun, who not only further advanced Tanabe's critique of Nishida but also developed unique philosophical answers to the problem of dialectics and mediation worth taking into consideration.

Tosaka and Nakai: "Three-Dimensional" Dialectic and "Technical Mediation"

Tosaka's critique of Nishida overlaps with Tanabe's in various aspects. For Tosaka, too, Nishida made the mistake of eventually "equat[ing] nothingness with being" in his thought.[19] According to Tosaka, for Nishida the contradiction between being and thought lies neither within thought nor within being but arises from the bottom of nothingness, in which the difference of thought and being itself is not yet conceived.[20] Nishida, Tosaka concluded, despite offering a very thorough inquiry into the origin of the meaning of contradiction, and thus of a possible "meaning" of dialectics, wanted to make his readers believe that "he found through this inquiry into its meaning, the cause of dialectic itself."[21] This equation of cause and meaning, however, necessitated an all-compassing "cosmological system of meanings" (*imi no uchū-ron taikei*), which—taken by itself, Tosaka admitted—might be considered as completely coherent. However, Tosaka argued, if one replaces the determination of being by a system of meanings, one "tacitly replaces the determination of being with an interpretation of the meaning of being." In this sense, Tosaka suggested, Nishida did not look at how things "really are" but was instead merely interested in the denomination of things and their respective meaning; in other words, instead of "being concerned with what society, history, and nature actually are," he inquired into the "meaning of concepts such as society, history, and nature" and the position they "occupy in a categorical system of meanings."[22] This becomes most obvious with regard to the question of the dynamics of Nishida's dialectic. From where, Tosaka asks, would Nishida's in fact merely interpretative "transdialectic" (*chō-benshōhō-teki*) gain its dynamic (*dōryoku*), namely its "dialectical contradiction" (*mujun*), if any "dialectical dynamic necessarily has its origin in this contradiction"?[23]

Eventually, the "logical instrumentarium" applied by Nishida was one of mere "metaphysical categories," by which he tried to interpret the meaning of dialectic, and not dialectic as such.[24] No different from a great deal of philosophy produced at academic institutions, Nishida's thought was, to Tosaka, an idealistic-metaphysical "bourgeois philosophy" that was merely an "ideational systematization and organization of fundamental concepts or categories of reality," an "interpretation of the world" (*sekai no kaishaku*), and therefore a kind of philosophy that, in its refusal to speak of the impetus to change it, was not interested in actual reality.[25] Instead of "clarifying the real order of things," Nishida applied a clever "trick" (*teguchi*) allowing him "to establish and maintain an order of meaning [*imi no chitsujo*] to correspond with reality."[26] In the final analysis, Nishida's philosophy, in Tosaka's view, turns out to be nothing other than a more refined sort of hermeneutic (and thus purely idealistic) philosophy.[27]

Naoki Sakai argues in his reading of Tosaka that the latter's "critique of [Nishida's] hermeneutics is inadequate" because it overemphasized existence over consciousness from a Materialist perspective and thus "did not pay attention to the poietic function of interpretation."[28] Although Tosaka *did* have a strong inclination toward Materialism, Sakai himself clearly overlooks the fact that Tosaka did not uncritically adopt a deterministic orthodox-Marxist viewpoint, which would argue that the latter was determined by the former. Rather, to Tosaka, the relationship of "individual consciousness" and "historical-social existence" was based on the fact that both progress "logically" in the broadest sense of the word. On the one hand, the mind worked cognitively in the idealistic sense of Kant or Hegel because "consciousness could only come into effect as consciousness by means of its capability to think logically."[29] On the other hand, however, existence progressed logically as well, because it was based on the (dialectical) "logic of existence" (namely historical materialism), which represented "existence's necessary structure." Hence, Tosaka declared that it was this twofold logic that "mediates" between existence and consciousness.[30] However, Tosaka emphasized, although the determination between the two was mutual, each had different qualities. He explained, "The way in which consciousness determines matter (existence) is partial, fragmentary, and noncosmological [*sekai hōsoku-teki de nai*]. On the contrary, matter (existence) can formatively determine the contents of consciousness. Only matter determines things in a universal, categorical, and cosmological way."[31] To put it in the words of Joachim Israel, Tosaka was not an "ontological" but a "methodological materialist," who begins his inquiry not from transcendental reflection, as Nishida did (despite the fact that the latter refused his labeling as an "idealistic" philosopher by Tosaka), but from the social-historical world.[32]

Having summarized Tosaka's own critique of Nishida's philosophy, I will now discuss the temporal and practical structure of mediation, which will lead us beyond Nishida's notion of a nonprocedural and static unmediated mediation.

The merely hermeneutic character of Nishida's thought becomes most obvious in his philosophy of time and history. Nishida understood time, diverging from the commonsensical linear understanding of time, as something evolving against the background of the "discontinuous continuity" (*hirenzoku no renzoku*) of "true time."[33] To him, this was the "self-determination of the present" or the "self-determination of the eternal now," out of which the three modes of time, and therefore time as it exists in our consciousness, come to the foreground. For Nishida, Tosaka argued, "the present is something . . . that can expand into eternity," whereby Nishida equated "the present with the past, the present, and the future."[34] In Nishida's own philosophical jargon this is formulated as follows: "Time, as the self-determination of the eternal now vanishes [*kie*] and emerges [*umareru*] everywhere. Therefore, time touches the eternal now at every moment. That is to say, time vanishes and emerges from moment to moment. Time has to be thought of as 'discontinuous continuity' [*hirenzoku no renzoku*]."[35] Nishida explains his understanding of history and how it corresponds to this idea of time only three years later in an essay titled "Self-Identity and Continuity of the World" (Sekai no jiko dō'itsu to renzoku): "History is not merely development, but metamorphosis. The different historical times can all be considered as metamorphoses of primordial history [*genrekishi*]. One can say that each time as a self-determination of the eternal now reflects the shadow of the [platonic] idea."[36] Tosaka harshly criticized this otherworldly understanding of time and history as a permutation of discontinuous continuity or primordial history by asking, "Why [does Nishida] explain time ensuing from its origin or a primordial time," if "this means an inversion of the order of things?"[37] For Tosaka, history, in contrast, had to be considered from the opposite direction, namely the end of time that is open and contingent: the future. In other words, he considered the "character [*seikaku*] of time" to lie not in its (assumed) origin, "but in the exactly opposite direction, namely the point from which time is moving towards us."[38]

Despite being critical of Tanabe's emphasis on religion and Christianity in particular (Tanabe repeatedly referred to the Holy Trinity to explain the relationship among the individual, the species, and the genus),[39] Tosaka was in general very sympathetic to Tanabe's logic of the species because the latter emphasized its meditated and temporal character. At some point, to explain his notion of dialectical "absolute mediation," Tanabe compared the mediating role of the species to the uniqueness of the present among the three temporal forms:

Nobody would deny that time is something which is absolutely mediated by the three modi past, present, and future, and that each of these three modes is essential for the mediation of the remaining two. . . . However, one would at the same time also not deny that the mediation by the present occupies a particularly unique place in the realization of time. . . . For us to be positioned in the present, the movement and the unity of time are related to each other. The mediating character of the present does not merely contradict the character of absolute mediation, it enables it. To doubt this would mean to consider the logic of absolute mediation not as dialectical, but to objectifyingly turn it into formal logic.[40]

In this regard, the species in Tanabe's Aristotelian thought occupied a unique twofold mediated middle position in-between the individual and the universal (genus)—namely, individual ↔ species ↔ genus. This is very different from Nishida's aforementioned notion of absolute mediation as the "interrelation among innumerable individuals." Tanabe's mediation of the present was absolute only in the sense that it was embedded in "a real dynamic of reciprocal dialectical negation and affirmation."[41] Tosaka, in his philosophy of time/history, further developed Tanabe's notion of dialectical (absolute) mediation and logic of the species in a Materialist direction.

PRAXIS AND THE THREE-DIMENSIONAL MEDIATION
OF ACTUAL REALITY AND PROJECTED FUTURES

For Tosaka, logical and temporal "three-dimensionality" signifies the contingency of history in the present toward the future. One cannot—as Nishida did—consider the future as the future in the present but rather as a future present in the sense of a "possibility not yet given to us," which can be shaped through contemporary praxis, since "society, or the social world, is . . . something . . . mediated, i.e., produced by man," and "something which is produced [that] can also be changed," as Joachim Israel put it.[42] Accordingly, Tosaka insisted, with a sharp-knifed attack on Nishida's one-dimensional "mediation" of primordial history, that a three-dimensional understanding of history has nothing to do with an idealistic utopia, because

only if we treat the historical, namely the historico-social, as a question of praxis, logic and the three-dimensionality of the now completely coincide (instead of merely corresponding to each other). . . . Although historical perspectives, namely [Nishida's] difference between before and after or fore- and background, might possess different logical values, it is nothing but a logical fallacy eventually inhibiting any praxis to consider the given reality and the future not yet given to us on the same plane as something nonquotidian or formal-logical. This is a logical fallacy usually described also as utopia.[43]

Among the three temporal forms, the present therefore occupies a particular position in Tosaka's thought as well, since it is the "centre of three-dimensional historical time," which can "expand and contract if necessary."[44] The necessity according to which the present time can "condense" even into the today (*kyō*) or the now (*ima*) is "the necessity of practical life" (*jissen-teki seikatsu*).[45] Eventually, the character of the present determines each single moment of time—both "are identical by their meaning."[46] Tosaka described this coincidence of the whole historical time in the now also as a basic principle of his philosophy of everydayness (*nichijō-sei no genri*).

Hence, one can understand Tosaka's philosophy of the everyday developed in the 1930s as an important attempt to take a stand against any teleological (modernistic or orthodox-Marxian) or metaphysical-idealistic interpretation of history, such as that of his mentor Nishida. Behind Tosaka's philosophical reappraisal of the "actuality" of the everyday lay the attempt to liberate Japanese academic philosophy, basically represented by idealism, phenomenalism, or the Kyōto School, from its dependence on religion, its otherworldliness, its celebration of the noneveryday, and its engagement with purely metaphysical terms such as *genjitsu* (reality). Tosaka, rejecting all purely phenomenological, psychological, or scientific explanations of time and history in particular, in an interesting move that combines Heidegger and historical materialism, located the logic of time not in individual consciousness but in history itself. It was his idea that "the present" (*genzai*) and "the now" (*ima*) represented the "kernel" of historical time, because the present as a period (*gendai*) was not just a historical period like any other, but, to Tosaka, something in which "the accent of total historical time" lay.[47] The now (which Nishida understood as the imperceptible moment in the foreground of an underlying "eternal now" or "primordial history" from which single historical periods would miraculously evolve) in Tosaka's thought represents the profane everyday that facilitates—despite being determined by current politico-economic conditions—(revolutionary) class praxis which dialectically mediates the actual present with a better possible future.

From the perspective of media philosophy, however, Tosaka seems to be entangled in a kind of moderate but still naïve mirror theory of representation. Despite acknowledging elsewhere that the "realization of mimetic representation [*mosha*] is by no means the result of direct, natural, and un-conditioned reflections but always involves the process of exerting endless mediation" and thus "is never like what one thinks of as [a] passive and con-templative mirror" and "nothing but a sign that indicates the goal of cognition gained through mimetic representation,"[48] a uniquely dialectical answer to the question of the epistemological function and temporal and practical structure of the medium qua mediation and in-betweenness was given only by Nakai Masakazu. Nakai described this structure of the dialectical media-tion of the actual present and possible futures as *gijutsu* (*téchne*, in the sense of "technology" or "technique"), which he understood neither as a purely physical means to an end nor as a Kantian-idealistic "cognitive-categorical medium" (*ninshiki hanchū-teki baikai*)[49] enabling the subject to perceive an object in the first place but rather—inspired by Martin Heidegger's philoso-phy—as an "existential-categorical medium" (*sonzai hanchū-teki baikai*) in the sense of a *poiesis* by which beings always somehow relate to their world. To Nakai, it is in the *present*, through the practico-poietic technique of the medium, that our perception or consciousness of the *past* ("representation") is mediated with a possible *future* (Heiddegerian) "projection" (*Entwurf*):

> Consciousness is not causally an agglomeration [*katamari*] yielding and grasping memory; rather, memory itself is already one phase of a projective structure inheriting the possibility to represent [*mosha*] many series of the world [*sekai keiretsu*]. Since these possible projec-tive structures provide all these worlds with a suspending and shift-ing target-aimed direction [*setsudan to dōza hyōteki hōkō*], the actual mode of "consciousness" thus lies in the transformation of memory, as a mediatory [*mediumu-teki*] possibility, into mediate [*mitteru-teki*] actual action. . . . In contrast to memory (or perception in a wide sense) being a static projective element, consciousness as a dynamic pivot or projecting moment being directed towards something, trans-forms these elements into subjective actual action. It transforms the projectiveness of the mediatory form into the projectiveness of the mediating form. In other words, consciousness thus possesses its own logical structure as that which transforms the mediatory mediation of the "spirit" spontaneously into the mediate mediation of "possibility."[50]

This relationship by which beings steadily relate to the surrounding world is a self-reflective and future-oriented mediated process that "allows people to err and, through the mediated observation of one's own actions, to spon-taneously create new modes of action based on the mistakes made."[51] For

Nakai, technique/technology hence was not something that enables humans to manipulate nature but rather a "medium" (*baikai*) through which beings are enabled to mediate the a posteriori reflection of one's relation to nature and constantly renew this relation. In other words, technique/technology is a moment of "praxis" (*jissen*) and thus "transformation" through which beings, within a process of "dialectical mediation" (*benshōhō-teki baikai*), can "actively transform the categories of impossibility into possibility, irreality into reality, and necessity into contingency—and vice versa."[52] Generally speaking, mediation is therefore—and here Nakai is in line with Tosaka's three-dimensional philosophy of history—a constant pendular movement between the reflection of the actual situation and the projection of a possible future. It is important to note, however, that this pendular movement mediating the past and the future in the present described by Nakai, despite being a very smooth, almost invisible mediation, and thus appearing as an almost "unmediated mediation," remains to be procedural and truly dialectical, very different from Nishida's idea of a nonmediated mediation.

FILM THEORY AS MEDIA PHILOSOPHY

The aforementioned perspectives of Tosaka and Nakai on the concept and temporality of mediation culminated in a fruitful philosophical discussion of the new medium of film among the two thinkers. Film having become one of the most important technological media in Japan by the 1930s, Nakai and Tosaka related this process of three-dialectical mediation qua poietic téchne particularly to film. Their approach was very different from contemporary discourse on film, which theorized film from the perspective of single media ontology, centering on the question of art in film, or film art, or compared the new technological capacities of film to previous media technologies. The approach to which Tosaka and Nakai had subscribed focused more on philosophical questions, mostly the question of the constitutive role of the medium qua mediation and in-betweenness within the epistemological process of perception or cognition in general. Although Tosaka and Nakai also dealt with the new capacity of film with regard to the visual perception of movement (a single media ontology), the larger share of their thought on film is of a philosophical nature. All in all, three aspects are of relevance to Tosaka and Nakai in their approach toward the new medium of film: (1) film as new "cognitive capacity" or "sensory formation," (2) the realistic actuality of film based on vision and movement, and (3) the collective reception in a state of "distraction" and the active/practical/kinetic character of film.

Tosaka from the outset stated that "within cinema, it is precisely 'film,' not 'art,' that is the question."[53] Although film, if seen from the perspective of "cultural history," might signify an "artistic" or "stylistic" means of cognition, from a philosophical viewpoint, it represents "a new human cognitive capacity" (*ningen no hitotsu atarashii ninshiki nōryoku*), and is thus just another "name for a *means of cognition* [*ninshiki shudan*] or a *function of cognition* [*ninshiki kinō*]."[54] Tosaka describes the difference between the artistic and philosophical perspective on film and its actual reality based on motion as follows:

> Let us leave the photography and reporting of natural or social events aside for a while and point out here that in other artistic modalities, the photographic effects of everyday natural phenomena often merely end up as a servile realism, trivialism, or mimicry, but within film, these same effects appear as the most outstanding and viciously incisive. In terms of natural phenomena, it is the screen that teaches humans the goodness of the materiality of the world, the joy of the *movement* of matter. By and large, we observe these things every day, but this element of goodness, this joy, actually occurs to us first when it appears on the screen. There was already the endearing nature of the photograph, and the attraction of the graph itself, but the screen is above all a photograph in *motion* and thus draws all the more attention to actual reality itself.[55]

The attention directed by the moving pictures toward actual reality, or simply "actuality,"[56] is not based on mass curiosity, Tosaka emphasizes. Rather, it is "something based on the journalistic instinct of the human being."[57] To Tosaka, journalism was, despite its rapid commercialization in the Taishō period, based from the outset on the "everyday life of the people," "inhabiting" a world that is "quotidian, social, external and sometimes as well profane." He continues, "Journalism, in contrast to academism, despite its internal antagonistic moments, is generally based on the principle of . . . actuality, a consciousness that originates in the activity of everyday social-life [*nichijō shakai seikatsu katsudō*]."[58] It is, according to Tosaka, "an immediate expression of how people see the world. Within journalism, the social circumstances [*sesō*] appear in a lively way."[59] Thus, for Tosaka, film, particularly newsreels and documentaries (though not the official propaganda films, or *bunka eiga*, of the 1930s and 1940s), was a new form of journalism based on a completely different means of cognition, vision, and movement.

Nakai, in a manner very similar to Tosaka, stated that film has created a new collective "sensory formation" (*atarashii kankaku-teki kōsei*), which, given the predominantly visual nature of the medium, "neither merely correspond[s] to conventional visuality, nor to written or spoken language."[60] However, it is not only what is depicted in film—social reality—but also the reception of the visuality of film itself, Nakai asserted, that is based on a socially constructed "convention" (konbenshon, yakusoku), which needed to be "practiced" by the audience, just as one practices a sporting technique.[61] Nakai thus finds himself in close intellectual proximity to Walter Benjamin, who similarly argued that the reception of media, namely "the manner in which human sense perception is organized, the medium in which it is accomplished," is "determined not only by nature" "but also by historical circumstances as well."[62]

However, this mode of filmic reception based on actuality and movement is not as new as one might suggest. Interestingly, Nakai and Benjamin both draw a parallel to the much earlier optical and tactile experience of architecture, which they consider analogous to the cinematic experience. Benjamin writes,

> Buildings are appropriated in a twofold manner: by use and by perception—or rather, by touch and sight. . . . On the tactile side there is no counterpart to contemplation on the optical side. Tactile appropriation is accomplished not so much by attention as by habit. As regards architecture, habit determines to a large extent even optical reception. The latter, too, occurs much less through rapt attention than by noticing the object in incidental fashion. This mode of appropriation, developed with reference to architecture, in certain circumstances acquires canonical value. For the tasks which face the human apparatus of perception at the turning points of history cannot be solved by optical means, that is, by contemplation, alone. They are mastered gradually by *habit*, under the guidance of tactile appropriation.[63]

Moving pictures, Tosaka also writes, thus possess a very particular materiality, a collectively experienced materiality of movement: film is a visual representation of movement, a "language in which matter speaks through a body." Whereas spoken language is based on hearing, the perception of movement is based on vision (in film *and* reality), and vision, in contrast to hearing, "possesses the characteristics of the touch, the caress. In contrast to the temporal continuity of hearing, it has a feeling of the tension of spatial continuity."[64]

For Nakai, not only vision itself, but particularly the fact that people bodily move through and live within buildings—Benjamin called this the "tactile side" of this mode reception—bears similarities to the reception of film, leading in both cases to a habitualized "collective" experience. It was particularly with the advent of glass and steel structures in modern times that this collective appropriation of architecture came to the fore, a time in which people started to observe the city through "glass walls," or "animated walls of painting, painting scrolls that unfold themselves without limitation, a revolving lantern that never repeats itself as time flows."[65] "Vision itself," Nakai writes, in reference to modern architecture, "has sunken into a collective character and an organized structure through the fragmentary vision that people have achieved from the glass walls."[66] Film, he suggests, has a similarly collective character: "Together the characters of the lens, film, and vacuum tubes possess a particular, collective character. This is not only in the sense that they possess a relational atmosphere as contemplative objects. Rather, it has to be stressed that they intrude into the senses themselves. They are, so to speak, the very nerve tissue of the social collective character [*shakai-teki shūdan-teki seikaku*]."[67]

According to Nakai, the viewer of a film—in contrast to the contemplative and hermeneutic reader of a book—watches a movie not mediated via the contemplative medium of their subjective consciousness but rather "sees through" the "order" of film in an "unpredictable" way,[68] just as he walks "through" a piece of architecture. Reception of film in a collective mode of distraction, according to Nakai, had already become a "standard" in the 1930s: it is "the vision and the nerves of the collective itself, it is one *action* [*kō'i*]. It is . . . , so to speak, the standardized form of one collective vision *providing action, or rather, with action attached to it.*"[69]

Tosaka concludes that "for the cognition of reality, vision, more than hearing, has a fundamental significance," because " 'seeing' is not merely *contemplation* [*kanshō*] but a practical measure [*jissai-teki shochi*] taken in relation to things."[70] The recipient of a film is hence not a "hermeneutic" subject, weaving together meaning or narration from single fragments of meaning, but a "kinetic" being,[71] projecting itself within cinematic space, just as it moves collectively through a piece of architecture. Film is not a tool or channel "through" which a message is transmitted to the receiver; rather, the viewers are located "within" the film by "seeing through" it. Thereby, their existence is "relativized"—in a very Latourian sense—into a "functional term" of the process of reception in its entirety.[72] Tactile and haptic movement, key components of Benjamin's "mode of reception in distraction [*Zerstreuung*]," replaces isolated contemplation: "A man who concentrates before a work of art is absorbed by it. . . . In contrast, the distracted mass absorbs the work of art."[73]

Nevertheless, it is important to emphasize that the process of mediation described here does not mean—either for Benjamin or for Nakai—that the viewer (subject) and the filmic representation (object), in idealist fashion, merge together within a field of "absolute nothingness" or "unmediated mediation," but rather that out of a process of dialectical mediation and habitualized reception a new dialectical tertium of distinct elements emerges, namely a social collective of massified film-viewers or viewer-films and their future projections. From the perspective of media philosophy, film is just another epistemological apparatus that is, in terms of its epistemological function, no different from any other media, and is understood as the mediation of representations of reality and possible futures. It is only because of the absorption or immersion of the film viewer into a realistic depiction of reality based on visuality and movement that film appears to be a gradually more "realistic" medium than language. That is to say, the medium qua mediation and in-betweenness does not disappear or stop—within the filmic reception the dialectical process of mediation is continuing but becomes invisible due to the proximity of subject and object. Therefore, an invisible mediation remains *as* mediation, which is something profoundly different from Nishida's unmediated mediation. The more "invisible they are, the more they stay below the threshold of perception [*Wahrnehmungsschwelle*]," and the more a medium fulfills its function as a realistic depiction of reality.[74] And this, Karatani Kōjin has taught us, is true not only for visual representations of reality but also for language. To Karatani, "realism" is a "semiotic constellation" that "requires the repression of the signification, or figurative language (Chinese characters) . . . , as well as the existence of a [phonocentric] language which is supposedly transparent," in order for us "to assume it to be natural that things exist and the artist merely observes them and copies them."[75]

Conclusion

One can draw the following conclusions from the aforementioned remarks on the thought of the Kyōto School. First, a revised reading of the thought produced by thinkers of the inner *and* outer circle of the school in the 1930s reveals a strand of media philosophy centering on the concepts of "mediation" and "dialectics," which contradicts the established understanding of the school as merely offering a meontological "philosophy of nothingness." One can argue that it was only based on this narrow reception of the school that it was possible to create an intellectually consistent picture of it as a *school* of philosophers of nothingness in the first place. Moreover, it was also based on this retrospectively constructed image that it was possible to bring the school's philosophy into a position in which it could be contrasted with Western philosophy as an allegedly genuine Eastern philosophy. In the case of the Kyōto School, this has often restricted research into possible conceptual contact points between philosophies in the West and in Japan concerning the concept of nothingness, which was most frequently studied in relation to Heidegger's philosophy or Derrida's deconstruction. Moreover, as we have seen through a close reading of the thought produced by the thinkers of the school particularly during the first half of the 1930s, this newly discovered strand of theorization can not only be fruitfully compared to and contextualized on a transnational level with other media philosophies in Europe but might also help widen the scope of theorizations of the medium within the intellectual discursive space of Japan in the 1930s, then dominated by newly emerging academic disciplines such as sociology and newspaper studies, and their rather functionalistic and vertical understanding of the role of the medium.[76]

Secondly, from a perspective internal to the discourse and its very mechanics, one could understand the thought of the proponents of the school presented here as a critical engagement with the concept of nothingness, representing a fruitful attempt to "fill" the "aching" conceptual emptiness that Nishida's philosophy left behind, by explaining, if not replacing, nothingness with the concepts of mediation (*baikai*), dialectic (*benshōhō*), or the in-between (*aida*). Instead of understanding Nishida's concept of nothingness in a pseudoreligious or esoteric Buddhist manner, these thinkers reinterpreted the idea of "absolute nothingness" as an intermediary medium (a field or place; *basho* in Nishida's terminology) of dialectical mediation, out of which something common (i.e., via a process of "commun-ication") or the negotiation of subjective perceptions and collective projections of reality could emerge. At the same time, this move avoided the pitfalls of essentializing the concept of the medium or nothingness without questioning Nishida's attempt to overcome the subject/object dualism produced by Western philosophy in general. Nakai, Tosaka, and Tanabe all gave answers to the philosophical question of overcoming, but not negating, the duality of subject/object, matter/spirit, and body/consciousness in Western correlationist philosophy by proposing various forms of media philosophy that manage to think of all of these dichotomies as dialectically coinciding in the process of mediation.

Third, on an entirely media-theoretical level, one has to welcome Tanabe and Tosaka's critique of Nishida's twisted use of the terms "mediation" and "dialectics," climaxing in the prelogical and paradoxical nonconcept of "unmediated mediation." As we have learned from the thinkers presented here, for mediation to qualify as mediation one necessarily needs to assume a (logical or fictional) intermediary third *tertium mediationis* mediating between the things mediated. Regardless of whether this tertium is the ethnical "species" (Tanabe), the proletarian "class" (Tosaka), or the "collective" of moviegoers (Nakai), the tertium of any process of mediation bears unique characteristics, is contextual, and cannot possibly be defined as a transhistoric/temporal and static "absolute nothingness." One can further argue that, in short, each of the three *tertia* presented here fulfill the function to construct—beyond any ideological valorization—imaginations of forms of a sensus communis based on fictions in the Kantian sense of "regulative ideas." It is the medium, as Nakai put it, with which future projections ("fictions") are negotiated with "contemporary representations" of "actual reality." Media—and Nakai recognized this all too well—are not just screens depicting one version of contemporary reality (all constructivist problematizations of the idea of reality in general set aside) but possess the constitutive power to open a "three-dimensional" (Tosaka) or dialectical space (*Freifläche*) for the negotiation of representations of the present and speculative projections of alternative future worlds. Put differently, one finds the most fundamental function of the medium qua dialectical mediation in the juxtaposition and mediation of visualized/imagined contrafactual and futuristic projections *and* "realistic" ("actual") representations of the present.

NOTES

1. Stefan Münker, "After the Medial Turn: Sieben Thesen zur Medienphilosophie," in *Medienphilosophie: Beiträge zur Klärung eines Begriffs*, ed. Stefan Münker, Alexander Roesler, and Mike Sandbothe (Frankfurt am Main: Fischer-Taschenbuch-Verl, 2003), 20.

2. Alexander Roesler, "Medienphilosophie und Zeichentheorie," in Münker, Roesler, and Sandbothe, *Medienphilosophie*, 35.

3. Georg Christoph Tholen, *Zur Ortsbestimmung analoger und digitaler Medien* (Bielefeld: Transcript, 2005), 151, 153; italics mine.

4. Sybille Krämer, "Erfüllen Medien eine Konstitutionsleistung? Thesen über die Rolle medientheoretischer Erwägungen beim Philosophieren," in Münker, Roesler, and Sandbothe, *Medienphilosophie*, 89.

5. Krämer, "Erfüllen Medien eine Konstitutionsleistung?," 89.

6. See James W. Heisig, *Philosophers of Nothingness: An Essay on the Kyoto School* (Honolulu: University of Hawai'i Press, 2001).

7. For a detailed account of the discourse on the press, please refer to Fabian Schäfer, *Public Opinion, Propaganda, Ideology: Theories on the Press and Its Social Function in Interwar Japan, 1918–1937* (Leiden: Brill, 2012).

8. Inaba Michio, *Komyunikēshon hattatsushi* [History of the development of communication] (Tokyo: Sōfūsha, 1989), 112.

9. Shimomura Toratarō rightly argues that Nishida in fact completed his intellectual development at the time he came up with the logic of place and that all subsequent shifts in terminology have to be considered as applications of the very same fundamental idea to other subjects such as history or society. See Shimomura Toratarō, *Nishida Kitarō: Hito to shisō* [Kitaro Nishida: The man and his thought] (Tokyo: Tōkai Daigaku Suppankai, 1977); and Nishida Kitarō, *An Inquiry into the Good*, trans. Masao Abe and Christopher Ives (New Haven CT: Yale University Press, 1990).

10. Nishida Kitarō, *Nishida Kitarō Zenshū*, new ed. (Tokyo: Iwanami, 2002), 1:9; Nishida, *An Inquiry into the Good*, 3.

11. Kitarō, *Nishida Kitarō Zenshū*, 4:215.

12. Nishida, *Nishida Kitarō zenshū*, 4:220.

13. Nishida, *Nishida Kitarō Zenshū*, 6:346–47; 11:73–74.

14. Nishida, *Nishida Kitarō Zenshū*, 7:313–14.

15. Nishida, *Nishida Kitarō Zenshū*, 6:386.

16. Hajime Tanabe, *Shu no roni* [Logic of the species], (Tokyo: Iwanami Bunko, 2010), 365–66.

17. Max Horkheimer and Theodor W. Adorno, *Dialectic of Enlightenment: Philosophical Fragments*, ed. Gunzelin Schmid Noerr, trans. Edmund Jephcott (Stanford, CA: Stanford University Press, 2002), 102.

18. Quentin Meillasoux, *Nach der Endlichkeit* (Zürich: diaphanes, 2008), 18.

19. Tosaka Jun, *Tosaka Jun zenshū*, (Tokyo: Keisōshobō, 1966), 3:75. See also Fabian Schäfer, *Tosaka Jun: Ideologie, Medien, Alltag: Eine Auswahl ideologiekritischer, kultur- und medientheoretischer und geschichtsphilosophischer Schriften* (Leipzig, Ger.: Leipziger Universitätsverlag, 2011), 208.

20. Schäfer, *Tosaka Jun*, 208.

21. Tosaka, *Tosaka Jun zenshū*, 3:77; Schäfer, *Tosaka Jun*, 210.

22. Tosaka, *Tosaka Jun zenshū*, 2:347; Schäfer, *Tosaka Jun*, 108.

23. Tosaka, *Tosaka Jun zenshū*, 3:75; Schäfer, *Tosaka Jun*, 207.

24. Tosaka, *Tosaka Jun zenshū*, 2:346.

25. Tosaka, *Tosaka Jun zenshū*, 2:343.

26. Tosaka, *Tosaka Jun zenshū*, 2:229.

27. Tosaka, *Tosaka Jun zenshū*, 3:77; Schäfer, *Tosaka Jun*, 210.

28. Naoki Sakai, *Translation and Subjectivity: On "Japan" and Cultural Nationalism* (Minneapolis: University of Minnesota Press, 1997), 202n7.

29. Tosaka, *Tosaka Jun zenshū*, 2:113, 114.

30. Tosaka, *Tosaka Jun zenshū*, 2:113, 114.

31. Tosaka, *Tosaka Jun zenshū*, 3:313.

32. Joachim Israel, *The Language of Dialectics and the Dialectics of Language* (Atlantic Highlands, NJ: Humanities Press, 1979), 43. Joachim Israel's words perfectly paraphrase Tosaka's perspective: "If society, or the social world, is not something which is immediately given, then it is mediated, i.e., produced by man. But something which is produced can also be changed. It can no longer be conceived as something existing independently of the producing man, or as imposing on him the inner lawfulness of its own goals. The notion of active forces in society to which man is submitted—e.g., the notion of technology imposing its inherent goals upon us—can be revealed as an appearance whose essence is the process of reification, i.e., the transformation of man into an object. Furthermore, if we comprehend reification as a process inherent in the capitalistic system of production, we can also begin to grasp how by overcoming the posed constraints to change it. This presupposes understanding of the given as something produced, produced through praxis in all its forms. 'When existence is revealed as mediated, it will be conceived as product.'" See Israel, *Language of Dialectics*, 69.

33. Kobayashi Toshiaki, *Denken des Fremden: Am Beispiel Kitaro Nishida* [Thinking the alien: The example of Kitaro Nishida] (Frankfurt am Main: Stromfeld/Nexus, 2002), 46.

34. Tosaka, *Tosaka Jun zenshū*, 3:100–101.

35. Nishida, *Nishida Kitarō Zenshū*, 6:342.

36. Nishida, *Nishida Kitarō Zenshū*, 8:94.

37. Tosaka, *Tosaka Jun zenshū*, 3:72.

38. Tosaka, *Tosaka Jun zenshū*, 3:72.

39. Tosaka, *Tosaka Jun zenshū*, 3:309.

40. Tanabe, *Shu no ronri*, 393–94.

41. Johannes Laube, "Westliches und östliches Erbe in der Philosophie Haijme Tanabe," *Neue Zeitschrift für systematische Theologie und Religionsphilosophie* 20 (summer 1978): 1–15.

42. Israel, Joachim, *The Language of Dialectics and the Dialectics of Language* (Atlantic Highlands, NJ: Humanities Press, 1979), 69.

43. Tosaka, *Tosaka Jun zenshū*, 3:103.

44. Tosaka, *Tosaka Jun zenshū*, 3:101.

45. Tosaka, *Tosaka Jun zenshū*, 3:101.

46. Tosaka, *Tosaka Jun zenshū*, 3:102.

47. Tosaka, *Tosaka Jun zenshū* , 3:101.

48. Tosaka, *Tosaka Jun zenshū*, 3:444.

49. Nakai, *Nakai Masakazu zenshū*, ed. Osamu Kuno (Tokyo: Bijutsu Shuppansha, 1964–81), 2:124.

50. This is a slightly modified version of Aaron Moore's translation. Nakai, *Nakai Masakazu zenshū*, 2:124–25.

51. Nakai, *Nakai Masakazu zenshū*, 2:128.

52. Nakai, *Nakai Masakazu zenshū*, 2:126–27.

53. Tosaka, *Tosaka Jun zenshū*, 4:468; Tosaka Jun, "Film as the Reproduction of the Present: Custom and the Masses," in *Tosaka Jun: A Critical Reader*, ed. Ken C. Kawashima, Fabian Schäfer, Robert Stolz, trans. Gavin Walker (Ithaca, NY: Cornell East Asia Series, 2013), 119.

54. Tosaka, *Tosaka Jun zenshū*, 4:469; Tosaka, "Film as Reproduction," 120; Tosaka, *Tosaka Jun zenshū*, 4:468; Tosaka, "Film as Reproduction," 119.

55. Tosaka, *Tosaka Jun zenshū*, 4:285–86; Tosaka, "Film as Reproduction," 108–9; italics mine.

56. Tosaka, *Tosaka Jun zenshū*, 4:286; Tosaka, "Film as Reproduction," 109. For an account of Tosaka's notion of the practical and temporal aspect of actuality please refer to Schäfer, *Tosaka Jun*.

57. Tosaka, *Tosaka Jun zenshū*, 4:285; Tosaka, "Film as Reproduction," 107–8.

58. Tosaka, *Tosaka Jun zenshū*, 3:131.

59. Tosaka, *Tosaka Jun zenshū*, 3:148.

60. Nakai, *Nakai Masakazu zenshū*, 3:149.

61. Nakai, *Nakai Masakazu zenshū*, 2:184.

62. Walter Benjamin, *Gesammelte Schriften*, vol. I.2 (Frankfurt: Suhrkamp Verlag, 1990), 478; italics mine.

63. Benjamin, *Gesammelte Schriften*, I.2:504–5.

64. Tosaka, *Tosaka Jun zenshū*, 4:286; Tosaka, "Film as Reproduction," 109.

65. Tosaka, "Film," 296.

66. Tosaka, "Film," 297–98.

67. Nakai, *Nakai Masakazu zenshū*, 3:153 (trans. Alex Zahlten).

68. Nakai, *Nakai Masakazu zenshū*, 3:153.

69. Nakai, *Nakai Masakazu zenshū*, 2:297–98.

70. Tosaka, *Tosaka Jun zenshū*, 4:283; Tosaka, "Film as Reproduction," 105.

71. Kitada Akihiro, "'Imi' e no aragai: Nakai Masakazu no 'baikai' gainen o megutte" [Against "meaning" on Nakai Masakazu's concept of "medium"], in *"Imi" e no aragai: Mediēshon no bunka seijigaku* (Tokyo: Serika Shobō, 2004), 58–59.

72. Nakai, *Nakai Masakazu zenshū*, 2:196; Kitada, "'Imi' e no aragai," 59.

73. Benjamin, *Gesammelte Schriften*, I.2:497, 503–4; italics in source.

74. Sybille Krämer, "Das Medium als Spur und als Apparat," in *Medien, Computer, Realität: Wirklichkeitsvorstellungen und Neue Medien*, ed. Sybille Krämer (Frankfurt am Main: Suhrkamp, 1998), 74.

75. Karatani Kōjin, *Origins of Modern Japanese Literature*, trans. and ed. Brett de Bary (Durham, NC: Duke University Press, 1993), 61.

76. See Stefanie Averbeck, *Kommunikation als Prozess: Soziologische Perspektiven in der Zeitungswissenschaft, 1927–1934* (Münster, Ger.: Lit, 1998); and Fabian Schäfer, *Public Opinion*.

13. KOBAYASHI HIDEO AND THE QUESTION OF MEDIA

KEISUKE KITANO

Kobayashi Hideo was once described in English as "the pivotal Japanese critic of his time, as crucial a presence in his own literary culture as, for example, Edmund Wilson, Walter Benjamin or Roland Barthes were in theirs."[1] In the twentieth—and even twenty-first—century in Japan, Kobayashi, initially trained in the study of French literature, has been energetically discussed within the context of letters, philosophy, social thought and many other intellectual fields, but his work has not often been examined from the viewpoint of media studies. Yet one can arguably state that Kobayashi was one of the first, if not the first, intellectual seriously engaged in considering the impact of the advent of mass media in society, which happened in 1920s and 1930s in Japan, as an important subject of intellectual commitment. In the way that Kobayashi appeared on an intellectual scene saturated with mass media culture, from print capitalism to radio to cinema, he can be reckoned as the first acclaimed writer to emerge within Japan's mass media culture.

How an intellectual giant of this sort conceived of media and media culture is then a crucial question to be tackled to understand the history, or histories, of media theories in Japan. This essay will focus on how Kobayashi approached media and media culture, in the process demonstrating his contribution both to the field of media studies in particular, and to the broader trajectory of intellectual activities within modern Japan.

Target, Scope, and Orientation

When exploring Kobayashi's complex theoretical practice we should be attentive to the way we contextualize Kobayashi's work with reference to media culture. Although an analytical comparison between Kobayashi and Benjamin, as indicated in the quotation cited above, might give one a sense of understanding the situation in question, it would be fatally misleading to take it literally. That would be merely a naïve comparative study of intellectual practices, leading to nothing but an instance of a new version of orientalism in the age of what might be called the *Empire* or some other slogan of globalization. Conducting a comparative study concerned with different intellectual practices in different cultures generally tends to transform what is happening, that which has been developing immanently, into what is translatable on the level of the receiver, ending up with a geopolitically biased production of the power of knowledge. Furthermore, Kobayashi was highly aware of such geopolitical tensions in modern Japan, which I will discuss later, and that awareness mobilized his singular writing practice. I am afraid that a naively formatted comparative approach might flatten out many issues of geopolitical dynamism potentially folded onto the signifying planes of discourse in such a work as Kobayashi's.

In addition, one has to be aware of the other side of the comparative study coin. It would be hopelessly optimistic to presume that an intellectual in Japan thinks in the same way that the original writer in the West did when one finds quotations from the latter's propositions and/or theories in the former's writings, which is another geopolitically naive approach toward consideration of discourses in different languages. Therefore, with this in mind, this paper attempts to organize its methodological orientation in the way that Kobayashi, in his early period, emerged in a society with a mass media culture *similar to* the one Benjamin saw in his time, almost contemporaneously, in Germany— which does not necessarily mean that Kobayashi was a Benjamin in the Japan of the time. Our consideration will be focused on how Kobayashi then approached the question of media and media culture, roughly speaking, in the period from the 1920s to the 1940s, in his early career.

In a roundtable discussion held in the early 1990s, some of the leading intellectuals of the time—namely Asada Akira, Karatani Kōjin, Hasumi Shigehiko, and Miura Masashi—met to reconsider the genealogies of intellectual practices in modern Japan under the rubric of the history of *hihyō*, a term most often translated into English as "criticism" or "critique."[2] During the discussion, the participants offered a synchronic and diachronic account of discursive practices in the 1920s and 1930s, and identified Kobayashi Hideo as the most important figure within this configuration (which surveyed events ranging from the impact of the introduction of Marxism, in particular the introduction of its Lukácsian iteration by Fukumoto Kazuo, who had become acquainted with those who would later be called the Frankfurt school, through to the advent of the phenomenology-oriented Kyoto school of philosophy and to the emergent Japanese Romantics led by Yasuda Yojūrō). Indeed, it has been more widely argued that it was Kobayashi—writing within a context in which Japanese society was undergoing its first exposure to a variety of modern mass media, from print capitalism to the gramophone and from radio to cinema—who elevated the literary genre of criticism in Japan to the point where it could vigorously address not only literature but also philosophy, political economy, civilization, and even science. Kobayashi led the intellectual orientation of the discursive sphere in Japan before, during, and after the Second World War. Arguably, although he died in 1983, he continues to do so even now.

In Kojin Karatani's understanding, hihyō refers to something more than literary criticism in the simple sense; it also names "the quintessence of the intellectual activities in modern Japan."[3] That is to say, Karatani argues that hihyō functions as a radical intellectual enterprise of skepticism toward both what stands in front of human beings as well as the very foundation of one's own thinking practices—and we might add toward the milieu of media, with language at the center. He adds that as such it resembles the work of Immanuel Kant's questioning of the foundation of metaphysics. While it might be said that, in the field of Japanese literature, this type of work began with Natsume Sōseki, Karatani argues, "It is in the work of Kobayashi Hideo that one finds in Japan the intellectual enterprise that truly compares with Kant's Die Drei Kritiken."[4] We might say that it was through Kobayashi that hihyō as we understand it today was created.

If, in the words of Japanese literature scholar Katō Shūichi, "it was Kobayashi who made criticism into a work of literature,"[5] then hihyō, as Kobayashi practiced it, was highly self-aware, attending to the materiality of language and its embeddedness within Japan's burgeoning mass media culture. Furthermore, Kobayashi was highly aware of contemporary geopolitical tensions surrounding Japan—a topic I will discuss later—and that keen awareness equally informed his singular writing practice. Indeed, much subsequent media theorization in Japan has taken place within this mode of hihyō, and as such, inherits from Kobayashi a reflexive attitude toward its own mediating and mediatized mechanisms, as well as the concept of media more broadly. Examining the work of this highly influential figure in both the pre- and postwar period—who therefore matured intellectually at an important moment within the history of media in Japan—is not only key to understanding the history of media *theory* in Japan; it is also clearly important to the understanding of *media* in Japan.

This chapter thus intends to demonstrate the most significant developments in Kobayashi's thought, and how this is reflected in his changing attitude toward the concepts of mediation and media. By first turning to the linguistic context in Japan in the 1920s and then proceeding to Kobayashi's conception of translation, we will lay the ground for an explication of his critical methodology, focusing, in particular, on his conception of verbal language as a form of mediation. From that, we will turn to Kobayashi's postwar writing, so as to demonstrate how he developed a more embodied theory of mediation following his encounters with the then new media of cinema and photography.

Linguistic Conditions of the Twentieth Century

One of the driving questions for Kobayashi throughout his career, argues Kojin Karatani, was "not simply that of modernity, but more crucially the question of the geopolitical and linguistic conditions surrounding Japan. No one can escape from that question even now."[6] That is to say, for Kobayashi, it was not simply a question of modernity per se, where even poetry was to be reformulated in each of the countries facing it in its early stages, but also specifically the question of *modernity in Japan* (forcefully introduced due to the geopolitical situation at the time).

We must therefore confront the problematic of the Genbun-icchi movement—a drastic transformation of the linguistic order during the Meiji period (1868–1912)—which attempted to unify the chaos of spoken and written languages in Japan into a single modern, secular, uniform language. While in a narrow sense it was largely a literary movement initiated and implemented by literary figures such as Futabatei Shimei and Yamada Bimyo, I would like to suggest that it reflects a much larger, radical restructuring process of the Japanese language as a whole.[7] Together with the chaotic circumstances involved in the construction of various institutions on the level of state government in the age of imperialism—namely the activity surrounding Japan's nation building—this language revolution lead to the elevation of a national consciousness within the minds of those living in a country only recently named "Japan." "Nation" here, then, designates the political-economic agenda of nation-state building.[8] In other words, Japan was undergoing the building process of what Benedict Anderson called an "imagined community."[9] In this sense, when confronting the question of the ontological and epistemological status of language, we also find that it is a part of the larger problematic of the intervention of media into the societal psyche within Japan during the height of the Genbun-icchi movement.

Although Kobayashi appeared on the intellectual scene in the 1920s after a significant portion of language restructuration had been achieved, it is arguable that, in fact, it was an agenda that had no end, once it had been extrinsically motivated and geopolitically exhorted.[10] Hasumi Shigehiko believed that the period from the 1910s to the 1920s—though roughly identifiable as "the Taisho period," it is more tellingly demarcated as lasting from the Japan-Russo War (1904–5) until the great Kanto Earthquake (1923)—can be characterized not only by the emergence of mass media culture and the ideological movement of "Taisho democracy" but, more importantly, by its slogan-like speeches and addresses in journalism and academia. These focused on idiosyncratically abstract words and phrases related to such nebulous notions as *sekai* (the world) and *shutai* (the subject).[11]

Kobayashi's Engagements

As long as the tensions generated by the interstate relations of world politics brought about a mediated and mediatized linguistic revolution, one cannot help but consider the problematic of translation in contemporary society, which is a key component of Kobayashi's conception of media. Even during Japan's period of international isolation (that is, before it opened its doors to the outside world around 1854 with Perry's Treaty of Kanagawa) the question of translation was already present in the form of the circulation of various forms of knowledge. After the doors opened, this question simply began to make one more conscious of the difference between what is to be translated and what *is* translated, or the here and the there, geopolitically and linguistically demarcated. Kobayashi, though belonging to a younger generation, was immersed in the problematic of translation in an unparalleled way. His commitment to it was so enormous that he devoted tremendous energy to translating works by Baudelaire, Rimbaud, and Gide. One can argue that he sought to cultivate his horizon of intellectual engagement through committing to the act of translation more profoundly than did other intellectuals—not in the sense of producing extensively, but of engaging in the question of how translation was practiced in Japan. His intense exploration of that question helped him find ways to critically work in and for Japan.

To grasp the significance of Kobayashi's thoughts concerning translation as mediation with regard to issues of selfhood and nation, we can refer to Sakai Naoki's theorization of the problematic of translation. Sakai contends that the process of translation occurs differently from what is generally assumed. That is to say, it does not simply entail a transfer of meaning from an "origin" to a "destination" language. On the contrary, it is the conception and act of translation that brings about the horizon of thinking where the different existential units of different languages are to be apprehended—and only after such apprehension can one engage oneself in translation. What is at work as a practical matter is the mobilization of what Sakai calls "the schema of configuration," the mechanism that configures the epistemological settings in which one language and another language could exist respectively and face each other so that someone—acting as a translator—could engage in the performance of mediating them. This would further effectuate the consciousness of the ontologically autonomous status of one language, leading to the realization of a national consciousness or identity.[12] Translation as mediation is thus inherently connected to the question of nation and self.

One can reasonably argue that, even in the late Edo period, the question of translation was what concerned many leading intellectuals working within the fields of philosophical consideration that considered what Japan was, is, and should be. Intellectual efforts to distinguish what was inherent to Japanese culture from what was historically imported from Chinese cultures, which were so dominant in the public sphere, were rooted in fervent polemics and debates centered around the question of how the Japanese language could be identified as distinct from the Chinese language. *Kokugaku* (national learning or, quite literally, "the study of our country"), conceived and refined by thinkers such as Ogyu Sorai and Motoori Norinaga in the eighteenth century and practiced most actively by the Mito school of thought, identified a distinction between the Japanese style and the Chinese style of aesthetics and exerted an influence on the modern history of Japan over many generations. Undoubtedly the question of translation was pivotal to the thinkers of the Edo period, as it helped them to constitute the idea of what it is to be Japanese.[13]

Yet, from the Meiji period onward, the problematic of translation came to be more seriously considered and energetically discussed. One can argue that even the form of the question of translation changed. When the government decided to modernize (i.e., Westernize) the country on many different levels, various issues relating to the question of translation—such as whether or not this or that Japanese culture could be translated or whether or not Western culture could be translated into a Japanese one—became *pressing and urgent* for those intellectuals concerned with the task of considering which direction Japan, as an emerging modern nation, should take. Which is to say that intellectuals, witnessing the process of modernization/Westernization (which can be interpreted as the process of translation in the broadest sense of the word) had to consider how they should and could place their own consciousness in an emerging and growing landscape of this kind. The question of translation found its locus, sometimes even its specific position, placed, with material intensity, in relation to this self-consciousness of intellectual life.

With Sakai's theoretical scheme, one may compare and distinguish these two historical stages of translation in the Edo and Meiji periods, understanding, of course, that the difference between them can be understood only in terms of degree.[14] Put simply, in the mid-Edo period thinkers were involved in their translation willingly, while in the Meiji period, intellectuals, including political elites as well as others, were pressed and impelled to do translation. This leads one to see more clearly that, theoretically speaking, the geopolitical demands of translation are more visible within a framework that emphasizes questions of medium production and circulation that are specifically, and materially, formatted. In other words, the act of translation, to someone like Kobayashi, was not just an intellectual practice of transmitting a message written in one language to those who could understand it only in another language. It instead existed as a sort of material process that could intervene in the conditions of ongoing patterns of thought. Kobayashi acutely recognized this asymmetric configuration of his own geopolitical situation, which is why, as we will see, he realized he could by no means be a Rimbaud in Japan.

However, Sakai's theoretical scheme is not sufficient in itself to capture the unique orbit within which Kobayashi's practice was situated, which concerned the domestic positioning of intellectuals in society at that time. In the 1920s and 1930s, after several stages of drastic efforts toward nation building—which began in 1867—intellectuals, in particular those not working in elite politics or for big trades or industries, were substantially alienated from what went on within the social mainstream.[15] For example, in 1933, Tanizaki Jun'ichiro, an already successful novelist contemporary to Kobayashi but belonging to a slightly older generation, wrote the following, to which, as we will see later, Kobayashi attentively responded:

It is true that adult taste runs mostly toward the Chinese classics, or else toward certain Japanese classics, though not toward modern writing. . . . Few can claim to have avid readers scattered widely throughout the population, among farmers and workers, for example. Of all arts, literature alone is trapped inside this narrow and cramped universe.[16]

Tanizaki lamented the shrinking of their generation's influence on society over the course of the Meiji period, later commenting that he and his contemporary artists should return to an Eastern cultural heritage.

In contrast to this, Kobayashi was well aware of the fact that little remained to be modernized/Westernized, that is, to be translated. In his perspective, there were no longer any substantial older customs or cultures that could be translated into Western languages. One of the reasons for this is that the Japanese language of his day was already adjusted to the Westernizing/modernizing forces to a significant degree. He emphatically remarked that nothing that the Japanese had experienced before Westernization existed any longer. Kobayashi was thus entangled not only with the question of translating, but also with the question of the impossibility of translation. This was the subject of his "Literature of the Lost Home" in 1933:

Some speak of the modern world as one beset by a common, universal social crisis, although I can only feel that contemporary Japanese society is collapsing in a quite distinctive way. Obviously, our modern literature (for all practical purposes we might substitute "Western" for "modern") would never have emerged without the influence of the West. But what is crucial is that we have grown so accustomed to this Western influence that we can no longer distinguish what is under the force of this influence from what is not.[17]

The difficulty that Kobayashi had to contend with was that, while he understood that "Mr. Tanizaki referred to a 'literature that will find a home for the spirit,'" for him "this is not a mere literary issue, since it is not at all clear that I have any real and actual home."[18] Instead, he had to explore how a Japanese person would "think" in a situation of this kind. To Kobayashi, all one could do was perform the act of translation as a mediating practice without any reliable recourse for implementing such a mediation—there was no point in returning in the past, no point in envisioning the future. This is why Kobayashi was not in agreement either with those who resisted or with those who naively welcomed the ongoing translation process. In this sense, it would be a mistake to evaluate his work with reference to the theory of "invented traditions." Tradition cannot be recovered and should not be re-lied upon. That was his comprehension, tinged with resignation.

It was giving himself up to the translation of the work of Arthur Rimbaud that most pointedly led Kobayashi to establish his own intellectual enterprise as a writer concerned with the issues of geopolitical-linguistic conditions in the Japanese context discussed above. Indeed, his study and translation of Rimbaud has been so influential it is still the most widely read work on the French poet in Japan. Kobayashi made some suggestive comments at a round-table discussion organized by the editorial board members of the most influential postwar journal, *Kindai bungaku* (Modern literature), just after the Second World War. The discussion concerned the manner in which Kobayashi should reflect on his own career as a critic, touching upon the issues of war responsibility and the emperor system. With regard to his own commitment to translation, he explains,

> I translated the work of Rimbaud because I thought translating could make me read his poetry all the better. Translating his work into Japanese and introducing it to the public was in no sense my motivation. . . . If you translate Rimbaud, it would unquestionably no longer be Rimbaud. But Rimbaud's influence on me, that is realized in a new form. . . . Which is what you can detect in any work of translation. In particular it is true in poetry. If you translate a poem into Japanese, then it would be a Japanese poem.[19]

Rimbaud, to Kobayashi, was unique. By translating his poetry and reading it better, Kobayashi hoped that he could gain an understanding of the philosophical import of individuality and modernity in the West, or of the individual's solitude in a homogenous civil society—the question of how one can reasonably live one's own singular life under the conditions of modernity. Yet what Kobayashi learned was the harsh truth that, while Rimbaud's work is fascinatingly instructive in this regard, it was by no means possible for a Japanese to become Rimbaud or to share an essential sympathy with his work. That is to say, in spite of and at the same time because of receiving and emulating the question of individuality in Western art, Japan, through approaching, receiving, and translating many instances and layers of Western modernity, always ends up realizing the logical truism that it is not a Western country. For Kobayashi, then, translation cannot but help emphasize the difference between Japan and Western countries: Rimbaud was a French poet, not a Japanese one.

Despite this realization, it was through this interaction that Kobayashi came to realize the possibility and potential of the Japanese language as *the* locus for his critical engagement. This enabled him to take into account the entire geopolitical condition of living in a country called Japan and of the ensuing domestic events. In a sense, his approach was very simple: language was something fundamentally tied to what it meant to be a human being; therefore, in Kobayashi's view, satisfactorily practicing criticism in language might lead to capturing the nature of one's own existence. He pointedly remarked that "unless you get married to language, you would not become visible in the world."[20] Kobayashi's commitment to language was so unparalleled that his achievement in the writing culture of the day surpasses that of any other intellectual—whether thinker, philosopher, theorist, or writer—in contemporary Japanese history.

In Kobayashi's view, it was an undeniable fact that people living in a country called "Japan" employed the Japanese language, conversed in this language, constituted their everyday experience in this language, and organized their thinking and sensibilities in this language. All the Japanese intellectuals could do, in Kobayashi's view, was to explore the potential of the ongoing Japanese language that existed specifically and concretely in plain view. To Kobayashi, the only way to engage in such an intellectual search was to entangle oneself with what went on in this language by way of double-folded skeptical criticism. One can embody double-folded criticism by simultaneously intervening in one aspect of language that constitutes the form of world experience—or the "life world" in the sense of Wittgenstein's philosophy—and in another that conditions one's own way of thinking. In other words, Kobayashi was engaged in the acrobatic task of investigating the position of Japanese language in its geopolitical relation to and distance from what went on outside the country while at the same time critically exploring the possibilities it offered for the future.

Kobayashi's Methodology: Its Contour and Background

As we have seen, Kobayashi's work took place in the context of a geopolitical conjuncture that was highly mediatized and destabilizing of every aspect of Japanese society. It now remains for us to articulate what double-folded skeptical criticism entails. To do so, we turn to one of Kobayashi's earliest essays, "Multiple Designs" (Samazamanaru Isho)—first published in the September 1929 issue of *Kaizo* monthly, as it illuminates some of his core methodological concerns, which will, in turn, help us to understand how, for Kobayashi, issues of language, translation, mediation, and geopolitics were intimately intertwined. This essay analyses contemporary ideological and theoretical undertakings in Japan in the early twentieth century, and so it is no surprise that Kobayashi begins by questioning what criticism is and what it should be:

> Just as poets and novelists inhabit a literary world, so too do literary critics. The poet's desire is to create a poem, a storyteller's to write a fiction. Does the literary critic have an analogous wish—to write literary criticism? This is a question rife with paradox.
>
> "How simple," it is said, "to practice criticism by just following one's own taste." But it is just as uncomplicated to practice criticism that follows an ideological yardstick. What is hard is to maintain tastes that are ever vital and alive, and to possess ever living and responsive ideas.[21]

Here, Kobayashi deliberately rejects any fixed, clear-cut formula to interpret this or that literary work. For him, such an approach cannot succeed because it does not allow the reader any intellectual excitement in experiencing the act of reading a work of criticism (*hihyō*). Instead, Kobayashi proposes to deconstruct the binary opposition between the subjective and objective, with particular reference to Baudelaire's work: "The magical power of Baudelaire's criticism derives from his awareness that to write criticism is to make oneself conscious. To say that the subject of criticism is the self and the other is to say there is but a single subject, not two. For is not criticism finally the skeptical narration of our dreams?"[22] In simple terms, one can summarize this passage by saying that Kobayashi understands criticism as an intellectual undertaking within language whose function is to critically mediate our experience of the world and oneself. This mediation targets not only the world around oneself but also what makes one who s/he is. In this view, all of the contemporary theoretical or ideological frameworks—what Kobayashi calls "designs"—from Marxism to "art for art's sake," from realism to symbolism—prove to be fatally ineffective because, it seems to him, none of them would succeed in identifying what positions and functions they serve in reality. Within the conditions of the society named "Japan," those "designs" were merely wholesale imports. As such, they simply could not touch upon the potentially questionable status of one's own intellectual foundation.

This is what Karatani tries to pin down with the term *hihyō*: a strategic methodology with which to critique one's own consciousness. What is to be mobilized in Kobayashi's critical methodology is the mechanism of what we have earlier called *double-folded critical skepticism*. It is a critical activity vis-à-vis a work of literature or art, a media object, or a historical situation, but it simultaneously uses that activity to perform a critique of its own foundations.

Let us take a closer look at how such a double-folded critical skepticism might function specifically in relation to thinking about media. Kobayashi produced a considerable number of essays and other writings demonstrating that he was intensely interested in media culture. Clearly his attention was caught by what was emerging in the then new mediums of photography, cinema, and the gramophone. He pointedly notes this later, some years after the Second World War, in "Letters from van Goh (Gohho no Tegami)":

> Reading literature in translation, listening to music on the gramophone, seeing paintings in reproduction. Everyone has done this. At least as far as modern arts are concerned. We first appreciate works through experiences of this sort. More often than not, people talk about translation culture rather pejoratively. That seems quite reasonable, but being excessively reasonable would lead to a lie. To say that the culture of modern Japan is nothing but translation culture is one thing, but to say that our joy and sorrow have been simply immersed in it and will continue to be so is another. Whatever the state of affairs may be, the real nature of culture stands out, not as problems or tasks we have to deal with, but, most importantly, as food given to us that is imperative for our living. Everybody lives on something that cannot be categorized, not on an abstract idea named "translation culture."[23]

Likewise in "Mozart" (Mootuaruto), one of Kobayashi's most popular essays, published just after the Second World War, he narrates how, before the war, the melody of Mozart's Symphony no. 40 sounded in his mind as he was walking in downtown Osaka and he rushed into a department store to buy a recording of the piece. This passage has often been cited to emphasize Kobayashi's romantically toned descriptions of his encounters with the beauty of such works of art.[24] Yet it is important to keep in mind the mediated nature of this encounter, as Kobayashi himself was incisively aware of his own interest in the reproduction culture produced by the mass media of the day.

In other words, Kobayashi, cognizant of his fond regard for media culture, oriented his critical involvement toward problems concerning the nature of the medium. This, considered together with Kobayashi's critical mechanism of double-folded critical skepticism, indicates that Kobayashi's hihyō harbors what we might call multidirectional signifying vectors toward readers, then and now. "Multidirectional" here does not refer to a psychoanalytical connotation associated with overdetermination lurking in the unconscious. Rather, it is a writing strategy. Kobayashi's conception of a medium is not something that transparently transmits a message or content; rather, it is something tactically embedded in his writing practices. Kobayashi thus established a highly reflexive critical method with language.

Kobayashi's Mediating Interventions

It is in the postwar period, when Kobayashi's attention shifts more explicitly to visual media, that his language-based model of mediation and intervention is destabilized. To understand that shift, we must turn to the question of how Kobayashi dealt with "media" and "media culture"—two terms that we might categorize as different kinds of mediating practices.

As we have seen, Kobayashi's critical methodology was firmly founded on the role of language in relation to the particular form of human existence within modernity. It was designed and conducted with a view of the geopolitical-linguistic conditions of Japan between the 1920s and the late 1940s, and during this time Kobayashi's understanding of language began to moderate his understanding of other mediums. To consider the question of media as such, it will be necessary to examine to what extent Kobayashi considered media culture to be similar to and different from literature or language practices more broadly.

Kobayashi was certainly sensitive to the question of whether language-based criticism needed to radically change its orientation in order to approach new media, especially visual mediums such as film. He clearly states this in an essay titled "On Film Criticism" (Eiga-hihyo nitsuite), written in 1939:

> To the general audience, watching a movie is a part of everyday life. Entertainment is something earnest, just like eating. None of them has any extra time to spare for watching a film in a special manner that a film critic might term pure appreciation of cinema. People watch movies simply because of the joys and pains, vitality and exhaustion in their lives. For the mass, or more precisely speaking, for human beings, entertainment in the true sense of the word is nothing but what exists in this sort of way.
>
> Their [peoples'] appreciation of cinema can be said to be impure, without any consistency, one may say. Yet, looking closely at the way it is, it is a disorder at surface value. Or it would be better to say that

they respond meekly to the attractiveness of cinema, which engenders a sort of ordered atmosphere. And the audience, holding their own impression, in a variety of shades, indulges itself in the atmosphere in the theatre.[25]

Referring to this essay and another essay, "On Theatre Criticism (Engeki-ni-tuite)" (1936), Kawakami Tetsutaro, a friend and critic contemporary to Kobayashi, explains that the latter perceived, within theatrical and cinematic practices, a specific "sociality" that went beyond language.[26]

It is a sociality of the same kind as that mentioned in Kobayashi's essay "On the 'I' Novel" (Shishosetsu-ron) and for which he perceived some critical possibilities (he even turned a negative gaze toward those plays straightforwardly adapting literary works in Shingeki, or modern theater). Kobayashi was able to observe distinctly different sorts of socialities, or mediations, engaging the spectator's mind and body, whether an audience member or a reader, and in different cultural practices, whether new or old. At the end of "On Film Criticism," Kobayashi laments that film criticism was becoming like literary criticism.[27]

Here Kobayashi touches upon the problem of material conditions, or the materiality of a medium. One can argue that his intervention into contemporary culture is essentially different from that of sociologist Gonda Yasunosuke, one of the founding figures of research on popular culture in Japan. In 1922, Gonda noted, "Last summer about 10 students from Waseda University visited me and asked me to introduce some Western books to which they could refer to because they had been thinking that they would like to deal with the subject of people's entertainment in their graduation thesis. However, there are no books on people's entertainment. So I suggested to them that 'there are no Western books of this kind in stores, but the topic of this sort of study could be readily apprehended in Asakusa.'" Asakusa is the name of a popular district full of amusements and attractions. Therefore, Gonda's advice was that those students do some field research in the entertainment district, and adopt a bottom-up approach toward cultural practices. As an established sociologist, Gonda believed that one was able to reach some sort of truth through on-the-spot knowledge production and positivistic sociological research.[28] In contrast to Gonda's positivistic approach, Kobayashi's notion of sociality was based on the fact that the conditions of language, which supported the fragile ontological state of self at that time, are unimpeachably embedded in the life form. That embeddedness, according to Kobayashi, should be considered when thinking about the concrete materializations of works of art, whether linguistic, theatrical, or cinematic.

How then can one understand Kobayashi's differentiation of medium(s) in terms of their material conditions? Let us turn to Kobayashi's narrativization of his own experience of photography. In a provocative essay titled "On the Photographs of Dead Bodies, or, The Dead Bodies" (Shitai-shashin aruiwa Shitai ni tsuite), written in 1949, Kobayashi describes what impressed him when he visited "the Exhibition of Real Images of Crimes" in Kamakura. He reports, "I felt so sick at heart and had pain in my stomach, and left the exhibition." He goes on to describe what he thinks is the most impressive scene in the exhibition: "A woman holding a baby on her back, watching the photographer, says 'look, strangled!' Fondling the baby, she says 'strangled!'"

> She obviously represents the audience in general. How else could they possibly react? The material traces of the dead bodies exposed outside of the context of criminal investigation do not necessarily tell you any story of what happened. . . . The objects displayed are nothing but material things that used to be human beings. Yet, looking more closely, they turn out to be low-grade material things, which one might not even call material things.[29]

Here Kobayashi is expressing more than an affect or affective response in the narrow sense of the word. Instead, he touches upon a media engagement outside of language, one that involves the material and the corporeal. Later in the text he compares photographic or filmic experience with that of theater:

> The audience by nature knows that cinema stands not as an extension of ordinary social life as theatre does. The audience, including me, are to be drawn, in silence, into this isolated mechanism. Everything goes on as predicted. All one has to do is sell one's soul to the devil. The mind rotates with the film. How can one call the mind rotating with the film the mind of a human being? Laughter and tears are merely mathematical functions of shadows in motion, which are not ours. It is hard to sniff the smell of the dead. We are so weak that being awake is the most difficult of difficulties.[30]

One is reminded of André Bazin's thoughts on the nature of photography, published in the late 1950s, though Kobayashi's essay was written in 1949. However, we need to read these words in the context of Kobayashi's life and the history of intellectual practices in Japan. As shown above, Kobayashi had previously examined the similarities and differences between literary criticism and film criticism in two earlier essays, and had also indicated that there were different strands of mediation process. Even compared with these essays, the postwar "On the Photographs of the Dead Bodies, or, the Dead Bodies" uses a noticeably different kind of phrase to describe photographic properties: "the smell of the dead." Here, photography as a mediating practice is considered similar to the change of material conditions in the act of confronting a dead body via one's eyes, nose, and body. At this point, Kobayashi, almost abandoning his exploration of the materiality of media experience, begins to incorporate his own experiences into his considerations. Indeed, he suddenly begins to talk about his experience visiting China as a war correspondent during the Second World War:

> As a war correspondent, I, having no scruples, looked continuously on a series of dead bodies, exposed under the bright sun, without feeling any poignancy. The senselessness of the dead bodies left my mind senseless. My memory prowls around the words saying that those were surely dead bodies. And I noticed some form of emotion coming out of it. If my mind were a dry plate, a photograph of dead bodies must have been taken. A photograph is able to do such a thing. A photograph does not express anything if one takes the word "expression" to signify its original meaning, that is to say, that of pressing things out.[31]

This is a key point that demonstrates the break in Kobayashi's linking of language and mediation, one that is deeply connected to the experience of the war. Witnessing the war led him to be unable to consider anything but the mediation of such *experiences*. However, we should be attentive to the fact that Kobayashi, in this paragraph, is commenting on a particular mechanism of perception at work between the viewer and the dead bodies. The materiality of the experience, described in this quotation, is to be rendered physically before the camera, optically reflecting from the object being shot. Yet this can be contrasted to what is also present in the aforementioned quotations regarding the exhibition of the dead bodies: in the latter essay, the material plane of photography was considered an experience to be constituted from the perspective of the viewer standing before the photograph.

Logically, this chapter argues, the working mechanism of the reproductive medium can be rendered as two distinct channels: that of the experiences of people in front of the camera, and that of the photograph or screen depicting those people. One may reformulate this, for instance, as the difference between the mechanically tangible representation of what might be called reality and a specifically sensed reality without any signification on the side of the spectator. After Kobayashi's travels as a war correspondent, it seems that these two channels began to overlap. Experience and photographic depiction became less distinguishable.

In other words, in the prewar period Kobayashi saw, within visual media, the potential to go beyond linguistic (in)capacity and to extend and expand people's sensibilities, imagination, and thinking. However, at some point during the war, Kobayashi, consciously or not, took this further, and began to rely on the possibilities and potentials of such visual media to transcendentally go beyond his own inability to identify and analyze—with his double-folded skepticism—the contemporary conjuncture in which dead bodies were lying on the field. Consequently, he began to intermix two experiential channels: that of the photographed and that of the viewer. By doing this, the mechanism of reproducing reality in such mediums as photography and cinematography could potentially, or romantically, overcome Kobayashi's critical incapacity to hold himself exposed in the Japanese language in confronting the war. It was at this point that Kobayashi became incapable of identifying the conjuncture of geopolitical tensions any longer.

NOTES

1. Paul Anderer, Introduction to *Literature of the Lost Home: Kobayashi Hideo—Literary Criticism, 1924–1939*, trans. and ed. Paul Anderer (Stanford, CA: Stanford University Press, 1995), i.

2. The roundtables were published first in the journal *Kikan Shicho* (Tokyo, Shinchosha) no. 5 (July 1989), no. 6 (October 1989), no. 7 (January 1990), and no. 8 (April 1990); and subsequently in *Hihyō-kūkan* (Tokyo: Fukutakeshoten) no. 1 (April 1991), no. 2 (July 1991), and no. 3 (October 1991). You can now find all of them in Karatani Kōjin, Asada Akira, Shigehiko Hasumi, and Masashi Miura, *Kindai Nihon no Hihyō I: Shōwa-hen* (Tokyo: Fukutake Shoten, 1990–91); and Karatani Kōjin, Asada Akira, Shigehiko Hasumi, and Masashi Miura, *Kindai Nihon no Hihyō II: Shōwa-hen* (Tokyo: Fukutake Shoten, 1992).

3. Karatani Kojin, "Bunkoban e no Jobun" [Introduction to the paperback edition], in *Kindai Nihon no Hihyō I: Shōwa-hen*, ed. Karatani Kojin (Tokyo: Kodansha, 1997), 8.

4. Karatani, "Bunkoban e no Jobun," 8–9.

5. Katō Shiuichi, *Nihon Bungakushi josetsu ge* (Tokyo: Chikuma Shobo, 1980), 489.

6. Karatani Kojin and Kenji Nakagami, "Beyond Kobayashi Hideo," in *Karatani Kōjin, Nakagami Kenji zen taiwa* [All dialogues between Karatani Kojin and Nakagami Kenji] (Tokyo: Kodansha, 2011), 62.

7. Many scholars, Suga Hidemi among them, have been engaging with this question since the 1980s, when problematizing the Japanese language and national consciousness began to be discussed. This is why I phrase this question as the problematic of the

Genbun-icchi. See Suga Hidemi, *Nihon kindai bungaku no tanjo: Genbun-icchi ūndo to nashonarizumu* (Tokyo: Ota Shuppan, 1995).

8. Karatani Kojin, "Karatani Kojin's Afterword to the English Edition (1991)," in *Origins of Modern Japanese Literature*, trans. and ed. Brett de Bary (Durham, NC: Duke University Press, 1993), 193–94.

9. See Benedict Anderson, *Imagined Communities: Reflections on the Origin and Spread of Nationalism* (New York: Verso, 1983).

10. In this sense, this chapter takes a different position from that of Carol Gluck, who argues that "by 1915 Japan possessed a public language of ideology that retained currency through the end of the Second World War" (*Japan's Modern Myths*, 247). However, even though Gluck understands that "ideology appeared as a conscious enterprise" and "a congeries of ideologies," it seems she misses the issue of the material conditions for ideologies in the beginning of the twentieth century. For more information on Gluck's position, see Carol Gluck, *Japan's Modern Myths: Ideology in the Late Meiji Period* (Princeton, NJ: Princeton University Press, 1985), 3, 16, 247.

11. See Shigehiko Hasumi, "'Taisho-teki' gensetsu to hihyō," in *Kindai nihon no Hihyō: Meiji-Taisho hen*, ed. Karatani Kojin (Tokyo: Kodansha, 1997), 146–76.

12. See Naoki Sakai, *Translation and Subjectivity: On "Japan" and Cultural Nationalism* (Minneapolis: University of Minnesota Press, 1997), 51–71.

13. For more on the question of translation, see chapter 4 of Sakai, *Translation and Subjectivity*, 472.

14. Sakai, in his dialogue with Nishitani Osamu, mentions that the problematic of translation in modern Japan should be considered not in relation to nationalism or national identity but to imperialism or expanding nationalism. See Naoki Sakai and Osamu Nishitani, *"Sekai-shi" no kaitai: Honyaku shutai rekishi* (Tokyo: Ibunsha, 1999).

15. Alain-Marc Rieu justifiably contends that the many knowledge circulation systems forming and working restricted the power and function of ideas and knowledge that intellectuals produced in their writings and dialogue in early twentieth-century Japan. In a sense, Japanese intellectuals who worked not in politics, trades, or other practical businesses but in writing activities were situated in circumstances in which what they wrote about could have efficacy only in a highly limited way. See Alain-Marc Rieu, *Savoir et pouvoir dans la modernisation du Japon* (Paris: PUF, 2001).

16. Junichiro Tanizaki, "'Gei' ni tsuite" [On art], *Kaizo* (March–April 1933), reprinted as "Geidan," in *Tanizaki Junichiro zenshu, vol. 20* (Tokyo: Shinchōsha, 1982), 442–44; the English translation is from the quotation in Kobayashi, "Literature of the Lost Home," 47.

17. Kobayashi, "Literature of the Lost Home," 53.

18. Kobayashi, "Literature of the Lost Home," 50.

19. Hideo Kobayashi, "Komedi literēru: Kobayashi Hideo o kakonde," *Kobayashi Hideo zenshū* 15 (Tokyo: Shinchōsha, 2001): 27–28.

20. Hideo Kobayashi, "X e no Tegami," in *Kobayashi Hideo zensakuhin* 4 (Tokyo: Shinchōsha, 2003), 78.

21. Hideo Kobayashi, "Multiple Designs," in *Literature of the Lost Home: Kobayashi Hideo—Literary Criticism, 1924–1939*, trans. and ed. Paul Anderer (Stanford, CA: Stanford University Press, 1995), 20–21.

22. Kobayashi, "Multiple Designs," 20–21.

23. Hideo Kobayashi, "Gohho no Tegami," in *Kobayashi Hideo zensakuhin* 20 (Tokyo: Shinchōsha, 2004), 14–15.

24. Hideo Kobayashi, "Mōtsuaruto" [Mozart], in *Kobayashi Hideo zensakuhin* 15 (Tokyo: Shinchōsha, 2003), 47–102.

25. Hideo Kobayashi, "Eiga-hihyō ni tsuite" [On film criticism], *Kobayashi Hideo zensakuhin* 11 (Tokyo: Shinchōsha, 2003), 56–57.

26. Kawakami Tetsutaro, "Kaisetsu," in *Kobayashi Hideo Zenshu, dai-yon-kan*, Shinchosha, 1978, 396.

27. Hideo Kobayashi "Eiga-hihyo ni tsuite" [On film criticism], *Kobayashi Hideo zensakuhin* 11 (Tokyo: Shinchōsha, 2003), 61.

28. Gonda's focus on popular culture is part of a larger context of intellectual activities that Watanabe Kazutami, an outstanding postwar French Literature scholar, describes when he notes that in the 1920s and 1930s, Marxism had seized the intellectual trend, leading "intellectuals to an excessively impetuous self-negation and the ideological placement of absolute trust in the people." See Watanabe Kazutami, "Sengo shiso no mitorizu," in *Sengo nihon no shiso-shi—sono saikento*, ed. Tetsuo Najita, Maeda Ai, and Kamishima Jiro (Tokyo: Iwanamishoten, 1988), 98. Kato Shuichi, for his part, argues that when attempting to criticize Marxist thought, Kobayashi's strategy was neither that of logical positivism nor that of establishing alternative social theories as typified in the work of Karl Popper; see Katō Shuichi, *Nihon bungakushi josetsu ge* (Tokyo: Chikuma Shobo, 1980), 484.

29. Hideo Kobayashi, "Shitai-shashin aruiwa Shitai nituite" [On the photographs of the dead bodies, or, the dead bodies], in *Kobayashi Hideo zensakuhin* 17 (Tokyo: Shinchōsha, 2004), 38–39.

30. Kobayashi, "Shitai-syashin aruiha Shitai ni tsuite," 42–43.

31. Kobayashi, "Shitai-syashin aruiha Shitai ni tsuite," 174.

14. MEDIA, MEDIATION, AND CRISIS

A History—and the Case for Media Studies
as (Postcultural) Anthropology

TOM LOOSER

The conscious thinking through of practices that mediate and organize life, including in terms of literal, even mechanical technologies, is not new in Japan. One might look back, for example, to the early modern Kabuki theater. Kabuki became one of the first theaters in the world to use complex mechanical technologies for staging, and also to then highlight those technologies as themselves subjects of life and action; this included plays that consisted of nothing more than quick changes of stage sets (as if to openly acknowledge that offering different technologies of space itself dramatized different modes of life), and an entire sub-era in which mechanical dolls and thereby mechanized life replaced living humans as the subjects of action onstage. The idea that there are technologies of life—*as* technologies that mediate life itself, and social life in particular—has been tied to Japanese modernity and capitalism for a long time.

The institutional form of media studies is of course much more specific, and the history of media, mediation, and social media theory in Japan is not simply framed by the generalized terms of modernity. To the extent that there is a disciplinary field of new media studies in Japan, it is really a post-war development, and, as other essays in this volume show, even in the more immediate history of the postwar period the changes within media studies have at times been dramatic. This chapter is concerned with changes in the assumptions underlying media studies that occurred during the post-bubble decades of crisis in Japan, roughly beginning in the 1990s—in particular the ways media studies engages with and proposes conceptions of mediation.

This is not meant to propose a theory of media studies that is ultimately defined in terms of historical crisis. But at the very least, times of real crisis may indicate a fundamental uncertainty within a given order of social life (perhaps; obviously crisis capitalism does not work quite that way, since it depends on crisis for its continuity). Further, periods of crisis may also be the points at which a very different order of social life and subjectivity becomes visible—and real. Media studies in Japan has been at the forefront of thinking about the fundamental questions of changing social life and social subjectivity, and changes in the discipline also reveal possibilities that have emerged from the lived conditions of crisis within contemporary Japan.

Reading the recent history of media studies in Japan along these lines is my primary aim, although this is just a single genealogy of one stream of thought within the field of media studies.[1] My focus is on changes within the work of Azuma Hiroki, with some reference to those writing around him. Azuma is one of the most prolific and influential figures in the field; he is thoughtful, and his influence symptomatically indicates the accuracy of some of his perceptions. He is not always systematic, however, and is at times content with suggestive description rather than rigorous analysis. But his work is not random. However much it may invoke seemingly contradictory positions, Azuma's work itself offers the reader an overview of the definitive terms of media and mediation within critical moments in contemporary Japanese history.

The trajectory outlined below highlights publications from two general periods: Azuma's work in the late 1990s (as in his *Dobutsuka suru posutomodan*), and writing that he produced in reaction to the Fukushima disasters of March 2011 (such as *Japan 2.0* and *General Will 2.0*).[2] As the general discourse moved first toward practices of the subcultural *otaku* and then toward governance and a broader vision of the social, one can see a change in the very idea and role of the (new) media studies field that implicates everything from the perceived grounds of mediation to the place of the political and cultural idea of Japan to the image of the social and the boundaries of animality and the self-making human.

Background

By the time Azuma published *Dobutsuka suru posutomodan* in 2001 (which was translated and published as *Otaku: Japan's Database Animals* in 2009), discussions concerning the deep changes felt to be occurring in Japanese society were well under way. New media studies had begun to take on a centrality in these dialogues, as a field that was ideally situated to address these changes. Social change was thus tied to epistemological change, and the turn away from other disciplines and toward new media studies implies a shift in thought as well as in social form. *Dobutsuka suru posutomodan* can be seen as a significant element in this shift—a pulling together of something new.

The constellation of thought that *Dobutsuka suru posutomodan* helped to concretize still included discussions of city form, artistic production, sociological analysis, and psychoanalytics, but media studies became a privileged arena within which these interests could come together in a critical concern with new social and cultural forms. This epistemological transition—which included a movement away from more traditionally constituted approaches to philosophy, literary criticism, and even anthropology—is evident in the institutional shift of focus from journals such as *Gendai shisô* (begun in 1973) and *Hihyô kûkan* (started in 1991) toward newer publications such as *Inter-Communication* (1992), *Ten Plus One* (1994), and, to varying degrees, the publications attached to Genron (2010).[3]

One can see the weaving of more traditional approaches and interests into Azuma's *Dobutsuka suru posutomodan*. He borrows heavily from Hegelian philosophy via Alexandre Kojève, and from the philosophy and literary theory of Jean-François Lyotard. His references span everything from the art history of Sawaragi Noi to the cultural theory of Roland Barthes, Jean Baudrillard and Walter Benjamin. He also retains a Lyotard-like interest in narrative form, and the transformation or loss of narrativity, as a basis for understanding contemporary culture. But with his focus shifted to the otaku as the subject of production, Azuma understands media technologies (the database and gamification) rather than economics to be the definitive conditions of consumption in *Dobutsuka suru posutomodan*.

In a sense, then, in this early iteration centered on the otaku's "database" methods of creation, mediation was conceived above all in terms of the materiality of media. Database modes of practice, and the otaku populations that went with them, are still concerned with consumption, but at this point consumption has more to do with these technologies of cultural production and consumption (the way a "database" of imagery operates for the otaku, including as the ground of consumption) than with the impetuses more strictly of capital. These arguments will be fleshed out below. For the moment, it will suffice to note that in this earlier breed of Japanese media studies articulated by Azuma, the effect was to locate the conditions for a new, historically unique order of human life within the practices of a specific population (the otaku) who were defined by their usages of new media technologies.

After the large-scale natural and nuclear disasters related to the earthquake and tsunami in March 2011 (or "3.11"), however, Azuma developed and published a very different kind of vision. He and others turned away from the otaku and the claim that Japan was effectively in a posthistorical condition. There is a return to politics—even constitutional politics, in some cases—and, at least for Azuma, the framing influences shift from the historical visions of society of Hegel and Lyotard toward the a priori individual, and the question of governance as figured by Rousseau and Freud. New media technologies, including the idea of the database, are still part of the discussion but are now more fully situated within the cultural, historical, and geographic conditions specific to Japan. Social signs of death seem to take on as much prominence as the possibility of an open and undetermined human (or animal) life.

Does this trajectory signal the end of media studies? And, furthermore, does it signal the end of the social subject of new media? Is this a return to the disciplinary perspectives, the visions of the social, and more traditional categories of nation, culture, and humanity that have defined modern social thought? Are we returning to more traditional understandings of mediation itself, and the outcomes of social mediation?

By answering these questions, I intend to offer a perspective on at least one stream of thought within Japanese media studies, and to provide a view of the changing grounds of what might be called "mediation." I will work with the two poles I have set up in these introductory comments: I take *Dobutsuka suru posutomodan* to be the concretization of elements already visible at the beginning of the 1990s, itself a time of crisis, and I view writing that has emerged post-3.11 as part of a second, if related, crisis moment. Although there is clear continuity between these times, and in the ongoing assumptions of media studies scholars writing about them, there are nonetheless new kinds of remediations of earlier thought in post-3.11 writing. That is to say, there is real history to contemporary Japanese media studies.

Azuma and Synthesis 1 (Post-1980s)

Media studies may have been a newly formed discipline in the postwar era, but it was certainly not new to look at media materialities in order to discern the specific grounds for the exchanges that produce social realities. Anthropology, for example, has tended to look at language as the basis for the cultural specificity of social worlds. In crude terms, if there is a distinguishing characteristic that defines media studies in Japan (as elsewhere), it has been a concern with the practical technologies that govern our everyday relation to the world—everything from digital photography to social media. But even the turn away from language has real effects on how one might conceptualize human social life. The vision of social life that Japanese media studies arrives at by the end of the twentieth century includes a theory of media technologies, but it is wide-ranging and eclectic.

The genealogy leading to contemporary Japanese media studies includes Nakai Masakazu in a critical early role. Taking up film as a primary medium of everyday life, Nakai attempted to understand both its material and aesthetic conditions in terms of the values and priorities of capitalism. Capitalism, for him, was thus the real materializing force and the ground of mediation in mid-twentieth-century modernity. The attempt to read film as an order of capitalism is not always entirely successful (Kitada Akihiro's reading is perhaps the best attempt to find success in Nakai's approach[4]), and it is not always clear how capitalism forms the specific structures of film discussed by Nakai. The result is neither an argument for media techno-determinism, nor a subsumption of technological conditions within the then popular Marxian interest in the mediating force of capitalism. One can see a real sensitivity to the particularities of specific media (along with Nakai's interest in film, his analysis of cataloging systems was predictive of conditions later described as digital), but it is never fully clear what mediates technologies such as film with economic forces such as capitalism in ways that define a historical era.

Much more recently, and contemporary to Azuma, Ōtsuka Eiji has been a pivotal figure in rethinking how best to conceive of the contemporary practices that materialize social form. Ōtsuka's seminal essay *Monogatari shôhiron* (Theory of narrative consumption, 1989)[5] brought together Baudrillard's insistence that by the 1980s people were consuming pure signs (and relations between signs) rather than things, with a renewed emphasis on consumption as the site at which the making of worlds happens. Although interested in narrative, Ōtsuka was no longer thinking in classic literary critical terms of the production of meaning, or of the tie of literary production to nation and culture. And despite emphasizing consumption in his study of the narratives of commodities (Bikkuriman chocolates in particular, and the stickers that went with them), his argument was not framed in classic economic terms.

More than the chocolate itself, what children were consuming, in Ōtsuka's view, was narrative, and the worlds of narrative that attached to individual commodities. These small worlds were ultimately driven by an underlying, larger narrative—what Ōtsuka called a "worldview." Somewhat utopically, Ōtsuka foresaw the possibility that consumers might eventually not only discern these larger worldviews but also break free from their messages (which in this way sounds almost like corporate advertising as ideology) and fully create their own worlds in the act of consumption. It is not without some irony that Ōtsuka already in 1989 saw the otaku—a social category at that time more typically thought of as unable to navigate social life at all—as the preeminent self-creating consumer-producer of worlds.

It is nonetheless difficult to identify the ground of mediation in Ōtsuka's analysis. Economic conditions are relevant, but not determinant. The same can be said of media specificity: without fully explaining why, Ōtsuka wrote that his model works for chocolates but not for the narratives of video games—so the type of medium is relevant, but also not determinant. Grand narratives and ideologies are still present, but we do not necessarily know what exactly constitutes them, or what really allows for their overcoming.

Ōtsuka understands the hyperconsumerist otaku to be the real agent of history, the place where something like a coming-into-conscious about the structures of consumption might happen. This is a potentially new kind of agency, not necessarily tied to modern frameworks of culture and nation but able to engage both in world making and to modulate across worlds.[6] This implies some kind of mediation, which allows the otaku to take on this role, even if we do not have an entirely clear view of what that is.

People such as Nakai and Ōtsuka were influential in pushing away from traditional disciplinary approaches, but a much fuller picture of a new media studies field is elaborated in works such as Azuma's iconic *Dobutsuka suru posutomodan*. With Ōtsuka, Azuma, and the wide circle around them (Miyadai Shinji, Morikawa Kaichiro, Okada Toshio, Osawa Masachi, etc.), by the start of the twenty-first century, otaku are taken as the new subject of history.[7] This signifies the end of the bourgeoisie, or the vast middle class, as Japan's postwar historical subject, and of the economistic readings of both culture and mass cultural consumption that went with that particular subject of history. The otaku are thus the subject that congeals within this moment of crisis, and the claim has tended toward reading their mode of consumption as not only different from and resistant to classic capitalist, mass cultural modes of consumption but also as pointing toward a reconfiguration of the social world more generally.[8]

One might say that labor is still part of the picture—in its materialist sense as the grounds of self-making (and the point at which mediation actually happens)—but it is now conflated with consumption; the latter is where productive and not just alienating self-creation happens. This includes the act of consuming and producing literature. Clearly "literature"—or more specifically, "fiction"—now means a somewhat transformed institution. It is the act of mediating what Azuma sees as the opposing poles of his time: a database that underlies everything (the equivalent of an earlier time's grand narrative, now without narrative structure—a kind of collective base, albeit one that is a value system only within itself and does not refer to larger, outside, "historical" meanings) and surface-level, localized affective elements (*moe*; these could be a visual character element, a narrative trope, etc.) that pull the reader into an open and creative relation with the database in a way that satisfies individual needs.[9] So there evidently *is* mediation, and in fact "fiction" (in this new guise) if anything takes on a newly important role. One might also see in this at least the possibility for an almost utopic mode of mediating production, with more radically individualized beings fully self-producing their own independent and self-fulfilling worlds out of a "database" commonality.[10] This moves us toward a different subject formation, but it is not yet the full picture.

It should also be pointed out that while Azuma characterized this practice as a form of postmodernism, it has little to do with the more pejorative readings of postmodernism, which describe a world of empty signs that leads to the impossibility of creative action. "Postmodernism," instead, is seen as a material situation of real potentiality (already visible in Ōtsuka Eiji's depiction of the world-producing capability of signs, described above) that lies within modernism, rather than as a kind of empty entropy deriving from the loss of grounding in narrative meaning.

At a simpler and more general level, Azuma tends to invoke a dualistic model that therefore begs for a theory of mediation. This includes not only the dividing of subjectivity into a relation between (common) database and (individual) affect, but also a relation between human and animal. Despite the fact that Azuma cites Kojève and is typically read along the lines of Kojève (some of this is appropriate, as described below), which might imply a Hegelian idealistic dialectics, his model of the world, although often described as post-Heideggerian, is in fact very close to a Heideggerian model of the modern world.

Heidegger not only felt that physical technologies do make a difference in our relation to the world (and Being)—for example, in our age reducing humanity to a "standing reserve"—he also ultimately sees life in a dualistic relation with humanity. That is to say, life in some ways is conceived of as external to humanity, in ways that one can also see in the more structuralist statements of Agamben and Foucault: life by itself (Agamben's "bare life," for example) is not only external to the human (and to technology),[11] it is that which humanity seeks to control; for Foucault, this is what biopolitics is (humanity's control of itself through the control of "life"). Azuma and others in Japanese media studies might be thought of as invoking this kind of model (with "life" being mediated by new technical modes of consumption), although, in fact, when it comes to the relation between life and the human, the lines are more blurred, and in interesting ways.

I will return to this latter question on the externality of life to the human—but first a little more on the dualisms that define this stage of media studies under Azuma—including the relation of human to animal. Azuma's formulation of animality and animal consumption, as well as his vision of history, are only lightly based on Kojève. In part, Azuma is simply laying out an opposition of modes of affect: the animal mode is defined by "satiable" cravings that have no larger meaning or implications attached to them, while the "human" mode always entails a search for meaning, which, being impossible to complete, means a mode of desire that is insatiable. In effect, Azuma is describing classic modern mass culture as the mode of the human, and this other, "postmodern" mode as the animal. This might sound like a historical trajectory—moving not only from classic mass culture to something else but also from human to animal—and Azuma at times is read that way, but that is only partially accurate.[12] Azuma largely retains the dualism of human versus animal, following Kojève.

The opposition that Azuma takes up most directly is that between a "snob" and an animal. For Kojève, the (human) snob is like the animal insofar as neither has anything to do with historical quests for meaning anymore. The epitome of the snob is one who in essence believes in and follows formalized values (value is form itself, and so one will follow that form, whatever the outcome—as in the example of "gratuitous" formal samurai suicide). This might be read as the outcome of bourgeois taste; Kojève then projects it into the "posthistorical" moment. And while the gratuitous human quality of snobbishness might oppose the snob to the animal (which has no snobbery), Kojève sees these as two sides of the same thing. Both can be part of the positive, posthistorical society that no longer involves the impossible desire for meaning (the "human" content that has previously structured history). Kojève locates the conditions for this posthistorical moment in both Japan and the United States: the countries are, in essence, the inverse of one another, and represent, respectively, the figure of the snob and the figure of animal that together populate posthistory. There is thus no more meaning sought or transferred in this posthistorical lifeworld. Human discourse is nothing more than "the language of bees."[13] This is a world of value distinctions, perhaps, but not of communication.

Azuma takes up the ambiguities and tensions of Kojève's posthistorical world, retaining some dual oppositions (the snob and the animal), but nonetheless resolves them into something either more open or utopic. For Azuma, it is clear that the database is not a meaning-based or classically literature-based order of consumption. So otaku are already either snobs or animals. Further, there is no mediation with the "real" world of historical human meanings in that sense.

Accordingly, there would be no hope in looking to narrative out of a classic desire for revolutionary politics—no hope for narrative to raise awareness of historical struggles, contradictions, or aims. However, the implication is that there is no need for that kind of meaning. Meaning goes with an older bourgeois subjectivity, which is itself hanging on to a categorization of the human, and the humanities, that is in fact a kind of entrapment of life into a falsely fixed concept. This is a different kind of politics, one that involves reevaluating the very category of the human, and this happens by breaking its tie to those orders of meaning.[14]

These relations are further clarified in Azuma's discussion of animality.[15] Here, too, Azuma cursorily adopts Kojève's model. The otaku are Japan's snobs, living now in posthistory, and by living at the level of pure form they are able to make a more radical break from the kinds of prescribed meanings, aims, and use-values that have hitherto helped to define what it means to be human. Azuma gives more weight to the role of the snob/Japanese otaku, and less importance to the American than Kojève (American animals quickly drop from Azuma's discussion), so that for Azuma, the otaku is itself both snob and animal. This animal being may have emerged out of Japan's "new human" (*shinjinrui*), the spoiled bourgeois youth of the wealthy 1980s, but it is now part of a world that is contented by the complete satisfaction of only immediate, "animal" needs, and refuses narration into anything larger (not even the narratives of commodity consumerism—so this is not mass culture).

Even in Azuma's depiction of a posthistorical world of a life freed from previous expectations and predefined desires, some categorizing dualities remain. Fiction remains opposed to reality, even while fiction takes over as the only realm of life. Similarly, while the new animal-human lives only at the level of form, unconcerned with the old contents that defined the good human life, the opposition of form and content remains. And while the category of the "human" is now intentionally blurred with the idea of the animal (as defined by animal needs),[16] not only does the distinction of human versus animal remain, but the category of the human itself remains a clearly defined object (the one quote Azuma pulls from Kojève indicates these points: "post-historical Man must continue to detach 'form' from 'content' . . . so that he may oppose himself as a pure form to himself and to others taken as a 'content' of any sort"[17]). Further, also following from Kojève, Azuma continues in an understated way to retain both culture and nation (privileging Japan as the location of the posthistorical) for this supposedly content-free posthistorical human, and ultimately therefore retains history itself.

In sum, Azuma's model in *Dobutsuka suru posutomodan* at once offers a vision of life that opens up to practices not set on predetermined paths—making human life a more unknown world of potential—and yet invokes the kind of oppositions that retain the boundaries of life and humanity, and even culture and nation, that we have known. For Hegel and Kojève, this was part of a dialectic, but for Azuma it is a little less clear—especially given that this dualism is part of the posthistorical world, so there would be no further resolution of these oppositional categories possible.

Azuma's analysis does work through and identify both economic forces (the bourgeois life that led to the otaku) and media constraints (databases, etc.). These both do seem to be grounds of mediation, and so deserve to be central to his form of media studies. But as Azuma moves toward the posthistorical as the heart of his understanding of the present, and therefore as media studies in this case moves closer to an analysis of life itself, his model seems to move toward a world of distinctions *only*—a world without mediation at all. Media studies without mediation—a kind of metaphysics without ontology.

As a postscript to this first position, it is worth pointing out that at this stage one can see the movement of media studies into a kind of anthropology—but one in which the foundation shifts from a relation between media and culture toward a relation between media and humanity (human life).

If the above can be taken as one concretization of media studies, as a central discipline for the analysis of social life in its post-bubble-era form—with the otaku as the centrally important subject of life—then the writings of Azuma and the orbit of writers and critics around him immediately after the events of 3.11 raise the possibility again of a different order of things.[18]

Azuma and Synthesis 2 (Post-Fukushima)

Azuma was only one of a very wide spectrum of writers and critics in Japan who saw the March 2011 events as not just part of repeating crises but as a catastrophe that was genuinely disclosing something new in Japan's postwar social life. In the first postdisaster issue of *Shisôchizu bêta*, Azuma immediately wrote that even the social criticism of the first decade of the 2000s—which was premised on finding new ways to maintain the image of Japan as largely homogenous, middle-class, and equal—was revealed as untenable.[19] In *Nihon 2.0*, he added that Japan needed a new "image," and a new mindset, because things had changed; "a new society requires a new mindset."[20] As Azuma therefore put it in his opening description of the overall Genron project, "For the next 5 to 10 years, Japan will become a sort of testing ground for diverse political, social and cultural undertakings."[21]

Azuma's circle of interlocutors changed, especially as institutionalized in the Genron-based journals, particularly *Shisôchizu bêta*. Some of Azuma's statements look different enough to raise the question whether, as a result of this observation, Azuma not only saw a revolution in Japanese society but also fundamentally transformed his own thinking (and what one might call "media studies" in the process); this raises further questions as to whether the terms of the field, therefore, have once again been reorganized as well.

There are some real continuities in Azuma's positions—at least one can see the development of ideas stated earlier—and he does at times note that the changes he is working with were in part already in motion before the March 2011 disasters. But to the extent that one can find a coherent outlook, there does seem to be a real shift in how Azuma's circle conceives of society and media studies as means of understanding the social. There are tremendous inconsistencies and contradictions even within Azuma's own publications, but again, his work is perhaps best taken as an expression of the landscape of thought in the immediate post-3.11 era. This includes some of the basic contradictions that have organized the field. A brief sketch of this landscape should start with Azuma's *Ippan ishi 2.0* (General will 2.0), a work that he began before the 2011 disasters, and which offers some of his fullest and most systematically conceptualized reworkings of earlier models.

If anything, *Ippan ishi 2.0* is even more of a conscious effort to rethink the very nature of the social, and the mediating grounds of what we call "society," than was *Dobutusuka suru posutomodan*. At least on the surface, it appears to return to some of the more traditional assumptions and categories of the social that *Dobutusuka suru posutomodan* had sought to move past—or perhaps it is trying to invoke but remediate those categories (it is worth leaving this as an open question for the moment). The otaku are no longer mentioned at all, for example, nor do subculture and subcultural consumption any longer play a central role; instead the book almost appears to return to the more mainstream bourgeois urbanite as the real subject of social life and of history.[22]

We are also returned to history. The present is no longer described as a posthistorical moment, and to the extent that there is a utopic quality to *Ippan ishi 2.0*, it is phrased as a world to come—a futurity (raising the question as to what will mediate or drive history). The book furthermore vaguely returns to Japan itself, and it specifies why the new vision of democracy and society might come uniquely from Japan. We are even told of something like the Japanese character,[23] which appears to be especially adept at sensing the general (and informational) "atmosphere" of social and political conditions.[24]

Azuma still retains a focus on a conception of the database, and on social media technologies as a critical site of mediation, but these are once again truly mass-media technologies and include Google, Twitter, television, and the video-sharing website Nico Nico Douga (Niconico). So in the same way that Azuma returns to a more mainstream and mass-oriented bourgeois subject, he also returns to mass mediation. There is also, therefore, a possibility that he is returning to mass culture as the model of society.

The book's aim is primarily to outline a new image of democracy, and thereby a new kind of state—a "state to come"—and media technologies are considered in that light. The "database" now refers to a collective unconscious (if there is a social whole, this would seem to be its defining characteristic) that also serves as the general will. This is the general will that for Azuma should drive what he calls "politics." Rejecting the politics of deliberation and debate, the role of media is in effect to collect a general sentiment, which politicians should follow more than guide. There is a visual component to Azuma's discussion as to how this practical mediation might work: Azuma dreams of a "giant visual screen" that would be placed in front of the national Diet building, revealing the general will in real time (*Ippan ishi 2.0*, 182); he also offers several televisual models, describing democracy in terms of performer-audience relations to the camera and screen. Although it might seem that Azuma is invoking something akin to screen theory—in which the screen is the equivalent of the unconscious—these visual components seem for the most part to act simply as a window for immediacy. There is no more concern with mass culture, or even a database of subcultural content, that then gets mediated by—or comes to the surface through—an otaku-like creative process of consumption. The database now is what you already see, on the surface, transparently and immediately.

Azuma does go on to offer us several possibilities for mass mediation. In television, a variety show is equivalent to populism, in which performers might pay attention to things such as viewer ratings, and so minimally act as representatives of viewers' wishes, but really the viewers are simply spectators. The performers (or politicians) act on their own, while viewers ultimately just listen, and lead an existence without power. The educational show, on the other hand, is worse. As in elitist politics, in educational shows scholars simply speak with one another, in a space entirely divorced from the viewer; the general public is entirely cut out of the process. Azuma's more ideal model comes from the live debate programs on the Niconico website. These are live broadcasts in which the performers continually interact with live comments from viewers posted on a real-time monitor (and sometimes that is all they do). In this case, the performer/politician principally reacts to the overall will of the fragmented viewership, and only occasionally tries to guide or rechannel it.

This is helpful, but these are only models (Azuma is not claiming that Niconico itself has become the site of democracy)—apparently for a future to come. It is not clear whether any of these models might be more definitive of conditions in the present than any other, or what holds them all together as part of the present. And even if Niconico could literally serve as the structure of governance in a future to come, it remains unclear how that future might come (as opposed to any of the other models taking precedence, for example) and what would mediate the present toward that future. Thus, in *Ippan ishi 2.0* Azuma gives even more weight to history itself as the grounds of mediation, but there is no real theory of history provided.[25] To the extent that Azuma does call up history, it is more the history of a primordial past, as figured by people such as Rousseau (more on this below).

More generally, in *Ippan ishi 2.0*, as in Azuma's previous work, his framework continues to return to and rely on dualisms. The democracy to come, he tells us, will be somewhere between populism and elitist governance, between purely rational and purely emotional action, between direct and indirect democracy, and it will be both human and animal (with "human" now abstractly standing for classic liberal idealism, and "animal" for selfish and anarchistic desires).[26] But, as in Azuma's earlier work, these are not really dialectical oppositions, and while they seem to beg for explanation as to what will mediate them, there is no clear indication of what will do so.

Those specific dualisms are important, and the uncertainty as to what really mediates between apparently opposed tendencies is symptomatic. But behind all of this, and perhaps more importantly, Azuma is really presenting us with two very different sets of assumptions, and two very different worlds in this later phase. To the extent that they are hoped-for dreams of the future, they are also perhaps two different utopias.

On the one hand, it is possible to see in Azuma's new "general will" a networked, connective sociality that is by no means a return to a more mainstream bourgeois image of society. It is largely an affectively formed and governed subject formation (a "sea of compassion"), neither fixed as a structured "society" by an overarching governing idea, nor made up of stable, monadic individuals acting in their own essential interest. By these terms, the "social," and the collective "unconscious" that defines it, seems to be a much more open, provisional formation that operates in relation to dispersed individualities, which come together in specific ways for specific reasons and in ways that are for the good of all. This would be the kind of cloudlike social subjectivity that is visible in new media studies elsewhere, premised on new media techniques (especially as in ubiquitous computing) and on some of the practices of global capital.[27] It is part of Azuma's new rejection of Hegel and of anything like idealism or deliberative social politics. As a reading of Rousseau, it is in this sense closest to the "general will," as something that is a collective unity and somehow always true to itself, as opposed to the "will of all," which is merely the sum of individual wills and may at times include elements that are not truly the will of the people.[28]

On the other hand, Azuma's turn away from Hegel and Lyotard and back to Rousseau also suggests a very different analysis of the present. In *The Social Contract*, Rousseau's vision anchors a more stable category of the human being, utopically, in nature and in a primordial past. Further, this stable subject is naturally a monadic individual (the social contract is, of course, a secondary formation, with individuals willingly ceding some of their rights in order to regain greater individual freedom out of a collectivity). So Rousseau, arguably, not only assumes an a priori, nature-based fixed category of the human as his starting point, he also can be used for more neoliberal socioeconomic views: that the individual should always come first.[29] It is not surprising that, if Azuma is thinking along these lines, he would also draw from Robert Nozick.

It is as if Azuma's underlying interest in and emphasis on animality as the full satisfaction of selfish needs serves as more of a guiding principle than is openly acknowledged. In this world, one does not seem to need an overarching guiding idea for the social because it is already there from the start. The origin really lies within the a priori individual, and even compassion is as much an innate quality of the individual as it is a fortuitous outcome of social mediation. There is, in other words, an unstated dependency on essentialisms, including the essential character of the human. The greater emphasis on the atomistic individual as apart from and prior to the social is then expressed when Azuma turns away from the visual realm of mass media and comments that, despite the massive scale of the world's current population, the real mode of connectivity is "friend of a friend of a friend of a friend" (*Ippan ishi 2.0*, 221). Thus, from this perspective, despite the world's massive population numbers, the scale and mode of connection is small rather than massive—this is not like television, with a mass cultural society collectively watching the same show, en masse—and even with its multiple connections the social form might be described more as a collection of individuals than a unified collective unconscious. It is therefore appropriate that, in this context, Azuma depicts the social as divided into myriad collectivities (*kyôdôtai*), or "island universes" (*Ippan ishi 2.0*, 221). Furthermore, these island universes themselves are akin to unique individuals, and the way Azuma describes them, they are composed simply of like-minded people; they are islands of sameness, apparently composed of individuals who are innately similar and so of like mind, without mediation and presumably more than just provisional unities.[30]

A tendency to reattach this naturalized individual to earlier essentialist categories is evident in other publications that Azuma produced around the same time. These include quick journalistic pieces, and the format may partially explain the reason for the less subtle modes of argument—as in Azuma's *New York Times* editorial "For a Change, Proud to Be Japanese," wherein he recounts a new patriotism and pride in the national government that was already visible almost immediately after the tsunami.[31] But the tendency is apparent in more carefully crafted work as well, as in Azuma's return to constitutional politics, and his joint drafting of a new constitution—which he believed would serve as the "central pillar" of a new Japan.[32] Along with the return to nation and nationalism, Azuma's politics change too: from the nonpolitics of an animalistic human, liberated precisely to the extent that it can no longer be identified by any earlier (grand) narratives at all, Azuma is again working with the narrative of fixed identities and historical meanings or ideals.

Accordingly, this starts to look like a *tenkô*—not only a reversal of outlook on the world, but a return to far more traditional visions of Japanese social form, and far more traditional disciplinary approaches to this social form. Is 3.11 therefore just a crisis for Azuma, rather than a moment of revolutionary change? Does it merely uncover the truth of an earlier social world? Might it even uncover the *lack* of importance of media studies altogether, as it had come to be constituted by the turn of this century?

Despite the reappearance of fixed categories such as the nation and even the human, and despite the turn back to earlier social theorists such as Rousseau and Freud, this is in some ways a new reformulation as much as it is a reinstatement of those older terms. As media studies has taken on the task of rethinking and remediating social and cultural theory in Japan's late postwar era in the face of new networking technologies, new alternative modes of capitalist consumption, and the fraying of older social fabrics, one can see in the work of Azuma himself and those around him distinctive and apparently new contradictions. Although perhaps unintended, these might be read as definitive contradictions of the moment. Again, Azuma and media studies are helping in this sense to give voice to the present.

Some of the contradictions and inconsistencies are clear. On the one hand, Azuma's later work implies a mass collective unconscious, or general will, that transcends any single individual (that is a subject formation in its own right),[33] but not any given moment (it is always only provisional, being only of the moment). This requires mass mediation, as in the public screen, or mass media, as with television—even if it is a kind of immediate or transparent mediation, in the sense of something that simply conveys rather than translates. On the other hand, one can also see an argument laid out for the undiminished primacy of atomized individuals, who can think and act rationally on their own behalf, whose very being stems mostly from essential qualities given to them by nature, and, if there is grouping of these, it tends toward unchanging communities of sameness.[34] This is not merely an opposition in which a new animalistic networked subject is opposed to an older vision of a society of humans brought together by a common ideal. Either way, there is apparently no need for real mediation—either the general will is simply a transparent reflection of a networked being, or it is the transparent expression of already-existing essentialisms. This is what both politics and society are reduced to.

But these really are contradictory images of the future, and both are manifest in Azuma's more recent examples of media studies. Azuma may be a voice of the era, but insofar as he is again producing a new approach to the social, he is really depicting two different materialities, two different subject formations, or two different worlds. At the risk of reduction, it is also possible to read into these two differing sets of assumptions a kind of affective openness on the one hand, and a rational and categorical closure on the other. If that is the case, then this is not such a new framework after all. It is this opposition that is closest to reviving a more classic modernist framework. Media studies, in other words, in this sense, ends up only replaying the older conceptual structures that it was ostensibly remediating, even if it is applying those conceptual structures to conditions that appear to be truly transformed. One can see the tremendous difficulty of escaping dependencies not only on received categories such as nation or culture but, more importantly, on the terms by which those categories are thought, or approached. If media studies was meant to rethink the order of things, and in the process to mediate and push history, the project clearly is complicated.

In Azuma's case, the post-Fukushima inclination has been toward closure and even essentialisms. To cite a final example, one might look to Azuma's own proposals for dealing with the aftermath of Fukushima. The idea is to bring Fukushima into the circulation of death tourism, and turn the nuclear disaster zone into a tourist park. Doing so, Azuma has said, will remind people of the reality (and tragedy) of death. In a crisis not only of economic and material infrastructure but of life itself, Azuma wants a true reconciliation with something we may once have been more easily able to think about, and with—reclaiming a stable understanding of the terms and limits of the human, and the measures of human life that once helped to describe them.

It may be that these are the definitive contradictions of the time, but if so, giving voice to them in this way nonetheless does not mean mediating them. Throughout Azuma's varied images and practices of media studies in works such as *Ippan ishi 2.0*, there is a thematic drive for immediacy. Even when Azuma is building the image of a more mass-oriented collective unconscious, the visual realm that helps pull things together into a collectivity functions ideally like a window, as noted above. It is a transparent graphing, without even the suggestion of a software interface that might play a mediating role.[35] And when Azuma turns toward the model of the Rousseauian individual, mediation seems to be unnecessary because the ultimate grounds of the social already lie within the individual as a naturally provided essentialism. There is a kind of social presence, or immediacy, without any need for mediation.

At worst, if there is a return to something in the post-Fukushima media studies projects it is a repetition of the old binarisms that have structured modernist thought on human life and social form (oppositional relations such as affective versus rational life), and a return to the categorical essentialisms (such as nation, culture, and humanity) that have given practical form to those modes of thought. It would make sense, then, that the crisis of 3.11 might result in death theme parks that enshrine stable notions of life, labor, consumption, and production.

If that were the case, it would lead to the end of media studies. In some ways, as I hope I have shown, that end is already visible. Yet even the contradictions that Azuma resorts to, as well as the specifically new conditions he outlines, show why a kind of media studies—perhaps as a kind of anthropology—is needed now as much as ever.

NOTES

1. Suggestions of other genealogies are evident even in other essays in this volume, as, for example, Marilyn Ivy's essay on the *InterCommunication* project.

2. Azuma Hiroki, *Dobutsuka suru posutomodan* (Tokyo: Kodansha, 2001); translated by Jonathan Abel and Shion Kono as *Otaku: Japan's Database Animals* (Minneapolis: University of Minnesota Press, 2009). Azuma Hiroki, *Nihon 2.0* [Japan 2.0] (Genron: Tokyo, 2012). Azuma Hiroki, *Ippan ishi 2.0: Rusô, Ruroito, Gûguru* [General will 2.0: Rousseau, Freud, Google] (Tokyo: Kodansha, 2011).

3. Genron is the company founded by Azuma Hiroki in 2010. Genron's focus is on publishing, in particular building on the *tankôbon* journal/book series *Shisôchizu*, edited by Azuma and Kitada Akihiro from 2008 to 2010 and published by NHK, and more recently, the triannual *Genron*, begun in 2015. Other Genron publications include *Shisôchizu beta*; *Genron etc.*, *Genron Tsûshin*, and *Kankôchika Mail Magazine*. The company also manages a café that holds lecture series; runs its own live streaming channel on the Niconico video sharing website; and coordinates the Genron Tomonokai paid members' group, which includes exclusive newsletters, online magazines and newspapers, and so on.

4. See Alexander Zahlten's translation of Kitada Akihiro, "An Assault on 'Meaning': On Nakai Masakazu's Concept of 'Mediation,'" in this volume.

5. Otsuka Eiji, *Monogatari shôhiron: "Bikkuriman" no shinwagaku* [Theory of narrative consumption: Myth analysis of "Bikkuriman"] (Tokyo: Shinyôsha, 1989). See also the annotated translation with translator's preface, "World and Variation," trans. Marc Steinberg, *Mechademia* 5 (2010): 99–116.

6. It is perhaps not surprising that Otsuka has viewed himself as above all an ethnographer.

7. The refocus onto the otaku is strong enough to leave open the possibility of an alternative subject-history for this era.

8. There is some tendency to read this new focus on the *otaku* as a turn from the mainstream to subculture, and from theory to pop cultural objects (e.g., anime). There may be some accuracy to this, but it is reductive and simplistic. Much of Japanese postwar mass culture has in fact been made up of subculture (it changes but is not a new formation in the 1990s), and "theory" may be refigured in the new media studies, but

thought is not lost. Rather, the more appropriate question has in part been, what is an otaku subcultural mode of thought, and how does it differ from a more bourgeois mode? As Azuma makes clear, this happens at all levels of critical practice, including obvious ones: the simple fact that he was writing for cheap paperback book editions to be read by a not-fully-academic readership already implies a different complex, and process, of "critical thought"; one sees here too a different thoughtful subject. This is a subject/readership that has long existed in postwar Japan, but in this context it takes on a new significance.

9. Azuma does seem to recognize the power of affective forces, saying that if anything it is the moe elements rather than the authors that become "gods," but he does not see these as adding up to anything like a coherent grand narrative—either of culture or of corporate advertising. See *Dobutsuka suru posutomodan*, chapter 2.

10. A commonality of social practice that also replaces the more determining concept of a collective unconscious. For a reading of this, see Marc Steinberg, "Review of *Otaku: Japan's Database Animals*: Japanese Postmodernity Reconsidered," *Mechademia*, last modified November 2011, http://mechademia.org/reviews/marc-steinberg-review -of-otaku/.

11. The clear separation of life as a distinct property or force has left this structuralist approach open to critique for invoking a kind of vitalism.

12. The possibility of a historical trajectory away from mass culture is more evident and comprehensible in Azuma's explanations. See especially chapter 2 of *Dobutsuka suru posutomodan*.

13. Alexander Kojève, *Introduction to Reading Hegel: Lectures on the Phenomenology of Spirit*, ed. Alan Bloom, trans. James H. Nichols, Jr. (Ithaca, NY: Cornell University Press, 1980), 160.

14. Here, too, one can see a different and subtler understanding of postmodernism than the plain notion of a world of signs that have lost their contents.

15. The attention given to Azuma's conception of animality is somewhat surprising, given the brief space he devotes to its explication (and perhaps the lack of rigor with which he pursues it). But it is critical to his larger view of mediation, and the fact that "animalization" is featured in the title of *Dobutsuka suru posutomodan* seems to indicate that he realizes that.

16. At times the opposition of animal and human seems to be reduced to a relation between passive and active consumption.

17. Azuma, *Otaku: Japan's Database Animals*, 69.

18. Azuma has been somewhat like Murakami Takashi, in the sense that he has drawn in people around him who are working on similar issues in similar ways but who are not always entirely in agreement (the incorporation of his company Genron— originally called Contectures—was in a sense the formalization of this process). A full survey would require discussion of the differences between some of these points of view, which space here does not allow. There are certain people with whom Azuma has continued to maintain dialogue, such as Murakami Takashi. In other ways, he has moved from discussions with those interested in subcultural content (Morikawa Kaichiro, for example) to close cooperation with media theorists such as Kitada Akihiro (his

coeditor of the first *Shisôchizu* journal project, which ran from 2008 to 2010), to a wider range of engagement that plays out across his media platforms (including the journal publications of *Shisôchizu beta*, *Genron Tsûshin*, and *Genron etc.* These include conversations with sociologists such as Miyadai Shinji, architects such as Fujimura Ryuji, philosophers such as Umehara Takeshi, science-oriented thinkers such as Kazutoshi Sasahara, and politicians such as former vice governor of Tokyo, Inose Naoki.

19. "We are not equal. . . . With the disaster, we became aware that we were fragmented"; Azuma Hiroki, "The Disaster Broke Us Apart," *Shisôchizu beta* 2 (2011): 222.

20. *Nihon 2.0*, E9.

21. This statement, dated May 10, 2011, is included on the online Genron portal: http://global.genron.co.jp/aboutus/ (accessed June 1, 2014).

22. As Naoki Matsumoto, Azuma's chief translator and "global outreach" point person, put it in a 2012 interview with Giant Robot, "The main point is that it's not about subculture per se. Subculture is becoming less of a focus. . . . It's more about the contemporary Japanese situation at large"; "Interview: Genron," Giant Robot, accessed October 2, 2014, http://www.giantrobot.com/blogs/giant-robot-store-and-gr2-news/15804763-interview -genron. Azuma does reference the earlier *Dobutsuka suru posutomodan* in *Ippan ishi 2.0*, so there is at least the implicit possibility that *otaku* now stands for all Japanese people rather than any subcultural group. But even in *Nihon 2.0*, Azuma was already writing that the otaku are no longer concerned with content at all (subcultural or otherwise), and were instead (like other Japanese) themselves interested in competing business models: "Things have completely changed . . . and otaku have become significantly more sociable" (E24). So there really is no need to use the term *otaku*.

23. Azuma does explicitly say that this is "not a theory of Japan" (*Ippan ishi 2.0*, 9), but he consistently returns to qualities and characteristics particular to Japan. He also, for example, suggests that Japan's "Galapagos syndrome" (having media practices that develop uniquely within its island geography) is an additional way in which the new universals of democracy might originate from within Japan.

24. *Ippan ishi 2.0*, 7.

25. The best that one might hope for is a kind of unstated deconstructive mode of history, in the way that one might read into Heidegger, but there is little reason to read Azuma in this way.

26. The closest Azuma comes to an actual example of the in-between figure is that of youth "going through the confusing rush of desire during puberty" (*Ippan ishi 2.0*, 198). In this work, amid all the dualities, Azuma tends to favor the affective over the rational, and suggests a world that operates through a "sea of compassion."

27. There are points in Azuma's description in which this general will seems to take on a life of its own, in ways that make it sound like a radical Durkheimian society (a collectivity that almost transcends the individuals that make it up). For example, Azuma cites Richard Rorty in saying that deliberation should be confined to the private sphere, while public nature is wholly of the unconscious will of the general public (*Ippan ishi 2.0*, 220). It is hard to see what practical relation there might be, then, between the private and the public. But Azuma does not generally suggest such a radical separation.

28. See *Ippan ishi2.0*, chapter 1.

29. It is also therefore not surprising that Azuma emphasizes that even the "general will," as opposed to just the "will of the people," is in his view a mathematical product of the population—in other words, it emerges simply out of the sum of the individuals that make up the collectivity. Thus, no government or other mode of representation or mediation is necessary. See, for example, *Ippan ishi 2.0*, 47–49.

30. This formulation is even more apparent in Nozick's writings, as in his idea that like-minded people might create geographically isolated communities. See Robert Nozick, *Anarchy, State, and Utopia* (New York: Basic Books, 1974).

31. Hiroki Azuma, "For a Change, Proud to Be Japanese," *New York Times*, March 16, 2011.

32. *Nihon 2.0*, E11. Even in *Ippan ishi 2.0*, Azuma writes that the Japanese people should give up on chasing a political system that is "not suitable for them" (*jibuntachi ni mukanai*); *Ippan ishi 2.0*, 7.

33. Even Azuma's use of Freud at some points functions in this way, working out a conception of the unconscious by these terms rather than as the inner anchor of an atomized and privatized individual.

34. These are clearly part of the more libertarian and neoliberal tendencies in Azuma's approach.

35. In many ways, this seems to be all that is meant by Azuma's privileging of an affective "democracy without communication."

AFTERWORD. THE DISJUNCTIVE KERNEL
OF JAPANESE MEDIA THEORY
MARK B. N. HANSEN

Situation Determines Our Media Theory

"Situation determines our media theory." It is with this reversal of the (in)famous opening statement of Friedrich Kittler's *Gramophone, Film, Typewriter* that Marc Steinberg and Alexander Zahlten announce the programmatic aim of their fascinating collection of essays on "media theory in Japan." At once the proclamation of an imperative to bring geocultural specificity to media studies in general and a concrete call to particularize media theory and development in Japan, this reversal—situation, not media, as determinant—furnishes a basis upon and a background against which to evaluate the stakes of Steinberg and Zahlten's project. At the same time, it serves as an anchor for interweaving what are, to be sure, highly diverse contributions whose commonality stems less from any shared commitment or claim than from a collectively singular, though highly disparate, engagement with the situation of Japan.

Informing Steinberg and Zahlten's reversal of Kittler's perspective is an ambivalent reception of the volume that I coedited with my then University of Chicago colleague W. J. T. Mitchell, *Critical Terms for Media Studies*. In our introduction to this volume, Tom and I also took up Kittler's infamous pronouncement by deforming it. "Rather than *determining* our situation," we wrote, "media *are* our situation."[1] By this, we meant that media permeate our lives so thoroughly as to be inseparable from our "situation," whatever that may be; in this perspective, any attempt to understand our situation must proceed through the media that inform it, although, to be sure, not narrowly or exclusively. For us, and in contrast to Kittler's strongly antihermeneutic thrust, media constitute "a perspective for understanding" that reinstates the "crucial and highly dynamic role of mediation—social, aesthetic, technical, and (not least) critical—that appears to be suspended by Kittler."[2]

Citing these very lines, Steinberg and Zahlten wholeheartedly endorse our central gesture to restore the dynamic role of mediation, as well as the general aim of our volume to historicize mediation well beyond current notions of digital media and canonical media forms. Yet they wonder—with some justification—"what happens if the very conditions of thinking mediation arise from the particular media and media-cultural forms with which we interact?"[3] Contending that the *Critical Terms* volume—here standing in for "the vast majority of writings on the subject"—largely "pass[es] over" questions of geographical and geocultural specificity, Steinberg and Zahlten position their volume as a remedy for such "silence." Specifically, they suggest that the contributions to *Media Theory in Japan*, despite their diversity and disparateness, each in their own way grapples with the "practical (and historically grounded) problem of how distinct cultural-media configurations give rise to distinct forms of mediation, and distinct kinds of media theorization."[4] This double call—to think media from the trenches and to (re)anchor theorization within concrete media practices—compels Steinberg and Zahlten to nuance their programmatic reversal of Kittler in an important way: it is always and necessarily *a specific situation*—"the situation of more or less temporally and spatially bounded media cultures and ecologies"—that determines our media theory.[5]

Far from a simple call to gather empirical facts about local media theories and developments, the task of excavating how media theory arises from the concrete geocultural realities of mediated life in twentieth- and early twenty-first-century Japan requires a dual trajectory. On one hand, Steinberg and Zahlten inform us, we must carry out a *transcultural* exploration of how Japanese reception *deforms* European and North American media theories; on the other, we must focus *intraculturally* on how media-theoretical framing modifies entrenched philosophical or critical movements *within Japan*. Positioned across such a double articulation, media theory operates both as an unstable set of practices subject to geocultural deformation and as a powerful set of agencies in the transformational rewriting of intranational intellectual history. What gives impetus to the deformations and transformations at issue in each case is *nothing other than Japan itself*—which is to say, nothing other than the concrete realities of media-cultural life in Japan at particular moments of its recent history. This impetus to deform and transform is precisely the double agency accorded the "in Japan" of Steinberg and Zahlten's title: Japan as both transformative assimilator of "universal" media theory and shifting medium for the ongoing, reiterated rearticulation of theory *after* media.

"... in Japan"

Taking up this double, *intra- and transcultural* agency of Steinberg and Zahlten's "in Japan," I shall dedicate my commentary here to exploring how these trajectories are in effect two components of a larger recursive correlativity between Japan and the West. Building on the findings of this exploration, I shall speculate about how the dual agency of "in Japan" might actually or potentially inflect or otherwise affect the "language of the universal" that is all too often held—either blindly or with critical eyes—to constitute the default, Euro–(North) American mode of media theory. To do this, I will adopt the same position Tom Mitchell and I took up with respect to the terms and categories with which we chose to structure *Critical Terms for Media Studies*: that of self-reflexive humility. Such a position begins by recognizing that any configuration, not least the one we settled on, is only one possible instantiation of a much broader field of potentiality and only one attempt to organize it categorically. As Tom and I noted in our introduction, many of our entries could perfectly well have been placed in different and indeed in multiple categories; and our three categories (aesthetics, society, and technology) are themselves nothing other than more or less contingent markers of tendencies *we* judged to be fundamental but that might well strike others as partial or misleading.[6] For their part, Steinberg and Zahlten recognize a similar contingency at the heart of their enterprise. They are keenly aware of the very disparate strata from which their contributors address media in Japan; the essays they have chosen range from "cultural histories of an encounter with media theory" to "philosophical questions" that urge us to rethink media theory as "mediation theory."[7] Steinberg and Zahlten are also self-conscious concerning the contingency of the organization of their volume. To see this, we would do well to consult the explanation they offer for their decision *not* to present the essays in the chronological order of their topics, but also—and in some sense, more significantly—their recognition of the viability of such a chronological reading strategy as one possible actualization of their volume.[8]

[370] MARK HANSEN

Exploiting the critical space opened by this contingency of organization, let me propose another actualization of—and another strategy for actualizing—the disparate themes and explorations constituting *Media Theory in Japan*. I propose that we substitute—as organizing categories for the volume as a whole—a different tripartite division: "Remediating the West," "Mediatizing Japan," and "Inter-izing (beyond) Japan." In place of the general topics Steinberg and Zahlten select (communication technologies, practical theory, and mediation and media theory), these categories name three distinct, though certainly overlapping, modes of relationality between Japan and the West: respectively, (1) remediating Western media theory from the Japanese perspective; (2) theorizing media within the intellectual traditions of Japan; and (3) positioning Japan within (which need not mean assimilating Japan to) an expanded international field. Not only do these modes collectively encompass the disparate investments *of all of the contributions to the volume*, but together, they allow us to reconfigure the significance of each contribution differentially in relation to a single critical problem: how to account for the nontrivial and always concrete and local agency of Japan as "*deformer-assimilator-perturber*" of globally circulating trends in media and media theory.

It is precisely their common, though to be sure disparate, engagement with this problem that unifies the contributions of the volume around a single venture: making good on the specificity of Japan. To see how this venture expresses Steinberg and Zahlten's animating aim, let me focus on Keisuke Kitano's account of the difficulties of translating between cultures. Rooted in his refusal to identify Japanese media theorist Hideo Kobayashi as the "Walter Benjamin of Japan," Kitano's argument foregrounds the crucial, indeed irreducible, role played by the resistance to translation *in any mediation between Japan and Western media theory*:

> Although an analytical comparison between Kobayashi and Benjamin . . . might give one a sense of understanding the situation in question, it would be misleading to take it literally. That would be merely a naïve comparative study of intellectual practices, leading to nothing but an instance of a new version of orientalism in the age of what might be called *Empire* or some other slogan of globalization. Conducting a comparative study concerned with different intellectual practices in different cultures generally tends to transform what is happening into what is to be translatable into the level of the receiver, ending up with a geopolitically biased production of the power of knowledge.

Furthermore, Kobayashi was highly aware of contemporary geopolitical tensions surrounding Japan . . . and that keen awareness equally informed his singular writing practice. I am afraid that a comparative approach naively formatted might flatten out many issues of geopolitical dynamism potentially folded onto their signifying planes of discourse written in such a work as Kobayashi's.[9]

Kitano's argument here gives a concise formula for taking stock of the "*deforming-transforming-reforming*" operationality of culture that Steinberg and Zahlten would like to introject into—or better, to discover retroactively to have always already been at the heart of—media theory, including (above all) media theory in the (Euro–North American) major key. Kitano's formula takes the form of an injunction to the media theorist: focus on the a-signifying resistances to cultural translatability, not its signifying successes.

Not surprisingly, this formula is itself a restatement—and a specification—of a central theme of recent media theory, namely, the disjunction of materiality from meaning. And this disjunction is, in its turn, also a restatement—or better, an extension—of the theoretical distinction that gives rise to media studies as a discipline: the distinction of media and communication. Steinberg and Zahlten cite Alexander Galloway, Eugene Thacker, and McKenzie Wark, who introduce a precise division of labor between the two: communication involves "things like senders and receivers, . . . encoding and decoding," whereas media attends to "questions of channels and protocols, . . . context and environment."[10] Together with the disjunction of materiality from meaning that it informs, this division of labor lies at the very heart of Friedrich Kittler's discipline-inaugurating "media-science" (*Medienwissenschaft*) and, through Kittler's wide-ranging influence, has come to inform much recent scholarship in Euro–(North) American media theory. Kittler, as is well known, extends Foucault's work on the archaeology of knowledge into the domain of media technics: if, for Foucault, what can be said (or seen or heard) at any given historical moment depends on a virtual archive of what is sayable (or seeable or audible), for Kittler, what is sayable (or seeable or audible) in turn depends on a technical archive, which is to say, on the concrete technical media that make available fluxes of letters, images, and sounds to human eyes and ears at a given historical moment. For Kittler, media operates to materialize the sensory fluxes that will subsequently become the raw material for meaning effects, which means that media is the empirico-transcendental condition of possibility for meaning. As such, media lies outside the scope of hermeneutics, and Kittler can mark the aporia within McLuhan's project to understand media: simply put, media *cannot* be understood.

What happens when this abstract and categorical disjunction of meaning and materiality is transposed to the terrain of transcultural difference? Itself the "experiment" *Media Theory in Japan* aims to perform, such a critical and cultural transposition operates by concretely and differentially embedding the disjunctive kernel of media theory—the categorical resistance of media to meaning—into a vast network of highly disparate sites of cultural production and contestation. As a result of such embedding, the abstraction of mediatic materiality is exploded into a potentially infinite number of concrete, practical operations, each of which has something singular to contribute to the encounter of Japan with media theory. Although Steinberg and Zahlten's collection can, in the end, include no more than a tiny share of this potentiality, what it does include provides a "fractal" image of the richness, diversity, and sheer messiness that characterizes media theory in Japan. By rendering commensurable quite disparate reference frames— from the advertising industry in 1960s Japan to the intellectual mode of *hihyō* (criticism), from governmental policies compelling women to service work to the television's assimilation into daily life—Steinberg and Zahlten's collection underscores how these operations, together with the three modes through which they engage the recursive coupling of Japan with the West, belong to a single continuum, the continuum of life in the age of global media.

Redistributing Media

Bearing in mind the sheer contingency of any possible actualization of this potentiality, I propose the following redistribution—a redistribution animated by my desire to capture both the disparity of the respective operationality of each frame of reference and their convergence around the media-inflected theme of resistance to (cultural) translatability:

REMEDIATING THE WEST:

- **Human-Animal:** Chapter 3: Takeshi Kadobayashi, "The Media Theory and Media Strategy of Azuma Hiroki, 1997–2003"
- **TakeMcLuhanism:** Chapter 5: Marc Steinberg, "McLuhan as Prescription Drug: Actionable Theory and Advertising Industries"
- **Double-Folded Critical Skepticism:** Chapter 13: Kitano Keisuke, "Kobayaski Hideo and the Question of Media"

- **General-Will-in-Real-Time:** Chapter 14: Tom Looser, "Media, Mediation, and Crisis: A History—and the Case for Media Studies as (Postcultural) Anthropology"
- **Man-Machine:** Chapter 2: Yuriko Furuhata, "Architecture as Atmospheric Media: The Tange Lab and Cybernetics"*
- **Lack-of-Copula:** Chapter 11: Akihiro Kitada, "An Assault on 'Meaning': On Nakai Masakazu's Concept of 'Mediation'"*
- **Mediation:** Chapter 12: Fabian Schäfer, "Much Ado about 'Nothing': The Kyōto School as 'Media Philosophy'"*

MEDIATIZING JAPAN:

- **Everydayness:** Chapter 1: Aaron Gerow, "From Film to Television: Early Theories of Television in Japan"
- **Exo-Data:** Chapter 10: Anne McKnight, "At the Source (Code): Obscenity and Modularity in Rokudenashiko's Media Activism"
- **Contingency:** Chapter 7: Tomiko Yoda, "Girlscape: The Marketing of Mediatic Ambience in Japan"
- **Performance:** Chapter 8: Alexander Zahlten, "1980s 'Nyū Aka': (Non)Media Theory as Romantic Performance"
- **National Public Sphere:** Chapter 9: Ryoko Misono, "Critical Media Imagination: Nancy Seki's T V Criticism and the Media Space of the 1980s and 1990s"
- **Lack-of-Copula:** Chapter 11: Akihiro Kitada, "An Assault on 'Meaning': On Nakai Masakazu's Concept of 'Mediation'"
- **Mediation:** Chapter 12: Fabian Schäfer, "Much Ado about 'Nothing': The Kyōto School as 'Media Philosophy'"
- **Double-Folded Critical Skepticism:** Chapter 13: Kitano Keisuke, "Kobayaski Hideo and the Question of Media"*

INTER-IZING (BEYOND) JAPAN:

- **Man-Machine:** Chapter 2: Yuriko Furuhata, "Architecture as Atmospheric Media: Tange Lab and Cybernetics"
- **(Inter)Translation:** Chapter 4: Marilyn Ivy, "The *InterCommunication* Project: Theorizing Media in Japan's Lost Decades"
- **Marxisms:** Chapter 6: Miryam Sas, "The Culture Industries and Media Theory in Japan"
- **Everydayness:** Chapter 1: Aaron Gerow, "From Film to Television: Early Theories of Television in Japan"*

- **TakeMcLuhanism:** Chapter 5: Marc Steinberg, "McLuhan as Prescription Drug: Actionable Theory and Advertising Industries"*
- **Performance:** Chapter 8: Alexander Zahlten, "1980s 'Nyū Aka': (Non)Media Theory as Romantic Performance"*

Little more than my own free associations to claims raised by the respective essays, my categories—and my naming exercise as such—are, to be sure, fraught with contingency. What I hope to capture with this eclectic mix of very local and specific terms (*TakeMcLuhanism, double-folded critical skepticism, general-will-in-real-time, exo-data, lack of copula*) and far more general, if not indeed abstract, terms (*everydayness, human-animal, contingency, performance, man-machine, mediation, Marxisms*) is the disparate texture, shifting scale, and wide range *of the resistances at issue in the encounter between media and Japan.* (Note that asterisks indicate entries that seem to straddle two categories; though these are only my associations, they serve to underscore the continuum linking the categories and exemplify a potentially quite numerous set of alternate distributions.)

Remediating the West

The essays grouped in "Remediating the West" all instantiate Kitano's argument against translation: "It was an undeniable fact that people living in a country called "Japan" employed the Japanese language, conversed in this language, constituted their everyday experience with this language and organized their thinking and sensibilities with this language."[11] The subject of his essay, the influential literary and media critic from the early twentieth century, Kobayashi Hideo, makes a similar point when he writes of his own translation work (in lines cited by Kitano): "If you translate Rimbaud, it would unquestionably no longer be Rimbaud. But Rimbaud's influence on me, that is realized in a new form. . . . Which is what you can detect in any work of translation. In particular it is true in poetry. If you translate a poem into Japanese, then it would be a Japanese poem."[12] What Kobayashi's translations bring home is a certain generic impossibility of translation, the fact that translation cannot overcome or eliminate the vast cultural differences it aims to bridge: "In spite of and at the same time because of receiving and emulating the question of individuality in Western art, Japan, through approaching, receiving and translating many instances and layers of Western modernity, always ends up realizing the logical truism that it is not a Western country. For Kobayashi, then, translation cannot but help emphasize the difference between Japan and Western countries."[13]

This cultural injunction against translation underpins Kitano's introduction of what he calls "double-folded critical skepticism": "a critical activity vis-à-vis a work of literature, art, a media object or a historical situation, but [one that] simultaneously uses that activity to perform a critique of its own foundations."[14] By reconstructing Kobayashi's intellectual career, Kitano is able to show how it is a certain deployment of language—of language embedded within everyday life—that makes such double-valenced criticism possible. It is through language, not solely or primarily as a medium of translation but rather *as the material core of life itself*, that we encounter the cultural world; and yet, because every such encounter is mediated by language, we meet the cultural world not as something external but, instead, *as a form of vital nourishment*: "food given to us that is imperative for our living."[15] For Kitano, two aspects of this digestive model of mediation deserve mention: on the one hand, Kobayashi's embeddedness within a robust media culture; on the other, Kobayashi's assimilation of medium to the mediation that is life-in-language.[16] The implication of this argument is profound: Japan can assimilate foreign media precisely and only because of the very impossibility of translation foregrounded by Kobayashi's model of mediation as digestion: for if reading literature in translation is akin to listening to music on the gramophone or seeing paintings in reproduction, as Kobayashi claims, that is because in all cases what is demanded is a material transformation of life-in-language. This "in-every-case-concrete" transformation—and not the abstract, if medium-specific, technical operations of modern media—is the site of mediation understood as a complex activity of materialization, indelibly connected to geopolitical realities, that at the same time marks a concrete resistance to translatability.

The two chapters devoted to the critical work of Hiroki Azuma—Kadobayashi's and Looser's—perfectly exemplify the specificity at issue in such materialization. Though they share a common focus on a controversial critic who is perhaps the foremost voice of media theory in Japan today, the two essays introduce terms, and develop arguments, that lie at opposite ends of the above-envisioned critical continuum. More than a mere paradox, this situation exemplifies the productivity involved in each and every concrete encounter between media theory and Japan.

Human-animal, the more abstract of the two terms in question here, is a distillation of the central claim animating Kadobayashi's reconstruction of Azuma's abandoned media theory (chapter 3): to wit, that the *différend* disjoining Azuma's transitional work on media theory from his subsequent celebration of *otaku* culture in *Otaku: Japan's Database Animals* can be traced to a dispute—a perspectival dispute pitting academic theory against fan practice—over how to understand the relation of animality and humanity. It is precisely a shift around this issue that explains Azuma's turn in his 2001 book *Database Animal* to an identification as a fan, a shift that ultimately explains why Azuma felt compelled to abandon his plans to publish a comprehensive theory of media. As Kadobayashi compellingly illustrates, this shift is motivated by Azuma's altered strategy for piercing the animal-human antinomy in the two bodies of work: if, in the work on media theory, and in particular in the text "On Information and Freedom," Azuma is committed to discovering a "human route" within the general tendency towards animality that constitutes the "lazy animal life of consumption" in the postmodern era, in *Otaku*, by contrast, Azuma goes back on his notion that "*otaku*'s animality is closed within the 'want-satisfaction circuit' of database consumption,"[17] in order to contend that it harbors a split subjectivity bridging the animal-human divide: "This subjectivity," Azuma writes, "is motivated by 'the need for small narratives' at the level of simulacra and 'the desire for a grand nonnarrative' at the level of database; while it is animalized in the former, it maintains a virtual, emptied-out humanity in the latter."[18]

General-will-in-real-time, the term I have chosen for Looser's essay (chapter 14), takes up this same conceptual problematic of the human and animal with the aim of tracing its dualism forward to Azuma's recent political theory in *General Will 2.0*, where the operation of mediation itself is superceded, or, we might better say, with a nod to Azuma's Kojève-mediated Hegelianism, *sublated*. For Looser, this means that we must reject the presentation of the human-animal as an implicit historical narrative, in which the rational, modern, meaning-seeking human cedes its place to the postmodern animal mode of consumption defined by "satiable" cravings without larger meaning. Such a historical trajectory is only "partially accurate," Looser specifies, for it fails to register the fact that Azuma "largely retains the dualism of human versus animal, following Kojève," and further that the animal is much closer kin to the snob than is usually recognized, since "neither has anything to do with historical quests for meaning anymore."[19] To this Looser adds an absolutely crucial claim, namely that as animal and/or snob, *otaku* have effectively given up the operation of mediation: "There is no mediation with the 'real' world of historical human meanings."[20] This same claim reappears in a new guise in Looser's account of Azuma's apparent rehabilitation of more traditional political categories in his post-Fukushima text, *General Will 2.0*. Though still articulated as a co-positing of contradictory tendencies—now the database qua collective unconsciousness (or "general will") and the individual as a neo-Rousseauesque essence that always already includes the social from its origin—Azuma's vision of a new politics, replete with his drafting of a new constitution for Japan, similarly marks the end of mediation, as Looser explains: "Rejecting the politics of deliberation and debate, the role of media is in effect to collect a general sentiment, which politicians would follow more than guide.... Azuma dreams of a 'giant visual screen' that would be placed in front of the national Diet building, revealing the general will in real time."[21]

This concept of *general-will-in-real-time* perfectly captures the shortcircuiting of mediation that occurs when meaning becomes something available only in a relation of immediacy without interface. In Azuma's figure of the giant visual screen, the immediacy central to the Rousseauesque individual, the implication of the social as the essence of the individual fuses with the immediacy provided by social media, Google, television genres such as the live debate and—in Azuma's favored example—the video sharing website Nico Nico Douga, such that the revelation of the social kernel of the individual, the crux of the general will, occurs spontaneously, *in-real-time*. Here, the contradictions between the animalistic drives of the social media sphere and the atomistic essence of the Rousseauesque individual are, similarly to the earlier case of the animal-human, not so much overcome as held together in an immediacy without outside: "It may be," concludes Looser, "that these are the definitive contradictions of the time, but if so, giving voice to them in this way nonetheless *does not mean mediating them....* Even when Azuma is building the image of a more mass-oriented collective unconscious, the visual realm that helps pull things together into a collectivity functions ideally like a window.... It is a transparent graphing, without even the suggestion of a software interface that might play a mediating role."[22] Likewise, in the case of Azuma's appropriation of Rousseau, where "mediation seems to be unnecessary because the ultimate grounds of the social already lie within the individual," there is "a kind of social presence, or immediacy, without any need for mediation."[23] The fusion of these conflictual components leads Looser to a double speculation: on one hand, with Azuma's double celebration of a contradictory immediacy, the end of media studies is "already visible"; on the other, the very contradictions Azuma resorts to show why media studies is "needed now as much as ever."[24]

Mediatizing Japan

Despite their concern with issues predating Azuma's post-Fukushima medi-tation on the Internet, the essays grouped in "Mediatizing Japan" all respond to this call for a revitalization of media studies in Japan. In one way or an-other, they each engage the problematic explored by Azuma—the paradox of "unmediated mediation"—and seek to think through media in order to theorize mediation. Following the pattern of Azuma's account of the In-ternet as the "general will," each of these studies trades in a focus on the medium as artifact or *techne* for a far broader concern with mediation as a practical activity of everyday social and cultural life. Whether this think-ing occurs through a reflection on the media of girl culture (Yoda), on the vagina as a medium of art (McKnight), or on the everydayness of televi-sion itself (Gerow), in each and every instance it is some specific feature of Japan—the legal status of women, the critical amnesia of postwar TV schol-ars, the gendering of the youth market—that takes center stage and operates in ways that fragment and pluralize the social impacts and cultural effects of media's mediation.

In his study of the Kyōto School as media philosophy—a study that would appear quite far removed from the just enumerated concerns of this section's essays—Fabian Schäfer proposes the contemporary German critical constel-lation of *Medienphilosophie* (media philosophy) as a promising avenue for theorizing this common critical project. For Schäfer, it is its buried poten-tial to give rise to a capacious concept of mediation, and not its canonical status as the "most prominent strand of modern Japanese philosophy," that accounts for the Kyōto School's importance.[25] The crux of Schäfer's revision-ist argument concerns the misappropriation of the Hegelian dialectic on the part of Kyōto School mainstay, Nishida Kitarō. For Nishida, writing at the end of the 1920s and beginning of the 1930s, dialectics meant the discovery of a "prelogical concept" capable of integrating all contradictions; in Nishi-da's understanding, "dialectic was the 'absolute contradictory self-identity' of the subject and object in particular, and of the universal and the individual in general."[26] The tacit connection Nishida here forges—the connection be-tween nothingness as encompassing all possible contradictions and media-tion as "interrelation among innumerable individuals"—yields what Schäfer dubs a "categorical mistake": the paradox of "unmediated mediation."[27]

In the hands of Nishida's colleagues (Hajime Tanabe) and disciples (To-saka Jun and, particularly, Nakai Masakazu), this paradox of "unmediated mediation" becomes the starting point for a fundamental reworking of the concepts of "media" and "mediation" that echoes the program of *Medienphilosophie*. For Tanabe, whose intervention initiates the medial transformation of nothingness, and for Tosaka, who follows his lead, what remains absent from Nishida's approach is the operation of a third term. Such a term is necessary, these critics argue, in order for Nishida's categories to be more than concepts forever trapped in a shadow play of mere meaning. Nakai brought this line of criticism to fruition by positioning technology as a third term: for him, technology furnishes not just a means for something, but "an 'existential-categorical medium' [*sonzai hanchū-teki baikai*] in the sense of a *poiesis* by which beings always somehow relate to their world."[28] Breaking with the conceptualism of Nishida, Nakai thus views technology as a resolutely practical domain, one that mediates not "by epistemological categories" but rather by "existential" ones.[29] Far from an abstract mediator between human consciousness and a reality outside it, technology is, in the words of Kitada Akihiro (chapter 11), "a (physical) thing that initiates the trial-and-error process of interaction between the human and nature, as well as, within this process, the transformation of its own functions/abilities." More than just a "tool enabling the human manipulation of nature," technology is "a medium that enforces both reflection on *and renewal of* the very relationship of humanity and nature."[30]

Central to this line of thinking is Nakai's concept of the *lack of copula* (my term for Kitada's intervention), which serves, in the narrow frame, to differentiate cinema medially from literature, but which also more broadly positions technology as a practical and nonrepresentational mediator between being and world. "Literature," Nakai observes, "possesses 'is'/'is not,' the copula that connects one representation to another. The sequentiality of film lacks this." What results from this concrete medial lack is a situation that quite literally exceeds the bounds of any hermeneutic contract between filmmaker and audience: "What this means," continues Nakai, "is that the filmmaker's subjectivity cannot attach conditions to an editing cut. It is the heart of the viewing public that establishes continuity between shots."[31] Together with the empowerment of the viewing public it produces, the lack of copula accounts for cinema's capacity to operate as a "new collective 'sensory formation,'"[32] which is precisely to say, as a technology in Nakai's understanding of the term. The lack of copula elicits a collective response—"common labor"—that places the cinematic audience in a practical, unmediated, and nonhermeneutic relationship with reality, and that positions cinema itself as a technology for renegotiating humanity's relationship with nature. As a medium constituted by the lack of copula, cinema becomes more than just one medium among others: cinema, that is, must be understood as *baikai* and not as *baizai*, as *Mittel* (means) and not just as *Medium* (medium), following Kitada's gloss on Nakai's well-known distinction.[33] For it is as *baikai/Mittel* that the medium of cinema becomes, or reveals itself to be, a technology; and it is as *baikai/Mittel* that cinematic mediation can be understood dialectically, as an "unmediated mediation" that, unlike Nishida's antidialectical concept of "nothingness," neither founders in nor simply encompasses (and thus levels) all contradiction.

Following his example of a boating competition, in which a direct and continuous connection of body, tool (oar), and water is subjected to ongoing practical negotiation by trial and error, Nakai's understanding of cinema as *baikai/Mittel* likewise foregrounds the practical: cinema in this view is not an apparatus for transmitting messages, meaning, or information through a channel, but rather "a site where humanity progressively renews/reestablishes/renegotiates the relationship with nature in the sense of *amidst* or *in*."[34] As if in response to sociologist Michio Inaba's 1989 criticism of the limitations of "newspaper studies" in prewar Japanese discourse on media— itself the pretext for Kitada's intervention—Nakai's theory views cinema as a cosmo-anthropo-logical activity that occupies a position at the very opposite extreme to any "single-medium" conceptualization.

If Nakai's view holds certain parallels with Walter Benjamin's roughly contemporaneous meditation on technical reproducibility and cinema as a mimetic, tactile, and in some sense cosmological technology, it is nonetheless flavored by the concrete institutional realities of media study in Japan. This geocultural specificity appears clearly in Inaba's critique of "newspaper studies": when Inaba bemoans the failure of Japanese newspaper studies to reflect on the being of the medium, he effectively foregrounds the need for a radically different ground on which to develop media philosophy in Japan. For Inaba, and for Kitada following him, it is precisely Nakai's standing as a heretic theorist of aesthetics within the Kyōto School, and thus as a critic situated outside the institutionalized system of journalism studies, that accounts for the value of his contribution to an ontological interrogation concerning media and mediation. As a Japanese philosopher reflecting on the role of media in mid-twentieth-century Japan, Nakai was not bound by the institutional constraints of media study then in force. Indeed, Nakai's eschewal of any medium-centered or "single-medium" approach—whether we view it as an unsolicited response to the limitations of newspaper studies or an anomalous development of his heretical aesthetic theory—serves both to differentiate him from Benjamin and to anchor him, indelibly if involuntarily, within the critical space of Japan and Japanese thinking on media.

Here again we confront the cultural injunction against translation foregrounded by Kitano, and once again it takes form in a refusal to identify a Japanese media theorist with the legendary figure of Walter Benjamin. According to Kitada, where Benjamin famously discovered the principle for his cosmosocial revelation of film's tactile and collective potential in a technical element of its mediality (technical reproducibility), Nakai pinpoints a certain disjunction between medium and mediation as the source for film's cosmo-anthropo-logical vocation. If film is a technology, in the sense Nakai lends the term, it is precisely because of its *failure* to operate as a self-contained and self-referential medium, which is equally to say, because it opens a practical space of contact between humanity and nature that offers a recompense of sorts for its inability to secure a hermeneutic contract with the viewer. Accordingly, although both Benjamin and Nakai shift the focus of film theory to the activity of reception, they do so in fundamentally different ways. Focusing on Nakai's contribution as an exemplar of a specifically Japanese inflection of media studies, what we find then is a strikingly original reformulation of Nishida's concept of "unmediated mediation" that appropriates dialectical thinking for a theory of humanity's practical imbrication with technology.

Inter-izing (beyond) Japan

If Kitada's exposition of Nakai's media theory emphasizes the "agency" of Japan, Yuriko Furuhata's account of Arata Isozaki's theorization of urban design (chapter 2) emphasizes the tension that emerges as Japanese architectural theory negotiates the "postmedium" condition. In a study that yields the term *man-machine*, Furuhata depicts Isozaki as a young architect and architectural theorist caught between the international forces of cybernetics and communication and the domestic legacy of Japan's colonial era urban planning. How Isozaki negotiates this tension marks his work as specifically Japanese but in a way that remains subordinate to the broader global forces informing the cybernetics revolution. For this reason, Furuhata's essay perfectly exemplifies the third and final clustering of essays I have proposed, namely "Inter-izing (beyond) Japan." By articulating the significance of cybernetics and communications specifically in relation to the program of his teacher, Tange Kenzo, Isozaki marks the break with Japanese colonial era reflections on biopolitical governance as crucial to his own reflections on architecture in the cybernetic age. In this formulation, the practices of Tange Lab—specifically, its allegiances to a structural paradigm and to a biopolitical mandate—constrain Isozaki's theorizing in ways that exemplify the force of the "inter-": here understood—perhaps exemplarily—as the agency that technically driven, international trends hold for the "cybernetic turn" of Japanese architecture.

To grasp the significance of Isozaki's contribution in all its singularity, let me turn briefly to Marilyn Ivy's account of *intertranslation* (chapter 4). Devoted to the Japanese journal *InterCommunication*, which ran from 1992 to 2008, Ivy's study focuses on the paradox of a journal devoted to intercommunication—literally "sharing in-between"—that has been placed out of communication (assuming that her own consultation of *literally unread* print copies in the Starr East Asian library at Columbia is indicative of the journal's reception fate). For Ivy, this paradoxical situation provides a compact "allegory" of the status of media theory in Japan, by which she means an allegory of the missed opportunity—or, alternatively, the latent potential—that the journal's interrogation of the "trope" of communication proffers to contemporary media theory. Simultaneously bemoaning the failure of the journal's desire to mediate the "inter"—the "place between" that would "allow communication to take place, in-between cities, technologies, critiques, dialogues"—and celebrating the critical potential of the journal's mission in the face of Japanese media theory's turn to pop culture, anime, and the Internet (largely synonymous with the name of Azuma Hiroki), Ivy urges a return to what she regards as a now lost vision of media theory in Japan: a vision that would take seriously *InterCommunication*'s allegiance to "internationalist high-theory and avant-gardist technocultural work" as the sole hope for a media theory that would not be "located simply within Japan."[35] Here "inter-izing" takes form as a countermeasure to the "containment of an exclusively Japanese *intra*communication"[36]—hence the aptness of *intertranslation* as a theme.

Regarded as a contribution to precisely such an "inter-izing" project, Isozaki's negotiation of the tension within Japanese architecture furnishes what I take to be a different model, one that marshals the forces of the international avant-garde toward a markedly different and, in some sense, "antiaesthetic" end. For Isozaki, as Furuhata's account underscores, it is the practical negotiation of urban space—and not the furtherance of an autonomous international aesthetic discourse—that is and must be at stake in any specifically Japanese negotiation of cybernetics. Consider Isozaki's analogy for negotiating the informationally mediated city of the cybernetic age: a pilot flying at night. Unable to trust his vision due to the darkness, the pilot must rely on signals received by his airplane's flight instruments in order to fly the plane. In a similar way, urban dwellers must increasingly rely on man-machine interfaces in order to maneuver effectively in the cybernetic city, and architecture must make use of computational modeling and data in order to design spaces as informational environments that are capable of supplementing human perceptual and cognitive capacities.

Notwithstanding its specific historical heritage, Isozaki's vision of the *man-machine* interface speaks to the role data plays in our world today. Indeed, once we factor in the possibilities for surveillance and control that any contemporary reliance on a machine interface affords—and to which we are certainly more attentive today than was Isozaki's generation—we discover a lingering trace of the colonial heritage of biopolitical governance at the very heart of Isozaki's program for a "symbolic" (as opposed to Tange's "structuralist") architecture. In one respect, this lingering agency of biopolitical governance resolves the "tension" that, for Furuhata, animates Isozaki's urban theory and architectural practice: specifically, it demonstrates how Japanese architecture can "sublate" its own contradictory heritage precisely by recontextualizing—and indeed, by "inter-izing"—the operationality of governance itself in a far broader, indeed global perspective—the perspective, precisely, of global media culture. Yet even as it does so, it leaves open the question of how the agency of governance—an agency concretized in the colonial era mandate to design for habitation—will exert itself in the context of the cybernetic turn in *international* architecture, and in culture more generally; and it also—and in some sense, more importantly—leaves open the question of how governance will acquire a specifically Japanese inflection, as the "inter-izing" movement is reentered into debates about Japanese media theory.

Media Theory . . . after Japan . . .

Let me close by suggesting one provisional "answer" to this line of thinking. In *General Will 2.0*, his 2011 study of Rousseau, democracy, and the Internet, Azuma Hiroki develops a quirky if compelling account of how the Internet can revitalize democracy. With its capacity to mine the behavioral nuances of the population, the Internet provides a concrete means to constitute Rousseau's general will—to transform it from the mere idea that it was and could only be in Rousseau's time into a materially instantiated and politically efficacious entity. Azuma announces his dream at the outset of his study: "In Rousseau's times, the general will was an entirely fictive construct. . . . He probably never dreamed that it would become possible to see and feel the texture of the 'general will.' Yet, two and a half centuries on, we've acquired the possibility of *technically 'implementing' his hypothesis* and doing away with any trace of mysticism. It is this kind of dream that I'm about to talk about."[37] In Azuma's vision, the capacity for direct, real-time monitoring of behavioral nuances and expressions allows us to concretize Rousseau's distinction between general will and "will of all," and, specifically, to fathom and indeed to make concrete the notion that the general will "never errs": as the direct, unmediated expression of the people (which is not equivalent to "public opinion"), the general will simply *is* the sum of data the Internet generates on the basis of user input.

As such, the Internet allows us to marshal Rousseau's general will toward a revitalization of democracy premised on a strict separation between private and public, and indeed on a startling reversal of their traditional functions. In the scenario Azuma sketches, and informed by the data made available by the Internet "governance," government will perforce be minimal government—he likens it to a waterworks utility—whose job is simply to ensure the basic conditions for life ("managing potentially violent relations with the exterior" and "managing violence in the interior"[38]). In this operation, the state becomes "an infrastructure service . . . that merely seeks to distribute resources with efficacy"; in the process, it loses its "political character." The state, that is, becomes the guarantor of animal life, and animal life becomes the basis of society, publicness, and solidarity. "In a society under democracy 2.0," Azuma explains, "it is precisely the aggregate of private, animal actions that shape the public realm (database), while public, human actions (deliberation) can only be established behind closed doors, that is to say, in the private realm."[39]

This startling reversal of the political inflection of private and public is certainly informed by Azuma's earlier theorization of the "database animal," in which he concluded (as we have seen) that contemporary subjectivity circa 2000—"motivated by the 'need for small narratives' at the level of simulacra and 'the desire for a grand nonnarrative' at the level of the database"—is a *database animal*: "animalized in the former," a "virtual, emptied-out humanity in the latter."[40] Despite the 2011 Fukushima disaster, which occasioned a partial disavowal of Azuma's "dream" for the renewal of democracy,[41] it is not hard to see in his theory the legacy of Isozaki's cybernetic renewal of architecture. Just as Isozaki focuses on the practical impact of the cybernetic revolution, on the way it transforms how we live and how we must design for living, Azuma discovers in the very animalization of culture, itself the contemporary legacy of cybernetics, the basis for political hope. If Fuku-shima shifted the tenor of this project—transforming it from a universal project instantiated by the example of Japan into a more tentative, specifi-cally Japanese project—Azuma's decision to publish the manuscript as is, which is to say, as a general argument for the contemporary materialization of the general will, and hence for the universal possibility of democracy, at-tests to the complexities of the "inter-." For who indeed—whether Japanese, American, or some other contemporary world citizen—could have foreseen what Azuma makes us see: the figure of Rousseau's general will reinvented in a specifically Japanese form as a model for future democracy worldwide?

As an instantiation of the complexities of the "inter-," the felicitous surprise occasioned by Azuma's text exemplifies the potential of each and every text in this collection to actualize the generativity of media theory "in Japan." If, in every case, the difference of Japan matters for how we concep-tualize media theory, and concrete theoretical approaches matter for how we understand Japan, each text's orchestration of a specific encounter yields an insight that is both singular and transformative. If my own experience is indicative of the collection's performative force, it attests to the significance of the collection as a contribution to media theory, as a collective mode of doing media theory: for in its wake, we will need to address media theory not simply as it operates "in Japan" but also as it itself is inflected by this operation—as, in short, media theory *after Japan* . . .

NOTES

1. W. J. T. Mitchell and Mark B. N. Hansen, *Critical Terms for Media Studies* (Chicago: University of Chicago Press, 2010), xxii.

2. Mitchell and Hansen, *Critical Terms*, xxi–xxii.

3. See introduction to this volume, Marc Steinberg and Alexander Zahlten, "Intro-duction," 6.

4. Steinberg and Zahlten, "Introduction," 6.

5. Steinberg and Zahlten, "Introduction," 6.

6. See, for example, John Durham Peters's remarks on our volume (to which he con-tributed) in his recent book, *The Marvelous Clouds*. Peters includes our volume as an example of what he considers to be an unfortunate trend in media studies to ignore the "social-scientific tradition of empirical research on people's attitudes, behavior, and cognition in a mainstream political context." With reference to Elihu Katz's 1987 parti-tion of media studies post-Lazarsfeld into three fiefdoms—critical approaches to media as battlefields of domination and resistance, historical accounts of how media tech-nologies shape underlying psychic and social order, and the above-named tradition

of empirical research—Peters advances the following indictment against the majority of humanistic treatments of media (again for which our volume stands as exemplar): "Most of the recent interest in media among humanists fits in this [historical] tradition . . . , and often ignores Katz's other two traditions, with their interests in audiences, institutions, and political economy, which can be a regrettable omission; I personally want no part of a media studies that has altogether lost the ballast of empirical investigation and common sense." In Peters's eyes, *Critical Terms* is "an otherwise strong collection that reinvents media studies *without regard to decades of social-scientific work*"; *The Marvelous Clouds: Toward a Philosophy of Elemental Media* (Chicago: University of Chicago Press, 2015), 17–18; italics mine. To this, all I would say is that to satisfy Peters, we would have had to have made different choices that would have resulted in a vastly different volume.

7. Steinberg and Zahlten, "Introduction," 17.

8. See Steinberg and Zahlten, "Introduction," note 33, for a recommended chronological ordering.

9. See chapter 13 of this volume, Kitano Keisuke, "Kobayashi Hideo and the Question of Media," 329.

10. Alexander Galloway, Eugene Thacker and McKenzie Wark, *Excommunication*, 2, cited in Steinberg and Zahlten, "Introduction," 12.

11. Kitano, "Kobayashi Hideo," 337.

12. Kitano, "Kobayashi Hideo," 336.

13. Kitano, "Kobayashi Hideo," 336.

14. Kitano, "Kobayashi Hideo," 338–39.

15. Kobayashi, cited in Kitano, "Kobayashi Hideo," 339.

16. "Indeed, it has been more widely argued that it was Kobayashi—writing within a context in which Japanese society was undergoing its first exposure to a variety of modern mass media, from print capitalism to the gramophone and from radio to cinema . . ."; Kitano, "Kobayashi Hideo," 330; "Kobayashi's conception of a medium is not something that transparently transmits a message or content; rather it is something tactically embedded in his writing practices"; Kitano, "Kobayashi Hideo," 340.

17. See chapter 3 of this volume, Kadobayashi, "The Media Theory and Media Strategy of Azuma Hiroki, 1997–2003," 94.

18. Azuma, cited by Kadobayashi, "Media Theory and Media Strategy," 94–95.

19. See chapter 14 of this volume, Tom Looser, "Media, Mediation, and Crisis: A History—and the Case for Media Studies as (Postcultural) Anthropology," 354.

20. Looser, "Media, Mediation, and Crisis," 355.

21. Looser, "Media, Mediation, and Crisis," 358.

22. Looser, "Media, Mediation, and Crisis," 363; italics mine.

23. Looser, "Media, Mediation, and Crisis," 363.

24. Looser, "Media, Mediation, and Crisis," 364.

25. See chapter 12 of this volume, Fabian Schäfer, "Much Ado about 'Nothing': The Kyōto School as 'Media Philosophy,'" 306.

26. Fabian Schäfer, "Much Ado about 'Nothing,'" 309.

27. Schäfer, "Much Ado about 'Nothing,'" 315, 311.

28. Schäfer, "Much Ado about 'Nothing,'" 317.

29. See chapter 11 of this volume, Kitada Akihiro, "Assault on 'Meaning': On Nakai Masakazu's Concept of 'Mediation,'" 287.

30. Kitada, "Assault on 'Meaning,'" 287; italics mine.

31. Nakai cited in Kitada, "Assault on 'Meaning,'" 291.

32. Schäfer, "Much Ado about 'Nothing,'" 319.

33. See Kitada, "Assault on 'Meaning,'" 288–89.

34. Nakai cited in Kitada, "Assault on 'Meaning,'" 289.

35. See chapter 4 of this volume, Marilyn Ivy, "The *InterCommunication* Project: Theorizing Media in Japan's Lost Decades," 115, 125.

36. Ivy, "*InterCommunication* Project," 125.

37. Hiroki Azuma, *General Will 2.0: Rousseau, Freud, Google*, trans. J. Person and N. Matsuyama (New York: Vertical, 2014), 7; italics mine.

38. Azuma, *General Will 2.0*, 205.

39. Azuma, *General Will 2.0*, 162.

40. Hiroki Azuma, *Otaku: Japan's Database Animals*, trans. Jonathan E. Abel and Shion Kono (Minneapolis: University of Minnesota Press, 2009 [2001]), 95.

41. As Azuma explains in his foreword to *General Will 2.0*, Fukushima installed a caesura between the world to which his dream belonged and the new reality facing Japan following the disaster: "After the disaster," he reports, "I grew unable to talk sincerely about a dream as a dream. I could only have written this book before the disaster" (xi). Although he gives some hints concerning how he would have written the book after the disaster, he recounts his decision to publish it "as is," which is to say, as a document belonging to a time now past, and in some way, to an obsolete "version" of the author—to Azuma 1.0.

Bibliography

Abel, Jonathan E. *Redacted: The Archives of Censorship in Transwar Japan*. Berkeley: University of California Press, 2012.
———. Translator's Introduction to *Otaku: Japan's Database Animals*, by Hiroki Azuma, xii–xxvi. Translated by Jonathan E. Abel and Shion Kono. Minneapolis: University of Minnesota Press, 2009.
Across Henshūshitsu, ed. *Ima, chōtaishū no jidai*. Tokyo: Parco Shuppan, 1985.
Allen, Samantha. "Japan's 'Vagina Kayak' Artist Fights Back against Obscenity Charges—and Misogyny." *Daily Beast*, January 13, 2015. http://www.thedailybeast.com/articles /2015/01/13/japan-s-vagina-kayak-artist-fights-back-against-obscenity-charges-and -misogyny.html.
Amano Yasukazu. *Kiki no ideorōgu: Shimizu Ikutarō hihan*. Tokyo: Hihyōsha, 1970.
Anderer, Paul. Introduction to *Literature of the Lost Home: Kobayashi Hideo—Literary Criticism, 1924–1939*. Translated and edited by Paul Anderer. Stanford, CA: Stanford University Press, 1995.
Anderson, Benedict. *Imagined Communities: Reflections on the Origin and Spread of Nationalism*. New York: Verso Books, 1983.
Andrew, Dudley. "The Core and the Flow of Film Studies." *Critical Inquiry* 35 (summer 2009): 879–915.
Appadurai, Arjun, ed. *Globalization*. Durham, NC: Duke University Press, 2001.
Arendt, Hannah. *The Human Condition*. Chicago: University of Chicago Press, 1958.
Arima Tetsuo. *Nihon terebi to CIA* [Japanese television and the CIA]. Tokyo: Shinchōsha, 2006.
Arvidsson, Adam. *Brand: Meaning and Value in Media Culture*. London: Routledge, 2006.
———. *Marketing Modernity: Italian Advertising from Fascism to Postmodernity*. London: Routledge, 2003.
Asada, Akira. "Infantile Capitalism and Japan's Postmodernism: A Fairy Tale." In *Postmodernism and Japan*, edited by Harry Harootunian and Masao Miyoshi, 273–78. Durham, NC: Duke University Press, 1989.
———. "Interview with Akira Asada." By Krystian Woznicki. Nettime Mailing Lists. Accessed July 9, 2014. http://www.nettime.org/Lists-Archives/nettime-1- 9802/msg00100 .html.

——. *Kōzō to chikara: Kigōron o koete* [Structure and power: Beyond semiotics]. Tokyo: Keisō Shobō, 1983.

——. *Tōsōron: Sukizo kizzu no bōken* [Escape theory: The adventures of the schizo kids]. Tokyo: Chikuma Bunko, 1986.

Asada Akira, Iwai Katsuhito, and Karatani Kōjin. "Marukusu kahei, gengo" [Marx, currency, language]. In *Tōsōron: Sukizo kizzu no bōken*, by Akira Asada, 151–239. Tokyo: Chikuma Bunko, 1986.

Asada Akira, Karatani Kōjin, and Kuno Osamu. "Kyōtō gakuha to sanjū-nindai no shisō." *Hihyō kūkan* [Critical space] *II* vol. 4 (1995).

Austin, J. L. *How to Do Things with Words*. Edited by J. O. Urmson and Marina Sbisá. Cambridge, MA: Harvard University Press, 1962.

Averbeck, Stefanie. *Kommunikation als Prozess: Soziologische Perspektiven in der Zeitungswissenschaft, 1927–1934*. Münster, Ger.: Lit, 1998.

Azuma Hiroki. "90 nendai o furikaeru: Atogaki ni kaete 2: Interview with Hiroki Azuma." [Looking back at the '90s: In place of postscript: Interview with Hiroki Azuma]. In *Cyberspace wa naze sō yobareru ka+*[Why is cyberspace called such?]: *Azuma Hiroki archives 2*. Tokyo: Kawade Bunko, 2011.

——. "About Us." *Genron*. Last modified May 10, 2011. Accessed June 1, 2014. (no longer active) http://global.genron.co.jp/aboutus/.

——. "The Disaster Broke Us Apart." *Shisōchizu beta* 2 (2011): 8–17.

——. *Dōbutsuka suru posutomodan* [Animalizing the postmodern]. Tokyo: Kodansha, 2001.

——. "For a Change, Proud to Be Japanese." *New York Times*, March 16, 2011.

——. *General Will 2.0: Rousseau, Freud, Google*, trans. John Person and Naoki Matsuyama. New York: Vertical, 2014.

——. *Ippan ishi 2.0: Rusō, Furoito, Gūguru* [General will 2.0: Rousseau, Freud, Google]. Tokyo: Kodansha, 2011.

——. *Jōhō jiyū ron: Html Version Index* [On information and freedom: HTML version index]. 2005. http://www.hajou.org/infoliberalism/.

——. *Nihon 2.0*. Tokyo: Genron, 2012.

——. *Otaku: Japan's Database Animals*. Translated by Jonathan E. Abel and Shion Kono. Minneapolis: University of Minnesota Press, 2009.

——. "Postmodern saikō: 'Gendai shisō' o hitotsu no ideology toshite saiseiri suru tame ni" [Rethinking the postmodern: In order to rearrange "contemporary thought" as an ideology]. *Asteion* 54 (2000): 203–17.

——. *Sonzairon teki, yūbin teki: Jacques Derrida ni tsuite* [Ontological, postal: On Jacques Derrida]. Tokyo: Shinchōsha, 1998.

——. "Sore ni shite mo mediaron wa naze konna ni konnnann na no ka?" [Why is it that media theory is so difficult?]. *InterCommunication* 14 (1995).

——. "Sōzōkai to dōbutsuteki tsūro: Keishikika no Derrida-teki shomondai" [The imaginary and the animal route: Derridean problems of formalization]. In *Hyōshō: Kōzō to dekigoto* [Representation: Structure and event], edited by Kobayashi Yasuo and Matsuura Hisaki. Tokyo: University of Tokyo Press, 2000.

——. "Superflat Speculation." In *Superflat*, edited by Takashi Murakami, 109–51. Tokyo: Madra, 2000.

Bao, Weihong. *Fiery Cinema: The Emergence of an Affective Medium in China*. Minneapolis: University of Minnesota Press, 2015.

Barshay, Andrew E. "Postwar Social and Political Thought, 1945–90." In *Modern Japanese Thought*, edited by Bob Tadashi Wakabayashi, 273–356. Cambridge: Cambridge University Press, 1998.

Baudrillard, Jean. *Consumer Society: Myths and Structures*. London: Sage, 1998.

———. "Requiem for the Media," trans. Charles Levin, in *For a Critique of the Political Economy of the Sign*, ed. Charles Levin, 164–84 (Saint Louis, MO: Telos Press, 1981).

———. *Symbolic Exchange and Death*. London: Sage Publication, 1993.

Benjamin, Walter. "Fukusei gijutsu jidai no geijutsu sakuhin." In *Benjamin korekushon I*. Translated by Kenjirō Asai. Tokyo: Chikuma Gakugei Bunkō, 1995.

———. "Gengo ippan oyobi ningen no kotoba ni tsuite." In *Benjamin Korekushon I*. Translated by Kenjirō Asai. Tokyo: Chikuma Gakugei Bunkō, 1995.

———. *Gesammelte Schriften*. Vol. I.2. Frankfurt: Suhrkamp Verlag, 1990.

———. "Shururearizumu." In *Benjamin Korekushon I*. Translated by Kenjirō Asai. Tokyo: Chikuma Gakugei Bunkō, 1995.

Blanchette, J.-F. "A Material History of Bits," *Journal of the American Society for Information Science and Technology* 62, no. 6 (2011): 1042–57.

Boorstin, Daniel. *The Image: A Guide to Pseudo-Events in America*. New York: Vintage Books, 1992.

Brodey, Warren M. "The Design of Intelligent Environment: Soft Architecture." *Landscape* 17, no. 1 (autumn 1967): 8–12.

Caldwell, John Thornton. "Introduction: Theorizing the Digital Landrush." In *Electronic Media and Technoculture*, edited by J. T. Caldwell, 1–31. New Brunswick, NJ: Rutgers University Press, 2000.

———. *Production Culture: Industrial Reflexivity and Critical Practice in Film and Television*. Durham, NC: Duke University Press, 2008.

Casanova, Pascale. *The World Republic of Letters*. Translated by M. B. DeBevoise. Cambridge, MA: Harvard University Press, 2004.

Cather, Kirsten. *The Art of Censorship in Postwar Japan*. Honolulu: University of Hawai'i Press, 2012.

———. "The Politics and Pleasures of Historiographic Porn." *positions: east asia cultures critique* 22, no. 4 (2014): 749–80.

Chen, Kuan-Hsing. *Asia as Method*. Durham, NC: Duke University Press, 2010.

Cho, Hyunjung. "Hiroshima Peace Memorial Park and the Making of Japanese Postwar Architecture." *Journal of Architectural Education* 66, no. 1 (2012): 72–83.

Chun, Jayson Makoto. *"A Nation of a Hundred Million Idiots"?: A Social History of Japanese Television, 1953–1973*. New York: Routledge, 2007.

Chun, Wendy Hui Kyong. "The Enduring Ephemeral, or The Future Is a Memory." In *Media Archaeology: Approaches, Applications, and Implications*, edited by Erkki Huhtamo and Jussi Parikka, 184–206. Berkeley: University of California Press, 2011.

———. "Introduction: Did Somebody Say New Media?" In *New Media, Old Media: A History and Theory Reader*, edited by Wendy Hui Kyong Chun and Thomas W. Keenan, 1–10. New York: Routledge, 2006.

———. *Programmed Visions: Software and Memory*. Cambridge, MA: MIT Press, 2011.

Clarke, Bruce. "Communication." In *Critical Terms for Media Studies,* edited by W. J. T. Mitchell and Mark B. N. Hansen, 131–44. Chicago: University of Chicago Press, 2010.

Coleman, Gabriella. *Coding Freedom: The Ethics and Aesthetics of Hacking*. Princeton, NJ: Princeton University Press, 2013.

Couldry, Nick. "Theorizing Media as Practice." *Social Semiotics* 14, no. 2 (2004): 115–32.

Dean, Jodi. *Blog Theory: Feedback and Capture in the Circuits of Drive*. Cambridge, UK: Polity Press, 2011.

Debord, Guy. *The Society of Spectacle*. Translated by Donald Nicholson-Smith. New York: Zone Books, 1994.

Deleuze, Gilles. *Cinema 2*. Translated by Hugh Tomlinson and Robert Galeta. Minneapolis: University of Minnesota Press, 1989.

———. "Postscript on the Societies of Control." *October* 59 (1992): 3–7.

Demachi Ryūji. *Taiken rupo: Zainichi gaikokujin josei no sekkusu 51-ka kuni-5000-nin o "seiha" shita otoko no nikki*. Tokyo: Kōbunsha, 2011.

Derrida, Jacques. "Architecture Where the Desire May Live." In *Rethinking Architecture: A Reader in Cultural Theory*, edited by Neil Leach, 300–28. London: Routledge, 1997.

———. "Hagaki yori" [From *The Post Card*]. *InterCommunication*, no. 0 (spring 1992): 34–39.

———. *Limited Inc*. Translated by Samuel Weber and Jeffrey Mehlman. Evanston, IL: Northwestern University Press, 1988.

———. *The Post Card: From Socrates to Freud and Beyond*. Translated by Alan Bass. Chicago: University of Chicago Press, 1987.

———. *Specters of Marx: The State of the Debt, the Work of Mourning, and the New International*. Translated by Peggy Kamuf. New York: Routledge, 1994.

———. "Structure, Sign, and Play in the Discourse of the Human Sciences." In *Writing and Difference*, 278–94. Chicago: University of Chicago Press, 1978.

Detleve, Zwick, and Julien Cayla. *Inside Marketing Practices, Ideologies, Devices*. Oxford: Oxford University Press, 2012.

Dickinson, Kay. *Arab Cinema Travels: Transnational Syria, Palestine, Dubai, and Beyond*. London: British Film Institute, 2016.

Doak, Kevin Michael. *Dreams of Difference: The Japanese Romantic School and the Crisis of Modernity*. Berkeley: University of California Press, 1994.

Driscoll, Mark. *Absolute Erotic, Absolute Grotesque: The Living, Dead, and Undead in Japan's Imperialism, 1895–1945*. Durham, NC: Duke University Press, 2010.

Dunne, Anthony, and Fiona Raby. *Speculative Everything: Design, Fiction, and Social Dreaming*. Cambridge, MA: MIT Press, 2013.

Ďurovičová, Nataša, and Kathleen Newman, eds. *World Cinemas, Transnational Perspectives*. New York: Routledge, 2010.

Eagleton, Terry. *After Theory*. New York: Basic Books, 2003.

Edwards, Paul N. *The Closed World: Computers and the Politics of Discourse in Cold War America*. Cambridge, MA: MIT Press, 1996.

Enzensberger, Hans Magnus. "Constituents of a Theory of the Media." In *The New Media Reader*, edited by Nick Montfort and Noah Wardrip-Fruin, 259–76. Cambridge, MA: MIT Press, 2003.

———. "Constituents of a Theory of the Media." *New Left Review* 64 (November/December 1970): 13–36.

Etō Jun. *Seijuku to sōshitsu* [Maturity and loss]. Tokyo: Kawade Shobo Shinsha, 1967.

Eto Kōichirō. *Niko Niko Gakkai Beta o kenkyū shite mita* [I went and studied Niko Niko Beta working group]. Tokyo: Kawade Shobō Shinsha, 2012.

Eyebeam. "About Eyebeam." Accessed March 7, 2016. http://eyebeam.org/about.

———. "Inter-Discommunication Machine." Accessed March 7, 2016. http://eyebeam.org/projects/inter-discommunication-machine.

Fabian, Johannes. *Time and Its Other: How Anthropology Makes Its Object*. New York: Columbia University Press, 1983.

Fan, Victor. *Cinema Approaching Reality*. Minneapolis: University of Minnesota Press, 2015.

Fingleton, Eamonn. "The Myth of Japan's Failure." *New York Times,* January 6, 2012.

Foucault, Michel. *Security, Territory, Population: Lectures at the Collège de France, 1977–1978*. Edited by Michel Senellart. Translated by Graham Burchell. New York: Palgrave Macmillan, 2007.

———. *"Society Must Be Defended": Lectures at the the Collège de France, 1975–1976*. Edited by Mauro Bertani and Alessandro Fontana. Translated by David Macey. New York: Picador, 2003.

Frank, Thomas. *The Conquest of Cool: Business Culture, Counterculture, and the Rise of Hip Consumerism*. Chicago: University of Chicago Press, 1997.

Frauenfelder, Mark. "Japanese Artist Goes on Trial over 'Vagina Selfies.'" *Boing Boing*, July 28, 2015. http://boingboing.net/2015/07/28/japanese-artist-goes-on-trial.html.

———. "Who's Afraid of Vagina Art?" *Broadly*, August 15, 2015. Accessed March 1, 2016. https://broadly.vice.com/en_us/video/whos-afraid-of-vagina-art?

Fujioka Wakao, ed. *Discover Japan 40nen kinen katarogu* [Discover Japan fortieth anniversary commemorative catalogue]. Tokyo: PHP Kenkyūsha, 2010.

———. *Karei naru shuppatsu: Discover Japan* [A splendid departure: Discover Japan]. Tokyo: Asahi Shuppan, 1972.

———. *Mōretsu kara biutifuru e* [From intense to beautiful]. Vol. 2 of *Fujioka Wakao zen purodūsu* [Fujioka Wakao's complete production]. Tokyo: PHP, 1988.

———. *Mōretsu kara byūtifuru e* [From gung-ho to beautiful]. Tokyo: Dentsū Shuppan, 1991.

———. *Sayonara taishū, bunshū no tanjō* [Goodbye mass, the birth of the segmented mass]. Tokyo: PHP Bunko, 1987.

Fujioka Wakao et al. "Zadankai: Discover Japan kyanpēn uraomote" [Roundtable discussion: Front and back of Discover Japan campaign]. *Senden kaigi* (January 1972): 14–23.

Fukasaku Mitsutada. *Shinjuku kōgengaku* [Shinjuku modernology]. Tokyo: Kadokawa Shuppan, 1968.

Furuhata, Yuriko. *Cinema of Actuality: Japanese Avant-Garde Filmmaking in the Season of Image Politics*. Durham, NC: Duke University Press, 2013.

———. "Multimedia Environments and Security Operations: Expo '70 as a Laboratory of Governance." *Grey Room* 54 (winter 2014): 56–79.

Gabrakova, Dennitza. "Archipelagic Thought and Theory's Other: Traveling Theory in Japan." *positions* 22, no. 2 (spring 2014): 461–87.

Galbraith, Patrick W., and Jason G. Karlin. "Introduction: The Mirror of Idols and Celebrity." In *Idols and Celebrity in Japanese Media Culture*, edited by Patrick W. Galbraith and Jason G. Karlin, 1–32. Basingstoke, UK: Palgrave Macmillan, 2012.

Galey, Alan, and Stan Ruecker. "How a Prototype Argues." *Literary and Linguistic Computing* 25, no. 4 (2010): 405–24.

Galloway, Alexander R., Eugene Thacker, and McKenzie Wark. *Excommunication: Three Inquiries in Media and Mediation.* Chicago: University of Chicago Press, 2014.

Gardner, William O. "The 1970 Osaka Expo and/as Science Fiction." *Review of Japanese Culture and Society* (December 2011): 26–43.

Gekkan *Across* Henshūshitsu, eds. *Kyanpēn obu Paruko: Paruko no senden senryaku* [Campaign of Parco: Parco's advertising strategy]. Tokyo: Parco Shuppan, 1984.

"Gender, Genitor, Genitalia—Rokudenashiko sapōto-ten." CAMPFIRE. Accessed July 12, 2015. http://camp-fire.jp/projects/view/2809.

Genosko, Gary. *McLuhan and Baudrillard: Masters of Implosion.* London: Routledge, 1999.

Geoghegan, Bernard Dionysius. "From Information Theory to French Theory: Jakobson, Lévi-Strauss, and the Cybernetic Apparatus." *Critical Inquiry* 38 (autumn 2011): 96–126.

Gerow, Aaron, ed. "Decentering Theory: Reconsidering the History of Japanese Film Theory." Special issue, *Review of Japanese Culture and Society* 22 (December 2010).

———. "Introduction: The Theory Complex." *Review of Japanese Culture and Society* 22 (December 2010): 1–13.

———. *Kitano Takeshi.* London: British Film Institute, 2008.

———. "The Process of Theory: Reading Gonda Yasunosuke and Early Film Theory." *Review of Japanese Culture and Society* 22 (2010): 37–43.

———. *Visions of Japanese Modernity: Articulations of Cinema, Nation, and Spectatorship, 1895–1925.* Berkeley: University of California Press, 2010.

Glander, Timothy. *Origins of Mass Communications Research during the American Cold War.* Mahwah, NJ: Lawrence Erlbaum Associates, 2000.

Gluck, Carol. *Japan's Modern Myths: Ideology in the Late Meiji Period.* Princeton, NJ: Princeton University Press, 1985.

Gonda Yasunosuke. *Katsudō shashin no genri oyobi ōyō* [The principles and applications of the moving pictures]. Tokyo: Uchida Rōkakuho, 1914.

———. "The Principles and Applications of the Moving Pictures (Excerpts)." Translated by Aaron Gerow. *Review of Japanese Culture and Society* 22 (2010): 24–36.

Gotō Kazuhiko. "Makurūhan no unda gensō" [The illusion produced by McLuhan]. *Asahi jyānaru* 9, no. 42 (October 8, 1967): 18–23.

———. "Makurūhan to Nihon no media" [McLuhan and the Japanese media]. *Chishiki* (April 1981): 190–96.

Gotō Shinpei. *Seiden: Gotō Shinpei, Mantetsu jidai, 1906–1908*. Vol. 4. Tokyo: Fujiwara Shoten, 2005.

Gramsci, Antonio. *Prison Notebooks*. Vol. 3. New York: Columbia University Press, 2010.

Grice, Paul. *Studies in the Way of Words*. Cambridge, MA: Harvard University Press, 1989.

Guillory, John. "Genesis of the Media Concept." *Critical Inquiry* 36, no. 2 (winter 2010): 321–62.

Habermas, Jürgen. *The Structural Transformation of the Public Sphere: An Inquiry into a Category of Bourgeois Society*. Translated by Thomas Burger with Frederick Lawrence. Cambridge, MA: MIT Press, 1991.

Hachiya, Kazuhiko. "Inter Dis-Communication Machine (1993)." YouTube. Accessed March 7, 2016. http://www.youtube.com/watch?v=JOzVzcmKoVU.

Hagimoto Haruhiko, Muraki Yoshihiko, and Konno Tsutomu. *Omae wa ada no genzai ni suginai: Terebi ni nani ga kanō ka* [You are nothing but the present: What is possible for television?]. Tokyo: Tabata Shoten, 1969.

Hakuhōdō Sōgō Seikatsu Kenkyūjo, ed. *Bunshū no* [The age of segmented mass]. Tokyo: Nihon Keizai Shinbunsha, 1985.

Hamano Satoshi. "Kaisetsu: Azuma Hiroki no jōhōronteki tenkai ni tsuite." In *Cyberspace wa naze sō yobareru ka+: Azuma Hiroki archives 2*, by Hiroki Azuma, 465–72. Tokyo: Kawade Bunko, 2011.

Hamano Yasuhiro. *Fasshonka shakai: Ryūdōkashakai, fasshon bijinesu, kyōkan bunka* [Fashionizing society: Society in flux, fashion business, and the culture of sympathy]. Tokyo: Bijinesusha, 1970.

Hani Susumu and Okada Susumu. "Eiga ni okeru henkakuki to wa nanika." [What would be a revolutionary period in cinema]. In *Besuto obu Kinema junpō*, 882–85. Tokyo: Kinema Junpōsha, 1994.

Hansen, Mark B. N. *Feed-Forward: On the Future of Twenty-First-Century Media*. Chicago: University of Chicago Press, 2015.

Hansen, Miriam. "Vernacular Modernism: Tracking Cinema on a Global Scale." In *World Cinemas, Transnational Perspectives*, edited by Nataša Ďurovičová and Kathleen Newman, 287–314. New York: Routledge, 2010.

Hardt, Michael, and Antonio Negri. *Multitude: War and Democracy in the Age of Empire*. New York: Penguin Press, 2004.

Harootunian, Harry. *Overcome by Modernity*. Princeton, NJ: Princeton University Press, 2001.

Hasumi Shigehiko. *Hyōsō hihyō sengen* [Declaration of surface criticism]. Tokyo: Chikuma Bunko, 1985.

———. "'Taisho-teki' gensetsu to hihyō." In *Kindai nihon no hihyō:—Meiji-Taishō hen*, edited by Kōjin Karatani, 146–76. Tokyo: Kodansha, 1997.

Hasumi Shigehiko and Yoshimoto Taka'aki. "Hihyō ni totte sakuhin to wa nani ka" [What is a work according to criticism?]. *Umi* 12, no. 7 (1980): 236–66.

Hayashi Shūji. *Ryūtsū kakumei: Seihin, keiro, oyobi shōhisha* [A revolution in distribution: Products, pathways, and consumers]. Tokyo: Chūō Kōron Shinsho, 1962.

Hayashi Yūjirō. *Jōhōka shakai: Hādo na shakai kara sofuto na shakai e* [Information society: From hard society to soft society]. Tokyo: Kōdansha Gendai Shinsho, 1969.

Hayashi Yūjirō and Kagaku Gijutsu to Keizai no Kai [Japan Techno-Economics Society], eds. *Chō gijutsu shakai e no tenkai: Jōhōka shisutemu no ningen* [Developing a super-technological society: Humans in the information system]. Tokyo: Daiyamondo Sha, 1969.

Hayles, Katherine. "Cybernetics." In *Critical Terms for Media Studies*, edited by W. J. T. Mitchell and Mark B. N. Hansen, 145–56. Chicago: University of Chicago Press, 2010.

Heidegger, Martin. *The Fundamental Concepts of Metaphysics: World, Finitude, Solitude*. Translated by William McNeill and Nicholas Walker. Bloomington: Indiana University Press, 2001.

Heisig, James W. *Philosophers of Nothingness: An Essay on the Kyoto School*. Honolulu: University of Hawai'i Press, 2001.

Hidaka Rokurō. "Terebijon kenkyū no hitotsu no zentei." *Shisō* 413 (November 1958): 23–29.

Hills, Matt. "Strategies, Tactics and the Question of *Un Lieu Propre*: What/Where Is 'Media Theory'?" *Social Semiotics* 14, no. 2 (2004): 133–49.

Hirabayashi Ichi. "'Bi-hihyō' 'Sekai bunka' to 'Doyōbi.'" In *Senjika teikō no kenkyū* I, Vol. 1, 239–75. Tokyo: Mizusu Shobō, 1968.

Hochschild, Arlie. *The Managed Heart: The Commercialization of Human Feeling*. Berkeley: University of California Press, 1973.

Honda, Masuko. "The Genealogy of Hirahira: Liminality and the Girl." In *Girl Reading Girl in Japan*, edited by Tomoko Aoyama and Barbara Hartley, 19–37. Oxford: Routledge, 2010.

Horkheimer, Max, and Theodor W. Adorno. *Dialectic of Enlightenment: Philosophical Fragments*. Edited by Gunzelin Schmid Noerr. Translated by Edmund Jephcott. Stanford, CA: Stanford University Press, 2002.

Howe, Jeff. "The Two Faces of Takashi Murakami." *WIRED*, November 1, 2003. http://www.wired.com/2003/11/artist/.

Illouz, Eva. *Consuming the Romantic Utopia: Love and the Cultural Contradictions of Capitalism*. Berkeley: University of California Press, 1997.

Imai Yasuo. *Benjamin no kyōiku shisō*. Tokyo: Seori Shobō, 1998.

Imamura Taihei. "Geijutsu keishiki to shite no eiga." [Film as art form] In *Eiga geijutsu no keishiki*, 129–62. Tokyo: Ōshio Shoin, 1938.

Inaba Michio. *Komyunikēshon hattatsushi* [History of the development of communication]. Tokyo: Sōfūsha, 1989.

———. "Nakai Masakazu no 'baikai'-ron shōkai." *Shinbungaku hyōron* 18 (1989): 111–18.

Inokuchi Ichirō. *Masu komyunikēshon: Dono you ni taishū e hataraki kakeru ka* [Mass communication: How to influence the masses]. Tokyo: Kōbunsha, 1951.

Ishikawa Hiroyoshi. "Bijinesuman dokusho hakusho" [White paper on the businessman's reading]. *Eguzekutibu* [Executive] (December 1967): 4–10.

Isozaki Arata. "Ātisuto-Ākitekuto no jidai: Osaka banpaku no sōzōryoku o hokan shita āto shin: Interview with Arata Isozaki." By Yasuko Imura, Yuriko Furuhata, and Shigeru Matsui. *Tokyo Geijutsu Daigaku Eizōkenkyū Kiyō* (October 2012): 36–80.

———. "Haikyo ron." In *Kigō no umi ni ukabu "shima"* [Islands in the sea of signs], 22–40. Tokyo: Iwanami Shoten, 2013.

———. "Invisible City." In *Architecture Culture, 1943–1968: A Documentary Anthology*, edited by Joan Ockman, 403–97. New York: Columbia Books of Architecture, 1993.

———. "Konpō sareta kankyō" [Packaged environments]. In *Kūkan e* [To space], 414–28. Tokyo: Kajima Shuppanka, 1997.

———. "Mienai toshi" [The invisible city]. In *Kūkan e* [To space], 370–91. Tokyo: Kajima Shuppankai, 1997.

———. "Tange Kenzō no 'kenchiku=toshi=kokka' kyōdōtai to shite no Nihon." In *Sahshutsu sareta modanizumu: "Nihon" to iu mondai kikō*, 173–202. Tokyo: Iwanami Shoten, 2005.

———. "Toshi dezain no hōhō" [Methods of urban design]. In *Kūkan e* [To space], 88–121. Tokyo: Kajima Shuppankai, 1997.

———. "Yami no kūkan" [Space of shadows]. In *Kūkan e* [To space], 136–54. Tokyo: Kajima Shuppankai, 1997.

Isozaki Arata and Asada Akira, eds. *Any Kenchiku to tetsugaku o meguru sesshon, 1991–2008* [*Any*: Sessions on architecture and philosophy, 1991–2008]. Tokyo: Kajima Shuppan, 2010.

Isozaki Arata and Hino Naohiko. "*Kūkan e*, Omatsuri Hiroba, *Nihon no toshi kūkan*: 1960 nen dai ni okeru toshiron no hōhō o megutte." *10+1* 45 (2006): 187–97.

———. "Tāningu pointo: Kūkan kara kankyō e" [Turning point: From space to environment]. *10+1* 48 (2007): 193–205.

Isozaki Arata and Jaques Derrida. "*Anywhere*: Dikonsutorakushon to wa nanika" [*Anywhere*: What is deconstruction?]. In *Any: Kenchiku to tetsugaku o meguru sesshon, 1991–2008*, 81–100. Tokyo: Kajima Shuppan, 2010.

———. Isozaki Arata and Tōno Yoshiaki. "'Kankyō' ni tsuite." Special Issue on *Kūkan kara kankyō e*, *Bijutsu techō* [Art notebook] 275 (November 1966): 91–105.

Isozaki Atelier. "Sofuto ākitekuchua: Ōtōba to shite no kankyō." *Kenchiku bunka* 279 (January 1970): 65–93.

Israel, Joachim. *The Language of Dialectics and the Dialectics of Language*. Atlantic Highlands, NJ: Humanities Press, 1979.

Ivy, Marilyn. "Critical Texts, Mass Artifacts: The Consumption of Knowledge in Postmodern Japan." In *Postmodernism and Japan*, edited by Masao Miyoshi and Harry D. Harootunian, 21–46. Durham, NC: Duke University Press, 1989.

———. *Discourses of the Vanishing: Modernity, Phantasm, Japan*. Chicago: University of Chicago Press, 1995.

Iwamoto Kenji, ed. *Nihon eiga to modanizumu, 1920–1930*. Tokyo: Ribropōto, 1991.

Johnson, Barbara. *The Barbara Johnson Reader: The Surprise of Otherness*. Edited by Melissa Feuerstein, Bill Johnson González, Lili Porten, and Keja L. Valens. Durham, NC: Duke University Press, 2014.

Joselit, David. *Feedback: Television against Democracy*. Cambridge, MA: MIT Press, 2007.

Kadobayashi, Takeshi. "Umesao Tadao's Theory of Information Industry and 1960s Japanese Media Theory." Paper presented at the Histories of Film Theories in East Asia conference, University of Michigan, September 29, 2012.

———. *Watcha Doin, Marshall McLuhan? An Aesthetics of Media*. Tokyo: NTT Shuppan, 2009.

Kadoyama Nobu. "Māketingu kihon genri ni arazu" [These are not the basic principles of marketing]. *Kindai keiei* [Modern management] (September 1967): 57–65.

"Kaisetsu." "Towards the Development of a Theory of the Information Industries." *Hōsō Asahi* (December 1964): 10–11.

Kaizen, William. "Steps to an Ecology of Communication: *Radical Software*, Dan Graham, and the Legacy of Gregory Bateson." *Art Journal* 67, no. 3 (fall 2008): 87–107.

Karatani Kōjin. *Architecture as Metaphor: Language, Number, Money*. Edited by Michael Speaks. Translated by Sabu Kohso. Cambridge, MA: MIT Press, 1995.

———. "Bunkoban e no jobun." In *Kindai Nihon no Hihyō I: Shōwa-hen*, edited by Kōjin Karatani, 193–94. Paperback ed. Tokyo: Kodansha, 1997.

———. *Hihyō to posutomodān* [Criticism and the postmodern]. Tokyo: Fukutake Shoten, 1989.

———. *Hyūmoa to yuibutsu-ron* [Humor and materialism]. Tokyo: Kodansha Geijutsu Bunko, 1999.

———. *Inyu to shite no kenchiku* [Architecture as metaphor]. Tokyo: Kōdansha, 1989.

———. "Karatani Kōjin's Afterword to the English Edition (1991)." In *Origins of Japanese Literature*, translation by Brett de Bary, 190–96. Durham, NC: Duke University Press, 1993.

———. *Origins of Modern Japanese Literature*. Translation by Brett de Bary. Durham, NC: Duke University Press, 1993.

Karatani Kōjin and Nakagami Kenji. "Beyond Kobayashi Hideo." In *Karatani Kōjin, Nakagami Kenji zen taiwa* [All dialogues between Karatani Kojin and Nakagami Kenji], 62. Tokyo: Kodansha, 2011.

Karatani Kōjin and Takahashi Genichirō. "Gendai bungaku o tatakau."[Fighting against contemporary literature] *Gunzō* 47, no. 6 (May 1992): 6–50.

Karatani Kōjin, Asada Akira, Hasumi Shigehiko, and Miura Masashi. *Kindai Nihon no Hihyō I: Shōwa-hen* [Modern Japanese Criticism vol. 1: Showa]. Tokyo: Fukutake Shoten, 1990–91.

———. *Kindai Nihon no Hihyō II: Shōwa-hen* [Modern Japanese Criticism vol. 2: Showa]. Tokyo: Fukutake Shoten, 1992.

Karatani Kōjin, Asada Akira, Fukuda Kazuya, Kamata Tetsuya, and Azuma Hiroki. "Ima hihyō no basho wa doko ni aru no ka" [Where is the place of criticism now?]. *Hihyō kūkan II* 21 (1999): 6–32.

Katō, Hidetoshi. "The Development of Communication Research in Japan." In *Japanese Popular Culture*, edited by Hidetoshi Katō, 29–44. Rutland, VT: Charles Tuttle, 1959.

———. *Jōhō shakai kara no chōsen* [The challenge issued by the information society]. Tokyo: Tōyō Keizai Shinpō-sha, 1971.

————. "Terebijon to goraku." [Television and entertainment] *Shisō* 413 (November 1958): 43–47.

Katō Shuichi. *Nihon bungakushi josetsu e* [Prolegema for a history of Japanese literature]. Tokyo: Chikuma Shobō, 1980.

Katsura Eishi. "Automaton Kompurekkusu" [Automaton complex]. In *20 seiki no media 3 maruchimedia no hoos to media porichikkusu*, edited by Eishi Katsura, 5–22. Tokyo: Jasuto Shisutemu, 1996.

Kawabe Kazuo, and Fujita Shigeya, directors. *Nippon Zeronen* [Nippon Year Zero]. Tokyo: Paionia LDC, 1969. DVD.

Kayama Rika. *Poketto no naka 80 nendai ga ippai* [My pockets are filled with the 1980s]. Tokyo: Bajiriko, 2008.

Keizai Shingikai Jōhō Kenkyū Iinkai. *Nihon no Jōhōka shakai: Sono bijon to kadai* [Japan Information society: Its vision and challenges]. Tokyo: Daiyamondo Sha, 1969.

Kelty, Christopher. *Two Bits: The Cultural Significance of Free Software*. Durham, NC: Duke University Press, 2008.

Kido Hiroyuki. "Shōhi kigōron to wa nandatta no ka?" [What was the theory of consumer semiotics?], in *Wakamono ron o yomu*, ed. Kotani Satoshi, 86–109. Kyoto: Sekai Shisōsha, 1993.

Kinoshita Nagahiro. *Nakai Masakazu—Atarashii bigaku" no kokoromi* [Nakai Masakazu: Approaches to a new aesthetics]. Tokyo: Riburopōto, 1995.

Kishida Masao. "Porno eiga no heroinu wa naze furui onna ka?" [Why is the porn movie heroine so old-fashioned?]. *Onna erosu* no. 1 (1973): 170.

Kitada Akihiro. *"Imi" e no aragai: Mediēshon no bunka seijigaku* [An assault on "meaning": The cultural politics of mediation]. Tokyo: Serika Shobō, 2004.

————. "'Imi' e no aragai: Nakai Masakazu no 'baikai' gainen o megutte" [Against "meaning" on Nakai Masakazu's concept of "medium"]. In *"Imi" e no aragai: Mediēshon no bunka seijigaku*, 47–73. Tokyo: Serika Shobō, 2004.

————. "'Kansatsusha' to shite no ukete." *Masu komyunikēshon kenkyū* 53 (1993): 83–96.

————. *Kōkokutoshi Tokyo: Sono tanjō to shi* [Advertising city, Tokyo: Its birth and death]. Tokyo: Kōsaidō, 2002.

————. *Warau Nihon no nashonarizumu* [A sneering Japan's "nationalism"]. Tokyo: NHK Books, 2005.

Kittler, Friedrich. *Gramophone, Film, Typewriter*. Translated by Geoffrey Winthrop-Young. Stanford, CA: Stanford University Press, 1999.

————. *The Truth of the Technological World: Essays on the Genealogy of Presence*. Translated by Erik Butler. Stanford, CA: Stanford University Press, 2013.

Kobayashi Hideo. "Eiga hihyō ni tsuite" [On film criticism]. In *Kobayashi Hideo zensakuhin* 11. Tokyo: Shinchōsha, 2003.

————. "Gohho no tegami" [Letters from Van Gogh]. In *Kobayashi Hideo zensakuhin* 20, 14–15. Tokyo: Shinchōsha, 2004.

————. "Komedi riterēru: Kobayashi Hideo o kakonde" [*Comédie littéraire*: Around Kobayashi Hideo]. In *Kobayashi Hideo zenshū* 15 (Tokyo: Shinchōsha, 2001): 27–28.

———. "Literature of the Lost Home." In *Literature of the Lost Home: Kobayashi Hideo— Literary Criticism, 1924–1939*, translated and edited by Paul Anderer, 53. Stanford, CA: Stanford University Press, 1995.

———. *"Manshū" no rekishi* [History of "Manchuria"]. Tokyo: Kōdansha Gendai Shinsho, 2008.

———. *Mantetsu chōsabu: "Ganso shinku tanku" no tanjō to hōkai* [The Manchurian Railway Research Department: The birth and dissolution of the "original think tank"]. Tokyo: Heibonsha, 2005.

———. "Mootuaruto" [Mozart]. In *Kobayashi Hideo zensakuhin* 15, 47–102. Tokyo: Shinchōsha, 2003.

———. "Multiple Designs." In *Literature of the Lost Home: Kobayashi Hideo—Literary Criticism, 1924–1939*, translated and edited by Paul Anderer, 20–21. Stanford, CA: Stanford University Press, 1995.

———. "Shitai shashin arui wa shitai ni tsuite" [On the photographs of the dead bodies, or, the dead bodies]. In *Kobayashi Hideo zensakuhin* 17, 38–39. Tokyo: Shinchōsha, 2004.

———. "X e no tegami." In *Kobayashi Hideo zensakuhin* 4, 78. Tokyo: Shinchōsha, 2003.

Kobayashi, Toshiaki. *Denken des Fremden: Am Beispiel Kitaro Nishida* [Thinking the alien: The example of Kitaro Nishida]. Frankfurt: Stromfeld/Nexus, 2002.

Kojève, Alexandre. *Introduction to the Reading of Hegel: Lectures on the Phenomenology of Spirit*. Edited by Alan Bloom. Translated by James H. Nichols, Jr. Ithaca, NY: Cornell University Press, 1980.

Konno Tsutomu (Ben). "Kanōsei no teiji ni mukatte" [Toward the presentation of possibility]. *Geijutsu kurabu* [Art Club journal] (July 1973), 91–96.

Koolhaas, Rem, and Hans Ulrich Obrist, eds. *Project Japan: Metabolism Talks . . .* Cologne, Ger.: Taschen, 2011.

Kōzu Akira. *Bunka no keikō to taisaku* [The tendencies and countermeasures of culture]. Tokyo: Chijin Kan, 1984.

Krämer, Sybille. "Das Medium als Spur und als Apparat." In *Medien, Computer, Realität: Wirklichkeitsvorstellungen und Neue Medien*, edited by Sybille Krämer, 73–94. Frankfurt am Main: Suhrkamp, 1998.

———. "Erfüllen Medien eine Konstitutionsleistung? Thesen über die Rolle medientheoretischer Erwägungen beim Philosophieren." In *Medienphilosophie: Beiträge zur Klärung eines Begriffs*, edited by Stefan Münker, Alexander Roesler, and Mike Sandbothe, 78–90. Frankfurt: Fischer, 2003.

Krapp, Peter. "Hypertext *Avant La Lettre*." In *New Media, Old Media: A History and Theory Reader*, edited by Wendy Hui Kyong Chun and Thomas W. Keenan, 359–74. New York: Routledge, 2006.

Kropotkin, Petr Alekseevich. *The Conquest of Bread and Other Writings*. Edited by Marshall Shatz. Cambridge: Cambridge University Press, 1995.

Krueger, Myron W. "Responsive Environments." In *The New Media Reader*, edited by Noah Wardrip-Fruin and Nick Montfort, 379–89. Cambridge, MA: MIT Press, 2003.

"Kuia Japan, tokushū: Miwaku no busu." Special Issue, *Kuia Japan* 3 (October 2000).

Kuroda Raiji. *Nikutai no anākizumu: 1960nendai nihon bijutsu ni okeru pafōmansu no chika suimyaku* [Anarchy of the body: Undercurrents of performance art in 1960s Japan]. Tokyo: Grambooks, 2010.

Kuroishi, Izumi. "Mathematics for/from Society: The Role of the Module in Modernizing Japanese Architectural Production." *Nexus Network Journal: Architecture and Mathematics* 11, no. 2 (2009): 201–16.

Kurokawa Kishō. *Jōhō rettō Nihon no shōrai* [The future of information archipelago Japan]. Tokyo: Dai San Bunmei Sha, 1972.

Lamarre, Thomas. *Shadows on the Screen: Tanizaki Jun'ichirō on Cinema and "Oriental" Aesthetics.* Ann Arbor: University of Michigan Press, 2005.

Lash, Scott, and Celia Lury. *Global Culture Industry: The Mediatization of Things.* Cambridge, UK: Polity Press, 2007.

Laube, Johannes. "Westliches und östliches Erbe in der Philosophie Hajime Tanabe." *Neue Zeitschrift für systematische Theologie und Religionsphilosophie* 20 (summer 1978): 1–15.

Lazzarato, Maurizo. "Struggle, Event, Media." republicart. Accessed June 2015. www.republicart.net/disc/representations/lazzarato01_en.htm.

Lin, Zhongjie. *Kenzo Tange and the Metabolist Movement: Urban Utopias of Modern Japan.* New York: Routledge, 2010.

Lionnet, Françoise and Shu-mei Shih, "Introduction: The Creolization of Theory," in *The Creolization of Theory,* Françoise Lionnet and Shu-mei Shih, eds. Durham: Duke University Press, 2011.

lixil. "10+1." Accessed July 9, 2014. http://10plus1.jp/.

Lovink, Geert. "Enemy of Nostalgia: Victim of the Present, Critic of the Future: Interview with Geert Lovink." By Peter Lunenfeld. *PAJ: A Journal of Performance and Art* 70 24, no. 1 (January 2002): 5–15.

———. *Networks without a Cause: A Critique of Social Media.* Cambridge, UK: Polity Press, 2011.

Lury, Celia. *Brands: The Logos of the Global Economy.* London: Routledge, 2004.

Mabuchi Kōsuke. *"Zokutachi" no sengoshi* [A postwar history of the "tribes"]. Tokyo: Sanseidō, 1989.

Mackie, Vera C. *Feminism in Modern Japan: Citizenship, Embodiment, and Sexuality.* Cambridge: Cambridge University Press, 2003.

———. "Reading Lolita in Japan." In *Girl Reading Girl in Japan,* edited by Tomoko Aoyama and Barbara Hartley, 187–201. New York: Routledge, 2010.

Macnaughtan, Helen. "Womenomics for Japan: Is the Abe Policy for Gendered Employment Viable in an Era of Precarity?" *Asia-Pacific Journal: Japan Focus,* April 5, 2015. http://apjjf.org/2015/13/12/Helen-Macnaughtan/4302.html.

"Makurūhanizumu to kōkoku" [McLuhanism and advertising]. Special issue, *Brain* 42, no. 10 (October 1967): 6–35.

Manovich, Lev. *The Language of New Media.* Cambridge, MA: MIT Press, 2001.

———. "Postmedia Aesthetics." In *Transmedia Frictions: The Digital, the Arts, and the Humanities,* edited by Marsha Kinder and Tara McPherson, 34–44. Oakland: University of California Press, 2014.

————. *Software Takes Command*. New York: Bloomsbury, 2013.

Martin, Reinhold. *The Organizational Complex: Architecture, Media, and Corporate Space*. Cambridge, MA: MIT Press, 2003.

Marx, Karl. *Grundrisse*. Translated by Martin Nicolaus. London: Penguin Books, 1973.

Masuda Tsūji. *Kaimaku beru wa natta: Masuda shiatā e yōkoso* [The opening bell has rung: Welcome to Masuda theater]. Tokyo: Tokyo Shinbun, 2005.

————. "Sōzōteki paruko kyowakoku: Sono kyōkan konseputo" [Republic of creative PARCO, its concept of sympathy]. *Senden kaigi* (November 1976).

Masuda Yoneji. *Jōhō shakai nyūmono: Konpyūta wa ningen shakai wo kaeru* [Introduction to information society: Computers transform human society]. Tokyo: Pelican, 1968.

Masuda, Yoneji. *The Information Society as Post-Industrial Society*. Tokyo: Institute for the Information Society, 1980.

Matsuda Masao. *Fūkei no shimetsu* [The extinction of landscape]. Tokyo: Kōshisha, 2013.

————. "Media kakumei no tame no akushisu" [The axis of media revolution]. *Bijutsu techō* (May 1973): 51–60.

Matsui Shigeru. "Fukusei gijutsu no tenkai to media geijutsu no seiritsu: 1950 nendai no Nihon ni okeru terebi, shakai shinrigaku, gendai geijutsu no sōgo shintō" [The development of reproduction technology and the establishment of media arts: Interpenetrations among television, social psychology, and contemporary art of the 1950s]. *Eizō media gaku: Tokyo geijutsu daigaku daigakuin eizō kenkyūkai kiyō* 2 (March 2012): 35–79.

Matsumoto, Naoki. "Interview: Genron: Interview with Naoki Matsumoto." By Giant Robot. Accessed October 2, 2014. (no longer active). http://www.giantrobot.com/blogs/news/15804763-interview-genron.

Matsumoto Toshio. "A Theory of Avant-Garde Documentary." Translated by Michael Raine. *Cinema Journal* 51, no. 4 (2012): 148–54.

McKenna, Christopher D. *The World's Newest Profession: Management Consulting in the Twentieth Century*. Cambridge: Cambridge University Press, 2006.

McLuhan, Marshall. "The Relation of Environment to Anti-Environment." In *Marshall McLuhan Unbound*, edited by Eric McLuhan and W. Terrence Gordon, 5–19. Corte Madera, CA: Ginko Press, 2005.

————. *Understanding Media: The Extensions of Man*. Cambridge, MA: MIT Press, 1994.

Media Rebyū, ed. *Za messēji: McLuhan ikō no media kankyō*. Tokyo: Heibon Sha, 1982.

Meillasoux, Quentin. *Nach der Endlichkeit*. Zürich: diaphanes, 2008.

Minami Hiroshi. "Terebijon to ukete no seikatsu." *Shisō* 413 (November 1958): 103–15.

————. "Terebi to ningen." In *Kōza gendai masu komyunikēshon 2: Terebi jidai* [The age of television], edited by Hiroshi Minami, 7–16. Tokyo: Kawade Shobō Shinsha, 1960.

Mitchell, W. J. T., and Mark B. N. Hansen. *Critical Terms for Media Studies*. Chicago, University of Chicago Press, 2010.

Miura Atsushi. *Jiyū no jidai no fuan na jibun: Shōhi shakai no datsu shinwa* [The anxious self in the age of freedom: Demythologizing consumer society]. Tokyo: Shō Bunsha, 2006.

Miyamoto Mitsugu. "Kono chō-nankai sho ga ureru makafushigi." *Asahi Journal* 26, no. 15 (June 1984): 11–13.

Mizoguchi Akiyo, Saeki Yōko, and Miki Sōko, eds. *Shiryō Nihon ribu-shi.* Tokyo: Shōkadō, 1992.

Mizukoshi Shin. *Media no seisei.* Tokyo: Dōbunkan, 1993.

"Mōi no Makurūhan senpū" [The raging McLuhan whirlwind]. *Shūkan sankei* 16, no. 40 (September 1967): 98.

Monnet, Livia. "Montage, Cinematic Subjectivity and Feminism in Ozaki Midori's *Drifting in the World of the Seventh Sense*." *Japan Forum* 11, no. 1 (1999): 57–82.

Moore, Aaron. "Para-Existential Forces of Invention: Nakai Masakazu's Theory of Technology and Critique of Capitalism." *positions* 17, no. 1 (2009): 125–57.

Morley, David, and Kevin Robins. *Spaces of Identity: Global Media, Electronic Landscapes, and Cultural Boundaries.* London: Routledge, 1995.

Morris-Suzuki, Tessa. *Beyond Computopia: Information, Automation, and Democracy in Japan.* New York: Kegan Paul, 1988.

Mumford, Eric Paul. *The CIAM Discourse on Urbanism, 1928–1960.* Cambridge, MA: MIT Press, 2000.

Mumford, Lewis. *The City in History.* New York: Harcourt, 1961.

Münker, Stefan. "After the Medial Turn: Sieben Thesen zur Medienphilosophie." In *Medienphilosophie: Beiträge zur Klärung eines Begriffs*, edited by Stefan Münker, Alexander Roesler, and Mike Sandbothe, 16–25. Frankfurt am Main: Fischer, 2003.

Murayama Tomoyoshi. "Eiga no genkaisei" [The limits of film]. *Kinema Junpō* 507 (June 1, 1934): 67–68.

Nagai Kiyohiko. "Kaikaku to handō to—Entsenberugā no rainichi o megutte" [Reformation and backlash: On Enzensberger's visit to Japan]. *Sekai* (May 1973): 228–31.

Nakahira Takuma. *Mitsuzukeru hate ni hi ga* [Fire on the shore of continual looking]. Tokyo: Osiris, 2007.

———. *Naze shokubutsu zukan ka: Nakahira Takuma hihyō seishū, 1965–1977* [Why an illustrated botanical dictionary: Nakahira Takuma's critical writings, 1965–1977]. Tokyo: Chikuma Shobō, 2007.

———. "Nikusei no kakutoku wa kanō ka: Media-ron hihan e mukete" [Is it possible to capture the voice (*nikusei*): Toward a critique of media theory]. *Nihon dokusho shinbun*, March 19, 1973.

———. *Sākyurēshon: Hizuke, basho, kōi = Circulation: Date, Place, Events.* Translated by Franz Prichard. Tokyo: Oshirisu, 2012.

Nakai Masakazu. *Nakai Masakazu zenshū.* 4 vols. Edited by Osamu Kuno. Tokyo: Bijutsu Shuppansha, 1964–81.

———. "Shikisai eiga no omoide." In *Nakai Masakazu zenshū*, edited by Osamu Kuno, 3:232–35. Tokyo: Bijutsu Shuppan, 1964–81.

Nakamura Hideyuki. "Tobichitta gareki no naka o." In *Jōhō shakai no bunka 2: Imēji no naka no shakai*, edited by Ryūzō Uchida. Tokyo: Tokyo Daigaku Shuppankai, 1988.

Negroponte, Nicholas. *Soft Architecture Machines*. Cambridge, MA: MIT Press, 1976.

Ngai, Sianne. "Zany, Cute, Interesting: Sianne Ngai on Our Aesthetic Categories." Asian American Writers' Workshop, February 7, 2013. Accessed June 8, 2015. http://aaww .org/our-aesthetic-categories-zany-cute-interesting/.

NHK Nenkan: 1962 [NHK Yearbook: 1962]. Tokyo: Rajio Sābisu Sentā, 1962.

Nishida Kitarō. *An Inquiry into the Good*. Translated by Masao Abe and Christopher Ives. New Haven, CT: Yale University Press, 1990.

———. *Nishida Kitarō zenshū*, Vols. 1–24. New ed. Tokyo: Iwanami, 2002–9.

Nishidō Kōjin, "Enshutsuka no shigoto" [The work of the director], in *Enshutsuka no shigoto: 6onendai, enre, engeki kakumei*, eds. Nihon Enshutsusha Kyōkai and Nishidō Kōjin, 11–64. Tokyo: Renga Shobō Shinsha, 2006.

Nornes, Markus. *Cinema Babel: Translating Global Cinema*. Minneapolis: University of Minnesota Press, 2007.

———. *Forest of Pressure: Ogawa Shinsuke and Postwar Japanese Documentary*. Minneapolis: University of Minnesota Press, 2007.

———. *Japanese Documentary Film: The Meiji Era through Hiroshima*. Minneapolis: University of Minnesota Press, 2003.

———, ed. *The Pink Book: The Japanese Eroduction and Its Contexts*. Ann Arbor, MI: Kinema Club, 2014.

Nozick, Robert. *Anarchy, State, and Utopia*. New York: Basic Books, 1974.

NTT Intercommunication Center. Accessed July 9, 2014. http://www.ntticc.or.jp/index _e.html.

———. "Seeing Is Believing." Accessed July 9, 2014. http://www.ntticc.or.jp/Exhibition /2013/Openspace2013/Works/Seeing_Is_Believing.html.

Nulty, Timothy E. "Introductory Note." *Nippon Telegraph and Telephone Privatization Study: Experience of Japan and Lessons for Developing Countries*, World Bank Discussion Paper 179 (1992): vi–vii.

Obara Kazuhiro. *IT bijinesu no enre* [The principles of IT business]. Tokyo: NHK Shuppan, 2014.

Oguma Eiji. *Shimizu Ikutarō* [Shimizu Ikutarō]. Tokyo: Ochanomizu Shobō, 2003.

Okonogi Keigo. *Moratoriamu ningen no jidai* [The age of the moratorium human]. Tokyo: Chūō Kōron Shinsha, 1978.

Ōmae, Masaomi. *Makurūhan: Sono hito to riron* [McLuhan: The man and his theories]. Tokyo: Daikosha, 1967.

Ōnishi Wakato. "Āto to waisetsu—hasama de" [Between art and obscenity]. *Asahi shinbun*, July 23, 2014.

O'Reilly, Tim. "What Is Web 2.0: Design Patterns and Business Models for the Next Generation of Software." September 30, 2005. http://www.oreilly.com/pub/a/web2 /archive/what-is-web-20.html.

Ōsawa Masachi. *Denshi mediaron* [Theories of electronic media]. Tokyo: Shinyōsha, 1995.

Ōtsuka Eiji. *Monogatari shōhiron: "Bikkurima" no shinwagaku* [Theory of narrative consumption: Myth analysis of "Bikkuriman"]. Tokyo: Shinyōsha, 1989.

———. *Teihon monogatari shōhi-ron* [Theory of Narrative Consumption: Authoritative edition]. Tokyo: Kadokawa Shoten, 2001.

———. "World and Variation." Translated by Marc Steinberg. *Mechademia* 5 (2010): 99–116.

Ōya Sōichi. "'Ichioku sōhakuchika' meimei shimatsuki." [An account of the coining of the term "one hundred million idiots"]. In *Ōya Sōichi zenshū* [Ōya Sōichi collected works], 339–48. Tokyo: Eichōsha, 1975.

Ozeki Shūji. "Gendai no ningenkan o tō: Asada Akira-ra no 'ryūkō shisō' o hihan suru" [Inquiry into the contemporary idea of the human: Criticizing the Asada Akira group's "fashionable thought"]. *Bunka Hyōron* 279 (June 1984): 28–57.

Parikka, Jussi. *A Geology of Media.* Minneapolis: University of Minnesota Press, 2015.

Partner, Simon. *Assembled in Japan: Electrical Goods and the Making of the Japanese Consumer.* Berkeley: University of California Press, 2001.

Peters, John Durham. *The Marvelous Clouds: Toward a Philosophy of Elemental Media.* Chicago: University of Chicago Press, 2015.

Raunig, Gerald, Gene Ray, and Ulf Wuggenig, eds. *Critique of Creativity: Precarity, Subjectivity, and Resistance in the "Creative Industries."* London: Mayfly, 2011.

Rieu, Alain-Marc. *Savoir et pouvoir dans la modernisation du Japon.* Paris: PUF, 2001.

Rodowick, David. *Elegy for Theory.* Cambridge, MA: Harvard University Press, 2014.

Roesler, Alexander. "Medienphilosophie und Zeichentheorie." In *Medienphilosophie: Beiträge zur Klärung eines Begriffs*, edited by Stefan Münker, Alexander Roesler, and Mike Sandbothe, 34–52. Frankfurt: Fischer-Taschenbuch-Verl, 2003.

Rokudenashiko. *Megumi Igarashi (Rokudenashiko): Art and Obscenity: Did the Japanese Police Go Too Far with Her?* (Tokyo: Foreign Correspondents' Club, Tokyo, 2014), July 14, FCCJ channel. https://www.youtube.com/watch?v=u35rEg_nTV8.

———. "Rokudenashiko 'Decoman.'" *Niconico Dōga.* Accessed June 30, 2015. http://www.nicovideo.jp/watch/sm24004330.

———. "Support MK Boat Project!—The World's First 3D Scanned Peach on the Beach." YouTube, June 17, 2013. Accessed June 9, 2015. https://www.youtube.com/watch?v=sbQnzELycdI.

———. *Waisetsu tte nan desu ka?* [What is obscenity?]. Tokyo: Kinyōbi, 2015. An English version was translated by Graham Kolbeins and Anne Ishii and published as *What is Obscenity?: The Story of a Good For Nothing Artist and Her Pussy* (Toronto: Koyama Press, 2016).

———. *Watashi no karada ga waisetsu?!: Onna no soko dake naze tabū* [My body is obscene?!: Why is only my lady part taboo?]. Tokyo: Chikuma Shobō, 2015.

Ronell, Avital. *The Telephone Book: Technology, Schizophrenia, Electric Speech.* Lincoln: University of Nebraska Press, 1989.

Russell, Andrew L. "Modularity: An Interdiscplinary History of an Ordering Concept." *Information and Culture* 47, no. 3 (2012): 257–87.

Saitō Ryōsuke. *Omocha hakubutsushi* [A natural history of toys]. Tokyo: Sōjinsha, 1989.

Sakai, Naoki. *Translation and Subjectivity: On "Japan" and Cultural Nationalism.* Minneapolis: University of Minnesota Press, 1997.

Sakai Naoki, and Nishitani Osamu. *"Sekai-shi" no kaitai: Honyaku shutai rekishi.* Tokyo: Ibunsha, 1999.

Salazkina, Masha. "Introduction: Film Theory in the Age of Neoliberal Globalization." *Framework: The Journal of Cinema and Media*, Vol. 56, no. 2 (fall 2015): 325–49.

Sarkar, Bhaskar. "Tracking 'Global Media' in the Outposts of Globalization," in *World Cinemas, Transnational Perspectives*. Nataša Ďurovičová and Kathleen Newman, eds. New York: Routledge, 2009.

Sas, Miryam. "By Other Hands: Environment and Apparatus in 1960s Intermedia." In *The Oxford Handbook of Japanese Cinema*, edited by Daisuke Miyao, 383–415. Oxford: Oxford University Press, 2014.

———. *Experimental Arts in Postwar Japan: Moments of Encounter, Engagement, and Imagined Return*. Cambridge, MA: Harvard University Asian Centre, 2011.

Sasaki Atsushi. *Nippon no shisō* [Japanese thought]. Tokyo: Kondansha Gendai Shinsho, 2009.

Sasaki Kiichi. "Terebi bunka to wa nanika." [What is television culture?]. *Shisō* 413 (November 1958): 225–31.

Sawaragi Noi. *Sensō to banpaku* [World Expositions and war]. Tokyo: Bijutsu Shuppansha, 2005.

Schäfer, Fabian. "Public Opinion and the Press: Transnational Contexts of Early Media and Communication Studies in Prewar Japan, 1918–1937." *Social Science Japan Journal* 14:1 (winter 2011): 21–38.

———. *Public Opinion, Propaganda, Ideology: Theories on the Press and Its Social Function in Interwar Japan, 1918–1937*. Leiden: Brill, 2012.

———. *Tosaka Jun: Ideologie, Medien Alltag: Eine Auswahl ideologiekritischer, kulturund medientheoretischer und geschichtsphilosophischer Schriften*. Leipzig: Leipziger Universitätsverlag, 2011.

Schieder, Chelsea Szendi. "Two, Three, Many 1960s." *Monthly Review*, June 10, 2015. http://mrzine.monthlyreview.org/2010/schieder150610.html.

Schmitt, Carl. *Politische Romantik* [Political Romanticism]. Berlin: Dunker & Humbolt, 1998.

Schnapp, Jeffrey T., and Adam Michaels. *The Electric Information Age Book: McLuhan/Agel/Fiore and the Experimental Paperback*. New York: Architectural Press, 2012.

Sconce, Jeffrey. *Haunted Media: Electronic Presence from Telegraphy to Television*. Durham, NC: Duke University Press, 2000.

"Seiki datadotta sakuhin geijutsu ka waisetsu ka" [Is a decorated sex organ art or obscenity?]. *Asahi shinbun*, December 17, 2014.

Seki Nancy. "Kawai Shun'ichi wa ikiteru koto ga sunawachi rōdō de aru" [Kawai Shun'ichi's very act of being alive is labor]. *Terebi shōtō jikan 2*. Tokyo: Bunshu Bunko, 2000.

———. *Nani o ima sara* [What do you want now?]. Tokyo: Kadokawa Bunko, 1999.

———. "Otoko no chikubi ga kane ni natte, shin no danjo byōdō wa chikai" [Male nipples also earn money; the true equality of the sexes is close]. *Shūkan Bunshū*, July 1997. Reprinted in *Terebi shōtō jikan 2*. Tokyo: Bunshu Bunko, 2000.

———. *Terebi shōtō jikan 2*. Tokyo: Bunshu Bunko, 2000.

———. "'Wain de dekiteiru' Kawashima Naomi o rikai dekiru ka." *Shūkan Bunshū*, November 6, 1997. Reprinted in *Terebi shōtō jikan 2*. Tokyo: Bunshu Bunko, 2000.

Seki Nancy and Ōtsuki Takahiro. *Jogoku de Hotoke* [Like meeting my saviour in Hell]. Tokyo: Asahi Bunko, 1999.

Sherif, Ann. *Japan's Cold War: Media, Literature, and the Law.* New York: Columbia University Press, 2009.

Shibuya Tomomi. "Sekai no shio: Rokudenashiko taiho ga aburidasu shakai no jinken kankaku" [Winds of the world: Rokudenashiko's arrest shakes up the perception of human rights]. *Sekai* no. 860 (2014): 38.

Shigematsu, Setsu. "The Japanese Women's Liberation Movement and the United Red Army." *Feminist Media Studies* 12, no. 2 (June 1, 2012): 163–79.

———. *Scream from the Shadows: The Women's Liberation Movement in Japan.* Minneapolis: University of Minnesota Press, 2012.

Shimada Atsushi. "Terebi geijutu no kiso." *Shisō* 413 (November 1958): 232–39.

Shimizu Hikaru. *Eiga to bunka* [Film and culture]. Kyoto: Kyōiku Tosho, 1941.

Shimizu Ikutarō. "Terebi bunmeiron" [On TV civilization]. In *Besuto obu Kinema junpō,* 707–9. Tokyo: Kinema Junpōsha, 1994.

———. "Terebijon jidai" [The television age]. *Shisō* 413 (November 1958): 2–22.

———. "Terebi no honshitsu" [The essence of television]. *Asahi shinbun,* May 2, 1957 (morning ed.).

Shimokōbe Atsushi, ed. *Jōhōshakai to no taiwa: Mirai Nihon no jōhō nettowāku* [Dialogues with information society: Information networks for future Japan]. Tokyo: Tōyō Keizai Shinhōsha, 1970.

Shimomura Toratarō. *Nishida Kitarō: Hito to shisō* [Kitaro Nishida: The man and his thought]. Tokyo: Tōkai Daigaku Shuppankai, 1977.

Simons, Jan. "New Media as Old Media: Cinema." In *The New Media Book*, edited by Dan Harries, 231–41. London: BFI, 2002.

Spackman, Barbara. "Politics on the Warpath: Machiavelli's *Art of War.*" In *Machiavelli and the Discourse of Literature*, edited by Vicky Kahn and Albert Ascoli, 179–93. Ithaca, NY: Cornell University Press, 1993.

Sputniko. "Tranceflora: Amy's Glowing Silk." Sputniko! Accessed February 22, 2016. http://sputniko.com/2015/04/amyglowingsilk/.

Stearn, Gerald Emanuel. Introduction to *McLuhan: Hot and Cool*, edited by Gerald Emanuel Stearn, xiii–xvi. New York: Signet Books, 1967.

Steinberg, Marc. *Anime's Media Mix: Franchising Toys and Characters in Japan.* Minneapolis: University of Minnesota Press, 2012.

———. "Review of *Otaku: Japan's Database Animals*: Japanese Postmodernity Reconsidered." *Mechademia.* Last modified November 2011. http://mechademia.org/reviews/marc-steinberg-review-of-otaku/.

Stone, Allucquére Rosanne. *The War of Desire and Technology at the Close of the Mechanical Age.* Cambridge, MA: MIT Press, 1996.

Suga Hidemi. *Nihon kindai bungaku no tanjō: Genbun icchi ndo to nashonarizumu.* Tokyo: Ota Shuppan, 1995.

———. "'1968-nen' to 3.11 ikō o tsunagu shikō" [Thought that links 1968 to the aftermath of 3.11]. In *Tsumura Takashi seisen hyōronshū: 1968-nen igo*, edited by Suga Hidemi, 381–92. Tokyo: Ronsōsha, 2012.

Sugiyama Mitsunobu. *Sengo keimō to shakaikagaku no shisō.* Tokyo: Shinyosha, 1983.

Suzuki Shigesaburō. "Zakkan." *Eiga ōrai* (April 1928).

Suzuki Tadashi. *Nihon no gōri-ron: Kanō Kōkichi to Nakai Masakazu.* Tokyo: Gendai Shichōsha, 1961.

Tahara Sōichirō. "Nichijō kara no tonsō." [Flight from the Everyday]. *Tenbō* (October 1971): 74–78. Quoted in Yoshiyuki Niwa, "Dokyumentarī seishun jidai no shūen." In *Terebi da yo! Zen'in shūgō,* edited by Masato Hase and Shōichi Ōta, 80–103. Tokyo: Sekyūsha, 2007.

Takemura Ken'ichi. *Gonin no mōretsu na Amerikajin* [Five intense Americans]. Tokyo: Kodansha, 1967.

———. "Ima wadai no TV komāsharu o saiten suru" [Rating the most talked about current TV commercials]. In *CM Gurafiti.* Vol. 2, *Terebi 25 nen no kiroku,* edited by Yamamoto Kōji, 22–27. Tokyo: Sebundō Shinkōsha, 1970.

———. *Makurūhan no riron no tenkai to ōyō* [The development and application of McLuhan's theory]. Tokyo: Kodansha, 1967.

———. *Makurūhan no sekai: Gendai bunmei no taishitsu to sono miraizō* [McLuhan's World: The constitution of contemporary civilization and its future]. Tokyo: Kodansha, 1967.

———. *Makurūhan to no taiwa: Nihon bunka to Makurūhannizumu* [Conversations with McLuhan: McLuhanism and Japanese culture]. Tokyo: Kodansha, 1968.

———. *Media no karuwazashi tachi: Makurūhan de yomitoku gendai shakai* [Media acrobats: Reading contemporary society through McLuhan]. Tokyo: Bijinesu Sha, 2002.

———. *Nijū shikō no ōyō to tenkai* [The application and development of twofold thought]. Tokyo: Daiwa Shobo, 1970.

———. *Takemura Ken'ichi jisenshū: Makurūhan no sekai: Gendai bunmei no taishitsu to sono miraizō* [Takemura Ken'ichi's self-selected works: McLuhan's world: The constitution of contemporary civilization and its future]. Tokyo: Tokuma Shoten, 1980. Originally published as *Makurūhan no sekai: Gendai bunmei no taishitsu to sono miraizō* [McLuhan's world: The constitution of contemporary civilization and its future] (Tokyo: Kodansha, 1967).

———. "Terebi jidai no yogensha M. Makkurūhan: Jinbutsu shōkai" [M. McLuhan, the prophet of the television age: An introduction to his personality]. In *Makurūhan: Tanjō 100 nen media (ron) no kanōsei o tou,* 160–71. Tokyo: Kawade, 2011.

———. Uchū o nomu hitotsu me" [One eye that swallows the universe]. *Hōsō Asahi* (June 1967): 8–23.

Takeuchi Yō. *Media to chishikijin: Shimizu Ikutarō no haken to bōkyaku* [Media and intellectuals: The discovery and forgetting of Shimizu Ikutarō]. Tokyo: Chūō Kōronsha, 2012.

Taki Kōji. "Aru media no bohimei" [The epitaph of a certain media]. *Bijutsu techō* (May 1973): 38–50.

Tamura Norio. "'Atarashii Shinbungaku' no tanjō to 'Masu komi' ron no eikyō: Inokuchi Ichirō ni hajimaru sengo no 'Amerikashu' kenkyū no inyū" [The birth of "new newspaper science" and the impact of mass communication theory: The postwar introduction of the "American" style of research that began with Inokuchi Ichirō], *Komyunikēshon kagaku* 35 (2012): 123–33.

Tanabe Hajime. *Nihon Rettō no shōraizō: 21 seiki e no kenchiku* [The future of the Japanese archipelago: The formation of Tōkaidō megalopolis]. Tokyo: Kōdansha, 1966.

———. *Shu no ronri* [Logic of the species]. Tokyo: Iwanami Bunko, 2010.

Tanaka Mitsu, "Benjo kara no kaihō" [Liberation from the toilet]. *Onna erosu* no. 2 (1973): 178–90.

Tange Kenzō. *Kenchiku to toshi: Dezain oboegaki* [City as architecture: Notes on design]. Tokyo: Sekai Bunkusha, 1975. Reprint, Tokyo: Shōkokusha, 2011.

Tanizaki, Junichiro. "Gei ni tsuite" [On art]. *Kaizo* (March–April 1933), reprinted as "Geidan," in *Tanizaki Junichiro zenshu vol. 20*, 442–44. Tokyo: Shinchosha, 1982.

Tholen, Georg Christoph. *Zur Ortsbestimmung analoger und digitaler Medien*. Bielefeld, Ger.: Transcript, 2005.

Thummel, Thomas, and Max Thummel. "Privatization of Telecommunications in Japan." In *Limits to Privatization: How to Avoid Too Much of a Good Thing*, edited by Ernst Ulrich von Weizsäcker, Oran R. Young, and Matthias Finger, 76–78. London: Earthscan, 2005.

Tosaka Jun. "Eiga no ninshikironteki kachi to fuzoku byosha." [The representation of custom and the epistemological value of cinema]. *Nihon eiga* 2, no. 6 (June 1937): 13–19.

———. "Eiga no shajitsuteki tokusei to fūzokusei oyobi taishūsei." [The realistic qualities of cinema in relation to custom and mass culture]. In *Tosaka Jun zenshū*, 282–89. Tokyo: Keisō Shobō, 1966–67. Quoted in Naoki Yamamoto. "Realities That Matter: The Development of Realist Film Theory and Practice in Japan, 1895–1945." PhD diss., Yale University, 2012.

———. "Film as the Reproduction of the Present: Custom and the Masses." Translated by Gavin Walker. In *Tosaka Jun: A Critical Reader*, edited by Ken C. Kawshima, Fabian Schäfer, and Robert Stolz, 103–13. Ithaca, NY: Cornell East Asia Series, 2013.

———. *Tosaka Jun zenshū*. Vols. 1–5. Tokyo: Keisō Shobō, 1966–67.

Toyokawa Saikaku. "The Core System and Social Scale: Design Methodology at the Tange Laboratory." Translated by Hiroshi Watanabe. In *Kenzō Tange: Architecture for the World*, edited by Seng Kuan and Yukio Lippit, 15–28. Zürich: Lars Müler Publishers and the President and Fellows of Harvard College, 2012.

———. *Gunzō to shite no Tange Kenkyūshitsu: Sengo Nihon kenchiku toshi shi no meinsutorīmu* [The Tange Lab as a group: The mainstream of postwar Japanese architecture and the history of urban design]. Tokyo: Ohmsha, 2012.

Tsumura Takashi. "An·an kara no jūnen" [Ten years since *An·an*], *Waseda bungaku* (August 1981): 26–29.

———. "70nen bunka kakumei to 'hōkōtenkan' no shomondai" [The cultural revolution of the 70s and the problems of "changing course"]. *Shin nihon bungaku* (May 1972): 109–13.

———. "Toshi=soshikiron to shite no mediaron o kaku to suru jōhō kankyō-gaku e no kōsatsu" [Thoughts toward information-environment studies centered on urban=organizational theory]. *Hōsō hihyō* 4 (1973): 35–41.

Tsurumi Shunsuke. "Komyunikēshon shi e no oboegaki" [Notes on the history of communication]. In *Komyunikēshon shi: Kōza komyunikēshon* [The history of communication: A course on communication], edited by Fumio Etō, Shunsuke Tsurumi, and Akira Yamamoto, 3–21. Tokyo: Kenkyūsha, 1973.

Tsurumi Shunsuke et al. "Zadankai: Nakai Masakazu to wareware no jidai." *Shisō no kagaku* 14 (1983): 71–89.

Turkle, Sherry. *Life on the Screen: Identity in the Age of the Internet*. New York: Simon and Schuster, 1995.

Turner, Fred. *The Democratic Surround: Multimedia and American Liberalism from World War II to the Psychedelic Sixties*. Berkeley: University of California Press, 2014.

Uchikawa Yoshimi et al., eds. *Jōhō shakai* [Information society]. Tokyo: Tokyo Daigaku Shuppan-kai, 1974.

Ueno Chizuko. *Onna asobi* [Women's play]. Tokyo: Gakuyō, 1988.

———. "Onna to iu shisō" [A theory called woman]. In *Onna no nanajūnendai, 1969–1986: Parco posutā ten*, edited by Tsūji Masuda, 26–29. Tokyo: Disuku Emu, 2001.

———. *Watashi sagashi gēmu* [Search-myself game]. Tokyo: Chikuma Shobo, 1987.

Ueyama Shunpei. "Nakai Masakazu no 'Iinkai no ronri.'" *Shisō no kagaku* 23 (1960): 55–60.

Umesao Tadao. *Jōhō no bunmeigaku* [A civilization study of information]. Tokyo: Chūō Bunko, 1999.

Ura Tatsuya. "Oboccha-man Asada Akira" [Man-child Asada Akira]. *Ushio* 304 (August 1984): 106–14.

Uricchio, William. "Old Media as New Media: Television." In *The New Media Book*, edited by Dan Harries, 219–30. London: BFI, 2002.

van Dijk, Paul. *Anthropology in the Age of Technology: The Philosophical Contributions of Günther Anders*. Amsterdam: Rodopi, 2000. Originally published as *Die Antiquiertheit des Meschen* by Günther Anders. Munich, Ger.: C. H. Beck, 1980.

Virno, Paolo. *The Grammar of the Multitude: For an Analysis of Contemporary Forms of Life*. Los Angeles: Semiotext(e), 2004.

Wada Ben. *Engi to ningen* [Performance and humans]. Tokyo: Mainichi Shinbunsha, 1970.

Wark, McKenzie. *Molecular Red: Theory for the Anthropocene*. London: Verso Books, 2015.

Wartella, Ellen, and Byron Reeves. "Historical Trends in Research on Children and the Media: 1900–1960." *Journal of Communication* 35, no. 2 (June 1985): 118–33.

Watanabe Kazutami. "Sengo shisō no mitorizu" [A sketch of postwar thought]. In *Sengo nihon no shisō-shi—sono saikento*, edited by Tetsuo Najita, Ai Maeda, and Jiro Kamishima, 98. Tokyo: Iwanami Shoten, 1988.

Wiener, Norbert. *Cybernetics: Or, Control and Communication in the Animal and the Machine*. New York: J. Wiley, 1948.

Wigley, Mark. "Network Fever." In *New Media, Old Media: A History and Theory Reader*, edited by Wendy Hui Kyong Chun and Thomas Keenan, 375–98. New York: Routledge, 2006.

Winthrop-Young, Geoffrey. *Kittler and the Media*. Cambridge, UK: Polity Press, 2011.

Yamada Munemutsu. "'Bi hihyō,' 'Sekai bunka.'" [Aesthetic criticism, world culture] *Shisō* 470 (1963): 101–14.

Yamai Kazunori and Saitō Yayoi. *Taiken rupo: Nihon no kōrei-sha fukushi* [Experiential reportage: Social welfare for Japan's aged persons]. Tokyo: Iwanami Shoten, 1994.

Yamamoto, Naoki. "Realities That Matter: The Development of Realist Film Theory and Practice in Japan, 1895–1945." PhD diss., Yale University, 2012.

Yasumi Akihiro. "Optical Remnants: Paris, 1971, Takuma Nakahira." In *Sākyurēshon: Hizuke, basho, kōi = Circulation: Date, Place, Events*, by Takuma Nakahira, 310–17. Translated by Franz Prichard. Tokyo: Oshirisu, 2012.

Yatsuka Hajime. *Metaborizumu Nekusasu* [Metabolism Nexus]. Tokyo, Ohmsha, 2011.

———. " 'Metaborizumu nekusasu' to iu 'kindai no chōkoku' " [The overcoming modernity called Metabolism Nexus]. In *Metaborizumu no mirai toshi* [Metabolism: The city of the future], 10–16. Tokyo: Mori Bijutsukan, 2011.

Yokoda Masuo. *Hyōden Nancy Seki: "Kokoro ni hitori Nancy o"* [A critical biography of Nancy Seki: "Always keep Nancy in one's heart"]. Tokyo: Asahi Bunko, 2014.

Yoneyama, Lisa. *Hiroshima Traces: Time, Space, and the Dialectics of Memory*. Berkeley: University of California Press, 1999.

Yoshimi Shun'ya. *"Koe" no shihonshugi: Denwa rajio chikuonki*. Tokyo: Kōdansha, 1995.

———. " 'Made in Japan': The Cultural Politics of 'Home Electrification' in Postwar Japan." *Media, Culture and Society* 21, no. 2 (1999): 149–71.

———. "Terebi ga ie ni yatte kita." *Shisō* 956 (December 2003): 26–47.

———. "Terebijon jidai' kaidai." *Shisō* 956 (December 2003): 7–10.

———. *Toshi no doramaturugī: Tokyo sakariba no shakaishi* [Dramaturgy of the city: The social history of the entertainment district, Tokyo]. Tokyo: Kōbundo, 1987.

Yoshimi Shun'ya, Wakabayashi Mikio, and Mizukoshi Shin. *Media toshite no denwa* [Telephone as media]. Tokyo: Kobundō, 1992.

Yoshimoto, Mitsuhiro. "The Difficulty of Being Radical." *Boundary 2* 18, no. 3 (fall 1991): 242–57.

———. *Kurosawa: Film Studies and Japanese Cinema*. Durham, NC: Duke University Press, 2000.

Yoshimoto Taka'aki. *Hai imēji-ron* [High-image theory]. Tokyo: Fukutake Shoten, 1989.

Zahlten, Alexander. "The Role of Genre in Film from Japan: Transformations, 1960s–2000s." PhD diss., UMI, 2009.

Žižek, Slavoj. "Cyberspace, or How to Traverse the Fantasy in the Age of the Retreat of the Big Other." *Public Culture* 10, no. 3 (1998): 483–513.

———. "Cyberspace, or, the Unbearable Closure of Being." In *The Plague of Fantasies*, 161–213. London: Verso, 1997.

Contributors

YURIKO FURUHATA is associate professor and William Dawson Scholar of Cinema and Media History in the Department of East Asian Studies and World Cinemas Program at McGill University. She is the author of *Cinema of Actuality: Japanese Avant-Garde Filmmaking in the Season of Image Politics* (2013), which won the 2014 Best First Book Award from the Society of Cinema and Media Studies. She has published articles in journals such as *Grey Room, Screen, Animation, Semiotica,* and *New Cinemas.* She is currently working on a book, tentatively titled *The Rise of Control Room Aesthetics,* exploring the historical connections between Japanese expanded cinema, cybernetic art, and security technologies during the Cold War period.

AARON GEROW is professor of Japanese cinema in the Film Studies Program and the Department of East Asian Languages and Literatures at Yale University. He received an MFA in film studies from Columbia University in 1987, an MA in Asian civilizations from the University of Iowa in 1992, and a PhD in communication studies from Iowa in 1996. His book on Kitano Takeshi was published by the BFI in 2007; *A Page of Madness* came out with the Center for Japanese Studies at the University of Michigan in 2008; and *Visions of Japanese Modernity: Articulations of Cinema, Nation, and Spectatorship, 1895–1925* was published in 2010 by the University of California Press (the Japanese version is forthcoming). He also coauthored the *Research Guide to Japanese Film Studies* with Abe Mark Nornes (2009). He is currently working on books about the history of Japanese film theory and about Japanese cinema after 1980.

MARK HANSEN is professor of literature at Duke University, and author of numerous monographs on new media, such as *Bodies in Code: Interfaces with Digital Media* (2006); *New Philosophy for New Media* (2004); and *Feed-Forward: On the Future of Twenty-First-Century Media* (2015). He is the coeditor (with W. J. T. Mitchell) of the volume *Critical Terms for Media Studies* (2010).

MARILYN IVY is professor of anthropology at Columbia University. She is the author of numerous articles and essays concerning modernity, mass mediation, aesthetics, and politics in contemporary Japan, and her book *Discourses of the Vanishing: Modernity, Phantasm, Japan* (1995) won the 1996 Hiromi Arisawa Memorial Award for Japanese Studies from the American Association of University Presses. Professor Ivy is on the editorial board of the journal *positions: east asia cultures critique* and was an active member of the editorial board of *Public Culture* for many years.

TAKESHI KADOBAYASHI is associate professor at the Department of Film and Media Studies, Faculty of Letters, Kansai University, and received his PhD from the Graduate School of Arts and Sciences, University of Tokyo. He specializes in media theory, epistemology, and studies of culture and representation. He is author of the book *Watcha Doin, Marshall Mcluhan?: An Aesthetics of Media* (in Japanese; 2009), and coedited *SITE ZERO / ZERO SITE* 3 (2010), and *Hyosho: Journal of the Association for Studies of Culture and Representation* 8 (2014).

AKIHIRO KITADA is associate professor in the Gradate School of Interdisciplinary Information Studies at the University of Tokyo. His numerous publications include *Warau Nihon no "Nashionarizumu"* (2005) and *Kōkoku no Tanjō: Kindai Media Bunka no Rekishi-Shakaigaku* (2000). He has coauthored books with Yoshimi Shunya, Miyadai Shinji, Nakamasa Masaki, and Ōsawa Masachi, among others. He served as coeditor, with Azuma Hiroki, of the book series *Shisō Chizu* (2008~2010).

KEISUKE KITANO is professor of the College of Image Arts and Science, Ritsumeikan University, Kyoto, Japan. He has published numerous books and essays, including *Introduction to Theories on Visual Image* (in Japanese, 2009) and *Society of Control* (in Japanese, 2014).

THOMAS LOOSER is associate professor in the Department of East Asian Studies at New York University. He received his BA in cultural anthropology from the University of California, Santa Cruz (1979), and his MA and PhD in anthropology from the University of Chicago (1999). Previously, he taught at McGill University and Emory University as an assistant professor in East Asian Studies. Looser is the author of many articles on Japan's cultural and historical anthropology, cinema and new media, and globalization, and his book from the Cornell CEASS Series is titled *Visioning Eternity: Aesthetics, Politics, and History in the Early Modern Noh Theater* (2008). Works in progress include a coauthored book on anime and new media in Japan, and a volume on Superflat art and 1990s Japan.

ANNE MCKNIGHT is associate professor and teaches Japanese literature and comparative culture, as well as courses on public design and California studies, at Shirayuri College in Tokyo. She is the author of the monograph *Nakagami, Japan: Buraku and the Writing of Ethnicity* (2011) as well as essays in *camera obscura, positions,* and elsewhere.

AKIRA MIZUTA LIPPIT teaches literature and film at the University of Southern California. His books include *Ex-Cinema: From a Theory of Experimental Film and*

Video (2012); *Atomic Light (Shadow Optics)* (2005); *Electric Animal: Toward a Rhetoric of Wildlife* (2000); and, most recently, *Cinema without Reflection: Jacques Derrida's Echopoiesis and Narcissism Adrift* (2016).

RYOKO MISONO was associate professor in the College of Japanese Language and Culture at the University of Tsukuba. She is the author of *Film and the Nation State: 1930s Shochiku Melodrama Films* (in Japanese, 2012), which won the annual prize of the Association for Studies of Culture and Representation. She coedited the volume *Awashima Chikage: The Actress as Prism* (in Japanese, 2009) and published many essays on gender, on the history of film and of film criticism in Japan, and on directors such as Nagisa Oshima, Keisuke Kinoshita, and Kiju Yoshida.

MIRYAM SAS is Professor of Film and Media, Japanese and Comparative Literature at the University of California, Berkeley. Her most recent book is *Experimental Arts in Postwar Japan: Moments of Encounter, Engagement, and Imagined Return* (2010). Earlier work has explored models for thinking about avant-garde movements cross-culturally (*Fault Lines: Cultural Memory and Japanese Surrealism*, released 2001), butô dance (in *Butôs*, 2002), and technology and corporeality (in *Histories of the Future*, 2005). She has forthcoming articles on intermedia in Japan, experimental animation, and pink film, and she is working on a book about critical media practices and transcultural media theory in Japan from the 1960s to the present.

FABIAN SCHÄFER is professor of Japanese Studies at the Friedrich-Alexander University of Erlanger–Nuremberg. He is the author of *Public Opinion, Propaganda, Ideology: Theories on the Press and Its Social Function in Interwar Japan, 1918–1937* (2012), and the editor of *Tosaka Jun: A Critical Reader* (forthcoming) and *Tosaka Jun: Ideology, Media, Everydayness* (in German, 2011). His current research interests include Japanese cultural studies, media and cultural theory, and transnational intellectual history.

MARC STEINBERG is associate professor of Film Studies at Concordia University, Montreal. He is the author of *Anime's Media Mix: Franchising Toys and Characters in Japan* (2012) and *Why Is Japan a "Media Mixing Nation"?* (in Japanese, 2015). He has published essays in *Japan Forum*; *Animation: An Interdisciplinary Journal*; *Journal of Visual Culture*; *Theory, Culture & Society*; *Mechademia*; and *Canadian Journal of Film Studies*.

TOMIKO YODA is the Takashima Professor of Japanese Humanities in the Department of East Asian Languages and Civilizations. She received her PhD in Japanese from Stanford in 1996 and taught at Duke, Cornell, and Stanford before arriving at Harvard. She is a recipient of fellowships from NEH, SSRC, the Japan Foundation, and the National Humanities Center. She is the author of *Gender and National Literature: Heian Texts and the Constructions of Japanese Modernity* (2004) and coeditor, with Harry Harootunian, of *Japan After Japan: Social and Cultural Life from the Recessionary 1990s to the Present* (2006).

ALEXANDER ZAHLTEN is assistant professor in the Department of East Asian Languages and Civilizations at Harvard University. He received his PhD in film studies at Johannes Gutenberg University of Mainz, Germany. In 2011–12 he was assistant professor at the Department of Film and Digital Media of Dongguk University in Seoul, South Korea. He has curated film programs for institutions such as the German Film Museum and the Athénée Français Cultural Center, Tokyo, and was program director for the Nippon Connection Film Festival, the largest festival for film from Japan, in 2002–10.

Index

Hachiya, Kazuhiko, 121, 123–24
Hagimoto, Kinichi, 229
Hajime, Tanabe, 379
Hamano, Satoshi, 91, 217
Haniya, Yūtaka, 213
Hansen, Mark B. N., 5–6, 12, 24–25, 53
Hansen, Miriam 151, 167n1,
Harootunian, Harry, 42
Hasumi, Shigehiko, 3, 15, 202, 206, 329, 332
Hayashi, Shūji, 61–62
Hayashi, Yūjirō, 60, 63
Heidegger, Martin, 92, 94, 300n25, 301n31, 301n38, 316, 317, 323, 353
hihyō (criticism), 16, 18, 22–23, 81, 167, 208, 211–12, 256, 329–30, 338–39, 373
Hills, Matt, 11
Hirabayashi, Hatsunosuke, 42–43
Hollywood, 297
Hōsō Asahi (magazine), 136–37, 139, 148n21

Igarashi, Megumi, 251, 253. *See also* Rokudenashiko
Imamura, Taihei, 44
Inaba, Michio, 35, 286, 299n1, 307, 381
in-betweenness (*aidagara*), 306–7, 310, 317–18, 322
industrial capitalism, 34, 137
information age, 3, 120, 139. *See also* information society, information industry
information capitalism, 108
information industry (*jōhō sangyō*), 3, 27n5, 61–62, 137, 148n23, 223
information society (*jōhō shakai*), 27n5, 60, 201; and *Information Networks for Future Japan*, 62; and *Future of Information Archipelago Japan*, 63
information technologies, 52, 55, 62, 73, 83, 86, 89
Informatization (*jōhōka*), 61, 64
Inokuchi, Ichirō, 68
InterCommunication (journal), 19, 82, 96, 101–4, 126, 383; advertisements in, 109–13; first issue of, 114–16; founding of, 105–8; and InterCommunication Center, 121–24; and intercommunication, 114–19
InterCommunication Center (icc), 104, 108, 113–14, 120–22, 125

interfacial subjectivity, 84–89, 96
intermedia, 67, 208
International Congresses of Modern Architecture, 57
Internet, 9–12, 16, 81, 95–96, 108, 174, 297; and general will, 379, 383–85; and identification, 84, 89; temporality of, 142
intertitles, 292–94. *See also* subtitles
invisible city, 71
Ippan ishi 2.0 (General Will 2.0), 81, 348, 357–63
irony, 21, 194, 205–6, 214–17, 220n37
Isozaki, Arata, 18, 55, 58, 66, 78n78, 106
Itoi, Shigesato, 203–4, 210, 213, 231–32
Ivy, Marilyn, 19, 135, 218n10, 218n12, 278n15, 364n1, 383

Japan Society of Image Arts and Sciences, 15
Japanese publishing industry, 4, 222, 233–34, 236, 239–40

Kadokawa, Haruki, 208, 211
Kamimura, Shin'ichi, 36
kankyō (environment), 58, 65–67
Kant, Immanuel, 286, 300n19, 301n31, 308, 311, 313, 317, 324, 330
Karatani, Kōjin, 19, 21, 96, 106, 114, 202, 204, 220n37, 322, 329–31
Katō, Hidetoshi, 15, 35, 38, 49n34, 200
Katō, Kazuhiko, 121, 181
Katō, Shūichi, 330, 346n28
Kawanaka, Nobuhiro, 154, 166
Kitada, Akihiro, xii, 2, 10, 13, 22, 351, 365n18; and mediatization of consumer culture, 175, 201, 213, 380–81; and unmediated mediation, 43, 134
Kitano, Keisuke, xii, 16, 22–23, 208, 211, 371–72, 375–76, 382
Kitano, Takeshi, 234–35. *See also* Beat Takeshi
Kittler, Friedrich, 2, 6–8, 27n2, 71–72, 114, 298, 372; and *Gramophone, Film, Typewriter,* 368–69
Kobayashi, Hideo: and *hihyō* (criticism), 23, 328–31; and Japanese modernity, 331–37; and translation, 371, 375; and visual media, 340–44, 387n16